T0178294

Lecture Notes in Computer Science 11969

More information about this series at http://www.springer.com/series/7409

Dang Van Hung · Meenakshi D'Souza (Eds.)

Distributed Computing and Internet Technology

16th International Conference, ICDCIT 2020
Bhubaneswar, India, January 9–12, 2020
Proceedings

 Springer

Editors
Dang Van Hung
Vietnam National University
Hanoi, Vietnam

Meenakshi D'Souza
International Institute
of Information Technology
Bangalore, India

ISSN 0302-9743　　　　　　　ISSN 1611-3349　(electronic)
Lecture Notes in Computer Science
ISBN 978-3-030-36986-6　　　　ISBN 978-3-030-36987-3　(eBook)
https://doi.org/10.1007/978-3-030-36987-3

LNCS Sublibrary: SL3 – Information Systems and Applications, incl. Internet/Web, and HCI

This Springer imprint is published by the registered company Springer Nature Switzerland AG
The registered company address is: Gewerbestrasse 11, 6330 Cham, Switzerland

Preface

This volume contains the papers presented at the 16th International Conference on Distributed Computing and Internet Technology (ICDCIT 2020) held during January 9–12, 2020, in Bhubaneswar, India.

Since it was initiated in 2004, the ICDCIT conference series has become a global platform for Computer Science researchers to exchange research results and ideas on the foundations and applications of Distributed Computing and Internet Technology. An additional goal of ICDCIT is to provide an opportunity for students and young researchers to get exposed to topical research directions of Distributed Computing and Internet Technology.

ICDCIT 2020 received 110 full paper submissions. Each submission was reviewed by at least three Program Committee (PC) members with the help from reviewers outside the PC. Based on the reviews the PC had online, it was decided that 20 regular papers and 3 short papers would be accepted for presentation at the conference, with an acceptance rate of 21%.

We would like to express our gratitude to all the researchers who submitted their work to the conference. We are particularly thankful to all colleagues who served on the PC as well as the external reviewers, whose hard work in the review process helped us select the papers and prepare the conference program.

Special thanks go to the six invited speakers – Y.N. Srikant from the Department of Computer Science and Automation, Indian Institute of Science, Bangalore, India; Dale Miller from Laboratoire d'Informatique, LIX École Polytechnique, Route de Saclay, France; Bhubaneswar (Bud) Mishra from Courant Institute, New York University, USA; Nobuko Yoshida from Imperial College, UK; Adegboyega Ojo from National University of Ireland, Ireland; and Hrushikesha Mohanty from University of Hyderabad (now online at KIIT Deemed University), India. The papers of the invited talks are included in this volume.

A number of colleagues have worked very hard to make this conference a success. We wish to express our thanks to the Local Organizing Committee, organizers of the satellite events, and many student volunteers. The School of Computer Engineering Kalinga Institute of Industrial Technology, the host of the conference, provided various supports and facilities for organizing the conference and its associated events. Finally, we enjoyed institutional and financial support from the Kalinga Institute of Industrial Technology (KIIT), Bhubaneswar, who we thank. Particularly, we express our sincere thanks to Achyuta Samanta, the Founder of KIIT University for his continuous support to ICDCIT since its inception. We also expresses our appreciation to D.N. Dwivedy for his active participations in ICDCIT. Our thanks is due to the faculty members of the School of Computer Engineering, KIIT University for their timely supports.

The conference program and proceedings were prepared with the help of EasyChair. We thank Springer for continuing to publish the conference proceedings.

January 2020   Dang Van Hung
                                                               Meenakshi D'Souza

Organization

General Chair

Ratan K. Ghosh   IIT Kanpur, India

Program Committee Chairs

Dang Van Hung   UET-VNU, Vietnam
Meenakshi D'Souza   International Institute of Information Technology
                                     Bangalore, India

Conference Management Chair

Madhabananda Das   KIIT, India

Organizing Chair

Siddharth Swarup Rautaray   KIIT, India

Finance Chair

Santosh Kumar Pani   KIIT, India

Publicity Chair

Krishna Chakravarty   KIIT, India

Registration Chairs

Bhaswati Sahoo   KIIT, India
Ajay Kumar Jena   KIIT, India

Session Management Chairs

Harish Kumar Pattniak   KIIT, India
Sital Dash   KIIT, India

Publications Chair

Bindu Agarwalla   KIIT, India

Student Symposium Chairs

Subhasis Dash	KIIT, India
Chittranjan Pradhan	KIIT, India

Industry Symposium Chair

Manjusha Pandey	KIIT, India

Project Innovation Contest Chairs

Jagannath Singh	KIIT, India
Mamta Motwani	KIIT, India

Steering Committee

Maurice Herlihy	Brown University, USA
Gérard Huet	Inria, France
Bud Mishra	Courant Institute of Mathematial Sciences of New York University, USA
Hrushikesha Mohanty	KIIT, India
Raja Natarajan	TIFR, India
David Peleg	WIS, Israel
R. K. Shyamasundar	IIT Bombay, India
Laxmi Parida	IBM Research, USA

Program Committee

Ramkalyan Ayyagari	NIT Tiruchirapalli, India
Hoang Truong Anh	VNU-UET, Vietnam
A. K. Bhattacharjee	BARC Mumbai, India
Alpana A. Dubey	Accenture Labs Bangalore, India
Maunendra Sankar Desarkar	IIT Hyderabad, India
Chittaranjan Hota	BITS Pilani Hyderabad, India
Hemangee Kapoor	IIT Guwahati, India
Atul Negi	SCIS, University of Hyderabad, India
Srinath Srinivasa	IIIT Bangalore, India
P. S. V. S. Sai Prasad	University of Hyderabad, India
Koushik Sinha	Southern Illinois University, USA
Dimitar Guelev	Bulgarian Academy of Sciences, Bulgaria
Jay Bagga	Ball State University, USA
Cao Son Tran	New Mexico State University, USA
Tien Do Van	BME, Hungary
Nikolaj Bjorner	Microsoft, USA
Venkatesh Choppella	IIIT Hyderabad, India
Rajiv Bagai	Wichita State University, USA

Chiara Di Francescomarino	Fondazione Bruno Kessler, Italy
Christian Erfurth	University of Applied Sciences Jena, Germany
Marc Frincu	West University of Timisoara, Romania
Hacene Fouchal	University of Reims Champagne-Ardenne, France
Pasupuleti Syam Kumar	IDRBT Hyderabad, India
Swarup Kumar Mohalik	Ericsson Research Bangalore, India
Raoul Jetley	ABB Corporate Research Bangalore, India
Ramakrishnan Raman	Honeywell Technology Solutions Bangalore, India
Ulrike Lechner	Bundeswehr University Munich, Germany
Hrushikesha Mohanty	Kalinga Institute of Industrial Technology, India
Srabani Mukhopadhyaya	Birla Institute of Technology Mesra, India
Dmitry Namiot	Lomonosov Moscow State University, Russia
Raja Natarajan	Tata Institute of Fundamental Research Mumbai, India
Sathya Peri	IIT Hyderabad, India
Niladri Bihari Puhan	IIT Bhubaneswar, India
Rajendra Raj	Rochester Institute of Technology, USA
Ramaswamy Ramanujam	Institute of Mathematical Sciences Chennai, India
Sapna P. G.	Coimbatore Institute of Technology, India
Miao Miao Zhang	Tong Ji University, China
Meenakshi D'Souza	IIIT Bangalore, India
Dang Van Hung	UET-VNU, Vietnam

Additional Reviewers

Kumar Abhinav
Parwat Singh Anjana
Partha Sarathi Bishnu
Rohit Kamal Chatterjee
Deepak D'Souza
Hemalatha Eedi
Diep Hoang
Yogalakshmi Jayabal
Junali Jasmine Jena
Chirag Juyal
Chandrika K. R.

Manisha Kumari
Sweta Kumari
Avijit Mandal
Devina Mohan
Sambit Nayak
Surya Palavalasa
Gopal Pandurangan
Muktikanta Sa
Sinchan Sengupta
Nagender Suryadevara
Hieu Vo-Dinh

Contents

Cloud and Grid Computing

Social Networks, Machine Learning and Mobile Networks

Data Processing and Blockchain Technology

Short Papers

Invited Talks

Distributed Graph Analytics

Y. N. Srikant[✉]

Indian Institute of Science, Bengaluru 560012, India
srikant@iisc.ac.in,
http://www.csa.iisc.ac.in/~srikant

Abstract. Graph Analytics is important in different domains: social networks, computer networks, and computational biology to name a few. This paper describes the challenges involved in programming the underlying graph algorithms for graph analytics for distributed systems with CPU, GPU, and multi-GPU machines and how to deal with them. It emphasizes how language abstractions and good compilation can ease programming graph analytics on such platforms without sacrificing implementation efficiency.

Keywords: Graph analytics · Social networks · Parallel algorithms · Multi-core processors · GPU computation · Graph frameworks · Graph processing languages

1 Introduction

Usage of graph algorithms to determine relationships between objects in a graph and also the overall structural characteristics of the graph constitutes *graph analytics*. Compiler optimizations, job scheduling in operating systems, database applications, natural language processing, computational geometry etc., are among the traditional applications of this area, and they continue to be important. *Social network analysis* is a major business driver of this area in recent times. It identifies potential "network influencers" who, in turn, influence buying products and services by social network communities. However, many more important applications of graph analytics have been proposed of late.

1.1 Some Real World Use Cases for Graph Analytics

- Locating neighbor nodes in GPS systems to identify nearby places of interest (uses breadth-first search).
- Finding driving directions between two locations (uses all-pairs or single source shortest paths).
- Finding optimal location of new public services for maximum accessibility (uses closeness centrality).
- Determining how major epidemic diseases spread in a large community of people or animals (uses percolation centrality).

© Springer Nature Switzerland AG 2020
D. V. Hung and M. D'Souza (Eds.): ICDCIT 2020, LNCS 11969, pp. 3–20, 2020.
https://doi.org/10.1007/978-3-030-36987-3_1

- Finding individuals who influence the flow around a system (uses betweenness centrality).
- Identifying groups of interacting people in a social network (uses clustering).
- Ranking web pages (pagerank).
- Making product recommendations based on group affiliation (uses strongly connected components).
- Detecting fake bots. Popularity of a product as compared to its competitors may be assessed from the number of tweets related to the product. However, fake bots may bias such data. By constructing graphs and analyzing them fake bots may be detected (uses degree centrality).
- Fake bank accounts and circular money transfer in financial crimes. A graph showing links between accounts transferring money between them and sharing common information such as email address etc., is useful in detecting such crimes (uses connectivity analysis).

1.2   Special Features of Distributed Graph Analytics

Graphical Processing Units (GPUs) are also widely used for general purpose high performance computing, along with multi-core processors and distributed systems. GPUs have their own cores and memory, and are connected to a CPU via a PCI-express bus. Due to massive parallelism available on GPUs, threads are organized into a hierarchy of warps and thread blocks. All the threads within a warp execute in single-instruction multiple data (SIMD) fashion. A group of warps constitutes a thread block, which is assigned to a multi-processor for execution. GPUs are programmed using programming languages such as CUDA and OpenCL. Graph algorithms contain enough parallelism to keep thousands of GPU cores busy.

Social applications of graph analytics usually involve massive graphs that cannot fit into the memory of a single computer. Distributed computation is one important way of handling such graphs. The graphs are partitioned and distributed across computing nodes of a distributed computing system, and computation happens in parallel on all the nodes. A deep knowledge of the hardware, threads, processes, inter-process communication, and memory management are essential for efficient implementation of graph analytics on such platforms. Tuning a given graph algorithm for such platforms is always quite cumbersome. The programmer needs to worry both about *what* the algorithmic processing is, and *how* the processing would be implemented. Programming on these platforms using traditional languages along with message passing interface (MPI) and tools is therefore challenging and error-prone. There is little debugging support either.

Graph analytic algorithms are parallelized using multiple threads, which can be very beneficial on a multi-core processor. Such a multi-core processing approach can improve the efficiency of the underlying computation, since all the threads in a multi-core system share a common memory. A multi-core system is programmed using OpenMP and libraries such as pthreads.

Different kinds of hardware need different programming paradigms for parallelizing a given application. It is imperative to combine the benefits of these hardware types to achieve best results with large data sizes. Thus, both the graph data as well as the associated computation would be split across multi-core CPUs and GPUs, operating in a distributed manner. A programmer needs enormous effort to optimize the computation for three different platforms in multiple languages. It is often infeasible to debug such parallel code at large scale.

Domain specific languages (DSL) and graph analytic frameworks can address this problem. A DSL hides the hardware details from a programmer and allows her/him to concentrate only on the algorithmic logic. A DSL compiler should generate efficient code from the input DSL program. This paper describes briefly a few issues in parallel graph processing, some of the programming frameworks and domain specific languages for graph analytics for distributed systems with CPUs and GPUs.

2 Challenges in Distributed Graph Analytics

Parallelization of graph algorithms poses challenges due to inherent input-centric nature of these algorithms. We discuss such challenges below.

2.1 Classification of Graphs

Some properties of graphs such as diameter and variance in degree are very important to graph algorithms and their execution on different types of hardware. The difference in these properties make a program perform poorly or very well for input graphs of different types (road, random, R-MAT). Table 1 shows a comparison of different graph types based on the properties.

Table 1. Graph types and their properties

Type of the graph	Variance in degree	Diameter
Random	Low	Low
R-MAT	High	Low
Social N/W	High	Low
Road N/W	Low	High

Particular graph types require implementations using particular data structures in order to be efficient. An excellent example is the Δ-stepping algorithm [17] and its implementation on a multi-core processor. This algorithm uses a dynamic *collection* called *bucket* and has proved to be very efficient for road network graphs which have a very high diameter. However, implementations of the Δ-stepping algorithm on GPUs are generally not as efficient as on multi-cores.

2.2 Graph Partitioning Strategies

When a graph is too large to fit in the memory of a single computer, it is partitioned into subgraphs and these are distributed across the computing nodes of a cluster computing system. It is desirable for a good partition to have almost equal number of vertices in each subgraph and a minimum number of inter-partition edges. Finding such a partition is an NP-complete problem. Each subgraph is processed in parallel on a different node of the computing cluster, and *message passing* is used for communication between subgraphs in the nodes.

Many frameworks have adopted *random* partitioning, in which, each vertex of the graph is considered in turn, and is randomly assigned to a node of the computing cluster. This method achieves good balance in the number of nodes per partition, but there is no control on either the number of remote edges or the number of edges in each partition. *Vertex-cut* and *edge-cut* methods are two methods of graph partitioning that provide more control on these issues.

In vertex-cut partitioning, each edge $e \in E$ is assigned a random computing node. Vertex-cut partitioning provides good balance in the number of edges per node, but results in communication overhead as nodes can be shared between partitions. For example, two edges $e_1 : u \rightarrow v$ and $e_2 : u \rightarrow w$ with a common tail vertex u, can reside in different subgraphs, thereby sharing vertex u. When a vertex is shared between two or more nodes all the updates to the data in vertex u in any one of the nodes must be communicated to the other nodes that share the vertex u. See Fig. 1 for an example.

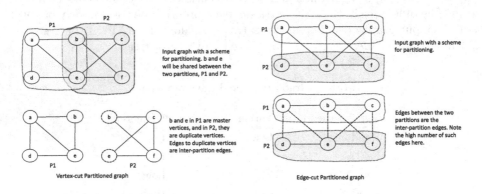

Fig. 1. Example vertex-cut and edge-cut graph partitioning

On the other hand, in *edge-cut* partitioning, a vertex $v \in V$ is assigned a random node, and all the edges $e \in E$ with *tail* $(e) = v$ are added to G_i, the subgraph stored at the node. This partitioning method can reduce inter-node communication overhead but may result in improper work balance among computing nodes. See Fig. 1 for an example. A vertex-cut partitioning algorithm that produces balanced partitions and also minimizes communication overheads is described in [22].

2.3   Heterogeneous Distributed Systems

A set of computers distributed geographically over many locations and are inter-connected with a not-so-fast communications constitutes a distributed system. Most of the time, components in a distributed system work independently, in parallel, and with little interaction between themselves. However, computers in a highly parallel machine are physically located very close to each other, and are connected by an extremely fast interconnection network. They work in unison to solve a single problem, such as a distributed version of a shortest path or a minimum spanning tree problem. The communication between such computers is usually using the Message Passing Interface (MPI) and parallelism within each computer is harnessed using threads. Each computer may be of a different type and hence the name *heterogeneous*. Such systems are also called *clusters* and these are the preferred platforms for distributed graph analytics.

Computing nodes of a cluster can be of different hardware architectures. Multiple Instruction Multiple Data (MIMD) architecture is used in multi-core processors and Graphical Processing Units (GPU) follow a Single Instruction Multiple Thread (SIMT) architecture. Due to the differences in the hardware architecture and programming aspects of CPUs and GPUs, a single program usually does not suffice for both and separate programs are required to be written for the same algorithm. A programmer should know the details of the hardware in order to obtain the best performance. It is a challenging task for a naive programmer with expertise in algorithm design but not in hardware architectures of multi-core CPUs and GPUs, to write and tune a program for a specific hardware.

2.4   Programming Libraries and APIs

Clusters of tightly coupled machines can be programmed using high level programming libraries, such as MPI for distributed processing, and OpenMP for multi-core processing. CUDA, Thrust, and OpenCL are the widely used frameworks for GPU implementations.

The OpenMP [7] application programming interface (API) is used to parallelize loops on a multi-core CPU with shared memory. It consists of compiler pragmas, a runtime library, and environment variables that influence runtime behavior. A loop can be parallelized if there is no data dependency between two or more iterations of a loop. Loop parallelization is carried out using the *omp parallel* pragma, which results in creation of multiple threads to execute the iterations concurrently. The compiler handles insertion of appropriate library routine calls into the code. However, ensuring the absence of data dependencies in a loop is the responsibility of the programmer.

CUDA [6], developed by Nvidia for programming Nvidia GPUs, is a popular parallel processing platform and application programming interface (API). Each GPU device has a private memory that is not shared with the host CPU. Allocating memory on GPU, copying data to and from the GPU, and making kernel calls, etc., are all handled by the CUDA library. CUDA extends the C++

language with additional keywords. Functions are executed in parallel on the GPU (known as *kernels*) and they are called from the CPU. CUDA kernel calls are asynchronous and the CPU continues execution after a kernel call. A *barrier* synchronization function forces the *host* to wait for the GPU to complete its operation.

The Message Passing Interface (MPI) [10] is a message passing library standard proposed by the MPI Forum. Many MPI libraries that are compliant with the specifications of MPI are available in public. The MPI library is used for communication between the nodes of a cluster with each computing node having private memory. Primarily, MPI focuses on the message-passing parallel programming model.

2.5   Irregular Computation

Data access or control patterns are unpredictable at compile time in irregular computations as opposed to these being predictable in the case of regular computations. For example, in dense matrix-matrix computation, which is regarded as a regular computation, a compiler can identify which elements get accessed (row elements of the first matrix along with the column elements of the second matrix). In contrast, in graph algorithms, without knowing the input graph, the edges along which, vertex attributes would be propagated, is not clear at compile time. In these situations, compilers make conservative assumptions about the input and these may forbid parallelization.

Therefore, in irregular computations parallelism decisions are deferred until runtime when the input graph is available. In addition, several real world graphs have arbitrary connectivity leading to load imbalance. It is possible that the thread operating on a low-degree vertex would have to wait for the other thread operating on a high-degree vertex, without performing useful work. In order to avoid idling of resources, such computations demand dynamic load balancing by way of efficient thread scheduling.

Graphs also pose synchronization challenges. Reading and writing of shared data by concurrent threads may lead to race conditions and usage of synchronization constructs (such as locks, barriers, atomics, etc.) is necessary to prevent such situations from occurring. Synchronization often implies slow-down of the overall algorithm.

2.6   Challenges in Programming

Programming distributed graph analytics algorithms targeting a cluster with CPUs and GPUs is very demanding and challenging. The programmer must have a good knowledge of various aspects of distributed computation such as, graph partitioning, parallel computation, dynamic memory management, thread management and communication between nodes, etc., for both multi-core CPUs and GPUs. The graph storage format should maximize cache locality and coalesced access to enable high throughput. Implementing distributed graph analytics applications in native languages such as C or CUDA with libraries such as OpenMP and MPI will lead to very large programs. Such programs will be error-prone, difficult to understand and modify, and are hard to debug. The complexity of programming graph analytics for clusters can be reduced by high level programming abstractions.

3   Programming Abstractions for Graph Analytics

Programming abstractions are used in many application domains, such as VHDL for hardware design, HTML for web programming, and MATLAB for scientific computations, and R for statistical computations. Such domain-specific frameworks or languages make the job of coding and debugging much easier than in the usual programming languages. More specifically, abstractions for heterogeneous hardware, graphs and distributed computation will help in programming graph analytics applications. This increases productivity and reliability.

3.1   Frameworks and Domain-Specific Languages for Graph Analytics

Graph analytics frameworks differ in multiple ways. Frameworks for single multicore CPU machines cannot be used with large graphs that do not fit into the memory of a single machine. Some frameworks support changes in graph topology during computation, some promise better performance using *speculative* execution, and some others support efficient worklist based implementations. A cluster of tightly coupled high-end CPUs and GPUs is required for processing large graphs. Different execution models have been proposed in the past for distributed execution on a CPU cluster. These include the Bulk Synchronous Parallel (BSP) model of execution, the *Gather-Apply-Scatter* execution model, and the asynchronous execution model. Frameworks deploy one of these models as their basis.

3.2   Bulk Synchronous Parallel (BSP) Model

In the BSP model of programming proposed by Valiant [24], input data is partitioned on the multiple compute nodes. Programs in the BSP model perform a sequence of iterations called *supersteps*. Each superstep has the following three phases.

1. *Computation*: Each compute node performs local computation independently on its partitioned data and is unaware of execution on other nodes. Nodes may produce data that needs to be sent to other nodes in the communication phase.
2. *Communication*: In the communication phase, data is exchanged as requested in the previous computation phase.
3. *Synchronization*: There is an implicit barrier at the end of communication phase. Each node waits for data which was transferred in communication phase to be available.

The BSP model simplifies programming in a distributed environment. During graph processing, each vertex behaves as a computing node, and vertices communicate among each other through edges of the graph. *Pregel* is a framework [16] based on the BSP model. Giraph [5] is an example of a framework that combines the benefits of Pregel and the *MapReduce()* framework [9] on the Hadoop distributed file system (HDFS) [26,27] for storing data.

3.3 Asynchronous Execution Model

BSP based systems are synchronous and hence may incur penalties when the compute nodes of the distributed system have varying speeds and/or the communication speeds between all nodes are not uniform. This is because synchronization waits for the *slowest* machine to finish. Imbalance in finishing times of nodes may also be due to the varying amount of computation in the nodes. For example, consider a power-law based graph that is randomly partitioned. Some nodes may have vertices which have a very large degree, thereby requiring more computation time than other nodes.

In such situations, resorting to asynchrony is useful. Asynchronous systems use the most recent parameter values as input in order to update parameters. Nodes do not always wait for all others to finish, and this may make the distributed computation execute faster. However, non-determinism may make asynchronous systems yield inconsistent results. Consistency control features must be carefully provided in such frameworks. Asynchronous execution systems also require work lists of active elements (vertices in case of graphs) that are scheduled appropriately. Examples of frameworks based on asynchrony are Graphlab [14] and Distributed Graphlab [15].

3.4 Gather-Apply-Scatter (GAS) Model

The GAS model of execution consists of a super step which is divided into three *minor* steps named *gather*, *apply* and *scatter*. The changes made to the graph properties are *committed* after each minor step, and this process requires transfer of vertex and/or edge property values between subgraphs stored in the nodes of a computer cluster. A set of *active* vertices are processed in each superstep, and new active vertices are created at the end of a superstep. The computation stops after reaching the *fixpoint*, which is apparent if no active vertices are created after a superstep. Execution is initiated with a set of algorithm-specific active points (e.g., the source node in the single-source-shortest-path algorithm). The GAS model supports both the BSP model and the asynchronous model of execution. [12] is an example supporting such an abstraction.

3.5 Frameworks Supporting GPUs

Many frameworks developed over the last decade support graph analytics on GPUs. Such frameworks usually support multiple-GPUs but only on a single machine. The communication overhead between GPUs on a multi-GPU machine is very low, if the GPUs are connected with a *peer-access* capability. Otherwise, it is very high. The communication cost between CPUs on different nodes of a cluster is very low compared to that between GPUs on different nodes. Therefore, proper graph partitioning assumes a great significance on such systems. Lones-tarGPU [2], IrGL [18], Totem [11] and Gluon [8] are graph analytics frameworks for GPU systems.

3.6   Domain Specific Languages

Graph analytics frameworks do not perform any semantic checks on programs. They also do not provide higher level abstractions which are available in a domain specific language (DSL). It is relatively easier to program algorithms using graph DSLs than using frameworks. Graph-specific data items such as *vertex*, *edge*, *graph*, *collection* and *set* along with operations on them, and parallel and synchronization constructs are provided directly in graph-theoretic DSLs. Syntax and semantic violations are caught by the DSL compiler. All this makes programming graph analytics easier and less error prone in such DSLs, thereby increasing productivity.

Some of the available Graph DSLs include Green-Marl [13], Elixir [21], Gluon [8], Falcon [3], and DH-Falcon [4]. An example of the shortest path algorithm written in *Falcon* is shown in Algorithm 1.1.

4   Major Issues in Programming Graph Analytics Algorithms

4.1   Parallelism and Atomicity

Most parallel graph algorithms parallelize only the outermost loop. That is, the outermost `foreach` statement is run in `parallel` mode, and any nested `foreach` statements are run in sequential mode. This is quite common in auto-parallelizing compilers as well. Efficient scheduling of iterations that balance work among threads is essential to exploit nested parallelism. In the case of regular nested loops, the number of iterations of an inner loop does not vary across the iterations of the outer loop. Hence, parallelization of regular nested loops can utilize thread- and block-based mapping. In the case of irregular nested loops, neither thread-based mapping nor block-based mapping offer advantages. Use of thread-based mapping on the outer-loop may cause warp divergence (i.e., different threads are assigned different amounts of work), while the use of block-based mapping will lead to uneven block utilization, which in turn may cause GPU underutilization.

The execution pattern of a parallel graph algorithm may vary for graphs of even the same size (number of vertices and/or edges). In an execution of a parallel graph algorithm implementation, two or more threads may try to update the same memory location at the same time. *Atomic operations* are provided by

---

Algorithm 1.1: Bellman-Ford SSSP code in Falcon

```
1  int changed=1;
2  relaxgraph( Point p, Graph g) {
3      foreach( t In p.outnbrs ){
4          MIN(t.distance,p.distance+g.getWeight(p,t),changed);
5          //MIN is an atomic operation. changed is set
6          //to 1, if t.distance changes.
7      }
8  }
9  SSSP(char *input_file) {
10     Graph given_graph; given_graph.addPointProperty(distance,int);
       given_graph.read(input_file);
11     foreach(t In given_graph.points)t.distance=9999999999;
12     given_graph.points[0].distance=0;
13     while( changed ){
14         changed=0;
15         foreach( t In given_graph.points ) relaxgraph( t,given_graph );
16     }
17     return;
18 }
19 main(int argc,char *argv[]) {
20     SSSP(argv[1]);
21 }
```

---

the hardware to handle such conditions. These atomic operations create *critical sections* that are executed by only one thread at a time. Table 2 shows a few variants of the atomic operations relevant to graph algorithms. The `atomic` language construct used to create such critical sections are implemented using atomic operations provided by the hardware. The atomic operations listed in the table are typically supported by both modern CPU and GPU. The old value in memory is returned by the operation. Some implementations also set/reset a flag on success/failure.

Table 2. Atomic operations

Operation	Processor	Inputs	Operation	Return
CAS	CPU & GPU	mem,x,y	if (mem.val==x) then mem.val = y;	mem.oldval
ADD	CPU & GPU	mem,y	mem.val += y;	mem.oldval
MIN	CPU & GPU	mem,y	if (mem.val > y) mem.val=y;	mem.oldval

4.2   Push vs. Pull Computation

Making graph algorithms run efficiently on GPUs required several factors. Synchronization and communication overheads must be reduced, in addition to having a coalesced memory access pattern. Push and pull versions of graph algorithms are two variations that must be used carefully in design. They have been explored in [1, 25]. We explain the push and pull computation models with the pagerank algorithm as an example.

A Brief Note on Pagerank. The Pagerank algorithm [25, 28] is used to index web pages, and decide the weight (read popularity) of a web page. The number of incoming links to a web page and the weight of each linking web page (i.e., *source* of the link) are used in computing the weight of a web page. It is also used for ranking text for entity relevance in natural language processing.

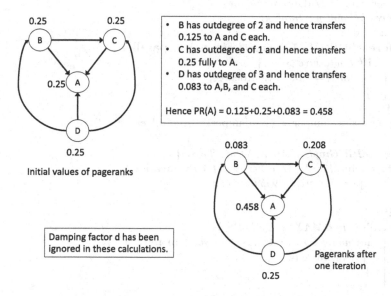

• B has outdegree of 2 and hence transfers 0.125 to A and C each.
• C has outdegree of 1 and hence transfers 0.25 fully to A.
• D has outdegree of 3 and hence transfers 0.083 to A,B, and C each.

Hence PR(A) = 0.125+0.25+0.083 = 0.458

Initial values of pageranks

Damping factor d has been ignored in these calculations.

Pageranks after one iteration

Fig. 2. Example of Pagerank computation

The page rank of a page or website A is calculated by the formula given below:

$$PageRank(A) = (1 - d) + d\left(\frac{PageRank(W_1)}{LinkNum(W_1)} + \ldots + \frac{PageRank(W_n)}{LinkNum(W_n)}\right)$$

where, W_1 to W_n correspond to the websites accessed by the user, PageRank(A) is the page rank of A, PageRank(W_1) to PageRank(W_n) are the page ranks of the pages which have *urls* linking to A, and LinkNum(W_1) to LinkNum(W_n) are the number of links on the sites W_1 to W_n respectively. The parameter d in the computation is called the damping factor and is typically set to 0.85. The probability at each page, that a "random surfer" will get bored and request another random page is called the *damping factor*. In the graph G in the pagerank algorithm: vertices are the websites accessed by the user, and an edge $A \rightarrow B$

represents the (multiple) outgoing *urls* from website A to B. The page rank of a vertex is high when it has more incoming edges. An example is shown in Fig. 2.

Pull-Based Pagerank. This algorithm is shown in Algorithm 1.2. Each vertex *p pulls* (reads) the *pagerank* value of all the neighbouring vertices with incoming edges to *p* (see lines 4–8), and updates its own pagerank. No **atomic** section is required in this type of parallel implementation, as each thread writes only its own updated pagerank value and not that of its neighbours (their pagerank values are just *read*).

Algorithm 1.2: Parallel Pagerank - Pull based

```
1  damper = 0.85; // damping factor
2  pagerank(Point p, Graph g) {
3      val = 0.0;
4      foreach( Point t In p.in_neighbours ) in parallel {
5          if( t.outdegree > 0 ){
6              | val += t.pr ÷ t.outdegree;
7          }
8      }
9      p.pr=val× damper + (1 - damper) ÷size(g.Vertex_set);
10 }
11 computePR(Graph g, MAX_NUM_ITRS) {
12     foreach( Point t In g.Vertex_set ) in parallel {
13         | t.pr = 1 ÷size(g.Vertex_set);
14     }
15     itr=1;
16     while( itr <MAX_NUM_ITRS ){
17         foreach( Point p In g.Vertex_set ) in parallel {
18             | pagerank(p, g);
19         }
20         itr++;
21     }
22 }
```

Push-Based Pagerank. The pagerank algorithm as a push-based algorithm is shown in Algorithm 1.3. Each vertex *p pushes* (updates) the pagerank value of all the neighbouring vertices with outgoing edges from *p*. The update operation is required to be **atomic**, as the pagerank of a vertex *t* can possibly be updated simultaneously by two of its neighbours corresponding to two incoming edges (see line 4, which is enclosed in an **atomic** section). Push-based algorithms may be slower than pull-based algorithms, due to the presence of **atomic** operations. However, appropriate scheduling may make a push-based algorithm faster than a pull-based algorithm, as demonstrated in [25].

Algorithm 1.3: Parallel Pagerank: Push Based

```
 1  damper = 0.85; // damping factor
 2  pagerank_val_update(Point p, Graph g) {
 3      foreach( Point t In p.outneighbours ) in parallel {
 4          atomic
 5          |   t.val+= p.pr ÷ p.outdegree;
 6          end
 7      }
 8  }
 9  pagerank_PR_update(Point p, Graph g) {
10      p.pr=p.val× damper +(1-damper)÷|g.V|;
11      p.val=0;
12  }
13  computePR(Graph g, MAX_ITERS) {
14      foreach( Point t In g.V ) in parallel {
15          |   t.pr=1÷|g.V|; t.val=0;
16      }
17      itr=1;
18      while( itr <MAX_ITERS ){
19          foreach( Point p In g.V ) in parallel {
20              |   pagerank_val_update(p,g);
21          }
22          foreach( Point p In g.V ) in parallel {
23              |   pagerank_PR_update(p,g);
24          }
25          itr++;
26      }
27  }
```

4.3 Topology Driven vs. Data Driven Nature of Algorithms

Manytimes it is possible to identify abstract operators in parallel graph algorithms which are applied iteratively to *active* nodes in the graph. As an example, the updating of pagerank after reading the pagerank values of the neighbours of a vertex in a graph is an abstract operator in a pull-based *pagerank* algorithm. Effect of an operator is generally local to a vertex, and affects only a small neighbourhood of the vertex. Therefore, several non-overlapping activities of operators may proceed in parallel.

Based on the application of operators to the vertices of a graph, parallel graph algorithms may be classified as *Topology-driven* or *Data-driven*. If all the nodes (vertices are also referred to as nodes) are considered as *active*, it is called a topology-driven implementation. This leads to the application of the operator at all nodes, even if there is nothing to do at some nodes. For example, in topology-driven BFS (see Algorithm 1.4), only the source node does some work in the first iteration and all other nodes have nothing to do. In the second iteration, all nodes at a distance of one from the source node have work to do and the others have nothing to do, and so on. However, in this case, threads would be assigned to each node irrespective of whether work needs to be done at the node or not.

Algorithm 1.4: Parallel Breadth-First Search (Topology-Driven)

```
1   Topology_BFS(Point src, Graph G) {
2       foreach( Point p In G ) in parallel {
3           p.dist = ∞; p.pred = NULL;
4       }
5       src.dist = 0;
6       while( 1 ){
7           changed = 0;
8           foreach( Point p In G ) in parallel {
9               foreach( Point t In p.outnbrs ){
10                  atomic
11                      if( t.dist > (p.dist + 1) ){
12                          t.dist = p.dist + 1; t.pred = p; changed = 1;
13                      }
14                  end
15              }
16          }
17          if( changed == 0 ){
18              break;
19          }
20      }
21  }
```

A topology-driven variant is easier to implement on GPUs than data-driven ones. GPUs can create a large number of threads very cheaply, since they have a huge number of cores. Each thread needs to perform only a small amount of work corresponding to the operator. Programming such kernels (threads) is also easy. However, efficiency of such implementations suffer. In contrast, multi-core CPUs often do not benefit from such implementations because they have much fewer cores than GPUs. Of special mention are very large and sparse graphs, on which topology-driven implementations on multi-cores perform poorly, due to relatively smaller number of edges (compared to the number of nodes).

Data-driven implementations apply the operator only at those nodes that may have some work to do. Active nodes are maintained in a queue and each thread applies the operator to a node after removing it from the queue. Application of the operator may activate some inactive nodes. Such nodes are inserted into the queue. Such parallel insertions and deletions to the queue (by the threads) require to be synchronized appropriately so that they do not interfere with each other. Data-driven implementations are the rule as far as multi-core CPUs are concerned. However, GPUs pose serious challenges to queue management and synchronization, and therefore, data-driven implementations on GPUs are generally inefficient. A library or a language feature providing a concurrent queue relieves programmers from the clumsy details of the underlying synchronization mechanism, and allows them to focus on algorithm development. Efficient data-driven implementations of BFS have been reported in literature [19,29] and have been excluded due to space limitations.

5 Compilation of Domain-Specific Languages for Graph Analytics

We now consider the challenges in the compilation of a high level domain-specific language: *Falcon*. *Falcon* is an explicitly parallel language, supports shared memory, and is based on C. It has the additional data types: Graph, Point, Edge, Set, and Collection. A special facility to add *properties* to Graph, Point, and Edge data types. A Set type supports a *Union-Find* data structure over disjoint set elements and a Collection type supports the usual add and delete operations. It supports parallel iterators over several data types, critical sections, and parallel sections. It supports mutation of graph objects. The compiler generates code that uses the Bulk Synchronous Parallel (BSP) model. The compiler is responsible for graph partitioning, any implicit and explicit synchronizations, and thread, memory, message, and global variable management. The compiler is flexible so that different partitioning strategies, and optimizations can be used as options. It has a multi-target code generator for CPU/GPU clusters [3,4], and also generates code for well known frameworks: Giraph and OpenCL [23].

5.1 Single GPU Compilation

The host CPU reads the graph and transfers it either wholly or in parts to the GPU device. Global variables are allocated in the GPU device. However, testing global variables and assignment to global variables happens in the host CPU and then the results are transferred to the GPU device. CUDA kernel code is generated by the compiler. Thrust library code is generated for for-iterators working on Collections.

5.2 Single Multi-core CPU Compilation

The graph is read and stored in the CPU shared memory. Global variables pose no special problem as they can be stored in the shared memory. OpenMP code is generated by the compiler and therefore, parallel sections, for-iterators, etc., can all be handled by easily since they are all supported directly by OpenMP. For iterating on a Collection, Galois worklist code is generated.

5.3 Distributed Processing on a Cluster

A large graph is automatically partitioned using vertex-cut partitioning and the partitions are read simultaneously by the nodes of the cluster. The compiler generates code assuming the model of computation to be BSP. There is one copy of each global variable in each node and they need to synchronize at the end of each superstep. They are synchronized by mutual send and receive by each machine, followed by local update. Such distributed synchronization code is automatically generated by the compiler. Properties of each vertex of the graph are updated only by its master. A process is created in each machine to handle its local computations. This process in turn may create several threads. Processes mutually send and receive messages for synchronization at the end of each superstep.

5.4   Performance of the Falcon Compiler

Many well known benchmarks such as SSSP, Boruvka's-MST, Pagerank, Connected Components, K-Core, BFS, and dynamic algorithms (Survey Propagation (SP), Delaunay Mesh refinement (DMR) and Dynamic-SSSP) have been used in testing the performance of the code generated by the Falcon compiler. Very large graphs of several types such as Random, R-Mat, Social network, and Road network of differing sizes ranging from 16 to 105 million vertices and 58 million to 3.7 billion edges, have been used as inputs in these experiments. The platforms used were:

1. Single Device: Machine with 12-core CPU, one Kepler-10 and 3 T GPUs.
2. Multi-GPU machine: Machine with 8 Kepler-40 GPUs.
3. Cluster: 16 Nodes with each node having a 24-core CPU and a Kepler-40 GPU.

The competitive frameworks against which Falcon was compared include the following:

1. Multi-core CPU: Galois [20], Green-Marl [13], and Totem [11].
2. Single GPU: LonestarGPU [2], and Totem [11].
3. Multi-GPU machine: Totem [11].
4. Distributed Systems: PowerGraph [12].

The results are very encouraging but could not be included here due to space limitations. The details are available in [3, 4, 23].

6   Conclusions

We have described the special features and challenges of distributed graph analytics. The frameworks and domain-specific languages supporting programming graph analytics applications and the major issues in programming such applications have been surveyed. A case study of compilation of a specific domain-specific language, *Falcon* was briefly described.

Acknowledgements. This survey paper was inspired by the ongoing collaborative book project co-authored by Dr. Unnikrishnan Cheramangalath of IIT Palakkad, Dr. Rupesh Nasre of IIT Madras, and the author of this paper. The author wishes to acknowledge their assistance in writing this paper.

References

1. Besta, M., Podstawski, M., Groner, L., Solomonik, E., Hoefler, T.: To push or to pull: on reducing communication and synchronization in graph computations. In: Proceedings of the 26th International Symposium on High-Performance Parallel and Distributed Computing, HPDC 2017, pp. 93–104. ACM, New York, NY, USA (2017). https://doi.org/10.1145/3078597.3078616. https://doi.acm.org/10.1145/3078597.3078616

2. Burtscher, M., Nasre, R., Pingali, K.: A quantitative study of irregular programs on GPUs. In: IEEE International Symposium on Workload Characterization (IISWC), pp. 141–151 (2012)

3. Cheramangalath, U., Nasre, R., Srikant, Y.N.: Falcon: a graph manipulation language for heterogeneous systems. ACM Trans. Archit. Code Optim. **12**(4), 54:1–54:27 (2015). https://doi.org/10.1145/2842618. http://doi.acm.org/10.1145/2842618

4. Cheramangalath, U., Nasre, R., Srikant, Y.N.: DH-Falcon: a language for large-scale graph processing on distributed heterogeneous systems. In: IEEE International Conference on Cluster Computing. IEEE (2017)

5. Ching, A., Edunov, S., Kabiljo, M., Logothetis, D., Muthukrishnan, S.: One trillion edges: graph processing at facebook-scale. In: Proceedings of the VLDB Endowment, pp. 1804–1815 (2015)

6. Cook, S.: CUDA Programming: A Developer's Guide to Parallel Computing with GPUs, 1st edn. Morgan Kaufmann Publishers Inc., San Francisco (2013)

7. Dagum, L., Menon, R.: OpenMP: an industry-standard API for shared-memory programming. IEEE Comput. Sci. Eng. **5**(1), 46–55 (1998). https://doi.org/10.1109/99.660313

8. Dathathri, R., et al.: Gluon: a communication-optimizing substrate for distributed heterogeneous graph analytics. In: Proceedings of the 39th ACM SIGPLAN Conference on Programming Language Design and Implementation (PLDI), pp. 752–768 (2018)

9. Dean, J., Ghemawat, S.: MapReduce: simplified data processing on large clusters. Commun. ACM **51**(1), 107–113 (2008). https://doi.org/10.1145/1327452.1327492. http://doi.acm.org/10.1145/1327452.1327492

10. Forum, M.P.: MPI: a message-passing interface standard. Technical report, Knoxville, TN, USA (1994)

11. Gharaibeh, A., Beltrão Costa, L., Santos-Neto, E., Ripeanu, M.: A yoke of oxen and a thousand chickens for heavy lifting graph processing. In: Proceedings of the 21st International Conference on Parallel Architectures and Compilation Techniques, PACT 2012, pp. 345–354 (2012)

12. Gonzalez, J.E., Low, Y., Gu, H., Bickson, D., Guestrin, C.: PowerGraph: distributed graph-parallel computation on natural graphs. In: 10th USENIX Symposium on Operating Systems Design and Implementation, OSDI 2012, pp. 17–30 (2012)

13. Hong, S., Chafi, H., Sedlar, E., Olukotun, K.: Green-Marl: A DSL for easy and efficient graph analysis. In: Proceedings of the Seventeenth International Conference on Architectural Support for Programming Languages and Operating Systems, ASPLOS XVII, pp. 349–362 (2012)

14. Low, Y., Bickson, D., Gonzalez, G.J., Guestrin, C., Kyrola, A., Hellerstein, J.M.: GraphLab: a new parallel framework for machine learning. In: Conference on Uncertainty in Artificial Intelligence (UAI) (2010)

15. Low, Y., Bickson, D., Gonzalez, J., Guestrin, C., Kyrola, A., Hellerstein, J.M.: Distributed GraphLab: a framework for machine learning and data mining in the cloud. In: Proceedings of the VLDB Endowment, pp. 716–727 (2012)
16. Malewicz, G., et al.: Pregel: a system for large-scale graph processing. In: Proceedings of the ACM SIGMOD International Conference on Management of Data, pp. 135–146 (2010)
17. Meyer, U., Sanders, P.: Delta-stepping: a parallel single source shortest path algorithm. In: Proceedings of the 6th Annual European Symposium on Algorithms, ESA 1998, pp. 393–404. Springer, London (1998). http://dl.acm.org/citation.cfm?id=647908.740136
18. Pai, S., Pingali, K.: A compiler for throughput optimization of graph algorithms on GPUs. In: Proceedings of the 2016 ACM SIGPLAN International Conference on Object-Oriented Programming, Systems, Languages, and Applications, OOPSLA 2016, pp. 1–19 (2016)
19. Pan, Y., Pearce, R., Owens, J.D.: Scalable breadth-first search on a GPU cluster. In: 2018 IEEE International Parallel and Distributed Processing Symposium (IPDPS), pp. 1090–1101 (2018). https://doi.org/10.1109/IPDPS.2018.00118
20. Pingali, K., et al.: The tao of parallelism in algorithms. SIGPLAN Not. **46**(6), 12–25 (2011). https://doi.org/10.1145/1993316.1993501. http://doi.acm.org/10.1145/1993316.1993501
21. Prountzos, D., Manevich, R., Pingali, K.: Elixir: a system for synthesizing concurrent graph programs. In: Proceedings of the ACM International Conference on Object Oriented Programming Systems Languages and Applications, OOPSLA 2012, pp. 375–394 (2012)
22. Rahimian, F., Payberah, A.H., Girdzijauskas, S., Haridi, S.: Distributed vertex-cut partitioning. In: Magoutis, K., Pietzuch, P. (eds.) DAIS 2014. LNCS, vol. 8460, pp. 186–200. Springer, Heidelberg (2014). https://doi.org/10.1007/978-3-662-43352-2_15
23. Upadhyay, N., Patel, P., Cheramangalath, U., Srikant, Y.N.: Large scale graph processing in a distributed environment. In: Heras, D.B., Bougé, L. (eds.) Euro-Par 2017. LNCS, vol. 10659, pp. 465–477. Springer, Cham (2018). https://doi.org/10.1007/978-3-319-75178-8_38
24. Valiant, L.G.: A bridging model for parallel computation. Commun. ACM **33**(8), 103–111 (1990)
25. Whang, J.J., Lenharth, A., Dhillon, I.S., Pingali, K.: Scalable data-driven PageRank: algorithms, system issues, and lessons learned. In: Träff, J.L., Hunold, S., Versaci, F. (eds.) Euro-Par 2015. LNCS, vol. 9233, pp. 438–450. Springer, Heidelberg (2015). https://doi.org/10.1007/978-3-662-48096-0_34
26. White, T.: Hadoop: The Definitive Guide, 1st edn. O'Reilly Media Inc., Sebastopol (2009)
27. Wikipedia contributors: Apache hadoop – Wikipedia, the free encyclopedia. https://en.wikipedia.org/w/index.php?title=Apache_Hadoop&oldid=918989758 (2019). Accessed 3 Oct 2019
28. Wikipedia contributors: PageRank – Wikipedia, the free encyclopedia. https://en.wikipedia.org/w/index.php?title=PageRank&oldid=907975070 (2019). Accessed 11 Aug 2019
29. Xia, Y., Prasanna, V.K.: Topologically adaptive parallel breadth-first search on multicore processors. In: Proceedings of 21st International Conference on Parallel and Distributed Computing Systems, PDCS 2009 (2009)

A Distributed and Trusted Web
of Formal Proofs

Dale Miller[(✉)]

Inria & LIX, École Polytechnique, Palaiseau, France
dale.miller@inria.fr

Abstract. Most computer checked proofs are tied to the particular technology of a prover's software. While sharing results between proof assistants is a recognized and desirable goal, the current organization of theorem proving tools makes such sharing an exception instead of the rule.
In this talk, I argue that we need to turn the current architecture of
proof assistants and formal proofs inside-out. That is, instead of having a few mature theorem provers include within them their formally
checked theorems and proofs, I propose that proof assistants should sit
on the edge of a web of formal proofs and that proof assistant should be
exporting their proofs so that they can exist independently of any theorem prover. While it is necessary to maintain the dependencies between
definitions, theories, and theorems, no explicit library structure should
be imposed on this web of formal proofs. Thus a theorem and its proofs
should not necessarily be located at a particular URL or within a particular prover's library. While the world of symbolic logic and proof theory
certainly allows for proofs to be seen as global and permanent objects,
there is a lot of research and engineering work that is needed to make
this possible. I describe some of the required research and development
that must be done to achieve this goal.

1 Introduction

A great triumph of the World Wide Web is the ease at which anyone can access
a great deal of diverse information. Such information spans a significant por-
tion of human activity, ranging from information that is continuously updating
(e.g., traffic information, flight schedules), to personal data (e.g., social networks,
home security), to academics (e.g., research papers, libraries). A glaring flaw of
the world wide web is that it provides few tools to help consumers of information actually trust the assertions that may be made in documents that are
retrieved from the web. While techniques such as digital signatures can be used
to determine the author of signed information and blockchains can be used to
manage the provenance and timing of sources of information, few techniques are
available to provide trust in what is actually claimed by information sources.

In many cases, we trust certain information sources since we trust the reputa-
tions of the corporations or individuals that generate and distribute that information. However, trust-based on reputation has serious problems since those

D. V. Hung and M. D'Souza (Eds.): ICDCIT 2020, LNCS 11969, pp. 21–40, 2020.
https://doi.org/10.1007/978-3-030-36987-3_2

agents may have their own reasons to make their assertions and this may have little to do with truth: e.g., there is no guarantee that past behavior of an entity forces continued trustworthy behaviors; entities may be wrong about the assertions they make; and many bad actors (e.g., criminals or nation-states) are ubiquitous in our modern networks and attempt to undermine reputable sources. Of course, trusting various agents is critical since trust leads to beliefs, and these can lead to a willingness to take action. For example, by trusting a particular engineering company, you might be willing to fly on the planes that they make. Similarly, trusting in the secure implementation of encryption software can lead one to use such software to communicate financial transactions.

Since so many of our actions today are informed by or rely on electronic and web-based services, trust in those services is a fundamental, societal need. Unfortunately, the news is full of reasons why we should, in fact, not trust our currently designed web-based systems. In particular, there are routine attacks on our information systems using computer viruses, malware, fake news, monitoring back doors, and phishing attacks. Such attacks cause a profound erosion of trust in our communication infrastructure and in the proper functioning of the many institutions (e.g., banks, governments, hospitals, etc.) that operate via that electronic infrastructure.

There are two significant and well-understood sources of permanent trust that have not yet been applied in any significant way to modern electronic infrastructure. One involves the notion of formal (mathematical) proof, and the other is the notion of reproducibility (replication) that is a critical component of the scientific method.

The First Anchor for Trust: Formal Proofs. Formal proofs have helped establish trust in two different epochs. In the late 1800s and early 1900s, there were various crises in the foundations of mathematics: the increasing use of both abstractions and infinitary methods were leading to inconsistencies and to a significant erosion of trust in some areas of mathematics [4]. The logicism project—dating back to Leibniz and continuing with Dedekind, Frege, Russell, and Whitehead—provided an approach to reducing mathematics to logic by insisting on using axioms, inference rules, and formal proofs. One may choose different sets of axioms (e.g., with or without the axiom of excluded middle or of choice) but the existence of a formal proof based on those axioms is a source of trust in mathematics. In the late 1900s and early 2000s, there have been numerous crises in the digital infrastructure used by society: the increasing use of computer systems to operate and control much of society's infrastructure has lead to serious system failures (e.g., Ariane 5, the 2015 Ukrainian power grid attack), data breaches, etc. Such incidents seriously erode the trust in our digital infrastructure and in the institutions built on it. The general topic of *formal methods* has been introduced and studied in order to provide some guarantees about some aspects of computer systems: most aspects of formal methods can be related to logic and formal proofs.[1] Formal proofs about the correctness

---

[1] Even the highly successful formal method of *model checking* can be given a foundation using formal proofs [27].

(or partial correctness) of computer hardware and software can greatly help us trust such hardware and software. While it is difficult to formally prove the full, functional correctness of complex hardware and software systems, it is possible to provide formal proofs of some aspects of such systems: for example, while it might be nearly impossible to prove that a video codex plugin correctly displays video, security concerns might be addressed by proving that plugin touches only narrowly constrained regions of memory (interpreters of binary data streams are typical places where software errors—particularly buffer overflows—can lead to exploits).

In this paper, we shall focus on formal proof and on how they might be shared and used. However, as we now observe, trust in formal proof is intimately tied to trust in proof checkers, which forces us to consider a second source of trust.

The Second Anchor for Trust: Reproducibility. The use of formal proofs as a font of trust faces, however, at least one serious challenge: how do you trust a formal proof? Except for toy examples, formal proofs are generated by computers and can only be checked by computers. Thus, it seems that we must necessarily trust in the correctness of proof checkers, which rely on the processors, operating systems, libraries, compilers, and linkers used to implement them [38]. Since our universal experience with computer programs is that they can be riddled with errors, we can easily doubt proof checkers and, consequently, doubt whether or not a given document is, in fact, a formal proof. This raises the familiar and ancient conundrum "Quis custodiet ipsos custodes?" (Who will guard the guards?). Fortunately, there is a modern approach to addressing this problem: make it possible for anyone and everyone to monitor and audit the guards (proof checkers, in our case). Thus, we need to explicitly invoke the second, foundational approach to trust, which we take directly from the *scientific method*: namely, proof checking needs to be *reproducible* in the sense that it is an activity that any skeptic should be able to undertake.

The seal of the Royal Society enshrines the creed "Nullius in verba" (take no one's word for it): that is, before trusting something, check it for yourself. The goal of this paper is to design an overlay for the World Wide Web that will enable the emergence of open, transparent, permanent, growing, and flexible collections of assertions and theorems. Both of these anchors for trust will be exploited in our design.

After surveying the state-of-the-art in Sect. 2, we briefly discuss the interplay between formal proof and trust in Sect. 3. In Sect. 4, we break down the problem of building a distributed and trusted web of formal proofs into five challenges, each of which is discussed in the next five sections. Finally, in Sect. 10, we describe some of the possible consequences of deploying the infrastructure described in those challenges.

2   State-of-the-Art

The proposal in this paper involves building an overlay on the internet that can be used to distribute formal proofs. At one level, of course, a formal proof is a document and such documents can be hosted and moved around the World Wide Web as if they were any other document, with extensions such as `html` or `pdf`. However, formal proofs do have additional properties that suggest that such an overlay can and should have additional structure. Before we describe this new structure for formal proofs, we first overview several aspects of the current state-of-the-art in the following topics: the World Wide Web, formal proof, and the modeling of trust.

2.1   The World Wide Web

In the matter of a couple of decades, the World Wide Web changed everything about how electronic documents were produced and shared. By designing some protocols and standards (e.g., `HTTP` and `HTML`) as well as some tools (e.g., web browsers), the sharing of documents created a revolution in the way people access information. We point out two lessons learned from the development of the World Wide Web that are particularly relevant to us here.

Standardization Versus Emergence. One of the strengths of the early web was that it developed some standards, but it did not standardize too much. Instead, many features that we now see as integral to our use of the web—ranging from curated sites like Wikipedia to programmable web content based on JavaScript—were left to evolve along their own trajectory. Thus a goal of early standards should be to allow for a diversity of new structures to *emerge* later.

Moving from a Cooperative to an Adversarial Environment. In the beginning, most users of the web were academics who were mainly using this distributed information system in a *cooperative* fashion. If someone found a bug in a protocol or implementation, that bug was reported so it could be fixed; back-doors existed to allow for testing; and information sources such as academic papers, user manuals, etc., communicated true and fact-based information. A decade after the invention of the world wide web, however, we have seen that the web must now defend against adversarial behaviors. Now, if someone finds a bug in a protocol or implementation, that bug can be sold in a market to people interested in exploiting it; back-doors are placed in systems to allow bad actors to infiltrate or remotely monitor those systems; information sources can be lies meant to manipulate voters. Many new techniques—many of them cryptographic in nature—have been invented and deployed in order to provide for authentication, privacy, and transparency.

2.2   Formal Proof

Completely formal proofs of significant theorems are produced by machines and are checked by machines: they are not meant for direct human consumption. Occasionally, a human can create and/or read a formal proof but that is the exception: formal proofs are meant for machines. Similarly, calculations can be done without machines, but far fewer would be done, and it would be hard to trust a human to do the correct sequence of steps every time. In the adversarial world of the World Wide Web, formal proofs can also be used to guarantee that certain classes of errors do not occur in software and hardware systems: sometimes, it is possible to declare a system to be *hacker-proof* [42].

Discovering and building formal proofs has often been considered a source of trust in both mathematics—as argued by Voevodsky [45]—and software systems—which is a theme of D. MacKenzie's book *Mechanizing Proof: Computing, Risk, and Trust* [31]. We describe here a few examples of how formal proofs and proof checking have been or are currently being used, supported, and standardized.

Proof-Carrying Code. The proof-carrying code (PCC) project [35] is an important precursor for our goals in this paper. The PCC project stressed that trust in programs distributed as byte code could be based on actual formal properties of the distributed file and not on the authority which may have signed it. While the PCC project targeted a narrow application (mobile code for insertion into operating system kernels) and had a narrow perspective on proofs (dependently typed λ-terms and oracle strings [36]), its use of formal proofs was, in large part, independent of the technology that created them: as such, their proof certificates could be checked by third-party checkers, which results in greater trustworthiness. Various follow-on efforts were also pursued where formal proofs and proof checking was attached to authentication [8], access control [12], and a file system [24].

Frameworks for Logics and Proofs. The exact nature of what is accepted as formal proofs has been a long-standing debate, and it has spawned lots of work on *logical frameworks* [37] as well as *mathematical knowledge management* systems and frameworks [20]. Clearly, certain well understood and flexible logics should be accepted by any framework: these include, for example, first-order classical and intuitionistic logics. Various additional axioms might well be added, accounting for set theory, arithmetic (Peano or Heyting), category theory, and even various type theories. Various people have built frameworks for expressing many logics in an ecumenical fashion [18,25,30,40]. The *QED manifesto* [6,26] described the value of formalizing a great deal of mathematics and proposed a vision in which the world's many theorem provers would work together to help construct that formalization.

Specialized and General-Purpose Proof Certificates. There have been a few attempts at defining computer-based representations of proofs that are output from theorem provers (automatic or interactive) for the expressed purpose of being checked by an independent proof checker. Such representations of proofs are often referred to as *proof certificates*: that is, documents that contain sufficient details for the complete construction of a formal proof. The SAT solver and term rewriting communities have developed special-purpose certificates for particular classes of theorems: DRUP/DRAT for SAT solvers [46] and CPF for term rewriting [23]. The Dedukti proof checker [10,11] targets provers working in intuitionistic arithmetic while the *Foundational Proof Certificate* (FPC) framework [21] targets more generally classical and intuitionistic logic and arithmetic.

2.3 Modeling Trust

As we shall discuss more in Sect. 3, a basic notion of *trust* is intertwined with formal proof. We mention here some topics related to trust below.

Chain-of-Trust. An important mechanism for ensuring trust in today's digital infrastructure uses the *chain-of-trust* ideas: here, a trusted principal (named by a *root certificate*) is used to anchor and to sign other principals that it deems as trustworthy. Two such chains-of-trust in use in systems today are the *public key infrastructure* (PKI) (used to secure web browser sessions) and the UEFI Secure Boot (used to secure the loading of trusted firmware and operating system components on computers). Although such an approach to trust is fundamental in today's world wide web architecture, this approach is based not on the content of signed documents but on reputation: e.g., in the UEFI secure boot framework, one trusts binaries not because we know them to be "safe" but because Microsoft has signed them.

Modal Logics for Modeling Trust Relations. It is possible to model more sophisticated organizations of trust relationships than those simply given by chain-like constructions. In particular, one might be interested in hypothetically trusting a principal and then see what flows from it. Such reasoning is required for the modular construction of software that could be part of a chain-of-trust. In fact, the notion that proof checking should be reproducible means that one presumably only trusts a theorem if *several* independent proof checkers are able to certify it: no one "root" proof checker is meant to be universally trusted. Modal logics, such as access control logic [2] and authorization logic [41], have been used to model such trusting relationships in a number of computer science settings.

Trust Management Systems. While the most basic notion of trust is central here, more general questions about how to manage trust will be left for elaboration in later work. We shall use formal method techniques as a way to *initiate* trust: this is in contrast to the work by, say Carbone, Nielsen, and Sassone [19], where formal methods are used to *manage* trust. We shall also not consider questions such as the *degree* of trust or whether or not trust is transitivity [39].

3   Formal Proof and Trust

In mathematics, a careful proof provides trust in a theorem. With such trust, we take actions such as publishing a paper, starting a new research effort, or building a physical object that we expect to work in a specific fashion. The checking of the correctness of a proof is a central activity of any discipline that makes use of proofs, particularly, mathematical proofs. Humans (e.g., reviewers) are often used as proof checkers. We have seen in recent years, important limits to what humans are capable of doing with proofs. Voevodsky [45] documents errors that were found in a series of mathematical papers. Also, many proofs are massive in size and complexity, and having humans check such proofs for correctness seems both impossible and counterproductive (would you really trust a group of humans to get every detail checked carefully in such large, technical proofs?).

Recent decades have witnessed a rise in the use of formal proofs for various purposes. One such use of formal proofs allows for large and complex mathematical proofs (of, say, the Feit-Thompson Theorem) to be checked with a level of detail not usually achieved by humans. Formal proofs have also been built for mathematical theorems that humans would find nearly impossible to check carefully (for example, the proof of the Kepler conjecture and of the four color theorem). Finally, it seems that only formal proof will allow us to prove various properties of software and hardware systems.

For our purposes here, a formal proof is a document (a computer file) that contains enough information so that a relatively simple proof checker can construct a fully formal proof in a well-established style of proof, such as Frege-style proofs, sequent calculus proofs, natural deduction proofs, tableaux proofs, or resolution refutations. If such documents are structured so that all the information needed to build explicit proofs are present, then proof checkers can be simple and small programs. On the other hand, if such documents contain only some information about a proof, then a proof checker will need to be able to reconstruct the missing details: such checkers are more complex pieces of software. In either case, however, formal proofs are documents that are produced by machines (sometimes as the result of interactions with humans) and that are checked by machines. In general, we do not expect humans to read, understand, and check a formal proof.

It seems that we must, therefore, trust in the correctness of proof checkers and the computer systems on which they are implemented. As we argued in Sect. 1, the reproducibility of proof checking is required. While proof checking depends on technology, it should not be dependent on any specific technology. Fifty years from now, when computer hardware and programming language technologies have radically changed, it should be possible to rebuild proof checkers on that newer technology so that a future skeptic can recheck proofs.

Of course, to communicate a proof to, say, a skeptic 50 years from now will require some carefully defined standards for describing formulas and their proofs need to exist. Both logical inference and formal proof have been studied extensively during the past several decades for first-order and higher-order versions of classical and intuitionistic logics. For example, the notion of a theorem in first-order logic can be described in multiple ways, including using model theory and using a variety of proof structures. Furthermore, there are numerous papers about and implementations of the basic algorithms that underlie proof search and proof checking. It is easy to find notions of formalized reasoning that are not ad hoc and temporary: anyone 50 years from now will be able to understand exactly the same notion of theorem as we understand today. That foundation provides the basis for writing a clear, flexible, and permanent definition of the structure of formulas and proofs.

Some communities within the computational logic field have already been establishing such standardize certificate formats. For example, researchers building systems that determine whether or not a propositional formula is satisfiable have designed various standardized proof certificate formats than their search programs can output. These formats have names such as DRUP [28] and DRAT [46], and anyone can build rather simple checkers that can check if a file in one of these formats actually describes a proof. Other researchers working in rewriting systems have designed the CPF proof certificate format [43] that can be used to check whether or not a given rewrite system is terminating or confluent. The logical framework LF [25,37] has been used by a number of projects as a general setting for storing and certifying proof structures [7,8,12,24,35,48].

In a distributed world of formal proofs, one must expect there to be a great diversity of proof systems that would be tied to different theorem provers, and those proof would like all have different structures. If we need to trust a large number of different proof checkers in order to treat a large number of proof formats, it is hard to see how we have improved trust in proof checking. Presently, there are at least two broad-spectrum proof certificates formats that are being developed. The Dedukti system [10,11] mixes functional programming style rewriting with dependently typed λ-calculus to provide a proof certificate for an increasing number of theorem provers working in higher-order intuitionistic logic. The *foundational proof certificates* framework [21,33] uses logic programming techniques to check a range of proof systems in classical and intuitionistic logics by allowing for proof reconstruction during proof checking. In both of these cases, the underlying proof checking technology is based on well-defined and understood computational logic frameworks: skeptics 50 years from now will be able to read the associated literature, build their own proof checker, and recheck any proof certificates written in these technology-independent formats.

4   A Web of Proofs and Its Challenges

A perspective on how to organize a global and distributed collection of formal proofs is given in Fig. 1. Several attributes of web-style distribution are listed on the left of that figure: these attributes are divided into two sets of rows. The first set of rows deals with infrastructure, and the second set of rows deals with emergent structures. The middle column describes the values given to those attributes when one considers the standard world wide web of documents. Hopefully, all the items listed in that column are familiar to the reader. The third column imagines how those attributes are changed in order to provide a possible treatment of a global and distributed collection of formal proofs. Our main goal here is to focus on describing an infrastructure that could support a global, distributed, and trustworthy treatment of formal proofs.

We now list five challenges that seem appropriate for attacking this problem of a global and distributed web of formal proofs.

Web	of documents	of formal proofs
Standards and infrastructure		
Documents	Files in various formats	Proofs in various formats
Standards	SGML, HTML, XML, etc	FPC, Dedukti, CPF, DRUP, etc
Naming	URI, DOI	Content addressable storage (CAS)
Transport	HTTP, FTP	In addition: IPFS
Trust	certificate authorities, open source code, encryption, public logs, etc	In addition: *reputation* (e.g., signed by Coq 8.1) and *reproducibility* (rechecking proof evidence)
Emergent structures		
Access	browsers, JavaScript	proof browsers, interaction with proofs
Curation	Wikipedia, etc	proof libraries, textbooks

Fig. 1. Comparing the World Wide Web for documents with what is proposed for proofs

Challenge 1: Permanent electronic documents. This challenge deals with supporting the signing of almost any kind of assertion and with making such a signed file globally available. A wide range of assertions should be treatable by any implementation of this challenge: for example, a news article (written in a natural language) could be signed by its author, and that article and its signature should be available universally. In that general setting, assertions are not assumed to be logical expressions, and formal proofs may not exist. None-the-less, it might be possible to have trust in such signed texts.

Challenge 2: Structuring libraries of theorems and their proofs. This challenge commits to representing assertions as logical expressions and addresses the issue of assembling and structuring collections of proved formulas into theories and libraries. The infrastructure underlying this challenge can be deployed in a setting where formal proofs are absent or where their structure is not used.

Challenge 3: Operating on proofs. This challenge proposes to develop tools and services—beyond proof checking—that can be applied to a range of proofs. This challenge requires working with details about the structure of formal proofs.

Challenge 4: Replication in experimental science. This challenge takes a particular aspect of formal proof, namely the direct specification of computation, and applies it to the problem of describing clearly the data and computations that are used within research in experimental mathematics and science. Formal proof checking could then be used to directly check and certify at least some of the computational and argumentative judgments that go into forming scientific conclusions from scientific observations.

Challenge 5: Deployment. This challenge considers the initial steps in attempting to deploy the framework we have proposed.

Each of these challenges will be addressed in the following five sections. These challenges have been sorted to reflect their dependency on the specifics of formal proofs. In particular, Challenge 1 needs little to no information about the structure of formal proofs, while Challenge 5 is specifically about implementing proof structure.

5   Challenge 1: Permanent Electronic Documents

Assume for the moment that we have suitable standards for capturing a formal proof in a computer file. Such a file will likely contain declarations of the constants and definitions and previously proved results that are needed in that proof. Since a foundational motivation for logic and proof is to be universal and technology-independent, such a file could exist outside of any specific library for a theorem prover or outside some specific tree structure based at some root URL. That is, a proof document could simply exist anywhere and everywhere. This leads us to the following task.

Task 1: Design a Global and Permanent Collection of Signed Documents. The usual approach to ensuring wide-spread access to a document is to locate them in a specific directory tree on a specific machine or web service using, say, a URL. Such a storage scheme has several problems: such machines or web services need to be trusted (so that they do not alter stored documents), and directory trees and servers often change over time. A different kind of storage mechanism which addresses those two issues is the so-called *content-addressable storage (CAS)* in which the hash of a file is its name. A start on an appropriate CAS facility can be found in the Interplanetary File System (IPFS) [13]. In such a system, one requests a file by using its hash. As a result, it is easy to confirm that the file that is retrieved from actually has the required hash: as a result, we can have a high assurance that the file was not modified during storage and transfer. Also, if that file is cached locally using its hash as its name, one never needs to return to the distribution system to check for a new version of the file: another version would, of course, have a different name (i.e., hash).[2]

Another key component of representing proof objects is the *assertion* that, in fact, a particular document contains a valid proof. It is the job of *proof checkers* to check a document and to assert that document contains a valid proof of the proposed theorem (also contained in the proof document). The act of an agent claiming to have proved a theorem or checked a proof can be modeled using cryptographic signing techniques (e.g., using public keys). Signing is usually done by a human or organization (collectively called *principals*). In particular, a given proof checker does not sign a document with its private key: instead, it would need to sign it with the private key of the principal that executes that checker. Since there is no way to be certain that a proof checker is not manipulated, we really need to trust the operator of the proof checker to be doing the appropriate

---

[2] We can assume that hashes are computed on the text contained in files: we do not rely on the more sophisticated notions of homomorphic hashes [9].

and trustworthy validation steps with a proof checker. A good starting point for such signing is employing the public key infrastructure of private/public asymmetric encryption: principals are identified with their public key, and any assertions that principals make are contained within cryptographically signed documents.

Assume that a principal has encryption key K. When K signs an assertion, say, A, we write $[P \ says \ A]$. Such an assertion is another (small) document that should be added to the CAS facility so that it is, in principle, available to anyone. The fact that such signed assertions are globally available plays an important role in the transparency of this system: if one eventually finds out that a principal asserted that a non-theorem is provable, the willingness of people to trust that principal would be questioned.

For our purposes here, we consider the following three kinds of assertions. The assertion $\vdash B$ is simply the statement that the formula B is provable. The assertion $\Xi \vdash B$ is the statement that the proof certificate Ξ was checked and lead to a formal proof of B. Finally, we should allow various kinds of meta-data M to be included in signed assertions, for example, $M, \Xi \vdash B$: such meta-data could include the time of the checking, the version number of the software used to do the checking, etc. If I have a file that encodes the signed file $[P_1 \ says \ \vdash B]$, do I trust that B is, in fact, a proper theorem? If I am skeptical, I could try to use a different theorem prover, say, P_2, and get it to prove B: in that case, the additional signed file $[P_2 \ says \ A]$ would appear. Having two theorem provers declare a formula to be a theorem might, in many cases, provide enough evidence to trust their assertion. Since theorem proving is a difficult task in most domains, it would be much more useful to attempt to reproduce signed documents of the form $[P_1 \ says \ \Xi \vdash B]$ since I could attempt to find another proof checker P_2 and use it to assert $[P_2 \ says \ \Xi \vdash B]$. On the other hand, meta-data is likely to be information that cannot be rechecked, and one either chooses to trust it or not.

Task 2: Select a Modal Logic for Tracking Trust. Critical to being able to use the global library of signed documents is the need to track principals, particularly, those which a given principal chooses to trust or not. I may choose to trust a particular authority: e.g., I might trust any theorem that I was able to prove using a particular version of the Coq theorem prover [15]. Clearly, one's rules for trusting some principals must be something that is made explicit and trackable. Within the general setting of epistemic logics for knowledge and belief [29], there are various modal logics that can be used for such tracking. The logics DCC (by Abadi [1]) and NAL (by Schneider et al. [41]) are candidates for initial development. The fundamental modal operator here will likely be $[P \ says \ A]$, meaning that principal P (identified by its public key) asserts the statement A. The global collection of signed documents provide precisely the semantics for that modal statement.

A consequence of Tasks 1 and 2 should be a permanent, transparent, and trackable infrastructure for publishing signed assertions. This framework will provide rudimentary support for trusting agents and the documents that they sign. Note that this infrastructure would work independently from the exact specification of formal proof.

6   Challenge 2: Structuring Libraries of Theorems and Their Proofs

Unlike most approaches to building proof assistants, we will view libraries of theorems and proofs as an *emergent* aspect of collecting theorems and proofs. In a similar fashion, Wikipedia is an emergent feature of the underlying structure of the basic protocols (URI, HTTP, HTML, etc.) of the web. Any number of people should be able to curate their own specific libraries or textbooks from the growing, dynamic collection of theorems and proofs. Andrews's commentary [5] on the QED manifesto [6] is worth repeating: many logics and proof systems should be allowed to exist, and future users of formalized proofs should be the ones to determine which logics and proof systems dominate (if any).

The dependency of one set of theorems to help establish another set of theorems can be captured (as a consequence of using CAS) as a Merkle tree, a structure that guarantees non-cyclic dependency [32]. A more crucial aspect of library building is the problem of *sharing*. When assembling a library (or a textbook), one wishes never to repeat the same theorem within a collection of theorems and one is willing to do significant work to ensure that as much proof structure and as many lemmas as possible are reused and not repeated. But libraries of theorems and proofs are not just *any* collection of theorems and proofs, and their large-scale structure needs to be understood.

Task 3: Understand the large scale structure of theories and proofs. One of the first emergent structures that will appear is that of *theory*. Several theories—set theory, type theory, higher-order logic—have already emerged within the study of the logical foundations of mathematics. Most existing theorem provers have one of these theories built into their foundation. To be liberated from their technologies, such theories must be clearly identified, categorized, and referenced consistently.

An important test of a good structuring of signed assertions is the possibility of rich notions of *sharing*. By sharing, we mean more than simply making theorems and proofs available to others: rather, we also mean that we will need to provide means for proofs to be *reused*. Since the late 1960's and the start of de Bruijn's Automath system [17], it has been recognized that libraries in mathematics can be seen as large-scale λ-terms. When λ-terms are used in writing computer programs (as in Lisp or ML), identifying sharing is generally seen as not worth the effort. As we mentioned above, when assembling a library or textbook, one often commits a great deal of energy into making certain that the same theorem or proof is not repeated. The use of Merkle trees within the CAS setting makes reuse of textually equal documents a triviality: we are, of course, interested in making certain that semantically equal assertions are reused.

Task 4: Determine how to do binding in highly distributed proof libraries. A key component of most sophisticated reasoning is the use of bound variables at the level of proof structures: these are called *eigenvariables* by Gentzen and λ-bound variables by most logical frameworks). While this concept of proof-level-binding is treated well in modern proof systems, when we need bindings to work in a highly distributed setting, an entirely new approach to such bindings must be taken. A good starting point for this kind of binding construction is the cryptographic constructions describe by Abadi, Fournet, and Gonthier in [3] and by Comon and Koutsos in [22].

These tasks will uncover the structure needed to organize large-scale permanent and trusted libraries of named documents. Some aspects of logic and proof—namely the need for uniquely naming assumptions and parameters—will be needed for here.

7   Challenge 3: Operating on Proofs

By viewing proofs as structures with well-defined properties, a rich collection of services on formal proofs can be provided. Computing directly with formal proofs can greatly increase their value beyond the initial intent of certifying their correctness.

Task 5: Develop support for foundation-independent proofs. During the past several decades, a number of different foundations for mathematical reasoning have been proposed and implemented. Foundations such as set theory, type theory, category theory, and higher-order logic have all played a role in anchoring mathematical reasoning to axioms and inference rules. In the choice of logic, there is also the familiar choice that needs to be made between classical and intuitionistic logics, particularly when dealing with infinity and undecidable propositions. In mathematical and computer science practice, however, there is a great deal of formal argumentation that can be done independent of exactly what foundations one picks: that is, much of mathematics can be established via "foundation-less proofs": for example, a proof in number theory of, say, Fermat's Little Theorem can be done without much regard to exactly which foundations one is using. Since such proofs are critical to preserve, we need to find ways to structure different proof environments to provide different ways to anchor such foundation-less proofs into different theories of foundations. It is also the case that the same theorem may have many different proofs and that these different proofs may have a range of different uses. For example, some proofs might be structured with interesting abstractions that make them easier for humans to read; other proofs might have a great deal of detail added to make them easier to check; still other proofs might be structured so that their constructive content is more apparent; and still other proofs might discard many details so that they become more like proof outlines that could also serve as proofs of related theorems.

This issue of "foundation-less proofs" is rather similar to the way software is often organized: computer programs are often organized around an application program interface (API). That is, an application program expects to use a particular interface with lower-level operating system features and is not expected to break the interface abstraction to code directly using low-level features of an operating system or run-time system. As a result of obeying that interface, the code could execute properly on many different hardware and operating systems.

Task 6: Demonstrate proof-checking-as-a-service. The proof certificates produced by theorem proving systems generally pose trade-offs for proof checkers. Certificates can provide a great deal of detail, which makes them simple to check but makes them large and hard to reuse. On the other hand, they can be compact and contain just essential details: in that case, proof checking requires doing some proof reconstruction [34], which can be computationally expensive. In either case, proof checking can be a challenge for many computer systems to perform: this could be particularly true of mobile phones. Of course, some principal, say Lib, could play the role of curating only assertions that its own proof checker can check. When a third-party vendor, say Vendor, wants to sell an application to a mobile phone customer who has certain (published) security requirements, the vendor may contract and pay Lib to certify its formal proofs that its applications meet those security requirements. The mobile phone would only then need to check the existence of a signed assertion from Lib that it has checked that the application satisfies the required security requirements. In such a setup, if, for some reason, Lib is not considered trustworthy (such as the discovery that Lib had once signed a non-theorem), another proof checking principal could be substituted.

Task 7: Develop a range of operations on proofs. Many valuable operations on proofs can be performed by proof checkers. For example, many proofs encode algorithms, and a proof checker can be used to execute those algorithms. For another example specific to the FPC style of proof certificate: during the process of checking an implicit proof certificate (one with few details), a proof checker must fill in all missing details, a step that usually requires sophisticated mechanisms such as unification and backtracking search [16]. The resulting detailed proof can then be check by a simple-to-write-and-trust proof checker, thereby alleviating the need to trust the more sophisticated proof checker. Distilling information from a proof (the converse of elaboration) is also an important service that proof checkers can provide: for example, distilling can extract the set of assumptions used in a proof, the number of times such assumptions have been used, the instances at which certain assumptions are used, etc.

Task 8: Develop tools for interacting with proofs. It is the rare formal proof that can be printed in such a way that beginners and experts can understand it. It seems much more likely, however, that people could learn from a formal proof by *interacting* with it via a *proof browser*: such a tool would allow a proof to be explored incrementally and partially. For example, someone might learn a lot from a proof if they could analyze only one of many cases, or use the proof to compute a specific witness given a user-provided input. Since proof checkers written using the FPC framework [21] are capable of elaborating proof certificates into fully detailed sequent calculus proofs, the rich meta-theory surrounding sequent calculus (in particular, the cut-elimination theorem) is available to provide for such dynamic and rich interactions.

8   Challenge 4: Replication in Experimental Science

In their most general setting, theorems and proofs can include both data and programs. Capturing reasoning steps as well as data and programs, is a major challenge today in what is often called the *replication crisis*. A treatment of formal proofs must necessarily provide a setting where this problem is addressed. Treating formal proofs is rather general and possibly naive, but it will provide a framework that can be elaborated and optimized. Central to the application of this framework to the experimental sciences is the ability to describe computations and data as parts of proofs (a concept familiar to such theorem provers as Coq, Agda, and Isabelle) as well as support novel kinds of inference such as those used in statistical reasoning. The modern view of *formal proof* makes it possible to incorporate all these aspects of reasoning in such scientific domains.

The *replication crisis*, a term coined in the early 2010s, arose when many researchers found it difficult or impossible to replicate the published results in areas of psychology, medicine, and computational and experimental mathematics [44]. Since replication of results is a cornerstone of our trust in science, the trustworthiness of these scientific areas has been called into question. Of the various methods for addressing this crisis, the one that is most directly related involves encouraging researchers to publish their experimental data and their software for analysis along with their papers announcing their results. For example, the Open Science Framework (osf.io) and the Life Sciences Protocol Repository (www.protocols.io) provide a platform for scientists to collaborate in an open setting and where various (proprietary) technologies (Dropbox, Google Drive, etc.) are linkable. While such a framework provides much-needed transparency, no technology-independent definition of computation and reasoning steps are provided.

Task 9: Address the replication problem in experimental science. Both the terms "reproducibility" and "replication" are used in the literature: we use the latter term here to mean redoing an experiment and gather new data; the former term will be targeted at rechecking the computations and arguments made on the results of an experiment. The modern view of formal proof is so general that it encompasses the specification of data and programs. The inference rules commonly used in scientific reasoning involving experimentation—for example, probabilistic and statistical reasoning—would need to be captured as inference rules in (mathematical) logic. In the end, the formal documents that are proofs can serve a dual purpose: they can be executed and validated by the many proof checkers we will have available, and they can serve as a simple, clear, and precise descriptions of data, computations, and reasoning steps. Given their formal encoding, such calculations and reasoning steps can be reproduced by others, even without reference to the large machinery of proof into which they sit.

Our formal proof setting will necessarily provide a transparent and permanent means of communicating the results, computations, and reasoning steps that represent the analysis of scientific experiments. As a result, this framework should, in principle, provide a formal approach to replication in the scientific setting.

9   Challenge 5: Deployment

A major challenge to this project is to make it possible for implementers and developers of theorem provers to export their proofs and libraries so independent systems can check them and import proofs from the global and permanent collection of checked assertions. We consider just one task associated with deployment.

Task 10: Build a prover that simply links other proofs. Design and build a theorem prover that does not have significant proof search methods of its own: its main job is to link proofs (via an established white-list of trusted agents) and make conclusions. Such a prover could be used to build large outlines in a distributed fashion. We might allow an agent, called "wild-guess" to sign a formula and, if we allow that agent to be trusted (at least temporarily), then we might be able to complete a large scale proof. Of course, one eventually wants to have additional proofs added so that anything signed by wild-guess is eliminated. Tracking provenance is central here.

10   Planned Versus Emergent Structures

The world wide web started with the deployment of a few extensions to internet protocols (e.g., the transport protocol HTTP and the document format HTML) and a few tools (e.g., browsers such as NCSA Mosaic and Netscape Navigator). It is a remarkable feature of the web that so many new structures have emerged that exploit the original standards (and their descendants). If Tim Berners-Lee had over-designed the early web systems so that it was just intended to be a large distributed hypertext library of research-oriented results and papers, then there would probably have been a significant delay in building what we now know as the web, especially since only a small community would have initially been interested in that particular application. By leaving much of the framework open, a great diversity of people and projects—far from providing a library of academic results—was able to flourish.

Linking formal proof and trust is not a new theme, of course. For example, it is part of the vision of the *semantic web* [14]. Two prior efforts at doing this over-specified their target application areas (at least in hindsight) and, as a result, their potential as a framework was limited. For example, the work on Proof-Carrying Code (PCC) [35], mentioned in Sect. 2.2, used formal proof to deal with trust but limited the application areas to the execution of untrusted code on mobile devices. Similarly, the 1984 QED manifesto [6,26] proposed the construction of a computer-based database of all mathematical knowledge, along with checked, formalized proofs. The intended audience for this manifesto was "working mathematicians". One of the reasons offered by Wiedijk [47] for why this project failed in this particular goal was that there is currently no compelling application for fully mechanized mathematics among working mathematicians. (As mentioned in Sect. 3, Voevodsky [45] is a recent counterexample, since he was a working mathematician with a compelling reason to mechanize parts of mathematics.)

Instead of over-designing, we should let things emerge (given that the right infrastructure is in place). Calling out the QED manifesto again, we can illustrate two examples of over-designing.

1. QED blended the need for formal proofs with concerns about the human readability of formal proofs. In contrast, this proposal makes the simplifying assumption that formal proofs are meant for machines. Human reading and understanding of formal proofs are left as an activity that should emerge (see Sect. 7). Also, having all proofs understood by humans in a "working mathematics" setting might be appropriate, it is certainly not desirable in a more general setting. For example, the proof that a specific device driver never touches memory outside certain boundaries might be extremely important to have in some settings, but one would not necessarily expect a human to read, check, or understand that proof.
2. The topics that get formalized within this framework should be expected to arise organically, from compelling community needs. At the end of the QED manifesto, however, the suggestion was that it might be good to work on ring theory. But it is hard to know what topics are compelling. For example, one might make the argument that formal proofs about cryptology might be an important starting point for building trust in our digital world. Such a focus on that might then lead organically to a need to formalize parts of number theory. The importance of ring theory might eventually arise, for example, as a useful way to organize some of the theorems and proofs surrounding number theory.

11 Concluding Remarks

In the areas of mathematics and software correctness, we might be tempted to say that trust begins with a formal proof. But the reality is that formal proofs are not known to be correct without the execution of a proof checker. Thus, trust must also be based on the correct execution of a possibly complex software and hardware system: that is, trust must also be based on *reputation* (in this case, on the computer system checking a proof). Thus, our starting point is that assertions are signed by a principal (an individual or an institution). Rudimentary forms of trust are then possible by simply providing a white-list of principals whom we may trust. While an approach to trust-based only on the reputation of principals is a requirement in the grand scheme, it also has serious weaknesses. A stronger form of trust arises by examining any *evidence of proof* (e.g., a formal proof or a proof certificate which can be elaborated into a formal proof), since it is possible for skeptics to write their own proof checker and check that the assertion is, in fact, a valid proof. Trust can thus be based on the *reproducibility* of checking.

Given this interplay between formal proof and trust, we have described a setting in which formal proofs can be distributed and trusted in a web-like network. This proposal attempts to turn the world of theorem proving inside-out: the provers that now form the center of the world for their users will be placed at the periphery of a web that will be focused on accumulating and reusing the results of those many provers. As a result, this framework should support any number of theorem provers since they only need to be able to export their proofs in a way that some trusted proof checkers can certify. In the process of reshaping that world, we needed to address also a number of issues—principals signing assertions, transparency, and global access—that provides an integrated infrastructure that might also be used in journalism as well as experimental sciences.

References

1. Abadi, M.: Access control in a core calculus of dependency. Electr. Notes Theor. Comput. Sci **172**, 5–31 (2007)
2. Abadi, M.: Variations in access control logic. In: van der Meyden, R., van der Torre, L. (eds.) DEON 2008. LNCS (LNAI), vol. 5076, pp. 96–109. Springer, Heidelberg (2008). https://doi.org/10.1007/978-3-540-70525-3_9
3. Abadi, M., Fournet, C., Gonthier, G.: Secure implementation of channel abstractions. Inf. Comput. **174**(1), 37–83 (2002)
4. Alexander, A.: Infinitesimal: How a Dangerous Mathematical Theory Shaped the Modern World. Oneworld Publications, London (2014)
5. Andrews, P.B.: Accept diversity, August 1994. http://mizar.org/qed/mail-archive/volume-2/0199.html
6. Anonymous: The QED manifesto. In: Bundy, A. (ed.) 12th International Conference on Automated Deduction, LNAI, vol. 814, pp. 238–251. Springer, Nancy, France, June 1994
7. Appel, A.W.: Foundational proof-carrying code. In: 16th Symposium on Logic in Computer Science, pp. 247–258 (2001)
8. Appel, A.W., Felten, E.W.: Proof-carrying authentication. In: Proceedings of the 6th ACM Conference on Computer and Communications Security, pp. 52–62. ACM (1999)
9. Armknecht, F., et al.: A guide to fully homomorphic encryption. Cryptology ePrint Archive, Report 2015/1192 (2015). https://eprint.iacr.org/2015/1192
10. Assaf, A., Burel, G.: Translating HOL to Dedukti. In: Kaliszyk, C., Paskevich, A. (eds.) Proceedings of the Fourth Workshop on Proof eXchange for Theorem Proving, PxTP 2015, EPTCS, Berlin, Germany, 2–3 August 2015, vol. 186, pp. 74–88 (2015). http://dx.doi.org/10.4204/EPTCS.186
11. Assaf, A., et al.: Expressing theories in the $\lambda\Pi$-calculus modulo theory and in the Dedukti system. In: TYPES: Types for Proofs and Programs. Novi Sad, Serbia (2016)
12. Bauer, L.: Access control for the web Via. Ph.D. thesis, Princeton University, 30 September 2003. http://www.ece.cmu.edu/lbauer/papers/thesis.pdf

13. Benet, J.: IPFS-content addressed, versioned, P2P file system (2014)
14. Berners-Lee, T.: Semantic Web road map. Technical report, W3C Design Issues (1998). http://www.w3.org/DesignIssues/Semantic.html
15. Bertot, Y., Castéran, P.: Interactive Theorem Proving and Program Development. Coq'Art: The Calculus of Inductive Constructions. Texts in Theoretical Computer Science. Springer, Heidelberg (2004). http://www.labri.fr/publications/l3a/2004/BC04
16. Blanco, R., Chihani, Z., Miller, D.: Translating between implicit and explicit versions of proof. In: de Moura, L. (ed.) CADE 2017. LNCS (LNAI), vol. 10395, pp. 255–273. Springer, Cham (2017). https://doi.org/10.1007/978-3-319-63046-5_16
17. de Bruijn, N.G.: A survey of the project AUTOMATH. In: Seldin, J.P., Hindley, R. (eds.) To H.B.Curry: Essays in Combinatory Logic, Lambda Calculus, and Formalism, pp. 589–606. Academic Press, New York (1980)
18. de Bruijn, N.G.: A plea for weaker frameworks. In: Huet, G., Plotkin, G. (eds.) Logical Frameworks, pp. 40–67. Cambridge University Press, Cambridge (1991)
19. Carbone, M., Nielsen, M., Sassone, V.: A formal model for trust in dynamic networks. In: SEFM, p. 54. IEEE Computer Society (2003)
20. Carette, J., Farmer, W.M.: A review of mathematical knowledge management. In: Carette, J., Dixon, L., Coen, C.S., Watt, S.M. (eds.) CICM 2009. LNCS (LNAI), vol. 5625, pp. 233–246. Springer, Heidelberg (2009). https://doi.org/10.1007/978-3-642-02614-0_21
21. Chihani, Z., Miller, D., Renaud, F.: A semantic framework for proof evidence. J. Autom. Reasoning 59(3), 287–330 (2017). https://doi.org/10.1007/s10817-016-9380-6
22. Comon, H., Koutsos, A.: Formal computational unlinkability proofs of RFID protocols. In: 2017 IEEE 30th Conference on Computer Security Foundations Symposium (CSF), pp. 100–114. IEEE (2017)
23. Certification problem format (2015). http://cl-informatik.uibk.ac.at/software/cpf/
24. Garg, D., Pfenning, F.: A proof-carrying file system. In: 2010 IEEE Symposium on Security and Privacy, pp. 349–364. IEEE (2010)
25. Harper, R., Honsell, F., Plotkin, G.: A framework for defining logics. J. ACM 40(1), 143–184 (1993)
26. Harrison, J., Urban, J., Wiedijk, F.: Preface: twenty years of the QED manifesto. J. Formaliz. Reasoning 9(1), 1–2 (2016)
27. Heath, Q., Miller, D.: A proof theory for model checking. J. Autom. Reasoning 63(4), 857–885 (2019). https://doi.org/10.1007/s10817-018-9475-3
28. Heule, M.J.H., Hunt, W.A., Wetzler, N.: Expressing symmetry breaking in DRAT proofs. In: Felty, A.P., Middeldorp, A. (eds.) CADE 2015. LNCS (LNAI), vol. 9195, pp. 591–606. Springer, Cham (2015). https://doi.org/10.1007/978-3-319-21401-6_40
29. Hintikka, J.: Knowledge and Belief: An Introduction into the Logic of the Two Notions. Cornell University Press, Ithaca (1962)
30. Kohlhase, M., Rabe, F.: QED reloaded: towards a pluralistic formal library of mathematical knowledge. J. Formaliz. Reasoning 9(1), 201–234 (2016)
31. MacKenzie, D.: Mechanizing Proof. MIT Press, Cambridge (2001)
32. Merkle, R.C.: A digital signature based on a conventional encryption function. In: Pomerance, C. (ed.) CRYPTO 1987. LNCS, vol. 293, pp. 369–378. Springer, Heidelberg (1988). https://doi.org/10.1007/3-540-48184-2_32
33. Miller, D.: A proposal for broad spectrum proof certificates. In: Jouannaud, J.-P., Shao, Z. (eds.) CPP 2011. LNCS, vol. 7086, pp. 54–69. Springer, Heidelberg (2011). https://doi.org/10.1007/978-3-642-25379-9_6

34. Miller, D.: Proof checking and logic programming. Formal Aspects Comput. **29**(3), 383–399 (2017). https://doi.org/10.1007/s00165-016-0393-z
35. Necula, G.C.: Proof-carrying code. In: Conference Record of the 24th Symposium on Principles of Programming Languages, vol. 97, pp. 106–119. ACM Press, Paris, France (1997)
36. Necula, G.C., Rahul, S.P.: Oracle-based checking of untrusted software. In: Hankin, C., Schmidt, D. (eds.) 28th ACM Symposium on Principles of Programming Languages, pp. 142–154 (2001)
37. Pfenning, F.: Logical frameworks. In: Robinson, J.A., Voronkov, A. (eds.) Handbook of Automated Reasoning, vol. 2, pp. 1063–1147. Elsevier and MIT Press, Cambridge (2001)
38. Pollack, R.: How to believe a machine-checked proof. In: Sambin, G., Smith, J. (eds.) Twenty Five Years of Constructive Type Theory. Oxford University Press, Oxford (1998)
39. Primiero, G., Raimondi, F.: A typed natural deduction calculus to reason about secure trust. In: Miri, A., Hengartner, U., Huang, N.F., Jøsang, A., García-Alfaro, J. (eds.) Twelfth Annual International Conference on Privacy, pp. 379–382. Security and Trust, Toronto, ON, Canada, 23–24 July (2014)
40. Rabe, F.: How to identify, translate and combine logics? J. Logic Comput. **27**(6), 1753–1798 (2017)
41. Schneider, F.B., Walsh, K., Sirer, E.G.: Nexus authorization logic (NAL): design rationale and applications. ACM Trans. Inf. Syst. Secur. **14**(1), 8:1–8:28 (2011). https://doi.org/10.1145/1952982.1952990
42. Shein, E.: Hacker-proof coding. Commun. ACM **60**(8), 12–14 (2017). https://doi.org/10.1145/3105423
43. Sternagel, C., Thiemann, R.: The certification problem format. In: Proceedings UITP 2014, pp. 61–72 (2014). https://doi.org/10.4204/EPTCS.167.8
44. Stodden, V., Bailey, D.H., Borwein, J., LeVeque, R.J., Rider, W., Stein, W.: Setting the default to reproducible: reproducibility in computational and experimental mathematics, February 2013. http://www.davidhbailey.com/dhbpapers/icerm-report.pdf
45. Voevodsky, V.: Univalent foundations. Talk given at the Institute for Advanced Study, March 2014. http://www.math.ias.edu/vladimir/sites/math.ias.edu.vladimir/files/2014_IAS.pdf
46. Wetzler, N., Heule, M.J.H., Hunt, W.A.: DRAT-trim: efficient checking and trimming using expressive clausal proofs. In: Sinz, C., Egly, U. (eds.) SAT 2014. LNCS, vol. 8561, pp. 422–429. Springer, Cham (2014). https://doi.org/10.1007/978-3-319-09284-3_31
47. Wiedijk, F.: The QED manifesto revisited. Stud. Logic Gramm. Rhetor. **10**(23), 121–133 (2007)
48. Wu, D., Appel, A.W., Stump, A.: Foundational proof checkers with small witnesses. In: Miller, D. (ed.) Proceedings of the 5th ACM SIGPLAN International Conference on Principles and Practice of Declaritive Programming, PPDP 2003, pp. 264–274. ACM, New York, NY, USA (2003)

Prospero's Books: A Distributed Architecture for AI

Invited Extended Abstract

Bhubaneswar (Bud) Mishra[✉]

Courant Institute, NYU, New York City, USA
mishra@nyu.edu

Abstract. This preliminary note and its sequels present a distributed architecture for AI (Artificial Intelligence) based on a novel market microstructure. The underlying game theory is based on Information-Asymmetric (Signaling) games, where deception is tamed by costly signaling. The signaling, in order to remain honest (e.g., *separating*), may involve crypto-tokens and distributed ledgers. Here, we will present a rough sketch of the architecture and the protocols it involves. Mathematical and computational analyses will appear in the subsequent sequels.

To my Recommenders and Verifiers: *Rekha's* and *Vera's*....

> *But release me from my bands − With the help of your good hands.*
> *Gentle breath of yours my sails − Must fill, or else my project fails,*
> *Which was to please. Now I want − Spirits to enforce, art to enchant;*
> *− Prospero in Shakespeare's* **The Tempest**

1 Minsky's Society of Mind

In 1986, in his book *Society of Mind*, AI pioneer Marvin Minsky wrote: "What magical trick makes us intelligent? The trick is that there is no trick. The power of intelligence stems from our vast diversity, not from any single, perfect principle." However, it has remained unclear how and whence these artificial agents congregate to form such a society of mind. Nonetheless, it has been argued that should such a society emerge from artificial computational building blocks, it will possess a great power as it would view "a mind as a society of agents, as opposed to the consequence of some basic principle or some simple formal system,... different agents can be based on different types of processes with different purposes, ways of representing knowledge, and methods for producing results."

We propose a game theoretic approach to establish and maintain such a society where the agents signal, interact strategically and maintain stable separating Nash equilibrium. In particular, we will also introduce two sets of non-strategic agents: namely, *Recommenders* and *Verifiers*, whose interactions are crucial for the system to reach and maintain "good" (honest, separating, desirable) Nash equilibria.

© Springer Nature Switzerland AG 2020
D. V. Hung and M. D'Souza (Eds.): ICDCIT 2020, LNCS 11969, pp. 41–49, 2020.
https://doi.org/10.1007/978-3-030-36987-3_3

The paper is meant to be widely accessible - primarily to computer, data, intelligence and finance engineers - and hence deeper mathematical treatment is relegated to subsequent sequels.

2   Turing's Artificial Intelligence

Classically, intelligence and its role in problem solving have been difficult to formalize. While computability has a widely-accepted model in terms of *Church-Turing thesis*, *Turing-reducibility* and *Turing-universality*, as a consequence of these, it remains impossible to define AI by its general problem solving capability, since there remain many useful and natural decision problems whose undecidability is straightforward: the classical decision problem represented by the Halting Problem or, equivalently, demonstrating computational equivalence of two "programs." In other words, given two programs: one genuine and other (presumably) imitative, there can be no decision procedure to determine if they are Turing equivalent. These statement have deep implications on how we may want to define Artificial Intelligence.

The solution Turing suggested was in terms of an Information-Asymmetric Signaling games: involving certain set of sender agents, some of which will have the type Oracles (e.g., humans) and the others the type Imitators (e.g., models). The senders send certain signals (e.g., conversational statements in English) to receivers (e.g., humans) who must act strategically by only responding to Oracles, while ignoring Imitators. Such a game may be called an *Imitation (Signaling) Game* and the receiver's test a *Turing Test*. Similarly, by also assigning types to receivers (i.e., Oracles and Imitators), one may extend the Imitation Game to also include *Reverse Turing Tests*. As a signaling game the classical Imitation Game and its extension both have Nash Equilibria: some trivial as Babbling or Pooling but others far more relevant to present discussion: namely, *separating*. A natural way to define Artificial Intelligence would be in terms of Imitators' ability to achieve a reasonably informative and stable pooling (non-separating) Nash Equilibrium when introduced into a society of human Oracles. In other words, the receiver must respond in exactly the same manner independent of whether the sender is an Oracle or Imitator.

Our approach involves extending the system to include additional non-strategic agents: namely, Recommenders and Verifiers. They will have no explicit utilities to optimize (or even, satisfies) other than those described in terms of betting and winning (or losing) certain tokens. These tokens may be implemented in terms of a cryptographic object, which must be "hard" to counterfeit (replicate or manufacture); transactions among recommenders and verifiers can be verified in terms of various local and global properties (expressed in terms of a model-checkable logic, e.g. propositional temporal logic), assuming that a non-tamperable model (e.g., a Kripke structure) is dynamically created by some other agents, who are additionally required to employ costly-signaling. While it will remain unspecified as to how the Recommenders and Verifiers and their models may be constructed and deployed, it is conjectured that as long as they satisfy certain system-wide distributed liveness (Recommender's responsibilities) and safety (Verifier's responsibilities) conditions, the game should result in and maintain a stable Nash equilibrium that will also be pooling (Imitators are indistinguishable from Oracles). The intuitions supporting this conjecture is out-of-scope of this introductory note. Since the work presented here combines various ingredients from Imitation Game, Society of Mind, Signaling Games, Turing Learning, Generative-Adversarial Networks, Approximate Bayesian Computation, Bayes and Empirical Bayes techniques and Causality Analysis, we will only briefly comment on these connections here, leaving more details to the full paper and additional sequels.

3   Sketch of an Architecture for AI

The architecture involves

1. Multiple AI modules ("Models" M's) in an ensemble working on multiple data sets ("Domains" D's). Such a set will be referred to as an "*Ecosystem*." There will be some effort to eliminate over-fitted models by using an empirical Bayes approach to control false-discovery rate in multiple hypotheses testing (described later in this paper).
2. *Ranking:* All models are assumed to be generative; the generated data can be compared to future data in order to provide a rank function ("Rank(M, D)").
3. *Oracle(s):* It is assumed that there exists a model M^* (perhaps not yet discovered) that on a data set D performs exactly, without any error. Namely, there is a distance function such that

$$\text{Distance}(D(M^*), D) = 0,$$

   where $D(M^*)$ is the data generated by M^*. Thus Rank(M^*, D) is superior to Rank(M, D) for any M in the ecosystem.
4. *Goal:* Use a recommender-verifier system in a signaling game to identify the best approximation to oracle M^* for a domain D.

As discussed earlier, we assume a set of agents who participate in the game to rank a model M (either an existing one, combination of existing ones or a new one). They will be referred to as Recommenders and Verifiers.

A recommender agent selects a domain and a data-set D associated with the domain and a model M. The recommender may publish hypotheses in support of M (e.g., why (M, D) may best approximate M^*, for instance, using qualitative reasoning, causal support, past history or new computational analysis on real or synthetic data.). The recommender stakes some utilities (e.g., tokens). If the recommended model is deemed to be ineligible for a competition the recommender loses the stake. The recommender also publishes an estimated rank Rank$_R(M, D)$.

One or many verifier-agents provide their estimated ranks of the model: Rank$_V(M, D)$.

A model eligible for competition may then be set up to test if the true rank $Rank(M, D)$ is above or below the median of the ranks estimated by the verifiers. If the competition occurs and the rank is above (resp. below) the median, then half of the agents who estimated a rank above (resp. below) the median win and the other half of the agents who estimated a rank below (resp. above) the median lose. All models found eligible for competition are included in the ecosystem, together with its computed rank (or its recommended rank, if no verifier challenges it).

Losers pay the winners a predetermined amount of utilities (e.g., tokens).

Suppose a recommender devises a strong Oracle-like model. He is then incentivized to contribute the model to the ecosystem as he is sure that it will be eligible for a competition and most likely attract sufficiently many verifiers (resulting in no loss of stake); he also expects a win from the verifiers who will underestimate the power of the model.

As a side effect, over time, weak recommenders whose models do not lead to competitions can get pruned out.

Note that independent of the result of the competition an Oracle-like model always gets evaluated and included in the ecosystem (if and only if it is eligible for competition). There may be further opportunities to earn rent from the future use of the model in the ecosystem.

A good recommender must avoid contributing weak random variations of an oracle model once it has been achieved, while the domain is stationary. In this case most strong verifiers will bet against him and win.

A recommender is also incentivized to work on a domain where the models can be further improved (instead of investing in a domain that already has an Oracle-model or a strong approximation to it.) This situation may arise as a result of the nonstationarity of data.

A weak recommender is deterred by the fact that his recommendations will not be eligible for competition and will result in loss of stake. In addition, just introducing black boxes without any reasoning (or domain-specific prior), may attract strong verifiers who will bet against him.

Similarly, a weak verifier will not be able to accumulate utilities as he will face more frequent losses than wins (assuming that there are other informed verifiers).

Intuitively, the system is designed to provide (1) liveness via Recommenders who are incentivized to introduce new models to the system as well as (2) safety via Verifiers who ensure that non-competitive (or non-verified) models accumulate in the system.

4   Building Utilities

The system also requires costly signaling in accordance with principles of game theory for signaling games as well as financial engineering. For this purpose, we assume existence of a cryptographic security token system that distributes tokens to Recommenders and Verifiers in exchange of financial investments.

These tokens are used in the dynamics of the game. In addition, there may be rent to be collected by allowing other agents (senders and receivers) to use the models in the ecosystem for other applications, where AI could be used productively. The rent for the models can be calculated by classical financial engineering approaches (e.g., CAPM, Capital Asset Pricing Models).

5   An Example System for FinTech

For the sake of concreteness, we use an example from FinTech, though the similar structures can be used for other domains *mutatis mutandis*. Modern FinTech builds on a wide range of disciplines: namely, from computer and data sciences, at one end of the spectrum, to finance, artificial intelligence, game theory and mathematics at the other. It is focused on a central aspect of modern economic life: namely, finance, a multi-faceted subject that draws on ideas from mathematics, economics, psychology and other social and political sciences, and increasingly, information technology and how it connects to society and social networks. In the last half of the century, with expanding data sources and increasing computing speed, finance has become more reliant on statistics, data and econometric models, slowly paving the way to newer forms of financial engineering and technologies as well as their management and regulation – often by computational means.

"FinTech" refers to financial sector innovations involving technology-enabled economic models that can eliminate market inefficiency, support synchronicity in the market and improve risks and liquidity, facilitate disintermediation, revolutionize how existing and emerging firms create and deliver products and services, address privacy, trust and personalization, regulatory and law-enforcement challenges, and seed opportunities for inclusive growth. Some of these innovations could substantially improve the economic life of a larger number of citizens, but would also require the development of new approaches to understand their opportunities and challenges.

Nonetheless, the evolving applications of FinTech has encountered a methodological problem, common to many domains using Data Science and Artificial Intelligence. Namely, (a) How does one quantitatively measure how much better an AI-based FinTech system performs in comparison to traditional approaches from statistical inference, econometrics, model-based (Bayesian) analysis, etc.; (b) How does one disentangle the improvements attributable to model selection, data size, special purpose computation (e.g., GPU or TPU), etc.? (c) How does one decide how to design future systems for a suitable application (e.g., ones with information asymmetry and illiquidity), a suitable computational infrastructure (e.g., clouds with special purpose software like Map-reduce or BigQuery) and a suitable data sets (e.g., social media data vs. cancer genomics data)?

A general goal is to carry out an empirical analysis with a prototype one may plan to build (more details are available in the full paper). This prototype will involve maintaining an ecosystem of models, with additional information such as how it was introduced, what information was given, a preliminary empirical

Bayesian evaluation of its goodness (e.g., rank), competition involving additional verifiers and the results. For succinctness, it may display an aggregated rank for each model in the ecosystem (specific to a particular domain).

The prototype could thus be used for evaluating Data Science, Machine Learning and AI based FinTech systems, to be used by the applied finance community. This prototype will be incorporating the essence of AI systems to detect statistical arbitrage, pricing models with metrics for *risks* and *liquidity* and the changes in the underlying market and regulatory microstructures[1]. This tool could be useful in gathering real time information about various FinTech and RegTech technologies in an international setting (US, India and China) and setting up the technology evaluation on a broader dataset. Its users may use this prototype environment to set up a base for economic, financial, mathematical and computational scientists to work together and solve complex fundamental problems in economics, computing, intelligence and learning.

5.1   Component 1

Rationale: Currently most powerful AI approaches are based on supervised learning. They are fairly simple in the formulation of the problems, but have performed surprisingly well in tasks that are mostly attributed to complex human skills: handwriting recognition, spam detection, image recognition, tagging humans in images, creating captions for images, language translation, etc., to name a few. It has been argued that such approaches, be they as successful as they may, only capture roughly one second of human cognition – roughly the tasks that can be performed by a large group of Mechanical Turks, engaged in labeling raw data.

Formally speaking, in the classical context, AI (more precisely, Machine Learning) deals with two fundamental spaces: The first space $\mathcal{D}$ consists of data points (e.g., point clouds in a high dimensional space) and the second space $\mathcal{M}$ consists of learning models (e.g., parameters of a distributions or weights of a multi-layer artificial neural net, etc.) In statistical learning, $\mathcal{M}$ is usually a space of statistical models $\{p(x, M) : M \in \mathcal{M}\}$ in the *generative* case or $\{p(y|x; M) : M \in \mathcal{M}\}$ in the *discriminative* case. The space $\mathcal{M}$ can be either a low dimensional parametric space or the space of all suitably sparse models in non-parametric space. While classical statistical estimation theory has focused on the former, there is a significant emphases on the later in machine learning – our primary focus here.

A machine learning algorithm selects a model $M \in \mathcal{M}$ based on a training sample $\{(x_i, y_i)_{i=1}^n \subseteq \mathcal{X} \times \mathcal{Y}\}$. Usually the selection of the model is formalized as an optimization problem in two parts: (i) guarding against underfitting:

---

[1] We will use AI to broadly refer to many diverse approaches that include Statistical Inference, Econometrics, Data Science, Big Data, Probably Approximate Computational (PAC) Learning, Shallow and Deep Neural Nets, Genetic Algorithms, Heuristics, Machine Learning, etc., all of which employ large-scale data and scalable computing.

by maximizing likelihood, margin, distance/divergence or utility (or minimizing a loss function) together with (ii) guarding against overfitting: by regularizing with shrinkage, entropy, information or sparsity (or a proxy such as L_1 norms), etc. There is generally a lack of an all-encompassing theory to compare various model selection approaches used by machine learning software (even in a specific domain such as FinTech) and nonconclusive anecdotal arguments based on empirical studies on benchmark data sets have been poor substitute for a deeper understanding.

Approach: The prototype allows one to study a wide class of AI algorithms developed specifically for FinTech. For this purposes, we may formalize our approach in the language of *multiple hypothesis testing*: namely, each model $m_i \in \mathcal{M}$ learned from a training data set $D_T = \{(x_i, y_i)_{i=1}^n \subseteq \mathcal{X} \times \mathcal{Y}$ corresponds to a hypothesis that it will perform with a specific "score" s_i on an unseen cross validating data set $D_V = \{(x_i', y_i')_{i=1}^m \subseteq \mathcal{X} \times \mathcal{Y}$. In particular, the prototype may use Efron's Empirical Bayes [1–3] approaches to control false discovery rates (fdr) and measure how well models from each family of machine learning algorithms is likely to win such a "horse race." This likelihood could be used to determine if a recommended model would be eligible for "competition," and thus included in the eco-system.

For our purposes, we may consider methods available in various AI open source platforms: e.g., WEKA, H2O, TensorFlow, OpenAI, Caffe, CNTK, Mahout, etc. We may deploy the prototype in a real setting, which is likely to closely follow various developments in AI that could be applied to finance data, and may implement most of the commonly used models (e.g., regressions, classification trees, neural nets (DNN and ENN: respectively Deep and Evolutionary Neural Nets), etc.). The data source the prototype may use would be derived from proprietary financial data collected by a large bank. The multiple hypotheses testing techniques, outlined earlier, would be applied to models derived from training data spanning several years with the cross validation applied to the last year of data. The overall success of the entire framework will be tested by applying only the truly successful machine learning models to financial data arriving in real-time over six months subsequent to the end of full analysis.

This prototype will support an ecosystem of models that have already been tried. When a new model is recommended this approach may be used to perform a preliminary analysis of the model being introduced and a competition is deemed eligible if and only if the proposed model passes the analysis outlined here.

5.2   Component 2

Rationale: Practically all machine learning algorithms currently in use suffer from several shortcomings that make them less than ideal for FinTech applications: (i) these algorithms assume a stationary distributions over $\mathcal{X} \times \mathcal{Y}$, and hence only capture an instantaneous response to the new incoming data; (ii) they are "black boxes," and are difficult to interpret or use in a strategic interventions [4,5]; and (iii) they are blind to "black swan events," costly adversarial events that are rare but plausible. In order to remedy these disadvantages, machine learning algorithms must understand the causal structures in the data and be amenable to stress testing that require causal generative models consistent with causal structures.

Approach: In order to address these issues, one may explore construction of graphical models that capture causal structures via a DAG (directed acyclic graphs), whose directed edges correspond to Suppes' notions of prima-facie causes. These models (SBCN: Suppes-Bayes Causal Nets) are regularized using BIC (Bayes Information Criterion) to eliminate spurious prima-facie causes and only retain genuine causes, supported by the training data.

Suppes notion of *probabilistic causation* is based on two ideas: (a) temporal priority (causes precede effect) and (b) probability raising (causes raise the conditional probability of the effect in the presence of the causes relative to its absence); these two notions are easily captured in a logic, called PCTL (probabilistic computational tree logic) [6, 7], which supports efficient polynomial time model checking algorithms.

Once an SBCN is constructed over financial factors (e.g., Fama French Five Factor Models), it is possible to traverse the graph to generate plausible adversarial rare trajectories that stress test a particular discriminative model (as the ones described earlier). Using these stress testing algorithms [8], we plan to analyze the best AI models selected earlier, to further identify robust profit-generating models.

If the recommended model enters a competition, the recommender may publish the results of the causal analysis.

6 Conclusion

These notes only sketch out a game theoretic model for creating AI of the future. These notes currently lack a detailed analysis (both theoretical and empirical) to ensure that the prototype may be competitive to the traditional approach. Also, although its connections to GAN, ABC and Turing Learning are fairly straightforward, they will be relegated to future sequels.

Nonetheless, since the fundamental research questions in the AI (with applications to FinTech) arena have not been well defined, we believe that the proposed research will create an opportunity for thought leadership.

Acknowledgement. We wish to thank Marti Subramanyam, Abhinav Tamskar and Vasant Dhar (all of NYU) for their questions and comments. We also wish to thank founders, members, investors and advisors of the startup Prospero.ai for their interest in creating a prototype to test out some of the core ideas in AI. We also acknowledge NYU for their financial support to carry out the research.

References

1. Efron, B., Hastie, T.: Computer Age Statistical Inference: Algorithms, Evidence and Data Science. Cambridge University Press, New York (2016)
2. Efron, B.: Bayes, oracle bayes, and empirical bayes (2017)
3. Wager, S., Hastie, T., Efron, B.: Confidence intervals for random forests: the jack-knife and the infinitesimal jackknife. J. Mach. Learn. Res. **15**(1), 1625–1651 (2014)
4. Goodfellow, I.J., Bengio, Y., Courville, A.C.: Deep Learning. Adaptive Computation and Machine Learning. MIT Press, Cambridge (2016)
5. Goodfellow, I.J.: NIPS 2016 tutorial: generative adversarial networks. CoRR, vol. abs/1701.00160 (2017)
6. Kleinberg, S., Mishra, B.: The temporal logic of token causes. In: Principles of Knowledge Representation and Reasoning: Proceedings of the Twelfth International Conference, KR 2010, Toronto, Ontario, Canada, 9–13 May 2010 (2010)
7. Kleinberg, S., Mishra, B.: The temporal logic of causal structures,. In: UAI 2009, Proceedings of the Twenty-Fifth Conference on Uncertainty in Artificial Intelligence, Montreal, QC, Canada, 18–21 June 2009, pp. 303–312 (2009)
8. Gao, G., Mishra, B., Ramazzotti, D.: Efficient simulation of financial stress testing scenarios with suppes-bayes causal networks. In: International Conference on Computational Science, ICCS 2017, Zurich, Switzerland, June 12–14 2017, pp. 272–284 (2017)

Trust: Anthropomorphic Algorithmic

Hrushikesha Mohanty[1,2]([✉])

[1] School of Computer and Information Sciences,
University of Hyderabad, Hyderabad, India
hmcs@uohyd.ac.in
[2] KIIT Deemed University, Bhubaneswar, India
h.mohanty@kiit.ac.in

Abstract. Computer Science often emulates humanlike behaviours
including intelligence that has taken to storms in every other domain
where human deals with. A computing system with a defined role and
goal is called an agent with humanlike capability for decision making in
dynamic and complex real world it is situated in. Largely this aspect of a
computing unit needs ability to learn, act and forecast. Broadly the study
in Artificial Intelligence (AI) also deals with such aspects. Researchers
of both the schools of computing viz. Intelligent Agents and AI systems,
propose several algorithms to emulate human like behaviours. These algorithms here, are labelled as anthropomorphic algorithms. In particular,
here our discussion is focussed on *trust*. The idea of trust as conceptu-
alised, computed and applied in different domains, is discussed. Further,
it points out the dimensions that need to be looked at, in order to endow
computing systems with trust as a *humanitics*.

Keywords: Autonomic computing · BDI agent · Anthropomorphic ·
Humanitics · Trust · Social networking

1 Introduction

Computation though started with number crunching but has gone to higher
realm of computing ranging from information based decision making to learning
of problem solving techniques. Researchers of artificial intelligence strive to make
computers qualify Turing Test so there will be no difference between man and
machine. This being the ultimate goal of computing there have been attempts to
develop computing models that mimics human decision making process. Other
than several bio-inspired soft computing models for variety of applications, artificial neural network model claims its operation similar to brain-neurons. Further, now for complex decision making, deep learning computing models are
being proposed. All these models mostly offer solutions to problems of classification, approximate learning and predicting. Whereas early artificial intelligence
systems addressed several problems in decision making, planning and learning.
Currently, machine intelligence has come to centre stage especially after renewed
industry interest in it. Thus researchers in computing are interested in designing models that manifest human traits into computing systems. Now in digital

D. V. Hung and M. D'Souza (Eds.): ICDCIT 2020, LNCS 11969, pp. 50–72, 2020.
https://doi.org/10.1007/978-3-030-36987-3_4

world, software bots and agents are positioned to provide services and to be appreciated by service consumers these cyber entities should exhibit human-like behaviour, that we term as *humanitics*. Before, classical computing systems also exhibit some human traits viz. greed, leadership, consensus and etc. as strategies for solving problems. Now, the trend is being followed further to endow systems with more and more human traits like believe, trust, predict, learn, emotive and etc.

In this paper we intend to survey the works on trust. We first discuss on autonomic computing and then agent based computing to position our point of discussion on computing systems exhibiting human-like behaviours. Particularly, we have a brief discussion on BDI agent model that uses three human behaviours viz. belief, desire and intention. Based on these descriptions we present the idea of trust, that computing science proposes for different applications, particularly in the field of social networking. In literature, belief is considered as information that may or may not be true. Whereas the information that is accepted without an iota of doubts is trust. The paper takes up some basic works on formulation as well as propagation of trust in a network of systems/users on cyberspace. In the sequence of presenting the idea, next section we briefly discuss on autonomic and agent based computing followed by an elaborate discussion on trust and its uses in different domains. Finally, we end with a concluding remark.

2 Autonomic Computing and Agent

In modern world while automation is prevalent in many domains, software is becoming complex for not only of its large code size but also of algorithmic complexity that is baffling for developers as well as decision makers those who depend upon such systems. In order to manage such complex systems running it is felt difficult for human so the trend is to manage by technology to avoid human errors and to provide just-in service with quality. Thus managing technology by technology is termed as autonomic computing [9]. However, another school of thought in computing may think of systems that reason on evolving situations and apply either common sense or deep reasoning for managing self and its ecosystems. We will look into such systems after review of the first kind i.e. autonomic computing system.

An autonomic computing system is built of several software components like a web service to perform a definite application. Such a system uses basic computing resources like software components, servers, database systems, storage and communication network. Typically, it gives an impression of distributed systems with services run at different servers connected over a computer network. These assembly units get assembled themselves based on the demand of an application. This requires interfaces for resources so they can communicate and work in collaboration towards a given work. The software units that orchestrate the basic units through interfaces (autonomic touchpoints) are autonomic managers capable of performing self-configuring, self-healing and self-optimising. These autonomic managers are characterised based on their domains of actions. Some such managers work within a domain discipline and some across several disciplines. A self-managing system monitors, analyses, plans and then executes planned actions on proper analysis of past performances. Such a system configures itself for a given goal by composing chosen components having compatible interfaces. These components during execution exchanges information over defined communication paths following specified protocol that components honour. Such systems are also designed to take decisions during exigencies and respond to undefined non-deterministic situations as and when they occur. For the purpose a system uses a knowledge base that stores required data, task-based domain policy, heuristics, optimisation policy, resiliency plan and learning rules. Thus, these systems are rather knowledge-driven than data-driven. Some of these systems at higher range of applications include command control communication and intelligence systems, space vehicle systems etc. and at lower end, applications may include web-services and systems for enterprise resource management.

Autonomic systems can be self-composed with capability of self-protection and self-healing based on the composition of required components guided by domain based policy of protection and healing. In a sense, system healing is before seen as system resiliency. However, here in case of an autonomic system, in case of failure the system reconfigures to upkeep its service delivery. In nutshell, such autonomic systems exhibit some anthropomorphic characters like autonomy making its own decision on collaboration of components for a purpose.

Later, computing science has got influenced with the idea of agency borrowed from business world. Agency is defined by a business goal, execution policy and monitoring mechanism for quality and in-time service. In computing world, an agent is a piece of software endowed with an agency i.e. a domain of operations. The paradigm of agent based computing is a higher version in terms of anthropomorphic characters. It is rational in making its work plan that's governed by certain principle like causal theory. It learns from its behaviour, collaborates with other agents for achieving common goals and negotiates for a better deal from other collaborators. It also turns to a benevolent samaritan by cooperating to other agents. This way agent based computing and later multi-agent based systems project a computing paradigm with many human-like behaviours. Particularly we will focus on (Belief-Desire-Intention) BDI agents as this paradigm is endowed with enough human-like behaviours and also widely researched.

2.1 Intelligent Agents

Autonomic computing offers a generic paradigm for composition of a system for a given purpose, from a given set of service modules. In addition to self-configuration, other human behaviours like self-protection and self-healing are found with autonomic systems. Autonomic systems being endowed with these features bear striking difference to classical computing system. Classical computing systems are developed to follow some particular algorithms, so as these systems start their execution, don't change their respective defined course of execution. So, it is also for autonomic systems as once such a system configured or composed then the same composite service gets executed. In run time the course of execution doesn't change. But can such a system be called agent though it has specific goal to achieve or service to perform? In answering this, computing paradigm has added a dimension called agency to it on inducting the concept of maximising self-interest while executing a service in the midst of constraints that are observed in real world. It's viewed in real world; the natural human tendency is to maximise its own interest. So, agent based computing paradigm essentially follows optimisation techniques for goal solving. Still, this doesn't confirm with the reality of human problem solving. So the researchers of agent based computing, have explored new avenues of research and development to induce human characteristics to agents so this software can offer solutions to ever changing dynamic worlds. The same question is answered by researchers of intelligent agents. The agents having capability to face dynamic and complex world and act accordingly are known as *intelligent agents*. Some of them have pursued an approach, i.e. first addressing a practical problem and then its characterisation from experiences gained. But, some other researchers have first gone for proposing a generic model explaining the way human mind works towards problem solving in dynamic complex worlds and then developing applications in following the model.

Among the first type of intelligent agents, Soar [23] has an admiring legacy in both research and development. A consortium of researchers from different universities had a unique attempt in emulating cognitive behaviour to software systems. Allen Newell a pioneer of Artificial Intelligence views AI systems as a confluence of micro theories of cognitive science in explaining human mind in problem solving, decision making, language, learning and memory. He is in view of unified theory of cognition [17] that provides basis for mechanistic approach for development of systems endowed with human cognitive behaviour. One such attempt is made in Soar to offer a generic problem solving paradigm that emulates human cognitive behaviour for solving problems of different domains.

Soar is a demonstrating artificial intelligence system designed for general problem solving including open ended problems. It takes the lead of cognitive behaviour in problem solving in seeing structures in problems in terms of tasks and subtasks, and designs execution plan, monitors different aspects of task executions and learns from these. In a seminal paper [24] Laird et al. presents Soar general architecture to demonstrate its features in comparison to other contemporary intelligent and learning systems. Tasks and associated methods are represented in both procedural as well as declarative forms. While a task is executed in a sequence, it also learns from its behaviour to refine its problem solving strategy. A generic learning strategy named "chunking" is used to learn from task execution. The other types of learning it supports are: problem solving strategy by explanation, generalisation and practice. However, other aspects like deliberate planning, new task representation techniques and interaction with external tasks are missing.

However, Soar has been successful in providing general problem solving strategy following cognitive behaviour towards general intelligence. Its structure to achieve general intelligence is based on eleven hypotheses. These are:

Goal structure hypothesis, Physical symbol system hypothesis, uniform representation of declarative knowledge, Problem solving by state space search, Goal directed behaviour, Uniform-learning, Hypothesis- chunking, Universal sub gaoling, Automatic sub-gaoling, Productions as long term knowledge, Control knowledge hypothesis, Weak method from task domain and Weak method emergence from task execution.

Though Soar and some of such contemporary systems are capable of offering general problem solving strategy based on several cognitive hypotheses towards general intelligence still are felt for not having enough capabilities to meet the challenges of dynamic world that needs to evaluate an evolving world to explore problem solving strategy. In search of such systems, researchers propose BDI: Belief Desire and Intention agents arguing its capability in meeting changing world. In the next section we will discuss on such agents.

2.2 BDI Agents

Agent based problem solving strategy is based on belief-desire-intention cognitive paradigm that though follows goal-oriented approach but different than Soar being able to reschedule its goals for execution on taking stock of the present situation prevailing in problem domain and limitation on its own resources. Like a knowledge based system it has capability to explain, reason and learn. Unlike Soar, before development of BDI agents, there has been a good deal of formal research work on specification, design verification, language and protocol for giving its rigour in engineering of BDI agents. In [15], authors have put BDI agents in clear perspectives in terms of research in agents.

Belief, Desire and Intention are three basic anthropomorphic characters a person follows for general problem solving. Belief is the information available to an agent. In a sense of programming, a belief is a variable with associated value; it can be a database record or can be a generic knowledge expressed in logic or/and in rules following if-then-else syntax. Belief constitutes both a partial view of agent world and an impression of past the agent has encountered in its domain. Because, of the resource limitation the past can't be totally remembered. Hence, belief is derived from past information. This derivation could be susceptible to imprecision while getting meta information from past views. Belief is usually expressed in logic giving semantics to express imprecise information. Desire of an agent can be viewed as a set of goals an agent can achieve with a given set of belief. Computationally a goal can be viewed as a variable, a data base record or a symbolic expression following some logic. Out of several possible goals, a goal is chosen for execution. Such a chosen goal is termed as an intention. However, unlike conventional task oriented computing, intention does not remain static. The classic theory of human decision making confirms of revision of executional plan weighing cost of execution at a given time and alternatives available with. It's reality to revise a plan in run time. It's also expected to draw a new plan from a given plan. But, runtime revising a plan could be expensive thus may turn impractical. In order to meet this challenge BDI agents store parameterised plans so the same can be reused as and when required at runtime. Thus BDI agent software exhibits belief, desire and intention, the three anthropomorphic characters in its behaviour.

It's essential to get the concept computationally feasible. From classical decision theory point of view, many possible worlds can be constructed from beliefs. Beliefs are considered as imprecise information. Possibility of achieving a goal is viewed as a goal tree that defines an order for execution of tasks represented by tree nodes. Each node is assigned with values showing the probability of achieving a goal and the cost associated to it. Each node in the tree exhibits a state that is achievable possibly by different ways that are represented by chance nodes from which arcs emanate to descend on a goal node. In order to generate a possible world, a copy of a given decision tree is created and then a chance node is replaced by a successor node that is a decision node in real world. This elimination of chance nodes continues till all the chance nodes are replaced by their respective successor nodes. The process generates a set of decision trees each consisting of decision and terminal nodes and each tree corresponds to some different possible worlds. With assigned pay-off values based on probability of happening and associated costs on each node of a tree, there could be several paths to the goal node with different costs. So for a given set of deliberation, a set of desire-accessible worlds is created where each has a set of decision trees. Trees are chosen based on a path choice criterion. Such a chosen tree is known as intention-accessible world. An algorithm implementing three anthropomorphic characters of BDI agents is presented in [2].

Implementing BDI agents with such three important cognitive behaviour is essential to realise a large scale application of agents in several applications. The implementation should be such that the basic characteristics agents that's autonomous, reactive, internally motivated and with capability of reacting to changing world are achievable. Researchers in [12] have proposed an agent engineering approach based on object oriented design methodology. It presents an agent from its external and internal views. External view on an application is obtained by looking into agency performing services. A service is an atomic activity carried out by an agent i.e. a unit of software using certain resources and possibly in exchange of a cost that's either taken from the problem domain or reached by run time based on dynamic situation of the environment that holds the problem. While looking for atomic service one may discover a hierarchy of services. For a service, roles, responsibilities as well as limitations are identified. Roles and responsibilities are refined to level by level in different granularities thus defining a hierarchy on roles. Such arrangement of roles and associated responsibilities give rise to a hierarchy of agents based on the roles at different levels of a hierarchy. This makes an external view of an agency. This hierarchy of agents resembles to a class hierarchy as one sees in case of object oriented analysis of an application. The other expect of agent oriented analysis in modelling of internal views of an agent. This internal views include belief, desire and intention. With respect to a goal, a set of initial beliefs or ground beliefs are identified during analysis. Ground beliefs could be of both types viz. variant and invariant beliefs. The former one are those who do not change during goal execution while the later one does. Further, an agent is designed not only to maintain its own beliefs consistent but also to see its beliefs on other agents are well defined with respect to their roles and responsibilities. This makes belief model of an agent. Internal view of an agent is made of three models viz. belief model, goal model and plan model. Goal model of an agent contains initial goal set, events and corresponding goals. While with respect to a goal, there is a defined sequence of actions by which a goal is achieved. Thus, a plan model of an agent is defined. Now programming for a goal with the above model is termed as agent oriented computing.

In case of classical computing paradigm, logical and physical distributions of data and functionalities have given rise to distributed computing. The same aspects are seen in case of agent based computing giving rise to plethora of research works in intelligent agents and the area is popularly known as DAI: Distributed Artificial Intelligence and also as Multi-Agent System (MAS). There could be subtle difference in between two types but both have many similar characteristics. Here, we are interested in humanitics of these paradigms. MAS draws ideas from philosophy, sociology and artificial intelligence while emulating human behaviour in agent societies. Agents perceive surrounding environment and accordingly solve problems individually or jointly being associated with other agents. In order to bring the notion of humanitics, some well-studied applications of agents are quoted below.

2.3   Applications

Let's consider an agent based system developed for automated landing of aircrafts on given runways of an airport. For the application there can be three types of agents viz. aircraft agents, runway agent and traffic-control agent. In order to achieve a goal i.e. safe landing of aircrafts these agents need to coordinate their activities to execute landing plans of aircrafts. Once an aircraft is located by the traffic-control agent, it signals for creation of an aircraft agent. At a given time, there could be several aircraft agents for many aircrafts scheduled to land at a given time. While a traffic control agent manages air space for aircraft agents and communicates them space allocations advices, at the same time aircraft agents communicate among themselves for coordinated landing keeping each other aware of air as well as runway scenarios. Similarly, a runway agent talks to the only aircraft that's scheduled to land on the run way. Once a landing is completed, the life time of the corresponding aircraft agent expires and updated runway status is communicated to traffic control agent to schedule next landings. Interestingly there are more humanlike behaviours, one can view in different evolving situations. The air scenarios being conveyed by different stake holders are trusted by all, so not only a common knowledge on air scenarios is perceived by all but also the knowledge is trusted. While beliefs are ground facts tagged with probability, trusts are the facts with very high probability of truth values assuring dependability of a system. In case of exigencies, a pilot can be assisted by a pilot agent that uses its episodic memory on exigency events and corresponding plans of actions for taking decisions towards resiliency when a landing plan is on trouble. Among a group of aircraft agents scheduled to land, one may wish to land out of turn. This requires deliberation and negotiation among aircraft agents. Agents need to share beliefs, goals, strategies, goal execution status and policies among themselves for changes in their goal state space. So the communication among agents are of interest as message passing and remote method invocation are to distributed computing; while the former has paradigm shift in communication adding both declarative as well as intensional programming paradigms. KQML: Knowledge Query and Manipulation Language proposed for agent communication uses a predefined set of performatives. However, such declarative language has limitation being minimal and closed. Researchers then look for intensional programming that can add context based communication performatives thus expanding communication capability of agents. This resembles to humanlike language learning capability [26]. This brief description of a case shows birth-death, communication, coordination, resiliency and trust among agents.

3 Trust

The word 'Trust' is being used in Computer Science with different semantics. In distributed computing, trusted systems mean the system nodes who perform and pass information without any loss. Because of faulty systems or transmission loss, maintaining consistency of information across different nodes in a distributed system, is a challenging issue. Classically, Byzantine quorum [25] is used to establish truth among faulty nodes or erroneous transmissions. It appears that in distributed computing paradigm, the systems trust each other when majority of systems have the same information i.e. the information that is known to the majority is true and are trusted by all in the system.

But, trust is seen in much wider dimension than consistency of information. A system is trusted if it rigorously follows rules, regulations and forms a knowledge base of its tested experiences. Further, a system is trusted based on elaborate risk analysis taking in account of gain and loss due to the system. Finally, trust has a cognitive dimension too. Often trust judgement is carried by emotion, feelings and impressions a trustee has. The last point may be a higher order humanitics on trust that computing may find challenging to realise. In search of trust models for its algorithmic implementations, a taxonomy for the building blocks of trust is discussed in [3].

The main components of trust include trust roles, worthiness factors, relations, metrics and operations. Actors involved in trust building are trustors, trustees and recommenders. A system can have a trust monitor for on-line computing of trust metrics of the actors associated with. Trustworthiness is a factor sometimes cognitive in nature. With internal factors, external factors also add to trust worthiness. Trust relations in a society provides an edifice towards trust building. It comes from direct relationship like one-to-one interactions and also indirect relationships that allow trust factors propagate making a web of trusts in a society. For computation we need to have a metric that transforms from narratives to digits usually in range of (0, 1). The network built with trust relationships is used for trust propagation. For the purpose, the operations required are trust initiation and propagation. Trust initiation at a trustor is computed by its prior information on a trustee, in case of digital world, it's like analysing trustee cyber foot prints. Trust inferencing is done using indirect relationships between truster and trustee. It is now being widely researched particularly for emergent social networking. Next we will discuss on some major works on trust inferencing.

3.1   Trust Inferencing

The concept trust has been defined in different ways in different areas of research in Computing Science, more or less confirming the semantics of the word trust. In a sense, trust is a form of dependable belief of higher order in comparison to others. In computer networks, a more dependable node is assigned with a strategic role or used as a guard for secured data repository. Such nodes are trusted nodes. In juxtaposed way, untrusted nodes, are those who either fail to adhere defined protocol or stealthily engaged in subversive acts like network traffic choking or data leaking. In case of web services trust has also been investigated to find out web-services those are dependable for service delivery. Now, the same problem is being studied in social networks. In all these three different domain types, there have been studies on trust. This is of interest to explore the general philosophy that computing world follows in dealing with trust.

Trust on social networking is a hot topic of research not only it's trendy but of use in many applications that transact on Internet. Social networking provides a platform for millions of users to interact, of them very few actually know each other. In such case, it's essentially useful to find trustworthiness of people from their digital presences. Ofcourse, affiliation of a person that we see on its digital profile brings a trust factor. This is trust by reference to a third party. But, finding trustworthiness between two unknown communicators is a challenge and required. Their profiles can be of some help only if those are genuine. In that sense, the means available to judge trustworthiness is finding the similarity in their respective activities and from the information flow in between. This common idea, many researchers have taken forward to design several schemes and develop algorithms to find trust among any two on social networking.

Users engaged in transactions are represented by a connected graph where users are nodes and their communications are represented by edges. The features of information passed over an edge is known as flow weight indicating quality of relation communicators have. Among a set of nodes, the pairs connected by high weight links, may be on similar context, are termed as trusted pairs. So, studying trust on social networking can be viewed as a graph theoretic problem. Deriving trust in a connected world is termed as trust inferencing. Here we will explore some prominent algorithms and ideas on trust inferencing.

[20] defines trust relation function from views two neighbouring vertices possess between themselves. With this assumption it presents a method based on trust transitivity. Though, in reality such transitivity property on trust can be

contested. Still, in case of social networking, trust propagation through transitive relation is accepted for its common acceptance and usages. This paper builds on this basic notion of transitivity to search trusted path in a social network graph. For trusted path discovery, an edge between two adjacent vertices with the highest degree of trust is selected. And then through the selected vertex the path extends to the next hop via a the most trusted edge. The process repeats till a trustor reaches at trustee. The found trusted path connecting the two is a basis of trust inferencing. However, there is a limit on the length of such a path showing there could be denudation of trust during its spread. With the concept, authors have presented two algorithms viz. TPS and TIM for trust path searching and trust inferencing. Before to it, trust literature finds an algorithm called TidalTrust that is backed by assumptions: First it says, transitivity in trust could be useful. Second, the shorter the path between trustor and trustee, better is the trust value. Third, to trust a remote trustee, it's always better to choose to reach through the most trusted neighbour. There are many heuristics based algorithms proposed by different groups of researchers.

TidalTrust is an algorithm [6] for trust inferencing. Considering a given weighted graph with values with ranging between $(0, 10)$ the algorithm proposes a formula that's ratio of summation of multiplicative trust values of all the chosen paths by the summation of the trust values of all the possible paths excluding the last hop of the edge to the trustee as seen in following formula:

$$t_{s \to d} = \frac{\sum_{j \in ADJ | t_{s \to j} > max} t_{s \to j} t_{j \to d}}{\sum_{j \in ADJ | t_{s \to j} > max} t_{s \to j}} \tag{1}$$

$t_{s \to d}$ is the trust inferred by applying the above equation recursively starting from node s to the node d representing trustor and trustee respectively. $t_{s \to j}$ is the direct trust labelled on the edge (s, j) when there is link from j landing on node s. ADJ of node s denotes a set of nodes from whom edges are landing on s. For a root of any length the equation is applied recursively from a trustor node to trustee node to infer trust of trustor on trustee. Looking at the above equation one needs to estimate max value that is used to filter out edges of choice for trust inference. The point of importance is to consider the nodes who are trusted more that's having trust value equal to or more than a threshold value. Threshold trust value finding could be domain specific. Ideally, for trust inferencing shortest paths between trustee and trustor are identified. From those paths a max trust value is obtained. For example, being very conservative the highest trust value of an edge can be considered as the max value. Or being too liberal, the minimum of direct values min can be considered as a threshold trust value.

The other trust inferencing scheme called RN-Trust algorithm [16] operates following the idea of electrical resistance for series and parallel connections. A basic concept of resistance between two adjacent nodes is based on principle of inverse relation between trust and resistance, means as trust value between two increases, resistance r between the two decreases. Given t a trust value between two neighbouring nodes, resistance is measured by $r = -\log(t)$. In case there is a multiple-hop path between nodes s and d, that is the trustor and trustee respectively then the resistance between the two is the summation of resistances due to the edges making the path. So, the resistance R for the path is computed by.

$$R(s,d) = r(s,i) + r(i,t)\dots + r(y,d) \tag{2}$$

In case of having two parallel paths say R_1 and R_2 between s and d nodes, the resistance inference value due to the paths is calculated following the paradigm of parallel electrical connections as shown below:

$$R(s,d) = \frac{R_1(s,d) \times R_2(s,d)}{R_1(s,d) + R_2(s,d)} \tag{3}$$

Having resistance between trustor and trustee computed, its trust value is computed as $t_{s \to d} = 10^{-R(s,d)}$. It is to be noted that unlike TidalTrust [6] algorithm, in this case all paths are considered for trust inferencing.

Another trust inferencing algorithm called SWTrust [10] proposes a simple frame-work to compute trust inference for a path by multiplying its direct trust values, that means trust values of edges are multiplied. Having multiple paths between a trustor and trustee an average of trust values of paths is considered as trust inference value for trustor on trustee.

The algorithms TidalTrust and SWTrust have conceptual similarity in computing trust inference values. TidalTrust is constrained with shortest path thus ignoring longer paths with greater direct trust values. Thus the algorithm is vulnerable of losing better trust worthiness paths. Further, the algorithm has unique path problem in case of having only one shortest path in between a truster and a trustee. The path problem may happen for considering the maximum direct trust as threshold value. For such a unique path the case becomes readily undesirable when the edge arriving at trustee has the highest direct trust value but that of at the trustor is very less. It raises a philosophical question of transitively trusting a most trusted person through the most untrusted person. Though RN-Trust algorithm [16] doesn't have such problem of unique path for considering all possible paths lying in between trustor and trustee but trust inference value may turn very low because of multiplication of decimal values of direct trusts. These problems are addressed in TISON [20].

TISON the algorithm for trust inferencing for social networks has two pronged strategies for computing trust inferencing following trust transitivity though it also considers asymmetry in trusting. A person called source node s intending to get trust inference on another node say d destination node, first finds all the trust paths leading from s to d nodes. This is a simple breadth first algorithm starting from the start node s. The algorithm takes inputs of user desired path length, trust matrix and the minimum trust required to consider admissibility of a direct truth. Trust matrix contains direct trust values of nodes with all other nodes. Usually, the maximum direct trust value of a path is considered as the threshold truth value a trusted path is to maintain. That means paths having less than the threshold trust are discarded. However, a user wishing to get strong trust reference may choose to increase minimum trust threshold and reduce trust path length. By traversing all the paths from a source to a sink and during the traversal it chooses the candidate trusted paths and labels their nodes and edges. It's to be noted that the edges leading to the destination node is not considered during traversal. This is rationalised to avoid the bias of the just friends of the destination node. The labelled nodes may give rise to a set of trusted paths i.e. the paths having trust values equal or more to the threshold trust value. Having trust paths then the second step is to compute inference trust value for each path. This computed by the following formula:

$$T_p = \alpha t_p + \beta(1 - v_p) + \gamma w_p \tag{4}$$

The inference trust T_p for path p from node s on node d' is due to three aspects viz. average trust value of a path, the variance of trust values, and path weight factor is multiplied with three multipliers α, β and γ specific to the path. Average trust value of a path is the average of the direct trust values of each node in a path. A path of high average trust signifies presence of trusted friends in the chain linking a source s to destination d. So, inferencing trust by a source on a sink is trusted when there are trusted people, more direct trusted values they have the better trusted chain they make and also the inferenced path truth value is better. The second parameter is on trust variance. When people on a chain are not too much divergent in their direct trust values, then they in a chain project consistent in truth inferencing. The third one is due to path weight. This is a fraction between the length of the shortest path to that of the current path. A hypothesis on length of a trust path is on its length i.e. a path with less people chain leads to a good path trust value. So, the current path trust value is viewed in relation to the shortest path. Formulas for the three are as follows

$$\overline{t_p} = \frac{1}{n} \sum_{i=1}^{n} t_i \tag{5}$$

where $\overline{t_p}$ is the average truth for path p of n edges and t_i is the direct trust value for an edge i. The variance v of truth for a path p is

$$v_p = \frac{1}{|n|} \sum_{i=1}^{|n|} (t_i - \overline{t_p})^2 \tag{6}$$

The metric path weight is computed as:

$$w_p = \frac{|n'|}{|n|} \tag{7}$$

where $|n'|$ is the length of the shortest path and $|n|$ is the length of the path under consideration p. A path is a perfect trust path when its inference trust value is 1 when its path average is 1, path variance is 0 and path weight is 1. The formula for computing T_p considers path from origin to the last intermediary nodes just neighbouring to destination. It's logical to consider the importance of the last person's direct trust on the trustee. Because the former has a bearing on path trust for he/she knows the trustee direct. Now having trust for a path, (just upto d' a neighbour of d the destination node) the impact due to direct trust value of the neighbour d' on trustee is taken into consideration to calculate the resultant trust value of the path p as:

$$T_{s \to d} = T_{s \to d'_p} \times t_{d'_p \to d} \tag{8}$$

where $T_{s \to d'_p}$ is the trust value of a path leading from s to d' just neighbour of trustee node d. $t_{d'_p \to d}$ denotes the direct trust value between the neighbour d' in path p and the d the trustee. [5] emphasizes the need of backbone for information flow in a social network. Network structure gives a graph model for flow of information among uses. Trust propagation in a social network is treated as a network flow problem. [11] finds trust propagation as a network flow problem by converting a trust evaluation task to a generalized network flow problem. Interesting point in decay of trust is also studied here.

The algorithms for trust inferencing mostly considers structure of networks. But all these miss to consider anthropomorphic characters of people. Mostly, people of similar background communicates with mutual trust. Mathematically, the familiarity of two is seen as a context similarity. This gives the basis of trust that we will discuss next.

3.2 Trust Basis

Putting trust on someone, largely depends on the commonality of interests both trustor and trustee have. More, the flow of trust not only depends on interest commonality but also on structure of a community that holds trustor and trustee connected. A classical algorithm as seen in the previous section finds a most trusted path for inferencing trust. Though it finds a structure i.e. a trusted path still while finding a path constituting edge at a given node, it considers one of the most trusted neighbour but does not consider the impact of the structure a node has on trust flow while calculating trust inference of a trustor on trustee. The nodes who pose trust are the in-degree nodes and the out-degree nodes are the trusted ones. The trust rates labelled with in-edges and out-edges of a node along with its positional structure bear importance on trust inference. Consideration of structure and context of a node in trust inferencing brings difference to classical ones [27].

The notion of trust rate on an edge is taken from context similarity between the nodes the edge connecting. A context of a node is defined by the topics of its interest, collected from the persons (nodes) comments, replies and postings on social media. Please note, here we are talking of trust inferencing between two unknowns on cyber world but connected by through common friends. Topic similarity turns a weak method in differentiating nodes when they have too many topics in common. So, the topics of low frequency is to be considered for weight of a topic. Frequency of a topic is calculated by number of times the topic appears as a topic of interest in different nodes. The weight of a topic j is defined as $w(tpc_j) = e^{-freq'_j}$ where $freq'_j = \frac{freq_j - freq_{min}}{freq_{max} - freq_{min}}$ The frequency of a topic j is normalized by the difference between the maximum and the minimum frequencies of topics of the domain of discussion by two nodes.

Trust flow on an edge of an inferencing chain depends on topic correlation between edge topics and common topics of trust and trustee nodes. Further it depends on correlation between edge topics and topics of trustee nodes. The notion is taken on common sense of human indulgence in speaking to people of similar interest though one could argue against with only some outlier examples.

Correlation of common topics at an intermediate node is the summation of the weights of its topics that are common to the topics common between trustor and trustee. Similarly, target topics correlation for an intermediate node with a target node is the summation of weights of topics $w(tpc)$ those are common between topics of the node and those of the trustee that's destination node on a path of trust inferencing. Both the correlations show the trust worthiness of a node with respect to trustor and trustee. For trust inferencing, we need the best paths between trustor (source) and trustee (target) nodes. The eligibility of a node to be chosen for the purpose is considered from its weighted topic similarity with both source and target nodes. The weighted topic similarity of a node is computed as weighted summation of two; one is the ratio of correlation of common topics of the node and summation of topic weights of common topics of source and target nodes; and the other is the ratio of correlation of target topics of a node and summation of topic weights of topics of the target node. The equations for computations of topic weights are as follows

$$wts(n_i) = \lambda \times \frac{C_c(n_i)}{sum(D_{com})} + (1 - \lambda) \times \frac{C_t(n_i)}{sum(D_{target})} \qquad (9)$$

$$sum(D_{com}) = \sum_{tpc \in D_{com}} w(tpc) \qquad (10)$$

$$sum(D_{target}) = \sum_{tpc \in D_{target}} w(tpc) \qquad (11)$$

$$C_c(n_i) = \sum_{tpc \cap D_i \cap D_{com}} w(tpc) \qquad (12)$$

where D_{com} D_{source} D_{target} are the common topics of source and target, topics of source and target nodes respectively. $C_c(n_i)$ and $C_t(n_i)$ are correlation of common topics and correlation of common target topics respectively when n_i is a intermediate node in a path.

Other than semantic similarity, the choice of a node in a trust inferencing path is also guided by the node's trust propagation ability that is governed by its structural position in social network. An intermediate node may have different trust rates for its incoming and outgoing neighbours. These trust rates could be due to perceptions derived from long interactions/supported by episodic goodness feelings. Trust propagating ability of a node is computed from trust rates of incoming and outgoing as square root of multiplied maximum trust rates of both incoming and outgoing nodes as shown below. Further priority of a node for being chosen for the best path is derived from its weighted topic similarity and trust propagation ability.

$$tpa(n_i) = \sqrt{max_{j=1}^{l}(t_{ij}) \cdot max_{j=1}^{m}(t'_{ij})} \tag{13}$$

Trust propagation ability of a node n_i is due to its both types of neighbours like the one whom the node trust and the other are the nodes who trusts it. The trust rates of these neighbours are termed as $t_{i,j}$ where l and m are number of inward and number of outward trust relations respectively. Then from a given node n_i its next node is to be chosen to construct trust path trustee. The choice of next in node in the path is done based of priority counts. The formula to compute priority is:

$$priority(n_j) = \sqrt{wts(n_j) \cdot tpa(n_j)} \tag{14}$$

Thus having trust rates on edges connecting chosen intermediate nodes on the basis of priority, inferencing trust value between trustor and trustee is calculated either by aggregation or concatenation. While the prior method computes average of trust rates in connecting edges, the later chose either minimum or maximum strategy in computing inferencing a trust value.

Trust propagation as studied in social network assumes the existence of web of trust in social network. However, in reality trust and distrust exist side by side. Philosophically, the question comes when trust value assumes zero then does it automatically imply distrust? Does one at the same breath, expresses trust and distrust both on a target? Again does a negative value to a trust rate be distrust? With a trust value on target, availability of distrust value on it, is of importance in taking decisions. For the purpose, along with propagation of trust, that of distrust is also important [28]. The paper uses matrix algebra for calculating inference truth of a set of people with given both belief and disbelief matrices respectively T, D representing trust and distrust of one with others. Along with distrust, the resultant trust matrix is $B = T - D$. Researchers while considering of trust and distrust propagation, first have defined (one step) atomic propagation with four types viz. direct propagation, co-citation, transpose and trust coupling with different semantics based on certain observed social behavioural patterns. Direct propagation exhibits transitive property on trust relation like when i trusts j and j trusts k then i trusts k. Transpose relation on trust essentially a symmetric relation telling i trusts j implies j trusts i. Co-citation trusting represents a tendency of joining with trustors on virtue of commonality in trusting like if i trust j and k and l trusts j then l also trusts k. Trust coupling says if two trust the same i.e. i and j both trust k then i trusts j too. The operations of such trusting on belief matrix is shown as below. Before discussing on atomic and iterative propagation of belief the terms used are defined in the following tables:

The author defines a kind of trust propagation as atomic propagation i.e. if i trusts j and j trusts k then we may guess i trusts j. This assumption helps us to avoid lengthy chain in trust propagation. The authors define four types of atomic belief propagation as showed in Tables 1 and 2:

Table 1. Terms on belief and disbelief

Name	Meaning
T	Trust matrix, T_{ij} i's trust on j
D	Distrust matrix, D_{ij} i's distrust on j
B	Beliefs, B is either T or $T - D$
$C_{B\alpha}$	Combined atomic propagation matrix
P^k	k step propagation matrix
F	Final belief, i' trust on j

Table 2. Types of atomic propagation of belief

Atomic propagation	Operator	Description
Direct propagation	B	i's trust on neighbour j
Co-citation	$B^T B$	Common trust should imply trust in all trustees
Transpose trust	B^T	If i trust j then j should trust i
Trust coupling	BB^T	If both trust the same then trust mutual

A composite trust matrix evolving due to all the above types of atomic propagations is given by

$$C_{B,\alpha} = \alpha_1 B + \alpha_2 B^T B + \alpha_3 B^T + \alpha_4 BB^T \qquad (15)$$

where $\alpha_1, \alpha_2, \alpha_3, \alpha_4$ are the weights to combine all four to composite belief. Then based on this composite trust matrix the propagation of trust is carried by iterative trust computation. Let's define $P(k)$ as the operator for sequence of k propagations.

$$B = T, P^{(k)} = C_{B,\alpha}^k \cdot (T - D) \qquad (16)$$

Consider distrust one atomic propagation. Because when one distrusts another the former discards all trust factors on the later. With this authors consider distrust propagation as atomic while trust propagates across the graph. With this: $B = T, P(k) = C_{B,\alpha}^k \cdot (T - D)$. But when both trust and distrust propagates across the network graph, in this case the authors propose $B = T - D, P(k) = C_{B,\alpha}^k$. The repeated propagation of trust/distrust is expressed as a matrix powering operation.

In comparison to [27] the algorithm proposed in [28] conceptually different by factoring distrust into trust flow. Computationally, the former performs cognitively simple by breadth first graph traversals while at every step on pruning outgoing paths based on trust worthiness of neighbours. However, the both the algorithms have option of restricting propagation of trust to k steps depending on domain requirements. While [28] algorithm is unique factoring distrust in trust propagation, the [27] factors both context and configuration in trust propagation.

3.3   Trust Graph

In general trust evaluation algorithms assume implicit existence of networks that span in a society connecting its people on social relationships derived from their social interactions. In social media, such networks also exist; for many applications evaluating trust between two connected on social media is found useful. For the purpose many algorithms are proposed but most of them have drawbacks in terms of size and its maintainability for changing contexts and in between malicious interventions of nodes. In answering to this challenge, some proposes limited length for computing trust propagation. But, the problem is with deciding on limited path length. A new approach in [10] proposes a method to build a trust network and generate a trusted graph. The approach is based on two fundamental ideas of Sociology. These are small world and weak ties phenomena. It's argued that in real world weak ties are more informative and at the same time if not all but each in the world is connected to other in smallest social distance that is proportional to logarithm of total number of people connected on a social network [7, 21]. The proposed algorithm for trust propagation follows two principles. One is it finds a long distance connecting a target node i.e. trustee using the concept of weak ties. And then the algorithm performs breadth-first to search the trustee node. As social media graph nodes are usually connected by hundreds of neighbours all being direct friends to a node, the algorithm at every step of search finds the best of those neighbours based on their target related or topic related degrees. The algorithm works in three phases. In the first phase it finds trust network following the concept of trust transitivity. It finds chains on domain based trusted acquaintance and thus size of neighbourhood graph is reduced by domain similarity. On building trust network, trusted graph is generated by choosing small and most trusted graph from a given trust network. The paper thus proposes a method for generating trusted graph with respect to a domain.

The models considered usually though based on Graph abstract model, still researchers look at different models. The next section presents a quantum like model that presents simultaneously both belief and disbelief on a trustee.

3.4   Quantum Model

Trust and distrust, as psychology researchers say, do exist simultaneously and impact human decision making based on the degree in trust or distrust. The concept of simultaneous existence of both paradoxical opposites is conceptually similar to quantum physics that provides a mathematical model to express a particle in dual states at a given instant based on the principle of uncertainties. The concept [3] proposes, follows quantum-like model. Quantum model is essentially a probabilistic model that is different than classical probability concept that operates with binary values. Rather quantum model uses Hilbert Space of trust vectors with defined inner products. Some of the basic concepts of quantum theory useful for the purpose is discussed in the paper.

A quantum system is known to have k basic distinguishable states; where each state is expressed with a probability amplitude say α, that is a complex number giving the probability amplitude of a state i in a system. The general representation of a quantum state of a system is a summation of probability amplitudes of all the states, that a system distinctly exhibits. In quantum model, probability of a system in a given state is the product of probability amplitude of the state and the complex conjugate of the probability amplitude of the state. This phenomenon is known as superposition axiom telling if a system is in one of the k given distinguishable states then the system can also be in any linear superposition of the states. But according to quantum theory when a system is measured, the system is collapsed to one of the distinct states and is made visible with certain probability. What it means, when a system is observed it's not viewed as superimposition of its distinct k states. Rather, the measurement of a system on orthogonal basis is a projection on to the basis vectors with certain probability. The probability is computed by inner product of row vector of system and column vector of the basis vector.

This idea of quantum model is taken here considering trust is a cognitive reading of a trustor on trustee where trustee is seen in two states that's belief and disbelief. That means a trustee is modelled as a superimposition of two distinct states with certain amplitudes. But, when a trustor views a trustee, it is measured to a new state that's the inner product of the basis vectors representing contexts on which belief and disbelief are conceived. One aspect that makes quantum model unique is about its ability to express trust on a trustee on different incompatible contexts. For each context a basis vector is defined. In order to compute trust on a trustee on certain context, its trust vector is projected on the basis vector of the context. This enables to compute trust of a trustor on a trustee in different contexts following a quantum model.

3.5   Soft Trust

Some researchers while exploring the source of trust, they realised that trust is a higher degree of belief. And also they realised numbers are not good representatives of trust because people usually don't use probability numbers but words like *yes, no, likely, most likely, quite true* etc. These semantics rather represent source of trust for qualifying degree of belief. These semantic in a sense provides cognitive mapping of a trustor on a trustee. The idea of using fuzzy set theory by qualitative description of uncertainty with associated semantics is shown in [4]. The model is built with assumption that degree of trust of a trustor on a trustee is derived from several factors the former is set in. For example a person may have both external and internal attributes that condition its belief system. Internal attribute may have several factors like ability, availability and not-harmfulness. These factors in different ways internally influence a person to believe. Opportunity and impediments are external factors to influence. All these in different combinations provide a graded belief system that can be well modelled by fuzzy set theory. The participations of different factors in context of a domain can assume fuzzy values. The authors with an example have shown the application of their model.

While the above talks of finding trustworthiness of a system state, the paper [22] takes up trusting of source of such expressions. In case of social networking trust on users is equally important along with trust on what do they say. The paper here is our of interest for being another example on trust modelling using fuzzy set theory. Mobile social networking is the domain the paper has addressed by projecting the importance of a user in a mobile social networking society. Mobile social networking is a reality for having users on move while using mobile devices like smart phones, laptops and palmtops. Users on move and the same time being connected to several mobile users create mobile social networks. These networks are unique in nature for their dynamic configurations for ongoing addition and deletion of users. Sometimes because of connectivity issues and at the same time context issues a user can be a part of several networks. This adds to another character to mobile social networks that is overlapping. The challenging problem in this mobile computing environment is user trustworthiness. The paper takes up the problem defining k-degree fuzzy relationships among users. It uses social trust context in determining fuzzy relationships. From the relationships it infers trust values between users based on social context based community structures. Then local trust values are propagated to compute global trust values spanning across a mobile social network.

The issue of sourcing information and from it inferring trust is the problem taken up in [13]. In a fast changing world, information change. At the same time, there are malicious information flow too. More it does happen in case of social media. The problem is, how does one trust postings on social media? The paper takes up the question offering a paradigm of trust evolution. The types of evolution include *entity-oriented, data-oriented* and *hybrid trust* models. The ingenuity of a message is ascribed by trust of the source, content consistency. Hybrid model takes both in account. For a domain relations, constraints and assertions are explored as model elements. Then operators are defined so that context based combinations of model elements can be made to judge the degree of belief associated to an information. The paper proposes Genetic programming approach to find different combinations while computing the degree of belief on a set of information. This provides soft computing approach to compute trust value of information. The authors have demonstrated the application of their method to compute trust worthiness of data evolving from mobile vehicular adhoc networks.

4   Trust and Service

Anonymity while is a requirement. At the same time finding trustworthiness of a anonymous person is also essential. It's more so when many services are gradually being delivered on Internet. Social networking now provides platforms for people to socialise and collaborate. Unknowns meet on web and exchange messages. This digital life, has profound impact on both social life as well as governance. So, for transacting services in digital society trust evaluation is needed. This section presents some representative applications but doesn't claim as complete.

Recommender systems use collaborating filtering in finding relevant items for users. For the purpose they use online ratings of items and their associations. But, at times the required inputs to recommender systems may not be available in enough. This sparsity of data is a challenge for recommender systems. The challenge has been addressed by using user relationships represented by multi-graphs for multi-relationships. A unified model is proposed in [14] that uses both the relationships of users as well as items. While item relation graph is defined by some aspect similarities, user relation graph is defined by trust values among users. Users trust others who are found to hold similar opinions consistently. Trust from direct relationships spread across social network to derive global trust values. Based on item associations and global trust values, the paper presents a model to develop collaborating filters that recommender systems use to suggest items to users.

Query processing on Internet for retrieving information from web sources is essentially different than that of relational databases. It is so not only for heterogeneous repository but also of multiple information sources. Deep web-based search returns many results to a given query on web. Currently, web search engines order query results and labels a rank to each. But the point is, the present query processing doesn't consider the trustworthiness of information sources. The work in [18] addresses the issue. The paper is based on a conjecture i.e. the agreement of query results certify trustworthiness of information sources. The researchers consider recommendation to a web source as the input to compute trust. The agreement is not collected from users. Agreement on results is implicit by their similarities. Thus an agreement is taken a mutual recommendation. They construct an agreement graph where vertices and edges represent sources and agreement respectively. Two heuristics the paper uses in deciding trust of a source. One is: the node with higher degree of in-degree represents higher degree of trust and the endorsement from a high in-degree carries higher recommendation than that of less in-degree. Query results ranking is augmented by edge trust worthiness as computed from agreement graph.

In another work [8], issue of trust in providing services on web is reported. Usually, customer feedback has been a method in realising trust in web market where customers are largely anonymous and so also are the service providers. In such cases though feedback has been a traditional method still this mechanism is not appreciated for inherent biases and artificial swell ups. Hence the paper proposes an integrated approach that along with feedback considers recommendations as well as associations. The third factor *association* is unique in a sense indicating trustworthy associations of an entity increases its trustworthiness. Its utility is shown in case of web services as services delivered to a user may be composed one with several other atomic web services. The proposed model is implemented in **jUUDI** an open source software for universal description, discovery and integration of webservices. It's shown trust can be used for service selection as well as composition.

Another example of trust usages is taken from systems paradigm particularly in case of wireless sensor networks having tiny sensors communicating with each other. In this case there could be case of malicious sensors that need to be identified and isolated for operational correctness and continuity. This requires trust management in wireless sensor networks. In addition to energy saving routes, message routing follows trusted nodes in the path. The paper [1] takes up the problem and proposes Energy-aware Trust-based Gravitational Search protocol for message routing. The routing protocol uses trust-based energy-aware routing algorithm. It considers direct and indirect trust of nodes and energy saving issue in designing optimised routing function metric that governs choice of nodes in finding paths for routing.

5   Conclusion

Trust as commonly understood is a human character that is always dependable. Other than dependability, no fear of loss is also a factor for trust initiation between a trustor and a trustee. Further, behaviour and consistency are also factors that initiate trust. A person is trusted being recommended by another trusted person. That way, a recommender is a third party that helps in establishing trust. Association is a contributing factor in initiation and maintenance of trust. A person having trusted professionalism and social relationships is usually assumed as a trusted person. Thus, there are many aspects considered for initiation of trust. In society trust is an essential factor, helps in transacting personal affairs and running professional activities.

The issue of trust is getting importance for increasing secluded life opting socialising on cyberspace being a member in different social networks. Anonymous individuals located geographically distant places but connected on cyberspace set up friendship on trust observing each others' digital presences. In business domain, industry houses transacting services over Internet need a trusted atmosphere that ensures successful transactions for both service providers as well as consumers. In governance sector, for successful implementation of government programmes, trust of people is required. In case of eGovernance and emerging digital society, trust management is necessary. More it's required due to increasing automation in decision makings by artificial intelligence systems. Non-deterministic systems providing heuristic based soft-solutions are vulnerable to miscalculations and misjudgements which may generate lack of trust among users. This has generated concerns among researchers and interest in trust artificial intelligence [19].

As told earlier, the trend being towards developing humanoid systems, the need is also to enshrine qualitative human behaviour in making of systems for public. We call those anthropomorphic characters as *Humanitics* like trust, love, compassion, collaboration, socialization and etc. Among those, this paper presents a systematic review of works on *Trust* reported in literature. We don't claim of completeness in this survey. A recent tour on this subject can also be found in [29].

This paper has taken a long walk from autonomic computing via intelligent agent based systems in order to show the related developments along a timeline.

Then it has dealt with social networking for its importance in the recent life style of people in digital society. In order to emphasize the recent trend in study of humanitics in software systems, some representative applications from sensor networking, webservice, web based query system and recommender system are discussed.

The challenge of computing trust remains as of now because a generic framework for trust computation is still not visible. Researchers define a trust metric with respect to a given problem domain. But, the question is, can there be generic framework for trust management in software systems? Do we need a third party in cyberspace who can monitor cyberspace to ensure trust on cyber-systems for users? How lost trusts can be revived? Once trust accreditation algorithm is public, then there could be artificial trust synthesis that needs to be identified and curtailed. There are many such philosophical questions to be addressed by the researchers. While software systems are gradually dominating human life, these need to have humanitics into it. Endowing humanitics into software systems needs a holistic research on Psychology, Social and Computer sciences in developing anthropomorphic algorithms.

References

1. Zahedi, A., Parma, F.: An energy-aware trust-based routing algorithm using gravitational search approach in wireless sensor networks. Peer-to-Peer Netw. Appl. **12**(1), 67–176 (2009)
2. Rao, A.S., Georgeff, M.: Modelling rational agents within BDI architecture. In: Proceedings of Second International Conference on Knowledge Representation and Reasoning, San Mateo, CA (1991)
3. Ashtiani, M., Azgomi, M.A.: A novel trust evolution algorithm based on a quantum-like model of computational trust. Cogn. Technol. works **21**, 1–24 (2018)
4. Castelfranch, C., Falcone, R., Pezzulo, G.: Trust in information sources as a source for trust: a fuzzy approach. In: Proceedings of AAMAS, pp. 89–96 (2003)
5. Kossinets, G., Kleinberg, J., Watts, D.: The structure of information pathways in a social communication network. In: Proceedings of ACM SIGKDD, pp. 435–443 (2008)
6. Golbeck, J.A.: Computing and Applying Trust in Web-Based Social Networks. Ph.D. dissertation, College Park, MD, USA, University of Maryland at College Park (2005)
7. Granovetter, M.: The strength of weak ties: a network theory revisited. Sociol. Theory **1**, 201–233 (1983)
8. Mohanty, H., Prasad, K., Shyamasundar, R.K.: Trust assessment in web services: an extension to jUDDI. In: Proceedings IEEE e-Business Engineering, pp. 759–762 (2007)
9. An architectural blueprint for autonomic computing, IBM White Paper (2006)
10. Jiang, W., Wang, G., Wu, J.: Generating trusted graphs for trust evaluation in online social networks. Future Gener. Comput. Syst. **31**, 48–58 (2014)
11. Jiang, W., Wu, J., Li, F., Wang, G., Zheng, H.: Trust evaluation in online social networks using generalized network flow. IEEE Trans. Comput. **65**(3), 952–963 (2016)

12. Kinny, D., Georgeff, M., Rao, A.: A methodology and modelling technique for systems of BDI agents. In: Van de Velde, W., Perram, J.W. (eds.) MAAMAW 1996. LNCS, vol. 1038, pp. 56–71. Springer, Heidelberg (1996). https://doi.org/10.1007/BFb0031846

13. Aslan, M., Sen, S.: Evolving trust formula to evaluate data trustworthiness in VANETs using genetic programming. In: Kaufmann, P., Castillo, P.A. (eds.) EvoApplications 2019. LNCS, vol. 11454, pp. 413–429. Springer, Cham (2019). https://doi.org/10.1007/978-3-030-16692-2_28

14. Mao, M., Zhang, G., Zhang, J.: Multirelational social recommendations via multi-graph ranking. IEEE Trans. Cybern. **47**(12), 4049–4061 (2017)

15. Georgeff, M., Pell, B., Pollack, M., Tambe, M., Wooldridge, M.: The belief-desire-intention model of agency. In: Müller, J.P., Rao, A.S., Singh, M.P. (eds.) ATAL 1998. LNCS, vol. 1555, pp. 1–10. Springer, Heidelberg (1999). https://doi.org/10.1007/3-540-49057-4_1

16. Taherian, M., Amini, M., Jalili, R.: Trust inference in web-based social networks using resistive networks. In: Proceedings ICIW, pp. 233–238 (2008)

17. Newell, A.: Unified Theories of Cognition. Harvard University Press, Cambridge (1990)

18. Balakrishnan, R., Kambhampati, S.: SourceRank: relevance and trust assessment for deep web sources based on inter-source agreement. In: Proceedings of WWW, vol. 1, pp. 227–236 (2011)

19. Cohen, R., Schaekermann, M., Liu, S., Cormier, M.: Trusted AI and the contribution of trust modeling in multiagent system. In: Proceedings of AAMAS, pp. 1644–1648 (2019)

20. Hamdi, S., Gancarski, A.L., Bouzeghoub, A., Yahia, A.B.: TISON: trust inference in trust-oriented social networks. ACM Trans. Inf. Syst. **34**(3), 17 (2016)

21. Schnettler, S.: A structured overview of 50 years of small-world research. Soc. Netw. **31**(3), 165–178 (2009)

22. Chen, S., Wang, G., Jia, W.: k-FuzzyTrust: efficient trust computation for large-scale mobile social networks using a fuzzy implicit social graph. Inf. Sci. **318**, 123–143 (2015)

23. Laird, J.E.: The Soar Cognitive Architecture. MIT Press, Cambridge (2012). ISBN 978-0262122962

24. Laird, J.E., Newell, A., Rosenbloom, P.S.: SOAR: an architecture for general intelligence. Artif. Intell. **33**, 1–64 (1987)

25. Malkhi, D., Reiter, M.K.: Byzantine quorum systems. Distrib. Comput. **11**(4), 203–213 (1998)

26. Alagar, V.S., Paquet, J., Wan, K.: Intensional programming for agent communication. In: Leite, J., Omicini, A., Torroni, P., Yolum, I. (eds.) DALT 2004. LNCS (LNAI), vol. 3476, pp. 239–255. Springer, Heidelberg (2005). https://doi.org/10.1007/11493402_14

27. Mao, C., Xu, C., He, Q.: A cost-effective algorithm for inferring the trust between two individuals in social networks. Knowl.-Based Syst. **164**, 122–138 (2019)

28. Guha, R., Kumar, R., Raghavan, P., Tomkins, A.: Propagation of trust and distrust. In: Proceedings of WWW, pp. 403–412 (2004)

29. Ruan, Y., Durresi, A.: A survey of trust management systems for online social communities-trust modelling, trust inference and attacks. Knowl.-Based Syst. **106**, 150–163 (2016)

A Very Gentle Introduction
to Multiparty Session Types

Nobuko Yoshida[✉] and Lorenzo Gheri

Imperial College London, London, UK
{n.yoshida,l.gheri}@imperial.ac.uk

Abstract. Multiparty session types (MPST) are a formal specification
and verification framework for message-passing protocols without central control: the desired interactions at the scale of the network itself
are specified into a session (called *global type*). Global types are then
projected onto *local types* (one for each participant), which describe the
protocol from a local point of view. These local types are used to validate
an application through type-checking, monitoring, and code generation.
Theory of session types guarantees that local conformance of all participants induces *global conformance* of the network to the initial global
type. This paper provides a very gentle introduction of the simplest version of multiparty session types for readers who are not familiar with
session types nor process calculi.

Keywords: Multiparty session types · Process calculi · Distributed
systems · Type safety · Progress

1 A Gentle Introduction to Multiparty Session Types

Backgrounds. Session types were introduced in a series of papers during the
1990s [8,10,18] in the context of pure concurrent processes and programming.
Session types have since been studied in many contexts over the last decade—see
the surveys of the field [4,13].

A basic observation underlying session types is that a communication-based
application often exhibits a highly structured sequence of interactions involving,
for example, sequencing, choices and recursion, which as a whole form a natural
unit of *session*. The structure of a session is abstracted as a *type* through an
intuitive syntax, which is then used for validating programs through associated
language primitives.

Multiparty session types generalise the binary session type theory to the
multiparty case, preventing deadlock and communication errors in more sophisticated communication protocols involving any number (two or more) of participants. The central idea is to introduce global types, which describe multiparty conversations from a global perspective and provide a means to check

Work partially supported by EPSRC projects EP/K034413/1, EP/K011715/1,
EP/L00058X/1, EP/N027833/1 and EP/N028201/1.

© Springer Nature Switzerland AG 2020
D. V. Hung and M. D'Souza (Eds.): ICDCIT 2020, LNCS 11969, pp. 73–93, 2020.
https://doi.org/10.1007/978-3-030-36987-3_5

protocol compliance. The theory [11,12] was born by transforming the industry idea developed during designing a protocol description language, Scribble [17], which was presented by Kohei Honda in [9] (see the historical background [20]). This original work was extended in various ways and applied to many different programming languages and tools, some of which use Scribble. The reader who is interested in programming languages can find the tools and papers at *Mobility Reading Group Home Page.*

Binary Session Types. As a first example, consider a scenario where a customer tries to conclude a deal with a travel agency. We associate a process with the *customer* (`Customer`) and one with the *agency* (`Agency`). The task involves synchronisation in the communication between the customer and the agency. Synchronisation is obtained through the exchange of messages.

Specifically, the protocol works as follows.

1. The customer sends an order to the agency, namely the place they desire to visit in their next travel (let us say *Hawaii*). On receiving the request, the agency looks up the price relative to that travel and sends a quote (*quote*) back to the customer.
2. When the customer receives the *quote*, they make a decision (choice): either to *accept* or to *reject* the offer. The customer communicates their decision to the agency, which is waiting for such a message.
3. In case of acceptance, the agency waits that the customer communicates their address (*address*), then sends a confirmation date (*date*) for the trip back to the customer and the protocol terminates.
4. In case of rejection, the deal is not made and the protocol immediately terminates.

The multiparty session types methodology is as follows. First, define a *global type* that gives a shared contract of the allowed pattern of message exchanges in the system. Second, *project* the global type to each end-point participant to obtain a *local type*: an obligation on the message sends and receipts for each process that together ensure that the pattern of messages are allowed by the global type. Finally, check that the implementation of each process conforms to its local type.

In our protocol, from a global perspective, we expect to see the following pattern of message exchanges, encoded as a *global type* for the communication:

$$\text{Customer} \rightarrow \text{Agency}: \textit{Hawaii}(\texttt{bool}).\text{Agency} \rightarrow \text{Customer}: \textit{quote}(\texttt{nat}).$$
$$\text{Customer} \rightarrow \text{Agency} : \{$$
$$\qquad \textit{accept}(\texttt{bool}).$$
$$\qquad\qquad \text{Customer} \rightarrow \text{Agency}: \textit{address}(\texttt{nat}). \qquad\qquad (1)$$
$$\qquad\qquad \text{Agency} \rightarrow \text{Customer}: \textit{date}(\texttt{nat}).\texttt{end},$$
$$\qquad \textit{reject}(\texttt{bool}).\texttt{end}$$
$$\}$$

The type describes the global pattern of communication between `Customer` and `Agency` using message exchanges, sequencing, and choice. The basic pattern

Customer → Agency: $m(S)$ indicates a message with label m sent from the Customer to the Agency, together with an element of sort S. The communication starts with the customer sending the message *Hawaii* to the agency, then the agency sends the *quote* label together with a natural number and at this point the customer either sends an *accept* or a *reject* message. In case of *reject*, the protocol ends (type **end**); otherwise, the communication continues with the sequential exchange of an *address* (from the customer to the agency) and a *date* (from the agency to the customer). The operator "." denotes sequencing, the "," separates possible continuations for the protocol.

The global type states what are the valid message sequences allowed in the system. When we implement Customer and Agency separately, we would like to check that their composition conforms to the global type. Since there are only two participants, projecting to each participant is simple. From the perspective of the Customer, the communication can be described by the type:

$$?Hawaii(\texttt{bool}).!quote(\texttt{nat}).$$
$$((\ !accept(\texttt{bool}).!address(\texttt{nat}).?date(\texttt{nat}).\texttt{end} \ ) \oplus (\ !reject(\texttt{bool}).\texttt{end} \ )) \quad (2)$$

where $!m$ denotes a message with label m sent to Agency, $?m$ denotes a message with label m received from Agency, and $\oplus$ denotes an internal choice. Thus the type states that, Customer after sending the message with label *Hawaii*, waits for a natural number for the *quote* and, after receiving it, decides either to send $!accept(\texttt{bool})$. $!address(\texttt{nat})$, wait for a natural number for the *date* and then exit, or to send just *reject*(**bool**) and exit.

From the viewpoint of Agency, the same global session is described by the dual type

$$Hawaii(\texttt{bool}).!quote(\texttt{nat}).$$
$$((\ ?accept(\texttt{bool}).?address(\texttt{nat}).!date(\texttt{nat}).\texttt{end} \ ) \ \& \ (\ ?reject(\texttt{bool}).\texttt{end} \ )) \quad (3)$$

in which & means that a choice is offered externally.

We can now individually check that the implementations of the customer and the agency conform to these local types.

Multiparty Session Types. In the case of two parties, the safety can be checked given the local type (2) since its dual (3) is unique (up to unfolding recursions).

However, for applications involving *multiple parties*, the global type and its projection to each participant are essential to provide a shared contract among all participants.

For example, consider a simple ring protocol, where, after the customer's acceptance, the agency needs to forward some details to the hotel, before a direct communication starts between the hotel and the customer. Namely, Customer sends a message *details* to Agency, which forwards the message to Hotel. After receiving the message, Hotel sends an acknowledgement *ok* to Customer. We start by specifying the global type as:

$$\text{Customer} \rightarrow \text{Agency}: details(\texttt{nat}).\text{Agency} \rightarrow \text{Hotel}: details(\texttt{nat}).$$
$$\text{Hotel} \rightarrow \text{Customer}: ok(\texttt{bool}).\texttt{end} \quad (4)$$

As before, we want to check each process locally against a local type such that, if each process conforms to its local type, then the composition satisfies the global type. The global type in (4) is *projected* into the three local types:

Customer's endpoint type: Agency!*details*(nat).Hotel?*ok*(bool).end

Agency's endpoint type: Customer?*details*(nat).Hotel!*details*(nat).end

Hotel's endpoint type: Agency?*details*(nat).Customer!*ok*(bool).end

where Agency!*details*(nat) means "send to Agency a *details* message," and Hotel?*ok*(bool) means "receive from Hotel an *ok* message." Then each process is type-checked against its own endpoint type. When the three processes are executed, their interactions automatically follow the stipulated scenario.

If instead we only used three separate binary session types to describe the message exchanges between Customer and Agency, between Agency and Hotel, and between Hotel and Customer, respectively, without using a global type, then we lose essential sequencing information in this interaction scenario. Consequently, we can no longer guarantee deadlock-freedom among these three parties. Since the three separate binary sessions can be interleaved freely, an implementation of the Customer that conforms to Hotel?*ok*(bool).Agency!*details*(nat).end becomes typable. This causes the situation in which each of the three parties blocks indefinitely while waiting for a message to be delivered.

In what follows we will start from giving more examples in Sect. 2, which will be used as running examples throughout the whole paper. In Sect. 3 we will introduce a formal process calculus powerful enough to describe multiparty communication protocols, such as the ones from above. Finally in Sect. 4, we will introduce a type system; we will show how multiparty session types work by examples and present the key properties of typed processes.

2   Examples, Intuitively

Multiparty session types are aimed at enabling compositional reasoning about communication among different parties. In this section we present informally some essential communication protocols that can be handled with this methodology.

Let us for example consider the basic protocol from the previous section. This simple protocol for a travel agency is synthetically displayed by Fig. 1a. A more interesting protocol could be the one shown in Fig. 1b. Here the customer is allowed to try *again and again* to obtain the new quote, should they not like the first one. We will see that our calculus (Sect. 3) is endowed with recursion, which can model an indefinite number of iterations.

Let us consider a specification in Fig. 2, which describes a simple communication protocol among three parties. Bob is waiting for a message from Alice, *non-deterministically* allowing for messages with two different labels (*l1* and *l2*). Alice sends the message with label *l1* and the communication continues with Bob sending a message message1 to Carol and finally Carol returning a message answer to Alice, which depends on the previous communication, including the choice of the label for the original message from Alice to Bob.

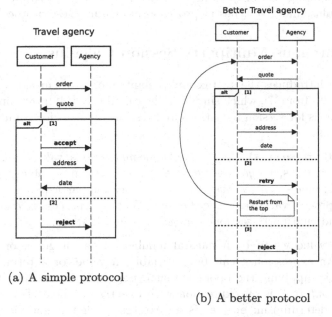

(a) A simple protocol

(b) A better protocol

Fig. 1. Communication protocols for a travel agency

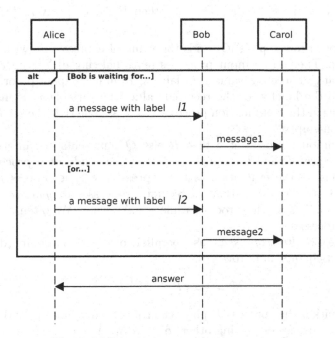

Fig. 2. Multiparty communication protocol

In the following sections, we model these protocols by a simple multiparty session calculus, and give types to processes modelling these protocols.

3   Synchronous Multiparty Session Calculus

This section introduces the syntax and semantics of a synchronous multiparty session calculus from [7], which simplifies the calculus in [14] by eliminating both shared channels for session initiations and session channels for communications inside sessions.

Notation 01 (Base sets). *We use the following base sets:* values, *ranged over by* $v, v', \ldots$; expressions, *ranged over by* $e, e', \ldots$; expression variables, *ranged over by* $x, y, z \ldots$; labels, *ranged over by* $\ell, \ell', \ldots$; session participants, *ranged over by* $p, q, \ldots$; process variables, *ranged over by* $X, Y, \ldots$; processes, *ranged over by* $P, Q, \ldots$; and multiparty sessions, *ranged over by* $\mathcal{M}, \mathcal{M}', \ldots$.

Syntax. A value v can be a natural number n, an integer i, or a boolean true/false. An expression e can be a variable, a value, or a term built from expressions by applying the operators $\text{succ}, \text{neg}, \neg, \oplus$, or the relation $>$. An *evaluation context* $\mathcal{E}$ is an expression with exactly one hole. The operator $\oplus$ models non-determinism: $e_1 \oplus e_2$ is an expression that might yield either e_1 or e_2.

The processes of the synchronous multiparty session calculus are defined by:

$$P ::= p!\ell\langle e \rangle.P \quad | \quad \sum_{i \in I} p?\ell_i(x_i).P_i \quad | \quad \text{if } e \text{ then } P \text{ else } P \quad | \quad \mu X.P \quad | \quad X \quad | \quad \mathbf{0}$$

The output process $p!\ell\langle e \rangle.Q$ sends the value of expression e with label ℓ to participant p. The sum of input processes (external choice) $\sum_{i \in I} p?\ell_i(x_i).P_i$ is a process that can accept a value with label ℓ_i from participant p, for any $i \in I$. According to the label ℓ_i of the received value, the variable x_i is instantiated with the value in the continuation process P_i. We assume that the set I is always finite and non-empty.

The conditional process if e then P else Q represents the internal choice between processes P and Q. Which branch of the conditional process will be taken depends on the evaluation of the expression e. The process $\mu X.P$ is a recursive process. We assume that the recursive processes are *guarded*. For example, $\mu X.p?\ell(x).X$ is a valid process, while $\mu X.X$ is not. We often omit $\mathbf{0}$ from the tail of processes.

We define a *multiparty session* as a parallel composition of pairs (denoted by $p \triangleleft P$) of participants and processes:

$$\mathcal{M} ::= p \triangleleft P \quad | \quad \mathcal{M} \mid \mathcal{M}$$

with the intuition that process P plays the role of participant p, and can interact with other processes playing other roles in $\mathcal{M}$. A multiparty session is *well formed* if all its participants are different. We consider only well-formed multiparty sessions.

Example 1. We now show how to encode, in the above calculus, processes respecting the protocols informally presented in Fig. 1. Note that we picked one different label for each destination (that can be either Hawaii or France), as well as for each action (as "accept", "reject", ...).

Let us start with processes in Fig. 1a.

$P'_{\text{Customer}} = \mathsf{Agency!}\textit{Hawaii}\langle\mathsf{true}\rangle.\mathsf{Agency?}\textit{quote}(x).$
$\quad\quad\quad\quad$ if $\ (x > 1000)$
$\quad\quad\quad\quad$ then $\ \mathsf{Agency!}\textit{reject}\langle\mathsf{true}\rangle.\mathbf{0}$
$\quad\quad\quad\quad$ else $\ \mathsf{Agency!}\textit{accept}\langle\mathsf{true}\rangle.\mathsf{Agency!}\textit{address}\langle 42\rangle.\mathsf{Agency?}\textit{date}(y).\mathbf{0}$
$P'_{\text{Agency}} \ = \mathsf{Customer?}\textit{Hawaii}(x).\mathsf{Customer!}\textit{quote}\langle 5000\rangle.$
$\quad\quad\quad\quad$ $(\mathsf{Customer?}\textit{accept}(y).\mathsf{Customer?}\textit{address}(z).$
$\quad\quad\quad\quad\quad$ $\mathsf{Customer!}\textit{date}\langle 25122019\rangle.\mathbf{0}$
$\quad\quad\quad\quad$ $+\mathsf{Customer?}\textit{reject}(y).\mathbf{0})$
$\quad\quad\ + \mathsf{Customer?}\textit{France}(x).\mathsf{Customer!}\textit{quote}\langle 1000\rangle.$
$\quad\quad\quad\quad$ $(\mathsf{Customer?}\textit{accept}(y).\mathsf{Customer?}\textit{address}(z).$
$\quad\quad\quad\quad\quad$ $\mathsf{Customer!}\textit{date}\langle 25122019\rangle.\mathbf{0}$
$\quad\quad\quad\quad$ $+\mathsf{Customer?}\textit{reject}(y).\mathbf{0})$

The customer here would ask for Hawaii as a destination, they will receive a quote that will be too expensive ($5000 > 1000$) and, thus, they will end up rejecting the offer (via sending true with label *reject*).

In what follows instead we will extend the above processes, giving to the customer the opportunity to retry, as suggested by the diagram in Fig. 1b.

$P_{\text{Customer}} = \mathsf{Agency!}\textit{Hawaii}\langle\mathsf{true}\rangle.\mathsf{Agency?}\textit{quote}(x).$
$\quad\quad\quad\quad$ if $\ (x > 1000)$
$\quad\quad\quad\quad$ then $\ \mathsf{Agency!}\ \boxed{\textit{retry}\langle\mathsf{true}\rangle}\ .\mathsf{Agency!}\textit{France}\langle\mathsf{true}\rangle.\mathsf{Agency?}\textit{quote}(y).$
$\quad\quad\quad\quad\quad$ if $\ (y > 1000)$
$\quad\quad\quad\quad\quad$ then $\ \mathsf{Agency!}\textit{reject}\langle\mathsf{true}\rangle.\mathbf{0}$
$\quad\quad\quad\quad\quad$ else $\ \mathsf{Agency!}\textit{accept}\langle\mathsf{true}\rangle.\mathsf{Agency!}\textit{address}\langle 42\rangle.\mathsf{Agency?}\textit{date}(z).\mathbf{0}$
$\quad\quad\quad\quad$ else $\ \mathsf{Agency!}\textit{accept}\langle\mathsf{true}\rangle.\mathsf{Agency!}\textit{address}\langle 42\rangle.\mathsf{Agency?}\textit{date}(y).\mathbf{0}$
$P_{\text{Agency}} \ = \boxed{\mu X.}\ \mathsf{Customer?}\textit{Hawaii}(x).\mathsf{Customer!}\textit{quote}\langle 5000\rangle.$
$\quad\quad\quad\quad$ $(\mathsf{Customer?}\textit{accept}(y).\mathsf{Customer?}\textit{address}(z).$
$\quad\quad\quad\quad\quad$ $\mathsf{Customer!}\textit{date}\langle 25122019\rangle.\mathbf{0}$
$\quad\quad\quad\quad$ $+ \boxed{\mathsf{Customer?}\textit{retry}(y).X}\ + \mathsf{Customer?}\textit{reject}(y).\mathbf{0})$
$\quad\quad\ + \mathsf{Customer?}\textit{France}(x).\mathsf{Customer!}\textit{quote}\langle 1000\rangle.$
$\quad\quad\quad\quad$ $(\mathsf{Customer?}\textit{accept}(y).\mathsf{Customer?}\textit{address}(z).$
$\quad\quad\quad\quad\quad$ $\mathsf{Customer!}\textit{date}\langle 25122019\rangle.\mathbf{0}$
$\quad\quad\quad\quad$ $+ \boxed{\mathsf{Customer?}\textit{retry}(y).X}\ + \mathsf{Customer?}\textit{reject}(y).\mathbf{0})$

In the example above, we have highlighted the syntactic construct allowing the customer to retry the purchase and obtain a new quote. In P_{Customer} the only occurrence of the label *retry* is within a deterministic choice (if _ then _ else _ construct): if the quote is too high, the customer will communicate to the agency that they would like a different quote for a different destination. More interesting

Table 1. Expression evaluation.

$$\mathsf{succ}(n) \downarrow (n+1) \qquad \mathsf{neg}(i) \downarrow (-i) \qquad \neg\mathsf{true} \downarrow \mathsf{false} \quad \neg\mathsf{false} \downarrow \mathsf{true} \qquad \mathsf{v} \downarrow \mathsf{v}$$

$$(i_1 > i_2) \downarrow \begin{cases} \mathsf{true} & \text{if } i_1 > i_2, \\ \mathsf{false} & \text{otherwise} \end{cases} \qquad \frac{e_1 \downarrow \mathsf{v}}{e_1 \oplus e_2 \downarrow \mathsf{v}} \qquad \frac{e_2 \downarrow \mathsf{v}}{e_1 \oplus e_2 \downarrow \mathsf{v}} \qquad \frac{e \downarrow \mathsf{v} \quad \mathcal{E}(\mathsf{v}) \downarrow \mathsf{v}'}{\mathcal{E}(e) \downarrow \mathsf{v}'}$$

is how P_{Agency} handles the *retry* request, namely by recursion on X: the recursive call is activated each time the agency receives a *retry* request from the customer.

Operational Semantics. *The value* v *of expression* e (notation e $\downarrow$ v) is computed as expected, see Table 1. The successor operation succ is defined only on natural numbers, the negation neg is defined on integers, and $\neg$ is defined only on boolean values. The internal choice $e_1 \oplus e_2$ evaluates either to the value of e_1 or to the value of e_2.

The *computational rules of multiparty sessions* are given in Table 3. They are closed with respect to the structural congruence defined in Table 2. In rule [R-COMM], the participant q sends the value v choosing the label ℓ_j to participant p, who offers inputs on all labels ℓ_i with $i \in I$. In rules [T-CONDITIONAL] and [F-CONDITIONAL], the participant p chooses to continue as P if the condition e evaluates to true and as Q if e evaluates to false. Rule [R-STRUCT] states that

Table 2. Structural congruence.

[S-REC]   [S-MULTI]
$$\mu X.P \equiv P\{\mu X.P/X\} \qquad P \equiv Q \Rightarrow \mathsf{p} \triangleleft P \mid \mathcal{M} \equiv \mathsf{p} \triangleleft Q \mid \mathcal{M}$$

[S-PAR 1]   [S-PAR 2]   [S-PAR 3]
$$\mathsf{p} \triangleleft \mathbf{0} \mid \mathcal{M} \equiv \mathcal{M} \qquad \mathcal{M} \mid \mathcal{M}' \equiv \mathcal{M}' \mid \mathcal{M} \qquad (\mathcal{M} \mid \mathcal{M}') \mid \mathcal{M}'' \equiv \mathcal{M} \mid (\mathcal{M}' \mid \mathcal{M}'')$$

Table 3. Reduction rules.

[R-COMM]
$$\frac{j \in I \qquad e \downarrow \mathsf{v}}{\mathsf{p} \triangleleft \sum_{i \in I} \mathsf{q}?\ell_i(x).P_i \mid \mathsf{q} \triangleleft \mathsf{p}!\ell_j\langle e\rangle.Q \mid \mathcal{M} \longrightarrow \mathsf{p} \triangleleft P_j\{\mathsf{v}/x\} \mid \mathsf{q} \triangleleft Q \mid \mathcal{M}}$$

[T-CONDITIONAL]
$$\frac{e \downarrow \mathsf{true}}{\mathsf{p} \triangleleft \mathsf{if}\ e\ \mathsf{then}\ P\ \mathsf{else}\ Q \mid \mathcal{M} \longrightarrow \mathsf{p} \triangleleft P \mid \mathcal{M}}$$

[F-CONDITIONAL]
$$\frac{e \downarrow \mathsf{false}}{\mathsf{p} \triangleleft \mathsf{if}\ e\ \mathsf{then}\ P\ \mathsf{else}\ Q \mid \mathcal{M} \longrightarrow \mathsf{p} \triangleleft Q \mid \mathcal{M}}$$

[R-STRUCT]
$$\frac{\mathcal{M}'_1 \equiv \mathcal{M}_1 \quad \mathcal{M}_1 \longrightarrow \mathcal{M}_2 \quad \mathcal{M}_2 \equiv \mathcal{M}'_2}{\mathcal{M}'_1 \longrightarrow \mathcal{M}'_2}$$

the reduction relation is closed with respect to structural congruence. We use $\longrightarrow^*$ with the standard meaning.

We adopt some standard conventions regarding the syntax of processes and sessions. Namely, we will use $\prod_{i \in I} \mathsf{p}_i \triangleleft P_i$ as short for $\mathsf{p}_1 \triangleleft P_1 \mid \ldots \mid \mathsf{p}_n \triangleleft P_n$, where $I = \{1, \ldots, n\}$. We will sometimes use infix notation for external choice process. For example, instead of $\sum_{i \in \{1,2\}} \mathsf{p}?\ell_i(x).P_i$, we will write $\mathsf{p}?\ell_1(x).P_1 + \mathsf{p}?\ell_2(x).P_2$.

Example 2. We now show the operational semantics in action. Consider the following multiparty session with three participants, Alice, Bob and Carol :

$$\mathcal{M} = \texttt{Alice} \triangleleft P_{\texttt{Alice}} \mid \texttt{Bob} \triangleleft P_{\texttt{Bob}} \mid \texttt{Carol} \triangleleft P_{\texttt{Carol}}$$

where

$$P_{\texttt{Alice}} = \texttt{Bob}!\ell_1\langle 50 \rangle.\texttt{Carol}?\ell_3(x).0$$
$$P_{\texttt{Bob}} = \texttt{Alice}?\ell_1(x).\texttt{Carol}!\ell_2\langle 100 \rangle.0 + \texttt{Alice}?\ell_4(x).\texttt{Carol}!\ell_2\langle 2 \rangle.0$$
$$P_{\texttt{Carol}} = \texttt{Bob}?\ell_2(x).\texttt{Alice}!\ell_3\langle \text{succ}(x) \rangle.0$$

This multiparty session reduces to

$$\texttt{Alice} \triangleleft 0 \mid \texttt{Bob} \triangleleft 0 \mid \texttt{Carol} \triangleleft 0$$

after three communications occur. First, Alice sends to Bob natural number 50 with the label ℓ_1. Bob is able to receive values with labels ℓ_1 and ℓ_4. Next, the only possible communication is between Bob and Carol. So, Carol receives natural number 100 from Bob. The value 100 is substituted in the continuation process. Finally, since $\text{succ}(100) \downarrow 101$, Carol sends 101 to Alice. We can then reduce the session to, for example, $\texttt{Alice} \triangleleft 0$, but not further.

Exercise 1. Prove the following:

1. $\texttt{Customer} \triangleleft P'_{\texttt{Customer}} \mid \texttt{Agency} \triangleleft P'_{\texttt{Agency}}$ reduces to $\texttt{Customer} \triangleleft 0 \mid \texttt{Agency} \triangleleft 0$;
2. $\texttt{Customer} \triangleleft P_{\texttt{Customer}} \mid \texttt{Agency} \triangleleft P_{\texttt{Agency}}$ reduces to $\texttt{Customer} \triangleleft 0 \mid \texttt{Agency} \triangleleft 0$.

From the end of Example 2, we can see that a session $\mathcal{M}$ always has at least one participant, since we do not have neutral element for the parallel composition. In Sect. 4, we will introduce a type system ensuring that if a well-typed multiparty session has only one participant, then the corresponding process is 0 — hence, the participant's process has no inputs/outputs to perform.

The most crucial property is that when a multiparty session contains communications that will never be executed.

Definition 1. *A multiparty session $\mathcal{M}$ is* stuck *if $\mathcal{M} \not\equiv \mathsf{p} \triangleleft 0$ and there is no multiparty session $\mathcal{M}'$ such that $\mathcal{M} \longrightarrow \mathcal{M}'$. A multiparty session $\mathcal{M}$ gets* stuck, *notation* $\text{stuck}(\mathcal{M})$, *if it reduces to a stuck multiparty session.*

The multiparty session $\mathcal{M}$ in Example 2 does not get stuck. A similar multiparty session, where instead of $P_{\texttt{Alice}}$ we take $P'_{\texttt{Alice}} = \texttt{Bob}!\ell_1\langle 50 \rangle.\texttt{Carol}?\ell_5(x).0$, gets stuck because of label mismatch.

4 Type System

This section introduces a type system for the calculus presented in Sect. 3 (the formulation is based on [7]). We formalise types and projections (Sect. 4.1), the subtyping relation (Sect. 4.2), and the typing rules and their properties (Sect. 4.3). All stated results in this paper are proved in [7].

4.1 Types and Projections

Global types provide global conversation scenarios of multiparty sessions, with a bird's eye view describing the message exchanges between pairs of participants.

Definition 2 (Sorts and global types). *Sorts, ranged over by S, are defined as:*

$$S \ ::= \ \texttt{nat} \mid \texttt{int} \mid \texttt{bool}$$

Global types, *ranged over by* G, *are terms generated by the following grammar:*

$$\mathsf{G} \ ::= \ \texttt{end} \mid \mu \mathsf{t}.\mathsf{G} \mid \mathsf{t} \mid \mathsf{p} \to \mathsf{q} : \{\ell_i(S_i).\mathsf{G}_i\}_{i \in I}$$

We require that $\mathsf{p} \neq \mathsf{q}$, $I \neq \emptyset$, *and* $\ell_i \neq \ell_j$ *whenever* $i \neq j$, *for all* $i, j \in I$. *We postulate that recursion is guarded. Unless otherwise noted, global types are closed: a recursion variable* t *only occurs bounded by* $\mu \mathsf{t}$....

In Definition 2, the type $\mathsf{p} \to \mathsf{q} : \{\ell_i(S_i).\mathsf{G}_i\}_{i \in I}$ formalises a protocol where participant p must send to q one message with label ℓ_i and a value of type S_i as payload, for some $i \in I$; then, depending on which ℓ_i was sent by p, the protocol continues as G_i. Value types are restricted to sorts, that can be natural (`nat`), integer (`int`) and boolean (`bool`). The type `end` represents a terminated protocol. Recursive protocol is modelled as $\mu \mathsf{t}.\mathsf{G}$, where recursion variable t is bound and guarded in G — e.g., $\mu \mathsf{t}.\mathsf{p} \to \mathsf{q} : \ell(\texttt{nat}).\mathsf{t}$ is a valid global type, whereas $\mu \mathsf{t}.\mathsf{t}$ is not. We take the equi-recursive viewpoint, i.e. we identify $\mu \mathsf{t}.\mathsf{G}$ and $\mathsf{G}\{\mu \mathsf{t}.\mathsf{G}/\mathsf{t}\}$.

We define the *set of participants of a global type* G, by structural induction on G, as follows:

$$\mathsf{pt}\{\mu \mathsf{t}.\mathsf{G}\} = \mathsf{pt}\{\mathsf{G}\} \qquad \mathsf{pt}\{\texttt{end}\} = \mathsf{pt}\{\mathsf{t}\} = \emptyset$$

$$\mathsf{pt}\{\mathsf{p} \to \mathsf{q} : \{\ell_i(S_i).\mathsf{G}_i\}_{i \in I}\} = \{\mathsf{p}, \mathsf{q}\} \cup \mathsf{pt}\{\mathsf{G}_i\} \ (i \in I)$$

We will often write $\mathsf{p} \in \mathsf{G}$ instead of $\mathsf{p} \in \mathsf{pt}\{\mathsf{G}\}$.

A *local session type* describes the behaviour of a single participant in a multiparty session.

Definition 3 (Local Session Types). *The grammar of session types, ranged over by* T, *is:*

$$\mathsf{T} \ ::= \texttt{end} \mid \&_{i \in I}\mathsf{p}?\ell_i(S_i).\mathsf{T}_i \mid \oplus_{i \in I}\mathsf{q}!\ell_i(S_i).\mathsf{T}_i \mid \mu \mathsf{t}.\mathsf{T} \mid \mathsf{t}$$

We require that $\ell_i \neq \ell_j$ *whenever* $i \neq j$, *for all* $i, j \in I$. *We postulate that recursion is always guarded. Unless otherwise noted, session types are closed.*

Note that, according to the previous definition, labels in a type need to be pairwise different. For example, $\mathsf{p}?\ell(\mathtt{int}).\mathtt{end}\&\mathsf{p}?\ell(\mathtt{nat}).\mathtt{end}$ is not a type.

The session type **end** says that no further communication is possible and the protocol is completed. The *external choice* or *branching type* $\&_{i\in I}\mathsf{p}?\ell_i(S_i).\mathsf{T}_i$ requires to wait to receive a value of sort S_i (for some $i \in I$) from the participant p, via a message with label ℓ_i; if the received message has label ℓ_i, the protocol will continue as prescribed by T_i. The *internal choice* or *selection type* $\oplus_{i\in I}\mathsf{q}!\ell_i(S_i).\mathsf{T}_i$ says that the participant implementing the type must choose a labelled message to send to q; if the participant chooses the message ℓ_i, for some $i \in I$, it must include in the message to q a payload value of sort S_i, and continue as prescribed by T_i. Recursion is modelled by the session type $\mu t.\mathsf{T}$ We adopt the following conventions: we do not write branch/selection symbols in case of a singleton choice, we do not write unnecessary parentheses, and we often omit trailing **end**s.

The set $\mathsf{pt}\{\mathsf{T}\}$ of participants of a session type T is defined inductively as follows

$$\mathsf{pt}\{\&_{i\in I}\mathsf{p}?\ell_i(S_i).\mathsf{T}_i\} = \mathsf{pt}\{\oplus_{i\in I}\mathsf{p}!\ell_i(S_i).\mathsf{T}_i\} = \{\mathsf{p}\}\cup\bigcup_{i\in I}\mathsf{pt}\{\mathsf{T}_i\}$$
$$\mathsf{pt}\{\mu t.\mathsf{T}\} = \mathsf{pt}\{\mathsf{T}\} \quad \mathsf{pt}\{t\} = \mathsf{pt}\{\mathtt{end}\} = \emptyset.$$

In what follows we introduce the concept of *projection* of a global type onto a participant, didactically into two steps: first we give the simpler version of the projection from [11,12], then we extend it with the *merging* operation. The second definition will extend the domain of the projection as a partial function on global types, i.e., the second version of the projection will be well-defined on a wider range of global types.

Definition 4. *The* projection (no-merging version) *of a global type onto a participant* r *is defined by recursion on* G:

- $\mathtt{end}{\upharpoonright}r = \mathtt{end};$ [PROJ-END]

- $t{\upharpoonright}r = t;$ [PROJ-VAR]

- $(\mu t.\mathsf{G}){\upharpoonright}r = \mu t.(\mathsf{G}{\upharpoonright}r)$ *if* $r \in \mathsf{pt}\{\mathsf{G}\};$ [PROJ-REC-1]

- $(\mu t.\mathsf{G}){\upharpoonright}r = \mathtt{end}$ *if* $r \notin \mathsf{pt}\{\mathsf{G}\};$ [PROJ-REC-2]

- $\mathsf{p} \to r : \{\ell_i(S_i).\mathsf{G}_i\}_{i\in I}{\upharpoonright}r = \&_{i\in I}\mathsf{p}?\ell_i(S_i).\mathsf{G}_i{\upharpoonright}r;$ [PROJ-IN]

- $r \to \mathsf{q} : \{\ell_i(S_i).\mathsf{G}_i\}_{i\in I}{\upharpoonright}r = \oplus_{i\in I}\mathsf{q}!\ell_i(S_i).\mathsf{G}_i{\upharpoonright}r;$ [PROJ-OUT]

- $\mathsf{p} \to \mathsf{q} : \{\ell_i(S_i).\mathsf{G}_i\}_{i\in I}{\upharpoonright}r = \mathsf{G}_{i_0}{\upharpoonright}r$ *where* $i_0 \in I,$ [PROJ-CONT']
  if $r \notin \{\mathsf{p},\mathsf{q}\}$ *and, for all* $i,j \in I$, $\mathsf{G}_i{\upharpoonright}r = \mathsf{G}_j{\upharpoonright}r;$

- *undefined otherwise.*

We describe the clauses of Definition 4:

[PROJ-END,PROJ-VAR] give the behaviour of projections on **end** and type variables;

[PROJ-REC-1,PROJ-REC-2] give the behaviour of projections on recursive types; in particular [PROJ-REC-2] is needed: if we applied only [PROJ-REC-1] to any recursive type, we will obtain $(\mu t.p \to q : \ell(nat).t) \restriction r = \mu t.t$, namely we will allow for unguarded occurrences of t, which we do not accept as valid;

[PROJ-IN] (**resp.** [PROJ-OUT]) states that a global type G starting with a communication from p to r (resp. from r to q) projects onto an external (resp. internal) choice $\&_{i \in I} p?\ell_i(S_i).G_i \restriction r$ (resp. $\oplus_{i \in I} q!\ell_i(S_i).G_i \restriction r$), provided that the continuations of $\&_{i \in I} p?\ell_i(S_i).G_i \restriction r$ (resp. $\oplus_{i \in I} q!\ell_i(S_i).G_i \restriction r$) are also projections of the corresponding global type continuations $G_i \restriction r$.

[PROJ-CONT'] states that if G starts with a communication between p and q, and we are projecting G onto a third participant r, then we need to make sure that continuation is *the same* on all branches; just below we will see how this restriction can be relaxed.

Example 3. We now show an example of some projections of global types. Consider the global type (where p, q and r are pairwise distinct):

$$G = p \to q : \{\ell_1(nat).G_1, \ell_2(bool).G_1\} \text{ where } G_1 = q \to r : \{\ell_3(int), \ell_4(nat)\}$$

We have:

$$G \restriction p = q!\ell_1(nat).(G_1 \restriction p) \oplus q!\ell_2(bool).(G_1 \restriction p)$$
$$= q!\ell_1(nat).end \oplus q!\ell_2(bool).end$$

$$G \restriction q = p?\ell_1(nat).(G_1 \restriction q) \& p?\ell_2(bool).(G_1 \restriction q)$$
$$= p?\ell_1(nat).(r!\ell_3(int) \oplus r!\ell_4(nat)) \& p?\ell_2(bool).(r!\ell_3(int) \oplus r!\ell_4(nat))$$

$$G \restriction r = G_1 \restriction r = (q?\ell_3(int) \& q?\ell_4(nat))$$

Note that $G \restriction r$ is well defined only because the continuation of the communication after the exchange $p \to q$ is equal, namely G_1, in both branches.

In the following Definition 5, we give a more permissive definition of projection, that handles also cases in which the continuation is not the same in all branches, but the types are somehow "compatible", namely they can be merged. Our definition follows [7], which extends [11,12], along the lines of [19] and [2]. i.e., it uses a *merging operator* $\sqcap$.

Definition 5. *The* projection *of a global type onto a participant r is defined by recursion on* G:

- $end \restriction r = end$;   [PROJ-END]

- $t \restriction r = t$;   [PROJ-VAR]

- $(\mu t).G \restriction r = \mu t.(G \restriction r)$ *if* $r \in pt\{G\}$;   [PROJ-REC-1]

- $(\mu t).G \restriction r = end$ *if* $r \notin pt\{G\}$;   [PROJ-REC-2]

- $p \to r : \{\ell_i(S_i).G_i\}_{i \in I} \restriction r = \&_{i \in I} p?\ell_i(S_i).G_i \restriction r$;   [PROJ-IN]

- $r \to q : \{\ell_i(S_i).G_i\}_{i \in I} \restriction r = \oplus_{i \in I} q!\ell_i(S_i).G_i \restriction r$;   [PROJ-OUT]

- $p \to q : \{\ell_i(S_i).G_i\}_{i \in I} \restriction r = \sqcap_{i \in I}(G_i \restriction r)$ *if* $r \notin \{p,q\}$;   [PROJ-CONT]

- *undefined otherwise.*

Above, $\bigsqcap$ *is the* merging operator, *that is a partial operation over session types defined as:*

$$T_1 \bigsqcap T_2 = \begin{cases} T_1 & \textit{if } T_1 = T_2 & \text{[MRG-ID]} \\ T_3 & \textit{if } \exists I, J : \begin{cases} T_1 = \&_{i \in I} p'?\ell_i(S_i).T_i & \textit{and} \\ T_2 = \&_{j \in J} p'?\ell_j(S_j).T_j & \textit{and [MRG-BRA]} \\ T_3 = \&_{k \in I \cup J} p'?\ell_k(S_k).T_k \end{cases} \\ \textit{undefined otherwise.} \end{cases}$$

Proposition 1. *The merging operation is associative, i.e.:* $T \sqcap (T' \sqcap T'') = (T \sqcap T') \sqcap T''$.

By Definition 5, merging a type with itself results in itself (rule [MRG-ID]). Moreover, Definition 5 allows to combine different external choices (rule [MRG-ID]) *if and only if* common labels have identical sorts and identical continuations, as formalised in Proposition 2 below and illustrated in Examples 4 to 6.

Proposition 2. *For two types* $T' = \&_{i \in I} p'?\ell_i(S_i).T_i$ *and* $T'' = \&_{j \in J} p''?\ell_j(S_j).T_j$, *we have that* $T' \sqcap T''$ *is defined if and only if* $p' = p''$ *and, whenever* $\ell_i = \ell_j$ *(for some* $i \in I$ *and* $j \in J$), $S_i = S_j$ *and* $T_i = T_j$.

Example 4. We now give some small examples that illustrate the definition of the merging operator (here, $i \neq j$ implies $\ell_i \neq \ell_j$):

$q!\ell(\mathtt{nat}) \sqcap q!\ell(\mathtt{nat}) = q!\ell(\mathtt{nat})$

$p!\ell(\mathtt{nat}) \sqcap q!\ell(\mathtt{nat})$ undefined: outputs to different participants

$q!\ell_3(\mathtt{nat}) \sqcap q!\ell_4(\mathtt{nat})$ undefined: outputs with different labels

$(q?\ell_3(\mathtt{int})\&q?\ell_5(\mathtt{nat})) \sqcap (q?\ell_4(\mathtt{int})\&q?\ell_5(\mathtt{nat}))$
$\qquad\qquad = q?\ell_3(\mathtt{int})\&q?\ell_4(\mathtt{int})\&q?\ell_5(\mathtt{nat})$

$q?\ell_3(\mathtt{nat}) \sqcap q?\ell_3(\mathtt{nat}).q?\ell_3(\mathtt{nat})$
$\qquad$ undefined: same prefixes, but different continuations

$q?\ell(\mathtt{nat}) \sqcap q?\ell(\mathtt{int})$ undefined: the payload sorts do not match

Now we understand better how clause [PROJ-CONT] works: it states that if G starts with a communication between p and q, and we are projecting G onto a third participant r, then we need to *(1)* skip the initial communication, *(2)* project all the continuations onto r, and *(3) merge* the resulting session types, using the *merging operator* $\sqcap$.

As a result, clause [PROJ-CONT] of Definition 5 allows participant r to receive different messages (from a same participant p') in different branches of a global type, as shown in Example 5 below.

Example 5. We demonstrate interesting points of Definition 5. First, we show some projections of global types. Consider the global type:

$$G = p \rightarrow q : \{\ell_1(\mathtt{nat}).G_1, \ell_2(\mathtt{bool}).G_2\} \quad \text{where} \quad \begin{cases} G_1 = q \rightarrow r : \{\ell_3(\mathtt{int}), \ell_5(\mathtt{nat})\} \\ G_2 = q \rightarrow r : \{\ell_4(\mathtt{int}), \ell_5(\mathtt{nat})\} \\ r \neq p \end{cases}$$

We have:

$$G{\upharpoonright}p = q!\ell_1(\text{nat}).(G_1{\upharpoonright}p) \oplus q!\ell_2(\text{bool}).(G_2{\upharpoonright}p)$$
$$= q!\ell_1(\text{nat}).\text{end} \oplus q!\ell_2(\text{bool}).\text{end}$$

$$G{\upharpoonright}q = p?\ell_1(\text{nat}).(G_1{\upharpoonright}q) \,\&\, p?\ell_2(\text{bool}).(G_2{\upharpoonright}q)$$
$$= p?\ell_1(\text{nat}).(r!\ell_3(\text{int}) \oplus r!\ell_5(\text{nat})) \,\&\, p?\ell_2(\text{bool}).(r!\ell_4(\text{int}) \oplus r!\ell_5(\text{nat}))$$

$$G{\upharpoonright}r = G_1{\upharpoonright}r \sqcap G_2{\upharpoonright}r = (q?\ell_3(\text{int})\&q?\ell_5(\text{nat})) \sqcap (q?\ell_4(\text{int})\&q?\ell_5(\text{nat}))$$
$$= q?\ell_3(\text{int})\&q?\ell_4(\text{int})\&q?\ell_5(\text{nat})$$

Note that in G, q could output different messages towards r, depending on whether p sends ℓ_1 or ℓ_2 to q; therefore, in $G{\upharpoonright}r$, the possible inputs of r in G_1 and G_2 are merged into a larger external choice that supports all possible outputs of q.

Importantly, by Definition 5, there exist global types that *cannot* be projected onto all their participants. This is because G might describe meaningless protocols, that cause the merging operation $\sqcap$ in clause [PROJ-CONT] to be undefined, as shown in Example 6 below.

Example 6. We show two global types that cannot be projected according to the Definition 5. Consider the global type $G = p \to q : \{\ell_1(\text{nat}).G_1, \ell_2(\text{bool}).G_2\}$, with $G_1 = r \to q : \ell_3(\text{nat})$ and $G_2 = r \to q : \ell_4(\text{nat})$. Then,

$$G{\upharpoonright}p = q!\ell_1(\text{nat}) \oplus q!\ell_2(\text{bool})$$
$$G{\upharpoonright}q = p?\ell_1(\text{nat}).r?\ell_3(\text{nat}) \,\&\, p?\ell_2(\text{bool}).r?\ell_4(\text{nat})$$
$$G{\upharpoonright}r = q!\ell_3(\text{nat}) \sqcap q!\ell_4(\text{nat}) \;(\textbf{undefined if } \ell_3 \neq \ell_4)$$

Intuitively, when $\ell_3 \neq \ell_4$, $G{\upharpoonright}r$ is undefined because in G, depending on whether p and q exchange ℓ_1 or ℓ_2, r is supposed to send either ℓ_3 or ℓ_4 to q; however, r is not privy to the interactions between p and q, and thus, G provides an invalid specification for r. Instead, if $\ell_3 = \ell_4$, then by Definition 5 we have $G{\upharpoonright}r = q!\ell_3(\text{nat}) \sqcap q!\ell_3(\text{nat}) = q!\ell_3(\text{nat})$.

Now, consider the global type $G' = p \to q : \{\ell_1(\text{nat}).G_1', \ell_2(\text{bool}).G_2'\}$, with $G_1' = q \to r : \ell_3(\text{nat})$ and $G_2' = q \to r : \ell_3(\text{nat}).q \to r : \ell_3(\text{nat})$. Then,

$$G'{\upharpoonright}p = q!\ell_1(\text{nat}) \oplus q!\ell_2(\text{bool})$$
$$G'{\upharpoonright}q = p?\ell_1(\text{nat}).r!\ell_3(\text{nat}) \,\&\, p?\ell_2(\text{bool}).r!\ell_3(\text{nat}).r!\ell_3(\text{nat})$$
$$G'{\upharpoonright}r = q?\ell_3(\text{nat}) \sqcap q?\ell_3(\text{nat}).q?\ell_3(\text{nat}) \;(\textbf{undefined})$$

Here, $G'{\upharpoonright}r$ is undefined because in G', depending on whether p and q exchange ℓ_1 or ℓ_2, r is supposed to receive either one or two messages ℓ_3 from q; however, as in the previous example, r is not aware of the interactions between p and q, and thus, G provides an invalid specification for r. This example could be fixed, e.g., by replacing ℓ_3 with $\ell' \neq \ell_3$ in G_2', or by letting $G_1' = G_2'$: both fixes would make $G'{\upharpoonright}r$ defined, similarly to Example 5.

4.2 Subtyping

The subtyping relation $\leqslant$ is used to augment the flexibility of the type system (introduced in Sect. 4.3): by determining when a type T is "smaller" than T′, it allows to use a process typed by the former whenever a process typed by the latter is required.

Definition 6 (Subsorting and subtyping). *Subsorting* $\leq:$ *is the least reflexive binary relation such that* nat $\leq:$ int.

Subtyping $\leqslant$ *is the largest relation between session types coinductively defined by the following rules:*

$$[\text{SUB-END}] \qquad \text{end} \leqslant \text{end}$$

$$
\frac{\text{SUB-IN}}{\&_{i \in I \cup J}\text{p?}\ell_i(S_i).\text{T}_i \leqslant \&_{i \in I}\text{p?}\ell_i(S_i').\text{T}_i'}{\forall i \in I: \quad S_i' \leq: S_i \quad \text{T}_i \leqslant \text{T}_i'}
$$

<!-- SUB-IN -->
$$
\frac{\forall i \in I: \quad S_i' \leq: S_i \quad \text{T}_i \leqslant \text{T}_i'}{\&_{i \in I \cup J}\text{p?}\ell_i(S_i).\text{T}_i \leqslant \&_{i \in I}\text{p?}\ell_i(S_i').\text{T}_i'}
$$

<!-- SUB-OUT -->
$$
\frac{\forall i \in I: \quad S_i \leq: S_i' \quad \text{T}_i \leqslant \text{T}_i'}{\oplus_{i \in I}\text{p!}\ell_i(S_i).\text{T}_i \leqslant \oplus_{i \in I \cup J}\text{p!}\ell_i(S_i').\text{T}_i'}
$$

Intuitively, the session subtyping $\leqslant$ in Definition 6 says that T is smaller than T′ when T is "less liberal" than T′ — i.e., when T allows for less internal choices, and demands to handle more external choices.[1] A peculiarity of the relation is that, apart from a pair of inactive session types, only inputs and outputs from/to a same participant can be related (with additional conditions to be satisfied). Note that the double line in the subtyping rules indicates that the rules are interpreted *coinductively* [15, Chapter 21]

[SUB-END] says that end is only subtype of itself.

[SUB-IN] relates external choices from the same participant p: the subtype must support all the choices of the supertype, and for each common message label, the continuations must be related, too; note that the carried sorts are contravariant: e.g., if the supertype requires to receive a message $\ell_i(\text{nat})$ (for some $i \in I$), then the subtype can support $\ell_i(\text{int})$ or $\ell_i(\text{nat})$, since nat $\leq:$ int and nat $\leq:$ nat.

[SUB-OUT] relates internal choices towards the same participant p: the subtype must offer a subset of the choices of the supertype, and for each common message label, the continuations must be related, too; note that the carried sorts are covariant: e.g., if the supertype allows to send a message $\ell_i(\text{int})$ (for some $i \in I$), then the subtype can allow to send $\ell_i(\text{int})$ or $\ell_i(\text{nat})$, since int $\leq:$ int and nat $\leq:$ int.

Lemma 1. *The subtyping relation* $\leqslant$ *is reflexive and transitive.*

---

[1] Readers familiar with the theory of session types might notice that our subtyping relation is inverted w.r.t. the original binary session subtyping, introduced in the works of [3,6]. In such works, smaller types have less internal choices, and more external choices: this is because they formalise a "channel-oriented" notion of subtyping, while we adopt a "process-oriented" view. For a thorough analysis and comparison of the two approaches, see [5].

4.3 Type System

We now introduce a type system for the multiparty session calculus presented in Sect. 3. We distinguish three kinds of typing judgments:

$$\Gamma \vdash e : S \qquad \Gamma \vdash P : \mathsf{T} \qquad \vdash \mathcal{M} : \mathsf{G}$$

where Γ is the *typing environment*:

$$\Gamma ::= \emptyset \mid \Gamma, x : S \mid \Gamma, X : \mathsf{T}$$

i.e., a mapping that associates expression variables with sorts, and process variables with session types.

We say that *a multiparty session $\mathcal{M}$ is well typed* if there is a global type G such that $\vdash \mathcal{M} : \mathsf{G}$. If a multiparty session is well typed, we will sometimes write just $\vdash \mathcal{M}$.

Table 4. Typing rules for expressions.

$$\Gamma \vdash \mathsf{n} : \mathsf{nat} \qquad \Gamma \vdash \mathsf{i} : \mathsf{int} \qquad \Gamma \vdash \mathsf{true} : \mathsf{bool} \qquad \Gamma \vdash \mathsf{false} : \mathsf{bool} \qquad \Gamma, x : S \vdash x : S$$

$$\frac{\Gamma \vdash e : \mathsf{nat}}{\Gamma \vdash \mathsf{succ}(e) : \mathsf{nat}} \qquad \frac{\Gamma \vdash e : \mathsf{int}}{\Gamma \vdash \mathsf{neg}(e) : \mathsf{int}} \qquad \frac{\Gamma \vdash e : \mathsf{bool}}{\Gamma \vdash \neg e : \mathsf{bool}}$$

$$\frac{\Gamma \vdash e_1 : S \quad \Gamma \vdash e_2 : S}{\Gamma \vdash e_1 \oplus e_2 : S} \qquad \frac{\Gamma \vdash e_1 : \mathsf{int} \quad \Gamma \vdash e_2 : \mathsf{int}}{\Gamma \vdash e_1 > e_2 : \mathsf{bool}} \qquad \frac{\Gamma \vdash e : S \quad S \leq: S'}{\Gamma \vdash e : S'}$$

The typing rules for expressions are given in Table 4, and are self-explanatory. The typing rules for processes and multiparty sessions are content of Table 5:

[T-SUB] is the *subsumption rule*: a process with type T is also typed by the supertype T';

[T-0] says that a terminated process implements the terminated session type;

[T-REC] types a recursive process $\mu X.P$ with T if P can be typed as T, too, by extending the typing environment with the assumption that X has type T;

[T-VAR] uses the typing environment assumption that process X has type T;

[T-INPUT-CHOICE] types a summation of input prefixes as a branching type. It requires that each input prefix targets the same participant q, and that, for all $i \in I$, each continuation process P_i is typed by the continuation type T_i, having the bound variable x_i in the typing environment with sort S_i. Note that the rule implicitly requires the process labels ℓ_i to be pairwise distinct (as per Definition 3);

[T-OUT] types an output prefix with a singleton selection type, provided that the expression in the message payload has the correct sort S, and the process continuation matches the type continuation;

[T-CHOICE] types a conditional process with T if its sub-processes can be typed by T and expression e is boolean.

[T-SESS] types multiparty sessions, by associating typed processes to participants. It requires that the processes being composed in parallel can play as participants of a global communication protocol: hence, their types must be projections of a single global type G. The condition $pt\{G\} \subseteq \{p_i \mid i \in I\}$ allows to also type sessions containing $p \triangleleft 0$: this is needed to assure invariance of typing.

Example 7. We show that the multiparty session $\mathcal{M}$ from Example 2 is well typed. Consider the following global type:

$$G = \texttt{Alice} \rightarrow \texttt{Bob} :$$
$$\{\ell_1(\texttt{nat}).\texttt{Bob} \rightarrow \texttt{Carol} : \ell_2(\texttt{nat}).\texttt{Carol} \rightarrow \texttt{Alice} : \ell_3(\texttt{nat}).\texttt{end},$$
$$\ell_4(\texttt{nat}).\texttt{Bob} \rightarrow \texttt{Carol} : \ell_2(\texttt{nat}).\texttt{Carol} \rightarrow \texttt{Alice} : \ell_3(\texttt{nat}).\texttt{end}\}.$$

We show that participants Alice, Bob and Carol respect the prescribed protocol G, by showing that they participate in a well-typed multiparty session. Applying rules from Table 5, we derive

$$\vdash P_{\texttt{Alice}} : \mathsf{T}_{\texttt{Alice}} \qquad \vdash P_{\texttt{Bob}} : \mathsf{T}_{\texttt{Bob}} \qquad \vdash P_{\texttt{Carol}} : \mathsf{T}_{\texttt{Carol}}$$

where:

$\mathsf{T}_{\texttt{Alice}} = \texttt{Bob}!\ell_1(\texttt{nat}).\texttt{Carol}?\ell_3(\texttt{nat}).\texttt{end}$

$\mathsf{T}_{\texttt{Bob}} = \texttt{Alice}?\ell_1(\texttt{nat}).\texttt{Carol}!\ell_2(\texttt{nat}).\texttt{end} \ \& \ \texttt{Alice}?\ell_4(\texttt{nat}).\texttt{Carol}!\ell_2(\texttt{nat}).\texttt{end}$

$\mathsf{T}_{\texttt{Carol}} = \texttt{Bob}?\ell_2(\texttt{nat}).\texttt{Alice}!\ell_3(\texttt{nat}).\texttt{end}$

Now, let:

$$\mathsf{T}'_{\texttt{Alice}} = \texttt{Bob}!\ell_1(\texttt{nat}).\texttt{Carol}?\ell_3(\texttt{nat}).\texttt{end} \oplus \texttt{Bob}!\ell_4(\texttt{nat}).\texttt{Carol}?\ell_3(\texttt{nat}).\texttt{end}$$

Since it holds that $\mathsf{T}_{\texttt{Alice}} \leqslant \mathsf{T}'_{\texttt{Alice}}$, and the projections of G to the participants are

$$G{\upharpoonright}\texttt{Alice} = \mathsf{T}'_{\texttt{Alice}} \qquad G{\upharpoonright}\texttt{Bob} = \mathsf{T}_{\texttt{Bob}} \qquad G{\upharpoonright}\texttt{Carol} = \mathsf{T}_{\texttt{Carol}}$$

Table 5. Typing rules for processes and sessions.

[T-SUB]
$$\dfrac{\Gamma \vdash P : \mathsf{T} \quad \mathsf{T} \leqslant \mathsf{T}'}{\Gamma \vdash P : \mathsf{T}'}$$

[T-0]
$$\Gamma \vdash 0 : \texttt{end}$$

[T-REC]
$$\dfrac{\Gamma, X : \mathsf{T} \vdash P : \mathsf{T}}{\Gamma \vdash \mu X.P : \mathsf{T}}$$

[T-VAR]
$$\Gamma, X : \mathsf{T} \vdash X : \mathsf{T}$$

[T-INPUT-CHOICE]
$$\dfrac{\forall i \in I \quad \Gamma, x_i : S_i \vdash P_i : \mathsf{T}_i}{\Gamma \vdash \sum_{i \in I} q?\ell_i(x_i).P_i : \&_{i \in I} q?\ell_i(S_i).\mathsf{T}_i}$$

[T-OUT]
$$\dfrac{\Gamma \vdash e : S \quad \Gamma \vdash P : \mathsf{T}}{\Gamma \vdash q!\ell\langle e \rangle.P : q!\ell(S).\mathsf{T}}$$

[T-CHOICE]
$$\dfrac{\Gamma \vdash e : \texttt{bool} \quad \Gamma \vdash P_1 : \mathsf{T} \quad \Gamma \vdash P_2 : \mathsf{T}}{\Gamma \vdash \texttt{if } e \texttt{ then } P_1 \texttt{ else } P_2 : \mathsf{T}}$$

[T-SESS]
$$\dfrac{\forall i \in I \quad \vdash P_i : G{\upharpoonright}p_i \quad pt\{G\} \subseteq \{p_i \mid i \in I\}}{\vdash \prod_{i \in I} p_i \triangleleft P_i : G}$$

we conclude:

$$\vdash \texttt{Alice} \lhd P_{\texttt{Alice}} \mid \texttt{Bob} \lhd P_{\texttt{Bob}} \mid \texttt{Carol} \lhd P_{\texttt{Carol}} : \texttt{G}.$$

Example 8. Let us consider processes $P_{\texttt{Customer}}$ and $P_{\texttt{Agency}}$ from Example 1. As a suitable global type for the session

$$\texttt{Customer} \lhd P_{\texttt{Customer}} \mid \texttt{Agency} \lhd P_{\texttt{Agency}}$$

we pick the following.

> $\texttt{G} = \mu\texttt{t}.\ \texttt{Customer} \to \texttt{Agency} : \{Hawaii(\texttt{bool}).\texttt{G}_1, France(\texttt{bool}).\texttt{G}_1\}$
> where
> $\texttt{G}_1 = \texttt{Agency} \to \texttt{Customer} : \{\ quote(\texttt{nat}).\texttt{Customer} \to \texttt{Agency} : \{$
> $\qquad accept(\texttt{bool}).\texttt{Customer} \to \texttt{Agency} : address(\texttt{nat}).$
> $\qquad\qquad\qquad\qquad\qquad \texttt{Agency} \to \texttt{Customer} : date(\texttt{nat}).\texttt{end},$
> $\qquad retry(\texttt{bool}).\texttt{t},$
> $\qquad reject(\texttt{bool}).\texttt{end}\ \}\}$

Observe the recursive behaviour over $\texttt{t}$. Now, let us project $\texttt{G}$ onto its participant $\texttt{Agency}$ (there is no need to merge types here, namely we can use Definition 4):

> $\texttt{G}{\restriction}\texttt{Agency} = \mu\texttt{t}.\ (\texttt{Customer}?Hawaii(\texttt{bool}).\texttt{G}_1{\restriction}\texttt{Agency}$
> $\qquad\qquad\qquad \oplus\ \texttt{Customer}?France(\texttt{bool}).\texttt{G}_1{\restriction}\texttt{Agency})$
> and
> $\texttt{G}_1{\restriction}\texttt{Agency} = \texttt{Customer}!quote(\texttt{nat}).($
> $\qquad\qquad\qquad (\texttt{Customer}?accept(\texttt{bool}).\texttt{Customer}?address(\texttt{nat}).$
> $\qquad\qquad\qquad\qquad\qquad\qquad \texttt{Customer}!date(\texttt{nat}).\texttt{end})$
> $\qquad\&\ (\texttt{Customer}?retry(\texttt{bool}).\texttt{t})$
> $\qquad\&\ (\texttt{Customer}?reject(\texttt{bool}).\texttt{end})\ )$

Also this projection presents a recursive behaviour as expected. The reader will now be able to derive:

$$\vdash \texttt{Customer} \lhd P_{\texttt{Customer}} \mid \texttt{Agency} \lhd P_{\texttt{Agency}} : \texttt{G}.$$

Exercise 2. This exercise is intended to guide the reader to obtain the final result (using the same notation as in Examples 1 and 8):

$$\vdash \texttt{Customer} \lhd P_{\texttt{Customer}} \mid \texttt{Agency} \lhd P_{\texttt{Agency}} : \texttt{G}$$

Let us proceed step by step following Example 7.

1. Given the global type $\texttt{G}$ and its projection $\texttt{G}{\restriction}\texttt{Agency}$, derive $\texttt{G}{\restriction}\texttt{Customer}$.
2. Then derive $\vdash P_{\texttt{Customer}} : \texttt{G}{\restriction}\texttt{Customer}$ and $\vdash P_{\texttt{Agency}} : \texttt{G}{\restriction}\texttt{Agency}$.

Hint 1. The reader might want to use the identification of $\mu\texttt{t}.\texttt{G}$ and $\texttt{G}\{\mu\texttt{t}.\texttt{G}/\texttt{t}\}$ (this holds both for global and session types), namely the possibility to unfold any recursive construct for types.

Hint 2. In order to prove points 2. and 3. the reader might want to proceed in two steps: first, finding appropriate session types T_{Customer} and T_{Agency} for processes P_{Customer} and P_{Agency} respectively, and second, proving $T_{\text{Customer}} \leqslant$ $G\lceil\text{Customer}$ and $T_{\text{Agency}} \leqslant G\lceil\text{Agency}$.

Exercise 3. Prove that: $\vdash \text{Customer} \lhd P'_{\text{Customer}} \mid \text{Agency} \lhd P'_{\text{Agency}} : G$.

The proposed type system for multiparty sessions enjoys two fundamental properties: typed sessions only reduce to typed sessions (subject reduction), and typed sessions never get stuck. The remaining of this section is devoted to the proof of these properties.

In order to state subject reduction, we need to formalise how global types are modified when multiparty sessions reduce and evolve.

Definition 7 (Global types consumption and reduction). *The* consumption *of the communication* $p \xrightarrow{\ell} q$ *for the global type* G *(notation* $G \setminus p \xrightarrow{\ell} q$*) is the global type coinductively defined as follows:*

$$\left(p \to q : \{\ell_i(S_i).G_i\}_{i \in I}\right) \setminus p \xrightarrow{\ell} q = G_k \qquad \text{if } \exists k \in I : \ell = \ell_k$$

$$\left(r \to s : \{\ell_i(S_i).G_i\}_{i \in I}\right) \setminus p \xrightarrow{\ell} q = r \to s : \{\ell_i(S_i).G_i \setminus p \xrightarrow{\ell} q\}_{i \in I}$$

$$\text{if } \begin{cases} \{r,s\} \cap \{p,q\} = \emptyset \\ \forall i \in I : \{p,q\} \subseteq G_i \end{cases}$$

The reduction of global types *is the smallest pre-order relation closed under the rule:* $G \implies G \setminus p \xrightarrow{\ell} q$

Example 9. We show that a projection of a global type before the consumption might require to support more external choices than the projection after the consumption. Take G, its subterm G_1, from Example 5, and their types denoted as G and G_1, respectively. Also take the projection:

$$G\lceil r = q?\ell_3(\text{int})\&q?\ell_4(\text{int})\&q?\ell_5(\text{nat})$$

and recall the explanation on how $G\lceil r$ above merges all the possible inputs that r might receive from q, depending on whether p first sends ℓ_1 or ℓ_2 to q. We have:

$$G \setminus p \xrightarrow{\ell_1} q = G_1 = q \to r : \{\ell_3(\text{int}), \ell_5(\text{nat})\}$$

$$(G \setminus p \xrightarrow{\ell_1} q)\lceil r = G_1\lceil r = q?\ell_3(\text{int})\&q?\ell_5(\text{nat})$$

and we obtain $G\lceil r \leqslant (G \setminus p \xrightarrow{\ell_1} q)\lceil r$. The reason is that, after the transition from G to G_1, there is no possibility for q to send ℓ_4 to r, hence r does not need to support such a message in its projection.

Note that a process that plays the role of r in G, and is therefore typed by $G\lceil r$, has to support the input of ℓ_4 from q, by rule [T-INPUT-CHOICE] in Table 5. After the transition from G to G_1, the same process is also typed by $G_1\lceil r$, by rule [T-SUB] — but will never receive a message ℓ_4 from q.

We can now prove subject reduction.

Theorem 1 (Subject Reduction). *Let* $\vdash \mathcal{M} : G$. *For all* $\mathcal{M}'$, *if* $\mathcal{M} \longrightarrow \mathcal{M}'$, *then* $\vdash \mathcal{M}' : G'$ *for some* G' *such that* $G \Longrightarrow G'$.

Theorem 2 (Progress). *If* $\vdash \mathcal{M} : G$, *then either* $\mathcal{M} \equiv \mathsf{p} \triangleleft \mathbf{0}$ *or there is* $\mathcal{M}'$ *such that* $\mathcal{M} \longrightarrow \mathcal{M}'$.

As a consequence of subject reduction and progress, we get the safety property stating that a typed multiparty session will never get stuck.

Theorem 3 (Type Safety). *If* $\vdash \mathcal{M} : G$, *then it does not hold* $\mathsf{stuck}(\mathcal{M})$.

Proof. Direct consequence of Theorems 1, 2, and Definition 1.

Finally the reader wishes to learn more about the full asynchronous multiparty session types (which includes channel passing, asynchrony (FIFO queues), shared names and parameterised recursion) can proceed to [1]. The article [16] also discusses type soundness of various MPST calculi.

Acknowledgements. We would like to thank Fangyi Zhou for their carfeul proofreading and detailed comments on the paper.

References

1. Coppo, M., Dezani-Ciancaglini, M., Padovani, L., Yoshida, N.: A gentle introduction to multiparty asynchronous session types. In: Bernardo, M., Johnsen, E.B. (eds.) SFM 2015. LNCS, vol. 9104, pp. 146–178. Springer, Cham (2015). https://doi.org/10.1007/978-3-319-18941-3_4
2. Deniélou, P., Yoshida, N., Bejleri, A., Hu, R.: Parameterised multiparty session types. Log. Methods Comput. Sci. **8**(4) (2012). https://doi.org/10.2168/LMCS-8(4:6)2012
3. Gay, S., Hole, M.: Subtyping for session types in the pi calculus. Acta Informatica **42**(2/3), 191–225 (2005). https://doi.org/10.1007/s00236-005-0177-z
4. Gay, S., Ravera, A. (eds.): Behavioural Types: From Theory to Tools. River Publishers (2017)
5. Gay, S.J.: Subtyping supports safe session substitution. In: Lindley, S., McBride, C., Trinder, P., Sannella, D. (eds.) A List of Successes That Can Change the World. LNCS, vol. 9600, pp. 95–108. Springer, Cham (2016). https://doi.org/10.1007/978-3-319-30936-1_5
6. Gay, S., Hole, M.: Types and subtypes for client-server interactions. In: Swierstra, S.D. (ed.) ESOP 1999. LNCS, vol. 1576, pp. 74–90. Springer, Heidelberg (1999). https://doi.org/10.1007/3-540-49099-X_6
7. Ghilezan, S., Jaksic, S., Pantovic, J., Scalas, A., Yoshida, N.: Precise subtyping for synchronous multiparty sessions. J. Log. Algebr. Meth. Program. **104**, 127–173 (2019). https://doi.org/10.1016/j.jlamp.2018.12.002
8. Honda, K.: Types for dyadic interaction. In: Best, E. (ed.) CONCUR 1993. LNCS, vol. 715, pp. 509–523. Springer, Heidelberg (1993). https://doi.org/10.1007/3-540-57208-2_35

9. Honda, K., Mukhamedov, A., Brown, G., Chen, T.-C., Yoshida, N.: Scribbling interactions with a formal foundation. In: Natarajan, R., Ojo, A. (eds.) ICDCIT 2011. LNCS, vol. 6536, pp. 55–75. Springer, Heidelberg (2011). https://doi.org/10.1007/978-3-642-19056-8_4
10. Honda, K., Vasconcelos, V.T., Kubo, M.: Language primitives and type discipline for structured communication-based programming. In: Hankin, C. (ed.) ESOP 1998. LNCS, vol. 1381, pp. 122–138. Springer, Heidelberg (1998). https://doi.org/10.1007/BFb0053567
11. Honda, K., Yoshida, N., Carbone, M.: Multiparty asynchronous session types. In: POPL, pp. 273–284. ACM Press (2008). https://doi.org/10.1145/1328438.1328472
12. Honda, K., Yoshida, N., Carbone, M.: Multiparty asynchronous session types. J. ACM **63**, 1–67 (2016)
13. Hüttel, H., et al.: Foundations of session types and behavioural contracts. ACM Comput. Surv. **49**(1) (2016). https://doi.org/10.1145/2873052
14. Kouzapas, D., Yoshida, N.: Globally governed session semantics. In: D'Argenio, P.R., Melgratti, H. (eds.) CONCUR 2013. LNCS, vol. 8052, pp. 395–409. Springer, Heidelberg (2013). https://doi.org/10.1007/978-3-642-40184-8_28
15. Pierce, B.C.: Types and Programming Languages. MIT Press (2002)
16. Scalas, A., Yoshida, N.: Less is more: multiparty session types revisited. ACM Program. Lang. POPL (2019). https://doi.org/10.1145/3290343
17. Scribble home page. http://www.scribble.org
18. Takeuchi, K., Honda, K., Kubo, M.: An interaction-based language and its typing system. In: Halatsis, C., Maritsas, D., Philokyprou, G., Theodoridis, S. (eds.) PARLE 1994. LNCS, vol. 817, pp. 398–413. Springer, Heidelberg (1994). https://doi.org/10.1007/3-540-58184-7_118
19. Yoshida, N., Deniélou, P.-M., Bejleri, A., Hu, R.: Parameterised multiparty session types. In: Ong, L. (ed.) FoSSaCS 2010. LNCS, vol. 6014, pp. 128–145. Springer, Heidelberg (2010). https://doi.org/10.1007/978-3-642-12032-9_10
20. Yoshida, N., Hu, R., Neykova, R., Ng, N.: The scribble protocol language. In: Abadi, M., Lluch Lafuente, A. (eds.) TGC 2013. LNCS, vol. 8358, pp. 22–41. Springer, Cham (2014). https://doi.org/10.1007/978-3-319-05119-2_3

Constructing Knowledge Graphs from Data Catalogues

Adegboyega Ojo[1]([✉]) [iD] and Oladipupo Sennaike[2] [iD]

[1] Insight Centre for Data Analytics, Data Science Institute, NUI Galway, Galway,
Republic of Ireland
adegboyega.ojo@nuigalway.ie

[2] Department of Computer Sciences, Faculty of Science, University of Lagos, Lagos, Nigeria

Abstract. We have witnessed about a decade's effort in opening up government institutions around the world by making data about their services, performance and programmes publicly available on open data portals. While these efforts have yielded some economic and social value particularly in the context of city data ecosystems, there is a general acknowledgment that the promises of open data are far from being realised. A major barrier to better exploitation of open data is the difficulty in finding datasets of interests and those of high value on data portals. This article describes how the implicit relatedness and value of datasets can be revealed by generating a knowledge graph over data catalogues. Specifically, we generate a knowledge graph based on a self-organizing map (SOM) constructed from an open data catalogue. Following this, we show how the generated knowledge graph enables value characterisation based on sociometric profiles of the datasets as well as dataset recommendation.

Keywords: Open data · Knowledge graphs · Self-organising maps · Dataset recommendation · Dataset value

1 Introduction

Many government institutions around the world have publicly published data about their services, performance and programmes on open data portals. These data portals are built on a myriad of open data platforms including CKAN, DKAN, Socrata, PublishMyData, Information Workbench, Enigma, Junar and OpenDataSoft. Despite the increasing number of datasets in these data portals, there has been limited use of the data by the public. While these islands of data resources have been exploited to create some economic and social value particularly in the context of city data ecosystems [1], there is a general acknowledgement the promises of open data are far from being realised [2]. In fact, usage of and engagement around open data has been and remains poor even with mediated use through apps. This problem could be associated with a number of factors. The first includes the failures of government to advertise available datasets and benefit obtained from their use [3]. The second factor is related to how the data are published on the data portals and the limited features on the underlying open data platforms to simplify access and consumption of data by ordinary users.

D. V. Hung and M. D'Souza (Eds.): ICDCIT 2020, LNCS 11969, pp. 94–107, 2020.
https://doi.org/10.1007/978-3-030-36987-3_6

Current generation of open data platforms essentially provide basic dataset search capabilities and features for filtering search results. These platforms do not provide capabilities for discovering related or important datasets. Without prior knowledge of what to search for, a typical user finds it very difficult to get any meaningful information out of these data portals. Users have no way of discovering how datasets are related or what other datasets could be of interest or potentially valuable to them. Prototypes of next-generation open data platforms are beginning to emerge with features to support the recommendation of datasets [4], social engagement around data [5, 6] and automatic extraction of facts from datasets in form data stories that are more meaningful for users [7].

Some of the recent ideas in unlocking the knowledge embedded within the vast amount of data on open data portals include the use of knowledge graphs [8]. Knowledge graphs which were popularised by Google in 2012 and now increasingly available in different forms [9] have enabled richer information search experience on the web. They allow entities in different domains to be described along with their interrelations in the form of a graph [10].

In this paper, we show how knowledge graphs could be constructed from open data catalogs to reveal latent relationships (including relatedness) among datasets and also the inherent values of these datasets based on their sociometric profiles. Our approach comprises two basic steps. The first step involves computing dataset relatedness on a Self-organising map (SOM) constructed in [4]. The second step entails the transformation of the SOM to a knowledge graph using the topological distances between datasets on the map. The resulting SOM-based knowledge graph enables the discovery of clusters and themes in datasets, enables the discovery of interesting datasets and enhances the recommendation of related datasets.

2   Knowledge Graphs

There are several definitions of Knowledge Graphs (KG). It may be defined as an object for describing entities and their interrelations, by means of a graph which are usually large in which arbitrary entities may be interrelated, thus covering various topical domains [8, 10]. One of the most detailed characterisation of KG is provided by the participants of the Dagstuhl Seminar 18371, Sept. 2018 [10]. The collective understanding of a KG is: *"(1) a graph-structured knowledge-base, (2) any dataset that can be seen through the lens of a graph perspective, (3) something that combines data and semantics in a graph structure, (4) structured data organisation with formal semantics and labels that is computationally feasible and cognitively plausible, (5) defined by examples such as Bablenet, OpenCyc, DBpedia, Yago, Wikidata, NELL and their shared features"*. A very similar definition is provided in [9] and also indicates that KG defines possible classes and relations of entities in a schema.

Since the popularization of knowledge graphs by Google in 2012, major companies including AirBnB, Facebook, Microsoft, Yahoo!, Elsevier and Ebay have adopted this idea and developed their own variant [10]. These industry variants all employ graph abstraction as the underlying data structure. Other examples of knowledge graphs in academic literature include a knowledge graph of connected things [11], product knowledge graph to support sales assistants [12], open research KG [13].

However, knowledge graphs are distinguished from conventional web-based publishing schemes such as linked data [14]. Specifically, some contributors to [10] argue that KGs are products of collaborative efforts and brings together techniques from scientific disciplines such as Knowledge Representation, Machine Learning, Semantic Web, Databases, Natural Language Processing, Multimedia Processing and Information Extraction, amongst others [10].

Similar to our approach in this work to KG development, many works report on automatically building knowledge graphs out of textual medical knowledge and medical records [14]. Lastly, Knowledge graphs need to be able to evolve and capture the changes made to the knowledge it contains [10].

3 Self-organizing Map (SOM)-Based Dataset Relatedness

3.1 Self-organising Maps

The self-organising map is an unsupervised artificial neural network proposed by Kohonen [15] that projects high dimensional data to two or three-dimensional map while preserving the topological order in the data. The map consists of an array of units or nodes arranged in a regular rectangular or hexagonal grid. Each node has an associated n-dimensional model vector $m_k = [m_{k1}, \ldots \ldots, m_{kn}] \in \mathbb{R}^n$ that approximates the set of input data, where n is the dimension of the input space. The SOM is trained by iteratively presenting the input data to the nodes in parallel with a winning node emerging based on some distance metric, usually the Euclidean distance metric. The model vectors of the best matching node and its neighbors are adjusted to better match the input data.

$$m_k(t+1) = m_k(t) + h_{c(x),k}(t)[x(t) - m_k(t)], \tag{1}$$

where t is a time step and $h_{c(x),k}(t)$ is the neighborhood function [16], and

$$c(x) = \arg \min_k \{\|x - m_k\|\}, \tag{2}$$

is the best matching unit.

The neighborhood function is usually a Gaussian function

$$h_{c(x),k}(t) = \alpha(t) \exp\left(-\frac{\|r_k - r_{c(x)}\|^2}{2\sigma^2(t)}\right), \tag{3}$$

where $0 < \alpha(t) < 1$ is the learning-rate, $r_k \in \mathbb{R}^2$ and $r_{c(x)} \in \mathbb{R}^2$ are vectorial locations on the display grid, and $\sigma(t)$ corresponds to the width of the neighborhood function. Both $\alpha(t)$ and $\sigma(t)$ decreases monotonically with the time steps.

Some applications of SOM include Image Compression, Image Segmentation, Density Modeling, Gene Expression Analysis and Text Mining [17].

3.2 Dataset Relatedness

Relatedness defines an established or discoverable connection or association between two concepts. The study of relatedness spans a number of domains including genetics [18], management [19], computational linguistics [20], etc. Of particular interest to us is semantic relatedness, which considers how much two concepts are associated via any type of relationship between them [20]. Semantic relatedness is used in word sense disambiguation [21], information extraction [22], biomedical informatics [23], etc. Semantic relatedness goes beyond semantic similarities because it explores other kinds of relationships (beyond hyponymy/hyperonymy) between concepts.

A number of approaches have been used to measure semantic relatedness between concepts. In [20], Budanitsky and Hirst gave an overview of lexical resource-based approaches to measuring semantic relatedness. Other approaches include Latent Semantic Analysis (LSA) [24], Extended Semantic Analysis (ESA) [25], Title vector Extended Semantic Analysis (ESA) [26].

Two datasets are related if they share some concepts in common. Dataset relatedness is a measure of the proportion of shared concepts between two datasets in a catalog. Two datasets are related if they are associated by a shared concept. An attempt can be made to explicitly relate two datasets by assigning them the same theme or tagging them with the same keywords. However, explicit methods can sometimes be subjective and incomplete. In a number of cases, these tags or themes are absent.

3.3 Computing Dataset Relatedness Using SOM

The SOM is an ordered map, thus nodes close on the map are more similar than nodes further away and by extension, datasets that report to them. We used this ordering property of the SOM as the basis of computing dataset relatedness. A node A is in the neighborhood of another node B if nodes A and B are adjacent to the SOM grid. A dataset X is related to another dataset Y if the node that Y belongs to on the SOM is in the neighborhood of the node that X belongs. The degree of relatedness is defined as the neighborhood size, thus, a degree of zero means that the datasets are in the same node while a degree of 1 means that the datasets are in the node under consideration and nodes that are immediate neighbors.

The SOM was used to cluster the Dublin City Council (DubLinked)[1] instance of the CKAN platform. The data portal contains 205 datasets for the Dublin region (www.dublinked.ie). Metadata for these datasets, along with the field names of underlying data were extracted and saved in a csv file. The data was transformed into a term frequency-inverse document frequency (tf-idf) matrix after removing stop words from the documents and stemming. The resulting matrix was a 205 by 1026 matrix, with 205 datasets and 1026 terms which serves as input to a 20 by 20 SOM. The resulting SOM is shown in Fig. 1.

From the generated map, related datasets can easily be determined based on a specified neighborhood radius. Increasing the radius increases the number of related datasets. Determining the optimal radius requires experimentation like a typical model selection problem.

---

[1] http://dublinked.ie/.

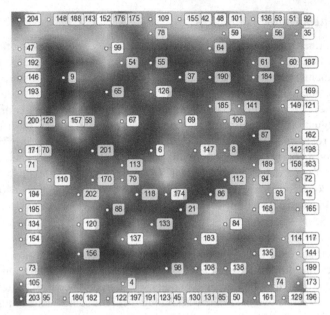

Fig. 1. The SOM

This SOM-based relatedness procedure has already been implemented as extensions to instances of the CKAN data platform with very good results [6]. The number of datasets returned is based on the degree of relatedness specified. When a high degree of relatedness is specified, datasets that are members of the same node with the dataset of interest are returned. However, when the relatedness is relaxed, datasets associated with neighbouring nodes (within a given radius) on our SOM map are also included. The model has been extended to the Dutch Language with equally good results. It is also been used as a basis for identifying datasets that can be merged [6].

4 Generating the SOM-Based Knowledge Graph

4.1 Graph Schema

The graph schema is designed to capture salient relationships among datasets in an open data catalogue - a collection of datasets descriptions or metadata. We highlight the set of important properties and relations of datasets that we consider in our graph schema specification as follows. One or more resources (in a variety of formats) are attached to each dataset in the catalogue. A dataset is associated with one or more themes usually specified by the its publisher. These themes are either associated explicitly or derived from the dataset. A dataset may also be associated with a set of *entities* (names, places, organisations, etc.). A dataset can be used in queries or visual artefacts, which are saved. Facts can be produced from a dataset. A dataset can be derived from one or more dataset, for example, a dataset can be split to form two or more datasets, or two datasets merged to form a new dataset. A dataset can also be related to another dataset. Datasets are used in sessions. Our proposed graph schema for our knowledge graph is presented in Fig. 2.

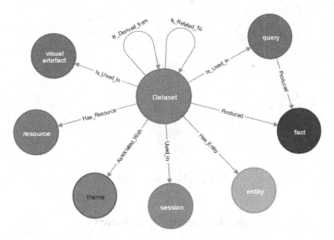

Fig. 2. The open data knowledge graph schema

4.2 Generating the Graph

The knowledge graph is generated from the SOM by eliciting the relatedness among the datasets and modeling it on a graph. The graph creation is broken down into three phases. In phase one, an initial graph is created strictly based on data relatedness information elicited from the SOM. In phase two, the graph is augmented to include relations between pairs of datasets that are very similar based on some distance metric (the Euclidean distance metric). In phase three, the graph is pruned to remove relationships between pairs of nodes with a distance exceeding a threshold.

For our experiment, we focused only on the dataset and the *is_related_to* relationship in Fig. 2. We chose a degree of 1 for our dataset relatedness, thus two datasets are related if their best matching nodes are in a neighborhood of radius 1 on the SOM. Each dataset in the catalog is represented by a node while the edges represent the relatedness between a pair of nodes. We had 205 nodes and 956 edges. Each node is labelled with the serial number of the dataset as used in the SOM from 0 to 204. Properties of the node include the title and the extracted features. Each edge connecting a pair of related dataset and is labelled "RELATED_TO" and has the following properties: the distance between the datasets, and the common terms between the datasets. Figure 3 shows an example graph with three nodes and six relationships. Table 1 summarises the parameters used in the experiment. The complete graph is presented in Fig. 4.

4.3 Structural Properties of the Graph

To analyse the generated KG, we compute some sociometric measures for each node of the knowledge graph. Specifically, we compute the degree of centrality, betweenness centrality and closeness centrality. The results of our analyses are below.

Degree of Centrality - assigns an importance score based purely on the number of links held by each node. Table 2 shows the top ten datasets in terms of degree centrality while Fig. 5 shows the subgraph containing the dataset with the highest degree centrality labelled 155.

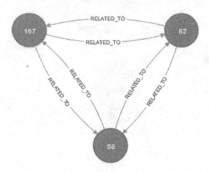

Fig. 3. Sample graph

Table 1. Summary of parameters

SOM size	20 by 20
Inclusion threshold	1.15
Exclusion threshold	1.4
No of graph nodes	205
Number of relationships	956

Fig. 4. Graph generated from SOM

Betweenness Centrality - measures the number of times a node lies on the shortest path between other nodes. Table 3 shows the top ten datasets in terms of betweeness centrality while Fig. 6 shows the subgraph containing the dataset with the highest betweeness centrality labelled 75.

Closeness Centrality - *This measure scores each node based on their 'closeness' to all other nodes within the network. This measure calculates the shortest paths between all nodes, then assigns each node a score based on its sum of shortest paths.*

Table 4 shows the top ten datasets in terms of closeness centrality while Fig. 7 shows the subgraph containing the dataset with the highest closeness centrality labelled 56.

Table 2. Datasets with highest Degree Centrality

Sn	Label	Degree	Title
1	155	14	Planning Register
2	52	13	DLR Goatstown Local Area Plan
3	150	13	Parking Meters location tariffs and zones in Dublin City
4	56	13	DLR Martello Towers - Location & Gun Range
5	40	12	Dublin City Council Development Planning
6	39	12	Development Planning
7	14	11	DLR - Blackrock LAP
8	48	11	DLR Cherrywood SDZ
9	38	11	Dun Laoghaire-Rathdown Development Planning
10	26	11	Citizens Information Centres

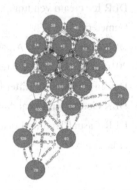

Fig. 5. Subgraph for dataset with highest degree centrality

Table 3. Datasets with highest Betweeness Centrality

Sn	Label	Betweeness	Title
1	75	2179.299417	Dublin City Council Administrative Area Maps
2	23	1802.105915	Cemeteries
3	56	1461.044824	DLR Martello Towers - Location & Gun Range
4	73	1383.155299	Dublin City Centre Litter Bin Survey
5	169	1325.938235	National Transport Authority Public Transport Information
6	90	1301.547113	Roads and Streets in Dublin City
7	51	1220.452887	DLR Cycle Counter Data
8	0	974.8005196	2010–2016 Amenities Areas
9	136	914.2101601	DLR Local Electoral Areas
10	52	878.0981247	DLR Goatstown Local Area Plan

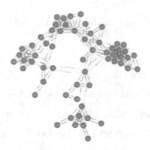

Fig. 6. Subgraph for dataset with highest betweeness centrality

Table 4. Datasets with highest Closeness Centrality

Sn	Label	Closeness	Title
1	56	0.013577496	DLR Martello Towers - Location & GunRange
2	75	0.013570882	Dublin City Council Administrative Area Maps
3	53	0.013570882	DLR Ice cream vending permits
4	23	0.013569937	Cemeteries
5	136	0.013568049	DLR Local Electoral Areas
6	0	0.013565217	2010–2016 Amenities Areas
7	73	0.013554845	Dublin City Centre Litter Bin Survey
8	52	0.013550136	DLR Goatstown Local Area Plan
9	46	0.013539786	DLR Casual Trading Locations
10	10	0.01353133	Arts Centres

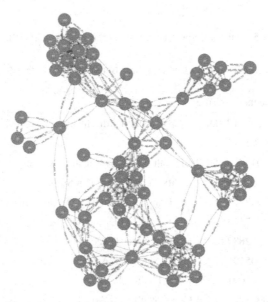

Fig. 7. Subgraph for dataset with highest closeness centrality

Clusters - A total of 32 clusters were obtained from the graph. An example cluster shown in Fig. 8 contains the labels 45, 56, 123, 10, 31, 130, 97, 67, 66, 98, 131, 1, 65, 85 and 9. The corresponding titles of these datasets are 'DLR Arts Venues', 'DLR Martello Towers - Location & Gun Range', 'Heritage Venues', 'Arts Centres', 'South Dublin Council Offices', 'Libraries', 'DLR Libraries', 'DLR WW1 Hospitals', 'DLR War Memorials', 'DLR Offices and Depots', 'Locations of Libraries and Mobile Libraries in Fingal', 'ACA Boundaries', 'DLR Sculpture Trail Map', 'Dublin City Councils Libraries November Adult Fiction Issues & Renewals List', 'Art in the Parks - A Guide to Sculpture in Dublin City Council Parks'. This cluster coherently contains datasets that are strongly related to "Culture" including arts, heritage and leisure.

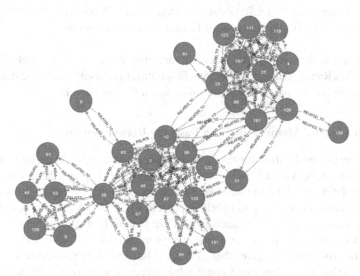

Fig. 8. Example cluster

5 Using the Generated Knowledge Graph

5.1 Dataset Centrality as an Indication of Its Value

We discuss here how the sociometric metrics above can inform the inherent value of datasets. Our notion of value here is related to the extent to which the dataset is related to or can be combined with other datasets. The dataset with the highest degree centrality has the highest number of dataset it is related to. Most of the datasets with the highest degree centrality in Table 2 are in the same cluster, so this is not very useful when considering the entire dataset, However, when the different clusters are considered, the dataset with highest degree centrality for each cluster serves as entry point to the different clusters through which majority of other datasets can be reached. These datasets can be recommended to users as entry points for their search and their exploration.

The datasets with the highest betweenness centrality are datasets that provide a bridge for two apparently different concepts. From our experiment, the dataset labelled 75, Dublin City Council Administrative Area Maps has the highest betweenness degree. It bridges dataset on:

- *Roads* - Road Collisions, Roads Maintenance Annual Works Programme, Winter Salting Routes, DLR Road Sweeping Schedule,
- *Bin locations* - Dublin City Centre Litter Bin Survey, DLR Refuse Bins Locations, Enterprise Centres,
- *Plans* - DLR Goatstown Local Area Plan, DLR Documentation for Local Area Plans, DLR Cherrywood SDZ, DLR Proposed Plan Areas,
- *Locations of amenities* - DLR Local Electoral Areas, 2010–2016 Amenities Area, DLR Ice cream vending permits, DLR Casual Trading Locations.

The datasets with the highest closeness centrality is the DLR Martello Towers - Location & Gun Range dataset labelled 56. This dataset is closely related to datasets on arts and heritage on one hand, and locations of amenities on the other.

5.2 Graph Segment Membership as a Basis for Recommendation

The second area of application for the developed knowledge graph is in the recommendation of related datasets to end-users. Based on our knowledge graph design, three types of recommendations could be potentially supported - content-based recommendation, collaborative recommendation and hybrid approaches [27, 28]. A content-based recommendation entails recommending datasets that are similar to a dataset being explored. In cases where user profiles are available, recommendations could consider datasets explored in the past. However given that most data platforms are explored or used anonymously (this is also true for our case), content-based recommendations will only consider current activities. For collaborative recommendation, users are recommended datasets that have been explored in the past by the same category of users. Hybrid collaboration combines both content and collaborative filtering methods. Against this background, we proceed to describe how the content-based recommendation works in our case.

In our content-based recommendation, we note two possible strategies. The first entails cluster membership-based recommendation and the second is based on artefacts shared by datasets including visual artefacts, queries and entities. For the cluster-based recommendations, members of cluster of the reference dataset are offered as recommendations to users. For instance, suppose the reference dataset $d*$ is titled *"Multi-story car parking space availability"* (see Table 5 below) belonging to Cluster 12 of the 32 clusters identified in Sect. 4. The set of recommendations for this dataset are the other datasets in *cluster 12* e.g. *Accessible Parking Places, DCC Derelict Site Register, Disabled Parking spaces, etc.* Cluster membership relations are implemented through the `is_related_to` relation on the graph. Therefore, the recommendations for reference dataset $d*$, is simply the result of the query `to produce the other members of the set/cluster in which d* belongs.`

Table 5. Datasets in cluster 12 of 32

• Accessible Parking Places
• DCC Derelict Site Register
• Disabled Parking Spaces
• DLR Commercial Parking Locations Numbers and Charges
• DLR County Council Parking Meters
• DLR Landscape Maintenance & Additional Sites
• DLR Parking Tag Information
• Dublin City Council Clamping Appeals
• **Multi Story Car Parking Space Availability**
• On Street Disabled Parking Bay in Dublin City Council area
• Parking Meters location tariffs and zones in Dublin City
• Parking Tag Weekly Reports
• Parks
• Play Areas
• Residential Parking permits for Dublin City Council Area
• Residential Permit Parking Area in Dublin City Council
• Suspension of Parking Bays in Dublin City Council Area

In the case of shared artefacts, recommendations for the reference dataset d^* is simply obtained by combining the results from querying the graph for the sets $is\_used\_in(d^*)$ and $has\_entity(d^*)$.

6 Conclusions

We have shown how a Knowledge graph could be constructed from a self-organising map guided by the KG schema. Albeit, our KB could potentially include all the relationships shown in Fig. 2, we have only chosen for the purpose of illustration, the relatedness relation. In some other work, we have laid the foundation for writing facts generated from datasets directly into the KB in terms of data stories [7]. What we have shown in particular is how our KG can be generated based on a single relationship between the datasets. Since there is yet no specific prescribed procedure in literature for developing a KG [10], our approach is simply one of the possible ways to construct one. In terms of the quality of the results from our experimentations, we note that the use of knowledge graphs constitutes a very promising approach for discovering some of the latent values and similar datasets. Richer KG can be generated automatically by considering all the relationships shown in Fig. 2.

Ultimately, our vision is that the islands of open data portals on the web be meaningfully connected into a web-scale knowledge graph to truly open up open data. However, there are several research challenges that must be tackled to fully harness knowledge graphs. These challenge among others include: how to efficiently manage the evolution of the knowledge graphs, providing explanations for information retrieved from knowledge graph, and how to effectively evaluate KGs.

Acknowledgment. This publication has emanated from research supported in part by a research grant from Science Foundation Ireland (SFI) under Grant Number SFI/12/RC/2289_P2, co-funded by the "European Regional Development Fund".

References

1. Ojo, A., Curry, E., Zeleti, F.A.: A tale of open data innovations in five smart cities. In: 2015 48th Hawaii International Conference on System Sciences, pp. 2326–2335 (2015)
2. Ojo, A., et al.: Realizing the innovation potentials from open data: stakeholders' perspectives on the desired affordances of open data environment. In: Afsarmanesh, Hamideh, Camarinha-Matos, Luis M., Lucas Soares, António (eds.) PRO-VE 2016. IAICT, vol. 480, pp. 48–59. Springer, Cham (2016). https://doi.org/10.1007/978-3-319-45390-3_5
3. Hogan, M., et al.: Governance, transparency and the collaborative design of open data collaboration platforms: understanding barriers, options, and needs BT. In: Ojo, A., Millard, J. (eds.) Government 3.0 – Next Generation Government Technology Infrastructure and Services: Roadmaps, Enabling Technologies & Challenges, pp. 299–332. Springer, Cham (2017). https://doi.org/10.1007/978-3-319-63743-3
4. Sennaike, O.A., Waqar, M., Osagie, E., Hassan, I., Stasiewicz, A., Ojo, A.: Towards intelligent open data platforms, pp. 414–421, September 2017
5. Scarano, V., et al.: Fostering citizens' participation and transparency with social tools and personalization. In: Ojo, A., Millard, J. (eds.) Government 3.0 – Next Generation Government Technology Infrastructure and Services: Roadmaps, Enabling Technologies & Challenges, pp. 197–218. Springer, Cham (2017). https://doi.org/10.1007/978-3-319-63743-3
6. Ojo, A., et al.: A comprehensive architecture to support Open Data access, co-creation, and Dissemination. In: ACM International Conference Proceeding Series, pp. 0–1 (2018)
7. Janowski, M., Ojo, A., Curry, E., Porwol, L.: Mediating open data consumption - identifying story patterns for linked open statistical data. In: ACM International Conference Proceeding Series, vol. Part F148155, pp. 156–163 (2019)
8. Musa Aliyu, F., Ojo, A.: Towards building a knowledge graph with open data – a roadmap. In: AFRICOMM 2017: International Conference on e-Infrastructure and e-Services for Developing Countries, pp. 157–162 (2018)
9. Noy, N., Paulheim, H.: Knowledge graph refinement: a survey of approaches and evaluation methods. Semant. Web **8**, 489–508 (2016)
10. Bonatti, P.A., Decker, S., Polleres, A., Presutti, V.: Knowledge graphs: new directions for knowledge representation on the semantic web. Report from Dagstuhl Seminar, vol. 8, no. 9, pp. 29–111 (2019)
11. Le-Phuoc, D., Nguyen Mau Quoc, H., Ngo Quoc, H., Tran Nhat, T., Hauswirth, M.: The Graph of Things: a step towards the Live Knowledge Graph of connected things. J. Web Semant. **37–38**, 25–35 (2016)
12. Halaschek-wiener, C., Kolovski, V.: Towards a sales assistant using a product knowledge graph. Web Semant. Sci. Serv. Agents World Wide Web **6**, 171–190 (2017)
13. Jaradeh, M.Y., et al.: Open Research Knowledge Graph: Next Generation Infrastructure for Semantic Scholarly Knowledge (2019)

14. Kejriwal, M.: What is a knowledge graph? Springer Briefs in Computer Science, pp. 1–7 (2019)
15. Kohonen, T.: The self-organizing map. Proc. IEEE **78**(9), 1464–1480 (1990)
16. Kohonen, T., et al.: Self organization of a massive text document collection. Kohonen Maps **11**(3), 171–182 (1999)
17. Yin, H.: The self-organizing maps: background, theories, extensions and applications. Stud. Comput. Intell. **115**, 715–762 (2008)
18. Weir, B.S., Anderson, A.D., Hepler, A.B.: Genetic relatedness analysis: Modern data and new challenges. Nat. Rev. Genet. **7**(10), 771–780 (2006)
19. Nocker, E., Bowen, H.P., Stadler, C., Matzler, K.: Capturing relatedness: comprehensive measures based on secondary data. Br. J. Manag. **27**, 197–213 (2016)
20. Budanitsky, A., Hirst, G.: Evaluating WordNet-based measures of lexical semantic relatedness. Comput. Linguist. **32**(1), 13–47 (2006)
21. Patwardhan, S., Banerjee, S., Pedersen, T.: Using measures of semantic relatedness for word sense disambiguation. In: Gelbukh, A. (ed.) CICLing 2003. LNCS, vol. 2588, pp. 241–257. Springer, Heidelberg (2003). https://doi.org/10.1007/3-540-36456-0_24
22. Stevenson, M., Greenwood, M.A.: A semantic approach to IE pattern induction. In: Proceedings of the 43rd Annual Meeting on Association for Computational Linguistics - ACL 2005 (2005)
23. Zhu, Y., Yan, E., Wang, F.: Semantic relatedness and similarity of biomedical terms: examining the effects of recency, size, and section of biomedical publications on the performance of word2vec. BMC Med. Inform. Decis. Mak. **17**, 95 (2017)
24. Lee, M.D., Pincombe, B., Welsh, M.: An empirical evaluation of models of text document similarity. In: Proceedings of the Annual Meeting of the Cognitive Science Society, pp. 1254–1259 (2005)
25. Gabrilovich, E., Markovitch, S.: Computing semantic relatedness using wikipedia-based explicit semantic analysis. IJCAI Int. Jt. Conf. Artif. Intell. **7**, 1606–1611 (2007)
26. Rybinski, M., Aldana-Montes, J.F.: tESA: a distributional measure for calculating semantic relatedness. J. Biomed. Semantics **7**, 67 (2016)
27. Adomavicius, G., Tuzhilin, A.: Toward the next generation of recommender systems: a survey of the state-of-the-art and possible extensions. IEEE Trans. Knowl. Data Eng. **17**(6), 734–749 (2005)
28. Shambour, Q., Lu, J.: Government-to-business personalized e-services using semantic-enhanced recommender system. In: Andersen, K.N., Francesconi, E., Grönlund, Å., van Engers, T.M. (eds.) EGOVIS 2011. LNCS, vol. 6866, pp. 197–211. Springer, Heidelberg (2011). https://doi.org/10.1007/978-3-642-22961-9_16

Concurrent and Distributed Systems Modelling and Verification

Round-Message Trade-Off in Distributed Steiner Tree Construction in the CONGEST Model

Parikshit Saikia[✉] and Sushanta Karmakar

Department of Computer Science and Engineering,
Indian Institute of Technology Guwahati, Guwahati 781039, India
{s.parikshit,sushantak}@iitg.ac.in
https://www.iitg.ac.in/

Abstract. The *Steiner tree* problem is one of the fundamental optimization problems in distributed graph algorithms. Recently Saikia and Karmakar [27] proposed a deterministic distributed algorithm for the Steiner tree problem that constructs a Steiner tree in $O(S + \sqrt{n}\log^* n)$ rounds whose cost is optimal upto a factor of $2(1 - 1/\ell)$, where n and S are the number of nodes and *shortest path diameter* [17] respectively of the given input graph and ℓ is the number of *terminal* leaf nodes in the optimal Steiner tree. The message complexity of the algorithm is $O(\Delta(n - t)S + n^{3/2})$, which is equivalent to $O(mS + n^{3/2})$, where Δ is the maximum degree of a vertex in the graph, t is the number of terminal nodes (we assume that $t < n$), and m is the number of edges in the given input graph. This algorithm has a better round complexity than the previous best algorithm for Steiner tree construction due to Lenzen and Patt-Shamir [21]. In this paper we present a deterministic distributed algorithm which constructs a Steiner tree in $\tilde{O}(S + \sqrt{n})$ rounds and $\tilde{O}(mS)$ messages and still achieves an approximation factor of $2(1 - 1/\ell)$. Note here that $\tilde{O}(\cdot)$ notation hides polylogarithmic factors in n. This algorithm improves the message complexity of Saikia and Karmakar's algorithm by dropping the additive term of $O(n^{3/2})$ at the expense of a logarithmic multiplicative factor in the round complexity. Furthermore, we show that for sufficiently small values of the shortest path diameter ($S = O(\log n)$), a $2(1 - 1/\ell)$-approximate Steiner tree can be computed in $\tilde{O}(\sqrt{n})$ rounds and $\tilde{O}(m)$ messages and these complexities almost coincide with the results of some of the singularly-optimal minimum spanning tree (MST) algorithms proposed in [9,12,23].

Keywords: Steiner tree · Distributed approximation algorithm · Singularly-optimal

1 Introduction

The MST problem has been widely studied in the CONGEST model of distributed computing since the celebrated work of Gallager, Humblet, and

D. V. Hung and M. D'Souza (Eds.): ICDCIT 2020, LNCS 11969, pp. 111–126, 2020.
https://doi.org/10.1007/978-3-030-36987-3_7

Spira [10]. Recently a few *singularly-optimal* distributed algorithms have been proposed for the MST problem [9,12,23] beating the long standing time-message trade-off. Note here that a distributed algorithm is said to be *singularly-optimal* if it achieves the optimal round and message complexities simultaneously. The term singularly-optimal was first introduced by Pandurangan, Robinson, and Scquizzato [23]. The round and message complexities of the singularly-optimal MST algorithms are $\tilde{O}(D + \sqrt{n})$ and $\tilde{O}(m)$ respectively, where D is the *unweighted diameter* of the network and both are optimal upto a polylogarithmic factors in n.[1] In this work we investigate the round-message trade-off in a generalized version of the MST problem known as the *Steiner tree* problem in the CONGEST model of distributed computing. It is defined as follows.

Definition 1 (Steiner tree (ST) problem). *Given a connected undirected graph $G = (V, E)$ and a weight function $w : E \rightarrow \mathbb{R}^+$, and a set of vertices $Z \subseteq V$, known as the set of terminals, the goal of the ST problem is to find a tree $T' = (V', E')$ such that $\sum_{e \in E'} w(e)$ is minimized subject to the conditions that $Z \subseteq V' \subseteq V$ and $E' \subseteq E$.*

It is known that the MST problem is polynomially solvable. However the ST problem is one of the original 21 problems proved NP-complete by Karp [14] in the centralized setting. The best known (polynomial time) approximation ratio for solving the ST problem in the centralized setting is $\ln(4) + \epsilon \approx 1.386 + \epsilon$, for $\epsilon > 0$ due to Byrka et al. [3]. It is also shown that in general the ST problem can not be solved in polynomial time with an approximation factor $\leq \frac{96}{95}$ [6] unless $P = NP$.

There are many variations of the ST problem such as directed Steiner tree, metric Steiner tree, euclidean Steiner tree, rectilinear Steiner tree, and so on. Hauptmann and Karpinaski [13] provide a website with continuously updated state of the art results for many variants of the problem.

Applications of the ST Problem. It finds applications in numerous areas such as VLSI layout design, communication networks, transportation networks, content distribution (video on demand, streaming multicast) networks, phylogenetic tree reconstruction in computational biology etc. Moreover the ST problem appears as a subproblem or as a special case of many other problems in network design such as Steiner forest, prize-collecting Steiner tree etc.

---

[1] Das Sarma et al. [8] showed that approximating (for any factor $\alpha \geq 1$) MST requires $\Omega(D + \sqrt{n/(B \log n)})$ rounds (assuming B bits can be sent through each edge in each round). For convention we assume that $B = O(\log n)$. Kutten et al. [19] established that $\Omega(m)$ is the message lower bound for leader election in the KT_0 (**K**nowledge **T**ill radius **0**) version of the CONGEST model, which holds for both the deterministic as well as randomized Monte Carlo algorithms even if the network parameters D, n (number of nodes), and m (number of edges) are known, and all the nodes wake up simultaneously. Since a distributed MST algorithm can be used to elect a leader, the above message lower bound in the KT_0 version of the CONGEST model also applies to the distributed MST construction.

Motivation. In literature a number of distributed algorithms have been proposed for the ST problem [2,4,5,21] which are mainly based on the MST heuristic and all of them achieved an approximation factor upto 2 of the optimal. Recently Bacrach et al. [1] showed that the lower bound round complexity in solving the ST problem exactly in the CONGEST model is $\Omega(n^2/\log^2 n)$. In the approximate sense on the other hand, no immediate lower bound result is known for the ST problem in the CONGEST model. However, since the ST problem is a generalized version of the MST problem, we believe that in the approximate sense the lower bound results for the MST problem also hold for the ST problem in the CONGEST model. Note that the lower bound round and message complexities for solving the MST problem in the CONGEST model are $\Omega(D + \sqrt{n/(\log^2 n)})$ [8] and $\Omega(m)$ [19] respectively. Regarding singular optimality results, till date, no result is known for the ST problem even in the approximate sense. Lenzen and Patt-Shamir [21] proposed a deterministic distributed algorithm (henceforth, it will be denoted by LP-algorithm) for the ST problem in the CONGEST model that constructs an ST whose cost is optimal upto a factor of 2 and the round complexity is $\tilde{O}(S + \sqrt{min\{St, n\}})$, where S is the *shortest path diameter* (the definition is deferred to Sect. 2), $t = |Z|$, and $n = |V|$. Since $1 \leq D \leq S \leq n$, the round complexity of the LP-algorithm is close to the near-optimal round complexity $(\tilde{O}(D + \sqrt{n}))$ of the MST algorithms [9,12,23]. But Lenzen and Patt-Shamir do not explicitly specify the message complexity of their algorithm: however, it is apparent from their proposed algorithm that the message complexity is $O(mn)$.[2] Recently Saikia and Karmakar [27] proposed a deterministic distributed $2(1 - 1/\ell)$-factor approximation algorithm that constructs an ST in $O(S + \sqrt{n}\log^* n)$ rounds which is close to the best known round complexity of the deterministic distributed MST algorithm $(O(D + \sqrt{n}\log^* n)$ [20]); however, the message complexity of the algorithm proposed in [27] is $O(mS + n^{\frac{3}{2}})$. Therefore an intriguing question is:

"Can we achieve a distributed algorithm for the ST problem in the CONGEST model whose round and message complexities coincide with that of the singular optimality results of the MST algorithms [9,12,23] while maintaining an approximation factor of at most 2?"

Our Contribution. Our work in this paper is one step towards addressing the above question. We propose a deterministic distributed approximation algorithm for the ST problem in the CONGEST model (henceforth, it will be denoted as

---

[2] **Message complexity of the LP-algorithm** [21]. The LP-algorithm consists of four steps. The step 1 uses Bellman-Ford algorithm to compute the Voronoi decomposition of G w.r.t. Z. Since the message complexity of the Bellman-Ford algorithm is $O(mn)$, the step 1 incurs $O(mn)$ messages. The steps 2 to 4 simulate the GKP (Garay, Kutten, and Peleg [11,20]) algorithm which has the message complexity of $O(m + n^{\frac{3}{2}})$. Since G is connected, therefore $O(mn)$ is the dominating term over $O(m+n^{\frac{3}{2}})$; therefore the overall message complexity of the LP-algorithm is $O(mn)$.

DSTC algorithm). The main result of the DSTC algorithm is summarized in the following theorem.

Theorem 1. *Given a connected undirected weighted graph $G = (V, E, w)$ and a terminal set $Z \subseteq V$, there exists a deterministic distributed approximation algorithm in the CONGEST model which computes an ST in $\tilde{O}(S + \sqrt{n})$ rounds and $\tilde{O}(mS)$ messages with an approximation factor of $2(1 - 1/\ell)$, where ℓ is the number of terminal leaf nodes in the optimal ST.*

As a by-product of the above theorem, for sufficiently small values of the shortest path diameter (where $S = O(\log n)$) we show the following corollary.

Corollary 1. *If $S = O(\log n)$ then a $2(1 - 1/\ell)$-approximate ST can be deterministically computed with the round and message complexities of $\tilde{O}(\sqrt{n})$ and $\tilde{O}(m)$ respectively in the CONGEST model.*

The above round and message complexities for the ST construction almost coincide with the results of some of the singularly-optimal distributed MST algorithms [9,12,23] and the approximation factor of the resultant ST is at most $2(1 - 1/\ell)$ of the optimal.

Related Work. There is a long line of study of polynomial time approximation algorithms [3,15,18,25,26,28–30] for the ST problem in centralized setting.

Chen et al. [5] proposed the first MST heuristic based deterministic distributed algorithm for the ST problem with the round and message complexities of $O(n(n - t))$ and $O(m + n(n - t + \log n))$ respectively and achieved an approximation factor of $2(1 - 1/\ell)$. Chalermsook et al. [4] presented a 2-factor distributed approximation algorithm for the ST problem in the synchronous model (which allows a bounded message size only) with round and message complexities of $O(n \log n)$ and $O(tn^2)$ respectively. Khan et al. [16] presented a $O(\log n)$-factor randomized distributed approximation algorithm for the ST problem in the CONGEST model with the round and message complexities of $O(S \log^2 n)$ and $O(Sn \log n)$ respectively. Lenzen and Patt-Shamir [22] presented two distributed algorithms for the Steiner forest problem (a more generalized version of the ST problem) in the CONGEST model: one is deterministic and the other one is randomized. The former one finds, a $(2 + o(1))$-approximate Steiner forest in $\tilde{O}(\sqrt{\min\{D, k\}}(D + k) + S + \sqrt{\min\{St, n\}})$ rounds, where k is the number of terminal components in the input graph. The latter one finds a $(2 + o(1))$-approximate Steiner forest in $\tilde{O}(\sqrt{\min\{D, k\}}(D + k) + \sqrt{n})$ rounds with high probability. Note that if $k = 1$ then the Steiner forest problem reduces to the ST problem. In this case the round complexities of the two algorithms in [22], in which one is deterministic and the other one is randomized reduce to $\tilde{O}(S + \sqrt{\min\{St, n\}})$ and $\tilde{O}(D + \sqrt{n})$ respectively. Furthermore, they showed that a 2-approximate ST can be computed deterministically in $\tilde{O}(S + \sqrt{\min\{St, n\}})$ rounds (Corollary 4.2 in [21]). Recently Saikia and Karmakar [27] proposed a deterministic distributed $2(1 - 1/\ell)$-factor approximation algorithm for the ST problem in the CONGEST model with the round and message complexities of

$O(S + \sqrt{n} \log^* n)$ and $O(mS + n^{3/2})$ respectively. Performances of some of the distributed algorithms for the ST problem mentioned above, together with that of our work, are summarized in Table 1.

Table 1. Summary of results for Steiner tree problem in distributed setting. DT = deterministic, RM = randomized, $n = |V|$, $m = |E|$, $t = |Z|$, S and D are the shortest path diameter and the unweighted diameter respectively of the given connected undirected weighted graph G. Here "–" indicates that the corresponding parameter is not discussed in the respective paper.

References	Type	Round complexity	Message complexity	Approximation
Chen et al. [5]	DT	$O(n(n - t))$	$O(m + n(n - t + \log n))$	$2(1 - 1/\ell)$
Chalermsook et al. [4]	DT	$O(n \log n)$	$O(tn^2)$	2
Khan et al. [16]	RM	$O(S \log^2 n)$	$O(Sn \log n)$	$O(\log n)$
Lenzen et al. [22]	DT	$\tilde{O}(S + \sqrt{min\{st, n\}})$	–	$2 + o(1)$
	RM	$\tilde{O}(D + \sqrt{n})$	–	$2 + o(1)$
Lenzen et al. [21]	DT	$\tilde{O}(S + \sqrt{min\{St, n\}})$	–	2
Saikia et al. [27]	DT	$O(S + \sqrt{n} \log^* n)$	$O(mS + n^{3/2})$	$2(1 - 1/\ell)$
This paper	DT	$\tilde{O}(S + \sqrt{n})$	$\tilde{O}(mS)$	$2(1 - 1/\ell)$

Regarding the singularly-optimal distributed algorithms for the MST problem, Pandurangan et al. [23] proposed a randomized distributed algorithm with the round and message complexities of $\tilde{O}(D + \sqrt{n})$ and $\tilde{O}(m)$ respectively. The polylogarithmic factors involved with the round and message complexities of this algorithm are $O(\log^3 n)$ and $O(\log^2 n)$ respectively.[3] Elkin [9] proposed a simple deterministic distributed algorithm with the near-optimal round and message complexities of $O((D + \sqrt{n}) \log n)$ and $O(m \log n + n \log n \cdot \log^* n)$ respectively. Recently Haeupler et al. [12] proposed a singularly-optimal distributed algorithm for the MST problem which is deterministic in nature but they do not explicitly specify the polylogarithmic factors involved with the round and message complexities. However, it is apparent from their analysis that the rounds and messages incurred by their algorithm are $O((D + \sqrt{n}) \log^2 n)$ and $O(m \log^2 n)$ respectively.

Paper Organization. In Sect. 2 we define the system model and notations. Section 3 contains some preliminaries related to the proposed DSTC algorithm. The proposed DSTC algorithm and its analysis are given in Sect. 4. A description of the Elkin's singularly-optimal MST algorithm and the pseudo-code of the shortest path forest algorithm, which are used in designing the DSTC algorithm, are deferred to the Appendix A and B respectively. We conclude the paper in Sect. 5.

---

[3] This analysis can be found in [9].

2 Model and Notations

System Model. We consider the CONGEST model as specified in [24]. A communication network is modelled as a connected undirected weighted graph $G = (V, E, w)$, where V is the set of nodes, E is the set of communication links, and $w : E \to \mathbb{R}^+$ is a non-negative weight function. The weight of each edge e is polynomially bounded in n and therefore polynomially many sums of weights can be encoded with $O(\log n)$ bits. Each node knows its unique identity (ID) (can be represented using $O(\log n)$ bits) and the weight of each edge incident on it. Nodes communicate and coordinate their actions with their neighbors by passing messages (of size $O(\log n)$ bits) only. In general, a message contains a constant number of edge weights, node IDs, and arguments (each of them is polynomially bounded in n).

An execution of the system advances in synchronous rounds. In each round, nodes receive messages that were sent to them in the previous round, perform some local computation, and then send (possibly different) messages. The time complexity is measured by the number of rounds required until all nodes (explicitly) terminate. The message complexity is measured by the number of messages sent until all nodes (explicitly) terminate.

Notation. We use the following terms and notations.

- $w(e)$ denotes the weight of an edge e.
- $s(v)$ denotes the *source* node of a node v.
- $\pi(v)$ denotes the *predecessor* or *parent* node of a node v.
- $d(v)$ denotes the *shortest distance* from a node v to $s(v)$.
- $d(u, v)$: (weighted) shortest distance between nodes u and v.
- The term *shortest path diameter* (denoted by S for short) was first introduced by Khan and Pandurangan [17]. Let $\rho(u, v)$ be the number of edges in the minimum-length shortest path from u to v. Then $S = \max_{u,v \in V} \rho(u, v)$. Note here that $1 \le D \le S \le n$.

3 Preliminaries

Definition 2 (Shortest path forest (SPF) [5]). *Let $G = (V, E, w)$ be the connected undirected weighted graph, where V is the vertex set, E is the edge set, and $w : E \to \mathbb{R}^+$ is the non-negative weight function. Given a subset $Z \subseteq V$, a SPF for Z in G is a sub-graph $G_F = (V, E_F, w)$ of G consisting of disjoint trees $T_i = (V_i, E_i, w)$, $i = 1, 2, ..., |Z|$ such that*

- *for all i, V_i contains exactly one node z_i of Z.*
- *if $v \in V_i$ then its $s(v)$ in G is $z_i \in Z$.*
- *$V_1 \cup V_2 \cup ... V_{|Z|} = V$ and $V_i \cap V_j = \phi$ for all $i \ne j$.*
- *$E_1 \cup E_2 \cup ... E_{|Z|} = E_F \subseteq E$.*
- *The shortest path between v and $s(v) = z_i$ in T_i is the shortest path between v and $s(v)$ in G.*

3.1 SPF Construction

Chen et al. [5] presented a deterministic distributed algorithm that constructs a SPF for $Z \subseteq V$ of a graph $G = (V, E, w)$ with the round and message complexities of $O(n(n-t))$ and $O(m + n(n-t))$ respectively, where $n = |V|, t = |Z|$, and $m = |E|$. Recently Saikia and Karmakar [27] proposed a deterministic distributed SPF algorithm (henceforth, it will be denoted by SPF algorithm) that constructs a SPF for $Z \subseteq V$ of $G = (V, E, w)$ with the round and message complexities of $O(S)$ and $O(\Delta(n-t)S)$ respectively. Here we assume that $t < n$. The SPF algorithm will be used as a subroutine in the proposed DSTC algorithm.

The SPF algorithm (the pseudo-code is deferred to the Appendix B) essentially partitions the input graph $G = (V, E, w)$ with a given terminal set $Z \subseteq V$ into $|Z|$ disjoint trees: Each partition contains exactly one terminal and a subset of non-terminals. A non-terminal v joins a partition containing the terminal $z \in Z$ if and only if $\forall x \in Z \setminus \{z\}, d(z,v) \leq d(x,v)$.

Lemma 1 (Saikia and Karmakar [27]). *There exists a deterministic distributed algorithm in the CONGEST model which computes a shortest path forest for $Z \subseteq V$ of a given graph $G = (V, E, w)$ in $O(S)$ rounds and $O(\Delta(n-t)S)$ messages, where $t < n$.*

3.2 ST Approximation via Complete Distance Graph

Definition 3 (Complete Distance Graph). *A graph K_Z is called a complete distance graph on the node set Z of G only if for each pair of nodes $u, v \in Z$, there is an edge (u,v) in K_Z and the weight of the edge (u,v) is the length of the shortest path between u and v in G.*

The approximation factor of the proposed DSTC algorithm directly follows from the correctness of a centralized algorithm due to Kou et al. [18] (Algorithm H). For a given connected undirected weighted graph $G = (V, E, w)$ and a set of terminal $Z \subseteq V$, the following centralized algorithm (Algorithm H) proposed by Kou et al. [18] computes an ST T_Z as follows.

1. Construct a complete distance graph K_Z.
2. Find an MST T_A of K_Z.
3. Construct a sub-graph G_A of T_A by replacing each edge of T_A with its corresponding shortest distance path in G.
4. Find an MST T_B of G_A.
5. Construct an ST T_Z, from T_B by deleting edges of T_B so that all leaves of T_Z are terminal nodes.

The running time and the approximation ratio of the Algorithm H are $O(tn^2)$ and $2(1-1/\ell)$ respectively. The time complexity of the Algorithm H is relatively higher due to the need of explicit construction of the complete distance graph K_Z. Following the principles of both Prim's and Krushkal's algorithms, Wu at el. [29] proposed a faster centralized algorithm (Algorithm M) which improves the time complexity to $O(m \log n)$, achieving the same approximation ratio as that of the Algorithm H. Algorithm M bypasses the explicit construction of K_Z and realizes it by constructing a sub-graph called *generalized MST* T_Z for Z of G which is defined as follows.

Definition 4 (Generalized MST [29]**).** *Let* $G = (V, E, w)$ *be a connected undirected weighted graph and* Z *be a subset of* V. *Then a generalized MST* T_Z *is a sub-graph of* G *such that*

- *there exists an MST* T_A *of the* K_Z *such that for each edge* (u, v) *in* T_A, *the length of the unique path in between* u *and* v *in* T_Z *is equal to the weight of the edge* (u, v) *in* T_A.
- *all leaves of* T_Z *are in* Z.

It is clear that T_Z is an ST for Z in G and is the actual realization of T_A.

3.3   ST Approximation via Generalized MST

The Algorithm M [29] constructs a generalized MST T_Z for Z of G as follows. Initially, the set of nodes in Z are treated as a forest of $|Z|$ separate trees and successively merge them until all of them are in a single tree T_Z. A priority queue Q is used to store the frontier vertices of paths extended from the trees. Each tree gradually extends its branches into the node set $V \setminus Z$. When two branches belonging to two different trees meet at some node then they form a path through that node merging these two trees. The algorithm always guarantees to compute only such paths of minimum length for merging trees.

Note that the Algorithm M computes an ST T_Z (generalized MST) for Z of G without explicitly computing the complete distance graph K_Z in the centralized setting. In this paper we propose a deterministic distributed approximation algorithm that computes a generalized MST T_Z for Z of G without explicitly computing the complete distance graph K_Z in the CONGEST model of distributed computing.

4   DSTC Algorithm and Its Analysis

Saikia and Karmakar [27] proposed a deterministic distributed algorithm for the ST problem (henceforth, it will be denoted by DST algorithm) that computes an ST in $O(S + \sqrt{n} \log^* n)$ rounds and $O(mS + n^{\frac{3}{2}})$ messages and the approximation factor is $2(1 - 1/\ell)$ of the optimal. The asymptotic term $O(n^{\frac{3}{2}})$ involved with the message complexity of the DST algorithm always exists even for sparse graphs ($m = O(n)$) or for graphs with small values of the shortest path diameter ($S = O(\log n)$). To get rid of the asymptotic term $O(n^{\frac{3}{2}})$ from the message complexity we propose the DSTC algorithm, which is a modification of the DST algorithm. We show that the round and message complexities of the proposed DSTC algorithm are $\tilde{O}(S + \sqrt{n})$ and $\tilde{O}(mS)$ respectively achieving the same approximation ratio as that of the DST algorithm. Specifically we replace the step 3 of the DST algorithm[4] by the singularly-optimal (upto a polylogarithmic

---

[4] The DST algorithm [27] consists of four major steps.

factors in n) MST algorithm proposed by Elkin [9] (henceforth, it will be denoted by Elkin's algorithm) which helps us achieve the aforementioned round and message complexities and still achieve a very good approximation factor.

DSTC Algorithm. We assume that a breadth first search (BFS) tree rooted at some terminal node ($r \in Z$) of G is available at the start of the algorithm (any node $v \in V$ can be considered as the root of the BFS tree). The root node r initiates the algorithm. There are four steps (small distributed algorithms) involved with the DSTC algorithm. Note that an ordered execution of the steps (from step 1 to step 4) is necessary for the correct working of the DSTC algorithm. We assume that the root node r ensures the ordered execution of the steps and initiates the step $i + 1$ after the step i is terminated. The outline of the DSTC algorithm is as follows.

Step 1 (SPF construction). Construct a SPF $G_F = (V, E_F, w)$ for Z in G by applying the SPF algorithm proposed by Saikia and Karmakar [27]. This produces $|Z|$ number of disjoint *shortest path trees*. Each tree has exactly one terminal node $z \in Z$ and a set of non-terminal nodes whose distances are minimum to z than any other terminal node.

The graph G_F yields a crucial information on the MST T_A of the complete distance graph K_Z for $Z \subseteq V$ of G. Let (u, v) be an edge in T_A, where $u, v \in Z$. Let T_u and T_v are two shortest path trees in G_F, where u and v are in T_u and T_v respectively. To realize the edge (u, v) of T_A using T_u and T_v, which are disjoint in G_F, they must be merged in such a way that u is connected to v by the shortest possible path in G. Towards this the following two steps (in order) *Edge weight modification* and *MST construction* are necessary.

Step 2 (Edge weight modification). With respect to the SPF $G_F = (V, E_F, w)$, each edge $e \in E$ of the graph $G = (V, E, w)$ is classified as any one of the following three types.
  (a) *tree* edge: if $e \in E_F$.
  (b) *inter_tree* edge: if $e \notin E_F$ and end points are incident in two different trees of the G_F.
  (c) *intra_tree* edge: if $e \notin E_F$ and end points are incident in the same tree of the G_F.
  Now transform $G = (V, E, w)$ into $G_c = (V, E, w_c)$. The cost of each edge $(u, v) \in E$ is computed as follows.
  (a) $w_c(u, v) = 0$ if (u, v) is a *tree* edge.
  (b) $w_c(u, v) = \infty$ if (u, v) is an *intra_tree* edge.
  (c) $w_c(u, v) = d(u) + w(u, v) + d(v)$ if (u, v) is an *inter_tree* edge. In this case $w_c(u, v)$ realizes the weight of a path from the source node $s(u)$ to the source node $s(v)$ in G that contains the *inter_tree* edge (u, v).
  The classification of the edges of G and the transformation to G_c can be done as follows. Each node v of G sends a message (say $\langle set\_category(v, s(v), d(v), \pi(v)) \rangle$) to all of its neighbors. Let a node v receives $\langle set\_category(u, s(u), d(u), \pi(u)) \rangle$ message on an incident edge

(v, u). If $s(v) \neq s(u)$ then v sets (v, u) as an *inter_tree* edge and $w_c(v, u)$ to $d(v) + w(v, u) + d(u)$. On the other hand if $s(v) = s(u)$ then (v, u) can be either a *tree* edge or an *intra_tree* edge: if $v = \pi(u)$ or $\pi(v) = u$ then node v sets (v, u) as *tree* edge and $w_c(v, u)$ to 0. Otherwise, v sets (v, u) as *intra_tree* edge and $w_c(v, u)$ to ∞.

Assuming that the root (r) of the BFS tree initiates this step, it is clear that the step 2 can be performed in $O(D)$ rounds. Also on each edge of G, the message $\langle set\_category \rangle$ is sent exactly twice (once from each end). Therefore, the message complexity of the step 2 is $O(m)$.

Step 3 (MST construction). Construct an MST T_M of G_c. This resultant T_M always guarantees the following.

 - it includes all the edges of G_F, i.e., all the *tree* edges of G_c. This is because during the MST construction the weight of the *tree* edges in G_c are considered equal to 0.
 - it selects $|Z| - 1$ *inter_tree* edges of G_c.
 - each *inter_tree* edge in T_M, say (a, b), merges two neighboring shortest path trees, say T_1 and T_2 of G_F such that $d(s(a), s(b)) = w_c(a, b)$, where, $s(a), s(b) \in Z$ and $s(a)$ and $s(b)$ are terminals in T_1 and T_2 respectively.

   Specifically, in this step, we apply the Elkin's algorithm [9] to construct an MST of G_c. Note that the Elkin's algorithm is the best known singularly-optimal (upto a polylogarithmic factors in n) deterministic distributed MST algorithm with the round and message complexities of $O((D + \sqrt{n}) \log n)$ and $O(m \log n + n \log n \cdot \log^* n)$ respectively. A brief description of the Elkin's algorithm is deferred to Appendix A.

Step 4 (Pruning). Construct a generalized MST T_Z from T_M. This is accomplished by performing a *pruning* operation in T_M. The pruning operation deletes edges from T_M until all leaves are terminal nodes. Pruning starts at all the non_terminal leaf nodes. A non_terminal leaf node v prunes itself from T_M and instructs its neighbor u to prune the common edge (v, u) from the T_M. This process is repeated until no further non_terminal leaf nodes remain and we get the final T_Z which contains $|Z| - 1$ *inter_tree* edges and all leaf nodes are in Z. Now edge weights of the T_Z are restored to w.

   Since pruning starts in parallel at all the non_terminal leaf nodes of the T_M and any non_terminal leaf node v can be at most S hops away from its $s(v)$ (which is a terminal node), the step 4 can be performed in $O(S)$ rounds. Also, in pruning, at most one message is sent on each edge of T_M. Since the T_M has exactly $n - 1$ edges, this ensures that the message complexity of the step 4 is $O(n)$.

The algorithm terminates with the step 4.

The correctness of the DSTC algorithm directly follows from the correctness of the algorithm proposed by Kou et al. [18]. Let $cost(X)$ and T_{opt} denote the sum of weights of all the edges of a sub-graph X and the optimal ST respectively. Now if we substitute the T_H of the Theorem 1 in Kou et al. [18] by T_Z then we get the following theorem.

Theorem 2 (Kou et al. [18]). $cost(T_Z)/cost(T_{opt}) \leq 2(1 - \frac{1}{\ell}) \leq 2(1 - \frac{1}{|Z|})$.

Round Complexity. By Lemma 1, the step 1 of the DSTC algorithm takes $O(S)$ rounds. The step 2 and 3 of the DSTC algorithm take $O(D)$ and $O((D + \sqrt{n}) \log n)$ rounds respectively. Since the step 4 also takes $O(S)$ rounds, the overall round complexity of the DSTC algorithm is $O(S + (D + \sqrt{n}) \log n)$. We know that $1 \leq D \leq S \leq n$. Therefore $O(S + (D + \sqrt{n}) \log n) = \tilde{O}(S + \sqrt{n})$. Note that the polylogarithmic factor involved with the round complexity is $\log n$.

Message Complexity. By Lemma 1, the message complexity of the step 1 of the DSTC algorithm is $O(\Delta(n - t)S)$. The message complexities of the steps 2, 3, and 4 are $O(m)$, $O(m \log n + n \log n \cdot \log^* n)$, and $O(n)$ respectively. It is clear that the overall message complexity of the DSTC algorithm is dominated by steps 1 and 3. Combining these two steps we get that the message complexity of the DSTC algorithm is $O(\Delta(n - t)S + m \log n + n \log n \cdot \log^* n)$. Note that $\log^* n \leq \log n$. Since the graph G is connected, $m \geq n-1$. Therefore we can write $O(\Delta(n - t)S + m \log n + n \log n \cdot \log^* n) = \tilde{O}(m + \Delta(n - t)S)$, where $t < n$. The polylogarithmic factor involved with the message complexity is at most $\log^2 n$. We also know that $\Delta(n - t) = O(\Delta n)$ and Δn is upper bounded by $O(m)$. This implies that $\tilde{O}(m + \Delta(n - t)S) = \tilde{O}(mS)$.

If we assume $S = O(\log n)$ then the round and message complexities incurred by the DSTC algorithm are $\tilde{O}(\sqrt{n})$ and $\tilde{O}(m)$ respectively. This implies that for sufficiently small values of the shortest path diameter (where $S = O(\log n)$) the round and message complexities of the DSTC algorithm coincide with the results of some of the singularly-optimal MST algorithms proposed in [9,12,23] and the cost of the resultant ST is at most $2(1 - 1/\ell)$ of the optimal.

DSTC Algorithm is Free from Deadlock. The deadlock freeness of the step 1 (SPF construction) of the DSTC algorithm directly follows from the work of Saikia and Karmakar [27]. In step 2, each node independently sends a message (containing its own state) to all of its neighbors only once. Upon receiving messages from all of its neighbors, a node performs some local computation and then terminates itself. Therefore, in step 2 nodes are free from any possible circular waiting. The correctness of the deadlock freeness of the step 3 essentially follows from the work of [9]. In step 4, the pruning operation is performed on a tree structure (T_M) and a node never requests and waits for resources holding by any other node in the network. This implies that during the pruning operation, nodes are free from any possible circular waiting. Therefore, the deadlock freeness of all the four steps together ensure the deadlock freeness of the proposed DSTC algorithm.

5 Conclusion

In this work we have proposed DSTC, a deterministic distributed approximation algorithm that computes a $2(1-1/\ell)$-approximate ST in $\tilde{O}(S+\sqrt{n})$ rounds and $\tilde{O}(mS)$ messages. The polylogarithmic factors involved with the round and message complexities are $O(\log n)$ and $O(\log^2 n)$ respectively. The proposed DSTC algorithm has improved the message complexity of Saikia and Karmakar's algorithm [27] by dropping the additive term of $O(n^{3/2})$ at the expense of a logarithmic multiplicative factor in the round complexity. We have also shown that for sufficiently small shortest path diameter networks (where $S=O(\log n)$) the proposed DSTC algorithm computes a $2(1-1/\ell)$-approximate ST in $\tilde{O}(\sqrt{n})$ rounds and $\tilde{O}(m)$ messages. This round and message complexities for ST construction almost coincide with the results of some of the singularly-optimal distributed MST algorithms [9,12,23] and the approximation factor of the resultant ST is at most $2(1-1/\ell)$ of the optimal. It will be interesting to improve the approximation factor further while maintaining the round and message complexities as that of this work.

A   Elkin's Algorithm [9]

This algorithm starts with the construction of an auxiliary BFS tree T_B rooted at some root node r. It consists of two parts. The first part constructs an $(O(n/D), O(D))$-MST forest[5] which is termed as the *base* MST forest. In the second part, the algorithm in [23] is applied on top of the base MST forest to construct the final MST. Specifically in the second part, the Boruvka's algorithm is applied in such a way that merging of any two fragments requires $O(D)$ rounds.

The first part of the algorithm runs for $\lceil \log D \rceil$ phases. At the beginning of a phase i, (i varies from 0 to $\lceil \log D \rceil - 1$), the algorithm computes $(n/2^{i-1}, O(2^i))$-MST forest $(\mathcal{F}_i)$. Each node updates its neighbors with the identity of its fragment. This requires $O(1)$ rounds and $O(m)$ messages. Every fragment $F \in \mathcal{F}_i$ of diameter $O(2^i)$ computes the MWOE e_F. For each $e_F = (u,v)$, $u \in V(F)$, $v \in V \setminus V(F)$, a message is sent over e_F by u and the receiver v notes down u as a *foreign-fragment* child of itself. In case the edge (u,v) is the MWOE for both the neighboring fragments F_u and F_v, the endpoint with the higher identity fragment becomes the parent of the other endpoint. This defines a *candidate fragment graph* $\mathcal{G}'_i = (\mathcal{F}'_i, \mathcal{E}_i)$, where $\mathcal{F}'_i$ is the set of fragments whose diameter is $O(2^i)$ and each such fragment is considered as a vertex of $\mathcal{G}'_i$ and $\mathcal{E}_i$ is the set of MWOE edges of all the fragments in $\mathcal{F}'_i$. The computation of the *candidate fragment graph* $\mathcal{G}'_i$ requires $O(2^i)$ rounds and $O(n)$ messages. Then a *maximal matching* of $\mathcal{G}'_i$ is built by using the Cole-Vishkin's 3-vertex coloring algorithm [7]. The computation of a maximal matching of $\mathcal{G}'_i$ requires $O(2^i \cdot \log^* n)$ rounds and $O(n \cdot \log^* n)$ messages. The phase i ends at the computation of a maximal

---

[5] For a pair of parameters α, β, an (α, β)-MST forest is an MST forest with at most α fragments, each of diameter at most β.

matching of the candidate fragment graph $\mathcal{G}'_i$. Hence the running time of a phase i is $O(2^i \cdot \log^* n)$ which requires $O(m + n \cdot \log^* n)$ messages. Since the first part runs for $\lceil \log D \rceil$ phases, the overall time and message complexities to construct a base MST forest are $O(D \cdot \log^* n)$ and $O(m \log D + n \log D \cdot \log^* n)$ respectively.

In the second part, the algorithm in [23] is applied on the top of the $(O(n/D), O(D))$-MST forest $(\mathcal{F})$. This part maintains two forests: one is the base MST forest $\mathcal{F}$ which is already computed in the first part of the algorithm and the other one is the MST forest $\hat{\mathcal{F}}$ obtained by merging some of the base fragments into the fragments of $\hat{\mathcal{F}}$ via Boruvka's algorithm. The second part of the algorithm requires $O(\log n)$ phases. In any phase $j + 1$, it does the following. In every base fragment $F \in \mathcal{F}$, the MWOE $e = (u, v)$ is computed (in parallel in all base fragments) that crosses between $u \in V(F)$ and $v \in V \setminus V(\hat{F})$, where $\hat{F} \in \mathcal{F}_j$ is the larger fragment that contains F. This step requires $O(D)$ rounds and $O(n)$ messages. Once all $O(n/D)$ MWOEs are computed, all of these information are sent to r of T_B. This is done using pipelined convergecast procedure over T_B, in which each vertex u of T_B forwards to its parent in T_B the lightest edge for each fragment $\hat{F} \in \mathcal{F}_j$. This step requires $O(D + |\mathcal{F}_j|)$ rounds and $O(D \cdot |\mathcal{F}_j|)$ messages. Then the root node r does the following: (i) computes MWOE $e_{\hat{F}}$ for every $\hat{F} \in \mathcal{F}_j$, (ii) computes a graph whose vertices are fragments of $\mathcal{F}_j$ and edges are the MWOEs, and (iii) computes the MST forest $\mathcal{F}_{j+1}$. After that r sends $|\mathcal{F}|$ messages over T_B using pipelined broadcast where each message is of the form $(F, \hat{F}')$, and $F \in \mathcal{F}$ and $\hat{F}' \in \mathcal{F}_{j+1}$. The root r_F of the base fragment F (each base fragment has a root node) receives this information $(F, \hat{F}')$ and broadcasts the identity of $\hat{F}'$ as the new fragment identity to all the vertices of F. This takes $O(D)$ rounds and $O(n)$ messages. Finally each vertex v updates its neighbors in G with the new fragment identity. This requires $O(1)$ rounds and $O(m)$ messages. Combining both the parts, the overall round and message complexities of Elkin's algorithm are $O((D + \sqrt{n}) \log n)$ and $O(m \log n + n \log n \cdot \log^* n)$ respectively.

B   Pseudocode for the SPF Algorithm

Let Z be the set of terminals, U be the set of ⟨update⟩ messages received by node v in a round, $\delta(v)$ denotes the set of edges incident on a node v, $SN(v)$ denotes the state of a node v (which can be either *active* or *sleeping*), $t\pi(v)$ denotes the tentative predecessor of v, $tf(v)$ denotes the *terminal_flag* of v (which can be either *true* or *false*), and $ES(e)$ denotes the state of an edge e (which can be either *basic* or *blocked*).

SPF algorithm at node v upon receiving a set of $\langle update \rangle$ messages or no message.

Initially, $SN = sleeping, t\pi = nill, ts = nill, tf = false, td = \infty, U = \phi$, and $ES(e) = basic$ for each edge $e \in \delta(v)$.

```
 1: UPON RECEIVING NO MESSAGE
 2: if v = r and v ∈ Z then                    ▷ spontaneous awaken of the root node r
 3:     SN ← active; tf ← true; ts ← v; td ← 0;
 4:     for each e ∈ δ(v) do
 5:         send ⟨update(v, ts, td, tf)⟩ on e
 6:     end for
 7: end if

 8: UPON RECEIVING A SET OF ⟨update⟩ MESSAGES                              ▷ U ≠ φ
 9: if v ∈ Z and SN = sleeping then      ▷ v receives ⟨update⟩ messages for the first
    time
10:     SN ← active; tf ← true; ts ← v; td ← 0;
11:     for each ⟨update(idn(e), tsn(e), tdn(e), tfn(e))⟩ ∈ U such that e ∈ δ(v)  do
12:         if tfn(e) = true then
13:             ES(e) ← blocked;
14:         end if
15:     end for
16:     for each e ∈ δ(v) do
17:         if ES(e) ≠ blocked then
18:             send ⟨update(v, ts, td, tf)⟩ on e
19:         end if
20:     end for
21: else if v ∉ Z then
22:     if SN = sleeping then          ▷ v receives ⟨update⟩ messages for the first time
23:         SN ← active;
24:     end if
25:     for each ⟨update(idn(e), tsn(e), tdn(e), tfn(e))⟩ ∈ U such that e ∈ δ(v)  do
26:         if tfn(e) = true then
27:             ES(e) ← blocked;
28:         end if
29:         if tdn(e) + w(e) < td then     ▷ update the tentative source, distance, and
    predecessor
30:             update_flag ← true;       ▷ update_flag is a temporary boolean variable
31:             td ← tdn(e) + w(e); t\pi ← idn(e); ts ← tsn(e);
32:         end if
33:     end for
34:     if update_flag = true then
35:         for each e ∈ δ(v) such that ES(e) ≠ blocked do
36:             send ⟨update(v, ts, td, tf)⟩ on e
37:         end for
38:         update_flag ← false;
39:     end if
40: end if
```

References

1. Bacrach, N., Censor-Hillel, K., Dory, M., Efron, Y., Leitersdorf, D., Paz, A.: Hardness of distributed optimization. In: Proceedings of the 2019 ACM Symposium on Principles of Distributed Computing, PODC 2019, pp. 238–247 (2019). https://doi.org/10.1145/3293611.3331597
2. Bauer, F., Varma, A.: Distributed algorithms for multicast path setup in data networks. IEEE/ACM Trans. Netw. **4**(2), 181–191 (1996). https://doi.org/10.1109/90.490746
3. Byrka, J., Grandoni, F., Rothvoß, T., Sanità, L.: An improved LP-based approximation for Steiner tree. In: Proceedings of the Forty-Second ACM Symposium on Theory of Computing, STOC 2010, pp. 583–592 (2010). https://doi.org/10.1145/1806689.1806769
4. Chalermsook, P., Fakcharoenphol, J.: Simple distributed algorithms for approximating minimum Steiner trees. In: Wang, L. (ed.) COCOON 2005. LNCS, vol. 3595, pp. 380–389. Springer, Heidelberg (2005). https://doi.org/10.1007/11533719_39
5. Chen, G.H., Houle, M.E., Kuo, M.T.: The Steiner problem in distributed computing systems. Inf. Sci. **74**(1–2), 73–96 (1993). https://doi.org/10.1016/0020-0255(93)90128-9
6. Chlebík, M., Chlebíková, J.: The Steiner tree problem on graphs: inapproximability results. Theoret. Comput. Sci. **406**(3), 207–214 (2008). https://doi.org/10.1016/j.tcs.2008.06.046
7. Cole, R., Vishkin, U.: Deterministic coin tossing with applications to optimal parallel list ranking. Inf. Control **70**(1), 32–53 (1986). https://doi.org/10.1016/S0019-9958(86)80023-7
8. Das Sarma, A., et al.: Distributed verification and hardness of distributed approximation. In: Proceedings of the Forty-Third Annual ACM Symposium on Theory of Computing, STOC 2011, pp. 363–372 (2011). https://doi.org/10.1145/1993636.1993686
9. Elkin, M.: A simple deterministic distributed MST algorithm, with near-optimal time and message complexities. In: Proceedings of the ACM Symposium on Principles of Distributed Computing, PODC 2017, pp. 157–163 (2017). https://doi.org/10.1145/3087801.3087823
10. Gallager, R.G., Humblet, P.A., Spira, P.M.: A distributed algorithm for minimum-weight spanning trees. ACM Trans. Program. Lang. Syst. **1**, 66–77 (1983). https://doi.org/10.1145/357195.357200
11. Garay, J.A., Kutten, S., Peleg, D.: A sublinear time distributed algorithm for minimum-weight spanning trees. SIAM J. Comput. **27**(1), 302–316 (1998). https://doi.org/10.1137/S0097539794261118
12. Haeupler, B., Hershkowitz, D.E., Wajc, D.: Round- and message-optimal distributed graph algorithms. In: Proceedings of the 2018 ACM Symposium on Principles of Distributed Computing, PODC 2018, pp. 119–128 (2018). https://doi.org/10.1145/3212734.3212737
13. Hauptmann, M., Karpinski, M.: A Compendium on Steiner Tree Problems (2015). http://theory.cs.uni-bonn.de/info5/steinerkompendium/netcompendium.html
14. Karp, R.M.: Reducibility among combinatorial problems. In: Miller, R.E., Thatcher, J.W., Bohlinger, J.D. (eds.) Complexity of Computer Computations. The IBM Research Symposia Series. Springer, Boston (1972). https://doi.org/10.1007/978-1-4684-2001-2_9

15. Karpinski, M., Zelikovsky, A.: New approximation algorithms for the Steiner tree problems. J. Comb. Optim. **1**(1), 47–65 (1997). https://doi.org/10.1023/A:1009758919736
16. Khan, M., Kuhn, F., Malkhi, D., Pandurangan, G., Talwar, K.: Efficient distributed approximation algorithms via probabilistic tree embeddings. In: Proceedings of the Twenty-Seventh ACM Symposium on Principles of Distributed Computing, PODC 2008, pp. 263–272 (2008). https://doi.org/10.1145/1400751.1400787
17. Khan, M., Pandurangan, G.: A fast distributed approximation algorithm for minimum spanning trees. Distrib. Comput. **20**(6), 391–402 (2008). https://doi.org/10.1007/s00446-007-0047-8
18. Kou, L., Markowsky, G., Berman, L.: A fast algorithm for Steiner trees. Acta Informatica **15**(2), 141–145 (1981). https://doi.org/10.1007/BF00288961
19. Kutten, S., Pandurangan, G., Peleg, D., Robinson, P., Trehan, A.: On the complexity of universal leader election. J. ACM **62**(1), 7:1–7:27 (2015). https://doi.org/10.1145/2699440
20. Kutten, S., Peleg, D.: Fast distributed construction of small k-dominating sets and applications. J. Algorithms **28**(1), 40–66 (1998). https://doi.org/10.1006/jagm.1998.0929
21. Lenzen, C., Patt-Shamir, B.: Improved distributed Steiner forest construction. In: Proceedings of the ACM Symposium on Principles of Distributed Computing, PODC 2014, pp. 262–271 (2014). https://doi.org/10.1145/2611462.2611464
22. Lenzen, C., Patt-Shamir, B.: Fast partial distance estimation and applications. In: Proceedings of the 2015 ACM Symposium on Principles of Distributed Computing, PODC 2015, pp. 153–162 (2015). https://doi.org/10.1145/2767386.2767398
23. Pandurangan, G., Robinson, P., Scquizzato, M.: A time- and message-optimal distributed algorithm for minimum spanning trees. In: Proceedings of the 49th Annual ACM SIGACT Symposium on Theory of Computing, STOC 2017, pp. 743–756 (2017). https://doi.org/10.1145/3055399.3055449
24. Peleg, D.: Distributed computing: a locality-sensitive approach. SIAM Discrete Math. Appl. (2000). https://doi.org/10.1137/1.9780898719772
25. Promel, H.J., Steger, A.: A new approximation algorithm for the Steiner tree problem with performance ratio 5/3. J. Algorithms **36**(1), 89–101 (2000). https://doi.org/10.1006/jagm.2000.1086
26. Robins, G., Zelikovsky, A.: Improved Steiner tree approximation in graphs. In: Proceedings of the Eleventh Annual ACM-SIAM Symposium on Discrete Algorithms, SODA 2000, pp. 770–779 (2000)
27. Saikia, P., Karmakar, S.: A simple $2(1 - 1/\ell)$ factor distributed approximation algorithm for Steiner tree in the congest model. In: Proceedings of the 20th International Conference on Distributed Computing and Networking, ICDCN 2019, pp. 41–50 (2019). https://doi.org/10.1145/3288599.3288629
28. Takahashi, H., Matasuyama, A.: An approximate solution for the Steiner problem in graphs. Math. Japan **24**, 573–577 (1980)
29. Wu, Y.F., Widmayer, P., Wong, C.K.: A faster approximation algorithm for the Steiner problem in graphs. Acta Informatica **23**(2), 223–229 (1986). https://doi.org/10.1007/BF00289500
30. Zelikovsky, A.: An 11/6-approximation algorithm for the network Steiner problem. Algorithmica **9**(5), 463–470 (1993). https://doi.org/10.1007/BF01187035

An Efficient Message Transmission and Verification Scheme for VANETs

Kunal Bajaj[1], Trupil Limbasiya[1], and Debasis Das[2]([✉])

[1] BITS Pilani, Goa Campus, Sancoale, India
kunalsbajaj@gmail.com, limbasiyatrupil@gmail.com
[2] Indian Institute of Technology (IIT) Jodhpur, Jodhpur, India
debasis@iitj.ac.in

Abstract. The vehicular ad-hoc network (VANET) is used for communication between vehicles in the same vicinity and road-side-units (RSUs). Since they communicate over a public channel, a secure data transmission protocol is necessary to exchange confidential information. Moreover, the number of vehicles is increasing day-by-day and thus, the receiver gets myriad messages from nearby RSUs and vehicles. As a result, the verification time plays a major role in vehicular communication scheme. Further, providing anonymous communication between vehicles is also a challenging task. To overcome these concerns, in this paper, we propose an identity-based signature protocol using the batch verification concept for VANETs. This paper aims to decrease the computational time (during the communication), and the proposed scheme resists various security attacks, i.e., man-in-the-middle, impersonation, replay, Sybil, and password guessing. Moreover, the proposed protocol achieves better performance results (for computational time, communication overhead, and storage cost) on Raspberry Pi 3B+ compared to other existing data transmission schemes.

Keywords: Batch verification · Tamper-proof-device · VANET · RSU

1 Introduction

The vehicular ad-hoc network (VANET) is a temporary network in which vehicles and road-side-units (RSUs) transmit messages using dedicated short-range communication (DSRC). VANETs are a crucial part of the Intelligent Transportation Systems (ITS) framework. In VANETs, there are two types of communications as vehicle-to-RSU (V2R) and vehicle-to-vehicle (V2V). In V2R, a vehicle exchanges messages with the nearby RSUs and in V2V, a vehicle transmits messages to the nearby vehicles. Based on these data transmission techniques, VANET finds its application in various real-life situations. Some of them are automatic light management in traffic signals, sending safety messages and traffic status to nearby vehicles, cooperative collision warning to both the vehicles, parking availability in the vicinity of a vehicle, value-added advertisement

© Springer Nature Switzerland AG 2020
D. V. Hung and M. D'Souza (Eds.): ICDCIT 2020, LNCS 11969, pp. 127–143, 2020.
https://doi.org/10.1007/978-3-030-36987-3_8

[1]. However, there are different shortcomings (fixed storage, continual change in the communication range, and limited computing power) associated in VANETs. Thus, this architecture should be managed adequately; otherwise, V2V and V2R communications can pose a threat to the lives of people and may also result in severe damages to properties. It is also challenging to ensure the authenticity of vehicular data transmission due to public channel communication in a mobility environment. Further, the network load varies in rural and urban areas. High traffic may lead to a possibility of collision in the network. Besides, there can be social issues, for example, a consumer may not like such type of monitoring of its vehicle as they may consider it as a hindrance to their privacy. Another issue in VANET is that vehicles/RSUs receive a huge number of messages regularly, and thus, it is a tough job to verify each message separately [2].

The VANET architecture is a temporary network and data is sent through DSRC standard. Thus, vehicle users may face various challenges during communication. The first challenge is encountered as the establishment and management of the public and the private keys efficiently. Because vehicles always move on the road, and thus, it is important to complete the verification process and data transmission procedure within a limited time. Another challenge is to maintain the confidentiality, integrity, and privacy of the transmitted messages [3]. If the communication scheme fails to fulfill security requirements for messages, then there are high chances for attackers to interrupt and tamper the transmitted messages between vehicles. Besides, it is also important to check the sender of the messages transmitted. There are another some limitations like communication between high-speed vehicles, the required time to transfer a message from one vehicle to other is high which can introduce delays, maintaining the security of messages and network mobility. These challenges are also necessary to be taken care of while designing the communication protocol for VANETs [4].

To overcome various communication issues, a secure and efficient vehicular communication system is required [5,6]. The efficiency of the system can be analyzed using different parameters as follows. To deal with security challenges and to increase the verification speed, this paper introduces an efficient ID based signature scheme for batch verification in VANETs. The proposed scheme has the following features: (1) A batch of signatures is verified instead of authenticating each signature one by one. By doing so, vehicle authentication speed can be increased significantly. (2) An ID based scheme uses bi-linear pairing along with hashing and small-scale multiplication. The use of bi-linear pairing reduces the signature signing overhead and due to the use of hashing, the user's identity is not revealed to the public. (3) This scheme supports conditional privacy, which ensures that only the road transport authority (RTA) can know a vehicle's original identity from its pseudo-identities.

Contributions: The main motive to design a protocol for communication in VANETs is that the present vehicular communication systems are not effective in both (performance and security). If the protocol computes all necessary operations quickly and confirms the authenticity and integrity by preserving messages confidentiality, then vehicle users can communicate securely and efficiently on the road. Further, compromising on the security of messages must not be done to increase the performance of the protocol. Hence, keeping the focus on these objectives, in this paper, we propose a rapid and secure communication protocol as described in Sect. 3. The receiver frequently gets messages from different senders and thus, it is important to reduce the verification overhead at the receiver side. Hence, the proposed scheme is designed using the bi-linear pairing concept to verify a large number of messages at the same time. Further, we do a security and performance analysis of the proposed scheme to check its efficiency and security strengths in Sect. 4 and Sect. 5.

Paper Organization: In Sect. 2, we discuss different features and drawbacks of existing vehicular communication protocols. In Sect. 3, we propose a secure and efficient vehicular communication system for V2R and V2V communications. In Sect. 4, we do efficiency analysis of the proposed protocol using several parameters like computation cost, storage cost, and communication overhead. Section 5 presents a security analysis of the suggested model to check its resistance against different security attacks. Finally, Sect. 6 concludes this paper and also contains prospects in this field.

2   Related Works

VANETs employ IEEE 802.11p standard instead of IEEE 802.11 to add Wireless Access in Vehicular Environments (WAVE), and this standard typically uses channels of 10 MHz bandwidth in the 5.9 GHz band using DSRC for communication as it has flexibility and fewer collisions of signals [7]. Raya et al. [8] carefully deliberated numerous security issues in VANETs like non-repudiation, authentication of messages, user anonymity. Further they [8] proposed a scheme for V2V data transmissions using anonymous public and private key pairs. Therefore, an on-board unit (OBU) needs abundant storage space to save numerous public/private key pairs. Moreover, the scheme [8] could not be readily applied to the VANET structure.

Researchers [9] designed a communication method for VANETs using digital signatures to improve security, user privacy, and non-traceability. However, the verification speed for a pairing operation is slower rather than the multiplication operation. The scheme in [9] focuses on sequential verification of messages but occasionally, the messages received by an RSU became large ultimately, and thus, it leads to scalability issues. To overcome these problems and to occupy less storage, anonymous batch authentication and key agreement (ABAKA) scheme was proposed in [10]. To avoid any pitfalls, they used batch verification to simultaneously authenticate multiple requests and establish different session keys with vehicles. The scheme [11] stated that the ABAKA scheme [10] is prone to a signature repudiation attack. The scheme proposed in [11] designed to overcame [9]'s weaknesses by not being prone to a replay attack, but also achieving signature non-repudiation. A major inadequacy of [9] was having no V2V scheme described, which was fulfilled by [12]. This scheme also accounted for non-repudiation and replaying resistance which was plausible attacks for [9]'s scheme. When the batch verification scheme faced an illegal signature, it loses its efficacy. In [13], a new CPAV authentication scheme was proposed for Internet of things (IoT) devices to achieve anonymous authentication along with less certificate and signature verification cost. It also improves conditional user privacy and involves a tracking mechanism to reveal the original identity of a malicious vehicle, which enhances system efficiency.

Zhang et al. in [14] included V2V and V2R communications to improve the scheme [9]. [14] asserted that their scheme fulfills the necessary and emerging design requirements for security and privacy preservation by addressing denial of service (DoS) and message jamming attacks. Researchers [15] indicated that AKABA scheme [10] is merely devised to entertainment service, and thus, they proposed an efficient privacy-preserving authentication scheme (EPAS) for VANETs. Experimental results have proved that the scheme proposed in [15] solves the bottleneck problem of one-by-one message verification. However, it is not very robust due to its performance results. In [16], it is explained that the scheme mentioned in [11] is insecure against an impersonation attack. Further, they suggested an improved vehicular communication method.

Authors [17] proposed a message verification scheme for V2V communication to improve the security of transmitted messages over a common channel, but it comparatively takes more computational resources because they used the public key cryptography concept in the design of a V2V communication protocol. Malhi et al. [18] introduced the concept of multiple authorities to verify the identity of a vehicle so that a single authority cannot solely locate the actual identity of a vehicle. Besides, they used bloom filters to reduce message dropping during busy traffic hours. Kang et al. [19] used the identity-based signature with cipher-text policy attribute-based encryption (CP-ABE) to protect the sender's privacy and authenticate the messages. Nkenyereye et al. [20] proposed a protocol to broadcast safety message (BSM) to the roadside cloud. In [20], they also mined BSM data broadcasted by vehicles using density and flow estimator methods.

In [21], it is shown that [16] and [11] are still vulnerable to a modification attack. After that, they proposed an identity-based message authentication using proxy vehicles (ID-MAP) for VANETs. Moreover, they [21] discussed that it is secure against the above-mentioned attacks and constitutes message authenticity. There are different vehicular communication methods to exchange important information on the road over a public channel. However, most of them are not effective to fulfill security requirements and better performance results. Hence, we come up with an efficient and secure data transmission method for VANETs.

3   The Proposed Vehicular Communication System

This section illustrates details of the proposed scheme including initialization with the road transport authority (RTA), communication with an RSU, and communication with other vehicles. Firstly, a vehicle user will register his/her vehicle itself with the RTA and during this process, the RTA installs an OBU along with a tamper-proof device (TPD) in a vehicle. After that, a vehicle can transmit messages with nearby VANET components. It also explains how the signature verification process takes place, and all the steps involved in it during the communication phase. The receiver gets more messages at the same time and it is tough to verify all messages one-by-one. Thus, the proposed protocol follows the batch verification process during the communication phase.

3.1   Network Model

This section presents a brief explanation of the network model to have a clear picture of the vehicular communication scheme. In this paper, a two-layer vehicular network model is proposed. The first layer comprises of vehicles and RSUs. The communication between them uses DSRC protocol. Every vehicle has their private and public keys which they use to sign a message and send them to RSU and/or other vehicles. Each vehicle receiving any message from other vehicles is required to first verify their signature before interpreting the message.

The second layer (top layer) is comprised of the RTA. Vehicles communicate with the RTA only when they enter in a different region (e.g., province) to obtain their new private and public keys. Vehicles also need to communicate with the RTA to change their ID or PW (password) of a TPD. The RTA is responsible for tracking the original identity of vehicles using pseudo-identities. This system consists of three entities, i.e., the RTA, RSUs, and vehicles. Figure 1 shows the network model for vehicular communications.

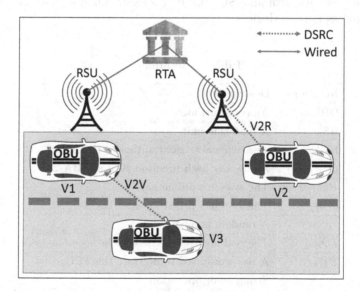

Fig. 1. The proposed scheme network model

1. **RTA:** This is the central authority, which is responsible for registering a new vehicle and it installs an OBU in the vehicle for future communication.

Besides, the RTA is a trusted entity. The RTA saves the certificate issued to vehicles in different memory devices (OBU, TPD, and its database) during the registration stage. Here, private credentials are saved in a TPD to ensure the confidentiality of the credentials, and nobody can access these credentials because it is saved in the secure TPD. This certificate is issued to the vehicles once in a lifetime.

2. **Vehicle:** Vehicles act as nodes to communicate with nearby VANET components. Firstly, a vehicle applicant registers his/her vehicle with the RTA. In this process, an OBU is installed in a vehicle to complete the registration procedure legally. An OBU mainly includes a GPS module, a TPD, and a wireless communication module. A TPD is considered as a non-damageable device by an adversary/individual and only the RTA can do changes in a TPD during the registration phase. As a TPD contain sensitive data (i.e. private keys) about the individual's identity, its safety should be the topmost priority. Hence, when someone tries to corrupt the data in a TPD, the keys are automatically destroyed. An OBU is used to confirm the authenticity of the owner of a vehicle. It is also responsible for receiving a message request or sending a message response during the communication.

3. **RSU:** An RSU is a crucial part of the VANET architecture because it acts as a receiver and confirms the legitimacy of a sender vehicle, thereby only legal vehicles are allowed to interact with it. RSUs are deployed on the road for exchanging messages with the nearby vehicles. The RTA shares data of newly registered vehicles with all RSUs through a secure channel and all RSUs are considered as trusted devices.

Table 1. Notations

Notations	Description
OBU	An on-board-unit
RSU	A road-side-unit
RTA	The regional trusted authority (RTA)
$h(\cdot)$	A one way hash function such as SHA-256
Pub_1/Pub_2	The system's public key
q_1/q_2	The system's private master key
s_i	A random number
ID_i	The real identity of the vehicle
PW_i	A password used to activate the TPD
$\oplus$	String ex-or operation
T_1	Transmission time of message at sender
T_2	Received time of message at receiver
ΔT	Time period to validate message

3.2   The Proposed Initialization Phase

In this scheme, there are two random keys assigned to the RTA, which are q_1 and q_2. Further, bi-linear maps are used so we describe them as follows. Let G_1, G_2, G_t be cyclic groups of same order. A bi-linear map from $G_1 \times G_2$ to G_t is a function $e: G_1 \times G_2 \rightarrow G_t$ such that for all $u \in G_1$, $v \in G_2$, $a, b \in Z$, $e(u^a, v^b) = e(u, v)^{ab}$. Bi-linear maps are called pairings because they associate pairs of elements from G_1 and G_2 with elements in G_t. This scheme uses elliptic curve cryptography (ECC) to produce two public keys, i.e. $Pub_1 = q_1 \cdot P$ and $Pub_2 = q_2 \cdot P$, where P is the generator of the cyclic group G [22]. These keys (Pub_1 and Pub_2) are stored in each vehicle at the time of initialization. Here, each vehicle has a TPD to impregnable against any attempt to break the scheme. It is authenticated using an identity and a password, which are defined by the user at the time of installation of a OBU in a vehicle. While registration of the vehicles, the RTA randomly pre-assigns two keys s_1 and s_2, where s_1, s_2 are $\in Z_p^*$. Here p is the generator of the group and the size of s_1 and s_2 is 12 bytes each. As s_1 and s_2 are very large, guessing them is not possible practically. Table 1 describes different used notations.

3.3   The Proposed Pseudo-Identifiable Key Generation Phase

The TPD initializes by the user id and password given by TA and subsequently generates two pseudo keys p_1 and p_2 where $p_1 = h(ID_i)$ and $p_2 = h(Salt(h(ID_i) \oplus h(PW_i)))$ and $a_1 = q_1 \cdot p_1$, $a_2 = q_2 \cdot p_2$. Also, $b_1 = s_1 \cdot p_1$, $b_2 = s_2 \cdot p_2$ are calculated and stored in TPD. Here, we also store two keys i.e. Pub_1 and Pub_2 at the time of initialization. The pseudo-identifiable key generation process is also shown in Fig. 2.

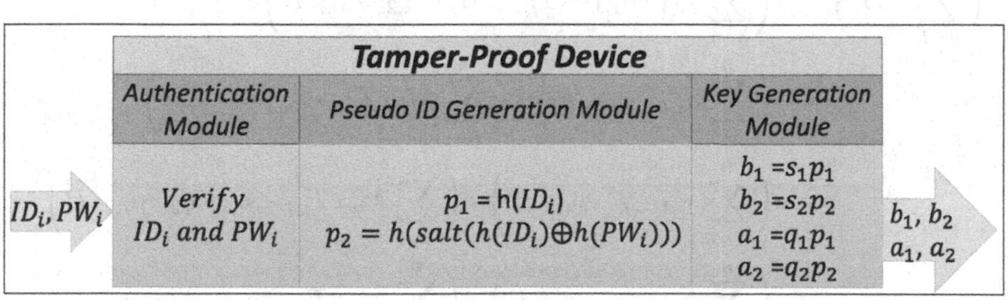

Fig. 2. The proposed scheme: Tamper proof device (TPD)

3.4   The V2R and V2V Authentication Phase

V2R communication is necessary to provide reliability, safety and comfort. V2V authentication facilitates vehicles to communicate with each other to support different applications and services such as cooperative driver assistance.

V2R Communication: When vehicles move on the road, they transmit meaningful information with nearby RSU using DSRC based on the following protocol.

1. The V2R communication is necessary for the execution of V2V communication. In this, a vehicle sends $<b_1, b_2, M, T_1, \sigma>$ to nearby RSU, where $M = m \oplus T_1$, m is the transmitted message, $T_1 =$ current time-stamp, $\sigma = s_1 \cdot a_1 + T_1 \cdot M \cdot s_2 \cdot a_2$.
2. An RSU does the following to confirm a received message from an OBU. Firstly, it checks that $\Delta T < T_2 - T_1$ and then, it checks the signature.

$$
\begin{aligned}
e(\sigma, P) &= e(s_1 \cdot a_1 + T_1 \cdot M \cdot s_2 \cdot a_2, P) \\
&= e(s_1 \cdot a_1, P) \cdot e(T_1 \cdot M s_2 \cdot a_2, P) \\
&= e(s_1 \cdot q_1 \cdot p_1, P) \cdot e(T_1 \cdot M \cdot s_2 \cdot q_2 \cdot p_2, P) \\
&= e(s_1 \cdot p_1, q_1 \cdot P) \cdot e(T_1 \cdot M \cdot s_2 \cdot p_2, q_2 \cdot P) \\
&= e(b_1, Pub_1) \cdot e(T_1 \cdot M \cdot b_2, Pub_2)
\end{aligned}
$$

3. If $e(\sigma, P)$ is equal to $e(b_1, Pub_1) \cdot e(T_1 \cdot M \cdot b_2, Pub_2)$, then an RSU returns $<RSUID, RSUkey>$ to that OBU which has sent its certificate for the verification. If both the terms are not equal, then an RSU verifies the signature individually. After that, an OBU uses these values for V2V communication. Here, $RSUkey$ is a key fixed of a particular RSU, which will be used by vehicles further in V2V communication.

The batch verification (for V2R communication) process is done as the following:

$$
\begin{aligned}
e\left(\sum_{i=1}^{n} \sigma_i, P\right) &= e\left(\sum_{i=1}^{n} s_{i,1} \cdot a_{i,1} + T_{i,1} \cdot M_i \cdot s_{i,2} \cdot a_{i,2}, P\right) \\
&= e\left(\sum_{i=1}^{n} s_{i,1} \cdot a_{i,1}, P\right) . e\left(\sum_{i=1}^{n} M_i \cdot T_{i,1} \cdot s_{i,2} \cdot a_{i,2}, P\right) \\
&= e\left(\sum_{i=1}^{n} s_{i,1} \cdot q_1 \cdot p_{i,1}, P\right) . e\left(\sum_{i=1}^{n} M_i \cdot T_{i,1} \cdot s_{i,2} \cdot q_2 \cdot p_{i,2}, P\right) \\
&= e\left(\sum_{i=1}^{n} s_{i,1} \cdot p_{i,1}, q_1 \cdot P\right) . e\left(\sum_{i=1}^{n} M_i \cdot T_{i,1} \cdot s_{i,2} \cdot p_{i,2}, q_2 \cdot P\right) \\
&= e\left(\sum_{i=1}^{n} b_{i,1}, Pub_1\right) . e\left(\sum_{i=1}^{n} M_i \cdot T_{i,1} \cdot b_{i,2}, Pub_2\right)
\end{aligned}
$$

V2V Communication: In V2V communication, only vehicles (with the same range of an RSU) can communicate with each others using DSRC technology, and this process is performed as follows.

1. An OBU sends $<b_1, b_2, RSUID, M, T_1, \sigma>$ to nearby vehicles via a public channel. Here, $M = m \oplus T_1$, m is the transmitted message, $T_1 =$ current time-stamp, $a_3 = a_2 \cdot RSUkey$, and $\sigma = s_1 \cdot a_1 + T_1 \cdot M \cdot s_2 \cdot a_3$.

2. A receiver OBU firstly checks whether the $RSUID$ matches or not. If equal, then it confirms the freshness by computing $\Delta T < T_2 - T_1$. After that, A receiver OBU verifies the signature as follows.

$$
\begin{aligned}
e(\sigma, P) &= e(s_1 \cdot a_1 + T_1 \cdot M \cdot s_2 \cdot a_3, P) \\
&= e(s_1 \cdot a_1, P).e(T_1 \cdot M \cdot s_2 \cdot a_3, P) \\
&= e(s_1 \cdot q_1 \cdot p_1, P).e(T_1 \cdot M s_2 \cdot q_2 \cdot p_2 \cdot RSUkey, P) \\
&= e(s_1 \cdot p_1, q_1 \cdot P).e(T_1 \cdot M \cdot s_2 \cdot p_2 \cdot RSUkey, q_2 \cdot P) \\
&= e(b_1, Pub_1).e(T_1 \cdot M \cdot b_2 \cdot RSUkey, Pub_2)
\end{aligned}
$$

The batch verification process is done as follows to verify a large number of messages.

$$
\begin{aligned}
e\Big(\sum_{i=1}^{n}\sigma_i, P\Big) &= e\Big(\sum_{i=1}^{n} s_{i,1} \cdot a_{i,1} + T_{i,1} \cdot M_i \cdot s_{i,2} \cdot a_{i,3}, P\Big) \\
&= e\Big(\sum_{i=1}^{n} s_{i,1} \cdot a_{i,1}, P\Big).e\Big(\sum_{i=1}^{n} M_i \cdot T_{i,1} \cdot s_{i,2} \cdot a_{i,3}, P\Big) \\
&= e\Big(\sum_{i=1}^{n} s_{i,1} \cdot q_1 \cdot p_{i,1}, P\Big).e\Big(RSUkey \cdot \sum_{i=1}^{n} M_i \cdot T_{i,1} \cdot s_{i,2} \cdot q_2 \cdot p_{i,2}, P\Big) \\
&= e\Big(\sum_{i=1}^{n} s_{i,1} \cdot p_{i,1}, q_1 \cdot P\Big).e\Big(RSUkey \cdot \sum_{i=1}^{n} M_i \cdot T_{i,1} \cdot s_{i,2} \cdot p_{i,2}, q_2 \cdot P\Big) \\
&= e\Big(\sum_{i=1}^{n} b_{i,1}, Pub_1\Big).e\Big(RSUkey \cdot \sum_{i=1}^{n} M_i \cdot T_{i,1} \cdot b_{i,2}, Pub_2\Big)
\end{aligned}
$$

In this way, receivers can verify more messages at the same time and this leads to saving of computational resources and does a quick verification of received messages from nearby RSUs and OBUs in V2V and V2R communications.

4   Efficiency Analysis and Comparison

In this section, we focus on the computational time, storage and communication cost of the proposed scheme. Further, a comparison of the proposed scheme is done with existing communication schemes.

4.1   Computational Time

Vehicles perform some operations before transmitting data to sign the message. Besides, vehicles verify different signatures doing some operations. This time is required to sign a message and verify other vehicles message, and it is known as computational time. Bi-linear pairing is a function $e\colon G_1 \times G_2 \to G_t$. As Bi-linear pairing is used in the scheme to verify signatures, we can verify n signatures simultaneously instead of verifying them individually. It will reduce the time overhead drastically. Further, different cryptographic operations are executed at the sender and receiver ends. Here, we implement the proposed scheme on Raspberry pi 3B+ model (1 GB LPDDR2 SDRAM memory, 2.4 GHz and 5 GHz IEEE 802.11.b/g/n/ac wireless LAN and Bluetooth 4.2/BLE) to know the execution time for each cryptographic operations. On this platform, the execution time of (one-way hash ($h(\cdot)$), EC_{SM}, EC_{MP}, and par) is 9.6901 milliseconds (ms), 22.5820 ms, 61.84 ms, and 238.9267 ms respectively. Here, $EC_{SM} = $ EC smal-scale multiplication, $EC_{MP} = $ EC map-to-point multiplication, and par = Bi-linear pairing. Accordingly, the proposed scheme requires 3 bi-linear pairing operations and 3 multiplication operations ($T_1 \cdot M \cdot b_2 \cdot RSU\,key$) to verify a single signature. In another case (to verify n signature), it requires 3 bi-linear pairing operations and (2n+1) multiplication operations. Similarly, we have calculated the computational cost for [9, 18–21]. Table 2 and Fig. 3 show the comparison of the proposed scheme with different schemes with respect to their computational cost and time. In Table 2, it is shown that scheme requires less cost for verifying a batch of signatures rather than most of other existing message verification protocols. Figure 3 displays the verification time (in milliseconds) for different vehicular communication methods by considering the number of transmitted messages (i.e., 0, 10, 20, 30, 40, 50, 60, 70, 80, 90, and 100).

Table 2. Performance efficiency analysis comparison

Schemes	For one signature	To verify one signature	To verify n signatures
Zhang et al. [9]	$1T_{EC-MP}$	$3T_{par} + 1T_{EC-SM} + 1T_{h(\cdot)}$	$3T_{par} + nT_{EC-SM} + nT_{h(\cdot)}$
Malhi and Batra [18]	$3T_{EC-SM}$	$3T_{par} + 3T_{EC-SM}$	$3T_{par} + 3nT_{EC-SM}$
Kang et al. [19]	$3T_{EC-SM} + 2T_{h(\cdot)} + 3T_{EC-MP}$	$1T_{EC-SM} + 2T_{h(\cdot)} + 3T_{par} + 3T_{EC-MP}$	$nT_{EC-SM} + 2nT_{h(\cdot)} + 3T_{par} + 3nT_{EC-MP}$
Nkenyereye et al. [20]	$1T_{EC-SM}$	$3T_{par}$	$(n+2)T_{par}$
Asaar et al. [21]	$2T_{h(\cdot)} + 2T_{EC-MP} + 3T_{EC-SM}$	$1T_{h(\cdot)} + 3T_{EC-SM} + 10T_{EC-MP}$	$nT_{h(\cdot)} + 3nT_{EC-SM} + 10nT_{EC-MP}$
Proposed	$3T_{EC-SM}$	$3T_{par} + 3T_{EC-SM}$	$(2n+1)T_{EC-SM} + 3T_{par}$

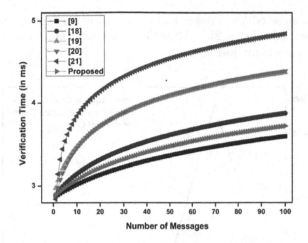

Fig. 3. Computational time analysis using batch verification

4.2   Communication Cost and Storage

During the communication phase, a vehicle sends some parameters and the size of these all values (sent to other OBUs/RSUs) is known as the communication cost. Next, the system saves different parameters in different devices (e.g., the RTA, OBU, and RSU) and for this, some memory is required, which is known as the storage cost.

We consider that a time-stamp requires 8 bytes, an identity/password/variable requires 12 bytes, a bi-linear pairing requires 64 bytes, a one-way hash using SHA-256 requires 32 bytes, an ECC small scale multiplication requires 32 bytes and a generator of ECC requires 48 bytes.

In the proposed method, the sender transfers $<b_1, b_2, RSUID, M, T_1, \sigma>$ during the communication phase, and thus, the communication cost of the proposed model will contain 1 (Time-stamp), 2 (variables: M and RSUID), 3 (ECC small scale multiplication: b_1, b_2 and σ). Hence, the total communication cost for the proposed scheme is 128 bytes. For storage in the proposed scheme, an OBU stores ID_i, PW_i, b_1, b_2, a_1, a_2, s_1, s_2, p_1, p_2 and the generator of EC group. Thus, the OBU storage comprises of 4 (variables: ID_i, PW_i, s_1, s_2), 4 (EC small scale multiplication: a_1, a_2, b_1 and b_2), 1 (Generator of EC), 2 (hash: p_1 and p_2). As a result, the OBU storage cost is 288 bytes. In the proposed protocol, an RSU also has its $RSUID$ and $RSUkey$. The total storage required in RSU is 2 (variables: $RSUID$ and $RSUkey$), 1 (Generator of EC), and this sums to 72 bytes. We also need to store some information about a vehicle in the RTA for enabling backward traceability of a vehicle given its parameters, which is sent during the communication phase. For this, the RTA stores ID_i, PW_i, b_1, b_2 of a vehicle. Accordingly, the storage required for RTA is 2 (variables: ID_i, PW_i), 2 (EC small scale multiplication: b_1 and b_2), 1 (Generator of EC). The total storage required in an RTA is 136 bytes. The total storage cost which is the sum of OBU storage, RSU storage and RTA storage is 496 bytes. In a similar way, we have calculated the storage and communication costs of relevant data transmission methods ([9, 18–21]). After that, we have compared these methods with the proposed scheme in Fig. 4.

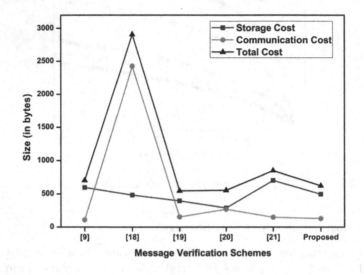

Fig. 4. Communication and storage cost

5   Security Analysis

We describe how the proposed scheme resist different attacks like replay, man-in-the-middle (MITM), impersonation, Sybil, and unauthorized backward trace-ability for preserving integrity, confidentiality, authentication, non-repudiation, user anonymity.

5.1   Strong User Anonymity

The signature helps in keeping the identity of the user confidential. During registration, a_1 and a_2 are saved in an OBU, which are used during the creation of the signature. The user's identity is hidden in p_1 and p_2, which are never directly transmitted to other vehicles during the communication phase. For ensuring additional security, p_1 and p_2 do not directly use the user's ID and password. First SHA-256 and salting on user's ID and password are done to make it more secure, and then, they are used to calculate b_1 and b_2, which are sent during the authentication phase. Hence, if an attacker wants to mock a user by sending another σ, s/he needs a_1 and a_2 to calculate new σ along with other parameters. The vehicle sends $<b_1, b_2, RSUID, M, T_1, \sigma>$ to other vehicles, but calculating a_1 and a_2 is not possible using the parameters sent by a vehicle. Hence, strong user anonymity is maintained in this scheme.

5.2 Impersonation Attack

If an unauthorized user sends messages on behalf of a registered user by imitating his/her identity without knowing his/her user ID and password, then it is called an impersonation attack. In the proposed scheme, σ is calculated as $\sigma = s_1 \cdot a_1 + T_1 \cdot M \cdot s_2 \cdot a_3$. Besides, b_1 and b_2 are sent to other vehicles along with σ. To calculate σ, s_1 and s_2 are required, which are random keys for a specific vehicle, and they are not sent via a communication channel. As s_1 and s_2 are 128 bits keys, it is difficult for a third person to guess them by a brute force attack. Thus, it is really difficult for an attacker to impersonate the sender. We consider that an attacker has these values ($<b_1$, b_2, RSUID, M, T_1, $\sigma>$) sent by the vehicle during communication, and s/he wants to send a fake message to another vehicle. Thus, s/he will alter M, but while calculating σ, s/he would not be able to alter it, as s/he does not know a_1 or a_3 of the vehicle, for which s/he is trying to impersonate. Hence, an attacker would be detected by other vehicles. Thus, the proposed scheme resists an impersonation attack.

5.3 Replay Attack

A replay attack means that a message transmitted by the sender can be transmitted again by the attacker at a later point of time. During the proposed communication phase, σ is computed as $\sigma = s_1 \cdot a_1 + T_1 \cdot M \cdot s_2 \cdot a_3$. Here, as time-stamp is sent for verification along with other parameters, another vehicle will first verify that $\Delta T < T_2 - T_1$ and if it matches, then it will check the signature. As discussed recently, it is not feasible to impersonate anyone in the proposed scheme, if an attacker changes the time-stamp and sends the message again, the signature verification will fail because the signature is calculated using the time-stamp. Besides, if an attacker sends the message again after some time, $\Delta T < T_2 - T_1$ will not hold, and the receiver will discard the message as it receives it. Hence, due to the use of time-stamp in generating σ, the suggested scheme is protected against a replay attack.

5.4 Unauthorized Backward Traceability

In the proposed method, the user's identity is not revealed during the V2V or V2R authentication. Hence tracking the sender of the message without the help of an RTA is not possible. Since, the sender's identity is unknown, it is not possible to collect any history related to the sender's daily routine or about the type of messages s/he transmits. The RTA knows s_1, s_2, p_1 and p_2 of the vehicle, as this information is recorded by the RTA during vehicle's registration. Hence, if b_1 and b_2 are known to the RTA, and thus, vehicle's identity can be known by the RTA by using s_1, s_2, p_1 and p_2. Tracing back using RTA stands helpful to trace a vehicle which is found creating chaos or sending false messages. Hence, this scheme resists unauthorized backward traceability.

5.5   Man-in-the-Middle Attack

In a MITM attack, the attacker secretly reads and modifies the transmitted messages between two users, who are unaware of the presence of the attacker. As explained earlier, an attacker cannot impersonate another user, and the attacker is not able to alter the information. Further, s_1, s_2, p_1 and p_2 are not directly transmitted, and therefore, s/he cannot create a third key using b_1 and b_2 of two different messages as they are calculated as $b_1 = s_1 \cdot p_1$, $b_2 = s_2 \cdot p_2$ using ECC. Thus, it is not possible to create new b_1 and b_2 using two different vehicle's b_1 and b_2, and due to use of time-stamp, the existing σ becomes useless later. Hence, the proposed scheme is efficient enough and cannot be attacked using a MITM attack.

5.6   Non-repudiation

Once the RTA has traced the ID of a vehicle, the vehicle cannot deny that the message was not sent by it as the RTA uses b_1 and b_2 for tracing a vehicle, which is created using the private keys of the same vehicle. The signature is traced as it is calculated using formula $\sigma = s_1 \cdot a_1 + T_1 \cdot M \cdot s_2 \cdot a_3$ and as shown above, the proposed protocol can defend replay, man-in-the-middle, and impersonation attacks. When the signature matches with the bi-linear pairing results, it is assured that the signature is sent by that vehicle only. Besides, the signature is sent along with b_1 and b_2, so the user cannot refuse that the message is not sent from its vehicle. Hence, the scheme supports non-repudiation. Thus, the sender cannot decline the fact, that s/he has not sent the specified message.

5.7   Sybil Attack

The reputation system of a network is disrupted by an attacker by creating multiple false identities in this attack. Here, for calculating σ, pseudonyms are used as $a_1 = q_1 \cdot p_1$, $a_3 = q_2 \cdot p_2 \cdot RSUkey$, $\sigma = s_1 \cdot a_1 + T_1 \cdot M \cdot s_2 \cdot a_3$. q_1 and q_2 are master keys which are only known to the RTA. To create a pseudo-identity, the attacker will require master keys, which are not available to an attacker. The proposed scheme is secure against a Sybil attack as master keys are required to create identity, which are only with the RTA. Therefore, the proposed scheme resists a Sybil attack.

5.8   Password Guessing

If an adversary can check the correctness of a guessed password, then s/he can apply a password guessing attack on the system. For the proposed protocol, a sender sends $<b_1, b_2, M, T_1, \sigma>$ to an RSU (V2R communication) and $<b_1, b_2, RSUID, M, T_1, \sigma>$ (for V2V communication). Therefore, an attacker has only one way to confirm a guessed password $(\overline{PW_i})$ with b_2. However, an adversary needs s_2 to compute b_2' using $\overline{PW_i}$, but s/he does not have s_2 because it is only saved in a TPD of a vehicle user. Thus, an attacker does not have an opportunity to verify $\overline{PW_i}$. Hence, a password guessing attack is not feasible in the proposed method.

A security comparison of different message transmission schemes ([9, 18–21]) is done with the proposed scheme in terms of security attributes in Table 3. Referring to Table 3, it can be observed that the proposed scheme is more secure agianst various attacks than the existing schemes.

Table 3. Security analysis for different communication protocols

Security aspects/schemes	[9]	[18]	[19]	[20]	[21]	Proposed
User Anonymity	✓	✓	✓	✓	✓	✓
Resists Impersonation attack	✓	✓	✗	✓	✓	✓
Resists Replay Attack	✗	✓	✗	✓	✓	✓
Resists MITM Attack	✗	✗	✗	✗	✗	✓
Non Repudiation	✓	✓	✗	✓	✓	✓
Resists Sybil Attack	✓	✓	✗	✓	✓	✓
Resists Password guessing Attack	✓	✓	NA	NA	NA	✓

6   Conclusion and Future Work

We have proposed a new scheme for authentication for vehicle users to transmit vital information through V2V and V2R communications securely and efficiently. The security analysis of the suggested scheme is discussed to understand its security strengths against various known attacks, i.e., replay, man-in-the-middle, impersonation, and password guessing. Moreover, the proposed scheme provides user anonymity, confidentiality, confidentiality, integrity, authentication, and conditional backward traceability. Besides, the performance analysis of the proposed scheme dictates that it requires less communication overhead compared to existing relevant data transmission methods.

In our future work, we shall work to reduce the execution time to identify false messages (transmitted over a public channel). As in the batch verification concept, if one message is false, then the scheme gives a result as a failure for verification, and then it needs to traverse through the messages to find the faulty signature(s). This takes a lot of time and spoils the advantage of batch verification to increase speed by verifying more message signatures simultaneously. Besides, we shall also improve the security strengths for the vehicular communication protocol to resist against side-channel attacks.

References

1. Al-Sultan, S., Al-Doori, M.M., Al-Bayatti, A.H., Zedan, H.: A comprehensive survey on vehicular ad hoc network. J. Netw. Comput. Appl. **37**, 380–392 (2014)
2. Limbasiya, T., Das, D.: Identity based proficient message verification scheme for vehicle users. Pervasive Mob. Comput. **60**(101083), 1–12 (2019)
3. Tangade, S.S., Manvi, S.S.: A survey on attacks, security and trust management solutions in VANETs. In: 2013 Fourth International Conference on Computing, Communications and Networking Technologies (ICCCNT), pp. 1–6. IEEE (2013)
4. Limbasiya, T., Das, D.: Lightweight secure message broadcasting protocol for vehicle-to-vehicle communication. IEEE Syst. J. 1–10 (2019). https://ieeexplore. ieee.org/document/8816679
5. Samara, G., Al-Salihy, W.A., Sures, R.: Security issues and challenges of vehicular ad hoc networks (VANET). In: 2010 4th International Conference on New Trends in Information Science and Service Science (NISS), pp. 393–398. IEEE (2010)
6. Raw, R.S., Kumar, M., Singh, N.: Security challenges, issues and their solutions for VANET. Int. J. Netw. Secur. Appl. **5**(5), 95 (2013)
7. Jiang, D., Delgrossi, L.: IEEE 802.11 p: Towards an international standard for wireless access in vehicular environments. In: Vehicular Technology Conference, VTC Spring 2008, pp. 2036–2040. IEEE (2008)
8. Raya, M., Hubaux, J.P.: Securing vehicular ad hoc networks. J. Comput. Secur. **15**(1), 39–68 (2007)
9. Zhang, C., Lu, R., Lin, X., Ho, P.H., Shen, X.: An efficient identity-based batch verification scheme for vehicular sensor networks. In: The 27th Conference on Computer Communications, INFOCOM 2008, pp. 246–250. IEEE (2008)
10. Huang, J.L., Yeh, L.Y., Chien, H.Y.: ABAKA: an anonymous batch authenticated and key agreement scheme for value-added services in vehicular ad hoc networks. IEEE Trans. Veh. Technol. **60**(1), 248–262 (2011)
11. Lee, C.C., Lai, Y.M.: Toward a secure batch verification with group testing for VANET. Wirel. Netw. **19**(6), 1441–1449 (2013)
12. Tzeng, S.F., Horng, S.J., Li, T., Wang, X., Huang, P.H., Khan, M.K.: Enhancing security and privacy for identity-based batch verification scheme in VANETs. IEEE Trans. Veh. Technol. **66**(4), 3235–3248 (2017)
13. Vijayakumar, P., Chang, V., Deborah, L.J., Balusamy, B., Shynu, P.G.: Computationally efficient privacy preserving anonymous mutual and batch authentication schemes for vehicular ad hoc networks. Futur. Gener. Comput. Syst. **78**, 943–955 (2018)
14. Zhang, C., Ho, P.H., Tapolcai, J.: On batch verification with group testing for vehicular communications. Wirel. Netw. **17**(8), 1851–1865 (2011)
15. Jia, X., Yuan, X., Meng, L., Wang, L.M.: EPAS: efficient privacy-preserving authentication scheme for VANETs-based emergency communication. JSW **8**(8), 1914–1922 (2013)
16. Bayat, M., Barmshoory, M., Rahimi, M., Aref, M.R.: A secure authentication scheme for VANETs with batch verification. Wirel. Netw. **21**(5), 1733–1743 (2015)
17. Limbasiya, T., Das, D.: Secure message transmission algorithm for Vehicle to Vehicle (V2V) communication. In: 2016 IEEE Region 10 Conference (TENCON), pp. 2507–2512. IEEE (2016)
18. Malhi, A., Batra, S.: Privacy-preserving authentication framework using bloom filter for secure vehicular communications. Int. J. Inf. Secur. **15**(4), 433–453 (2016)

19. Kang, Q., Liu, X., Yao, Y., Wang, Z., Li, Y.: Efficient authentication and access control of message dissemination over vehicular ad hoc network. Neurocomputing **181**, 132–138 (2016)
20. Nkenyereye, L., Park, Y., Rhee, K.H.: Secure vehicle traffic data dissemination and analysis protocol in vehicular cloud computing. J. Supercomput. **74**(3), 1024–1044 (2018)
21. Asaar, M.R., Salmasizadeh, M., Susilo, W., Majidi, A.: A secure and efficient authentication technique for vehicular ad-hoc networks. IEEE Trans. Veh. Technol. **67**(6), 5409 (2018)
22. Hankerson, D., Menezes, A.J., Vanstone, S.: Guide to Elliptic Curve Cryptography. Springer, New York (2006). https://doi.org/10.1007/b97644

Generalised Dining Philosophers as Feedback Control

Venkatesh Choppella[1], Arjun Sanjeev[1(✉)], Kasturi Viswanath[1],
and Bharat Jayaraman[2]

[1] International Institute of Information Technology, Hyderabad, India
arjun.sanjeev@research.iiit.ac.in
[2] University at Buffalo (SUNY), New York, USA

Abstract. We examine the mutual exclusion problem of concurrency through the systematic application of modern feedback control theory, by revisiting the classical problem involving mutual exclusion: the Generalised Dining Philosophers problem. The result is a modular development of the solution using the notions of system and system composition in a formal setting that employs simple equational reasoning. The modular approach separates the solution architecture from the algorithmic minutiae and has the benefit of simplifying the design and correctness proofs.

Two variants of the problem are considered: centralised and distributed topology with N philosophers. In each case, solving the Generalised Dining Philosophers reduces to designing an appropriate feedback controller.

Keywords: Feedback control · Modular concurrency · Generalised Dining Philosophers

1 Introduction

Resource sharing amongst concurrent, distributed processes is at the heart of many computer science problems, specially in operating, distributed embedded systems and networks. Correct sharing of resources amongst processes must not only ensure that a single, non-sharable resource is guaranteed to be available to only one process at a time (safety), but also starvation-freedom – a process waiting for a resource should not have to wait forever. Other complexity metrics of interest (though outside the scope of this paper) are average or worst case waiting time, throughput, etc. Distributed settings introduce other concerns: synchronization, faults, etc.

In this paper, we carry out a systematic application of control systems theory to revisit one of the classical problems in concurrency - the Generalised Dining Philosophers problem.

Mutual exclusion problems are stated in terms of global properties on the combined behaviour of multiple actors running concurrently. One way of solving the mutual exclusion problem is to define a more complex dynamics that

© Springer Nature Switzerland AG 2020
D. V. Hung and M. D'Souza (Eds.): ICDCIT 2020, LNCS 11969, pp. 144–164, 2020.
https://doi.org/10.1007/978-3-030-36987-3_9

each actor (process) implements so as to ensure the required behaviour hold. In the control approach, however, additional actors, *controllers*, are employed that restrain the main actors' original actions in some specific and well-defined way so as to achieve the same. The role of a controller is to issue *commands* to the main actors controlling their behaviour. At the same time, the control exercised on an actor should be not overly constraining: a philosopher should be allowed to exercise his/her choice about what to do next as long as it does not violate the safety conditions.

The objective of this paper is to demonstrate the usefulness of the idea of control, particularly that which involves feedback. Feedback control, also called supervisory control, is the foundation of much of engineering science and is routinely employed in the design of embedded systems. However, its value as a software architectural design principle is only insufficiently captured by the popular "model-view-controller" (MVC) design pattern [1], usually found in the design of user and web interfaces. For example, MVC controllers implement open loop instead of feedback control. Furthermore, they are elements of an architectural design pattern that is not designed to address liveness properties.

A key motivation for the controller based approach is modularity of design. Composition is defined with respect to an interconnect that relates the states and inputs of the two systems being composed [2]. Viewed from this perspective, the Dining Philosophers form systems consisting of interconnected subsystems. A special case of the interconnect which relates inputs and outputs yields modular composition and allows them to be treated as instances of feedback control. The solution then reduces to designing two types of components, the main actors and the controller and their interconnections (the system architecture), followed by definitions of their transition functions.

The compositional approach encourages us to think of the system in a modular way, emphasising the interfaces between components and their interconnections. One benefit of this approach is that it allows us to define multiple types of controllers that interface with a fixed model system. The modularity in architecture also leads to modular correctness proofs of safety and starvation freedom. For example, the proof of the distributed solution to the dining philosophers is reduced to showing that the centralised controller state is reconstructed by the union of the states of the distributed local controllers[1]. That said, however, subtle issues arise even in the simplest variants of the problem. These have to do with non-determinism, timing and feedback, but equally, from trying to seek a precise definition of the problem itself[2].

2 Systems Approach

The main idea in control theory is that of a *system*. Systems have *state* and exhibit behaviour governed by a *dynamics*. A system's state undergoes change

---

[1] Due to page limit constraints, all proofs are delegated to a technical report [3].

[2] "In the design of reactive systems it is sometimes not clear what is given and what the designer is expected to produce." Chandy and Misra [4, p. 290].

due to input. Dynamics is the unfolding of state over time, governed by laws that relate input with the state. A system's dynamics is thus expressed as a relation between the current state, the current input and the next state. Its output is a function of the state. Thus inputs and outputs are connected via state. The system's state is usually considered hidden, and is inaccessible directly. The observable behaviour of a system is available only via its output. A schematic diagram of a system is shown in Fig. 1.

In control systems, we are given a system, often identified as the *plant*. The plant exhibits a certain *observable behaviour*. In addition to the plant, we are also given a *target behaviour* that is usually a restriction of the plant's behaviour.

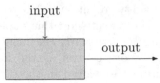

Fig. 1. System with input and output

The control problem is to determine *what additional* input(s) have to be supplied to the plant, such that the resulting dynamics as determined by a new relation between states and inputs now exhibits output behaviour that is as close as possible to the target behaviour specified in the problem. The additional input is usually called the *forced* or *control input*. The plant's dynamics may need to be altered to take into account the combined effect of the original input and the control input.

The second design question is *how* should the control input be computed. Often the control input is computed as a function of the output of the plant (now extended with the control input). Thus we have another system, the controller, one of whose inputs is the output of the plant and whose output is (one of) the inputs to the plant. This architecture is called *feedback control*. The relation between the controller's input and its state and output is called a *control law*. The principle of feedback control is well studied and is used extensively in building large-scale engineering systems of wide variety. Figure 2 is a schematic diagram representing a system with feedback control.

In the rest of the paper, we follow the formal notion of a system and system composition as defined by Tabuada [2]. A complex system is best described as a composition of interconnected subsystems. We employ the key idea of an *interconnect* between two systems, which is a relation that relates the states and the inputs of two systems. While interconnects can, in general, relate states, the interconnects designed in this paper are *modular*: they relate inputs and outputs. Defining a modular interconnect is akin to specifying a wiring diagram between two systems. Modular interconnects drive modular design.

We also illustrate the approach of modular design using feedback control by formulating solutions to the well-known mutual exclusion problem - the generalized dining philosophers, which is an allegorical example of the mutual exclusion problem on an arbitrary graph of processes. This problem is used to introduce the idea of a centralised (hub) controller and also local controllers for the distributed case.

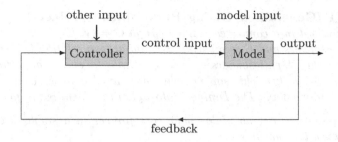

Fig. 2. Feedback control system

3   The Generalised Dining Philosophers Problem

The Dining Philosophers problem, originally formulated by Edsger Dijkstra in
1965 and subsequently published in 1971 [5] is a celebrated thought experiment in concurrency control. A generalization of this problem was suggested
and solved by Dijsktra himself [6]. later, the Generalised Dining Philosophers
problem was discussed at length by Chandy and Misra's [4]. Each philosopher
denotes a process running continuously and forever that is either waiting (*hungry*) for a resource (like a file to write to), or using that resource (*eating*), or
having relinquished the resource (*thinking*). A philosopher may either eat or
think, but can also get hungry in which case she needs to ensure mutual exclusion: that no adjacent philosopher is eating. The problem consists of designing
a protocol by which no philosopher remains hungry indefinitely, the *starvation-
freeness* condition, assuming each eating session lasts only for a finite time In
addition, *progress* means that there should be no deadlock: at any given time,
at least one philosopher that is hungry should move to eating after a bounded
period of time. Note that starvation-freedom implies progress.

Individual Philosopher Dynamics: Consider a single philosopher who may
be in one of three states: thinking, hungry and eating. At each step, the philosopher may *choose* to either continue be in that state, or switch to the next state
(from thinking to hungry, from hungry to eating, or from eating to thinking
again). The dynamics of the single philosopher is shown in Fig. 3. Note that the
philosophers run forever.

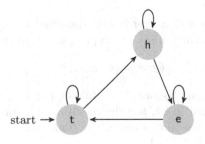

Fig. 3. Philosopher states and transitions

Definition 1 (Generalised Dining Philosophers problem). *N philoso-phers are arranged in a connected conflict graph $G = \langle V, E \rangle$ where V is a set of $N = |V|$ philosophers and E is an irreflexive adjacency relation between them.*

If each of the N philosophers was to continue to evolve according to the dynamics in Fig. 3, two philosophers sharing an edge in E could be eating together, violating safety. The Dining Philosophers problem is the following:

Problem: *Assuming that no philosopher eats forever in a single stretch, con-struct a protocol that ensures*

1. **Safety:** *No two adjacent philosophers eat at the same time.*
2. **Starvation-freedom:** *A philosopher that is hungry eventually gets to eat.*
3. **Non-intrusiveness:** *A philosopher that is thinking or eating continues to behave according to the dynamics of Fig. 3.*

In the subsequent sections, we design solutions to the problem by designing appropriate controller systems and composing them with the philosophers form-ing feedback loops. The solutions may be broadly classified as either centralised or distributed. The centralised approach assumes a central controller that com-mands the philosophers on what to do next. The distributed approach assumes no such centralised authority; the philosophers are allowed to communicate to arrive at a consensus on what each can do next. In both the approaches, it is interesting to note that the definition of the philosopher system does not change.

3.1   The Philosopher System

A philosopher can be in 3 states: t (thinking), h (hungry) or e (eating). We denote the set of states of the philosopher by *Act* (also called the *activity* set).

$$Act = \{t, h, e\}$$

The philosopher is designed in such a way that the non-determinism involved in the decision of the philosopher to either stay in the same state or switch to a new one is encoded as a *choice input*, and is captured as a binary input b of type B to the system, where

$$B = \{0, 1\}$$

The resultant system is deterministic with respect to the choice input. On choice $b = 0$ the system stays in the same state; on $b = 1$ it switches to the new state.

The interface of the philosopher is also modified to accommodate the addi-tional control input (or *command*) c of type *Cmd* from the controller, where

$$Cmd = \{\mathsf{pass}, !1, !0\}$$

With command c equal to pass, the philosopher follows the choice input b. With the command equal to ! b, the choice input is ignored, and the command prevails in determining the next state of the philosopher according to the value of b: stay if $b = 0$, switch if $b = 1$.

The deterministic and transparent philosopher system S may then be defined as follows:

$$S = \langle a : X = Act, a^0 : X^0 = \{\mathsf{t}\}, (b, c) : U = B \times Cmd, f_S \rangle$$

where $f_S : Act \times B \times Cmd \to Act$ is defined as

$$f_S(a, b, \mathsf{pass}) = f_P(a, b) \tag{1}$$
$$f_S(a, \_, !\, b) = f_P(a, b) \tag{2}$$

where $f_P : Act \times B \to Act$ is defined as

$$f_P(a, 0) = stay(a) \tag{3}$$
$$f_p(a, 1) = switch(a) \tag{4}$$

and $stay : Act \to Act$ and $switch : Act \to Act$ are given by

$$stay(a) = a$$
$$switch(\mathsf{t}) = \mathsf{h}$$
$$switch(\mathsf{h}) = \mathsf{e}$$
$$switch(\mathsf{e}) = \mathsf{t}$$

3.2   N Dining Philosophers with Centralised Control

We now look at the centralised controller solution to the problem. We are given a graph $G = \langle V, E \rangle$, with $|V| = N$ and with each of the N vertices representing a philosopher and E representing an undirected, adjacency relation between vertices. The vertices are identified by integers from 1 to N.

Each of the N philosophers are identical and modeled as instances of the system S described in the previous section. These N vertices are all connected to a single controller (called the hub) which reads the activity status of each of the philosophers and then computes a control input for that philosopher. The control input, along with the choice input to each philosopher computes the next state of that philosopher (Fig. 4).

Notation 31. *Identifiers $j, k, l \in V$ denote vertices.*

An activity map $\bar{a} : V \to A$ *maps vertices to their status, whether hungry, eating or thinking.*

A choice map $\bar{b} : V \to B$ *maps to each vertex a choice value.*

A command map $\bar{c} : V \to Cmd$ *maps to each vertex a command.*

If v is a constant, then $\bar{v}$ denotes a function that maps every vertex to the constant v.

The data structures and notation used in the solution are described below:

1. $G = (V, E)$, the graph of vertices V and their adjacency relation E. G is part of the hub's internal state. G is constant throughout the problem.
   We write $\{j, k\} \in E$, or $E(j, k)$ to denote that there is an undirected edge between j and k in G. We write $E(j)$ to denote the set of all neighbours of j.

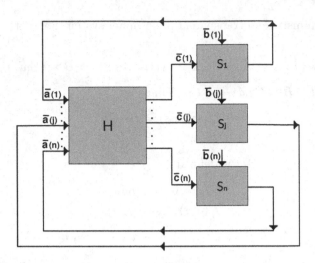

Fig. 4. Wiring diagram describing the architecture of centralised controller.

2. $\bar{a} : V \to \{\mathsf{t}, \mathsf{h}, \mathsf{e}\}$, an activity map. This is input to the hub controller.
3. $D : (j, k) \in E \to \{j, k\}$, is a directed relation derived from E. D is called a *dominance map* or *priority map*. For each edge $\{j, k\}$ of E it returns the source of the edge. The element $\{j, k\} \mapsto j$ of D is indicated $j \mapsto k$ (j dominates k) whereas $\{j, k\} \mapsto k$ is indicated $k \mapsto j$ (j is dominated by k). If $\{j, k\} \in E$, then exactly one of $j \mapsto k \in D$ or $k \mapsto j \in D$ is true.
   $D(j)$ is the set of vertices dominated by j in D and is called the set of *subordinates* of j. $D^{-1}(j)$ denotes the set of vertices that dominate j in D and is called the set of *dominators* of j.
4. $top(D)$, the set of maximal elements of D. $top(D)(j)$ means that $j \in top(D)$. This is a derived internal state of the hub controller.
5. $\bar{c} : V \to Cmd$, the command map. This is part of the internal state of the hub controller and also its output.

Informal Introduction to the Control Algorithm. Initially, at cycle $t = 0$, all vertices in $G = (V, E)$ are thinking, so $\bar{a}[0] = \bar{\mathsf{t}}$. Also, $D[0]$ is D^0, $top(D)[0] = \{j \mid D^0(j) = E(j)\}$ and $\bar{c}[0] = \overline{\mathsf{pass}}$.

Upon reading the activity map, the controller performs the following sequence of computations:

1. (Step 1): Updates D so that (a) a vertex that is eating is dominated by all its neighbours, and (b) any hungry vertex also dominates its thinking neighbours.
2. (Step 2): Computes *top*, the set of top vertices.
3. (Step 3): Computes the new control input for each philosopher vertex: A thinking or eating vertex is allowed to pass. A hungry vertex that is at the top and has no eating neighbours is commanded to switch to eating. Otherwise, the vertex is commanded to stay hungry.

Formal Structure of the Hub Controller. The centralised or hub controller is a deterministic system $H = \langle X, X^0, U, f, Y, h \rangle$, where

1. $X_H = (E \rightarrow \mathbb{B}) \times (V \rightarrow Cmd)$ is the cross product of the set of all priority maps derived from E with the set of command maps on the vertices of G. Each element $x_H : X_H$ is a tuple $(D, \overline{c})$ consisting of a priority map D and a command map $\overline{c}$.
2. $X_H^0 = (D^0, \overline{c}^0)$ where $D^0(\{j, k\}) = j \mapsto k$ if $j > k$ and $k \mapsto j$ otherwise for $\{j, k\} \in E$, and $\overline{c}^0(j) = \overline{\text{pass}}$. Note that D^0 is acyclic.
3. U_H is the set of activity maps. $\overline{a} : U_H$ represents the activity map that is input to the hub H.
4. $f_H : X, U \rightarrow X$ takes a priority map D, a command map $\overline{c}$, and an activity map $\overline{a}$ as input and returns a new priority map D' and a new command map. $f_H((D, \overline{c}), \overline{a}) = (D', g_H(D', \overline{a}))$ where

$$D' = d_H(D, \overline{a}) \tag{5}$$

$$d_H(D, \overline{a}) \overset{\text{def}}{=} \{d_H(d, \overline{a}) \mid d \in D\} \tag{6}$$

$$d_H(j \mapsto k, \overline{a}) \overset{\text{def}}{=} (k \mapsto j) \quad \text{if } \overline{a}(j) = \mathsf{e} \tag{7}$$

$$\overset{\text{def}}{=} (k \mapsto j) \quad \text{if } \overline{a}(j) = \mathsf{t} \text{ and } \overline{a}(k) = \mathsf{h} \tag{8}$$

$$\overset{\text{def}}{=} (j \mapsto k) \quad \text{otherwise} \tag{9}$$

Note that the symbol d_H is overloaded to work on a directed edge as well as a priority map. d_H implements the updating of the priority map D to D' mentioned in (Step 1) above. The function g_H computes the command map (Step 3). The command is pass if j is either eating or thinking. If j is hungry, then the command is !1if j is ready, i.e., it is hungry, at the top (Step 2), and its neighbours are not eating. Otherwise, the command is !0.

$$g_H(D, \overline{a})(j) \overset{\text{def}}{=} \mathsf{pass}, \quad \text{if } \overline{a}(j) \in \{\mathsf{t}, \mathsf{e}\} \tag{10}$$

$$\overset{\text{def}}{=} \mathsf{!1}, \quad \text{if } ready(D, \overline{a})(j) \tag{11}$$

$$\overset{\text{def}}{=} \mathsf{!0}, \quad \text{otherwise} \tag{12}$$

$$ready(D, \overline{a})(j) \overset{\text{def}}{=} \mathsf{true}, \quad \text{if } \overline{a}(j) = \mathsf{h} \wedge \tag{13}$$
$$j \in top(D) \wedge$$
$$\forall k \in E(j) : \overline{a}(k) \neq \mathsf{e}$$

$$top(D) \overset{\text{def}}{=} \{j \in V \| \forall k \in E(j) : j \mapsto k\} \tag{14}$$

5. $Y_H = V \rightarrow Cmd$: The output is a command map.
6. $h_H : X_H \rightarrow Y_H$ simply projects the command map from its state: $h_H(D, \overline{c}) \overset{\text{def}}{=} \overline{c}$.

Note that an existing priority map D when combined with the activity map results in a new priority map D'. The new map D' is then passed to g_H in order to compute the command map.

Wiring the Hub Controller and the Philosophers. Consider the interconnect $\mathcal{I}$ between the hub H and the N philosopher instances s_j, $1 \le j \le N$.

$$\mathcal{I} \subseteq X_H \times U_H \times \Pi_{j=1}^N s_j.X \times s_j.U$$

that connects the output of each philosopher to the input of the hub, and connects the output of the hub to control input of the corresponding philosopher.

$$\mathcal{I} = \{(x_H, u_H, s_1.x, s_1.u \ldots s_n.x, s_n.u) \mid$$
$$u_H(j) = h_S(s_j.x) \wedge h_H(x_H)(j) = s_j.u,$$
$$1 \le j \le N\}$$

The composite N Diners system is the product of the $N + 1$ systems.

Dynamics of the Centralised N Diners System. The following are the equations that define the dynamics of the centralised N Diners system.

$$\bar{a}^0 = \bar{t} \tag{15}$$
$$\bar{c}^0 = \overline{\mathsf{pass}} \tag{16}$$
$$D^0 = \{j \mapsto k \mid E(j,k) \wedge j > k\} \tag{17}$$

$$\bar{c} = g_H(D, \bar{a}) \tag{18}$$
$$\bar{a}' = f_S(\bar{a}, \bar{b}, \bar{c}) \tag{19}$$
$$D' = d_H(D, \bar{a}') \tag{20}$$

Asynchronous Interpretation of the Dynamics. It is worth noting that the dynamics of the system as shown above can be interpreted as asynchronous evolution of the philosopher system. A careful examination of the equations yields temporal dependencies between the computations of the variables involved in the systems. Consider the equations, consisting of indexed variables $\bar{a}$, $\bar{c}$ and D:

$$\bar{a}[0] = \bar{t}$$
$$D[0] = D^0$$
$$\bar{c}[i] = g_H(D[i], \bar{a}[i])$$
$$\bar{a}[i+1] = f_S(\bar{a}[i], \bar{b}[i], \bar{c}[i])$$
$$D[i+1] = d_H(D[i], \bar{a}[i+1])$$

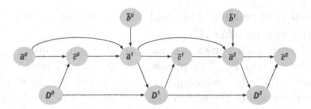

Fig. 5. Dependencies between $\bar{a}$, $\bar{c}$ and D, along with input $\bar{b}$, shown for three calculations.

The asynchronous nature of the system dynamics tells us that the ith value of $\bar{c}$ requires the ith values of $\bar{a}$ and D to be computed before its computation happens, and so on. This implicitly talks about the temporal dependency of the ith value of $\bar{c}$ on the ith values of $\bar{a}$ and D. Similarly, the $(i+1)^{th}$ value of $\bar{a}$ depends on the ith values of $\bar{a}$, $\bar{c}$ and D, and the $(i+1)^{th}$ value of D depends on the ith value of D and the $(i+1)^{th}$ value of $\bar{a}$. Note that they only talk about the temporal dependencies between variable calculations, and do not talk about the clock cycles, nor when the values are computed in physical time. The following figure depicts the dependencies between the variables (Fig. 5).

It is also worth noting that the asynchronous dynamics can be converted to synchronous by composing each system with a global clock and introducing appropriate delays between consecutive computations. This has been discussed in detail in the tech report.

3.3   N Dining Philosophers with Distributed Control

In the distributed version of N Diners, each philosopher continues to be connected to other philosophers adjacent to it according to E, but there is no central hub controller. Usually the problem is stated as trying to devise a protocol amongst the philosophers that ensures that the safety and starvation freedom conditions are met. The notion of devising a protocol is best interpreted as designing a collection of systems and their composition.

Architecture and Key Idea. The centralised architecture employed the global maps $\bar{a}$, $\bar{b}$, $\bar{c}$ and D. While the first three map a vertex j to a value (activity, choice input, or control) the last maps an edge $\{j, k\}$ to one of the vertices j or k.

The key to devising a solution for the distributed case is to start with the graph $G = \langle V, E \rangle$ and consider its distributed representation. The edge relation E is now distributed across the vertex set V. Let α_j denote the size of the set of neighbours $E(j)$ of j. We assume that the neighbourhood $E(j)$ is arbitrarily ordered as a vector $\overrightarrow{E_j}$ indexed from 1 to α_j. Let j and k be distinct vertices in V and let $\{j, k\} \in E$. Furthermore, let the neighbourhoods of j and k be ordered such that k is the mth neighbour of j and j is the nth neighbour of k. Then, by definition, $\overrightarrow{E_j}(m) = k$ and $\overrightarrow{E_k}(n) = j$.

In addition, with each vertex j is associated a philosopher system S_j and a *local* controller system L_j. The philosopher system S_j is an instance of the system S defined in 3.1. In designing the local controllers, the guiding principle is to distribute the state of the centralised controller to N local controllers. The state of the centralised controller consists of the directed graph D that maps each edge in E to its dominating endpoint and the map $\bar{c} : V \longrightarrow Cmd$ which is also the output of the hub controller.

The information about the direction of an edge $\{j, k\}$ is distributed across two *dominance vectors* $\overrightarrow{d_j}$ and $\overrightarrow{d_k}$. Both are boolean vectors indexed from 1 to α_j and α_k, respectively. Assume that $k = \overrightarrow{E_j}(m)$ and $j = \overrightarrow{E_k}(n)$. Then, the value of $D(\{j, k\})$ is encoded in $\overrightarrow{d_j}$ and $\overrightarrow{d_k}$ as follows: If $D(\{j, k\}) = j$ then $\overrightarrow{d_j}(m) = $ true and $\overrightarrow{d_k}(n) = $ false. If $D(\{j, k\}) = k$, then $\overrightarrow{d_j}(m) = $ false and $\overrightarrow{d_k}(n) = $ true.

In the next subsection we define the local controller as a Tabuada system.

Local Controller System for a Vertex j. The controller system L_j has $\alpha_j + 1$ input ports of type A which are indexed 0 to α_j. The output of L_j is of type Cmd.

The local controller L_j is a Tabuada system

$$L_j = \langle X, X^0, U, f, Y, h \rangle$$

where

1. $X = ([1..\alpha_j] \longrightarrow \mathbb{B}) \times Cmd$. Each element of X is a tuple $(\overrightarrow{d_j}, c_j)$ consisting of a *dominance vector* $\overrightarrow{d_j}$ indexed 1 to α_j and a command value c_j. $\overrightarrow{d_j}(m) = $ true means that the there is a directed edge from j to its mth neighbour k; false means that there is an edge from its mth neighbour to j.

2. X^0 is defined as follows: $X^0 = \langle \overrightarrow{d_j^0}, c_j^0 \rangle$ where $c_j^0 = $ pass and $\overrightarrow{d_j^0}(m) = $ true if $\overrightarrow{E_j}(m) = k$ and $j > k$, false otherwise. In other words, there is an edge from j to k if $j > k$.

3. $U = [0..\alpha_j] \longrightarrow A$: We denote the input to L_j as a vector $\overrightarrow{a_j}$, the activities of all the neighbours of the jth philosopher, including its own activity. $\overrightarrow{a_j}(m)$ denotes the value of the mth input port.

4. $f_L : X, U \longrightarrow X$ defines the dynamics of the controller and is given below.

5. $Y = Cmd$, and

6. $h : X \rightarrow Y$ and $h(\overrightarrow{d_j}, c_j) = c_j$. The output of the controller L_j is denoted c_j.

The function f_L takes a dominance vector $\overrightarrow{d}$ of length M, a command c and an activity vector $\overrightarrow{a}$ of length $M + 1$ and returns a pair consisting of a new dominance vector $\overrightarrow{d'}$ of length M and a new command c'. f_L first computes the new dominance vector $\overrightarrow{d'}$ using the function d_L. The result $\overrightarrow{d'}$ is then passed along with $\overrightarrow{a}$ to the function g_L, which computes the new command value c'. The functions f_L and d_L are defined below:

$$f_L((\overrightarrow{d}, c), \overrightarrow{a}) = (\overrightarrow{d'}, c') \quad \text{where}$$

$$\overrightarrow{d'} = \overrightarrow{d_L}(\overrightarrow{d}, \overrightarrow{a}), \text{ and} \tag{21}$$

$$c' = g_L(\overrightarrow{d'}, \overrightarrow{a}) \tag{22}$$

$$\overrightarrow{d_L}(\overrightarrow{d}, \overrightarrow{a})(m) \stackrel{\text{def}}{=} d_L(\overrightarrow{d}(m), \overrightarrow{a}(0), \overrightarrow{a}(m)) \quad \text{where } m \in [1..M] \tag{23}$$

$d_L(d, a_0, a)$ is defined as

$$d_L(d, \mathsf{t}, \mathsf{t}) = d \tag{24}$$
$$d_L(d, \mathsf{t}, \mathsf{h}) = \mathsf{false} \tag{25}$$
$$d_L(d, \mathsf{t}, \mathsf{e}) = \mathsf{true} \tag{26}$$
$$d_L(d, \mathsf{h}, \mathsf{e}) = \mathsf{true} \tag{27}$$
$$d_L(d, \mathsf{h}, \mathsf{h}) = d \tag{28}$$
$$d_L(d, \mathsf{e}, \mathsf{h}) = \mathsf{false} \tag{29}$$
$$d_L(d, \mathsf{e}, \mathsf{t}) = \mathsf{false} \tag{30}$$
$$d_L(d, \mathsf{h}, \mathsf{t}) = \mathsf{true} \tag{31}$$
$$d_L(d, \mathsf{e}, \mathsf{e}) = d \tag{32}$$

$d_L(\overrightarrow{d}(m), \overrightarrow{a}(0), \overrightarrow{a}(m))$ takes the mth component of a dominance vector $\overrightarrow{d}$ and computes the new value based on the activity values at the 0th and mth input ports of the controller.

The function g_L takes a dominance vector $\overrightarrow{d}$ of size M and an activity vector $\overrightarrow{a}$ of size $M + 1$ and computes a command. It is defined as follows:

$$g_L(\overrightarrow{d}, \overrightarrow{a}) \stackrel{\text{def}}{=} \mathsf{pass}, \quad \text{if } \overrightarrow{a}(0) \in \{\mathsf{t}, \mathsf{e}\}$$
$$\stackrel{\text{def}}{=} !1, \quad \text{if } ready_L(\overrightarrow{d}, \overrightarrow{a}) = \mathsf{true}$$
$$\stackrel{\text{def}}{=} !0, \quad \text{otherwise}$$

$$ready_L(\overrightarrow{d}, \overrightarrow{a}) \stackrel{\text{def}}{=} \mathsf{true}, \quad \text{if } \overrightarrow{a}(0) = \mathsf{h} \text{ and } top_L(\overrightarrow{d}) \text{ and } \forall m \in [1..M] : \overrightarrow{a}(m) \neq \mathsf{e}$$
$$\stackrel{\text{def}}{=} \mathsf{false}, \quad \text{otherwise}$$

$$top_L(\overrightarrow{d}) \stackrel{\text{def}}{=} \mathsf{true}, \quad \text{if } \forall m \in [1..M] : \overrightarrow{d}(m) = \mathsf{true}$$
$$\stackrel{\text{def}}{=} \mathsf{false}, \quad \text{otherwise}$$

Wiring the Local Controllers and the Philosophers. Each philosopher S_j is defined as the instance of the system S defined in Sect. 3.1. Let the choice input, control input and output of the philosopher system S_j be denoted by the variables $S_j.c$, $S_j.b_\perp$ and $S_j.a$, respectively. The output of L_j is fed as the control input to S_j. The output S_j is fed as 0th input of L_j. In addition, for each vertex j, if k is the mth neighbour of j, i.e., $k = \overrightarrow{E_j}(m)$, then the output of S_k is fed as the mth input to L_j. (See Fig. 6).

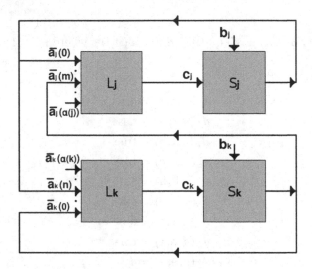

Fig. 6. Wiring between the systems of adjacent philosophers j and k where k and j are respectively the mth and nth neighbour of each other.

The wiring between the N philosopher systems and the N local controllers is the interconnect relation $\mathcal{I} \subseteq \Pi_j S_j.X \times S_j.U \times L_j.X \times L_j.U$, $1 \leq j \leq N$ defined via the following set of constraints:

1. $c_j = S_j.c$: The output of the local controller L_j is equal to the control input of the philosopher system S_j.
2. $S_j.a = \overrightarrow{a_j}(0)$: the output of the philosopher S_j is fed back as the input of the 0th input port of the local controller L_j.
3. $S_k.a = \overrightarrow{a_j}(m)$, where $1 \leq m \leq \alpha_j$ and $k = \overrightarrow{E_j}(m)$: the output of the philosopher S_k is connected as the input of the mth input port of the local controller L_j where k is the mth neighbour of j.
4. $\overrightarrow{d_j}(m) = \neg\overrightarrow{d_k}(n)$, where $k = \overrightarrow{E_j}(m)$ and $j = \overrightarrow{E_k}(n)$. The dominance vector at j is compatible with the dominance vectors of the neighbours of j.

Dynamics of the Distributed N Diners System. Now we can write down the equations that define the asynchronous dynamics of the philosopher system.

Consider any arbitrary philosopher j and its local controller L_j:

$$a_j^0 = \mathsf{t} \tag{33}$$

$$\text{For } m \in [1..\alpha_j] : \quad \vec{d_j}^0(m) = \mathsf{true}, \quad \text{if } \vec{E_j}(m) = k \text{ and } j > k$$
$$= \mathsf{false}, \quad \text{otherwise} \tag{34}$$

$$c_j = g_L(\vec{d_j}, \vec{a_j}) \tag{35}$$

$$a_j' = f_S(a_j, b_j, c_j) \tag{36}$$

$$\vec{d_j}' = d_L(\vec{d_j}, \vec{a_j'}) \tag{37}$$

From Eq. 36, it can be seen that the philosopher dynamics has not changed - it is the same as that of the centralised case. A close examination of the equations help us deduce that the dynamics we obtained in the distributed case are very much comparable to that of the centralised case. This identical nature of the dynamics form the foundation for the correctness proofs.

Correctness of the Solution to the Distributed Case. The correctness of the solution for the distributed case rests on the claim that under the same input sequence, the controllers and the philosopher outputs in the distributed and centralised cases are identical. This claim in turn depends on the fact that the centralised state may be reconstructed from the distributed state. The detailed proof is given in the technical report [3].

4   Related Work

This section is in two parts: the first is a detailed comparison with Chandy and Misra's solution, the second is a survey of several other approaches.

4.1   Comparison with Chandy and Misra Solution

Chandy and Misra [4] provides the original statement and solution to the Generalised Dining Philosophers problem. There are several important points of comparison with their problem formulation and solution.

The first point of comparison is architecture: in brief, shared variables vs. modular interconnects. Chandy and Misra's formulation of the problem identifies the division between a *user* program, which holds the state of the philosophers, and the *os*, which runs concurrently with the user and modifies variables shared with the *user*. Our formulation is based on formally defining the two main entities, the philosopher and the controller, as formal systems with clearly delineated boundaries and modular interactions between them. The idea of feedback control is explicit in the architecture, not in the shared variable approach.

Another advantage of the modular architecture that our solution affords is apparent when we move from the centralised solution to the distributed solution.

In both cases, the definition of the philosopher remains exactly the same; additional interaction is achieved by wiring a local controller to each philosopher rather than a central controller. We make a reasonable assumption that the output of a philosopher is readable by its neighbours. In Chandy and Misra's solution, the distributed solution relies on three shared boolean state variables per edge in the *user*: a boolean variable *fork* that resides with exactly one of the neighbours, its status *clean* or *dirty*, and a *request token* that resides with exactly one neighbour, adding up to $3|E|$ boolean variables. These variables are not distributed; they reside with the *os*, which still assumes the role of a central controller. In our solution, the distribution of philosopher's *and* their control is evident. Variables are distributed across the vertices: each vertex j with degree j has $\alpha(j)+1$ input ports of type *Act* that read the neighbours' plus self's activity status. In addition, each local controller has, as a boolean vector $\vec{d}_j$ of length $\alpha(j)$ as part of its internal state, that keeps information about the direction of each edge with j as an endpoint. A pleasant and useful property of this approach is that the centralised data structure D may be reconstructed by the union of local data structures $\vec{d}$ at each vertex.

The second point of comparison is the algorithm and its impact on reasoning. Both approaches rely on maintaining the dominance graph D as a partial order. As a result, in both approaches, if j is hungry and has priority over k, then j eats before k. In Chandy and Misra's algorithm, however, D is updated only when a hungry vertex transits to eating to ensure that eating vertices are sinks. In our solution, D is updated to satisfy an additional condition that hungry vertices always dominate thinking vertices. This ensures two elegant properties of our algorithm, neither of which are true in Chandy and Misra: (a) a top vertex is also a maximal element of the partial order D, (b) a hungry vertex that is at the top remains so until it is ready, after which it starts eating. In Chandy and Misra's algorithm, a vertex is at the top if it dominates only (all of its) hungry neighbours; it could still be dominated by a thinking neighbour. It is possible that a hungry top vertex is no longer at the top if a neighbouring thinking vertex becomes hungry (Table 1). This leads us to the third property that is true in our approach but not in Chandy and Misra's: amongst two thinking neighbours j and k, whichever gets hungry first gets to eat first.

4.2   Comparison with Other Related Work

Literature on the Dining Philosophers problem is vast. Our very brief survey is slanted towards approaches that—explicitly or implicitly—address the modularity and control aspects of the problem and its solution. [7] surveys the effectiveness of different solutions against various complexity metrics like response time and communication complexity. Here, we leave out complexity theoretic considerations and works that explore probabilistic and many other variants of the problem.

Table 1. Example demonstrating two properties of Chandy and Misra's algorithm: (a) a top hungry vertex no longer remains top, and (b) In step 3, Vertex 1, which was at the top, is hungry, but no longer at the top.

i	G	D	Top	Remarks
0	$\{1:t, 2:t, 3:t\}$	$\{2 \mapsto 1, 3 \mapsto 1\}$	$\{2,3\}$	initial
1	$\{1:h, 2:t, 3:h\}$	ditto	$\{2,3\}$	3 at top
2	$\{1:h, 2:t, 3:e\}$	$\{2 \mapsto 1, 1 \mapsto 3\}$	$\{1,2\}$	1 is at the top
3	$\{1:h, 2:h, 3:e\}$	ditto	$\{2\}$	2 is at the top

Early Works. Dijkstra's Dining Philosophers problem was formulated for the five philosophers seated in a circle. Dijsktra later generalized it to N philosophers. Lynch [8] generalised the problem to a graph consisting of an arbitrary number of philosophers connected via edges depicting resource sharing constraints. Lynch also introduced the notion of an interface description of systems captured via external behaviour, i.e., execution sequences of automata. This idea was popularized by Ramadge and Wonham [9] who advocated that behaviour be specified in terms of language-theoretic properties. They also introduce the idea of control to affect behaviour.

Chandy and Misra [4,10] propose the idea of a dynamic acyclic graph via edge reversals to solve the problem of fair resolution of contention, which ensures progress. This is done by maintaining an ordering on philosophers contending for a resource. The approach's usefulness and generality is demonstrated by their introduction of the Drinking Philosophers problem as a generalisation of the Dining Philosophers problem. In the Drinking Philosophers problem, each philosopher is allowed to possess a subset of a set of resources (drinks) and two adjacent philosophers are allowed to drink at the same time as long as they drink from different bottles. Welch and Lynch [11,12] present a modular approach to the Dining and Drinking Philosopher problems by abstracting the Dining Philosophers system as an I/O automaton. Their paper, however, does not invoke the notion of control. Rhee [13] considers a variety of resource allocation problems, include dining philosophers with modularity and the ability to use arbitrary resource allocation algorithms as subroutines as a means to compare the efficiency of different solutions. In this approach, resource managers are attached to each resource, which is similar in spirit to the local controllers idea.

Other Approaches. Sidhu et al. [14] discuss a distributed solution to a generalised version of the dining philosophers problem. By putting additional constraints and modifying the problem, like the fixed order in which a philosopher can occupy the forks available to him and the fixed number of forks he needs to occupy to start eating, they show that the solution is deadlock free and robust. The deadlock-free condition is assured by showing that the death of any philosopher possessing a few forks does not lead to the failure of the whole network, but instead disables the functioning of only a finite number of philosophers.

In this paper, the philosophers require multiple (more than 2) forks to start eating, and the whole solution is based on forks and their constraints. Also, this paper discusses the additional possibility of the philosophers dying when in possession of a few forks, which is not there in our paper.

Weidman et al. [15] discuss an algorithm for the distributed dynamic resource allocation problem, which is based on the solution to the dining philosophers problem. Their version of the dining philosophers problem is dynamic in nature, in that the philosophers are allowed to add and delete themselves from the group of philosophers who are thinking or eating. They can also add and delete resources from their resource requirements. The state space is modified based on the new actions added: adding/deleting self, or adding/deleting a resource. The main difference from our solution is the extra option available to the philosophers to add/delete themselves from the group of philosophers, as well as add/delete the resources available to them. The state space available to the philosophers is also expanded because of those extra options - there are total 7 states possible now - whereas our solution allows only 3 possible states (thinking, hungry and eating). Also, the notion of a "controller" is absent here - the philosophers' state changes happen depending on the neighbours and the resources availability, but there is no single controller which decides it.

Zhan et al. [16] propose a mathematical model for solving the original version of the dining philosophers problem by modeling the possession of the chopsticks by the philosophers as an adjacency matrix. They talk about the various states of the matrix which can result in a deadlock, and a solution is designed in Java using semaphores which is proven to be deadlock free, and is claimed to be highly efficient in terms of resource usability.

Awerbuch et al. [17] propose a deterministic solution to the dining philosophers problem that is based on the idea of a "distributed queue", which is used to ensure the safety property. The collection of philosophers operate in an asynchronous message-driven environment. They heavily focus on optimizing the "response time" of the system to each job (in other words, the philosopher) to make it polynomial in nature. In our solution, we do not talk about the response time and instead we focus on the modularity of the solution, which is not considered in this solution.

A distributed algorithm for the dining philosophers algorithm has been implemented by Haiyan [18] in Agda, a proof checker based on Martin-Lof's type theory. A precedence graph is maintained in this solution where directed edges represent precedences between pairs of potentially conflicting philosophers, which is the same idea as the priority graph we have in our solution. But unlike our solution, they also have chopsticks modelled as part of the solution in Agda.

Hoover et al. [19] describe a fully distributed self-stabilizing[3] solution to the dining philosophers problem. An interleaved semantics is assumed where only one philosopher at a time changes its state, like the asynchronous dynamics in our solution. They use a token based system, where tokens keeps circling the

---

[3] Regardless of the initial state, the algorithm eventually converges to a legal state, and will therefore remain only in legal states.

ring of philosophers, and the possession of a token enables the philosopher to eat. The algorithm begins with a potentially illegal state with multiple tokens, and later converges to a legal state with just one token. Our solution do not have this self-stabilization property, as we do not have any "illegal" state in our system at any point of time.

The dining philosophers solution mentioned in the work by Keane et al. [20] uses a generic graph model like the generalized problem: edges between processes which can conflict in critical section access. Modification of arrows between the nodes happens during entry and exit from the critical section. They do not focus on aspects like modularity or equational reasoning, but on solving a new synchronization problem (called GRASP).

Cargill [21] proposes a solution which is distributed in the sense that synchronization and communication is limited to the immediate neighbourhood of each philosopher without a central mechanism, and is robust in the sense that the failure of a philosopher only affects its immediate neighbourhood. Unlike our solution, forks are modelled as part of their solution.

You et al. [22] solve the Distributed Dining Philosophers problem, which is the same as the Generalized Dining Philosophers problem, using category theory. The phases of philosophers, priority of philosophers, state-transitions etc. are modelled as different categories and semantics of the problem are explained. They also make use the graph representation of the priorities we have used in our paper.

Nesterenko et al. [23] present a solution to the dining philosophers problem that tolerates malicious crashes, where the failed process behaves arbitrarily and ceases all operations. They talk about the use of stabilization - which allows the program to recover from an arbitrary state - and crash failure locality - which ensures that the crash of a process affects only a finite other processes - in the optimality of their solution.

Chang [24] in his solution tries to decentralise Dijkstra's solution to the dining philosophers problem by making use of message passing and access tokens in a distributed system. The solution does not use any global variables, and there is no notion of "controllers" in the solution like we have in ours. Forks are made use of in the solution.

Datta et al. [25] considers the mobile philosophers problem in which a dynamic network exists where both philosophers and resources can join/leave the network at any time, and the philosophers can connect/disconnect to/from any point in the network. The philosopher is allowed to move around a ring of resources, making requests to the resources in the process. The solution they propose is self-stabilizing and asynchronous.

Supervisory Control. The idea of using feedback (or supervisory) control to solve the Dining Philosophers program is not new. Miremadi et al. [26] demonstrate how to automatically synthesise a supervisory controller using Binary Decision Diagrams. Their paper uses Hoare composition but does not describe the synthesised controller, nor do they attempt to prove why their solution is correct. Andova et al. [27] use the idea of a central controller delegating part of its control to local controllers to solve the problem of self-stabilization: i.e., migrating a deadlock-prone configuration to one that is deadlock-free using distributed adaptation.

Similar to our solution, Vaughan [28] presents centralised and distributed solutions to the dining philosophers problem. The centralised solution does not have a hub controller, but has monitor data structures, which store information like the number of chopsticks available to each philosopher, the claims made by a philosopher on his adjacent chopsticks, etc. In his distributed solution, the chopsticks are viewed as static resources and there are manager processes, like we have controllers, to control them. But unlike our solution, the local manager processes only control the chopsticks (with the help of a distributed queue to sequentialize access to the chopsticks for the philosophers) and not the philosophers, and the access to the resources is scheduled by the philosophers by passing messages between themselves.

Siahaan [29], in his solution, proposes a framework containing an active object called "Table" which controls the forks and the state transitions of the philosophers. The other active objects in the framework are the philosophers and the timer controller (which issues timeout instructions to the philosophers to change state). The table manages the state-change requests of the philosophers depending on the state of forks, hence serving a purpose similar to the controllers in our solution. The timer object sends instructions to the philosophers for state change, but our paper does not involve a timer to do so.

Feedback control has been used to solve other problems too. Wang et al. [30] model discrete event systems using Petri nets and synthesise feedback controllers for them to avoid deadlocks in concurrent software. Mizoguchi et al. [31] design a feedback controller of a cyber-physical system by composing several abstract systems, and prove that the controlled system exhibits the desired behaviour. Fu et al. [32] model adaptive control for finite-state transition systems using elements from grammatical inference and game theory, to produce controllers that guarantee that a system satisfies its specifications.

Synchronous Languages. Synchronous languages like Esterel, SIGNAL and Lustre [33] are popular in the embedded systems domain because synchronicity allows simpler reasoning with time. Gamatie [34] discusses the N Dining Philosophers problem with the philosophers seated in a ring. The example is presented in the programming language SIGNAL, whose execution model uses synchronous message passing. The SIGNAL programming language also compiles the specifications to C code. The solution uses three sets of processes: one for the philosophers, one for the forks, and one for the main process used for coordination. Communication between the philosophers and the forks happens via signals that are clocked. In this respect, the solution is similar to the one described in this paper. However, in the solution, each signal has its own clock (polysynchrony), all derived from a single master clock.

5 Conclusion and Future Work

This work has three objectives: first, to apply the idea of feedback control to problems of concurrency; second, to systematically apply the notion of Tabuada systems and composition when constructing the problem statement and its solution, and third, to ensure that the solution is as modular as possible. In the process, we have also come up with a different solution in the case of the Generalised Dining Philosophers problem, one which reveals how the distributed solution is a distribution of the state in the centralised solution.

The solutions discussed in this paper using this approach leads us to believe that this is a promising direction to explore in the future, the formalisation of software architectures for other sequential and concurrent systems.

References

1. Gamma, E., Helm, R., Johnson, R., Visslides, R.: Design Patterns: Elements of Reusable Object-Oriented Software. Addisson-Wesley, Reading (1994)
2. Tabuada, P.: Verification and Control of Hybrid Systems: A Symbolic Approach. Springer, Boston (2009). https://doi.org/10.1007/978-1-4419-0224-5
3. Choppella, V., Viswanath, K., Sanjeev, A.: Generalised dining philosophers as feedback control. arXiv preprint arXiv:1805.02010 (2018)
4. Chandy, M., Misra, J.: Parallel Program Design: A Foundation. Addison–Wesley, Reading (1988)
5. Dijkstra, E.W.: Hierarchical ordering of sequential processes. Acta Informatica **1**, 115–138 (1971). Also published as EWD 310
6. Dijkstra, E.W.: Two starvation-free solutions of a general exclusion problem. Circulated privately (1977)
7. Papatriantafilou, M.: On distributed resource handling: dining, drinking and mobile philosophers. In: Proceedings of the First International Conference on Principles of Distributed Systems (OPODIS), pp. 293–308(1997)
8. Lynch, N.: Upper bounds for static resource allocation in a distributed system. J. Comput. Syst. Sci. **23**, 254–278 (1981)
9. Ramadge, P., Wonham, W.: The control of discrete event systems. Proc. IEEE **77**(1), 81–98 (1989)
10. Chandy, K.M., Misra, J.: The drinking philosophers problem. ACM Trans. Program. Lang. Syst. **6**(4), 632–646 (1984)
11. Welch, J.L., Lynch, N.A.: A modular drinking philosophers algorithm. Distrib. Comput. **6**(4), 233–244 (1993)
12. Lynch, N.: Distributed Algorithms. Morgan Kaufmann, Burlington (1996)
13. Rhee, I.: A fast distributed modular algorithm for resource allocation. In: Proceedings of the 15th International Conference on Distributed Computing Systems, 1995, pp. 161–168, May 1995
14. Sidhu, D.P., Pollack, R.H.: A robust distributed solution to the generalized dining philosophers problem. In: 1984 IEEE First International Conference on Data Engineering, pp. 483–489. IEEE (1984)
15. Weidman, E.B., Page, I.P., Pervin, W.J.: Explicit dynamic exclusion algorithm
16. Zhan, J., Guo, Y., Liu, C.: A deadlock prevention using adjacency matrix on dining philosophers problem, vol. 121–126 (2012)

17. Awerbuch, B., Saks, M.: A dining philosophers algorithm with polynomial response time. In: Proceedings of the 31st Symposium on Foundations of Computer Science (FOCS), pp. 65–74 (1990)
18. Haiyan, Q.: A Distributed Algorithm in Agda: The Dining Philosophers (1999)
19. Hoover, D., Poole, J.: A distributed self-stabilizing solution to the dining philosophers problem. Inf. Process. Lett. **41**(4), 209–213 (1992)
20. Keane, P., Moir, M.: A general resource allocation synchronization problem. In: 21st International Conference on Distributed Computing Systems, 2001, pp. 557–564. IEEE (2001)
21. Cargill, T.A.: A robust distributed solution to the dining philosophers problem. Softw. Pract. Exp. **12**(10), 965–969 (1982)
22. You, Z., Xue, J., Ying, S.: Categorial semantics of a solution to distributed dining philosophers problem. In: Lee, D.-T., Chen, D.Z., Ying, S. (eds.) FAW 2010. LNCS, vol. 6213, pp. 172–184. Springer, Heidelberg (2010). https://doi.org/10.1007/978-3-642-14553-7_18
23. Nesterenko, M., Arora, A.: Dining philosophers that tolerate malicious crashes. In: Proceedings on the 22nd International Conference on Distributed Computing Systems, 2002, pp. 191–198. IEEE (2002)
24. Chang, E.: n-philosophers: an exercise in distributed control. Comput. Netw. (1976) **4**(2), 71–76 (1980)
25. Datta, A.K., Gradinariu, M., Raynal, M.: Stabilizing mobile philosophers. Inf. Process. Lett. **95**(1), 299–306 (2005)
26. Miremadi, S., Akesson, K., Fabian, M., Vahidi, A., Lennartson, B.: Solving two supervisory control benchmark problems in Supremica. In: Proceedings of the 9th International Workshop on Discrete Event Systems, pp. 131–136. IEEE (2008)
27. Andova, S., Groenewegen, L.P.J., de Vink, E.P.: Distributed adaption of dining philosophers. In: Barbosa, L.S., Lumpe, M. (eds.) FACS 2010. LNCS, vol. 6921, pp. 125–144. Springer, Heidelberg (2012). https://doi.org/10.1007/978-3-642-27269-1_8
28. Vaughan, J.G.: The dining philosophers problem and its decentralisation. Microprocess. Microprogr. **35**(1–5), 455–462 (1992)
29. Siahaan, A.P.U.: Synchronization in dining philosophers problem using lock & release algorithm
30. Wang, Y., Kelly, T., Kudlur, M., Mahlke, S., Lafortune, S.: The application of supervisory control to deadlock avoidance in concurrent software. In: 9th International Workshop on Discrete Event Systems, WODES 2008, pp. 287–292. IEEE (2008)
31. Mizoguchi, M., Ushio, T.: Output feedback controller design with symbolic observers for cyber-physical systems. arXiv preprint arXiv:1612.04974 (2016)
32. Fu, J., Tanner, H.G., Heinz, J., Chandlee, J.: Adaptive symbolic control for finite-state transition systems with grammatical inference. IEEE Trans. Autom. Control. **59**(2), 505–511 (2014)
33. Halbwachs, N.: Synchronous Programming of Reactive Systems. Kluwer Academic Publishers, Dordrecht (1993)
34. Gamatié, A.: Designing Embedded Systems with the Signal Programming Language: Synchronous, Reactive Specification. Springer, New York (2009). https://doi.org/10.1007/978-1-4419-0941-1

Verifying Implicitly Quantified Modal Logic over Dynamic Networks of Processes

Anantha Padmanabha⦿ and R. Ramanujam(✉)

Institute of Mathematical Sciences, HBNI, Chennai, India
{ananthap,jam}@imsc.res.in

Abstract. When we consider systems with process creation and exit, we have potentially infinite state systems where the number of processes alive at any state is unbounded. Properties of such systems are naturally specified using modal logics with quantification, but they are hard to verify even over finite state systems. In [11] we proposed IQML, an implicitly quantified modal logic where we can have assertions of the form *every live agent has an α-successor*, and presented a complete axiomatization of valid formulas. Here we show that model checking for IQML is efficient even when we consider systems with infinitely many processes, provided we can efficiently present such collections of processes, and check non-emptiness of intersection efficiently. As a case study, we present a model checking algorithm over systems in which at any state, the collection of live processes is regular.

Keywords: Implicitly quantified modal logic · Unbounded agents · Model checking · Finite specification

1 Introduction

Modal and temporal logics [3,7] play a central role in the formal specification and verification of reactive systems [12]. In the last two decades, these techniques have been extended to the verification of infinite state systems, and in this context model checking of first order modal logics (FOML) has become relevant. For instance, Abdulla et al. [1] introduce a framework for dynamic database systems, whose reachability properties can be expressed in FOML with transitive modal operators.

When verifying distributed systems, multi-modal logics are used, with modalities indexed by the set of agents. Van Benthem et al. [2] show the close correspondence between processes, transition systems, verification and modal logic. In general, the underlying set of agents is assumed to be finite and fixed for the logical language. Thus when we specify a property we know the set of agents beforehand.

However there are many situations when we do not know the agent set beforehand when we describe system properties. An obvious instance is a dynamic network of processes, where a process can *fork*, splitting into two processes, or *join*

ⓒ Springer Nature Switzerland AG 2020
D. V. Hung and M. D'Souza (Eds.): ICDCIT 2020, LNCS 11969, pp. 165–176, 2020.
https://doi.org/10.1007/978-3-030-36987-3_10

combining processes, or *spawn* child processes. In such systems, even determining the number of live processes at any particular system state can be difficult. In fact, every time the system configuration changes, some processes may be terminated and some new processes may be created, and reasoning about such changes is challenging.

In server-client systems, a server typically handles requests from many clients. If we want to model such systems, once again we cannot bound the number of clients beforehand. Moreover, the set of clients keeps changing dynamically. Once a server has handled a client's request, that client becomes deactivated but during this time there may be new clients who have issued requests.

Another instance is that of *social networks*. Suppose that we want to model how information spreads over a social network. We cannot place a limit on the number of agents in the network at any time; we cannot even place an upper bound on the number of friends of a particular agent. Moreover, agents do not know all the other agents in the network; in other words, the names of agents is not "common knowledge" [6].

In *action indexed* modal and temporal logics [9] we could index modalities by events or actions that cause change of state. But here again, typically the set of actions is assumed to be fixed and finite. Once the set of potential actions is unbounded, we are left with the same problem.

A natural question arises in such contexts: how do we specify properties of systems in which the set of agents is dynamic, changing from state to state? We not only want the set of agents to be unbounded, but also the facility to refer to agents whose names are not available when formulating the specification. Such agents can only be referred to by their properties.

When the agent set is unbounded, we may use variables to index over agents and quantifi over them. This leads us to the realm of Term-modal logics (TML, [4]) introduced by Fitting, Thalmann and Voronkov. In TML we can express properties of the form *for every agent x*, $\Box_x \alpha$ or *there is some agent x such that* $\Box_x \alpha$. Indeed we can go further and specify properties like $\forall x.\exists y.\Box_x \Diamond_y \alpha$ etc. As TML includes first-order logic, it is highly expressive.

If we confine our attention only to the kind of properties above where the quantification over x immediately precedes the modality indexed by x, we can eliminate the variable x altogether. For instance the x-properties above can be represented as modal operators $[\forall]\alpha$ and $[\exists]\alpha$ respectively. In [11], we introduce such a variable free logic of this kind. Since the modalities are *implicitly quantified*, we call it *implicitly quantified modal logic* (IQML).

In an epistemic setting, IQML coincides with the notion of *somebody knows* and *everybody knows*, when the set of reasoners is not fixed a priori. Grove and Halpern [5,6] discuss such a logic where the agent set is not fixed and the agent names are not common knowledge. Wang [14] introduced a fragment of FOML as an epistemic logic in which quantifiers and modalities occur together. Khan et al. [8] use a logic similar to IQML to study approximations in the context of rough sets.

In [11] we presented a complete axiomatization for IQML. In this paper we study the extended model checking problem for IQML. Typically, we have two inputs for model checking: a finite system model and a property to be checked. However, once we are given a finite system model, the set of agents in it is finite and we can translate the property to be checked to a formula of multi-modal logic and use the well known model checking algorithm. But then, as we have observed, in dynamic networks of processes, we have unbounded sets of agents, which are really infinite state systems. Essentially we want to check a modal property of an infinitely branching tree. The real interest in model checking then is this: given a finite presentation of the infinitely branching tree, and a property, we wish to know whether the property holds on the tree. We therefore need a way of specifying such models. Typically we wish to finitely specify the set of live agents at any state, and for each live agent, the set of successor states and the agents live in each of those states.

In this paper, we show that model checking for IQML extended with reachability is efficient over finitely specified models with unboundedly branching. IQML itself can only force models of bounded depth, but for system verification we crucially need reachability. With this extension, we can force models with unbounded branching as well as unbounded depth. The main observation of this paper is that model checking is yet in polynomial time. Since IQML cannot refer to agent names, it suffices to know at each state whether the set of agents that are live at that state has a nonempty intersection with each potential subset of agents undergoing transition. As long as checking such nonemptiness can be performed efficiently, IQML model checking is efficient as well.

As an illustration, we define a class of systems where agent names are synthesised from regular expressions. For this class we consider the model checking problem and present an efficient algorithm for it.

2   Implicitly Quantified Modal Logic

In modal logic we have a modal operator $\Diamond$ that asserts the existence of a successor state. When the successor relation is indexed by an agent identity i, we can correspondingly use a modality $\Diamond_i$ in the syntax. However, since we do not have agent identities in our reasoning we propose a modality $\langle \exists |$ to assert that some agent indexes a successor state. Its dual modality $[\forall |$ would range over the successor states indexed by all agents. Another modality $\langle \forall \rangle$ asserts the existence of a successor state for each agent index. As observed above, since reachability property is crucial in system verification, we introduce an additional modality $\Box^* \alpha$ which ranges over all reachable states.

Definition 1 (IQML syntax). *Let $\mathcal{P}$ be a countable set of propositions. The syntax of IQML is given by:*

$$\varphi := p \in \mathcal{P} \mid \neg \varphi \mid \varphi \wedge \varphi \mid \langle \exists | \ \varphi \mid [\forall | \ \varphi \mid \Box^* \varphi$$

The boolean connectives $\vee$ and $\supset$ are defined in the standard way. The dual modalities of $[\exists]$ and $[\forall]$ are respectively defined by $\langle\forall\rangle\varphi = \neg[\exists]\neg\varphi$ and $\langle\exists\rangle\varphi = \neg[\forall]\neg\varphi$. The dual of $\square^*$ is given by $\lozenge^*\varphi = \neg\square^*\neg\varphi$. We use $\top$ and $\bot$ to denote the boolean constants 'True' and 'False' respectively: they can be coded by $p \vee \neg p$, and $p \wedge \neg p$, for some fixed atomic proposition p.

The set of subformulas of a formula φ is defined inductively where $\mathsf{SF}(p) = \{p\}$; $\mathsf{SF}(\neg\varphi) = \{\neg\varphi\} \cup \mathsf{SF}(\varphi)$; $\mathsf{SF}(\varphi \wedge \psi) = \{\varphi \wedge \psi\} \cup \mathsf{SF}(\varphi)$; $\mathsf{SF}([\exists]\varphi) = \{[\exists]\varphi\} \cup \mathsf{SF}(\varphi)$ and $\mathsf{SF}([\forall]\varphi) = \{[\forall]\varphi\} \cup \mathsf{SF}(\varphi)$.

The semantics of modal logics is given by Kripke structures $M = (W, \mathcal{R}, \rho)$ where W is referred to as a set of *worlds*, $\mathcal{R} \subseteq (W \times W)$ is called the accessibility relation and $\rho : W \mapsto 2^{\mathcal{P}}$ gives the valuation of propositions at worlds. In propositional multi-modal logics over n agents, the Kripke structure is given by $M = (W, \mathcal{R}_1, \cdots, \mathcal{R}_n, \rho)$ where each $\mathcal{R}_i \subseteq (W \times W)$ is the accessibility relation for the corresponding index. But in case of IQML, the agent set is not fixed. Moreover, the set of *relevant agents* changes from one world to the other. Thus, along with the set of worlds W, every model comes with a potential set of agents $\mathcal{I}$. Further, $\delta : W \mapsto 2^{\mathcal{I}}$ specifies the set of relevant agents at every world. The accessibility relation is now given by $\mathcal{R}_i \subseteq (W \times W)$ for every $i \in \mathcal{I}$. To ensure that only *live agents* can change the system state, we impose the condition that whenever $(w, u) \in \mathcal{R}_i$ we have $i \in \delta(w)$. The formal definition follows.

Definition 2 (IQML structure). *An IQML structure is given by the tuple $M = (W, \mathcal{I}, \mathbb{R}, \delta, \rho)$ where W is a non-empty set of worlds, $\mathcal{I}$ is a non-empty countable index set, $\mathbb{R} : \mathcal{I} \to 2^{W \times W}$ (with R_i denoting the relation $\mathbb{R}(i)$), $\delta : W \mapsto 2^{\mathcal{I}}$ such that whenever $(w, u) \in \mathcal{R}_i$ we have $i \in \delta(w)$ and $\rho : W \mapsto 2^{\mathcal{P}}$ is the valuation function.*

For any model $\mathcal{M}$ and any $w, u \in W$ we say that u *is reachable from* w if there is a path of the form $v_0 \xrightarrow{i_0} v_1 \xrightarrow{i_1} \ldots \xrightarrow{i_n} v_n$ where $v_0 = w$ and $v_n = u$ and every $(v_j, v_{j+1}) \in \mathcal{R}_{i_j}$. Note that $w = u$ when $n = 0$. Let $\mathsf{Reach}(w) = \{u \mid u$ is reachable from $w\}$. Clearly, every transition along the path is by an active agent.

The semantics is defined naturally as follows:

Definition 3 (IQML semantics). *Given a IQML model $\mathcal{M} = (W, \mathcal{I}, \mathbb{R}, \delta, \rho)$, an IQML formula φ and $w \in W$, define $\mathcal{M}, w \models \varphi$ inductively as follows:*

$$
\begin{aligned}
&\mathcal{M}, w \models p && \Leftrightarrow p \in \rho(w) \\
&\mathcal{M}, w \models \neg\varphi && \Leftrightarrow \mathcal{M}, w \not\models \varphi \\
&\mathcal{M}, w \models (\varphi \wedge \psi) && \Leftrightarrow \mathcal{M}, w \models \varphi \text{ and } \mathcal{M}, w \models \psi \\
&\mathcal{M}, w \models [\exists]\varphi && \Leftrightarrow \text{there is some } i \in \delta(w) \text{ such that for all } u \in W \\
& && \quad \text{if } (w, u) \in R_i \text{ then } \mathcal{M}, u \models \varphi \\
&\mathcal{M}, w \models [\forall]\varphi && \Leftrightarrow \text{for all } i \in \delta(w) \text{ and for all } u \in W \\
& && \quad \text{if } (w, u) \in R_i \text{ then } \mathcal{M}, u \models \varphi \\
&\mathcal{M}, w \models \square^*\varphi && \Leftrightarrow \text{for all } u \in W \\
& && \quad \text{if } (w, u) \in \mathsf{Reach}(w) \text{ then } \mathcal{M}, u \models \varphi
\end{aligned}
$$

The model checking problem is to consider an IQML structure $\mathcal{M}$, $w \in W$ and a formula φ and decide whether $\mathcal{M}, w \models \varphi$. When $\mathcal{M}$ is finite, $\mathcal{I}$ is finite as well. Suppose $|\mathcal{I}| = k$. Now, it is easy to see that we can translate φ into a formula φ_k of multi-modal logic with k modal indices. The crucial steps in the translation are: $[\exists]\alpha$ gets translated to a disjunction of $\square_i \alpha'$ with i ranging over the finite index set I (and α' being the inductive translation of α). The translation for $[\forall]$ is similarly a conjunction. Now we can employ the well known model checking procedure for multi-modal logic.

However, when we consider models which are potentially infinite, we first need a finite representation of such models that can be provided as input for the model checking algorithm. We consider one such specification motivated by regular dynamic networks of processes.

Example 1. Consider an operating system which can execute many processes at a time. A configuration of the system is given by the states of its active processes. Any active process can change the system state by making a move. Any move by a process can create one or more new processes (threads), thus making the active set dynamic and potentially unbounded.

In this setting, consider the following assertions:

- The system never halts
  $\square^*(\langle\exists\rangle\top)$.
- Whenever p holds, there is always a process that is guaranteed to change the system state such that q holds.
  $\square^*(p \supset [\exists]q)$.
- There are at least two active processes[1]:
  $[\exists]p \wedge \langle\exists\rangle\neg p$.
- There is a reachable state in which the system halts:
  $\Diamond^*([\forall]\bot)$.

It is clear that similar specifications can be written in the case of communicating distributed processes, as well as processes in server client systems.

3   Model Specification

In multi-threaded dynamic systems, the names of processes (id) can be thought of as strings over a finite alphabet. We assume that the processes come from a *regular set* and thus, the system itself can be specified as a *transition system* with finitely many states and edges between the states labelled by *regular expressions* (which denote live agents participating in the transition). Further, every state also comes with its own regular expression that specifies the set of processes that can be active at that state.

---

[1] The witnesses for the two conjuncts cannot be the same and hence at least two processes are required.

Let Σ be a finite alphabet and $Reg(\Sigma)$ be the set of all regular expressions over Σ. For all $r \in Reg(\Sigma)$ let L_r denote the regular language generated by the expression r. If $s, t \in \Sigma^*$ then $s \cdot t$ denotes the concatenation of strings s and t, often written as st. We say that a string $s \in \Sigma^*$ matches regular expression $r \in Reg(\Sigma)$ if $s \in L_r$.

In the manner in which we fix a finite alphabet Σ and consider finite state automata operating on alphabet Σ, we fix $\Lambda \subseteq_{fin} Reg(\Sigma)$, a finite set of regular expressions over Σ and consider systems operating over these regular languages. This is also for reasons of efficiency for system modelling and verification, since we can pre-compute many properties of them as needed in processing. Since Λ can be a large set, with each member denoting a finite or infinite regular language there is no loss of generality in modelling.

Definition 4 (Regular agent transition system). *Let $\mathcal{P}$ be a countable set of propositions. A* regular agent transition system *over Λ is given by $\mathcal{T} = (\mathcal{Q}, \gamma, \mu, \rho)$ where:*

- *$\mathcal{Q}$ is a finite set of states.*
- *$\gamma \subseteq (\mathcal{Q} \times \Lambda \times \mathcal{Q})$ is the set of transitions labelled by regular expressions.*
- *$\mu : \mathcal{Q} \mapsto \Lambda$ where $\mu(q)$ describes the potential set of new processes that may be created at q.*
- *$\rho : \mathcal{Q} \to 2^{\mathcal{P}}$ is the valuation of propositions at states.*

A regular agent transition system is a succinct representation of the configuration space of a dynamic system of processes. The configuration of the system is given by a state along with the set of processes that are currently active. At every state q the function $\mu(q)$ acts as a guard for the set of processes that are live. If the system configuration is in state q then all active process ids should belong to $L_{\mu(q)}$. From the regular agent transition system, we can obtain the configuration space of the network as follows.

For any regular expression r if there is an r edge from q to q' in the transition system, then any process with id s matching the regular expression r that is currently active can change the system configuration with the state being updated from q to q'. Each new string (new process id) that is created is of the form st in the updated configuration which indicates that the new child thread is created when the parent process s makes a transition. The number of threads newly created is constrained to be finite, but yet we cannot bound the size beforehand. The language of regular expressions is rich enough to enable modelling of tree structures of concurrent and sequential threads with forking, as well as process threads created within loops, perhaps while waiting for an external event to occur.

Formally a configuration of $\mathcal{T}$ is a pair (q, A) where $q \in Q$ is a state and $A \subseteq L_{\mu(q)}$ is a finite set of id's of processes active at q. Let $\mathcal{W}$ denote the configuration space of $\mathcal{T}$.

Let $L_1, L_2 \subseteq \Sigma^*$. We say that L_1 and L_2 are compatible if $(L_1 \cap L_2) \neq \emptyset$. We say that L is compatible with $\{L_1, \ldots, L_k\}$ if $L \cap \bigcap_{i=1}^{k} L_i$ is nonempty.

We say that L_2 partially extends L_1 if for all $s \in (L_2 - L_1)$, there exists $t \in L_1$ such that $s = t \cdot t'$ for some $t' \in \Sigma^*$. Thus every 'new' string in L_2 extends a string in L_1.

Definition 5. *Given a regular agent transition system $T = (\mathcal{Q}, \Lambda, \gamma, \mu, \rho)$ and an initial configuration $(q_0, A_0) \in \mathcal{W}$, define the* **configuration graph of** T *is defined to be $C_T = (\mathcal{W}, \mathcal{R})$, the smallest tree rooted at (q_0, A_0) such that for every $(q, A) \in \mathcal{W}$, if $\big((q, A), \ s, \ (q', A')\big) \in \mathcal{R}$ then, A' extends A, and for some $r \in \Lambda$, $(q, r, q') \in \gamma$ such that $L_{\mu(q)}$ and L_r are compatible.*

For any configuration graph $C_T = (\mathcal{W}, \mathcal{R})$ define the corresponding induced IQML model $\mathcal{M}_T = (\mathcal{W}, \Sigma^*, \mathcal{R}, \delta, \rho)$ where for all $(q, A) \in \mathcal{W}$ define $\delta((q, A)) = A$ and $\rho((q, A)) = \rho(q)$.

3.1 Example

Consider the regular agent transition system $T = (\mathcal{Q}, \Lambda, \gamma, \mu, \rho)$ defined in Fig. 1. The regular expressions on the edges denote the set of processes that can change the corresponding system state. The regular expressions inside a state q given by $\mu(q)$ states denote the potential pool of processes that can be active when the system enters the state q.

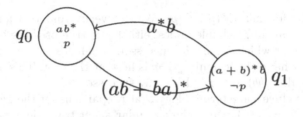

Fig. 1. Illustration of a regular agent transition system.

Suppose the system starts at initial state q_0 and active processes $\{a, ab, abb\}$, then the corresponding configuration graph of the system is described in Fig. 2. Note that ab is the only process that can make a move from the root since it is the only string that matches a^*b. However, ab itself can have unboundedly many branches. In every such branch, the process a cannot remain active since it does not match $(a + b)^*b$. The processes ab and abb may either survive or not. Further, there are some finitely many new processes added at every new branch which are of the form $ab \cdot s$ for some $s \in \Sigma^*$ such that $ab \cdot s$ matches $(a + b)^*b$. The figure highlights three such possible branches.

At the second level, consider the state where the set of live processes is $\{ab, abb, abab\}$ (the middle state). The possible processes that can make a move from this state are ab and $abab$ since these are the only strings that match $(ab + ba)^*$. Further, in the successors of $abba$, there are no new processes since there cannot be a string of the form $abba \cdot s$ that matches a^*b. On the other hand, the successors of ab are unbounded since there are infinitely many extensions of ab that match ab^*.

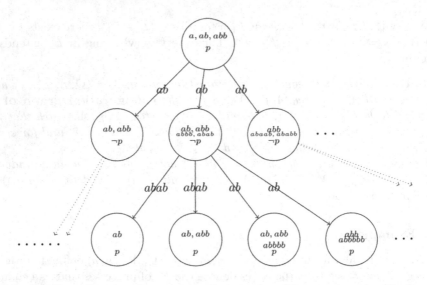

Fig. 2. Configuration graph corresponding to transition system in Fig. 1 with $(q_0, \{a, ab, ba\})$ as the initial configuration. The dotted lines indicate the presence of more successors.

Consider the formula $\Box^*(p \vee [\exists]p)$. We can verify that this formula is true at the root since at all reachable nodes, either p is true or there is at least one successor where for which, at all the successors, $\neg p$ holds.

On the other hand the formula $\langle \forall \rangle \neg p$ is false at the root. This is because the process a (and also abb) does not have any successor.

Now we introduce some terminology that prepares us for the model checking procedure. Let $\mathcal{T} = (\mathcal{Q}, \Lambda, \gamma, \mu, \rho)$ be a regular agent transition system, and let $C_\mathcal{T} = (\mathcal{W}, \mathcal{R})$ be its configuration graph. Then a transition $(q, r, q') \in \gamma$ is said to be **live** if $L_{\mu(q)}$ and L_r are compatible, and $L_{\mu(q')}$ extends $L_{\mu(q)}$. In this case, we refer to q' as a *live successor* of q.

Proposition 1. *For any $(q, A) \in \mathcal{W}$, $C_\mathcal{T}$ has a successor configuration (q', A') from (q, A) iff q' is a live successor of q.*

Further, let $q \in \mathcal{Q}$ and $(q, r_1, q_1), \ldots, (q, r_k, q_k) \in \gamma$ be live at q. Let J be a maximal subset of $\{1, \ldots, k\}$ such that $L_{\mu(q)}$ is compatible with $\{L_j \mid j \in J\}$. Then we call the set $\{q_j \mid j \in J\}$ the set of *local live successors* of q.

Proposition 2. *For any $(q, A) \in \mathcal{W}$, and any $s \in L_{\mu(q)}$, the set $\{q' \mid ((q, A), s, (q', A')) \in \mathcal{R}\}$ is the set of local live successors of q.*

We say that q' is live reachable from q if $q' = q$ or there exists a path $(q_0, r_1, q_1), (q_1, r_2, q_2), \ldots, (q_{k-1}, r_k, q_k)$ in γ such that q_i is a live successor of q_{i-1}, $0 < i \leq k$, $q_0 = q$ and $q_k = q'$.

Proposition 3. *For any $(q, A) \in \mathcal{W}$, a configuration (q', A') is reachable from (q, A) in the configuration graph iff q' is live-reachable from q.*

4   Model Checking Algorithm

Given $(\mathcal{T}, q_0, A_0)$ and an IQML formula φ as inputs, the regular model checking problem asks whether $\mathcal{M}_\mathcal{T}, (q_0, A_0) \models \varphi$.

Note that for any regular agent transition system $\mathcal{T}$ the corresponding $\mathcal{M}_\mathcal{T}$ is an unbounded branching model that describes the configuration space of the run of the system starting from the initial configuration.

To check whether an IQML formula is true in the configuration graph, it appears as if need to check properties on the infinite graph, which is problematic. However, as we show below, it suffices for the algorithm to label the states of the given finite transition system with subformulas carefully.

The algorithm essentially follows in the spirit of model checking propositional multi-modal logics. The difficult part is to pick witnesses for the $[\exists]$ and $\langle \forall \rangle$ operators, since these involve potentially unbounded search.

To recall the model checking procedure for propositional multi-modal logic, we first enumerate all subformulas of the given formula in increasing order of structure and evaluate each at all worlds. The propositions and are evaluated by reference to the ρ function. To evaluate $\neg \varphi$ and $\varphi \wedge \psi$ at a world w, we refer to the inductively evaluated smaller formulas at w. To evaluate $\Box_i \varphi$ at w we check if φ is evaluated to true at all i-successors of w.

For IQML over regular agent systems, we use the same idea. However when evaluating $[\exists]\varphi$, we first need to choose some witness. Note that if the current state is q then the currently active strings are in $L_{\mu(q)}$. Suppose q has successors with edge labels $r_1, \ldots r_k$, then it is sufficient to pick one string $s \in L_{\mu(q)} \cap L_{r_j}$ for some $j \leq k$ such that φ holds at all r_j successors of q. Similarly for the $[\forall]\varphi$ case, we need to ensure that φ is true at all successors for all strings in $L_{\mu(q)} \cap L_{r_j}$ for all $j \leq k$. Finally for $\Box^* \psi$ we need to verify that ψ is true at all reachable states.

Note that checking for non-emptiness of intersection of regular expressions can be done in polynomial time [13]. Hence the procedure terminates in polynomial time. Moreover we can preprocess and calculate the reachability set from each state of the model.

We now describe the algorithm formally.

For any IQML formula φ, let $\mathsf{SF}(\varphi)$ denote the set of subformulas of φ. Note that the size of $\mathsf{SF}(\varphi)$ is linear in the size of φ. Further, fix an enumeration $E_\varphi = \{\psi_1, \psi_2 \ldots, \psi_n\}$ of $\mathsf{SF}(\varphi)$ such that if $\psi_i \in \mathsf{SF}(\psi_j)$ then $i \leq j$.

For any system $(\mathcal{T}, q_0, A_0)$, since A_0 is a finite set of strings, we can define $\hat{r}$, a regular expression such that $A_0 = L_{\hat{r}}$. (This is the initial set of live processes specified in the model.)

Let $(\mathcal{T}, q_0, A_0)$ and φ_0 be input to the model checking algorithm. Let SF denote $\mathsf{SF}(\varphi_0)$ and E denote E_{φ_0}.

Now for every state q in $\mathcal{T}$ and every proposition $\psi \in E$ we define $N(q, \psi)$ to be either $\mathbf{T}$ or $\mathbf{F}$ by induction on ψ.

For the base case, if ψ is a proposition p, then define $N[q, p] = \mathbf{T}$ iff $p \in \rho(q)$.

For the induction step, we have several cases. For the boolean connectives, $N[q, \neg \psi] = \mathbf{T}$ iff $N[q, \psi] = \mathbf{F}$ and $N[q, \psi \wedge \psi'] = \mathbf{T}$ iff $N[q, \psi] = N[q, \psi'] = \mathbf{T}$.

For the case $[\forall]\psi$, define $N[q, [\forall]\psi] = \mathsf{T}$ iff for all *live* successors q' of q, we have $N[q', \psi] = \mathsf{T}$.

For the case $[\exists]\psi$, we first compute $LS(q)$ the set of *local live* successors of q. Then define $N[q, [\exists]\psi] = \mathsf{T}$ iff for all $q' \in LS(q)$, we have $N[q', \psi] = \mathsf{T}$.

For the case $\Box^*\varphi$ define $N[q, \Box^*\varphi] = \mathsf{T}$ iff $N[q', \varphi] = \mathsf{T}$ for every q' live-reachable from q in $\mathcal{T}$.

Finally output yes iff $N[q_0, \varphi] = \mathsf{T}$.

Correctness. To prove correctness of the algorithm, we need to verify that the checking done by the algorithm suffices to generate a valid model and that the formula labelling achieved by the construction of N is correct. The first of these is independent of formulas and follows from the propositions relating transition systems and their configuration graphs, involving live successors and local successors.

Lemma 1 (Correctness of labelling). *Given $(\mathcal{T}, q_0, A_0)$ and an IQML formula φ as inputs we have: $N[q_0, \varphi] = \mathsf{T}$ iff $\mathcal{M}_{\mathcal{T}}, (q_0, A_0) \models \varphi$.*

Proof. To show this, we prove for all $\psi \in \mathsf{SF}(\varphi)$, for all q and for any $A \subseteq L_{\mu(q)}$, we have: $N[q, \psi] = \mathsf{T}$ iff $\mathcal{M}_{\mathcal{T}}, (q, A) \models \varphi$.

This can be verified by induction on the structure of φ. The propositional case follows since $N[q, p] = \mathsf{T}$ iff $p \in \rho(q)$ iff $\mathcal{M}_{\mathcal{T}}, (q, A) \models p$ for all $A \subseteq L_{\mu(q)}$. The case of $\neg$ and $\wedge$ are standard.

For the case $[\forall]\psi$, note that in the model, ψ must hold at every successor configuration (q', A') independent of the agent label on the transition. But as we observed earlier, such a successor configuration exists exactly when q' is a live successor of q. By induction hypothesis this amounts to checking that $N[q', \psi] = \mathsf{T}$ for every live successor q' in the agent transition system, which follows by definition of N.

For the case $[\exists]\psi$, note that for any $s \in L_{\mu(q)}$, the set $\{q' \mid ((q, A), s, (q', A')) \in \mathcal{R}\}$ is the set of local live successors of q. Thus if $\mathcal{M}_{\mathcal{T}}, (q, A) \models [\exists]\psi$, then there exists $s \in L_\mu(q)$ such that for all (q', A'), if $((q, A), s, (q', A')) \in \mathcal{R}$ then $\mathcal{M}_{\mathcal{T}}, (q', A') \models \psi$. By induction hypothesis $N[q', \psi]$ is true for every such q'. Since these are exactly the set of local live successors at q, by definition of N, we get that $N[q, [\exists]\psi] = \mathsf{T}$. The other direction is argued similarly.

Finally for the case $\Box^*\psi$, if $N[q, \Box^*\varphi] = \mathsf{T}$ then $N[q', \varphi] = \mathsf{T}$ for all q' live-reachable from q in $\mathcal{T}$. In the configuration graph, all nodes reachable from (q, A) are of the form (q', A') where q' is live-reachable from q in $\mathcal{T}$. Now, by induction hypothesis $\mathcal{M}_{\mathcal{T}}, (q', A') \models \psi$ and hence we have $\mathcal{M}_{\mathcal{T}}, (q, A) \models \Box^*\psi$. The other direction is argued similarly.

Complexity. Firstly note that the size of N is at most $|\mathcal{T}| \cdot |\varphi|$. Secondly, given regular expressions r_1 and r_2 we need to check if L_{r_1} and L_{r_2} have a non-empty intersection and we need to look for extension of regular languages when we check live successors. These can all be done in polynomial time. Thirdly, we need to compute the set of local live successor states at each state, which involves computing a maximal subset of regular expressions whose intersection is non-empty. Checking unbounded intersection of regular languages is hard, but the set of regular expressions in the transition system is fixed by Λ and hence these can be pre-computed so that the checking in the algorithm can be efficient. Thirdly, the set of live-reachable states from the initial state can be computed in time linear in the number of transitions. Hence the algorithm runs in PTIME (in the size of N).

Corollary 1. *The* regular model checking problem *for* IQML *is in polynomial time.*

5   Discussion

We have discussed IQML, a logic suitable for the specification of properties of systems with unboundedly many and dynamic agents. Since these systems are potentially infinite state, we have suggested a finite specification of models based on regular agent transition systems. We showed that over such specifications, the model checking problem for IQML is in polynomial time.

In [10], we have considered a similar class of models and shown that model checking the "monodic" fragment of propositional term modal logic (PTML) is decidable. PTML is a logic used to reason about unbounded number of agents but involves variables and explicit quantification over them. Variables add expressive power and model checking PTML takes exponential time.

Note that the algorithm presented here works for any finite specification as long as the 'local' checking for live successors at a state is efficiently computable. We have illustrated this using regular expressions to denote the agents. The same algorithm can be modified appropriately if the set of agents were specified using semi-linear sets or counter automata, but this requires some technical work.

When we defined the class of models, we fixed Λ, a finite "alphabet" of regular expressions and considered models over them. However, we could also consider this alphabet specified with each model. Then the model checking algorithm would be polynomial in all other parameters but singly exponential in the size of the alphabet. Thus the result presented here can be seen as fixed-parameter tractability of model checking IQML with size of the regular expression set as the parameter.

This paper is intended as an initial attempt towards model checking systems with unbounded branching with dynamic sets of agents. Adding temporal operators like in LTL and CTL will make the logic more expressive and the model checking problem would then have a wider range of applications.

References

1. Abdulla, P.A., Aiswarya, C., Atig, M.F., Montali, M., Rezine, O.: Recency-bounded verification of dynamic database-driven systems. In: Proceedings of the 35th ACM Symposium on Principles of Database Systems (2016)

2. van Benthem, J., van Eijck, J., Stebletsova, V.: Modal logic, transition systems and processes. J. Log. Comput. **4**(5), 811–855 (1994). https://doi.org/10.1093/logcom/4.5.811
3. Blackburn, P., de Rijke, M., Venema, Y.: Modal Logic (Cambridge Tracts in Theoretical Computer Science). Cambridge University Press, Cambridge (2001)
4. Fitting, M., Thalmann, L., Voronkov, A.: Term-modal logics. Studia Logica **69**(1), 133–169 (2001)
5. Grove, A.J.: Naming and identity in epistemic logic Part II: a first-order logic for naming. Artif. Intell. **74**(2), 311–350 (1995)
6. Grove, A.J., Halpern, J.Y.: Naming and identity in epistemic logics Part I: the propositional case. J. Log. Comput. **3**(4), 345–378 (1993)
7. Hughes, M., Cresswell, G.: A New Introduction to Modal Logic. Routledge, Abingdon (1996)
8. Khan, M.A., Patel, V.S.: A formal study of a generalized rough set model based on relative approximations. In: Nguyen, H.S., Ha, Q.-T., Li, T., Przybyła-Kasperek, M. (eds.) IJCRS 2018. LNCS (LNAI), vol. 11103, pp. 502–510. Springer, Cham (2018). https://doi.org/10.1007/978-3-319-99368-3_39
9. Lamport, L.: The temporal logic of actions. ACM Trans. Program. Lang. Syst. **16**(3), 872–923 (1994). https://doi.org/10.1145/177492.177726
10. Padmanabha, A., Ramanujam, R.: Model checking a logic over systems with regular sets of processes. Developmental Aspects of Intelligent Adaptive Systems (Innovations in Software Engineering), CEUR Workshop Proceedings, vol. 1819 (2017)
11. Padmanabha, A., Ramanujam, R.: Propositional modal logic with implicit modal quantification. In: Khan, M.A., Manuel, A. (eds.) ICLA 2019. LNCS, vol. 11600, pp. 6–17. Springer, Heidelberg (2019). https://doi.org/10.1007/978-3-662-58771-3_2
12. Pnueli, A.: The temporal logic of programs. In: 18th Annual Symposium on Foundations of Computer Science (SFCS 1977), pp. 46–57. IEEE (1977)
13. Sipser, M.: Introduction to the Theory of Computation, vol. 2. Thomson Course Technology Boston (2006)
14. Wang, Y.: A new modal framework for epistemic logic. In: Proceedings Sixteenth Conference on Theoretical Aspects of Rationality and Knowledge, TARK 2017, Liverpool, UK, 24–26 July 2017, pp. 515–534 (2017)

Cloud and Grid Computing

Secure Content-Based Image Retrieval Using Combined Features in Cloud

J. Anju[1](✉) and R. Shreelekshmi[2]

[1] Department of Computer Science and Engineering,
College of Engineering Trivandrum, Thiruvananthapuram, Kerala, India
anjuj@cet.ac.in
[2] Department of Computer Science and Engineering,
Government Engineering College, Thrissur, Kerala, India
shreelekshmir@gmail.com

Abstract. Secure Content-Based Image Retrieval (SCBIR) is gaining enormous importance due to its applications involving highly sensitive images comprising of medical and personally identifiable data such as clinical decision-making, biometric-matching, and multimedia search. SCBIR on outsourced images is realized by generating secure searchable index from features like color, shape, and texture in unencrypted images. We focus on enhancing the efficiency of SCBIR by combining two visual descriptors which serve as a modified feature descriptor. To improve the efficacy of search, pre-filter tables are generated using Locality Sensitive Hashing (LSH) and resulting adjacent hash buckets are joined to enhance retrieval precision. Top-k relevant images are securely retrieved using Secure k-Nearest Neighbors (kNN) algorithm. Performance of the scheme is evaluated based on retrieval precision and search efficiency on distinct and similar image categories. Experimental results show that the proposed scheme outperforms the existing state of the art SCBIR schemes.

Keywords: Secure content-based image retrieval · Locality Sensitive Hashing · Secure kNN · Secure searchable index · Encrypted images

1 Introduction

Images generated using devices like smart-phones, cameras, and medical imaging devices render very large image databases. These databases contain petabytes of data that need to be processed and indexed to enable effective searching. Since this huge amount of data demand more storage space and computational power, they are outsourced to the cloud storage. Images stored in the cloud can be accessed from anywhere through the Internet using any resource-constrained devices that relieve users from the burden of carrying entire image repositories with them. These images include sensitive information like personally identifiable data, medical images, financial data, biometric information, etc. So outsourcing

© Springer Nature Switzerland AG 2020
D. V. Hung and M. D'Souza (Eds.): ICDCIT 2020, LNCS 11969, pp. 179–197, 2020.
https://doi.org/10.1007/978-3-030-36987-3_11

such data in the plain to a third party cloud server is not secure. Once the data is in cloud, the owner loses control over the data and is unaware of the kind of processing it undergoes. In order to secure sensitive data from incidents of any security breach, storing data in cryptographic storage is highly desirable. Several searchable encryption schemes have been proposed to enable efficient search over an encrypted domain. Such schemes enable cloud server to perform search on the user's behalf without losing privacy of data. Secure content-based image retrieval (SCBIR) gains enormous importance due to its application in clinical decision-making process, multimedia search, biometric matching, etc. Since these images include sensitive information, they are to be protected before being outsourced. SCBIR users expect retrieved results that are more close to the query image based on the similarity of different contents in it. Moreover, retrieval of precise results outperforming keyword searches is also intended. SCBIR on encrypted images without revealing its actual content has been a major research challenge and several schemes have been proposed to improve its privacy and efficiency.

The remaining part of this paper is organized as follows: Sect. 2 discusses related works relevant to the proposed scheme and Sect. 3 illustrates the proposed scheme in detail. Experimental results and analysis of the proposed scheme are discussed in Sect. 4 followed by a conclusion in Sect. 5.

2 Related Works

Several SCBIR schemes have been proposed to ensure the privacy of outsourced images. Enabling efficient CBIR without compromising security is a challenging task. Generally, SCBIR schemes automate search by employing a searchable index generated using features extracted from images. These features include color descriptors, shape descriptors, etc. that aid effective representation of an image. While querying these searchable indices, corresponding features from query images are extracted to find matching ones. To ensure the privacy of these extracted features in the index as well as query, they are further encrypted or protected. These encrypted images and searchable index are outsourced to the cloud server to accomplish SCBIR.

In 2016, Xia et al. proposed an efficient and privacy-preserving CBIR scheme (EPCBIR) in cloud computing [11]. In this scheme, they have used two MPEG-7 visual descriptors [5] Color Layout Descriptor (CLD) and Edge Histogram Descriptor (EHD) for representing images. For enabling search over encrypted images, they use a one-to-one map index that maps each image to its feature vector. They construct pre-filter tables by applying Locality Sensitive Hashing (LSH) on these features to enhance search efficiency. The features are further protected by Secure k-Nearest Neighbor (kNN) algorithm to ensure secure retrieval of top-k relevant images. In this scheme, images are encrypted using a chaotic map before outsourcing to the cloud. Query users generate a trapdoor based on the features extracted from query image and sent to the cloud server. Using pre-filter tables and one-to-one map index, the cloud server retrieves top-k relevant encrypted images to the query users.

In 2016, Xia et al. proposed another privacy-preserving CBIR with copy deterrence [10] over encrypted images. In this scheme, four MPEG-7 visual descriptors namely Color Structure Descriptor (CSD), Scalable Color Descriptor (SCD), CLD and EHD are compared. This scheme also uses LSH to generate pre-filter tables and secure kNN to securely retrieve top-k similar results. In addition to this, they proposed a copy deterrence mechanism to find illegal query users by embedding watermarks in retrieved images. These watermarks are specific to each query user and once image owner finds an illegal copy of an image, he can extract the watermark and identify the illegal query user.

In 2018, Wang et al. proposed a SCBIR scheme to retrieve feature-rich data [8] like images, audio, video, etc. in the cloud. This scheme automates CBIR by using color histograms extracted from images as feature vectors. They also employ LSH to generate M feature-to-file indices based on extracted features. Each hash value generated by LSH is mapped to an Inverted File Vector (IFV) which specifies the corresponding images. In addition, adjacent IFVs are propagated by calculating the union of two neighboring IFVs. This improves the probability of finding more images similar to the query image. In this scheme, Homomorphic Encryption and Pseudo-Random Functions (PRF) are used to protect the feature-to-file index. The IFVs are encrypted using Paillier Homomorphic encryption which enables the cloud server to aggregate M intermediate IFVs from each feature-to-file index in the encrypted form itself. This reduces the communication cost of sending all encrypted IFVs to the user for getting them decrypted and aggregated by the user. They also propose another method to secure IFVs using a one-time pad generated by PRF. These IFVs secured by PRF can only be decrypted by the user having a secret key which incurs an extra communication overhead between the cloud server and user.

In 2018, Xia et al. proposed a privacy-preserving CBIR scheme [12] to outsource image databases and CBIR services to the cloud. They use local features like Scale Invariant Feature Transform (SIFT) features to represent images. In this scheme, bag of words model is employed in which local features extracted from images are clustered and image signatures are generated based on it. Image signatures uniquely identify each image based on the clusters they fall into and the associated weight. LSH is also applied on these image signatures to generate a pre-filter index. To compute the similarity between two image signatures, Earth Mover's Distance (EMD) is used. While searching the image database, the cloud server will first return a subset of similar images obtained from pre-filter index. For enabling the cloud server to calculate the similarity between the query images and retrieved images, query user securely transforms EMD problem to linear programming (LP) problem. Cloud server solves the transformed problems and uses resulting offset values to compute EMDs in an order-preserving way to rank the resulting images. Thus the scheme incurs an extra communication cost between the cloud server and user for transforming EMD problem securely.

In 2019, Anju and Shreelekshmi proposed a SCBIR scheme [2] that aims at improving retrieval precision of Xia et al.'s [10] scheme. They have used five MPEG-7 visual descriptors namely CSD, SCD, CLD, EHD, and Dominant

Color Descriptor (DCD) [5] as features and combined the retrieved results of two descriptors to improve retrieval precision. The scheme also uses LSH for generating pre-filter tables and secure kNN to facilitate retrieval of top-k similar results. The retrieval precision of the scheme is more compared to other schemes at the cost of more search time.

The existing SCBIR schemes in the encrypted domain differ in the features used to represent the images. Retrieval precision of SCBIR schemes greatly depend on the feature descriptors being used. Most of the schemes use LSH for generating pre-filter index for relieving the burden of searching entire image databases [2,8,10,11]. Secure kNN is used by some of the SCBIR schemes [2,10,11] for enabling secure ranked search based on Euclidean similarity without losing privacy. In addition, it is more desirable to have schemes that do not require user intervention to complete the retrieval process which results in extra communication and computation overhead at the user end. SCBIR schemes with high retrieval precision and efficiency without compromising privacy are required in cloud applications at the cost of low computation and communication overhead.

3   Proposed SCBIR Scheme

3.1   Framework of SCBIR Scheme Proposed by Xia et al. [10]

A framework of SCBIR scheme according to Xia et al. [10] is shown in Fig. 1. It mainly consists of three entities: Image owner, Image/Query user and Cloud Server.

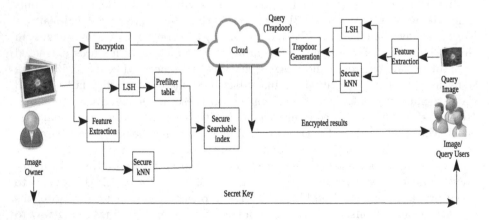

Fig. 1. SCBIR framework proposed by Xia et al. [10]

Image Owner. Image owner outsources a large number of images to the cloud server after encryption using a secret key. To enable search on these images, image owner will generate a secure searchable index which will also be stored in cloud server. In Xia et al. [10] SCBIR scheme, secure searchable index is generated using LSH and secure kNN. LSH is employed to generate pre-filter tables which improves search efficiency. The image owner provides access privileges to users by sharing secret keys used for encryption. The image owner also authorizes the image users and provides authorization information to the cloud server for validating them.

Image User/Query User. Image user is the one who queries the cloud server to retrieve desired results. Users extract features from the query image and generate a trapdoor using LSH and secure kNN for searching the secure index. Trapdoors preserve privacy of the query image and prevent any information leakage through it. Image users retrieve top-k relevant encrypted images from cloud which are later decrypted using secret keys shared by the image owner.

Cloud Server. Cloud server is responsible for storing encrypted image databases and provides SCBIR services to image users. On getting a query, the cloud server will first authenticate the query user based on the authorization information shared by the image owner. After validating the user, the cloud server will search the secure searchable index to retrieve similar images matching the query trapdoor. Ciphertexts of these similar images are sent to the image user.

3.2 Basic Terminologies

Locality-Sensitive Hashing (LSH). LSH has the property that close items will collide with a higher probability than distant ones, which can be used for searching near neighbors [4]. It is used in SCBIR schemes [8,10,11] for improving the search efficiency. For hashing feature vectors of d dimension, the dot product of each feature vector with a random vector a of the same dimension d is computed. Then a random real number b is added to it. The resulting value projects the d dimensional vector to a point in the real line. If two vectors are close to each other their dot products will also be close. This real line is then cut into equidistant segments of size 'r' and each hash values are assigned based on these segments. All image features that map to the same segment generates the same hash, consequently close images collide with higher probability. The hash functions can be varied based on a and b being used.

MPEG-7 Visual Descriptors. MPEG-7 is a multimedia content description standard that offers a comprehensive set of descriptors for multimedia data description [5].

1. Color Structure Descriptor (CSD) identifies local color structure in an image using an 8×8 window. For different quantized colors, each bin contains a number of pixels in the structuring window having that specific color.
2. Scalable Color Descriptor (SCD) uses hue saturation value (HSV) histogram followed by Haar transform to solve scalability issues in image representation.
3. Color Layout Descriptor (CLD) is a compact descriptor that uses a representative grid followed by DCT and encoding of the colors on resulting coefficients. It is widely used for content-based searches.
4. Edge Histogram Descriptor (EHD) captures the spatial distribution of edges. The distribution of edges is a good texture signature for the image matching even when the underlying texture is not homogeneous.
5. Dominant Color Descriptor (DCD) clusters colors in a region into a small number of representative colors. The feature descriptor consists of these colors, their percentages in the region, spatial coherency of the dominant colors, and color variances for each dominant color. Its dimension varies depending on the images.

These descriptors can be represented as feature vectors and the image similarity could be measured by Euclidean distance between the feature vectors [2,10,11].

Secure kNN. Secure kNN finds k-nearest neighbors closest to the query image in encrypted domain [9]. This enables a third party like cloud server to compute the distance between two encrypted data and finds closest items based on Euclidean similarity without compromising privacy. The steps involved in secure kNN encryption are illustrated in Sect. 3.3.

Inverted File Identifier Vector (IFV). IFV is used to represent the images in pre-filter tables [8]. Each row of the pre-filter table maps the hash value generated by images to an IFV of length same as total number of images. A '1' in the ith position of the vector indicates that i^{th} image generated the corresponding hash bucket and '0' otherwise.

3.3   Proposed Scheme

Figure 2 shows the framework of proposed SCBIR scheme. The main contribution of the proposed scheme is to enhance the retrieval precision of SCBIR scheme by combining the effect of two feature descriptors. For this, a new feature descriptor is generated by fusing feature vectors of two descriptors extracted from the image. This modified descriptor combines the effect of both feature descriptors in a single shot. For grouping similar images based on feature descriptors, LSH is performed on this fused feature descriptor. On hashing feature vectors using hash functions belonging to LSH family, close images tend to generate the same hashes [8,10,11]. These hashes along with the set of corresponding IFVs are stored in pre-filter tables. These pre-filter tables serve as a first-level searchable index to improve efficacy of SCBIR scheme. Each IFV in the pre-filter table is

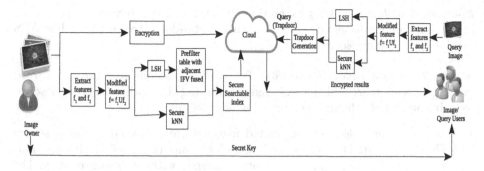

Fig. 2. Framework of the proposed SCBIR scheme

further joined with two adjacent IFVs to improve retrieval precision. The hashes are protected by performing XOR with a pseudo-random sequence generated by a secret key. The feature descriptor of each image is encrypted using secure kNN as in [2,10,11] and stored in a feature vector index which facilitates retrieval of ranked results. For searching, users extract the same features from the query image to generate a fused feature vector. LSH is performed on these fused feature vectors followed by XOR of resulting hashes with the same pseudo-random sequence to find the subset of similar images from pre-filter tables. A trapdoor consisting of this hash and the encrypted query feature vector is sent to the cloud server to enable search. Cloud server uses this hash to find the subset of similar images from pre-filter tables and their corresponding feature vectors are compared with that of the query in trapdoor to find top-k similar images.

Steps Involved in the Proposed SCBIR Scheme

Key Generation. Secret keys are required for encrypting images and extracted features. Since features are secured by secure kNN, its parameters are also generated in this step. Secret key, K = (S, M_1, M_2, k_{image}, k_{hash}, LSH functions h_i where $i = 1, .., L$) is generated in this step. Here, first three parameters S, M_1 and M_2 are used for performing secure kNN where S is a binary vector of size '$d+1$' bits for feature vector of dimension d and M_1 and M_2 are two invertible matrices with the size $(d+1) \times (d+1)$. $[h_i]$ is the set of L hash functions belonging to LSH family. k_{hash} is the key used for generating pseudo-random sequence to protect hash values. k_{image} is the secret key for encrypting images.

Feature Extraction. Feature descriptors are used to represent images. Two features f_1 and f_2 are extracted from each image I. Depending on the features being extracted, they vary in dimension and characteristics. A modified feature descriptor f is generated by fusing f_1 and f_2, $f = f_1 \cup f_2$. The f so generated is of size $d = d_1 + d_2$ where d_1 and d_2 are the length of feature vector of f_1 and f_2 respectively.

Encryption of Images. After extracting the features, the images are encrypted before outsourcing to cloud server. For this, a standard stream cipher like AES can be applied using secret key k_{image}.

Secure Searchable Index Generation. For enabling search over the outsourced images, a secure searchable index is generated using the modified feature descriptors. It consists of a feature vector index and pre-filter tables.

1. Feature vector index: The extracted features are protected by using secure kNN as in [2,10,11]. Secure kNN enables computation of Euclidean similarity between query image and other images without losing privacy. For this, feature vector of ith image, $f_i = (f_{i,1}, f_{i,2}, .., f_{i,d})^T$ is modified into $\hat{f}_i = (f_{i,1}, f_{i,2}, .., f_{i,d}, ||f_i||^2)^T$ where, $||f_i||$ is the Euclidean norm. Split $\hat{f}_i$ into two random vectors $(\hat{f}_{ia}, \hat{f}_{ib})$ according to secret parameter S. If $S[j] = 0$, $\hat{f}_{ia}[j] = \hat{f}_{ib}[j] = \hat{f}_i[j]$; otherwise $\hat{f}_{ia}[j] = r_1$ and $\hat{f}_{ib}[j] = r_2$ where r_1 and r_2 are chosen randomly such that $r_1 + r_2 = \hat{f}_i[j]$. Then encrypted feature vector is computed as: $f'_i = (M_1^T \hat{f}_{ia}, M_2^T \hat{f}_{ib})$. In feature vector index, these encrypted feature vectors f'_i of each image are mapped to corresponding image identifiers.

2. Pre-filter tables: To improve search efficiency, pre-filter tables are also employed on top of feature vector index by using LSH. These pre-filter tables consist of hashes generated by images and corresponding set of image identifiers that generate those hashes. For this, λ LSH functions are chosen at random : $h_1, h_2, .., h_\lambda$. This results in λ hashes per image which is considered as a hash bucket of λ dimension. Images that generate same λ dimensional hash bucket are having close features based on Euclidean similarity [10]. LSH is repeated L times to generate L pre-filter tables for getting more probable results. The hash buckets thus generated by each image is further protected by performing XOR operation with a pseudo-random sequence generated by a secret key, k_{hash}. Each entry in the pre-filter table consists of these encrypted hash buckets and corresponding IFV. The ith entry of the IFV is 1 if i^{th} image generates that hash bucket; otherwise 0. For improving the chances of retrieving more probable results, IFVs in each ith hash bucket is combined with those of $(i-1)^{th}$ and $(i+1)^{th}$ hash buckets and these joined IFVs are stored in pre-filter tables.

Trapdoor Generation. For performing search on secure searchable index, users generate a trapdoor based on query image to ensure query privacy. Users extract two feature vectors f_{q1} and f_{q2} from query images and combine them to generate $f_q = f_{q1} \cup f_{q2}$. Then hash functions $h_1, h_2, .., h_\lambda$ are applied on this f_q, to generate λ dimensional hash buckets. This is repeated L times, to generate L hash buckets as in index generation. These L hash buckets so generated are further encrypted by performing XOR operation with pseudo-random sequence generated by secret key, k_{hash} shared by the image owner. Cloud server matches this with corresponding L pre-filter tables stored in cloud to find a subset of similar images. To compare similarity of query image feature vector f_q with

Table 1. Parameters used in experiments

Visual descriptors	Parameters		
	L	r	d
CSD+SCD	12	14	256
CSD+CLD	12	14	248
CSD+EHD	12	14	208
CSD+DCD	12	14	Image dependent
SCD+CLD	5	6	248
SCD+EHD	8	4	208
SCD+DCD	8	4	Image dependent
CLD+EHD	4	4	200
CLD+DCD	4	4	Image dependent
EHD+DCD	4	4	Image dependent

features f_i of images in feature vector index, modify $f_q = (f_{q,1}, f_{q,2}, ..., f_{q,l})^T$ to $\hat{f}_q = (-2f_{q,1}, -2f_{q,2}, ..., -2f_{q,l})^T$. Then, split $\hat{f}_q$ into two random vectors $(\hat{f}_{qa}, \hat{f}_{qb})$ according to S. If $S[j] = 1$, $\hat{f}_{qa}[j] = \hat{f}_{qb}[j] = \hat{f}_q[j]$; otherwise $\hat{f}_{qa}[j] = r_1$ and $\hat{f}_{qb}[j] = r_2$ where r_1 and r_2 are chosen randomly such that $r_1 + r_2 = \hat{f}_q[j]$. This results in encrypted query vector: $f'_q = (\gamma M_1^{-1} \hat{f}_{qa}, \gamma M_2^{-1} \hat{f}_{qb})$ where γ is a random positive value.

Search. To perform search on encrypted images, cloud server uses the trapdoor generated by the user. Firstly, the cloud server fetches the subset of similar images from L pre-filter tables using encrypted hash buckets in the trapdoor. Then, to retrieve top-k images similar to the query image, cloud server compares the distance between encrypted query vector f'_q and encrypted feature vectors f'_i of images obtained from pre-filter tables. For this, cloud server computes $f_q^{T'} \cdot f_i' = \gamma(||f_q - f_i||^2) - (||f_q||^2)$. This gives the Euclidean distance between f_q and f_i hidden by a random positive value γ. On sorting these results in ascending order, cloud server can find top-k images relevant to the query. Finally, these encrypted images are sent to the query user.

Decryption of Retrieved Images. Image users can decrypt the resulting encrypted images from cloud server using secret key k_{image} shared by the image owner.

4   Experimental Results

In this section, the experimental evaluation of the proposed scheme on Corel Image dataset [1] is illustrated. This dataset consists of 10,000 images classified into 100 image categories in which each category comprises of 100 images. The proposed scheme is implemented using MATLAB R2017b on Ubuntu 16.04

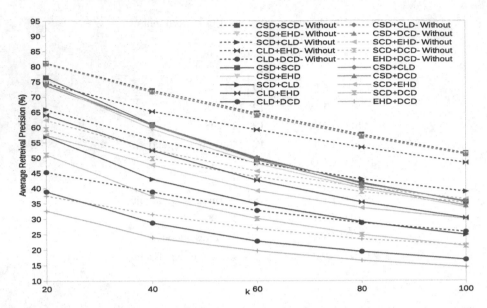

Fig. 3. Average retrieval precision of top-k retrieved images by each modified feature descriptors averaged over 40 queries in 20 distinct image categories.

LTS with Intel Core (TM) i5-7400 CPU 3 GHz. The MPEG-7 visual descriptors are extracted using feature extraction tool in [3]. The performance of the proposed scheme is evaluated using its retrieval precision and search efficiency. The parameters used in the experiments are shown in Table 1 where d is the dimension of the visual descriptor, L is the number of pre-filter tables generated per descriptor and r is the distance parameter input to LSH that restricts the images within a limit r to generate the same hash. The value of the parameter λ is fixed as 2 for all descriptors. The parameters L and r used in LSH are chosen empirically and cannot be claimed to be optimal ones as in schemes [8,10,11]. Table 1 shows the L and r values used in the proposed scheme that give better results with respect to retrieval precision and search efficiency. L and r values can vary depending on the application being considered [10].

4.1 Retrieval Precision

In the experiments, retrieval precision is computed as k'/k where k' is the number of relevant images retrieved and k is the total number of retrieved images [6]. The relevance of retrieved images for each query is determined by the image category they belong to in the standard dataset [7]. For analyzing the retrieval precision of the scheme on distinct and similar image categories, 20 distinct and similar image categories are chosen from the dataset. They contain 2000 images each and two queries from each image category are selected for performing search operation. Image categories like Tiger, Dinosaur, Pyramids, Africans, Fruits, Flowers, Ducks, etc. are used for evaluating the retrieval precision of

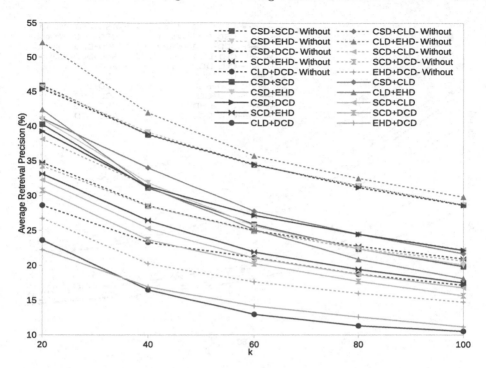

Fig. 4. Average retrieval precision of top-k retrieved images by each modified feature descriptors averaged over 40 queries in 20 similar image categories.

the proposed scheme on distinct image categories. Image categories like Ocean, Waterfall, Beaches, Lighthouse, Ships/boats in ocean, sky, flying airplanes, flying birds, etc. which have comparable semantics are chosen for evaluating the scheme's performance on similar images. The results are averaged over 40 (2 query × 20 categories) queries for distinct and similar image categories. The precision of the scheme over entire dataset having 100 categories is also evaluated to further validate the results. The retrieval precision over 200 queries (2 queries per category) is averaged for the entire image dataset.

Obviously, the retrieval precision in distinct image categories is more since the probability of identifying an image outside the category as relevant is very less. On the contrary, while using similar categories it is more difficult to identify the relevant images due to the ambiguity caused by similar images in different categories. A query image having an airplane can be matched to images in categories like flying birds, sky, etc. The relevance of such retrieved images may depend on user perception [7] and hence actual performance is relative to the users.

Figure 3 compares the average retrieval precision of k- retrieved images in 20 distinct image categories with and without pre-filter tables using the modified feature descriptors. Descriptor CSD with SCD gives the highest retrieval

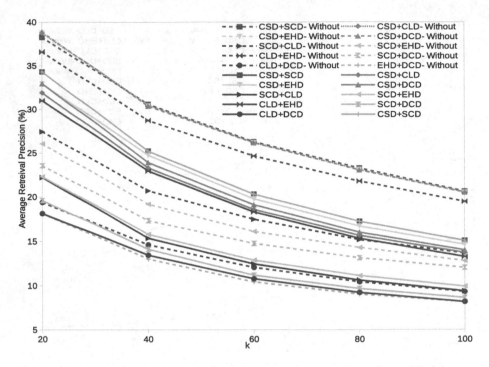

Fig. 5. Average retrieval precision of top-k retrieved images by each modified feature descriptors averaged over 200 queries in all 100 image categories.

precision of 81.125% without pre-filter tables and 76.375% with pre-filter tables at $k = 20$ on distinct image categories.

Figure 4 depicts the average retrieval precision of k- retrieved images in 20 similar image categories with and without pre-filter tables using the modified feature descriptors. For similar image categories, descriptor CLD with EHD gives the highest retrieval precision of 52.125% without pre-filter table and CLD with EHD gives 42.375% using the proposed scheme at $k = 20$.

Figure 5 compares the average retrieval precision of k- retrieved images in all 100 image categories with and without pre-filter tables using the modified feature descriptors. At $k = 20$, descriptor CSD with DCD gives the highest retrieval precision of 38.88% retrieval precision without pre-filter table and CSD with SCD gives 34.3% with pre-filter tables in the proposed scheme.

4.2 Search Efficiency

Search efficiency of the proposed scheme is evaluated based on the time consumed for search operation per query. In this scheme, pre-filter tables are generated using LSH to improve search efficiency. LSH on extracted image features cause similar images to generate the same hashes resulting in small groups of similar images which are stored in pre-filter tables. These images are similar based on

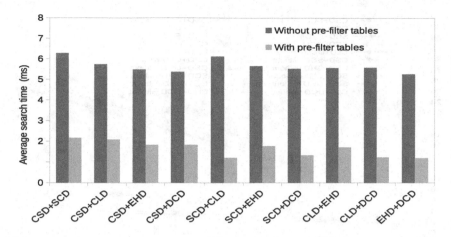

Fig. 6. Average search time consumed by the proposed scheme in 20 distinct image categories with and without pre-filter tables.

the Euclidean similarity of the extracted features. Using the hashes in trapdoor generated from the query image, cloud server retrieves the subset of relevant images from pre-filter tables and similarity of these images with the query is computed. This consumes less time compared with the time taken for performing similarity comparison with all images in the collection.

Figure 6 shows the time consumption for search per query in 20 distinct image categories averaged on 40 queries. In this figure, the time consumed for search operation by each descriptor using the proposed scheme is compared with that of without pre-filter table. Without pre-filter table, similarity of query image with all images in the dataset is compared to find top-k ranked results. All descriptors take around 6 ms on an average and CSD with SCD consumes the maximum search time of 6.27 ms without pre-filter table. In the proposed scheme, pre-filter tables generated by LSH filters off dissimilar images and hence query image needs comparison with much lesser number of images. Consequently, search time of the proposed scheme using pre-filter tables is less. CSD with SCD consumes a maximum search time of 2.16 ms and achieves the maximum retrieval precision of 76.375% when $k = 20$.

The scalability of the proposed scheme is evaluated by analyzing average search time consumed for different number of images as shown in Fig. 7. For each image collection, two random queries per image category is tested and the search time is averaged over these number of queries. As the number of images in the dataset increases, search time also increases proportionally. The time consumed by each descriptor without pre-filter table is much more compared with that of with pre-filter tables. Hence, the use of pre-filter table to improve search efficiency is evident from the above comparison. For 10,000 images, the maximum time consumed for search operation using the proposed scheme is 7.95 ms for descriptors CLD with EHD. This is much less compared to the maximum search time of 31.74 ms consumed without pre-filter tables. In the case of cloud storage

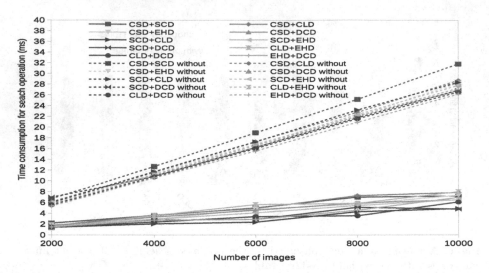

Fig. 7. Comparison of average search time consumed by the proposed scheme with and without pre-filter tables for different number of images.

which requires processing of a large number of images, the search time depends on the number of images in the storage.

4.3   Security Analysis

Data Privacy. Since the images are outsourced to a third party, data privacy is one of the major security concerns. It mainly consists of two issues: privacy of outsourced images and privacy of searchable index used to perform search operation. Since this data is vulnerable to different types of attacks, they are encrypted to ensure privacy. Only those who have access to secret key can view the images or perform search operation. In the proposed scheme, the images are encrypted using secret key before outsourcing to the cloud. Secure searchable index consists of encrypted feature vector index and pre-filter tables. The feature vector index maps each image to its feature descriptor which is protected by secure kNN. Secure kNN uses secret keys chosen by the image owner and is only shared with query users authorized by him. These encrypted feature vectors do not disclose any information regarding the images unless the secret keys are compromised. In the case of pre-filter tables, the hash buckets obtained by LSH are protected by performing XOR with a pseudo-random sequence generated by a secret key. Thus privacy of the outsourced secure searchable index and images are ensured.

Trapdoor/Query Privacy. Since queries made by the image user can reveal information regarding the content of the outsourced images, they are to be protected. The trapdoor mainly consists of the hash bucket generated from the feature descriptor of query image and the feature descriptor itself for computing the similarity of retrieved images with the query image. The hash bucket generated by LSH is protected by the same secret key used during index generation. If a different key is used, the hash bucket so obtained will not match the required bucket in the pre-filter table. In addition to this, the feature descriptor of the query image is protected by secure kNN which involve secret keys as described in Sect. 3.3 to enable ranking among the retrieved results. Thus, query privacy is ensured and only those users having the secret keys will be able to search the index.

Table 2. Comparison of average retrieval precision of the proposed scheme with Xia et al. [10] and Anju and Shreelekshmi [2] in 20 distinct image categories.

Scheme	Descriptors	L	r	$k = 20$	$k = 40$	$k = 60$	$k = 80$	$k = 100$
Xia et al. [10]	CSD	12	14	62.875	43.875	32.4583	25.59375	21.3
	SCD	5	6	47.5	36.4375	29.5833	24.5625	20.775
	CLD	4	4	49.5	39.3125	30.75	25.03125	20.925
	EHD	2	4	50.125	36.6875	27.916	23.15625	19.45
	DCD	8	4	26.25	20.3125	16.666	14.6875	13.075
Anju and Shreelekshmi [2]	CSD + SCD	12	14	73.375	59.75	48.5833	40.0625	33.675
	CSD + CLD	12	14	72.25	58.125	47.041667	38.375	32.175
	CSD +EHD	12	14	71.125	57.25	45.875	37.34375	31.5
	CSD + DCD	12	14	74.125	59.125	47.833	39.625	33.05
Proposed scheme	CSD + SCD	12	14	76.375	60.8125	49.583	41.71875	35.475
	CSD + CLD	12	14	73.75	60.75	49.95833	41.4375	35.7
	CSD + EHD	12	14	74.5	59.3125	47.95	39.84375	33.75
	CSD + DCD	12	14	74.625	60.5	49.208	40.59	34.275
	SCD + CLD	5	6	57	42.9375	34.91667	29	24.85
	SCD + EHD	8	4	57.5	47.5625	39.1667	33.59375	30
	SCD + DCD	8	4	51	37.375	30.167	24.906	21.25
	CLD + EHD	4	4	64	52.3125	42.541	35.40	30.275
	CLD + DCD	4	4	38.875	28.75	22.83	19.4375	16.825
	EHD + DCD	4	4	32.625	24	19.708	16.5625	14.4

4.4 Comparison with Other SCBIR Schemes

The performance of the proposed scheme is compared with Xia et al. [10] and Anju and Shreelekshmi [2] SCBIR schemes. The retrieval precision of these schemes on distinct image categories, similar image categories and entire 100 categories using the same queries are compared in Tables 2, 3 and 4 respectively. The retrieval precision at different k values and respective L, r values used in the experiments are shown in the tables. From Table 2, it is evident that at $k = 20$ proposed scheme achieves highest retrieval precision of 76.375% for descriptor CSD with SCD in distinct image categories compared with other schemes.

In case of similar image categories, the proposed scheme achieves a maximum retrieval precision of 42.375% for CLD with EHD which is comparable with the maximum retrieval precision obtained by Anju and Shreelekshmi [2] as shown in

Table 3. Table 4 shows that the proposed scheme achieves a maximum retrieval precision of 34.3% for CSD with SCD at $k = 20$ in all 100 image categories. In all 100 image categories, retrieval precision is less compared with distinct and

Table 3. Comparison of average retrieval precision of the proposed scheme with Xia et al. [10] and Anju and Shreelekshmi [2] in 20 similar image categories.

Scheme	Descriptors	L	r	$k = 20$	$k = 40$	$k = 60$	$k = 80$	$k = 100$
Xia et al. [10]	CSD	12	14	32.125	22	17	14.15625	12.5
	SCD	5	6	28.125	20.8125	17	14.96875	13.05
	CLD	4	4	29.5	22.625	18.75	15.6875	13.8
	EHD	2	4	32.25	24.1875	19.875	16.84	14.8
	DCD	8	4	17.875	14.375	12.625	11.09	10.075
Anju and Shreelekshmi [2]	CSD + SCD	12	14	42.63	31.25	24.70	21.18	18.45
	CSD + CLD	12	14	38	29.25	24.583	21.40	18.6
	CSD +EHD	12	14	38.75	29.25	3.75	20.53	18.225
	CSD + DCD	12	14	39.5	29.43	24.208	21.03	18.55
Proposed Scheme	CSD + SCD	12	14	40.25	31.125	25.875	22.375	19.85
	CSD + CLD	12	14	41.125	34	27.75	24.46	21.7
	CSD + EHD	12	14	41	31.875	25.66	22.375	20.075
	CSD + DCD	12	14	39.25	31.31	27.16	24.468	22.175
	SCD + CLD	5	6	32.25	25.31	21.04	18.718	16.8
	SCD + EHD	8	4	33.12	26.43	21.91	19.43	17.525
	SCD + DCD	8	4	30.75	23.6875	20.25	17.7	15.675
	CLD + EHD	4	4	42.375	31.25	25.125	20.875	18.125
	CLD + DCD	4	4	23.625	16.5	12.9583	11.312	10.525
	EHD + DCD	4	4	22.25	16.93	14.166	12.59	11.175

Table 4. Comparison of average retrieval precision of the proposed scheme with Xia et al. [10] and Anju and Shreelekshmi [2] in all 100 image categories in the dataset.

Scheme	Descriptors	L	r	$k = 20$	$k = 40$	$k = 60$	$k = 80$	$k = 100$
Xia et al. [10]	CSD	12	14	28.8	19.7	15.27	12.69	10.82
	SCD	5	6	18.85	13.26	10.51	8.91	7.91
	CLD	4	4	19.78	13.14	10.18	8.47	7.37
	EHD	2	4	17.55	11.38	8.78	7.28	6.39
	DCD	8	4	12.2	8.51	6.7	5.56	4.87
Anju and Shreelekshmi [2]	CSD + SCD	12	14	33.15	24.64	19.77	16.74	14.63
	CSD + CLD	12	14	32.23	24.05	19.31	16.26	14.16
	CSD +EHD	12	14	31.08	22.06	17.38	14.58	12.71
	CSD + DCD	12	14	32.13	23.95	19.18	16.41	14.3
Proposed Scheme	CSD + SCD	12	14	34.3	25.2	20.31	17.25	15.07
	CSD + CLD	12	14	31.9	23.3	18.58	15.67	13.71
	CSD + EHD	12	14	32.93	24.74	19.79	16.72	14.62
	CSD + DCD	12	14	32.95	23.9	19.12	16.03	14
	SCD + CLD	5	6	22.2	15.35	12.45	10.62	9.38
	SCD + EHD	8	4	22.3	15.8	12.88	11.14	9.91
	SCD + DCD	8	4	19.6	14.11	11.18	9.67	8.63
	CLD + EHD	4	4	31	22.94	18.31	15.33	13.25
	CLD + DCD	4	4	18.13	13.44	10.78	9.22	8.17
	EHD + DCD	4	4	14.83	9.9	7.71	6.54	5.7

Table 5. Comparison of average search time of the proposed scheme with Xia et al. [10] and Anju and Shreelekshmi [2] in 20 distinct image categories.

Scheme	Descriptors	L	r	Average search time without pre-filter (ms)	Average search time with pre-filter table (ms)
Xia et al. [10]	CSD	12	14	5.4484	1.046
	SCD	5	6	5.278	0.98
	CLD	4	4	5.313	1.14
	EHD	2	4	5.110	1.26
	DCD	8	4	4.90	1.37
Anju and Shreelekshmi [2]	CSD + SCD	12	14	5.44	1.68
	CSD + CLD	12	14	5.44	1.90
	CSD +EHD	12	14	5.44	1.95
	CSD + DCD	12	14	5.44	2.06
Proposed Scheme	CSD + SCD	12	14	6.27	2.16
	CSD + CLD	12	14	5.73	2.09
	CSD + EHD	12	14	5.47	1.82
	CSD + DCD	12	14	5.36	1.82
	SCD + CLD	5	6	6.10	1.20
	SCD + EHD	8	4	5.65	1.76
	SCD + DCD	8	4	5.51	1.327
	CLD + EHD	4	4	5.55	1.70
	CLD + DCD	4	4	5.57	1.22
	EHD + DCD	4	4	5.247	1.18

similar image categories due to the retrieval of more related images from other image categories having similar semantics.

The search efficiency of the proposed scheme is compared with Xia et al. [10] and Anju and Shreelekshmi [2] SCBIR schemes in Table 5. This table shows average search time with and without pre-filter tables using each scheme in 20 distinct image categories averaged over 40 queries. The proposed scheme consumes more time for search compared to Xia et al.'s scheme because Xia et al. uses a single descriptor whereas the proposed scheme fuses two feature descriptors at a time. Moreover, joined IFV in pre-filter table aggregates IFVs of adjacent hash buckets which result in more number of images to be compared with the query image. From the experiments, it is evident that fusing two feature descriptors results in more search time and this goes on increasing if three or more feature descriptors are fused. Thus fusing more feature descriptors almost nullifies the purpose of using pre-filter tables and has same effect as searching the entire image database.

Xia et al. proposed another SCBIR scheme [12] in 2018 which achieves a maximum retrieval precision of 52.5% [12] at $k = 20$ for LSH parameters $r = 4$, $\lambda = 2$, and $L = 20$. The time for performing search by transforming EMD problems and its calculation require 1.4 s [12] on an average for 1000 images. In comparison, our proposed scheme achieves better retrieval precision than Xia et al. [12] at comparable search efficiency.

From the experiments, it is evident that the proposed scheme achieves better retrieval precision compared with Xia et al.'s [10], Anju and Shreelekshmi's [2] and Xia et al.'s [12] SCBIR scheme. The proposed scheme consumes more time compared with other schemes which is a trade-off for retrieval precision.

5   Conclusion

The proposed scheme aims at enhancing the retrieval precision of SCBIR using combined feature descriptors and joined IFVs. From the experimental evaluation and comparative analysis, it is evident that retrieval precision of the proposed scheme outperforms existing SCBIR schemes [2,10,12]. Combining the visual descriptors CSD and SCD gives better retrieval precision compared with other combinations for distinct and entire image categories. For similar image categories, CLD with EHD outperforms other combinations. The proposed scheme consumes more search time since joined IFVs causes more comparisons. It is observed that the presence of totally unrelated images in the retrieved results degrade retrieval precision. Due to the critical applications of SCBIR in cloud, the presence of such insignificant results affect usability of the scheme and for addressing these shortcomings future research is required.

Acknowledgment. Authors acknowledge Centre for Engineering Research and Development, Government of Kerala, for granting research fellowship.

References

1. Corel Image dataset (2019). http://www.ci.gxnu.edu.cn/cbir/Dataset.aspx. Accessed 1 Jan 2019
2. Anju, J., Shreelekshmi, R.: Modified feature descriptors to enhance secure content-based image retrieval in cloud. In: Proceedings of Second IEEE International Conference on Intelligent Computing, Instrumentation and Control Technologies (ICICICT - 2019), pp. 1260–1266. IEEE (2019). To be published in IEEE Xplore Digital Library
3. Bastan, M., Cam, H., Gudukbay, U., Ulusoy, O.: An MPEG-7 compatible video retrieval system with integrated support for complex multimodal queries. IEEE MultiMedia (2009)
4. Datar, M., Immorlica, N., Indyk, P., Mirrokni, V.S.: Locality-sensitive hashing scheme based on p-stable distributions. In: Proceedings of the Twentieth Annual Symposium on Computational Geometry, pp. 253–262. ACM (2004)
5. Manjunath, B.S., Ohm, J.R., Vasudevan, V.V., Yamada, A.: Color and texture descriptors. IEEE Trans. Circuits Syst. Video Technol. **11**(6), 703–715 (2001)
6. Müller, H., Müller, W., Squire, D.M., Marchand-Maillet, S., Pun, T.: Performance evaluation in content-based image retrieval: overview and proposals. Pattern Recogn. Lett. **22**(5), 593–601 (2001)
7. Wang, J.Z., Li, J., Wiederhold, G.: Simplicity: semantics-sensitive integrated matching for picture libraries. IEEE Trans. Pattern Anal. Mach. Intell. **9**, 947–963 (2001)
8. Wang, Q., He, M., Du, M., Chow, S.S., Lai, R.W., Zou, Q.: Searchable encryption over feature-rich data. IEEE Trans. Dependable Secure Comput. **15**(3), 496–510 (2018)

9. Wong, W.K., Cheung, D.W.L., Kao, B., Mamoulis, N.: Secure KNN computation on encrypted databases. In: Proceedings of the 2009 ACM SIGMOD International Conference on Management of Data, pp. 139–152. ACM (2009)

10. Xia, Z., Wang, X., Zhang, L., Qin, Z., Sun, X., Ren, K.: A privacy-preserving and copy-deterrence content-based image retrieval scheme in cloud computing. IEEE Trans. Inf. Forensics Secur. **11**(11), 2594–2608 (2016)

11. Xia, Z., Xiong, N.N., Vasilakos, A.V., Sun, X.: EPCBIR: an efficient and privacy-preserving content-based image retrieval scheme in cloud computing. Inf. Sci. **387**, 195–204 (2016). https://doi.org/10.1016/j.ins.2016.12.030

12. Xia, Z., Zhu, Y., Sun, X., Qin, Z., Ren, K.: Towards privacy-preserving content-based image retrieval in cloud computing. IEEE Trans. Cloud Comput. **6**(1), 276–286 (2018)

Design of a Scheduling Approach
for Budget-Deadline Constrained Applications
in Heterogeneous Clouds

Naela Rizvi and Dharavath Ramesh$^{(\boxtimes)}$ ⓘ

Department of Computer Science and Engineering, Indian Institute of Technology (ISM)
Dhanbad, Dhanbad 826004, Jharkhand, India
naela.17dr000330@cse.ism.ac.in, drramesh@iitism.ac.in

Abstract. The notion of seemingly infinite resources and the dynamic provisioning of these resources on rental premise fascinated the execution of scientific applications in the cloud. The scheduling of the workflows under the utility model is always constrained to some QoS (Quality of Service). Generally, time and cost are considered to be the most important parameters. Scheduling of workflows becomes more challenging when both the time and cost factors are considered simultaneously. Therefore, most of the algorithms have been designed considering either time or cost factor. Hence, to handle the scheduling problem, in this paper, a novel heuristic algorithm named SDBL (Sub-deadline and Budget level) workflow scheduling algorithm for the heterogeneous cloud has been proposed. The proposed methodology effectively utilizes the deadline and budget constrained workflows. The novel strategy of distributing deadline as the level deadline (sub-deadline) to each level of workflow and the mechanism of budget distribution to every individual task satisfies the given constraints and results the exceptional performance of SDBL. SDBL strives to produce a feasible schedule meeting the deadline and the budget constraints. The PSR (Planning Success Rate) is utilized to show the efficiency of the proposed algorithm. For simulation, real workflows were exploited over the methodologies such as SDBL (Sub-deadline and budget level workflow scheduling algorithm), BDSD, BHEFT (Budget Constraint Heterogeneous Earliest Finish Time), and HBCS (Heterogeneous Budget Constrained Scheduling). The comprehensive experimental evaluation demonstrates the effectiveness of the proposed methodology in terms of higher PSR in most cases.

Keywords: Workflow scheduling · Deadline · Budget · Sub-deadline · Budget level · Makespan · PSR

1 Introduction

The enhancement of analytical analysis and the ever-growing complexity of data instigated the researchers to explore the advantages of the cloud. The "pay-per-use" policy, elasticity, and auto-scaling capabilities of the cloud are much adequate to fit the requirement of extensive data and compute-intensive applications [1–3]. These applications

© Springer Nature Switzerland AG 2020
D. V. Hung and M. D'Souza (Eds.): ICDCIT 2020, LNCS 11969, pp. 198–213, 2020.
https://doi.org/10.1007/978-3-030-36987-3_12

can be formalized as workflows consisting of dependent and independent task modules. The workflows consist complex data process and require high computations have become the most important paradigm among researchers [4, 5]. Workflows can benefit from an unlimited virtual resource of cloud at minimum cost and therefore, with such advantages of cloud, workflows are shifted to the cloud environment for scheduling [6]. However, the scheduling of workflows in a cloud is also not a trivial task. The scheduling strategy involves the selection of virtual machine and the assignment of tasks to the virtual machine instances accompanied by the decision of the order of the task's execution based on the precedence constraint. This paper focusses the workflow scheduling problem, where the workflow scheduling problem comes under the class of NP-Complete problem [7]. The objective of workflow scheduling involves minimizing the makespan, cost reduction, robust scheduling, etc. Scheduling can be categorized as best-effort scheduling and QoS constrained scheduling. In best-effort scheduling, only one parameter is optimized either time/cost, where other parameters related to QoS are ignored. On the other hand, QoS constrained scheduling approach involves optimization of one parameter constrained to the others. QoS constraints can be single objective and multi-objective. The most important QoS constrained algorithms such as budget constrained workflow scheduling [8] and deadline constrained workflow scheduling [9] involve time and cost parameters. The budget constrained algorithms try to minimize the execution time of workflows while assigning constrained on budget, whereas the deadline constrained algorithms try to optimize the workflow scheduling cost having constraints on deadline. With the recent developments, excessive research considering budget constrained workflow scheduling and deadline constrained workflow scheduling have been explored with suitable prerequisites. However, there are only a few works addressing workflow scheduling that considers both budget and deadline constraints simultaneously.

To address the above-mentioned instances, a heuristic based approach named SDBL (Sub-deadline and budget level workflow scheduling algorithm) is proposed. The proposed SDBL considers both the time and cost parameters simultaneously. The proposed mechanism aims to produce a feasible schedule that satisfies both the deadline and budget constraints simultaneously. The proposed approach provides a distinct strategy of distributing deadline as sub-deadline and budget as budget level. Sub-deadline is the assigned deadline to each level of the workflow, whereas budget level is the budget constraint to each task of a workflow. Extensive experiments with real workflows such as Cybershake, Montage, Inspiral LIGO, SIPHT and Epigenomic have been performed to evaluate the efficacy of the proposed algorithm. The result analysis shows that the success rate of SDBL is higher than BDSD [20], HBCS [15], and BHEFT [17] in most of the cases.

The remainder of the paper is organized as follows. Section 2 is about related work Sect. 3 discusses system model and problem formulation. Section 4 introduces the proposed approach for workflow scheduling illustrated with suitable example. Section 5 is all about the experimental results and Sect. 6 provided the conclusion and future work.

2 Related Work

Workflow scheduling is categorized into best-effort scheduling and QoS constrained scheduling. On the other hand, QoS constrained scheduling can be a single QoS constraint and multi-QoS constraint. This section provides the literature gathering of QoS related constraint scheduling approaches. Reducing the execution time of the workflow by satisfying the budget constraint or minimizing the scheduling cost while meeting the deadline constraint falls under the category of single QoS constraints. Abrishami et al. [11] introduced a deadline distribution strategy based on the concept of Partial Critical Paths (PCP). This work is further extended in [12] which presents a one phase scheduling algorithm called IC-PCP (IaaS Cloud Partial Critical Path) and another two-phase algorithm called IC-PCPD2 (IaaS Cloud Partial Critical Path with Deadline Distribution) for IaaS clouds. The proposed approach aims to minimize the monetary cost of execution while satisfying the deadline constraints. The experimental result shows that the performance of IC-PCP is better than IC-PCPD2. Yuan et al. [13] designed an effective heuristic scheduling approach called DET (Deadline Early Tree). In this approach, all the tasks are grouped and categorized into critical and non-critical activities. Deadlines are segmented into time windows. For critical activities, dynamic programming optimizes the cost under the defined deadline constraints and for the non-critical activities, an iterative procedure is proposed to maximize the time window. Verma et al. [14] proposed a Deadline Constrained Heuristic based Genetic Algorithms (HGAs) for workflow scheduling that minimizes the schedule cost under the defined deadline constrained. A Heterogeneous Budget Constrained Scheduling (HBCS) approach is proposed by Arabnejad et al. [15] for scheduling of applications in the heterogeneous environment. The methodology guarantees the minimal time of execution of workflows for the defined budget. The processors are selected for the tasks according to the worthiness value of each processor. Worthiness value depends on the budget available and the finish time of task on the particular processor. However, HBCS proves to be unfair for the tasks of lower priority. Therefore, to give equal importance to every task and to remove the drawback of HBCS another algorithm named MSBL (minimizing the schedule length using the budget level) has been proposed by Chen et al. [16]. The proposed low time complexity algorithm converts the budget constraint of an application for each task using the budget level.

The scheduling problem becomes more challenging for the workflows considering time and cost constraints at the same time. Therefore, this paper presents an approach called SDBL that considers optimizing both time and cost under the defined deadline and budget constraints. Only a few strategies are proposed till date that considers both the time and cost factor simultaneously. Zheng et al. [17] introduced an algorithm named BHEFT (Budget Constraint Heterogeneous Earliest Finish Time) which is the extension of HEFT algorithm. This algorithm decides the task scheduling strategy based on two factors CTB (Current Task Budget) and SAB (Spare Application Budget). Verma et al. [18] designed Bi-Criteria priority based Particle Swarm Optimization (BPSO) that minimizes the cost and time under the defined budget and deadline. Another budget and deadline aware scheduling (BDAS) approach is proposed by Arabnejad et al. [19] for the e-Science workflows. Sun et al. [20] proposed a BDSD algorithm to schedule the workflows under the given budget and deadline constraints. The proposed approach uses SDL (sub-deadline) for each task to assign priority of each task. Arabnejad et al. [21] introduced a novel low time complexity algorithm that addresses both the deadline and budget constraints.

3   Scheduling System Model and Problem Definition

This section provides the IaaS cloud model, the application model and the scheduling objectives.

3.1   Cloud Model

The cloud model comprises of IaaS cloud provider to offer services to its customer. The IaaS cloud services comprise the heterogeneous virtualized resources of different costs and capabilities [10]. These heterogeneous resources are the virtual machines represented as $V = \{v_1, v_2, v_3........v_n\}$. Each virtual machine is associated with two parameters $<w, p>$, where w is the capability of the machine including the computational power, RAM size, I/O speed, and bandwidth. On the other hand, parameter p represents the unit cost of the virtual machine. Each virtual machine has a different unit cost because of their heterogeneity nature. Therefore, the total cost of a virtual machine depends on its capability and the time for being used for execution. However, in the proposed model, it has been assumed that the cost of a virtual machine depends only on the time of execution. Usually, the higher processing capability virtual machines are more expensive.

3.2   Application Model

Workflow application can be modelled as a directed acyclic graph G (T, E), where $T = \{t_0, t_1, t_2 .... t_n\}$ is the set of tasks and $E = \{e_{i,j}|t_i, t_j \in T\}$ is the set of edges representing dependencies between the tasks t_i and t_j. Each dependency consists of precedence constraint ensuring that the parent task (t_i) must complete its execution before its child task (t_j) starts. In a DAG, the tasks having no predecessor are called entry task and the tasks having no successor is the exit tasks. In the proposed model, DAG having only one entry and one exit task has been considered. However, for the DAG having multiple entries and exist tasks, dummy entry and exist task having the zero-dependency edge are added. In addition to this, it is required to define some parameters for task scheduling [22].

Schedule length or makespan is the actual finish time of the exit task, where it is the time when the last task of an application finishes its execution.

$$makespan = FT(t_{exit}) \tag{1}$$

ST (t_i, v_k) and $FT(t_i, v_k)$ denote the start time and finish time of task t_i on virtual machine v_k and computed as follows.

$$ST(t_i, v_k) = \max\{T_{avail[v_k]}, \max_{t_j \in pred(t_i)}(FT(t_j) + CT(t_j, t_i))\} \tag{2}$$

Where $pred(t_i)$ is the immediate predecessor of task $t_{i,}$ $avail[v_k]$ is the earliest time at which virtual machine v_k is ready for execution of the next task. CT is the communication time between t_i and t_j. CT will be zero if tasks are placed on same virtual machine. It is noted that for entry task, $ST(t_{entry})$ is zero.

$$FT(t_i, v_k) = ST(t_i, v_k) + w_{t_i,k} \tag{3}$$

Equation 3 denotes the finish time of t_i, where $w_{ti,k}$ is the execution time of task t_i on virtual machine v_k.

3.3 Scheduling Problem

For the given workflow application, scheduling is defined by a function $\{Sh(G): T \in V\}$ that assigns each task $t_i \in T$ to each desired virtual machine $v_k \in V$ subjected to:

- *Virtual machine constraints:* No virtual machine is allowed to execute more than one task at the same time.
- *Precedence constraints:* It determines the task precedence which is represented by dependency edges.
- *Budget constraints:* All tasks must be executed within the defined budget as;

$$Cost(G) \leq Budget \tag{4}$$

The total cost of executing an application is computed as

$$Cost(G) = \sum_{i=1}^{T} Cost(t_i, v_k) \tag{5}$$

The monetary cost $Cost(t_i, v_k)$ of task t_i on k^{th} virtual machine is defined as:

$$Cost(t_i, v_k) = w_{t_i,k} * p_{v_k} \tag{6}$$

Where p_{vk} is the unit cost of kth virtual machine.
- *Deadline constraints*: Execution time of all the tasks must be within the defined deadline.

$$makespan(G) \leq Deadline \tag{7}$$

The scheduling strategy must find the schedules that satisfy the user-defined QoS constraints. The schedule is said to be successful only if it is in the range of defined budget and deadline constraints. Budget and deadline constraints must be negotiated between the providers and users to obtain feasible scheduling solutions.

4 Proposed Algorithm: Sub-deadline and Budget Level (SDBL)

This section introduces the proposed sub-deadline and budget level algorithm (SDBL) which aims to find the schedules within the defined budget and deadline constraints. The SDBL is a heuristic list based scheduling approach, consisting of two phases, namely; a task selection phase and virtual machine selection phase. The detailed description of the proposed algorithm is described in the following manner.

Phase 1: Task selection phase
Tasks are selected priority wise and the priorities are assigned based on the *EST* value of each task of the fastest virtual machine. *EST* is defined as the earliest start time of a task on a fastest virtual machine [19] which is computed as;

$$EST(t_i) = \begin{cases} 0, & t_i = t_{entry} \\ \max\limits_{t_j \in pred(t_i)} \{EST(t_j) + w_{t_j,k} + CT_{i,j}\}, & otherwise \end{cases} \tag{8}$$

Where $w_{t_j,k}$ is the execution time of predecessor task t_j on fastest virtual machine k and $CT_{i,j}$ is the communication time of task t_i and t_j. However, for the entry task, *EST* is always zero.

Phase 2: Virtual machine selection phase
The virtual machine is to be selected for the execution of the current task is bounded by two constraints, namely; budget and deadline. Virtual machines have to satisfy the budget and deadline constraints for the successful execution of the current task, otherwise the schedule is considered as failure. The complete description of assigning deadline and budget constraints are discussed in the following manner.

Deadline Level Assignment: Provisioning of resources and subsequently, the execution of workflow application over these resources is one of the critical issues. Moreover, including the deadline constraints on workflows becomes even more challenging. Hence, for the earliest possible execution, different strategies satisfying the deadline has been emerged till date [23]. One approach is to distribute the deadline as sub deadline over the workflows to ensure more manageable deadline distribution, where each task of the workflow must be scheduled under the defined sub-deadline. The proposed methodology distributes the deadline among different levels of workflow and the execution of each task in a level must be completed before the assigned sub deadline.

Definition 1 (*Workflow partitioning*: Tasks of a workflow are categorized into different levels based on their respective dependencies. Subsequently, user defined deadline is distributed among different levels. There are two algorithms for deadline distribution named Deadline Bottom Level (DBL) [24] and Deadline Top Level (DTL) [25]. Both the algorithms assign levels to workflows in bottom to top and top to bottom approach respectively. In this paper, DTL algorithm is used to categorize the tasks into a different level.

The level of a current task can be described as maximum number of edges from a current task to the exit task. For the entry task, level number (l) is always 1 and level number for the other task is determined as:

$$l(t_i) = \max\nolimits_{t_j \in pred(t_i)}(l(t_j) + 1) \tag{9}$$

The level of each task has now been determined respectively, and the next step involves distribution of user deadline to each level of workflow. Deadline assigned to the level denoted as *subDL(l)* is the sub-deadline. Deadline of a level *subDL(l)*, can be computed from Eqs. 14 and 15 using DTL approach. Initially, the estimated deadline for each level is computed from the Eq. 10.

$$subDL(l) = \max_{t_i \in TTL(l)}\{EAT(t_i)\} \tag{10}$$

Where *EAT* is the Earliest Accomplishment Time of task t_i., *TTL(l)* denotes the total number of tasks assigned to the same level. *EAT* can be calculated from Eq. 11.

$$EAT(t_i) = \max_{l \in pred(t_i)}\{subDL(l), EST(t_i)\} + w_{t_i,k} \tag{11}$$

The maximum *EAT* of all tasks in a level determines the estimated sub deadline of level *l*. Subsequently, the user defined deadline is distributed to each level. The deadline distribution is dependent on *TTL* and deadline measure (*dm*). Therefore, there is non-uniform distribution of deadline to each level. Before computing of the deadline measure (*dm*), the deadline proportional (ϕ_d) is evaluated as;

$$\phi_d = \sum_{l=1}^{m} |subDL(l)| \times TTL(l) \tag{12}$$

Where |*subDL(l)*| is the difference of sub deadline of level *l* and *l-1*. Deadline measure (*dm*) is calculated as;

$$dm = \frac{D - subDL(l_n)}{\phi_d} \tag{13}$$

subDL(l_n) is the sub deadline of the level containing the exit task node. Afterwards, the length of each sub deadline of a level is updated using Eq. 14 and from the Eq. 15 the length of last level is updated.

$$U\_subDL(l) = dm \times |subDL(l)| \times TTL + subDL(l) \tag{14}$$

$$U\_subDL(l_n) = D \tag{15}$$

Budget Level Assignment: Tasks are selected according to their priority from the sorted task in a level and user defined budget is distributed to every task of an application. Each task has been associated with budget level (*bl*) value, where every task must satisfy the *bl* for the successful schedule. *bl* of each task can be computed as;

$$bl(t_i) = \frac{rb}{n} \tag{16}$$

$$rb = Budget \tag{17}$$

$$rb = rb - \cos t(t_i, v_k) \tag{18}$$

Where *rb* is the remaining budget and *n* denotes the remaining unscheduled task number. Initially, for the entry task, *rb* is the total budget assigned to the application.

Budget and deadline have been distributed to the respective task. Afterwards, those virtual machines that satisfies both the budget and deadline constraints as described in Eqs. 19 and 20 are eligible for the execution. However, tasks are scheduled only to that virtual machine that has earliest finish time computed from the Eq. 3.

$$\cos t(t_i, v_k) \leq bl(t_i) \tag{19}$$

$$FT(t_i, v_k) \leq U\_subDL(l) \tag{20}$$

SDBL Algorithm
Input: *A DAG, User defined budget and deadline*
Output: *A Schedule satisfying both budget and deadline constraint*
1. Compute the *EST* of every task using eq. (8)
2. Sort the tasks priority wise in according to *EST* value
3. Assign user-defined Budget (*B*) and Deadline (D)
4. Determine the level of every task using eq. (9)
5. Compute *subDL(l)* of each level using eq. (10)
6. *for (l=1,l<=m, l++)*   // m is the total number of level in a DAG
7.   Determine *TTL* value
8.   Compute the *U_subDL(l)* using eq. (14) and eq. (15)
9.   *While* (there are tasks in the level *(l)) do*
10.   select the task *t_i* having highest priority
11.   Calculate the *bl(t_i)* from eq. (16)
12.   *for (v_k=1, v_k<= V, v_k++)*
13.   Select the virtual machines that satisfies the eq. (19)
14.   Compute *FT(t_i,v_k)* on selected virtual machine using eq. (3)
15.   *If FT(t_i,v_k)* <=U_subDL(l)
16.   Select the virtual machine with minimum *FT*
17.   *end*
18.   *end*
19. Update the *rb* using eq. (18), update the n, *n=n*-1
20.   *end while*
21. *end for*
22. return schedule

4.1 Working Example

A working example is provided for better illustration of the proposed SDBL algorithm. A DAG consisting of 10 tasks is presented in Fig. 1. As shown in Fig. 1, the weighted edge between t_1 and t_4 is 29 which represents the communication time between the two tasks if they are assigned on different virtual machine, otherwise it is considered to be zero. Furthermore, the assumed execution time of these tasks on three different heterogeneous virtual machines is also shown in Table 1. The unit execution price of each virtual machine $V = \{0.92, 0.29, 0.4\}$ is assumed. The user defined budget and deadline is set to 95 and 200 for the evaluation.

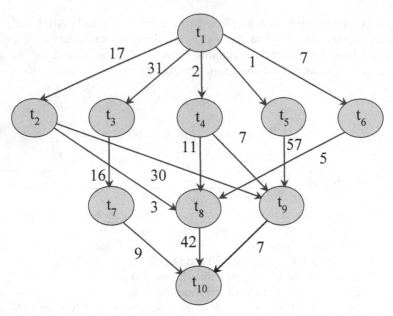

Fig. 1. DAG representation with 10 tasks

Table 1. Execution time of a DAG on three virtual machines

Tasks/VMs	V_1	V_2	V_3
t_1	22	21	36
t_2	22	18	18
t_3	32	27	43
t_4	7	10	4
t_5	29	27	35
t_6	26	17	24
t_7	14	25	30
t_8	29	23	36
t_9	15	21	8
t_{10}	13	16	33

Initially, all the tasks are assigned to their respective level, i.e., $\{l_1, l_2, l_3, l_4\}$ and tasks are sorted according to their *EST* value. *EST* and *EAT* of each task are shown in Table 2. In the proposed approach, the deadline is distributed level wise, whereas the budget is distributed among each task.

Estimated sub-deadline for each level l is evaluated as $subDL(l) = \{21, 79, 126, 146\}$ and then updated as $U\_subDL(l) = \{23.4025, 112.178, 142.1314, 200\}$. Afterwards, the budget level of each task is evaluated. Budget level for task t_1 is 9.5. As t_1 belongs to

Table 2. *EST* and *EAT* of tasks

Tasks	t_1	t_2	t_3	t_4	t_5	t_6	t_7	t_8	t_9	t_{10}
EST	0	38	52	50	34	28	95	65	118	133
EAT	21	56	79	54	67	45	109	102	126	146

level *1*, therefore, sub-deadline of t_1 is 23.4025. The virtual machine v_2 only satisfies both the constraints, hence opted for the scheduling of task t_1. Similarly, for the task t_6, $bl(t_6) = \frac{95-6.09}{9}$ and sub deadline is 112.178. Both v_1 and v_2 satisfies the constraints. However, only v_2 is selected for the scheduling because of the earliest finish time of task t_6 on v_2. In the same fashion, all the tasks are scheduled on the best virtual machine that provides a feasible schedule. The complete schedule along with tasks and budget level is shown in Table 3.

Table 3. Complete schedule of DAG of 10 tasks

Tasks	Budget level (bl)	V_1		V_2		V_3		$Cost(t_i, v_{sel})$
		EST	EFT	EST	EFT	EFT	EST	
t_1	9.5			0	21			6.09
t_6	9.8789			21	38	28	52	4.93
t_5	10.497			38	65			7.83
t_2	10.879			65	83	38	56	7.20
t_4	11.492	50	57	65	75	56	60	6.44
t_3	12.502			65	92			7.83
t_8	13.67			92	115			6.67
t_7	16.003	108	122	115	140	108	138	12.88
t_9	17.565	122	137	115	136	122	130	3.2
t_{10}	31.93	157	170	137	153	157	190	4.64

5 Performance Metrics and Experimental Analysis

This section presents the comparison and results of the proposed SDBL with BDSD [20] HBCS [15] and BHEFT [17] algorithms. Algorithms are evaluated through various simulation runs with scientific applications.

Performance Metrics: To evaluate the performance of every algorithm, the experiments are repeated several times such that planning success rate (PSR) is computed with suitable instances. If the given deadline and budget constraints are satisfied by the algorithms then the schedule is said to be successfully executed otherwise failed. PSR is computed as;

$$PSR = \frac{number\ of\ successful\ schedule}{number\ of\ simulation\ runs} * 100 \qquad (21)$$

For each DAG, constraints are assigned with a specific range of values. Constraints can be very strict or can be relaxed. For each parameter of constraints, PSR for the mentioned algorithm is evaluated. Constraints of budget and deadline are defined in the following manner.

$$BC = bf * LC \quad 1 < bf < 10 \qquad (22)$$

$$DC = df * FS \quad 1 < df < 10 \qquad (23)$$

Where BC and DC defines the budget and deadline constraints and bf and df are the budget and deadline factors that varies from very strict to relaxed value. LC is the lowest cost of execution, which can be obtained by scheduling all the tasks on the cheapest virtual machine. On the other hand, FS denotes the fastest schedule, i.e. executing all the tasks on the fastest virtual machine.

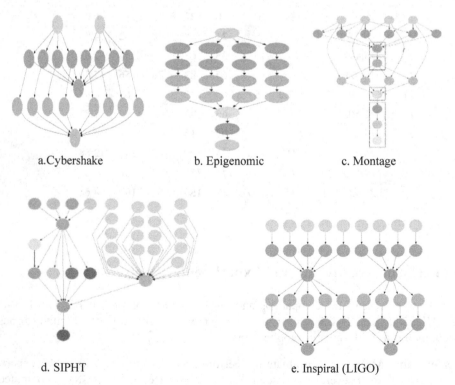

a.Cybershake   b. Epigenomic   c. Montage

d. SIPHT   e. Inspiral (LIGO)

Fig. 2. Types of real workflows

Datasets and Experimental Results: The proposed mechanism is tested over five benchmark workflows named; Cybershake, Epigenomic, Montage, SIPHT, and Inspiral (LIGO). Cybershake workflow consists of earthquake hazard dataset that is used by southern California earthquake center. Montage is used for astronomy whereas, Epigenomic and SIPHT is used in biology. Inspiral (LIGO) analyzes the data of the gravitational waveforms of compact binary system. These workflows are generated from Pegasus Workflow Generator [26].

Detailed characterization of these workflows is provided in [27] and structure of these workflows is shown in Fig. 2. On the other hand, the efficacy of proposed methodology SDBL has also been validated with the well-known existing methodology HBCS, BHEFT, and BDSD. To evaluate the performance, budget and deadline constraints of various parameters are considered. A combination of 10 different budget factor and 10 different deadline factors have been permuted by yielding 100 different cases. Due to the complexity in considering all 100 cases, only 10 different situations are shown. Constraints can vary from very strict to very relaxed. Workflows ranging from 30-1000 tasks size are considered. However, the results did not differ significantly; therefore, PSR of only workflows of size 1000 tasks is shown graphically.

The result of all workflows is depicted in Figs. 3, 4, 5, 6, and 7. Workflows are exploited over constraints of different parameters to obtain PSR. Figure 3 shows the PSR of Cybershake workflow, considering different parameters of budget and deadline. As shown in Fig. 3, when very strict budget and deadline factors (1, 3) are considered then the proposed SDBL shows 42% of success rate while the rest of the algorithms show 100% failure. However, SDBL, BDSD and BHEFT shows the consistent result, while the constraints are relaxed. The SDBL algorithm shows significant overall performance by achieving 92% success rate. On the other hand, HBCS shows only 26% success rate. Figure 4 shows the PSR of Epigenomic workflow. From Fig. 4, it is shown that at the factors (1, 3), (2, 2) and (3, 1) only BDSD is successfully executed and the rest of the algorithm shows 100% failure. The failure of most of the algorithms may be due to pipelined structure of Epigenomic. SDBL achieves a higher success rate than HBCS and lags behind the BDSD and BHEFT. As shown in Fig. 5, for the Montage workflow, BDSD outperforms other algorithms.

BDSD achieves a higher success rate when the strict constraints are assigned. At the factor of (2, 2) only BDSD shows 20% successful execution. BDSD proves to be more efficient when the constraints are relaxed. Whereas, proposed SDBL is more efficient than BHEFT and HBCS. BDSD, SDBL and BHEFT become consistent from the factor (8, 6) and the HBCS still needs to be improved. For the SIPHT workflow, SDBL achieves remarkable performance as shown in Fig. 6. When the strict budget factor is considered, only SDBL shows 20% success rate while all other algorithms show 100% failure. Moreover, when the budget constraint is relaxed to the factor (2, 2) SDBL shows 100% success rate. Overall, 90% of success rate is achieved by SDBL. As shown in Fig. 7, SDBL also shows the significant result for Inspiral (LIGO). At the factor of (1, 3), all the algorithms were failed in executing the related parameters. However, SDBL and BDSD achieves 32% and 25% of success rate when constraints are relaxed to (2, 2). On the other hand, BHEFT and HBCS still show 100% failure.

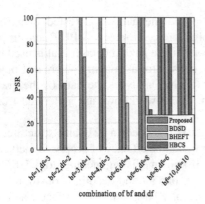

Fig. 3. PSR of Cybershake

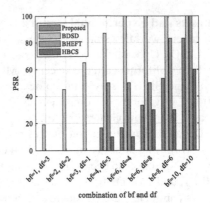

Fig. 4. PSR of Epigenomic

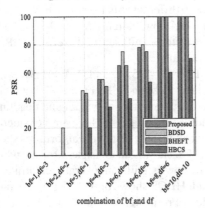

Fig. 5. PSR of Montage

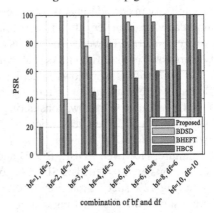

Fig. 6. PSR of SIPHT

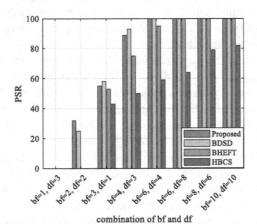

Fig. 7. PSR of Inspiral (LIGO)

Based on the above analysis, SDBL proves to be the best scheduling algorithm for Cybershake and SIPHT workflow. THE PSR achieved by the SDBL for Cybershake and SIPHT is greater than 90%. Moreover, for the Inspiral (LIGO), SDBL proves to be more efficient than BDSD for the strict constraints. However, the overall success rate for both the algorithm is nearly same. Finally, it can be concluded that, the novel methodology of budget and deadline distribution of SDBL results remarkable performance for most of the workflows.

6 Conclusion and Future Work

This paper presents an algorithm named sub-deadline and budget level (SDBL) workflow scheduling, which aims to satisfy the budget and deadline constraint and produce a feasible schedule. The novelty of the proposed work is to provide simple deadline and budget distribution strategy for the given workflow application. The mechanism of distributing user-defined deadline as sub-deadline and the approach of converting budget constraints of an application into task satisfies the given constraints and results in the satisfactory performance of SDBL. Moreover, the performance of the proposed SDBL has also been compared with the existing algorithms BDSD, BHEFT, and HBCS over different parameters of deadline and budget constraints.

PSR for each workflow has been evaluated for all the aforementioned algorithms. The experimental results show that SDBL behaves remarkably for the Cybershake and SIPHT workflow and achieves more than 90% of the successful schedule. SDBL also proves to be more efficient for Inspiral LIGO by satisfying strict constraints. Performance of SDBL is better than BHEFT and HBCS for the Montage workflow. On the other hand, BDSD proves to be a more efficient algorithm for Epigenomic and Montage. HBCS shows 100% failure for the strict constraints. Moreover, HBCS shows poor performance by achieving a minimal success rate for all the workflows. One of the advantages of SDBL is simplicity and low time complexity. Furthermore, from the exploited knowledge, it is the first algorithm in which deadline constraint of an application is distributed into level deadline (sub-deadline), and the budget constraint is distributed to the individual task. For the future work, enhancement of SDBL can be done such that the performance of Montage and Epigenomic workflows also get improved. Moreover, it is also intended to use the SDBL algorithm for multiple workflows.

Acknowledgment. This research work was supported by Indian Institute of Technology (ISM), Dhanbad, Govt. of India. The authors wish to express their gratitude and heartiest thanks to the Department of Computer Science & Engineering, Indian Institute of Technology (ISM), Dhanbad, India for providing research support.

References

1. Tsai, W.T., Sun, X., Balasooriya, J.: Service-oriented cloud computing architecture. In: 2010 Seventh International Conference on Information Technology: New Generations, pp. 684–689. IEEE, April 2010

2. Liu, H., Orban, D.: Gridbatch: cloud computing for large-scale data-intensive batch applications. In: 2008 Eighth IEEE International Symposium on Cluster Computing and the Grid (CCGRID), pp. 295–305. IEEE, May 2008
3. Avram, M.G.: Advantages and challenges of adopting cloud computing from an enterprise perspective. Procedia Technol. **12**, 529–534 (2014)
4. Liu, J., Pacitti, E., Valduriez, P., Mattoso, M.: A survey of data-intensive scientific workflow management. J. Grid Comput. **13**(4), 457–493 (2015)
5. Lin, C., Lu, S.: Scheduling scientific workflows elastically for cloud computing. In: 2011 IEEE 4th International Conference on Cloud Computing, pp. 746–747. IEEE, July 2011
6. Smanchat, S., Viriyapant, K.: Taxonomies of workflow scheduling problem and techniques in the cloud. Future Gener. Comput. Syst. **52**, 1–12 (2015)
7. Garey, M.R., Johnson, D.S.: A Guide to the Theory of NP-Completeness. Computers and Intractability, pp. 37–79 (1990)
8. Yu, J., Buyya, R.: Scheduling scientific workflow applications with deadline and budget constraints using genetic algorithms. Sci. Program. **14**(3–4), 217–230 (2006)
9. Rodriguez, M.A., Buyya, R.: Deadline based resource provisioningand scheduling algorithm for scientific workflows on clouds. IEEE Trans. Cloud Comput. **2**(2), 222–235 (2014)
10. Broberg, J., Venugopal, S., Buyya, R.: Market-oriented grids and utility computing: the state-of-the-art and future directions. J. Grid Comput. **6**(3), 255–276 (2008)
11. Abrishami, S., Naghibzadeh, M.: Deadline-constrained workflow scheduling in software as a service cloud. Scientia Iranica **19**(3), 680–689 (2012)
12. Abrishami, S., Naghibzadeh, M., Epema, D.H.: Deadline-constrained workflow scheduling algorithms for infrastructure as a service clouds. Future Gener. Comput. Syst. **29**(1), 158–169 (2013)
13. Yuan, Y., Li, X., Wang, Q., Zhu, X.: Deadline division-based heuristic for cost optimization in workflow scheduling. Inf. Sci. **179**(15), 2562–2575 (2009)
14. Verma, A., Kaushal, S.: Deadline constraint heuristic-based genetic algorithm for workflow scheduling in cloud. Int. J. Grid Util. Comput. **5**(2), 96–106 (2014)
15. Arabnejad, H., Barbosa, J.G.: A budget constrained scheduling algorithm for workflow applications. J. Grid Comput. **12**(4), 665–679 (2014)
16. Chen, W., Xie, G., Li, R., Bai, Y., Fan, C., Li, K.: Efficient task scheduling for budget constrained parallel applications on heterogeneous cloud computing systems. Future Gener. Comput. Syst. **74**, 1–11 (2017)
17. Zheng, W., Sakellariou, R.: Budget-deadline constrained workflow planning for admission control. J. Grid Comput. **11**(4), 633–651 (2013)
18. Verma, A., Kaushal, S.: Bi-criteria priority based particle swarm optimization workflow scheduling algorithm for cloud. In: Recent Advances in Engineering and Computational Sciences (RAECS), pp. 1–6. IEEE, March 2014
19. Arabnejad, V., Bubendorfer, K., Ng, B.: Budget and deadline aware e-science workflow scheduling in clouds. IEEE Trans. Parallel Distrib. Syst. **30**(1), 29–44 (2019)
20. Sun, T., Xiao, C., Xu, X.: A scheduling algorithm using sub-deadline for workflow applications under budget and deadline constrained. Cluster Comput. 1–10 (2018)
21. Arabnejad, H., Barbosa, J.G., Prodan, R.: Low-time complexity budget–deadline constrained workflow scheduling on heterogeneous resources. Future Gener. Comput. Syst. **55**, 29–40 (2016)
22. Topcuoglu, H., Hariri, S., Wu, M.Y.: Performance-effective and low-complexity task scheduling for heterogeneous computing. IEEE Trans. Parallel Distrib. Syst. **13**(3), 260–274 (2002)
23. Arabnejad, V., Bubendorfer, K., Ng, B.: Deadline distribution strategies for scientific workflow scheduling in commercial clouds. In: 2016 IEEE/ACM 9th International Conference on Utility and Cloud Computing (UCC), pp. 70–78, December 2016

24. Yuan, Y., Li, X., Wang, Q., Zhang, Y.: Bottom levelbased heuristic for workflow scheduling in grids. Chin. J. Comput. Chin. Ed. **31**(2), 282 (2008)
25. Yu, J., Buyya, R., Tham, C.K.: Cost-based scheduling of scientific workflow applications on utility grids. In: First International Conference on e-Science and Grid Computing (e-Science 2005), p. 8. IEEE, July 2005
26. Bharathi, S., Chervenak, A., Deelman, E., Mehta, G., Su, M.H., Vahi, K.: Characterization of scientific workflows. In: Third Workshop on Workflows in Support of Large-Scale Science, pp. 1–10. IEEE, November 2008
27. Juve, G., Chervenak, A., Deelman, E., Bharathi, S., Mehta, G., Vahi, K.: Characterizing and profiling scientific workflows. Future Gener. Comput. Syst. **29**(3), 682–692 (2013)

Resource Scheduling for Tasks of a Workflow in Cloud Environment

Kamalesh Karmakar[✉], Rajib K Das, and Sunirmal Khatua

Computer Science and Engineering, University of Calcutta, Kolkata, India
k.karmakar.ju@gmail.com, rajib.k.das@ieee.org, skhatuacomp@caluniv.ac.in

Abstract. In recent days most of the enterprises and communities adopt cloud services to deploy their workflow-based applications due to the inherent benefits of cloud-based services. These workflow-based applications are mainly compute-intensive. The major issues of workflow deployment in a cloud environment are minimizing execution time (*makespan*) and monetary cost. As cloud service providers maintain adequate infrastructural resources, workflow scheduling in the cloud environment becomes a non-trivial task. Hence, in this paper, we propose a scheduling technique where monetary cost is reduced, while workflow gets completed within its minimum makespan. To analyze the performance of the proposed algorithm, the experiment is carried out in WorkflowSim and compares the results with the existing well-known algorithms, *Heterogeneous Earliest Finish Time (HEFT)* and *Dynamic Heterogeneous Earliest Finish Time (DHEFT)*. In all the experiments, the proposed algorithm outperforms the existing ones.

Keywords: Cloud computing · Workflow scheduling · Monetary cost · Makespan

1 Introduction

In the traditional computing paradigm, workflow-based applications are scheduled on constrained resources of a server or a cluster. Thus, the performance of the scheduling techniques is measured either in terms of throughput or energy consumption. But in a cloud environment, the resources are not a constraint as huge infrastructural resources are maintained by service providers for fulfilling the growing needs of the users. Hence, job scheduling in the cloud environment receives high attention of the researchers for developing and analyzing workflow scheduling techniques for cloud environments, which are inherently scalable.

Most of the jobs in scientific and business applications are divisible into many independent tasks having some precedence relationships among them. A job having multiple tasks is considered as workflow while the relatively independent tasks can be executed in parallel. In a cloud environment, the tasks are executed in virtual machines (VMs), while the VMs are deployed in physical machines. Hence relatively independent tasks can be mapped to distinct VMs to run in

© Springer Nature Switzerland AG 2020
D. V. Hung and M. D'Souza (Eds.): ICDCIT 2020, LNCS 11969, pp. 214–226, 2020.
https://doi.org/10.1007/978-3-030-36987-3_13

parallel instead of sharing the resources of one VM. Thus, this research focuses on workflow scheduling in a cloud environment aiming maximization of resource utilization of the VMs and executing the workflow within its minimum *makespan*, where VM resources are not shared by multiple tasks simultaneously.

In this context, the rest of the paper is organized as follows. Related works are reviewed in Sect. 2, followed by the problem formulation in Sect. 3. A heuristic-based algorithm is presented in Sect. 4. The experimental results and their evaluation is demonstrated in Sect. 5. And finally, we conclude the wok in Sect. 6.

2   Related Work

Numerous research works are published in the recent past for job scheduling in cloud data centers. These works can be categorized in different aspects such as (i) minimization of the makespan (ii) energy-aware scheduling, (iii) dead-line-aware scheduling, and (iv) online scheduling.

Many works focus on the performance of the workflows concerning makespan [1–3] whereas an ant colony based multi-objective optimization technique is proposed in [4] aiming reduction of makespan and user's budget. An adaptive task scheduling algorithm is proposed in [5] for MapReduce jobs where tasks are dynamically provisioned considering completion time and size of map output. In [1] scheduling is performed using the Genetic Algorithmic approach whereas authors of [6] propose a Genetic Simulated Annealing algorithm to reduce makespan.

In contrast, energy-aware workflow scheduling techniques are investigated in [7–9]. In [7] a scheduling algorithm is proposed with the DVFS technique [8] energy and deadline aware data-intensive workflow-based task scheduling is proposed. In [9] a genetic algorithm based task scheduling technique is proposed considering different energy requirements.

In another context, researchers are focusing on online scheduling of workflow-based jobs [10–12]. Ge et al. proposed a genetic algorithm based task scheduling technique in [10] that gives reduced makespan compared to FIFO and delay scheduling policies. They have also shown that their proposed algorithm provides better load balancing compared to others. In [11] a rolling horizon scheduling architecture is proposed for real-time task scheduling aiming at the reduction of energy consumption. Liu et al. proposed a scheduling technique in [12] for I/O intensive workflows, in which extra cpu is shared in I/O interruption.

In [13], Zhu et al. proposed a two-step workflow scheduling technique, where resource utilization is maximized while the workflow is completed within a user-specified execution time-bound. In [14–18], authors proposed a scheduling technique for minimizing execution cost of a workflow by executing it within its deadline. Abrishami et al. proposed two polynomial-time heuristic algorithms in [14]. In their work, the first algorithm, namely IaaS Cloud Partial Critical Paths (IC-PCP) algorithm, runs in one phase, and the next one, namely, IaaS Cloud Partial Critical Paths with Deadline Distribution (IC-PCPD2) algorithm, runs in two phases. Calheiros et al. proposed an algorithm in [15], to use idle time

Table 1. List of symbols and descriptions

Symbol	Description	Symbol	Description
T	set of tasks in workflow W	ms	minimum makespan of the workflow
τ_a	a task of job W	κ^c	critical path
$M_{a,b}$	dependency of task τ_a on τ_b	κ^{nc}	non-critical path
τ_a^{es}	early start time of τ_a	T^{al}	allocated tasks
τ_a^{ef}	early finish time of τ_a	$Pre(\tau_a)$	set of predecessor tasks of τ_a
τ_a^{ls}	latest start time of τ_a	$Suc(\tau_a)$	successors of τ_a
		V	set of virtual machines
τ_a^{lf}	latest finish time of τ_a	v_i	i^{th} virtual machine
τ_a^{lt}	life-time of task τ_a	$A_{a,t}$	if τ_a is allocated at time t
τ_a^{st}	start-time of task τ_a	L	set of allocation lists
τ_a^{et}	end-time of task τ_a	L_i	list of tasks assigned to v_i

of provisioned resources and budget surplus to mitigate performance variation on soft deadlines of a workflow. In [16], the authors proposed a cloud-pricing model-based heuristic policy for workflow scheduling, where the scheduling policy runs in two phases. First, multiple tasks are aggregated into a common VM instance sequentially, and later, these tasks are merged in parallel. In [17], the authors proposed an algorithm, Multi-Cloud Partial Critical Paths (MCPCP), for minimizing the execution cost by satisfying deadline constraint. In [18], the authors proposed two algorithms where the prime focus is deadline constraint of the workflows, though the authors are able to reduce communication cost. Their proposed algorithms, Proportional Deadline Constrained (PDC) and Deadline Constrained Critical Path (DCCP), focus on task prioritization and backfilling respectively.

Most of the research works, where VM cost is reduced, the workflow is executed within its deadline. However, the makespan can be reduced further. Thus, this paper focuses on reducing the cost of VM while executing the workflow within its minimum makespan.

3   Problem Formulation

If all the tasks of a workflow are scheduled to run in one VM, execution time (makespan) becomes too high, which can be reduced by scheduling relatively independent tasks on different VMs simultaneously. Hence, we propose a scheduling policy where tasks of a workflow are deployed in different VMs of a cloud service provider's infrastructure.

3.1   Assumption

To construct a task allocation schedule for a workflow, the following assumptions are made:

1. Only one task can execute in one VM at a time. However multiple tasks may run in a single VM sequentially one after another.
2. Delayed start of a task is permitted if the job gets completed within minimum makespan.

3.2 Problem Definition

A workflow is represented as a graph $W = (T, E)$ where T is a set of tasks and E is a set of directed edges representing dependency among the tasks. Here, the set of tasks of the workflow W is represented by $T = \{\tau_1, \tau_2, \tau_3, \ldots, \tau_q\}$ and the set of dependency among tasks is represented by $E = \{e(\tau_a, \tau_b) | \tau_a, \tau_b \in T\}$.

Given a workflow W, containing a set of tasks represented as $T = \{\tau_1, \tau_2, \tau_3, \ldots \tau_q\}$ and given a set of VMs $V = \{v_1, v_2, v_3, \ldots, v_n\}$, determine a placement schedule $f : T \to V$ which minimizes peak demand of VM resources while minimum makespan of the workflow is ensured.

In this work, our objective is to reduce the total VM cost while execution time (i.e. makespan) of the workflow to be minimized. To achieve this objective, first, we determine minimum makespan. Then we prepare a schedule aiming reduction of peak VM demand by reusing the VMs for more than one task. Various symbols used in this paper are listed in Table 1.

Minimization of Makespan of a Workflow

The dependency among the tasks is represented by matrix M, which is defined as follow:

$$M_{a,b} = \begin{cases} 1 & \text{if } \tau_a \text{ is dependent on } \tau_b \\ 0 & \text{otherwise.} \end{cases} \tag{1}$$

Let us assume that the workflow is submitted at time 0. In order to reduce the makespan (ms), we need to

$$minimize \quad \max_{\tau_a \in T}(\tau_a^{et})$$

subject to the following constraints

$$(i) \quad \tau_a^{et} = \tau_a^{st} + \tau_a^{lt} \qquad \forall a$$

$$(ii) \quad \tau_a^{st} \geq \tau_b^{et} \times M_{a,b} \qquad \forall a, b$$

where constraint-(i) ensures that the tasks are non-preemptive, constraint-(ii) ensures that task τ_a starts after completion of the tasks on which it is dependent.

Minimization of Peak Resource Demand

The tasks are to be scheduled in such a way that the peak demand of VMs is reduced and the job gets completed within its minimum makespan, ms, as defined above.

Let us consider an allocation matrix A as defined below:

$$A_{a,t} = \begin{cases} 1 & \text{if } \tau_a \text{ is allocated at time, } t \\ 0 & \text{otherwise.} \end{cases} \tag{2}$$

Hence, $\sum_{a=1}^{m} A_{a,t}$ represents number of allocated tasks at clock t. In order, to reduce peak demand of VMs, we need to

$$minimize \quad \max_{t} \sum_{a=1}^{q} A_{a,t}$$

subject to the following constraints

$$(i) \qquad \tau_a^{et} = \tau_a^{st} + \tau_a^{lt} \qquad \forall a$$

$$(ii) \qquad A_{a,t} = 1 \qquad \forall t \in \tau_a^{st} \cdots \tau_a^{et} - 1$$

$$(iii) \qquad \sum_{t=1}^{ms} A_{a,t} = \tau_a^{lt} \qquad \forall a$$

$$(iv) \qquad \tau_a^{st} \geq \tau_b^{et} \times M_{a,b} \qquad \forall a, b$$

$$(v) \qquad \tau_a^{et} \leq ms \qquad \forall a$$

$$(vi) \qquad \sum_{t=1}^{\tau_a^{st}-1} A_{b,t} \geq \tau_b^{lt} \times M_{a,b} \qquad \forall a$$

Here, constraint-(i) and (iv) are the same as described earlier. Constraint-(ii) ensures that a task is scheduled for each clock within its start and end time. Constraint-(iii) ensures that a task gets executed for its lifetime. Constraint-(v) ensures that all the tasks are completed within its minimum *makespan*, which is determined in the makespan minimization phase. Constraint-(vi) ensures that all the tasks, on which the current task is dependent, are completed before the current task is started.

Finding an optimal solution, for this problem is NP-Hard. Thus, in the following section, we propose a heuristic algorithm to solve the problem in polynomial time.

4   Proposed Algorithm

In this task allocation, we prepare a schedule where a workflow gets completed within its minimum makespan. First, we determine a critical path consisting of a subset of tasks of the workflow. Then, the tasks on the critical path are allocated in one VM and they are scheduled according to the earliest start times. Later, we try to assign the tasks in such a way that the VM reservation cost is minimized. The proposed algorithm is discussed below.

The Algorithm 1 receives a DAG, $W(T, E)$, and returns a set of virtual machines and task allocation lists. First, we rearrange the tasks using *topological ordering*, so that the tasks can be processed from the beginning of the set T, which in turn reduces computational complexity. Topological ordering ensures that a task is not dependent on any task present on the right-hand side. A task can be dependent on one or more tasks present on the left-hand side.

Algorithm 1. Greedy Workflow Deployment

---

input : DAG, $W(T, E)$;
output: set of virtual machines, V; allocation list, L

1 initialize $L \leftarrow \phi$; allocated tasks $T^{al} \leftarrow \phi$; $V \leftarrow \phi$
2 rearrange T using *topological ordering*
3 **foreach** $\tau_a \in T$ **do**
4 | determine $< \tau_a^{es}, \tau_a^{ef}, \tau_a^{ls}, \tau_a^{lf} >$ of task τ_a

    `/* allocation of the tasks in the critical path`   `*/`
5 $\kappa^c \leftarrow GetCriticalPath(T)$
6 **foreach** $\tau_a \in \kappa^c$ **do**
7 | add $< \tau_a, \tau_a^{es} >$ to allocation list L_1
8 | $T^{al} \leftarrow T^{al} \cup \tau_a$

9 launch a new VM, v_1; assign allocation list L_1 to v_1; add v_1 to VM set, V
   `/* allocation of the tasks not in critical path`   `*/`
10 set $T^{ua} \leftarrow T - \{\tau_a | where\ \tau_a \in \kappa^c\}$
11 **while** $T^{ua} \neq \phi$ **do**
12   select task τ_a from the beginning of T^{ua}
13   set κ^{nc} as empty path; add τ_a to κ^{nc}
14     $\kappa^{nc} \leftarrow GetNonCriticalPath(\tau_a, T, T^{al}, \kappa^{nc})$
15     $v_i \leftarrow FindSuitableVM(V, \kappa^{nc}, L)$
16   **if** $v_i = null$ **then**
17 | launch a new VM, v_i; add the VM to V
18   **while** $\kappa^{nc} \neq \phi$ **do**
19   select τ_a from the begining of κ^{nc}
20   determine start time, τ_a^{st}, for deployment in v_i
21   add $< \tau_a, \tau_a^{st} >$ to allocation list L_i
22         $UpdateDependentTasks(\tau_a, T^{ua})$
23 | $T^{al} \leftarrow T^{al} \cup \tau_a$; remove τ_a from κ^{nc}
24 | $T^{ua} \leftarrow T^{ua} - \kappa^{nc}$

25 return V, L

Hence, first we calculate early start (τ_a^{es}), early finish (τ_a^{ef}), latest start (τ_a^{ls}) and latest finish (τ_a^{lf}) times of task τ_a. The τ_a^{es} and τ_a^{ef} times are calculated as

$$\tau_a^{es} \leftarrow \max\{(\tau_b^{es} + \tau_b^{lt}) \cdot M_{a,b}\} \quad \forall \quad \tau_b \in Pre(\tau_a)$$

and

$$\tau_a^{ef} \leftarrow \tau_a^{es} + \tau_a^{lt}.$$

After determining the early start and the early finish time of all the tasks in T, we calculate latest finish (τ_a^{lf}) and latest start (τ_a^{ls}) times as follow

$$\tau_a^{lf} \leftarrow \min\{(\tau_b^{ef} + \tau_b^{lt}) \cdot M_{a,b}\} \quad \forall \quad \tau_b \in Suc(\tau_a)$$

and

$$\tau_a^{ls} \leftarrow \tau_a^{lf} - \tau_a^{lt}.$$

Algorithm 2. GetCriticalPath

---

input : set of tasks, T
output: critical path, κ^c
1 initialize critical path, $\kappa^c \leftarrow \phi$
2 choose a task τ_a for which τ_a^{lf} is maximum
3 add τ_a to path κ^c
4 **while** $Pre(\tau_a) \neq null$ **do**
5 $\quad$ choose $\tau_b \in Pre(\tau_a)$ for which $\tau_a^{es} = \tau_a^{ls}$
6 $\quad$ add task τ_b at the begining of sequence κ^c
7 $\quad$ set $\tau_a \leftarrow \tau_b$
8 return κ^c

Algorithm 3. GetNonCriticalPath

---

input : task, τ_a; task sequence, T;
$\qquad\quad$ set of allocated task, T^{al} non-critical path, κ^{nc}
output: updated non-critical path, κ^{nc}
1 initialize $T' \leftarrow \phi$
/* determine dependent tasks $\qquad\qquad\qquad\qquad\qquad\qquad$ */
2 **foreach** $\tau_b \in T$ **do**
3 $\quad$ **if** τ_b is dependent on τ_a **then**
4 $\quad\quad$ $T' \leftarrow T' \cup \tau_b$
5 **if** $T' \cap T^{al} = \phi$ **then**
6 $\quad$ add τ_b at the end of non-critical path, κ^{nc}
7 $\quad$ call $GetNonCriticalPath(\tau_b, T, T^{al}, \kappa^{nc})$
8 return κ^{nc}

Later we determine a critical path of the workflow and deploy the tasks residing in the critical path to one VM. Then, we deploy the rest of the tasks (i.e. non-critical path tasks) to other VMs.

4.1 Critical Path Determination and Allocation

Here, the critical path is determined using Algorithm 2. This algorithm starts with the last task of the critical path and gradually adds the tasks until it reaches the starting task. Though a graph may have more than one critical path, this algorithm determines a path in a greedy approach.

After determining the critical path κ^c, the tasks are scheduled to the first VM, v_1. As the tasks on the critical path do not have any slack time, utilization of the VM instance is maximum.

Algorithm 4. FindSuitableVM

---

input : set of virtual machines, V; non-critical path, κ^{nc};
allocation list, L

output: suitable VM, v

1 set execution time, $et \leftarrow 0$
2 set start time, $st \leftarrow \min_{\tau_a \in \kappa^{nc}} \tau_a^{st}$
3 set finish time, $ft \leftarrow \max_{\tau_a \in \kappa^{nc}} \tau_a^{ft}$
4 **foreach** $\tau_a \in \kappa^{nc}$ **do**
5 $\quad\lfloor\ et = et + \tau_a^{lt}$

6 set temporary allocation, $L_i' \leftarrow \phi$
7 **foreach** $v_i \in V$ **do**
8 $\quad\vert\quad$ determine free time, ft, in L_i within es and lf
9 $\quad\vert\quad$ **if** $ft \geq et$ **then**
10 $\quad\vert\quad\vert\quad$ **foreach** $\tau_a \in \kappa^{nc}$ **do**
11 $\quad\vert\quad\vert\quad\vert\quad$ **if** τ_a *fits in* v_i *before* τ_a^{lf} **then**
12 $\quad\vert\quad\vert\quad\vert\quad\vert\quad$ determine τ_a^{st}
13 $\quad\vert\quad\vert\quad\vert\quad\lfloor\quad$ add $< \tau_a, \tau_a^{st} >$ to L_i'

14 $\quad\vert\quad\vert\quad\vert\quad$ **else**
15 $\quad\vert\quad\vert\quad\vert\quad\lfloor\quad$ break

16 $\quad\vert\quad$ **if** $|L_i'| = |\kappa^{nc}|$ **then**
17 $\quad\vert\quad\lfloor\quad$ return v_i

18 return *null*

4.2 Non-critical Path Determination and Allocation

The Algorithm 3 is used to determine a path starting at task τ_a which is not scheduled till now. Thus, this algorithm gradually adds the tasks to the non-critical path κ^{nc} recursively as shown in the algorithm.

Once a non-critical path κ^{nc} is determined, in Algorithm 4, first we search a VM from the list of VMs (i.e. V, virtual machines in use). If a VM in V has sufficient free time to execute all the tasks of κ^{nc}. Then the algorithm tries to find the free slots for feasible allocation. If all the tasks of κ^{nc} do not fit in any VM, the algorithm returns *null*, otherwise, the algorithm returns the VM in which tasks can be deployed.

After receiving the value returned by Algorithm 4 in Algorithm 1, it decides whether a new VM is to be added in active VM list or not. While allocating a task residing in κ^{nc}, if the task is not scheduled at it's early start time, early start time and early finish time of the dependent tasks are to be updated. Updation policy is shown in Algorithm 5.

Algorithm 5. UpdateDependentTasks

---

    input : task, τ_a;
                un-allocated tasks, T^{ua}
    output: updated tasks, T^{ua}
1 initialize $T' \leftarrow \phi$
    /* determine dependent tasks   */
2 **foreach** $\tau_b \in T^{ua}$ **do**
3   **if** $M_{b,a} = 1$ **then**
4         $T' \leftarrow T' \cup \tau_b$

    /* update early start and latest finish time   */
5 **foreach** $\tau_b \in T'$ **do**
6   **if** $\tau_b^{es} < \tau_a^{st} + \tau_a^{lt}$ **then**
7         $\tau_b^{es} \leftarrow \tau_a^{st} + \tau_a^{lt}$
8         $\tau_b^{ef} \leftarrow \tau_b^{es} + \tau_b^{lt}$
9         $UpdateDependentTasks(\tau_b, T^{ua})$

---

5   Implementation and Result Evaluation

In order to evaluate the performance of our proposed technique, we compare it with HEFT [19] and DHEFT techniques. We compare the result with HEFT because the technique is considered as a baseline in workflow scheduling for both in traditional and cloud environments. In this paper, we have used a standard simulation environment, WorkflowSim [20], developed on CloudSim [21].

The workflows used in this experiment are synthesized based on the sample workflows available in the simulation tool. To analyze the performance, many workloads are synthesized from each category, like *CyberShake*, *Epigenomics*, *Montage* and *Sipht*. And the results are presented by taking the average of multiple experiments for each category. Due to the significant variation in workflow size (makespan, number of tasks, etc.), we present the result in normalized form instead of taking a simple average to avoid domination of larger tasks over a smaller one.

5.1   Evaluation Metrics

For defining the evaluation metrics, let us consider a set of workflows $W = \{w_1, w_2.w_3, \ldots, w_m\}$.

Average Makespan. The average normalized makespan $(\overline{AM}^x)$ is calculated as:

$$\overline{AM}^x = \frac{1}{|W|} \sum_{w \in W} \frac{ms^x \text{ of } w}{ms^p \text{ of } w}$$

where, ms^x and ms^p are the makespan of a workflow w using algorithm x and proposed one respectively.

Average of Peak Resource Demand. The average normalized peak demands $\overline{PR}^x$ is calculated as:

$$\overline{PR}^x = \frac{1}{|W|} \sum_{w \in W} \frac{\max_t |A_t^x| \; of \; w}{\max_t |A_t^p| \; of \; w}$$

where, $|A_t^x|$ and $|A_t^p|$ are the peak demand of VM instances at time t in algorithm x and proposed one respectively.

Monetary Cost. Amazon EC2 on-demand instance price is calculated in terms of resource-hour. Thus, we calculate monetary cost based on the requirement of VM instances to execute the workflow.

5.2   Experimental Results and Discussion

Figure 1 depicts the average normalized makespan of the workflows. The results depict that the DHEFT algorithm performs better than the HEFT algorithm sometimes, but it is not consistent for each type of workflow. But our proposed algorithm gives a significant improvement in makespan. Moreover, as we use the well-known critical path method for determining the minimum makespan of the workflow. Our proposed algorithm gives an optimal solution in terms of makespan.

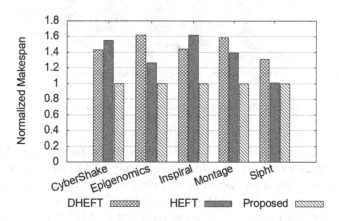

Fig. 1. Average makespan ($\overline{AM}$)

The average of normalized peak demands of VM instances is shown in Fig. 2. Here, we observe that the DHEFT algorithm outperforms the HEFT algorithm for every type of workflow. Furthermore, our proposed algorithm gives significant improvement over the DHEFT algorithm. The results also depict that the proposed algorithm improves the result significantly for *Cybershake* and *Epigenomics* workflows.

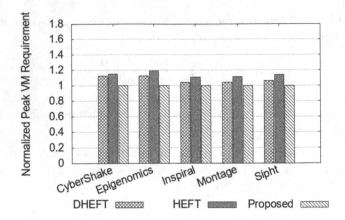

Fig. 2. Peak demand of VM instances $(\overline{PR})$

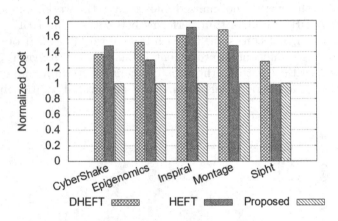

Fig. 3. Monetary cost of VM reservation

In this work, our prime objective is reducing the monetary cost of VM reservations. As Amazon charges for on-demand reserved VM instances on an hourly basis. We calculate the cost accordingly. Thus, we plot monetary cost in Fig. 3. The results show that neither of HEFT and DHEFT is consistent for every type of workflow. But our proposed technique gives noticeable improvement for every type of workflow.

6   Conclusion and Future Work

The Quality of Service of a workflow-based job is mainly measured in terms of the makespan of the workflow. At the same time, the monetary cost involved in workflow execution is a great concern to the cloud service users. Thus, in this paper, we present a workflow scheduling technique for the cloud environment where monetary cost is minimized while the workflow is executed in its minimum makespan. In this regard, the well known critical path method is used to determine the minimum makespan of the workflow-based job. The proposed algorithm is designed to execute the tasks on on-demand instances of Amazon Web Service. The performance of the proposed algorithm is analyzed with existing algorithms and correctness is verified with the standard and random workflows using *WorkflowSim* simulation tool. In the future, we would like to analyze prediction based resource allocation for the workflows, which are arriving at real-time.

Acknowledgments. This research is an outcome of the R&D work supported by the Visvesvaraya Ph.D. Scheme of Ministry of Electronics & Information Technology, Government of India, being implemented by the Digital India Corporation, Ref. No. MLA/MUM/GA/10(37)C.

References

1. Kumar, P., Verma, A.: Independent task scheduling in cloud computing by improved genetic algorithm. Int. J. Adv. Res. Comput. Sci. Softw. Eng. **2**(5), 111–114 (2012)
2. Mathew, T., Chandra Sekaran, K., Jose, J.: Study and analysis of various task scheduling algorithms in the cloud computing environment. In: 2014 International Conference on Advances in Computing, Communications and Informatics (ICACCI), pp. 658–664. IEEE (2014)
3. Zhan, Z.-H., Liu, X.-F., Gong, Y.-J., Zhang, J., Chung, H.S.-H., Li, Y.: Cloud computing resource scheduling and a survey of its evolutionary approaches. ACM Comput. Surv. (CSUR) **47**(4), 63 (2015)
4. Zuo, L., Shu, L., Dong, S., Zhu, C., Hara, T.: A multi-objective optimization scheduling method based on the ant colony algorithm in cloud computing. IEEE Access **3**, 2687–2699 (2015)
5. Tang, Z., Jiang, L., Zhou, J., Li, K., Li, K.: A self-adaptive scheduling algorithm for reduce start time. Futur. Gener. Comput. Syst. **43**, 51–60 (2015)
6. Gan, G., Huang, T., Gao, S.: Genetic simulated annealing algorithm for task scheduling based on cloud computing environment. In: 2010 International Conference on Intelligent Computing and Integrated Systems (ICISS), pp. 60–63. IEEE (2010)
7. Chia-Ming, W., Chang, R.-S., Chan, H.-Y.: A green energy-efficient scheduling algorithm using the DVFS technique for cloud datacenters. Futur. Gener. Comput. Syst. **37**, 141–147 (2014)
8. Zhao, Q., Xiong, C., Ce, Y., Zhang, C., Zhao, X.: A new energy-aware task scheduling method for data-intensive applications in the cloud. J. Netw. Comput. Appl. **59**, 14–27 (2016)
9. Shen, Y., Bao, Z., Qin, X., Shen, J.: Adaptive task scheduling strategy in cloud: when energy consumption meets performance guarantee. World Wide Web **20**(2), 155–173 (2017)
10. Ge, Y., Wei, G.: Ga-based task scheduler for the cloud computing systems. In: 2010 International Conference on Web Information Systems and Mining (WISM), vol. 2, pp. 181–186. IEEE (2010)

11. Zhu, X., Yang, L.T., Chen, H., Wang, J., Yin, S., Liu, X.: Real-time tasks oriented energy-aware scheduling in virtualized clouds. IEEE Trans. Cloud Comput. **2**(2), 168–180 (2014)
12. Liu, D., Han, N.: An energy-efficient task scheduler in virtualized cloud platforms. Int. J. Grid Distrib. Comput. **7**(3), 123–134 (2014)
13. Zhu, M., Wu, Q., Zhao, Y.: A cost-effective scheduling algorithm for scientific workflows in clouds. In: 2012 IEEE 31st International Performance Computing and Communications Conference (IPCCC), pp. 256–265. IEEE (2012)
14. Abrishami, S., Naghibzadeh, M., Epema, D.H.J.: Deadline-constrained workflow scheduling algorithms for infrastructure as a service clouds. Futur. Gener. Comput. Syst. **29**(1), 158–169 (2013)
15. Calheiros, R.N., Buyya, R.: Meeting deadlines of scientific workflows in public clouds with tasks replication. IEEE Trans. Parallel Distrib. Syst. **25**(7), 1787–1796 (2013)
16. Kang, D.-K., Kim, S.-H., Youn, C.-H., Chen, M.: Cost adaptive workflow scheduling in cloud computing. In: Proceedings of the 8th International Conference on Ubiquitous Information Management and Communication, p. 65. ACM (2014)
17. Lin, B., Guo, W., Chen, G., Xiong, N., Li, R.: Cost-driven scheduling for deadline-constrained workflow on multi-clouds. In: 2015 IEEE International Parallel and Distributed Processing Symposium Workshop, pp. 1191–1198. IEEE (2015)
18. Arabnejad, V., Bubendorfer, K., Ng, B.: Scheduling deadline constrained scientific workflows on dynamically provisioned cloud resources. Futur. Gener. Comput. Syst. **75**, 348–364 (2017)
19. Lin, C., Lu, S.: Scheduling scientific workflows elastically for cloud computing. In: 2011 IEEE International Conference on Cloud Computing (CLOUD), pp. 746–747. IEEE (2011)
20. Chen, W., Deelman, E.: WorkflowSim: a toolkit for simulating scientific workflows in distributed environments. In: 2012 IEEE 8th International Conference on E-science (e-science), pp. 1–8. IEEE (2012)
21. Calheiros, R.N., Ranjan, R., Beloglazov, A., De Rose, C.A.F., Buyya, R.: CloudSim: a toolkit for modeling and simulation of cloud computing environments and evaluation of resource provisioning algorithms. Softw. Pract. Exp. **41**(1), 23–50 (2011)

Bearing Fault Classification Using Wavelet Energy and Autoencoder

Sandeep S. Udmale[1,2]([✉])[iD] and Sanjay Kumar Singh[2][iD]

[1] Department of Computer Engineering and IT,
Veermata Jijabai Technological Institute (VJTI), Mumbai 400019, Maharashtra, India
ssudmale@it.vjti.ac.in
[2] Department of Computer Science and Engineering,
Indian Institute of Technology (BHU), Varanasi 221005, Uttar Pradesh, India
{ssudmale.rs.cse17,sks.cse}@iitbhu.ac.in

Abstract. Today's modern industry has widely accepted the intelligent condition monitoring system to improve the industrial organization. As an effect, the data-driven-based fault diagnosis methods are designed by integrating signal processing techniques along with artificial intelligence methods. Various signal processing approaches have been proposed for feature extraction from vibration signals to construct the fault feature space, and thus, over the years, the feature space has increased rapidly. Also, the challenge is to identify the promising features from the space for improving diagnosis performance. Therefore, in this paper, wavelet energy is presented as an input feature set to the fault diagnosis system. In this paper, wavelet energy is utilized to represent the multiple faults for reducing the requirement of number features, and therefore, the complex task of feature extraction becomes simple. Further, the convolutional autoencoder has assisted in finding more distinguishing fault feature from wavelet energy to improve the diagnosis task using extreme learning machine. The proposed method testified using two vibration datasets, and decent results are achieved. The effect of autoencoder on fault diagnosis performance has been observed in comparison to principal component analysis (PCA). Also, the consequence has seen in the size of the extreme learning machine (ELM) architecture.

Keywords: Autoencoder · Bearing · Fault diagnosis · Wavelet energy

1 Introduction

Recently, the rapid development of sensor technology as well as communication networks has helped to develop and deploy the cyber-physical system (CPS) in advanced industrial systems. The emergence of this CPS has made the data collection much easier for various processes conditions and a significant amount of data generated for the analysis of machinery health status [1–3]. The advances in artificial intelligence techniques have assisted in extracting useful information from the substantial amount of vibration data for mitigating the issues of

© Springer Nature Switzerland AG 2020
D. V. Hung and M. D'Souza (Eds.): ICDCIT 2020, LNCS 11969, pp. 227–238, 2020.
https://doi.org/10.1007/978-3-030-36987-3_14

fault diagnosis. As a practical means, it reduces the risk of unplanned shutdowns/breakdowns and assures the reliability as well as the safety of industrial systems. The majority of unexpected shutdowns occur due to the failure of rolling element bearing, and classifying the bearing fault as early as possible provides adequate time for maintenance planning and saves the time as well as money of industry [4–6].

Over the years, a significant amount of methods have been proposed for feature extraction and selection/transformation in bearing fault diagnosis. These approaches aim to enhance the characterization of fault features for improving fault diagnosis performance, and the remarkable advancement in the signal processing techniques has supported significantly for the various fault characterization. Therefore, the fault feature space has increased rapidly and become hybrid in nature in the last two decades due to the advancement in signal processing techniques. This advancement has introduced the various multi-domain features by the researchers to represent the multiple faults and fault severities [7–9].

Recently, a Neuro-Fuzzy system has been developed to identify the bearing health status by learning the resonant zones of vibration signals in the frequency domain [10]. The statistical feature space has been designed using the wavelet packet transform, and then distance-based criteria have been used to build the Bayesian inference fault information [11]. The Shannon entropy has assisted in choosing wavelet transform (WT) for designing the statistical feature space to calculate bearing health using artificial neural network and support vector machine [12,13]. A spectral kurtosis has assisted in extracting time-frequency energy density information to train the optimized extreme learning machine (ELM) [14]. The nonlinear and non-Gaussian characteristics of vibration data have captured using intrinsic mode function to develop the statistical feature space for expressing multiple fault pattern. Then the fault diagnosis task has been performed by the support vector machine [15]. The wavelet-spectrum method along with kurtosis ratio reference functions has assisted in calculating the health indicator for the monitoring of bearing based on Neuro-Fuzzy classifier [16].

Along with machine learning methods, recently, a deep learning approach has been broadly employed for fault classification. The kurtogram has been evaluated using a convolutional neural network (CNN) [17,18] and recurrent neural network [19] to enhance the fault diagnosis results. The statistical feature space has been designed by capturing the vibration data from multiple sources to develop a responsive fault diagnosis method using deep neural network [20]. The 2D input feature map has been constructed using time and frequency domain statistical features to train the CNN for fault diagnosis [21,22]. The various signal processing methods have served to establish the multi-domain feature set for the learning of stacked Gaussian-Bernoulli restricted Boltzmann machines [23]. A similar type of feature set has been developed by Chen et al. to examine the performance of bearing fault diagnosis using deep Boltzmann machines, deep belief network, and stacked autoencoders (AE) [24].

The above literature signifies that the various methods have been proposed to extract the fault features for improving fault diagnosis results. The different signal processing domain features have been analyzed by introducing new features along with existing features for identification of gear and bearing fault [25]. For developing the fault features spaces, one must be master in the signal processing and then determine the promising features from the space to express various defects by designing a robust feature selection routine. Therefore, in this paper, this complex task of identifying the fault features has been simplified by introducing the wavelet energy (WE) as a feature set to represent the various faults. In addition, to enhance the fault pattern representation capability of WE, convolutional AE has applied to the feature set. Then the efficient, as well as fast classifier like ELM, has been utilized for fault diagnosis. However, Haidong et al. have proposed a similar approach of fault diagnosis with wavelet as an activation function of AE [26]. The major difference between the proposed method and approach proposed by Haidong et al. is the use of convolutional layers for the extraction of significant fault information. This information is very crucial for differentiating the faults of short duration and low amplitude value such as ball fault and healthy bearing. The effect of AE has been analyzed for achieving small-size ELM architecture in the proposed method. The two vibration datasets have been used for testifying the proposed method and compared with existing alternatives.

2   Related Work

In this section, we briefly introduce the concepts of wavelet energy and autoencoder, which underlies the proposed method.

2.1   Wavelet Energy

The effective method to represent the signal in the time-frequency domain is a WT. The delightful property of WT is that at low frequencies, it presents the significant frequency information, and at high frequencies, it provides adequate information of time [9,27]. These characteristics are vital for fault diagnosis because the vibration signal contains the high frequencies as well as low frequencies components. Also, the non-gaussianity of vibration signal has been analyzed by WT to locate the transient present in the signal. The analysis using wavelet depends on the selection of the mother wavelet for the characterization of signal, and the unique decomposition of the signal provides the advantage in signal analysis [27,28].

The wavelet family set $\Psi_{n,j}(t)$ for multiresolution analysis in $L^2(\Re)$ is an orthogonal basic, and the idea of calculating the energy is derived from the Fourier theory. Initially, the mother wavelet $\Psi(t)$ is selected with the decomposition levels N [27,28]. At different decomposition levels, energy is expressed as the energy of wavelet coefficients $C_{n,j}$. Thus, the energy is defined at different decomposition levels with m number of wavelet coefficients as

$$E_n = \sum_{j=1}^{m} |C_{n,j}|^2 \tag{1}$$

where the jth wavelet coefficient of nth scale is $C_{n,j}$. Thus, the total energy is calculated by

$$E_{total} = \sum_n E_n = \sum_n \sum_j |C_{n,j}|^2 \tag{2}$$

The above equations provide essential information at different frequency bands for characterizing the vibration signal energy distribution.

2.2   Autoencoder

Autoencoder belongs to the family of deep learning architecture in which the dimension of input and output is the same so that it will reconstruct the input at the output stage through intermediate layers with a reduced number of hidden nodes. The basic idea of AE is to compress the input data into a latent-space representation, and then reconstruct the output from this representation. Therefore, the AE network consists of encoder and decoder parts for performing dimensionality reduction and data denoising tasks [29, 30].

In the proposed method, WE is treated as 2D data and therefore, to extract the more significant information for the fault representation by dimensionality reduction, convolutional AE has operated on WE E_i [29]. The encoder assists in determining the reduced hidden representation $\hat{E} \in R^{d_{\hat{E}}}$ by mapping the $E_i \in R^{d_E}$ with the help of the feed-forward process of the network as

$$\hat{E} = \varphi_L \left(\cdots \varphi_2 \left(\varphi_1 \left(E, \delta^{(1)} \right), \delta^{(2)} \right) \cdots, \delta^{(L)} \right) \tag{3}$$

where δ is the learning parameters of a network for each stage L and φ are the various convolutional and pooling operation performed by the network at each L. The decoder reconstructs the $E' \in R^{d_E}$ from $\hat{E}$ as

$$E' = \varphi_1 \left(\cdots \varphi_{L-1} \left(\varphi_L \left(\hat{E}, \delta^{(L)} \right), \delta^{(L-1)} \right) \cdots, \delta^{(1)} \right) \tag{4}$$

Finally, the training of AE is a minimization of error between E, and E' and it is given as

$$\underset{\varphi, \delta}{argmin} \left(E, E' \right) \tag{5}$$

AE illustrates a promising potential to study the meaningful features from E for fault diagnosis.

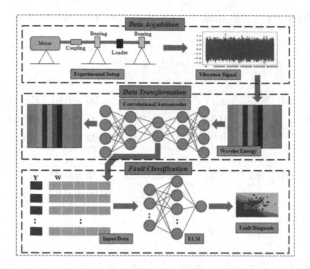

Fig. 1. Proposed method framework.

3 Proposed Method

Several signals generated through machines provide adequate information about the health state of the machine by analyzing them. Therefore, in this paper, a novel bearing fault classification method is proposed by incorporating WE and AE for identifying the distinguishing features, and then various fault patterns are learned by ELM. The proposed bearing fault classification method is manifested in Fig. 1, and it is consists of the following phases: (1) Data acquisition, (2) Feature transformation, and (3) Fault classification.

It has been found in the literature that the vibration data has been utilized extensively for the development of fault diagnosis solutions. As a result, a two bearing vibration set has assisted in testifying the proposed method. The detail information of data acquisition with experimental setup and dataset description as well as analysis is provided in [17, 19, 31–33].

The traditional signal processing methods could not able to handle a large amount of industrial data effectively for identifying the various fault patterns. As a result, it causes a bottleneck for precise and timely evaluation of bearing health conditions. In addition, assuming the idealization and simplifications of vibration data extend the inappropriate review of the bearing health. As an effect, the reliability of the overall bearing health diagnosis system reduces. Therefore, in this paper, to determine the various faults, WE have utilized it as a feature. Hence, in the second stage, the raw data has been transformed into WE. Further, to mine important information about the various defects and improve the fault diagnosis performance, the AE based dimension reduction technique has been operated on WE feature in the data transformation stage. It identifies the more distinguishing features to articulate the various features. The W contains the

Table 1. Performance analysis of the proposed method.

Algorithm	Training accuracy (%)	Testing accuracy (%)	F-score	Computational time (s.)
Dataset-1				
ELM (Sigmoid)	98.33 ± 1.17	96.34 ± 1.08	0.96 ± 0.01	170.11 ± 0.01
ELM (RBF)	98.61 ± 0.54	97.39 ± 0.77	0.97 ± 0.01	167.21 ± 0.01
MLP	96.11 ± 0.0	92.91 ± 0.0	0.92 ± 0.0	165.5 ± 0.01
Dataset-2				
ELM (Sigmoid)	98.13 ± 1.57	95.14 ± 3.27	0.95 ± 0.03	125.71 ± 0.01
ELM (RBF)	98.11 ± 1.1	95.94 ± 1.79	0.96 ± 0.02	125.24 ± 0.01
MLP	90.63 ± 0.0	86.75 ± 0.0	0.86 ± 0.0	125.24 ± 0.01

input data, and Y is the corresponding class label. In the final stage, ELM has trained using W and Y to study the different fault diagnosis patterns.

3.1 Benefits of Proposed Method

- The use of WE as an input feature has reduced the task of constructing the feature space using various signal processing methods.
- Further, there is no need to find promising features from the feature space. As a result, feature extraction and selection process become simple.
- The convolutional AE has assisted in dimension reduction of input data and identifies the more distinguishing feature to represent the fault.
- The use of AE helps in reducing the requirement of L, and hence, small size ELM architecture has been attained by preserving the accuracy of the model.
- In addition, AE has assisted in improving the fault diagnosis performance.

4   Results and Discussion

4.1 Simulation Environment

The two REB datasets are used to verify the effectiveness of the proposed fault diagnosis method. Dataset-1: The machine fault simulator is used to generate the vibration signal under different working conditions in a supervised manner [31] and Dataset-2: Publicly available bearing dataset from Case Western Reserve University (CWRU) [32]. The simulation environment (i7-CPU with the frequency of 3.6 GHz, 8.0-GB RAM, and Ubuntu 16.04 operating system) has setup to analyze the fault diagnosis results. The 50 trails are performed to calculate the average as well as standard deviation value for training and testing performance along with F-score and computational time. The K-fold cross-validation method has been employed to deliver the data partitioning exercise. The AE consists

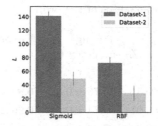

Fig. 2. Value of L for ELM the performance in Table 1.

Table 2. Performance analysis of the proposed method without autoencoder.

Algorithm	Training accuracy (%)	Testing accuracy (%)	F-score	Computational time (s.)
Dataset-1				
ELM (Sigmoid)	93.85 ± 0.81	90.48 ± 1.02	0.90 ± 0.01	2.29 ± 0.01
ELM (RBF)	91.69 ± 0.01	89.37 ± 0.01	0.88 ± 0.0	2.61 ± 0.01
MLP	85.83 ± 0.0	84.31 ± 0.0	0.84 ± 0.0	2.32 ± 0.01
Dataset-2				
ELM (Sigmoid)	90.14 ± 1.57	79.41 ± 2.24	0.79 ± 0.02	0.57 ± 0.01
ELM (RBF)	88.42 ± 0.01	84.11 ± 0.01	0.83 ± 0.0	0.36 ± 0.01
MLP	85.18 ± 0.0	80.81 ± 0.0	0.79 ± 0.0	0.16 ± 0.01

of six layers of convolutional and pooling. The first three layers are used for encoding and the last three for decoding. The bottom layer of encoding obtains the low-level features, and a top layer acquires the high-level features of faults to train the classifier [26]. For the comparison, the stopping RMSE is set to 0.2, and sigmoid as well as RBF type of nodes are considered in ELM [34].

4.2 Result Analysis

Table 1 illustrates the performance of the proposed method. For both the vibration datasets, the ELM demonstrate the training and testing performance respectively of 98.0% and 95.0% with RMSE equal to 0.2. The RBF types of nodes show the acceptable performance in comparison to the sigmoid type of nodes for both the datasets. The best performance of 97.39% has been recorded for the dataset-1 and, similarly, 95.94% for dataset-2. The SD value of performance is around 1.0 for dataset-1 and 2.0 for dataset-2. The F-score values of different algorithms are above 0.95.

Also, the hidden node requirement of a sigmoid node is high compared to RBF nodes, and it is almost 300.0% more in both the datasets as shown in Fig. 2. However, the SD value of L for a sigmoid node is better than RBF nodes, and it is approximately below 10. It is also noted that the computational time

Table 3. Performance analysis of the proposed method with PCA.

Algorithm	Training accuracy (%)	Testing accuracy (%)	F-score	Computational time (s.)
Dataset-1				
ELM (Sigmoid)	98.12 ± 0.51	95.75 ± 0.82	0.95 ± 0.01	5.16 ± 0.01
ELM (RBF)	95.13 ± 0.01	89.74 ± 0.01	0.90 ± 0.0	3.64 ± 0.01
MLP	90.03 ± 0.0	87.73 ± 0.0	0.86 ± 0.0	3.44 ± 0.01
Dataset-1				
ELM (Sigmoid)	92.64 ± 1.18	86.19 ± 0.06	0.86 ± 0.06	3.36 ± 0.01
ELM (RBF)	91.21 ± 0.01	88.16 ± 0.01	0.88 ± 0.0	3.16 ± 0.01
MLP	88.64 ± 0.0	84.16 ± 0.01	0.83 ± 0.0	2.59 ± 0.01

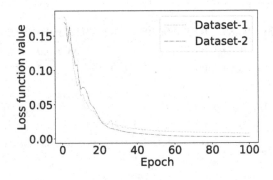

Fig. 3. Training speed comparison of the datasets for autoencoder.

requirement of RBF nodes is less as compared to sigmoid nodes. This impact has been observed due to the less demand for RBF hidden nodes in comparison to sigmoid nodes for achieving similar performance. This effect has been found in both the data sets. In addition, the proposed method has been compared with MLP. Table 1 indicates that the MLP performance is not acceptable in comparison to ELM and it is almost 5.0% to 9.0% less than ELM performance.

Further, to analyze the effect of AE, the WE has been presented as an input to the classifier, and L value for the ELM has been utilized from the Fig. 2 to illustrate the generalize performance for comparison. Table 2 demonstrates the results for the proposed method without the AE step. It has been found that the overall performance has decreased for all the types of nodes. The significant effect has been noticed for the dataset-2 as compared to dataset-1. The total decrement in the training performance is approximately 6.0% and 10.0%, respectively, for the dataset-1 and dataset-2. Similarly, for the testing performance, it has been 6.0% and 15.0%, respectively, for the dataset-1 and dataset-2. The effect of performance degradation has observed on the F-score value. Besides F-score,

Table 4. Statistical feature set performance comparisons of ELM and MLP.

Algorithm	Training accuracy (%)	Testing accuracy (%)	F-score	Computational time (s.)
Dataset-1				
ELM (Sigmoid)	72.83 ± 3.65	65.31 ± 3.92	0.65 ± 0.04	1.78 ± 0.4
ELM (RBF)	78.19 ± 0.28	76.45 ± 0.21	0.76 ± 0.01	1.69 ± 0.01
MLP	35.41 ± 0.18	34.58 ± 0.1	0.29 ± 0.01	1.32 ± 0.17
Dataset-2				
ELM (Sigmoid)	87.09 ± 2.34	78.64 ± 3.91	0.77 ± 0.03	1.18 ± 0.06
ELM (RBF)	87.5 ± 0.1	86.36 ± 0.1	0.85 ± 0.1	0.96 ± 0.02
MLP	39.77 ± 0.08	38.63 ± 0.04	0.38 ± 0.0	0.51 ± 0.1

the computational time of the method without AE is better than the routine with AE.

Further, PCA has been widely utilized to extract sensitive features and reduced feature size in bearing [35]. Therefore, to analyze the effect of AE, the WE has been presented as an input to principal component analysis (PCA), and then to the classifier. L value for the classifier has been utilized from the Table 1 to display the generalize performance for comparison. Table 3 illustrates the results for the proposed method with PCA as a dimension reduction step. It has been notified from the Tables 1, 2 and 3 that the AE and PCA improve the fault diagnosis performance. PCA based proposed method performance is not acceptable in comparison to AE based proposed method. Similar to AE, in PCA based approach, RBF provides better performance than sigmoid nodes. Also, the computational time of the PCA based method is better than the AE-based method. This effect of computational time has seen due to the utilization of various convolutional and pooling layers.

From Tables 1, 2 and 3, it can be concluded that the proposed method reduces the size of ELM architecture. With the same number of L, the method with PCA and without AE has unable to attain a similar performance. Thus, the combined effect of WE and AE has been seen on the overall performance of the system. Also, Fig. 3 demonstrates the training speed of the AE using both the datasets.

In addition, the fault diagnosis system development Samanta and Al-Balushi by utilizing statistical features have been analyzed for the comparison with WE feature set [36]. Tables 1 and 4 indicates that the performance of the proposed method is better than the statistical feature set, and it is improved by 20.0% [19]. Also, the result notifies that the proposed method illustrates the satisfactory results with wavelet energy.

5   Conclusion

In the modern industry, the rotating machinery has been broadly employed for various applications. Therefore, the health monitoring of equipment is an essential task for the overall functioning of the system. Hence, bearing fault classification performance has improved by introducing the wavelet energy as an input feature set in this paper. Also, it simplifies the feature extraction and selection process of fault diagnosis. In addition, it proves the wavelet energy as a useful input feature vector for fault diagnosis. Further, the use of autoencoder has assisted in identifying the promising features from wavelet energy to achieve the small size ELM design by preserving the accuracy of the solution.

Acknowledgement. Authors would like to acknowledge TEQIP-III and TEQIP-II (subcomponent 1.2.1) Centre of Excellence in Complex and Nonlinear Dynamical Systems (CoE-CNDS), VJTI, Mumbai-400019, Maharashtra, India for providing experimental environment.

References

1. Hossain, M.S., Muhammad, G.: Cloud-assisted industrial internet of things (IIoT) - enabled framework for health monitoring. Comput. Netw. **101**, 192–202 (2016)
2. Ren, L., Cheng, X., Wang, X., Cui, J., Zhang, L.: Multi-scale dense gate recurrent unit networks for bearing remaining useful life prediction. Future Gener. Comput. Syst. **94**, 601–609 (2019)
3. Kan, C., Yang, H., Kumara, S.: Parallel computing and network analytics for fast industrial internet-of-things (IIoT) machine information processing and condition monitoring. J. Manuf. Syst. **46**, 282–293 (2018)
4. Bellini, A., Filippetti, F., Tassoni, C., Capolino, G.A.: Advances in diagnostic techniques for induction machines. IEEE Trans. Ind. Electron. **55**(12), 4109–4126 (2008)
5. Henriquez, P., Alonso, J.B., Ferrer, M.A., Travieso, C.M.: Review of automatic fault diagnosis systems using audio and vibration signals. IEEE Trans. Syst. Man Cybern. Syst. **44**(5), 642–652 (2014)
6. Dai, X., Gao, Z.: From model, signal to knowledge: a data-driven perspective of fault detection and diagnosis. IEEE Trans. Ind. Inf. **9**(4), 2226–2238 (2013)
7. Kan, M.S., Tan, A.C., Mathew, J.: A review on prognostic techniques for non-stationary and non-linear rotating systems. Mech. Syst. Sign. Process. **62**, 1–20 (2015)
8. Choudhary, A., Goyal, D., Shimi, S.L., Akula, A.: Condition monitoring and fault diagnosis of induction motors: a review. Arch. Comput. Methods Eng. **26**(4), 1221–1238 (2018)
9. El-Thalji, I., Jantunen, E.: A summary of fault modelling and predictive health monitoring of rolling element bearings. Mech. Syst. Sign. Process. **60**, 252–272 (2015)
10. Marichal, G., Artés, M., Prada, J.G., Casanova, O.: Extraction of rules for faulty bearing classification by a neuro-fuzzy approach. Mech. Syst. Sign. Process. **25**(6), 2073–2082 (2011)
11. Zhang, S., Mathew, J., Ma, L., Sun, Y.: Best basis-based intelligent machine fault diagnosis. Mech. Syst. Sign. Process. **19**(2), 357–370 (2005)
12. Kankar, P., Sharma, S.C., Harsha, S.: Fault diagnosis of ball bearings using continuous wavelet transform. Appl. Soft Comput. **11**(2), 2300–2312 (2011)
13. Kankar, P., Sharma, S.C., Harsha, S.P.: Rolling element bearing fault diagnosis using wavelet transform. Neurocomputing **74**(10), 1638–1645 (2011)

14. Udmale, S.S., Singh, S.K.: A mechanical data analysis using kurtogram and extreme learning machine. Neural Comput. Appl. 1–13 (2019). https://doi.org/ 10.1007/s00521-019-04398-0
15. Soualhi, A., Medjaher, K., Zerhouni, N.: Bearing health monitoring based on Hilbert-Huang transform, support vector machine, and regression. IEEE Trans. Instrum. Meas. **64**(1), 52–62 (2015)
16. Liu, J., Wang, W., Golnaraghi, F.: An enhanced diagnostic scheme for bearing condition monitoring. IEEE Trans. Instrum. Meas. **59**(2), 309–321 (2010)
17. Udmale, S.S., Patil, S.S., Phalle, V.M., Singh, S.K.: A bearing vibration data analysis based on spectral kurtosis and ConvNet. Soft. Comput. **23**(19), 1–19 (2019)
18. Udmale, S.S., Singh, S.K., Singh, R., Sangaiah, A.K.: Multi-fault bearing classification using sensors and ConvNet-based transfer learning approach. IEEE Sens. J. 1–12 (2019). https://doi.org/10.1109/JSEN.2019.2947026
19. Udmale, S.S., Singh, S.K., Bhirud, S.G.: A bearing data analysis based on kurtogram and deep learning sequence models. Measurement **145**, 665–677 (2019)
20. Tao, J., Liu, Y., Yang, D.: Bearing fault diagnosis based on deep belief network and multisensor information fusion. Shock Vibr. **2016**, 9 (2016)
21. Chen, Z., Li, C., Sanchez, R.V.: Gearbox fault identification and classification with convolutional neural networks. Shock Vibr. **2015**, 10 (2015)
22. Lu, C., Wang, Z., Zhou, B.: Intelligent fault diagnosis of rolling bearing using hierarchical convolutional network based health state classification. Adv. Eng. Inf. **32**, 139–151 (2017)
23. Li, C., Sánchez, R.V., Zurita, G., Cerrada, M., Cabrera, D.: Fault diagnosis for rotating machinery using vibration measurement deep statistical feature learning. Sensors **16**(6), 895 (2016)
24. Chen, Z., Deng, S., Chen, X., Li, C., Sanchez, R.V., Qin, H.: Deep neural networks-based rolling bearing fault diagnosis. Microelectron. Reliab. **75**, 327–333 (2017)
25. Dhamande, L.S., Chaudhari, M.B.: Compound gear-bearing fault feature extraction using statistical features based on time-frequency method. Measurement **125**, 63–77 (2018)
26. Shao, H., Jiang, H., Li, X., Wu, S.: Intelligent fault diagnosis of rolling bearing using deep wavelet auto-encoder with extreme learning machine. Knowl. Based Syst. **140**, 1–14 (2018)
27. Zhang, X., Yan, Q., Yang, J., Zhao, J., Shen, Y.: An assembly tightness detection method for bolt-jointed rotor with wavelet energy entropy. Measurement **136**, 212–224 (2019)
28. Pan, Y., Zhang, L., Wu, X., Zhang, K., Skibniewski, M.J.: Structural health monitoring and assessment using wavelet packet energy spectrum. Saf. Sci. **120**, 652–665 (2019)
29. Goodfellow, I., Bengio, Y., Courville, A.: Deep Learning. MIT Press, Cambridge (2016)
30. Wang, W., Huang, Y., Wang, Y., Wang, L.: Generalized autoencoder: a neural network framework for dimensionality reduction. In: 2014 IEEE Conference on Computer Vision and Pattern Recognition Workshops, pp. 496–503, June 2014
31. Udmale, S.S., Singh, S.K.: Application of spectral kurtosis and improved extreme learning machine for bearing fault classification. IEEE Trans. Instrum. Meas. **68**(11), 1–12 (2019)
32. CWRU: Case Western Reserve University Bearing Data Center Website (2009). https://csegroups.case.edu/bearingdatacenter/home

33. Smith, W.A., Randall, R.B.: Rolling element bearing diagnostics using the Case Western Reserve University data: a benchmark study. Mech. Syst. Sig. Process. **64–65**, 100–131 (2015)
34. Huang, G.B., Chen, L., Siew, C.K.: Universal approximation using incremental constructive feedforward networks with random hidden nodes. IEEE Trans. Neural Netw. **17**(4), 879–892 (2006)
35. Dong, S., Luo, T.: Bearing degradation process prediction based on the PCA and optimized LS-SVM model. Measurement **46**(9), 3143–3152 (2013)
36. Samanta, B., Al-Balushi, K.: Artificial neural network based fault diagnostics of rolling element bearings using time-domain features. Mech. Syst. Sig. Process. **17**(2), 317–328 (2003)

Social Networks, Machine Learning and Mobile Networks

Community Detection in Social Networks Using Deep Learning

M. Dhilber[1] and S. Durga Bhavani[2]([⊠])

[1] School of Computer and Information Sciences,
University of Hyderabad, Telangana, India
dilber.dillu@gmail.com
[2] University of Hyderabad, Telangana, India
sdbcs@uohyd.ernet.in

Abstract. Community structure is found everywhere from simple networks to real world complex networks. The problem of community detection is to predict clusters of nodes that are densely connected among themselves. The task of community detection has a wide variety of applications ranging from recommendation systems, advertising, marketing, epidemic spreading, cancer detection etc. The two mainly existing approaches for community detection, namely, stochastic block model and modularity maximization model focus on building a low dimensional network embedding to reconstruct the original network structure. However the mapping to low dimensional space in these methods is purely linear. Understanding the fact that real world networks contain non-linear structures in abundance, aforementioned methods become less practical for real world networks. Considering the nonlinear representation power of deep neural networks, several solutions based on autoencoders are being proposed in the recent literature. In this work, we propose a deep neural network architecture for community detection wherein we stack multiple autoencoders and apply parameter sharing. This method of training autoencoders has been successfully applied for the problems of link prediction and node classification in the literature. Our enhanced model with modified architecture produced better results compared to many other existing methods. We tested our model on a few benchmark datasets and obtained competitive results.

Keywords: Community detection · Social networks · Deep learning · Modularity · Autoencoders

1 Introduction

In this increasingly interlinked world, studying and analyzing relationships and patterns in networks gains tremendous importance. Detecting community structures in networks is an important problem in social network analysis. There have been a fair number of approaches for achieving this task proposed in the literature. Traditional approaches to community detection can be broadly classified

© Springer Nature Switzerland AG 2020
D. V. Hung and M. D'Souza (Eds.): ICDCIT 2020, LNCS 11969, pp. 241–250, 2020.
https://doi.org/10.1007/978-3-030-36987-3_15

into node/link based [16] and matrix based methods [18]. These involve Hierarchical clustering, Cut-based partitioning and those that use properties of random walks. A comprehensive survey of these huge number of algorithms proposed in the literature have been presented by Fortunato in [7]. Newman [8] proposed a measure called modularity which is based on the difference between the number of edges within communities and expected number of edges in overall network. This is a widely accepted measure and has been used by most of the algorithms to evaluate the performance of the community prediction algorithms.

Recently a whole new approach is being taken to solve the problems of social network analysis, using deep neural networks (DNN) [4]. One of the major advantages of this approach is its novel and highly effective node as well as graph representation ability [10]. Deep neural networks help in learning a latent low-dimensional embedding for a node in a graph in such a way that two similar nodes in the graph would have vector representations that are closer in the embedding space. Perozzi et al. [17] use random walks to learn embedding by considering random walks as equivalent to sentences for language representation problem. DNN Autoencoders learn the hierarchical mappings between the original network and for example, the latent cluster structures, with implicit low-to-high level hidden attributes of the original network learnt in the intermediate layers in achieving community detection and related tasks [10,20,21]. Node embeddings have been applied for other important problems in social network analysis, namely, link prediction and node classification which have wide applications [20]. We focus on the problem of community detection. This problem finds major applications which include, detecting suspicious groups in a network, recommending products or services, targeted marketing, epidemic spread control, cancer detection etc.

Our work is closely related to that of Yang et al. [21], who used modularity matrix innovatively to propose a new method for community detection in which network embeddings have been used to detect communities. We adopt a stacked autoencoder architecture and a different training scheme that was successfully used for problems like link prediction. Further we apply parameter sharing across layers for a faster implementation of the deep neural network.

2   Related Literature

2.1   Background

Machine learning on graphs is one of the pivotal areas that has applications ranging across multiple domains. The interconnectivity of nodes in graphs, that models the real world interactions makes graphs ubiquitous in several applications. One of the primary challenges in this field is to transform graphs to formats which can then be directly used for downstream machine learning tasks. Several approaches including Matrix Factorization, Random Walk based and Graph Neural Networks have been proposed. The classical methods use traditional network statistical measures like centrality, closeness etc. and network embedding based methods use non-linear algorithms like deep neural networks.

2.2   Representation Based Methods

Recently there is a hype about network embedding based approaches in solving community detection and related problems.

Advent of Deepwalk in 2014 [17] has given a new face to graph representation learning. In Deepwalk, Perozzi et al. compare word sequences to random walks starting at a vertex. These random walks are used to learn network topology information. This work has inspired a lot of research since it gives key ideas that join language modelling and vertex representation. They model small random walks at graph vertices to learn representation. These learned representations include neighbourhood information, community membership and vertex resemblance. This information is encoded as a vector which is used for multiple machine learning tasks. In short, Deepwalk model takes a network as input and gives a representation vector with its information encoded. There are multiple advantages in using random walks. This representation gives the flexibility to explore different parts of the network and makes the model more adaptive to small changes without overall recomputation. Deepwalk uses skipgram as language model to calculate occurrence probability of words within a frame. Algorithm is also scalable to large datasets and performs exceptionally well on even sparse datasets.

An improved approach of Deepwalk called Node2vec [9] implements a biased random walk which explores diverse neighborhoods. The authors claim that a much richer representation can be learned by making the random walks biased. The key idea behind *Node2vec* is to learn the topological structure based on vertex network neighborhood. This is achieved by carefully organizing a bunch of biased random walks. This provides the flexibility of exploring diverse neighborhoods which in turn results in better representation.

Kipf et al. [14] apply convolutional neural networks (CNN) directly on graph structured data to encode features. Jia et al. [12] make use of Generative Adversarial Networks to obtain representations with membership strength of vertices in communities and solves overlapping community detection problem. Phi et al. [20] build autoencoders with tied weights for multitask learning of link prediction and node classification. Hamilton et al. [10] introduced an inductive framework to generate node embedding for unseen networks by modelling a neighborhood aggregation function.

3   Approaches to Community Detection Problem

Solutions to the problem of community detection can be broadly classified as those based on Modularity maximization model [6] and Stochastic model [4, 11, 13]. Modularity maximization model introduced by Newman in 2006 proposes to maximize the modularity function Q, where modularity Q is defined as difference between number of edges within community and the expected number of edges over all pair of vertices.

$$Q = \frac{1}{4m} \sum_{i,j} (A(i,j) - \frac{k_i k_j}{2m})(h_i h_j)$$

$$= \frac{1}{4m} h^T B h$$

Here h is the community membership vector with $h_i = 1$ or -1 to denote the two different communities, k_i denotes the degree of node i, B is the modularity matrix and m is the total number of edges in network.

In the Stochastic model approach, community detection is formulated as Non Negative Matrix Factorization problem (NMF). This approach aims to find a non-negative membership matrix H to reconstruct adjacency matrix A. Yang et al. [21] demonstrate that both Modularity maximization and Stochastic model formulations can be interpreted as finding low dimensional representations to best reconstruct new structure. They further show that mapping of networks to lower dimensions is purely linear, which makes them less practical for real world networks and hence propose a non-linear solution using autoencoders [4].

4   Deep Learning Approach to Community Detection

The basic idea adopted in the literature [20] is to substitute factorization based reconstruction methods with non-linear models like autoencoders. In the following sections we introduce autoencoder and discuss these models in detail.

4.1   Autoencoder

An autoencoder is a deep neural network architecture composed of encoder and decoder. The encoder part compresses the data to a lower dimension trying to preserve maximum information. On the other side, decoder expands the compressed code to reproduce output with maximum similarity as input. The main application of autoencoders is in dimensionality reduction and embedding learning. Here the autoencoders are used as non-linear reconstruction models. Figure 1 depicts a typical autoencoder architecture.

Autoencoders use backpropagation algorithm to learn the weights. For reconstruction, target values are set to be same as the input values and the error is backpropagated. Considering input modularity matrix $B = [b_{ij}]$, b_i represents vertex at column i. At encoder side for the encoded embedding E we have,

$$e_i = a(W_E b_i + d_E)$$

where W_E and d_E are the neural network weights (parameters) to be learnt, b_i is the input and a is the activation function.

At the decoder side for the decoded embedding D we have,

$$d_i = a(W_D e_i + d_D)$$

where W_D and d_D are the parameters, e_i is the encoded input and a is another activation function.

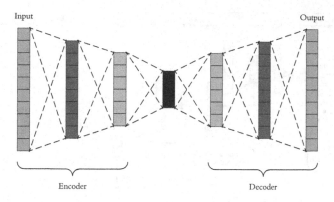

Fig. 1. Autoencoder architecture [2,4].

4.2 Model of Yang et al.

Yang et al. [21] are among the first researchers to apply deep learning (DL) approach to the community detection problem. Idea of reconstruction in both modularity maximization model and stochastic models is well explored by Yang et al. They chose autoencoder as a substitute tool for reconstruction mechanism required here. They construct a DL model by connecting autoencoders in series to obtain parameter optimization. They train the first autoencoder to reduce reconstruction error, take new representation obtained from the first autoencoder and give it to the next one and so on. Figure 2 depicts layer by layer training scheme model of Yang et al. In order to obtain communities in the final step, K-means algorithm is used to cluster the vertex embeddings.

5 Proposed Model

We follow a similar approach of Yang et al. as described above. The key differences between our model and that of [21] are, first, we stack the autoencoder layers together, not in series, and perform common training to all the layers instead of training each autoencoder separately. Secondly, we apply parameter sharing across layers to control the parameter growth and obtain optimization. This method of weight tying was successfully applied by [20] in solving link prediction and node classification problems simultaneously.

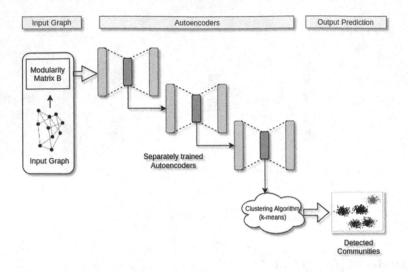

Fig. 2. Model of Yang et al.

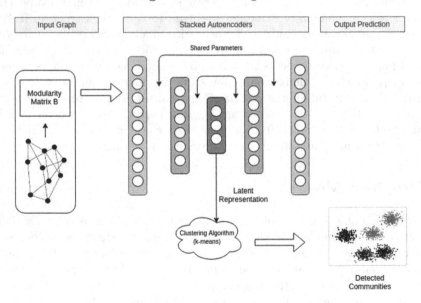

Fig. 3. Architecture of the proposed model.

5.1   Method

The architecture of the proposed method is given in Fig. 3 which is discussed in this section. First an autoencoder model with a common 2 layer architecture is built with varied layer configurations depending on datasets. We train the autoencoder for multiple iterations to reduce the reconstruction error. The modularity matrix of the input graph network is given as input to the autoencoder and a low dimensional representation of the corresponding network is obtained. Community detection is carried out by applying a clustering algorithm (K-means in this case) to the obtained representation. The intuition behind such an idea is, since we could reconstruct the entire network with this low dimensional representation, any downstream machine learning task applied to this low dimensional representation is equivalent in applying to the entire network. More importantly, the reconstructed network is supposed to better represent the latent structures of the original network.

In Yang et al. [21], each layer is pretrained one at a time to minimize the error. This training approach for parameter optimization is motivated from [19], where they stack the layers of denoising autoencoders, train them layer by layer and shows its efficiency. As an alternative to this, we chose weight tying (or parameter sharing) as optimization method, in which weights are shared across the layers and a common weight matrix will be updated during backpropogation.

5.2   Experimental Setup

For implementation[1] we used python 3.7 and chose keras as deep learning library. We used keras custom layer feature to build layers capable of weight tying. We considered *adam* as optimizer and *relu* as activation function. As loss function we chose *sigmoid-cross entropy* and added 20% dropout to each layer. We trained each autoencoder to atmost 50,000 iterations to reduce the reconstruction error. For each network, a layer configuration that fits in 2 layer architecture has been chosen, which in turn gave flexibility of adopting our model to networks of different ranges. For a particular network, a one-step training of stacked layer autoencoder is done instead of layerwise training of multiple autoencoders as done by [21]. This in fact reduces training time and effort. Figure 4 depicts the gradual decrease in loss with respect to the number of epochs for all datasets except *Polblogs*, in which the loss decreases exponentially.

5.3   Evaluation Measure

Normalized Mutual Information (NMI) is used as the evaluation measure here. NMI is the quality measure value between 0 and 1 which indicates how much two clusters are correlated. A 0 value indicates no mutual information and 1 indicates perfect correlation. NMI is defined as,

$$NMI(Y, C) = \frac{2 \times I(Y; C)}{H(Y) + H(C)}$$

where Y is the class label, C is the clustering label, H() is the entropy and I(Y;C) is the mutual information between Y and C. In our case, each of the output cluster of our model is compared with ground truth value of the network.

---

[1] https://github.com/dilberdillu/community-detection-DL.

Table 1. Comparative performance of the proposed deep architecture for community detection: NMI values obtained for the bench mark real world networks

Dataset	Layer configuration	N	m	K	SP	FUA	FN	DNR	This model
Polbooks	105-64-32	105	441	3	0.561	0.574	0.531	0.582	**0.600**
Polblogs	1490-256-128	1490	16718	2	0.511	0.375	0.499	0.517	**0.533**
Dolphin	62-32-16	62	159	4	0.753	0.516	0.572	0.818	**0.830**
Football	115-64-32	115	613	12	0.334	0.890	0.698	**0.914**	0.904

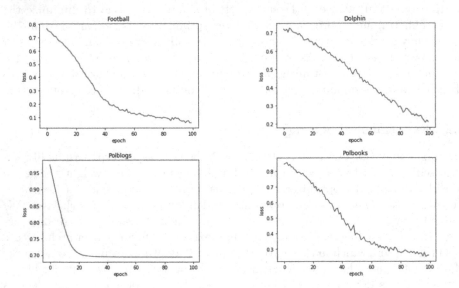

Fig. 4. Comparison of loss with respect to the number of epochs for different datasets

6   Results and Evaluation

We compared the NMI results obtained by the proposed model with the recent deep learning model DNR of Yang et al. [21]. Further the comparison is done with the other existing community detection methods like FN [5] and the spectral method SP of Newman et al. [6] and the fast unfolding of communities algorithm of Blondel et al. FUA [3]. Our model is tested on 4 benchmark datasets [1, 8, 15]. The standard measure of NMI is used as a quality measure to assess the clustering obtained. In Table 1, second column contains the layer configuration of the stacked autoencoder architecture, N and m refer to the number of nodes, edges respectively and K is the ground truth number of communities that we have used in the experiment.

From Table 1, it can be seen that for the datasets of *Polbooks*, *Polblogs* and *Dolphin* networks, the proposed model performs much better than the existing algorithms, and with slightly improved results over the deep learning model DNR of Yang et al. and we have a close margin on the *Football* network with DNR [21].

7 Conclusion

In this paper we proposed an improved method that solves the problem of community detection. Unlike existing methods that uses autoencoders, we use shared weights across layers and followed a common 2 layer architecture with one-step layer stacked training. Experiments on multiple datasets have shown that the proposed model performs better than the existing state of the art methods in community detection. Our work delivers a convenient framework with a flexibility of adopting the model to networks of different sizes with reduced training time for community detection. For future work, we plan to extend our model and apply it on larger datasets. Our focus will be on scaling as well as improving the model at the same time.

References

1. Adamic, L.A.: The political blogosphere and the 2004 U.S. election: divided they blog. In: Proceedings of the 3rd International Workshop on Link Discovery, April 2005
2. Baldi, P.: Autoencoders, unsupervised learning, and deep architectures. In: JMLR: Workshop and Conference Proceedings, vol. 27, pp. 37–50 (2012)
3. Blondel, V., Guillaume, J.L., Lambiotte, R., Lefebvre, E.: Fast unfolding of communities in large networks. J. Stat. Mech. Theory Exp. **2008** (2008)
4. Hinton, G.E., Zemel, R.S.: Autoencoders, minimum description length and Helmholtz free energy. In: Advances in Neural Information Processing Systems, vol. 6, February 1994
5. Newman, M.E.J.: Fast algorithm for detecting community structure in networks. Phys. Rev. E **69**, 066133 (2004). Statistical, nonlinear, and soft matter physics
6. Newman, M.E.J.: Modularity and community structure in networks. Proc. Natl. Acad. Sci. U.S.A. **103**, 8577–8582 (2006)
7. Fortunato, S.: Community detection in graphs. Phys. Rep. **486**, 3–5, 75–174 (2010)
8. Girvan, M., Newman, M.E.J.: Community structure in social and biological networks. Proc. Natl. Acad. Sci. **99**, 7821–7826 (2001)
9. Grover, A., Leskovec, J.: Node2vec: scalable feature learning for networks. In: Proceedings of the 22nd ACM SIGKDD International Conference on Knowledge Discovery and Data Mining, KDD 2016, pp. 855–864. ACM, New York, NY, USA (2016)
10. Hamilton, W.L., Ying, Z., Leskovec, J.: Representation learning on graphs: methods and applications. IEEE Data Eng. Bull. **40**, 52–74 (2017)
11. He, D., Liu, D., Jin, D., Zhang, W.: A stochastic model for detecting heterogeneous link communities in complex networks. In: AAAI (2015)
12. Jia, Y., Zhang, Q., Zhang, W., Wang, X.: CommunityGAN: community detection with generative adversarial nets, January 2019
13. Jin, D., Chen, Z., He, D., Zhang, W.: Modeling with node degree preservation can accurately find communities. In: AAAI (2015)
14. Kipf, T.N., Welling, M.: Semi-supervised classification with graph convolutional networks. CoRR (2016)
15. Lusseau, D., Newman, M.: Identifying the role that animals play in their social networks. Proc. Biol. Sci. **271**(Suppl 6), S477–S481 (2004)

16. Newman, M.: Networks: An Introduction. Oxford University Press, Oxford (2010)
17. Perozzi, B., Al-Rfou, R., Skiena, S.: Deepwalk: online learning of social representations. In: Proceedings of the ACM SIGKDD International Conference on Knowledge Discovery and Data Mining, March 2014
18. Psorakis, I., Roberts, S., Ebden, M., Sheldon, B.: Overlapping community detection using Bayesian non-negative matrix factorization. Phys. Rev. E **83**, 066114 (2011). Statistical, nonlinear, and soft matter physics
19. Vincent, P., Larochelle, H., Lajoie, I., Bengio, Y., Manzagol, P.A.: Stacked denoising autoencoders: learning useful representations in a deep network with a local denoising criterion. J. Mach. Learn. Res. **11**, 3371–3408 (2010)
20. Vu Tran, P.: Learning to make predictions on graphs with autoencoders. CoRR abs/1802.08352, pp. 237–245, October 2018
21. Yang, L., Cao, X., He, D., Wang, C., Wang, X., Zhang, W.: Modularity based community detection with deep learning. In: Proceedings of the Twenty-Fifth International Joint Conference on Artificial Intelligence, IJCAI 2016, New York, NY, USA, 9–15 July 2016, pp. 2252–2258, January 2016

Multi-Winner Heterogeneous Spectrum Auction Mechanism for Channel Allocation in Cognitive Radio Networks

Monisha Devi$^{(\boxtimes)}$, Nityananda Sarma, and Sanjib K. Deka

Department of Computer Science and Engineering, Tezpur University,
Tezpur 784028, Assam, India
mnshdevi@gmail.com, {nitya,sdeka}@tezu.ernet.in

Abstract. Fair allocation of unused licensed spectrum among preferable secondary users (SUs) is an important feature to be supported by Cognitive Radio (CR) for its successful deployment. This paper proposes an auction theoretic model for spectrum allocation by incorporating different constraints of a CR network and intents to achieve an effective utilization of the radio spectrum. We consider heterogeneous channel condition which allows SUs to express their preference of channels in terms of bid values. A sealed-bid concurrent bidding policy is implemented which collects bids from SUs while dealing with variation in availability time of the auctioned channels. The proposed model develops a truthful winner determination algorithm which exploits spectrum reusability as well as restraints to dynamics in spectrum opportunities amongst SUs. Allowing multiple non-interfering SUs to utilize a common channel significantly helps to achieve an improved spectrum utility. However, every SU acquires at most one channel. The proposed model also develops a pricing algorithm which helps the auctioneer to earn a revenue from every wining bidder. Simulation based results demonstrate the effectiveness in performance of the proposed model in terms of spectrum utilization compared to the general concurrent auction model.

Keywords: Cognitive Radio · Auction theory · Spectrum opportunities · Secondary user · Primary user

1 Introduction

Fast expansion in the deployment of wireless technologies creates insufficiency of radio spectrum amongst users. On the other side, Federal Communications Commission (FCC) [1] declares that a bulk of licensed spectrum are left unused by their legitimate owners which generates dynamically available spectrum holes. Therefore, both the spectrum scarcity and spectrum under-utilization problems demand a new technology which can efficiently utilize the radio spectrum. Advances in dynamic spectrum access (DSA) [2] techniques results in the development of a novel technology called Cognitive Radio (CR) [3–5]. With its opportunistic behaviour, CR permits the secondary users (or unlicensed users) to utilize the idle licensed spectrum without harming the primary users (or licensed

© Springer Nature Switzerland AG 2020
D. V. Hung and M. D'Souza (Eds.): ICDCIT 2020, LNCS 11969, pp. 251–265, 2020.
https://doi.org/10.1007/978-3-030-36987-3_16

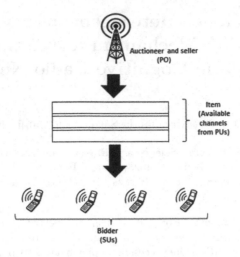

Fig. 1. Single-sided auction scenario in CRN

users) with destructive interference. To efficiently carry out spectrum allocation amongst secondary users (SUs), CR formulates different allocation models [6,7]. Among them, auction [8,9] has been widely accepted to provide a fair channel allocation since every bidder in the game gets an equal chance to win.

Auction-based approaches for spectrum allocation in a CR network (CRN) considers primary owner (PO) of the network as the auctioneer. In a single-sided auction, it is the PO who leases the channels of the primary users (PUs) to obtain some financial benefit. PUs are not involved in the game. As such, PO acts both as seller and auctioneer, whereas SUs act as bidders. Channels left unused are the items which are to be auctioned with proper valuation from SUs. Figure 1 shows a single-sided auction scenario in CRN. With a sealed-bid policy, SUs submit their bid values privately to the auctioneer. This reduces the communication overhead since no bidder gets to know the bidding strategies of other bidders. To refrain from market manipulations, it is necessary to design a truthful auction where no bidder can improve its utility with an untruthful bid. In CRN, dynamics in spectrum opportunities (SOPs) is an important concern due to which every SU may not sense the same set of available channels. Also, each channel at an SU may have a different channel availability time. If bid submission from the SUs takes into account the channel availability time, then disturbances during data transmission of SUs due to the return of PUs over their owned channels can be avoided. Previous research works on auction mechanism in CRN [10–19] do not incorporate the points for varying channel availability time and dynamics in SOPs. To improve the spectrum utilization and the profit of PO, spectrum reuse can be applied where non-interfering SUs are simultaneously assigned a common channel. Hence, with these motivations, we focus on developing a single-sided auction mechanism that supports CR network constraints and performs single-unit-multi-user allocation.

In this paper, we propose a multi-winner spectrum allocation mechanism which deploys a single-sided auction framework. The single-unit-single-user spectrum allocation discussed in [10] is extended in this work to provide a better utilization of the radio spectrum. Channels available for auction are considered to be heterogeneous with respect to their maximum allowable transmission power. SUs being the bidders in the game decide their true valuations for the channels while considering heterogeneous channel condition, dynamics in SOPs and availability time of channels. Accordingly, each SU shows a preference on submitting the bids for its available channels. Spectrum reusability in the model allows geographically separated SUs to access a common channel. As such, single-unit-multi-user allocation is applied where one channel can be allocated to more than one non-interfering SUs at a time, but one SU can get at most one channel at a time. Finally, the auctioneer develops the winner determination and pricing algorithms which can achieve an effective spectrum allocation amongst SUs and are proven to be individually rational and truthful. Simulations are carried out to evaluate the performance of the proposed auction model where a comparison with the general concurrent auction model is performed.

The rest of the paper is organized as follows. In Sect. 2, we perform a literature review of the existing works. Section 3 gives a brief description of the proposed auction model. Experimental analysis is discussed in Sect. 4. Finally, we conclude the paper in Sect. 5 along with future works.

2   Related Works

Auction provides a fair platform for allocation of the scarce radio resource. Both single-sided and double-sided auctions efficiently allow SUs to dynamically share the licensed spectrum. In double-sided auction [11,12], PUs act as sellers and they fix certain ask values to sell their channels. An SU can win a channel only if its bid is greater than the ask value. As such, certain channels may remain unassigned since ask values are not known to the SUs while bidding. This reduces the spectrum utilization in double-sided auction. In single-sided auction, almost all channels get assigned on satisfying the network constraints. Wang et al. in [13] designs an auction where bidders request for bandwidth from the PUs. Nash equilibrium can be achieved to obtain the solution of the auction game in both single-PU and multiple-PU scenarios. In [14], the auction model uses a bipartite graph to represent bidders and available heterogeneous channels. Maximal weight matching algorithm has been implemented to assign one channel to a single SU such that spectrum utilization is maximized. Another spectrum allocation model SATYA in [15] develops an auction algorithm for both shared and exclusive-use agents where bucketing and ironing techniques are deployed and right to access the channels are provided in discrete intervals of time. In another auction mechanism [16], Gao et al. introduces a quality discrimination spectrum trading where channels are characterized by their channel capacity and accordingly bidders offer quality-price combinations. A feasible contract is established that assigns channels to appropriate consumer types such that

PO's revenue is maximized. In [17], a multi-item highest price sealed auction is designed which formulates an algorithm based on first-price auction. Every SU in the game can bid and win only one channel at a time. To solve the revenue maximization problem, authors in [18] introduced a revenue generation approach where bidders follow virtual valuation to get to a sub-optimal solution. Chen et al. in their designed model in [19], applies the first-price and second-price auctions where SUs bid for transmission time slots to get the channels which differ due to fading and changing traffic conditions. Packet deadline checking and loser bonus schemes are combined with the auction mechanism to improve the system efficiency and revenue.

Literature study on single-sided auctions in CRN reveal that while developing the auction mechanisms for the channel allocation problem, researchers have not addressed the CR network constraints which would provide a better utilization of the spectrum in CR environment. However, authors in [10] designed a single-sided sequential bidding auction for single-unit-single-user allocation where channel availability time is taken care of for the homogeneous channels. By introducing the concept on spectrum reuse among non-interfering SUs, we can except a greater utility of the radio spectrum. Also, it is more practical to allow channels to be heterogeneous in their quality which then uses the concurrent bidding policy for the bid submission process. In this paper, we propose an auction model which handles different issues of the CR network and incorporates spectrum reuse to boost the overall spectrum utilization across the network.

3   Multi-winner Heterogeneous Spectrum Auction

In this section, we provide an overview of the proposed model and discuss the economic properties for truthfulness and individual rationality.

3.1   System Model

Auction applied for channel allocation in a CR environment takes SUs as bidders, PO as auctioneer and unused channels as the item offered for lease. We consider a CR network coexisting with a primary network where N number of SUs, $\mathcal{N} = \{1, 2, 3, ..., N\}$, are willing to obtain any of the M channels, $\mathcal{M} = \{1, 2, 3, ..., M\}$, left unused by PUs. We assume $N > M$. Owing to dynamics in SOPs, all available channels may not be sensed by every SU. This is due to differences in SU capabilities [20]. A channel availability matrix, $C = \{c_{ij} | c_{ij} \in \{0, 1\}\}_{N \times M}$, shows the channels sensed as available by the SUs. $c_{ij} = 1$ implies that idle channel j is available to SU i, otherwise $c_{ij} = 0$. To represent the geographically separated SUs, an interference matrix, $X = \{x_{ik} | x_{ik} \in \{0, 1\}\}_{N \times N}$, is used where $x_{ik} = 1$ if SUs i and k are within the interference range of each other and cannot be assigned a common channel simultaneously, otherwise $x_{ik} = 0$. In CRN, if a PU wants to get back to its licensed channel, the SU using the channel has to release it. Under such circumstance, transmission of the SU may get disturbed. To provide a seamless data transmission amongst SUs, channel availability time

[21] plays an essential role. For a channel, the availability time is approximately same for all SUs who can sense the channel. Considering $T_{A(j)}$ as the channel availability time of channel j and $T_{R(ij)}$ as the channel requirement time of SU i on using channel j, SU i bids for the channel j only when $T_{A(j)} \geq T_{R(ij)}$. We assume that the transmission time and the propagation delay together helps to compute the channel requirement time. To obtain the transmission time over channel j, message size of SU i and data rate used over channel j are considered. Distance to the receiver from SU i and propagation speed gives the propagation delay. Therefore, the bid value from an SU on auctioning some channel is the data rate which the SU would use for its transmission over the channel. Moreover, with the channels being heterogeneous with respect to their maximum allowable transmission power, $\mathcal{P}_j$ represents the power allowed over channel j. So, the channel capacity, $\mathcal{H}_{ij}$, of channel j for SU i can be computed as given in Eq. 1.

$$\mathcal{H}_{ij} = W \log_2(1 + \mathcal{P}_j \cdot \tfrac{P_{L(i)}}{I_i + \sigma^2}) \tag{1}$$

where, channel bandwidth, W, and noise variance σ^2 for all channels are same, $P_{L(i)}$ is the path loss factor between SU i's transmitter and the receiver and I_i is the interference from primary network. In previous works [14,16], the auctioneer selects the SU having highest channel capacity as the winner. But, the wining SU may not use a good amount of data rate from the channel. For instance, $S1$ and $S2$ are two SUs with channel capacity 5 Kbps and 4 Kbps respectively. Accordingly, $S1$ wins the channel. But, $S1$ uses a data rate of 2.5 Kbps whereas $S2$ would use a data rate of 2.8 Kbps. So, if the winner determination scheme chooses $S2$ as winner, spectrum utilization would be more. In this work, we therefore consider the data rate which SU will use for its transmission as the bid value. On auctioning the channels, SU i plans a valuation v_{ji} for a channel j by taking into consideration $T_{A(j)}$ and $T_{R(ij)}$. However, SU i bids for the channel j only when the channel is available at the SU. That is, when $c_{ij} = 1$. Initially, $T_{R(ij)}$ is computed using the channel capacity $\mathcal{H}_{ij}$ obtained from Eq. 1. Further, the data rate as v_{ji} is decided based on one of the following conditions given in Eq. 2.

$$v_{ji} = \begin{cases} 0 & \text{if } c_{ij} = 0 \\ 0 & \text{if } (c_{ij} = 1) \wedge (T_{R(ij)} > T_{A(j)}) \\ \mathcal{H}_{ij} & \text{if } (c_{ij} = 1) \wedge (T_{R(ij)} = T_{A(j)}) \\ < \mathcal{H}_{ij} & \text{if } (c_{ij} = 1) \wedge (T_{R(ij)} < T_{A(j)}), \text{ but } v_{ji} \text{ is} \\ & \text{chosen s.t. } T_{A(j)} \geq T_{R(ij)} \text{ continues to hold} \end{cases} \tag{2}$$

Since truthful bidding strategy has been incorporated to avoid any market manipulation, bid value b_{ji} from SU i for channel j is equal to the valuation v_{ji}, i.e., $b_{ji} = v_{ji}$. So, we get a bid vector $B_j = \{b_{j1}, b_{j2}, ..., b_{jN}\}$ for channel j. For M channels, bid vectors formed are B_1, B_2, ..., B_M. On applying concurrent bidding, every SU simultaneously submits the bids for all its available channels. This constructs a bid matrix, $\mathcal{B} = (B_1, B_2, ..., B_M)$, which holds the bid vectors of all channels. Concurrent bidding policy allows an SU to choose its most preferred channel in terms of its bid. When sequential bidding is followed as in [10], an SU bids for the auctioned channel and on winning the channel the SU-channel pair does not further participate in the auction. However, when channels are heterogeneous, a winner SU may find a more favourable channel in successive auction rounds, but it cannot bid for the channel since it has already won one. Such a situation can be handled using concurrent bidding. A reserve price, r, is chosen by the PO according to Eq. 3 so that PO can earn a minimal price value on leasing the channels.

$$r \leq \min\{b_{ji} \in \mathcal{B}\} \quad \text{s.t. } b_{ji} \neq 0, r \neq 0 \tag{3}$$

Every winning bidder (SU) i pays a price, p_i, to the auctioneer which is determined from the pricing algorithm. This gives a payment vector $P = (p_1, p_2, ..., p_N)$ where $p_i = 0$ when no channel is allocated to SU i. PO benefits from the auction by earning a revenue, $\mathcal{R}$, as given in Eq. 4.

$$\mathcal{R} = \sum_{i=1}^{N} p_i \tag{4}$$

An allocation matrix, $\mathcal{A} = \{a_{ij} | a_{ij} \in \{0,1\}\}_{N \times M}$, represents the channel allocation patterns among the SUs by restricting to single-unit-multi-user allocation. In $\mathcal{A}$, $a_{ij} = 1$ if channel j has been assigned to SU i, otherwise $a_{ij} = 0$. To obtain the utility u_i of SU i, the difference between valuation and price paid is used as shown in Eq. 5.

$$u_i = \begin{cases} v_{ji} - p_i & \text{if } a_{ij} = 1 \\ 0 & \text{otherwise} \end{cases} \tag{5}$$

So, the average utility, $\mathcal{U}_a$, among SUs can be determined using Eq. 6.

$$\mathcal{U}_a = \sum_{i=1}^{N} u_i / N \tag{6}$$

A count of the SUs who have acquired the channels can be obtained from the term user satisfaction, $\mathcal{U}_s$. This gives a measure of spectrum reusability in the network. So, $\mathcal{U}_s$ can be computed as the number of winner SUs divided by total number of SUs participating in the auction as shown in Eq. 7

$$\mathcal{U}_s = \sum_{j=1}^{M} \sum_{i=1}^{N} a_{ij} / N \tag{7}$$

Finally, spectrum utilization, $\mathcal{S}_u$, for the allocation $\mathcal{A} = \{a_{ij}\}_{N \times M}$ can be defined as the sum of winning bids for all available channels as given in Eq. 8.

$$\mathcal{S}_u = \sum_{j=1}^{M} \sum_{i=1}^{N} a_{ij} b_{ji} \tag{8}$$

Efficient channel allocation aims at maximizing the spectrum utilization which can be formulated as an optimization problem as shown in Eq. 9.

maximize

$$\mathcal{S}_u = \sum_{j=1}^{M} \sum_{i=1}^{N} a_{ij} b_{ji}$$

subject to

$$(i) \sum_{j=1}^{M} a_{ij} \leq 1, \ \forall i \tag{9}$$

$(ii) \ a_{ij} \leq 1, \text{ if } c_{ij} = 1$

$(iii) \ a_{ij} + a_{kj} \leq 1, \text{ if } x_{ik} = 1$

$a_{ij} \in \{0,1\}; \ i, k \in \mathcal{N}; \ j \in \mathcal{M}$

Therefore, considering different network constraints, we design the auction mechanism which efficiently utilizes the unused radio spectrum.

3.2   Auction Mechanism

To resolve the channel allocation problem in CRN, PO takes the responsibility of fairly leasing the unused channels among SUs by deploying an auction mechanism. For each channel j, a winner set $\mathcal{W}_j$ and an interfering set $\mathcal{Z}_j$ are formed during the allocation process. $\mathcal{W}_j \subseteq \{1, 2, 3, ..., N\}$ where an SU $i \in \mathcal{W}_j$ if $a_{ij} = 1$. $\mathcal{W}_{j(-i)}$ refers to the winner set excluding SU i. Similarly, $\mathcal{Z}_j \subseteq \{1, 2, 3, ..., N\}$ where an SU $k \in \mathcal{Z}_j$ if there exists some SU $i \in \mathcal{W}_j$ such that $x_{ik} = 1$ when $c_{kj} = 1$. To start the auction, PO announces the allowable transmission power of every channel auctioned simultaneously. Depending on dynamics in SOPs, an SU i initially computes the capacity of the channels using Eq. 1. On obtaining $T_{R(ij)}$ value for a channel j and comparing it with $T_{A(j)}$, SU i decides the valuation as per Eq. 2 and accordingly submits a truthful bid. Now, with all bids collected in the bid matrix, PO implements the Algorithm 1 for winner determination. Taking SU i, we check its highest bid by sorting the ith column of bid matrix $\mathcal{B}$ in descending order and storing it as $\mathcal{B}'_{(i)}$. b'_q in the sorted list $\mathcal{B}'_{(i)}$ represents the bid for channel q from SU i. And accordingly, the channel q corresponding to the sorted bids in maintained in $\mathcal{M}'_{(i)}$. Now if j is the channel with highest bid and is unallocated, then SU i gets channel j. Also, if channel j is allocated to some SUs who are non-interfering with SU i, channel j is assigned to SU i. But, if there exists winner SUs who interfere with SU i, then total bid value of the interfering SUs in $\mathcal{W}_j$, i.e. $\sum_{\substack{k \in \mathcal{W}_j \\ x_{ik}=1}} b_{jk}$, and bid value of SU i, b_{ji}, is compared. If the value b_{ji} is less, than SU i looks into $\mathcal{Z}_j$ to find if there exists any non-interfering SU g such that according to the algorithm SU i along with SU g can be included into $\mathcal{W}_j$. But if no such SU is present in $\mathcal{Z}_j$, then SU i gets the next highest channel and continues the same process. However, if b_{ji} is more than the total bid value of its interfering SUs in $\mathcal{W}_j$, then

---

Algorithm 1. Winner Determination Algorithm

Input: Bid matrix $\mathcal{B} = \{b_{ji}\}_{M \times N}$
Output: Allocation matrix $\mathcal{A}$, $\mathcal{W}_j$ and $\mathcal{Z}_j$ $\forall j \in \mathcal{M}$
1: $\mathcal{A} = \{0\}_{N \times M}$ and $\forall j \in \mathcal{M}$, $\mathcal{W}_j = \mathcal{Z}_j = \phi$
2: **for** $i \leftarrow 1$ **to** N **do**
3:    $\mathcal{B}'_{(i)} = \text{sort}(\mathcal{B}_{*,i})$ s.t. $\mathcal{B}'_{(i)} = \{b'_q\}_{1 \times M}$, $1 \leq q \leq M$ // in descending order
4:    Get corresponding channel q for each bid b'_q and store in $\mathcal{M}'_{(i)}$
5:    **for** $y \leftarrow 1$ **to** M **do**
6:      $j = \mathcal{M}'_{(i)}(y)$
7:      **if** $b'_j = 0$, then goto step 2. **else** goto step 8.
8:      **if** $\mathcal{W}_j = \phi$, then goto step 9. **else** goto step 10.
9:      $\mathcal{W}_j = \mathcal{W}_j \cup \{i\}$, $a_{ij} = 1$ and goto step 2.
10:     **if** $\forall k \in \mathcal{W}_j$, $x_{ik} = 0$, then goto step 9. **else** goto step 11.
11:     **if** $\sum_{\substack{k \in \mathcal{W}_j \\ x_{ik}=1}} b_{jk} < b'_j$, then goto step 12 and 13. **else** goto step 14.
12:     $\mathcal{W}_j = \mathcal{W}_j \setminus \{k\}$, $\mathcal{Z}_j = \mathcal{Z}_j \cup \{k\}$ and $a_{kj} = 0$. Also, $\mathcal{W}_j = \mathcal{W}_j \cup \{i\}$, $a_{ij} = 1$
13:     **if** $\exists g \in \mathcal{Z}_j, g \neq k$ s.t. $x_{ig} = 0$ and $\forall h \in \mathcal{W}_{j(-i)}$, $x_{gh} = 0$, then $\mathcal{Z}_j = \mathcal{Z}_j \setminus \{g\}$, $\mathcal{W}_j = \mathcal{W}_j \cup \{g\}$ and $a_{gj} = 1$.
14:     **if** $\exists g \in \mathcal{Z}_j$ s.t. $x_{ig} = 0$, the goto step 15. **else** goto step 5.
15:     **if** $x_{gk} = 1$ s.t. $k \in \mathcal{W}_j$, $x_{ik} = 1$ and $x_{gh} = 0$ s.t. $h \in \mathcal{W}_{j(-k)}$, then goto step 16. **else** goto step 5.
16:     **if** $\sum_{g \in \mathcal{Z}_j} b_{jg} + b'_j \geq \sum_{\substack{k \in \mathcal{W}_j \\ x_{ik}=1}} b_{jk}$, then $\mathcal{W}_j = \mathcal{W}_j \cup \{i, g\}$ and $a_{ij} = a_{gj} = 1$.
        Also, $\mathcal{W}_j = \mathcal{W}_j \setminus \{k\}$, $\mathcal{Z}_j = \mathcal{Z}_j \cup \{k\}$ and $a_{kj} = 0$. **else** goto step 5.
17:   **end**
18: **end**

SU i moves to the set of winners $\mathcal{W}_j$ on being assigned channel j and at the same time the SUs in $\mathcal{W}_j$ who are interfering with SU i are moved to $\mathcal{Z}_j$. Also, here we check if any SU from $\mathcal{Z}_j$ list can be brought back to $\mathcal{W}_j$ such that the overall spectrum utility gets enhanced. Thereafter, once the allocation matrix is obtained, every winner SU pays a price to the PO by following the pricing algorithm. For an SU i winning channel j, we look for SU $k \in \mathcal{Z}_j$ who interferes with SU i but it does not interfere with other winners of the channel. Payment p_i is chosen such that it is less than or equal to b_{ji}. Otherwise, if no SU satisfies the condition, then p_i is the reserve price. In brief, the proposed auction model eventually plans to improve the overall spectrum utilization while upholding the CR network constrains.

3.3 Auction Properties

Definition 1. *Individual Rationality: An auction is individually rational if every bidder i on wining the auction submits a price p_i which is not more than the bid value b_{ji} offered for the winning channel j, i.e., $p_i \leq b_{ji}$.*

Definition 2. *Truthfulness: An auction is truthful if the utility u_i of a bidder i on winning channel j can never improve by submitting an untruthful bid $b_{ji} \neq v_{ji}$, no matter how other bidders bid for the item.*

Algorithm 2. Pricing Algorithm

Input: $\mathcal{W}_j$ and $\mathcal{Z}_j$ when SU i wins channel j

Output: Payment p_i

1: $IList = \phi$

2: **if** $\exists k \in \mathcal{Z}_j$ s.t. $x_{ik} = 1$ and $\forall g \in \mathcal{W}_{j(-i)}$, $x_{gk} = 0$, then $IList = IList \cup \{bjk\}$. **else** no change in $IList$.

3: **if** $IList = \phi$, then $p_i = r$. **else** $IList' = \text{sort}(IList)$ // in descending order

4: $len = \text{length}(IList')$

5: **for** $i \leftarrow 1$ **to** len **do**

6:    $value = IList'(i)$ and $flag = 0$

7:    **if** $value \leq b_{ji}$, then $flag = 1$ and break. **else** goto step 5.

8: **end**

9: **if** $flag = 1$, then $p_i = value$. **else** $p_i = r$.

Theorem 1. *The proposed auction mechanism is individually rational.*

Proof. According to the pricing algorithm, a winner SU i considers the bid from an SU $k \in \mathcal{Z}_j$ as its payment p_i when SU k interferes with only SU i from the winner set $\mathcal{W}_j$ and bid value b_{jk} is less than the winning bid b_{ji}. That is, $p_i = b_{jk}$ if $b_{jk} \leq b_{ji}$, $x_{ik} = 1$ and $\forall q \in \mathcal{W}_{j(-i)}, x_{kq} = 0$. Otherwise, payment p_i is the reserve price r where $r \leq b_{ji}$ according to Eq. 3. Therefore, every winner SU pays a price which is less than or equal to its winning bid, implying $u_i \geq 0$. ∎

Lemma 1. *Given the bid matrix $\mathcal{B} = (B_1, B_2, ..., B_j, ..., B_M)$. If SU i wins channel j by bidding b_{ji}, then SU i also wins the same by bidding $b'_{ji} > b_{ji}$ (provided that all other conditions remain same).*

Proof. SU i wins channel j implies that SU i is non-interfering with all other SUs in winner set $\mathcal{W}_j$. There may exist some SU $k \in \mathcal{Z}_j$ where $b_{jk} > b_{ji}$ but SU k interferes with some winner SU from $\mathcal{W}_j$ resulting in a lower total valuation. In such case, SU i wins the channel according to the winner determination algorithm. Therefore, with $b'_{ji} > b_{ji}$, SU i still wins the game irrespective of any $b_{jk} \geq b'_{ji}$ or $b_{jk} < b'_{ji}$. ∎

Theorem 2. *The proposed auction mechanism is truthful.*

Proof. To prove truthfulness, we consider a bid $b_{ji} \neq v_{ji}$ from SU i for a channel j. Let u_i and u'_i be the utility on bidding v_{ji} and b_{ji} respectively. With untruthful bid submission $u_i \geq u'_i$. Two cases that can arise are as follows.

Case I: $b_{ji} > v_{ji}$

(1) If both b_{ji} and v_{ji} loses, then $u_i = u'_i = 0$ according to Eq. 5.

(2) If b_{ji} wins but v_{ji} loses, then $p_i = 0$ and $u_i = 0$. Bidding with v_{ji} loses when there exists some SU $k \in \mathcal{W}_j$ that interferes with SU i and total bid value, i.e. $\sum_{\substack{k \in \mathcal{W}_j \\ x_{ik}=1}} b_{jk}$ is greater than or equal to v_{ji}. With a bid $b_{ji} > v_{ji}$, SU i wins implying that every SU k is moved to $\mathcal{Z}_j$ and k is non-interfering

with every SU $q \in \mathcal{W}_{j(-i)}$. So, to make the payment p'_i, we apply pricing algorithm which takes the total bid value from every SU k as p'_i. As such, $p'_i \geq v_{ji}$ giving $u'_i \leq 0$.

(3) If b_{ji} loses but v_{ji} wins, then according to Lemma 1 this cannot be true.

(4) If both b_{ji} and v_{ji} wins, then $u_i = u'_i$. On winning with v_{ji} or b_{ji}, if there appears no interfering SU with SU i, then reserve price is being paid and $p_i = p'_i$. Otherwise, if there exists any SU k interfering with only SU i, then b_{ji} and v_{ji} wins when $b_{jk} \leq v_{ji}$. This makes $p_i = p'_i = b_{jk}$ giving $u_i = u'_i$.

Case II: $b_{ji} < v_{ji}$

(1) If both b_{ji} and v_{ji} loses, then $u_i = u'_i = 0$.

(2) If b_{ji} wins but v_{ji} loses, then according to Lemma 1 this cannot be true.

(3) If b_{ji} loses but v_{ji} wins, then $p'_i = u'_i = 0$. And according to Theorem 1, when SU i wins by bidding v_{ji}, $u_i \geq 0$.

(4) If both b_{ji} and v_{ji} wins, then $u_i = u'_i$. Reason is similar to Case I. Hence, with untruthful bidding, no SU in the game can achieve a better utility.

∎

3.4 Illustrative Example

To illustrate the proposed model, we present an example where 6 SUs, $\mathcal{N} = \{1, 2, 3, 4, 5, 6\}$, are competing for a single channel, $\mathcal{M} = \{1\}$. Channel availability matrix, interference matrix and bid matrix are shown in Tables 1, 2 and 3 respectively. According to the winner determination algorithm, SU 1 gets the channel since $\mathcal{W}_1$ is empty and enters $\mathcal{W}_1$. SU 2 has no bid for the channel. SU 3 interferes with SU 1 and since its bid is higher than SU 1, SU 3 enters $\mathcal{W}_1$ and SU 1 moves to $\mathcal{Z}_1$. Then, SU 4 interferes with SU 3 but bid of SU 4 is less than that of SU 3. Now in $\mathcal{Z}_1$, there is SU 1 who does not interfere with SU 4 but interferes with SU 3 present in $\mathcal{W}_1$ and total bid from SU 1 and SU 4 (1.9 + 1.5 = 3.4) is greater than bid of SU 3. So, SU 4 and SU 1 are moved to $\mathcal{W}_1$ and SU 3 goes to $\mathcal{Z}_1$. Again, SU 5 interferes with SU 4 and due to its higher bid it is shifted to $\mathcal{W}_1$. SU 4 goes to $\mathcal{Z}_1$. And finally SU 6 goes to $\mathcal{W}_1$ with no interference with other winners. So, the winner set comprises of $\mathcal{W}_1 = \{1, 5, 6\}$ as shown in Table 4 resulting in a total valuation of 5.7 and interfering set comprises of $\mathcal{Z}_1 = \{3, 4\}$ as shown in Table 5.

4 Performance Evaluation

This section demonstrates the network simulations performed to evaluate the performance of the proposed mechanism. SUs in the network are randomly distributed in an area of size 600 m × 600 m. Interference amongst SUs is modeled by considering the distance between the SUs. Maximum allowable transmission power of channels are selected from [0.01, 1] Watts with bandwidth of 1 KHz and noise variance of $\sigma^2 = 10^{-5}$ for all channels. We study the performance of

Table 1. Channel availability among SUs, 1: Available, 0: Unavailable

SU	1	2	3	4	5	6
Channel availability	1	0	1	1	1	1

Table 2. Interfering relations among SUs

SU	1	2	3	4	5	6
Interfering SUs	{2, 3}	{1, 4}	{1, 4, 6}	{2, 3, 5}	{4}	{3}

Table 3. Bids from the bidders

SU	1	2	3	4	5	6
Bids	1.9	0	2.0	1.5	2.1	1.7

Table 4. Winner set, $\mathcal{W}_1$

SU	1	5	6

Table 5. Interfering set, $\mathcal{Z}_1$

SU	3	4

the auction model under two different network scenarios. In the first scenario, number of SUs is varied from 20 to 60 while keeping the number of channels fixed at 6, and in the second scenario, the number of channels is varied from 4 to 14 while keeping the number of SUs fixed at 40. MATLAB based simulation investigates the model and averages all the results over 500 rounds.

To analyze the performance of the proposed model, we carry out a comparison with the general concurrent auction which uses Vickey Clarke Groves (VCG) auction [8] for simultaneous auctioning of multiple units. According to the VCG method, on biding for all available channels, the highest bid SUs are first chosen for each channel. Then to integrate spectrum reuse, the next highest SUs are picked, but by restraining to the interference and allocation constraints. This process continues till we visit the last SU who participated in the auction. Traditionally, VCG is suitable when the auctioned items are homogeneous and a single-unit allocation is to be performed. In the designed model, VCG cannot produce an adequate result, since for an auctioned channel, it does not always consider the winner set with high total valuation. Finally, to evaluate the network performance, we consider spectrum utilization (Eq. 8), revenue (Eq. 4), average utility (Eq. 6) and user satisfaction (Eq. 7) as the performance metrices.

In Fig. 2a, spectrum utilization is compared for the proposed model with general concurrent auction when number of SUs are varied. An increase of 48.646%

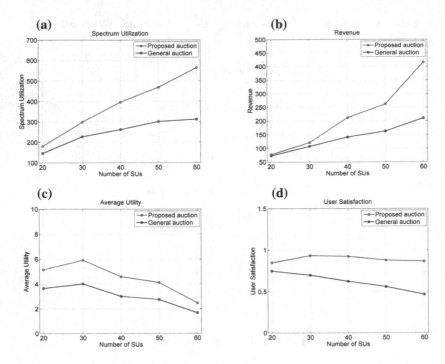

Fig. 2. a, b, c, d shows spectrum utilization, revenue, average utility and user satisfaction of proposed auction and general concurrent auction with respect to number of SUs respectively

can be observed in the proposed model since it chooses a winner set for an auctioned channel which can obtain high valuation. On applying the VCG method in general auction, the winner set generated takes highest bid SUs one-by-one by constraining to the network conditions. But in most of the cases, it cannot provide the winner set with a high valuation which in turn effects the spectrum utilization. On increasing the number of SUs, more users are now available to access the channels. Since one channel can be assigned to multiple users, therefore use of the radio bands significantly improves. Similarly in Fig. 2b, revenue earned in the proposed model shows at increase of 45.410% compared to general auction. But this mainly depends on the interference and allocation patterns of SUs. Figure 2c and 2d shows the average utility and user satisfaction respectively where an increase of 47.858% and 47.502% can be observed. However, with increase in number of SUs, utility and user satisfaction tends to decline because more number of SUs compete amongst themselves to acquire the same number of channels. But due to spectrum reuse, the decline appears to be moderate.

In Fig. 3a, a comparison for spectrum utilization is shown when the number of channels are varied. Due to the similar reason as stated above, we get an increase of 24.468% in spectrum utilization in the proposed model. When number of auctioned channels are increased, larger amount of radio spectrum

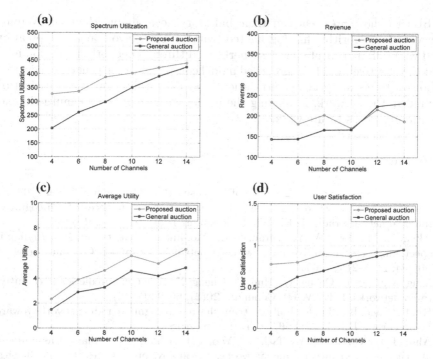

Fig. 3. a, b, c, d shows spectrum utilization, revenue, average utility and user satisfaction of proposed auction and general concurrent auction with respect to number of channels respectively

becomes available amongst the SUs. As such, SUs will now have more chance to win the auction which accordingly improves the utilization of the unused spectrum. In Fig. 3b, a rise of 14.865% can be noticed in the revenue of the proposed auction. However, depending upon the number of interfering SUs and the allocation pattern, if most of the winner SUs pay the reserve price, then a higher value of payment cannot be earned by the PO. For average utility and user satisfaction we take Fig. 3c and Fig. 3d respectively where an improvement of 35.340% and 23.984% reflects a better performance by the proposed model. This is because for same number of SUs more channels become available which allows the SUs to acquire some channel.

Hence, from the results obtained through the network simulation it can be stated that the proposed auction mechanism significantly contributes in the overall utilization of the radio spectrum.

5   Conclusion

In this paper, we have modelled the channel allocation problem in CRN with a concurrent bidding based auction framework which takes into account different CR network constraints along with single-unit-multi-user allocation to incorporate spectrum reuse amongst SUs. Heterogeneous channel condition has allowed the SUs to show preference in their bids for the available channels. Winner determination algorithm has formulated truthfulness to avoid any manipulation in bid values. Experimental analysis performed through network simulation indicated the effectiveness of the proposed model compared to the general concurrent auction in terms of spectrum utilization, revenue, utility and user satisfaction acquired in the network. Extending the model with provision for multi-channel allocation is left as future work.

References

1. FCC: ET Docket No 03-322 Notice of Proposed Rule Making and Order (2003)
2. Song, M., Xin, C., Zhao, Y., Cheng, X.: Dynamic spectrum access: from cognitive radio to network radio. IEEE Wirel. Commun. **19**(1), 23–29 (2012)
3. Akyildiz, I.F., Lee, W.-Y., Vuran, M.C., Mohanty, S.: Next generation/dynamic spectrum access/cognitive radio wireless networks: a survey. Comput. Netw. J. **50**(13), 2127–2159 (2006)
4. Xing, X., Jing, T., Cheng, W., Huo, Y., Cheng, X.: Spectrum prediction in cognitive radio networks. IEEE Wirel. Commun. **20**(2), 90–96 (2013)
5. Hu, F., Chen, B., Zhu, K.: Full spectrum sharing in cognitive radio networks toward 5G: a survey. IEEE Access **6**, 15754–15776 (2018)
6. Ahmed, E., Gani, A., Abolfazli, S., Yao, L.J., Khan, S.U.: Channel assignment algorithms in cognitive radio networks: taxonomy, open issues, and challenges. IEEE Commun. Surv. Tutor. **18**, 795–823 (2016)
7. Tragos, E.Z., Zeadally, S., Fragkiadakis, A.G., Siris, V.A.: Spectrum assignment in cognitive radio networks: a comprehensive survey. IEEE Commun. Surv. Tutor. **15**(3), 1108–1135 (2013)
8. Parsons, S., Rodriguez-Aguilar, J.A., Klein, M.: Auctions and bidding: a guide for computer scientists. ACM Comput. Surv. **43**, 1–66 (2011)
9. Zhang, Y., Niyato, D., Wang, P., Hossain, E.: Auction-based resource allocation in cognitive radio systems. IEEE Commun. Mag. **50**(11), 108–120 (2012)
10. Devi, M., Sarma, N., Deka, S.K., Chauhan, P.: Sequential bidding auction mechanism for spectrum sharing in cognitive radio networks. In: Proceedings of International Conference on Advanced Networks and Telecommunication Systems (IEEE ANTS), India. IEEE (2017)
11. Zhai, X., Zhou, T., Zhu, C., Chen, B., Fang, W., Zhu, K.: Truthful double auction for joint internet of energy and profit optimization in cognitive radio networks. IEEE Access **6**, 23180–23190 (2018)
12. Khairullah, E.F., Chatterjee, M.: PreDA: preference-based double auction for spectrum allocation in heterogeneous DSA networks. Comput. Commun. **133**, 41–50 (2019)
13. Wang, X., Li, Z., Xu, P., Xu, Y., Gao, X., Chen, H.-H.: Spectrum sharing in cognitive radio networks-an auction based approach. IEEE Trans. Syst. Man Cybern. **40**, 587–596 (2010)
14. Khaledi, M., Abouzeid, A.A.: Auction-based spectrum sharing in cognitive radio networks with heterogeneous channels. In: Proceedings of Information Theory and Applications Workshop (ITA) (2013)
15. Kash, I.A., Murthy, R., Parkes, D.C.: Enabling spectrum sharing in secondary market auctions. IEEE Trans. Mob. Comput. **13**, 556–568 (2014)

16. Gao, L., Wang, X., Xu, Y., Zhang, Q.: Spectrum trading in cognitive radio networks: a contract-theoretic modeling approach. IEEE J. Sel. Areas Commun. **29**, 843–855 (2011)

17. Shi, Z., Luo, G.: Multi-band spectrum allocation algorithm based on first-price sealed auction. Cybern. Inf. Technol. **17**(1), 104–112 (2017)

18. Jia, J., Zhang, Q., Zhang, Q., Liu, M.: Revenue generation for truthful spectrum auction in dynamic spectrum access. In: Proceedings of ACM International Symposium on Mobile Ad hoc Networking and Computing (MobiHoc) (2009)

19. Chen, B., Hoang, A.T., Liang, Y.-C.: Cognitive radio channel allocation using auction mechanisms. In: Proceedings of IEEE Vehicular Technology Conference, Singapore. IEEE (2008)

20. Xiang, J., Zhang, Y., Skeie, T.: Medium access control protocols in cognitive radio networks. Wirel. Commun. Mob. Comput., 1–18 (2009)

21. Kim, H., Shin, K.G.: Efficient discovery of spectrum opportunities with MAC-layer sensing in cognitive radio networks. IEEE Trans. Mob. Comput. **7**, 533–545 (2008)

A Hybrid Approach for Fake News Detection in Twitter Based on User Features and Graph Embedding

Tarek Hamdi[1](✉), Hamda Slimi[1,2](✉), Ibrahim Bounhas[2](✉), and Yahya Slimani[2]

[1] National School for Computer Science, Manouba, Tunisia
{tarek.hamdi,hamda.slimi}@ensi-uma.tn
[2] INSAT, LISI Research Laboratory, University of Carthage, Tunis, Tunisia
bounhas.ibrahim@gmail.com, yahya.slimani@gmail.com

Abstract. The quest for trustworthy, reliable and efficient sources of information has been a struggle long before the era of internet. However, social media unleashed an abundance of information and neglected the establishment of competent gatekeepers that would ensure information credibility. That's why, great research efforts sought to remedy this shortcoming and propose approaches that would enable the detection of non-credible information as well as the identification of sources of fake news. In this paper, we propose an approach which permits to evaluate information sources in term of credibility in Twitter. Our approach relies on node2vec to extract features from twitter followers/followees graph. We also incorporate user features provided by Twitter. This hybrid approach considers both the characteristics of the user and his social graph. The results show that our approach consistently and significantly outperforms existent approaches limited to user features.

Keywords: Fake news source detection · User credibility · Twitter network analysis · Graph embedding · Machine learning

1 Introduction

According to a recent survey [44], in 2017 there is approximately 224.3 million smartphone users in the United States and more than 2 billion worldwide. Factors such as the affordable price of mobiles markets, the development of wireless communications technology, and the competitive prices of internet providers facilitated the creation of various Online Social Networks (OSNs). Also, microblogging is considered as a bridge for people to share, coordinate and spread information about events instantly. However, the ease of information sharing allowed the spread of malicious and incorrect content. The absence of gatekeepers led to a need for a credibility evaluation of content shared on social media.

For instance, Twitter has more than half a billion users worldwide with more than 300 million active users [22] who produce approximately 170 million tweets

© Springer Nature Switzerland AG 2020
D. V. Hung and M. D'Souza (Eds.): ICDCIT 2020, LNCS 11969, pp. 266–280, 2020.
https://doi.org/10.1007/978-3-030-36987-3_17

per day, about 10,000 tweets per second. This increase of inter-connectivity and the massive data can be source of interest to a wide range of organizations. This can put the users at the mercy of fake news, misinformation and rumors which have critical consequences [30] that would imperil their personal safety and privacy. Businesses, governmental agencies, and political parties [33] can take the valuable information in tweets for different purposes, including policy formation, decision-making, advertising campaigns, and gauging people's awareness of governmental programs [18]. With an analysis of users data collected from OSNs, it is possible to predict users' future behavior [4,20].

Based on their different interests, Source Of Fake News (SOFNs) continue to disturb and fallacy people opinions. In politics, during the 2016 U.S. presidential election, Grinberg and his team came to the conclusion that fake news was most concentrated among conservative voters [14]. In the same way, Allcott and Gentzkow mention that the 2016 election might have been affected by several rumors and fake news that became viral on Facebook and Twitter [5]. Allcott, Gentzkow and Econ mentioned that 27% of people visited a fake news source in the final weeks before the election [5].

In the cryptocurrency domain, Aggarwa with his group underline the relationship between social factors and the way the stock market of Bitcoin and cryptocurrency behaves. They draw attention to the major impact that social media has on cryptocurrency value [2]. Such statement clearly shows that, in some cases, fake news can dictate the outcome of a stock market.

In 2018, crypto-investors lost more than $9.1 million a day on average to cryptocurrency fraud based on a survey done by Bitcoin.com News [34]. Fake news can affect badly the market and lead to heavy losses. In 2013, a fake tweet about explosion in White House claimed that Barack Obama was injured in this explosion caused $130 billion loss on the stock market [29]. Fake news are present during disaster event and terrorism attacks. In the Boston Marathon bombing during the spring of 2013, terrorist and fake sources terrified people with lies and rumors. Some twitter profiles and bots are established entirely with the intent to spread fabricated, unfounded and misleading information [36].

Those faceless and anonymous people play a major role on what becomes viral on a social media platform during a certain event. Therefore as a remedy to such malicious behavior, some researchers proposed various approaches to detect sources of fake news in Twitter.

2   Related Work

Automatic SOFNs detection can be regarded as a binary classification problem, that can be solved using feature extraction and machine learning algorithms. Our main focus is Twitter, where user credibility can be analyzed from three levels: post or tweet level, topic or event level, and user level.

The topological follow relationship in Twitter yields a social graph which is asymmetric. The Twitter follow graph is directed as the user being followed does not necessarily follow his/her follower. Many follows are built on social ties, which means that Twitter is primarily about information consumption based on the "follow" relationship [27]. Twitter follow graph represent an information and a social network based on its structural characteristics [27].

Twitter is considered as a news medium as well as a social network. The directed nature of the links between users distinguishes Twitter from other OSNs such as Facebook which is based on undirected links between users [6]. Nevertheless, symmetric relationships can exist on Twitter; two users can follow each other. Based on these features, we perceive Twitter to be more about the manner in which information propagates in reality [6].

Some of the various approaches that were proposed to tackle the issue of the sources of fake news detection are discussed below. Mainly we can distinguish the following categories: user-based features, graph-based features, NLP features and influence-based features.

Some of the first attempts to detect the source of information spread where focused on the node proprieties, they used various graph-theoretic measures such as degree of centrality, betweenness, closeness and eigenvector centrality. They assume that the node with the highest values is likely to be the source [10].

Gupta and Lamba [16] focused on tweets sharing fake images during Hurricane Sandy. They used two levels: user and tweet features. In the first level, they collected the followers graph between users. Then, they analyzed the role of Twitter social graph in propagating the fake tweet images. In the second level, they focused on the retweet graph and they found that 86% of tweets spreading the fake images were retweets. Hence, very few were original tweets. They also extracted the sources of tweets from the intersection of the followers graph and the tweet graph, then they relied on their classification model to detect if the picture shared by the source was fake or not. Their classification model attained 97% accuracy in detecting fake images. Finally, authors highlight that Tweet-based features are very effective in discovering fake images. Whereas, the performance of user based features is mediocre. They also discovered that the top 30 users (0.3% of the people) resulted in 90% of retweets of the fake images. Therefore, sources of fake news usually represent a minority compared to credible sources. Hence, Aditi and Hemank conclude that a handful of users contributed to the majority of the damage, via the retweeting activity on Twitter.

Caninin's group [9] focused their research on automatic ranking to measure the credibility of information resources on Twitter. For each given topic, tweet content and network structure acts as a prominent feature for the effective ranking of user credibility. Some research had focused on time snapshot of the infected nodes to construct a maximum likelihood estimator to identify a single source of rumor [35]. Canini et al., showed that by combining a basic text search with an analysis of the social structure of the network, it is possible to generate a ranked list of relevant users for any given topic. They found that the most important thing to identify relevant and credible users is the content-based topic analysis of the social network [9]. In the end, Canini et al. perceived that their algorithm could be more relevant by combining topic-based textual analyses with network-based information in order to identify interesting users to follow. This goal is only attainable if they have knowledge of the follower graph which is the biggest issue [6].

The ease of information sharing on a massive scale renders the detection of SOFNs a fastidious task, since Twitter permits almost anyone to publish their thoughts or share news about events they attended. Moreover, the scarcity and uniqueness of fake news encumbers the ability to learn a trend in data. Based on the aforementioned inconveniences, we believe it is crucial to appropriately deal with the atypical character of sources of fake news.

Other researchers used graph theory to assist in the detection of sources of fake news. In fact, Shu et al. [38] showed that network diffusion models can be applied to trace the provenance nodes and the provenance paths of fake news.

3   Methodology

We are motivated by the great success in applications of attention-based on graph machine learning. We consider extracting some useful features of users from Twitter social graph (followers/following) by using graph embedding which captures the irregular behavior of SOFNs. It takes into consideration the relationship between Twitter users. In this paper, we propose an efficient automated SOFNs detection model by combining user features and social features. As social feature contain important clues, our proposed model is expected to improve the performance of SOFNs detection.

In this section, we discuss our pipeline process and the data collection setup which consists in several different stages: (1) Searching for an appropriate twitter social graph to test our approach based on graph embedding. (2) For each user in the graph, we collect the topics he twitted about. (3) Calculate each user credibility based on topics credibility annotation. (4) We compare each user credibility to a fixed threshold in order to label each user as SOFNs or not. (5) Once the appropriate graph is selected, a graph embedding operation is applied in order to extract nodes feature. (6) We extract each user profile features from Twitter. (7) We apply feature selection to the resulted graph embedding vector. (8) We concatenate user profile features and user graph features. (9) We will try several binary machine learning models to classify correctly SOFNs. All those steps are clearly shown in Fig. 1.

Data Collection and Preprocessing. In general, most of the works related to SOFNs, rumors or fraud, are likely to face the problem of imbalanced data which renders the classification task tedious. Therefore, as a data source for our approach we refereed to published graph dataset, ego-Twitter[1] in SNAP[2] by McAuley and Leskovec [24]. Then, we tried to find a dataset which contains a list of Twitter users labeled as sources of fake news or source of reliable news. Moreover, to classify a user as a SOFNs or not, we need to evaluate their tweets and topic credibility. The collection of users tweets can be achieved by using

---

[1] https://snap.stanford.edu/data/ego-Twitter.html.
[2] snap-stanford/snap: Stanford Network Analysis Platform (SNAP) is a general purpose network analysis and graph mining library.

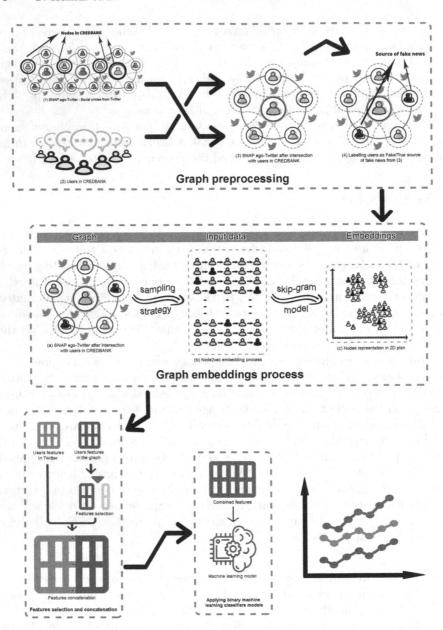

Fig. 1. The pipeline process.

Twitter API. Manually determining the veracity of tweets about news is a challenging task since only experts in the field are eligible for news annotation. These annotators perform careful analysis of claims and additional evidence, context, and reports from authoritative sources [39] to achieve a credible annotation of news content. However, there are no agreed upon benchmark datasets for the fake news detection problem, there is no way of determining whether or not news is fake or not [39], and if there was, it would not be a problem in the first place. Fortunately, in 2015, during the ninth International AAAI Conference on Web and Social Media (ICWSM), a Large-scale Social Media Corpus with Associated Credibility Annotations of approximately 60 million tweets that covers 96 days starting from October 2015 named CREDBANK[3] was announced by Mitra and Gilbert [26], so we used CREDBANK to determinate which user is SOFNs or not in the Labelling Users subsection.

3.1   Graph Selection and Preprocessing

We established an intersection between nodes in ego-Twitter network and the users in CREDBANK to retrieve the graph of users like shown in the graph preprocessing step in the Fig. 1. Also, we selected from ego-Twitter network only the edges which their node source and destination are in CREDBANK. However, an issue was accoutered during the establishment of the intersection, users in CREDBANK are identified with their screen names (string) on Twitter but users in ego-Twitter dataset are identified with their ID (integer). In order to handle this issue, we used Twitter API through Tweepy[4] library to extract each users screen name in ego-Twitter dataset to remedy the issue. The resulted graph contains the relationships between 11592 unique users in CREDBANK and 63108 edges. Then, we created this graph using NetworkX[5], a Python package for the creation, manipulation, and study of the structure, dynamics, and functions of complex networks. Figure 2 presents this graph using Gephi[6]: a software for network analysis and visualization. The zoomed graph is shown in the right part of the Fig. 2. Some nodes and edges can be seen clearly as white circles and white lines, the size of each node increases depending on his degree. This combination yielded a graph that will be used along with the users features to train credibility classification model. In the following, we will refer to the graph as CREDGRAPH.

3.2   Graph Embeddings

The central problem in machine learning on graphs is finding a way to incorporate information about the structure of the graph into the model [17]. Furthermore, graph data is represented in a non-linear manner and it is non-trivial to identify a "context" for any single node in the graph [37].

We start by defining an unweighted graph by synthesizing the two definitions of Wang et al. [43] and Abu-El-Haija et al. [1]. A graph $G(V, E)$ is a collection of

---

[3] http://compsocial.github.io/CREDBANK-data/.

[4] Tweepy is open-sourced, hosted on GitHub and enables Python to communicate with Twitter platform and use its API.

[5] https://networkx.github.io/.

[6] https://gephi.org/.

Fig. 2. The graph of credibility 'CREDGRAPH'

$V = \{v_1, \cdots, v_n\}$ vertices (a.k.a. nodes) and $E = \{e_{ij}\}_{i,j=1}^{n}$ edges. The adjacency matrix $\mathbf{A} \in \{0,1\}^{|V| \times |V|}$ of unweighted graph G can be constructed according to $A_{vu} = \mathbb{1}[(v,u) \in E]$, where the indicator function $\mathbb{1}[.]$ evaluates the values in the matrix to 1 if its boolean argument is true.

To solve graph-based problems using a model, there are two choices available. Either, operations may be directly applied on the original adjacency matrix or on a derived vector space. Working directly on the original adjacency matrix is time consuming and requires substantial memory space. Recently, the idea of representing a network in a vector space without losing their properties by automatically learning to encode graph structure into low-dimensional embedding, using techniques based on deep learning, Factorization, Random Walk and nonlinear dimensionality reduction have become widely popular [13,17,37]. In general, graph embedding methods minimize an objective:

$$\min_{\mathbf{Y}} \mathcal{L}(f(\mathbf{A}), g(\mathbf{Y}));$$

where $\mathbf{Y} \in \mathbb{R}^{|V| \times d}$ is a d-dimensional node embedding dictionary; $f : \mathbb{R}^{|V| \times |V|} \rightarrow \mathbb{R}^{|V| \times |V|}$ is a transformation of the adjacency matrix; $g : \mathbb{R}^{|V| \times d} \rightarrow \mathbb{R}^{|V| \times |V|}$ is a pairwise edge function; and $\mathcal{L} : \mathbb{R}^{|V| \times |V|} \times \mathbb{R}^{|V| \times |V|} \rightarrow \mathbb{R}$ is a loss function.

The idea behind these approaches is to learn a mapping that embeds nodes, as points in a low-dimensional vector space of features $\mathbb{R}^d$ [17]. Also, it maximizes the likelihood of preserving network neighborhoods of nodes [15] and translates the relationships between nodes from graph space to embedding space [37]. The goal is to optimize this mapping so that geometric relationships in this learned space reflect the structure of the original graph [17].

Our task is considered as a user classification, where analogy is applied with node embedding. Hence, we are on a node classification problem which is the most common benchmark task.

Some algorithms are able to generate node embeddings, such as DeepWalk [32], Line [41], SDNE [43], HOPE [28], Graph Factorization (GF) [3] and Laplacian Eigenmaps [7]. DeepWalk is a random walk based algorithm with a fixed return parameter and in-out parameter of 1.

The node2vec model extends DeepWalk by providing a more flexible way to train different combinations of these parameters. Grover and Leskovec [15], define node2vec as an semi-supervised algorithmic framework for scalable feature and for representational learning in networks [15,37]. Therefore, the sampling strategy provided by DeepWalk can be considered as a special case of node2vec. Line learn graph embedding with an efficient way by leveraging both first-order and second-order proximities [37]. However, there is a difficulty in learning feature representation with a balance between BFS and DFS in a graph network. According to a graph embedding survey paper by Cai [8], node2vec is the only work that takes into account both BFS and DFS in a biased random walk algorithm and leads to the learning of an enriched graph embedding [37]. Goyal and Ferrara [13] tested in their survey the performance of several graph embedding methods such as node2vec, GF, SDNE, HOPE and LE on the task of node classification with several datasets. Their results in Figs. 3 and 4 show that node2vec outperforms other methods in this task.

Indeed, node2vec is motivated and inspired by prior work on natural language processing. More specifically, the word2vec [25,37] model. There is an analogy between node2vec and word2vec as each node in the graph behaves as a single word in text. Also, a group of neighborhood nodes around a specific node are similar to the context around a word.

In general, as introduced by Shen et al. [37], these methods operate in two discrete steps. First, they prepare input data through a random walk based sampling strategy. Specifically, for graph data, node2vec takes two forms of equivalences into consideration: homophily [42] and structural equivalence [12,45]. For homophily equivalence, node2vec uses a breadth first search (BFS) algorithm to reach neighborhood nodes based on homogeneous clusters. For structural equivalence, node2vec leverages a depth first search (DFS) strategy to identify neighborhood nodes based on their structural roles (e.g., hub node or peripheral node). Node2vec makes a mixture of both equivalences and customizes a random walk algorithm to switch between BFS and DFS in a moderate way, in order to balance graph searching. Second, once the input data is ready, node2vec

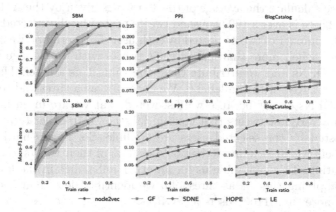

Fig. 3. Micro-F1 and Macro-F1 of node classification for different data sets varying the train-test split ratio (dimension of embedding is 128) [13]

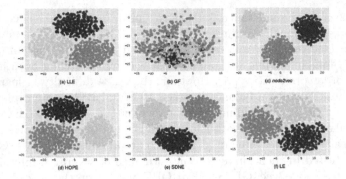

Fig. 4. Visualization of SBM using t-SNE (original dimension of embedding is 128). Each point corresponds to a node in the graph. Color of a node denotes its community [13] (Color figure online)

trains an embedding model using Skip-gram to learn representations that encode pairwise node similarities and generate node embeddings [1].

The hyperparameters used by node2vec are: embedding dimensions d, walks per node r, walk length l, context size k, return p, in-out q.

Therefore, we chose node2vec in this study for generating node embedding along with the hyper-parameters: $d = 128$, $r = 200$, $l = 5$, $p = 0.5$ and $q = 3$ applied to our CREDGRAPH. We tried the 256, 64, 32 and 16 but the 128 dimension attained the best results with the classifiers.

3.3 Users Labelling

The steps of this stage are: (1) Collecting from CREDBANK dataset all the tweets posted by the 11592 users. (2) Joining those results with their topics terms (an identifier of 3 words for each topic in CREDBANK) as a key. (3) For each tweet, we calculate the average of the 30 ratings given by the AMT[7] to the topic terms. There is over a 100 thousand tweets posted by the selected users. (4) Retrieving the number of tweets posted by each user. Furthermore, we considered users having reached more than 5% of their tweets with an average value less than one as SOFNs and we attribute them the value 1 as a label. The rest are considered as SORNs with the label 0. We chose 5% as a threshold to decide if the user is SOFNs or not because we discovered that we are in an imbalanced dataset with a very low tweets that contain fake news. In other terms, most of the news posted by the selected users are credible. So, it was hard to find a number of users which have more than 50% or 25% of their tweets less than one in average rating. This can guide us for an other imbalance in the level of user classes. By applying the 5% as threshold, we identified less than 500 users as SOFNs and more than 11000 users as SORNs.

---

[7] https://www.mturk.com/.

3.4 User Feature Extraction

Analyzing user-based features can provide useful information for SOFNs detection. Such features represent the profile characteristics of users who have interacted with news on social media. We extracted these features for the selected set of users from their corresponding accounts in Twitter. We referred to Twitter API through Tweepy to acquire the user-based features. Unfortunately, we were able to extract only 5536 accounts information from the 11592 CREDBANK users because some accounts were blocked or private. Finally, 468 users were deemed as SOFNs and 5068 users as SORNs after following the instructions in Subsect. 3.3. The extracted features are: followers, friends, created_at, name, default_profile, default_profile_image, favourites_count, statuses_count, description.

Once the user-based features are extracted, a standard feature engineering techniques was applied. It consist of the following steps (1) generate elaborate features based on the basic features extracted from Twitter; (2) normalization; and, (3) feature combination. These steps produced the following features: month and year extracted from created_at, Same_name_scrname which describes if the user handle is the same as user screen name, length_user_id: the number of digits in the user ID, length_description: presents the number of characters in the description, length_description_words: the number of words in the description and number of tweets tweeted by each user in the CREDBANK dataset.

We did not focus on the engineering process for user features since it is irrelevant to our study case. Also, user-based features are only considered as baseline for our approach. Finally, the main interest of our contribution is to show the impact of node embedding in the detection of users who spread fake news by combining it with the user-based features.

3.5 Node2vec Features Selection

One of the biggest challenges in node embedding is to find the optimal dimensions of the vector representation of nodes in the graph. The reconstruction precision of a graph depends on the number of dimensions. However, a high number of dimensions will increase the training time and decrease the precision in node classification.

First, an examination of the vector representation of nodes is performed in order to determine the importance of each dimension or feature in the vector. Then, features that reduce the vector dimensions and increase the performance of node classification are kept. We used Light GBM [21] model to evaluate the importance of each feature. It approaches the problem in two ways. The first one is "split" [21] which represents the number of times a feature is used in a model. The second one is "gain" [21] which the total gains of splits that use the feature.

The vector contains 128 dimensions and each dimension represents a feature. We relied on the gain value to select prominent features since the number of dimensions is fairly small. The process is: (1) Sort the 128 features that resulted from node2vec based on their gain importance. (2) Drop all features with zero gain value. (3) Drop features starting from the lowest gain value until the best dimensions size that yields the highest results in node classification is achieved. (4) Concatenate the selected node embedding features with user-based features. These steps are resulted in the Fig. 1.

4   Results and Discussion

To evaluate the performance of our approach, various metrics were used. In this section, we review the most widely used metrics for SOFNs detection. The choice of the appropriate evaluation metric plays a critical role in achieving an unbiased judgment of classifier performance. Also, a selection of the suitable evaluation metric is an important key for choosing the optimal classifier [19].

The classification problem was defined as follows: can we detect the sources of fake news on Twitter through a combination of users account features and features from the user social graph? Fitting and scoring time are used to show the duration of both the learning and the prediction process respectively. Whereas, the remaining measures showcase the performance and the ability of the proposed model to detect in an efficient and non-biased manner the sources of fake news.

Precision measures the fraction of all detected users as SOFNs that are annotated as SOFNs. It considers the important aspect of identifying which user is SOFNs. However, SOFNs datasets are often skewed, a high precision can be easily achieved by making fewer positive predictions [39]. Thus, recall is used to measure the sensitivity, or the fraction of annotated fake news sources that are predicted to be SOFNs. F1_score is used to combine precision and recall, which can provide an overall prediction performance for SOFNs detection. We note that for Precision, Recall, F1, and Accuracy, the higher the value, the better the performance. Like recall, the specificity metric should be maximized, although recall has a higher impact because falsely predicting that source of real news as SOFNs will not affect the trust placed in the sources predicted to be fake. The maximum value for the AUC is 1.0, which indicates a perfect test since it is 100% sensitive and 100% specific. An AUC value of 0.5 indicates there is no class separation capacity at all [11]. As our concatenated features are represented in a vector space, dimensionality reduction techniques like Principal Component Analysis (PCA) [31], t-distributed stochastic neighbor embedding (t-SNE) [23] and Truncated SVD [40] can be applied to visualize the disparity between different group of users (Fig. 6).

With our approach, SOFNs detection achieved optimal AUC-ROC and Recall equal to 0.99–0.99 with Linear Discriminant Analysis (LDA) algorithm which was equal to 0.79–0.79 respectively.

Based on the metrics shown in the Fig. 7, we can clearly notice that LDA outperforms other classifiers in Recall, f measure and AUC-ROC. By comparing results in Figs. 5 and 7, an improvement of classifier performance can be noticed. Amongst the derived subsets of features, we can clearly notice that the combination of Node2Vec and user features achieved the best results. In fact, LDA

	Model	Fitting time	Scoring time	Accuracy	Precision	Recall	F1_score	AUC_ROC
1	Decision Tree	0.021058	0.005143	0.927282	0.763939	0.781048	0.928625	0.781048
5	Random Forest	0.055438	0.012653	0.962021	0.971195	0.777273	0.956908	0.837866
6	K-Nearest Neighbors	0.005735	0.174906	0.962021	0.970186	0.777272	0.956850	0.800488
7	Bayes	0.002577	0.006412	0.953683	0.903566	0.768936	0.949074	0.850996
4	Quadratic Discriminant Analysis	0.006219	0.007759	0.952063	0.893392	0.765527	0.947408	0.849373
2	Support Vector Machine	0.922096	0.054136	0.960632	0.976600	0.765152	0.954811	0.840951
0	Logistic Regression	0.020959	0.005264	0.951367	0.947766	0.719696	0.942841	0.868336
3	Linear Discriminant Analysis	0.011431	0.007522	0.949284	0.956836	0.702146	0.939127	0.859261

Fig. 5. The classification results with only user-based features

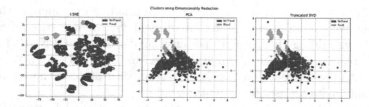

Fig. 6. Visualization of users with only user-based features using t-SNE, PCA and truncated SVD. Each point corresponds to a user. Color of a node denotes its class (Color figure online)

	Model	Fitting time	Scoring time	Accuracy	Precision	Recall	F1_score	AUC_ROC
3	Linear Discriminant Analysis	0.022635	0.005116	0.982165	0.913252	0.990264	0.982972	0.995939
7	Bayes	0.004685	0.006065	0.981931	0.915559	0.983825	0.982664	0.994182
0	Logistic Regression	0.082663	0.005081	0.980775	0.923681	0.959432	0.981186	0.996164
5	Random Forest	0.065707	0.010418	0.979619	0.930450	0.941499	0.979763	0.996508
1	Decision Tree	0.022734	0.004764	0.979393	0.933312	0.933950	0.979315	0.933950
2	Support Vector Machine	1.393793	0.115069	0.976142	0.917719	0.931954	0.976388	0.994190
4	Quadratic Discriminant Analysis	0.008879	0.006889	0.973819	0.934512	0.889141	0.973003	0.994963
6	K-Nearest Neighbors	0.018205	0.717797	0.971277	0.924146	0.883001	0.970531	0.980457

Fig. 7. The classification results using node embeddings with 30 features and user-based features

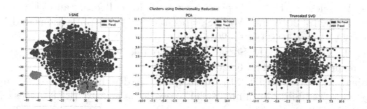

Fig. 8. Visualization of users using t-SNE, PCA and truncated SVD using node embeddings with 30 features and user-based features. Each point corresponds to a user. Color of a node denotes its community (Color figure online)

achieved the best results with a Recall equal to 0.98, an F1_score equal to 0.98 and AUC-ROC equal to 0.98. This can be explained by the fact that node2vec features encompasses information about user credibility that mere Twitter user features are unable to convey (Fig. 8).

5 Conclusion

In this paper, we proposed a hybrid approach which combines node embeddings and user-based features to enrich the detection of sources of fake news in Twitter. Our study showed that the extracted knowledge from the social network graph using node2vec is able to provide a generalized way to assist in detecting SOFNs. After the evaluation of classifiers performance, we conclude that features generated by graph embedding are efficient for the detection of SOFNs. Also, node embeddings features are powerful predictors of SOFNs that convey useful information about the credibility of a user in the social graph. We showed a significant improvements on SOFNs detection over state-of-the-art baseline which mainly relies on user-based features.

In future works, we intend to apply the aforementioned features in other domains related to source evaluation such as fraud, spam, rumor, and anomaly detection. Also, we will try to generate synthetic networks with real-world characteristics in order to study their evolution. Finally, link prediction and recommendation are a promising research tracks in the field of graph embedding.

References

1. Abu-El-Haija, S., Perozzi, B., Al-Rfou, R., Alemi, A.A.: Watch your step: learning node embeddings via graph attention. In: Advances in Neural Information Processing Systems, pp. 9180–9190 (2017). abs/1710.09599
2. Aggarwal, G., Patel, V., Varshney, G., Oostman, K.: Understanding the social factors affecting the cryptocurrency market (2019). arXiv preprint arXiv:1901.06245
3. Ahmed, A., Shervashidze, N., Narayanamurthy, S., Josifovski, V., Smola, A.J.: Distributed large-scale natural graph factorization. In: Proceedings of the 22nd International Conference on World Wide Web, pp. 37–48. ACM (2013)
4. Al-Qurishi, M., Al-Rakhami, M., Alrubaian, M., Alarifi, A., Rahman, S.M.M., Alamri, A.: Selecting the best open source tools for collecting and visualzing social media content. In: 2015 2nd World Symposium on Web Applications and Networking (WSWAN), pp. 1–6. IEEE (2015)
5. Allcott, H., Gentzkow, M.: Social media and fake news in the 2016 election. J. Econ. Perspect. **31**(2), 211–36 (2017)
6. Alrubaian, M., Al-Qurishi, M., Alamri, A., Al-Rakhami, M., Hassan, M.M., Fortino, G.: Credibility in online social networks: a survey. IEEE Access **7**, 2828–2855 (2018)
7. Belkin, M., Niyogi, P.: Laplacian eigenmaps and spectral techniques for embedding and clustering. In: Advances in Neural Information Processing Systems, pp. 585–591 (2002)

8. Cai, H., Zheng, V.W., Chang, K.C.C.: A comprehensive survey of graph embedding: problems, techniques, and applications. IEEE Trans. Knowl. Data Eng. **30**(9), 1616–1637 (2018)
9. Canini, K.R., Suh, B., Pirolli, P.L.: Finding credible information sources in social networks based on content and social structure. In: 2011 IEEE Third International Conference on Privacy, Security, Risk and Trust and 2011 IEEE Third International Conference on Social Computing, pp. 1–8. IEEE (2011)
10. Comin, C.H., da Fontoura Costa, L.: Identifying the starting point of a spreading process in complex networks. Phys. Rev. E **84**(5), 056105 (2011)
11. Fan, J., Upadhye, S., Worster, A.: Understanding receiver operating characteristic (ROC) curves. Can. J. Emerg. Med. **8**(1), 19–20 (2006)
12. Fortunato, S.: Community detection in graphs. Phys. Rep. **486**(3–5), 75–174 (2010)
13. Goyal, P., Ferrara, E.: Graph embedding techniques, applications, and performance: a survey. Knowl. Based Syst. **151**, 78–94 (2018)
14. Grinberg, N., Joseph, K., Friedland, L., Swire-Thompson, B., Lazer, D.: Fake news on twitter during the 2016 US presidential election. Science **363**(6425), 374–378 (2019)
15. Grover, A., Leskovec, J.: Node2vec: scalable feature learning for networks. In: Proceedings of the 22nd ACM SIGKDD International Conference on Knowledge Discovery and Data Mining, KDD 2016, pp. 855–864. ACM (2016). https://doi.org/10.1145/2939672.2939754
16. Gupta, A., Lamba, H., Kumaraguru, P., Joshi, A.: Faking sandy: characterizing and identifying fake images on twitter during hurricane sandy. In: Proceedings of the 22nd International Conference on World Wide Web, pp. 729–736. ACM (2013)
17. Hamilton, W.L., Ying, R., Leskovec, J.: Representation learning on graphs: methods and applications (2017). arXiv preprint arXiv:1709.05584
18. Hassan, N.Y., Gomaa, W.H., Khoriba, G.A., Haggag, M.H.: Supervised learning approach for twitter credibility detection. In: 2018 13th International Conference on Computer Engineering and Systems (ICCES), pp. 196–201. IEEE (2018)
19. Hossin, M., Sulaiman, M.: A review on evaluation metrics for data classification evaluations. Int. J. Data Min. Knowl. Manag. Process **5**(2), 1 (2015)
20. Jin, L., Chen, Y., Wang, T., Hui, P., Vasilakos, A.V.: Understanding user behavior in online social networks: a survey. IEEE Commun. Mag. **51**(9), 144–150 (2013)
21. Ke, G., et al.: LightGBM: a highly efficient gradient boosting decision tree. In: Advances in Neural Information Processing Systems, pp. 3146–3154 (2017)
22. Kim, J., Hastak, M.: Social network analysis: characteristics of online social networks after a disaster. Int. J. Inf. Manag. **38**(1), 86–96 (2018)
23. Maaten, L.V.D., Hinton, G.: Visualizing data using t-SNE. J. Mach. Learn. Res. **9**(Nov), 2579–2605 (2008)
24. Mcauley, J., Leskovec, J.: Discovering social circles in ego networks. ACM Trans. Knowl. Discov. Data **8**(1), 4:1–4:28 (2014). https://doi.org/10.1145/2556612
25. Mikolov, T., Chen, K., Corrado, G., Dean, J.: Efficient estimation of word representations in vector space (2013). arXiv preprint arXiv:1301.3781
26. Mitra, T., Gilbert, E.: CREDBANK: a large-scale social media corpus with associated credibility annotations. In: Ninth International AAAI Conference on Web and Social Media (2015)
27. Myers, S.A., Sharma, A., Gupta, P., Lin, J.: Information network or social network? The structure of the twitter follow graph. In: Proceedings of the 23rd International Conference on World Wide Web, pp. 493–498. ACM (2014)

28. Ou, M., Cui, P., Pei, J., Zhang, Z., Zhu, W.: Asymmetric transitivity preserving graph embedding. In: Proceedings of the 22nd ACM SIGKDD International Conference on Knowledge Discovery and Data Mining, pp. 1105–1114. ACM (2016)

29. Paluch, R., Lu, X., Suchecki, K., Szymański, B.K., Hołyst, J.A.: Fast and accurate detection of spread source in large complex networks. Sci. Rep. **8**(1), 2508 (2018)

30. Pastor-Satorras, R., Vespignani, A.: Epidemic spreading in scale-free networks. Phys. Rev. Lett. **86**(14), 3200 (2001)

31. Pearson, K.: LIII. On lines and planes of closest fit to systems of points in space. Lond. Edinb. Dublin Philos. Mag. J. Sci. **2**(11), 559–572 (1901)

32. Perozzi, B., Al-Rfou, R., Skiena, S.: Deepwalk: online learning of social representations. In: Proceedings of the 20th ACM SIGKDD International Conference on Knowledge Discovery and Data Mining, KDD 2014, pp. 701–710 (2014). https://doi.org/10.1145/2623330.2623732

33. Sáez-Mateu, F.: Democracy, screens, identity, and social networks: the case of Donald Trump's election. Am. Behav. Sci. **62**(3), 320–334 (2018)

34. Seth, S.: $9 million lost each day in cryptocurrency scams. Investopedia 13 (2018)

35. Shah, D., Zaman, T.: Rumor centrality: a universal source detector. In: Proceedings of the 12th ACM SIGMETRICS/PERFORMANCE Joint International Conference on Measurement and Modeling of Computer Systems, SIGMETRICS 2012, pp. 199–210 (2012). https://doi.org/10.1145/2254756.2254782

36. Shao, C., Ciampaglia, G.L., Varol, O., Flammini, A., Menczer, F.: The spread of fake news by social bots, pp. 96–104 (2017). arXiv preprint arXiv:1707.07592

37. Shen, F., et al.: HPO2Vec+: leveraging heterogeneous knowledge resources to enrich node embeddings for the human phenotype ontology. J. Biomed. Inform. **96**, 103246 (2019). https://doi.org/10.1016/j.jbi.2019.103246

38. Shu, K., Bernard, H.R., Liu, H.: Studying fake news via network analysis: detection and mitigation. In: Agarwal, N., Dokoohaki, N., Tokdemir, S. (eds.) Emerging Research Challenges and Opportunities in Computational Social Network Analysis and Mining. LNSN, pp. 43–65. Springer, Cham (2019). https://doi.org/10.1007/978-3-319-94105-9_3

39. Shu, K., Sliva, A., Wang, S., Tang, J., Liu, H.: Fake news detection on social media: a data mining perspective. ACM SIGKDD Explor. Newslett. **19**(1), 22–36 (2017)

40. Speer, R., Havasi, C., Lieberman, H.: Analogyspace: reducing the dimensionality of common sense knowledge. In: Proceedings of the 23rd National Conference on Artificial Intelligence, AAAI 2008, pp. 548–553 (2008)

41. Tang, J., Qu, M., Wang, M., Zhang, M., Yan, J., Mei, Q.: Line: large-scale information network embedding. In: Proceedings of the 24th International Conference on World Wide Web, WWW 2015, pp. 1067–1077 (2015). https://doi.org/10.1145/2736277.2741093

42. Tang, L., Liu, H.: Leveraging social media networks for classification. Data Min. Knowl. Disc. **23**(3), 447–478 (2011)

43. Wang, D., Cui, P., Zhu, W.: Structural deep network embedding. In: Proceedings of the 22nd ACM SIGKDD International Conference on Knowledge Discovery and Data Mining, pp. 1225–1234. ACM (2016)

44. Wu, L., Zhang, Y., Xie, Y., Alelaiw, A., Shen, J.: An efficient and secure identity-based authentication and key agreement protocol with user anonymity for mobile devices. Wirel. Pers. Commun. **94**(4), 3371–3387 (2017). https://doi.org/10.1007/s11277-016-3781-z

45. Yang, J., Leskovec, J.: Overlapping communities explain core-periphery organization of networks. Proc. IEEE **102**(12), 1892–1902 (2014)

Online Context-Adaptive Energy-Aware Security Allocation in Mobile Devices: A Tale of Two Algorithms

Asai Asaithambi, Ayan Dutta$^{(\boxtimes)}$, Chandrika Rao, and Swapnoneel Roy

School of Computing, University of North Florida, Jacksonville, USA
{asai.asaithambi,a.dutta,n01412075,s.roy}@unf.edu

Abstract. Cryptographic operations involved in securing communications are computationally intensive and contribute to energy drain in mobile devices. Thus, varying the level of security according to the user's location may provide a convenient solution to energy management. Context-adaptive energy-aware security allocation for mobile devices is modeled in this paper as a combinatorial optimization problem. The goal is to allocate security levels effectively so that user utility is maximized while bounding the maximum energy cost to a constant E. Although the offline version of the problem has been previously studied in the literature where both the security levels and the locations to which a user may travel to is known *a priori*, this is the first work that formulates and solves an online version of the problem where the locations may be known a priori but the security levels are revealed only upon reaching the locations. We provide two different algorithms for the solution of this online problem by mapping it to the online multi-choice knapsack problem. We study competitive ratios of our two algorithms by comparing the solutions they yield to the optimal solution obtained for the corresponding offline problem. We also present simulation experiments on realistic datasets to validate the scalability and efficiency of our approaches (taking in order of milliseconds for up to 100 locations and providing near-optimal competitive ratios).

Keywords: Green computing · Context-aware security · Energy-aware security · Allocation

1 Introduction

Energy management has become one of the foremost concerns in the design of mobile devices, due primarily to the increasing functionality of mobile applications, which rapidly drain battery power in these devices. The computation-intensive cryptographic operations involved in securing communications significantly contribute to energy drain. There is sufficient research reported in the literature confirming that energy use patterns are unique and driven by context (e.g. location of a user) [2,3,7,18]. However, current approaches to assure

© Springer Nature Switzerland AG 2020
D. V. Hung and M. D'Souza (Eds.): ICDCIT 2020, LNCS 11969, pp. 281–295, 2020.
https://doi.org/10.1007/978-3-030-36987-3_18

security do not adapt well to energy-security trade-offs that vary for individual user-contexts. As the benefits associated with the varying levels of security also vary, it will be useful to have the mobile device select the level of security adaptively and automatically so that the benefit is maximized while not exceeding its energy budget.

The real-life scenario we wish to consider is that of a single mobile device user traveling through different locations, each of which offers a set of security levels characterized by the energy requirements and the associated benefit quantified in some suitable manner. The challenges associated with this scenario are: (1) the user is constrained by a total energy budget such as the available battery charge; and (2) the available security levels are not known beforehand and only become available as the user travels to a new location. Thus, when a user reaches a new location, the device should be able to choose the appropriate level of security from the available choices and still ensure maximum benefit, while not exceeding the energy budget.

Several previous studies [1,4,6,9,10,16] on the importance of context for security in mobile environments have proposed adaptable mechanisms that configure security according to the needs of the environment. Our motivation for the present work comes from Roy et al. [14] in which the *offline* context-adaptive security problem (CONTEXT-SEC-OFFLINE), which assumes the security levels to be known beforehand, has been proved to be NP-Complete. We emphasize that the approaches used to solve the offline problem are not directly suitable to solve the online problem we wish to solve. On the other hand, the strategies used for the offline problem may be used. For instance, Roy et al. [14] mapped CONTEXT-SEC-OFFLINE to a variant of the classical knapsack problem known as the multiple-choice knapsack problem. In a similar manner, we map CONTEXT-SEC-ONLINE to the online multiple-choice knapsack (MULTIPLE-CHOICE-KNAPSACK-ONLINE) problem as described by [5], and develop two algorithms, which we call CONTEXT-SEC-ONLINE-GREEDY and CONTEXT-SEC-ONLINE-EFFICIENT. We study the competitive ratio, namely the ratio of the solution produced by an algorithm to the optimal solution. In this regard, we note that the optimal solution will correspond to a competitive ratio of 1. Higher the ratio for an algorithm is, the farther will be the solution obtained by the algorithm from the optimal solution. We have empirically demonstrated that under no simplifying assumptions our proposed approaches provide, on the average, near-optimal competitive ratios ranging from 1 to 2.63, while scaling easily to 100 locations. Our contributions in this paper are as follows:

- We formulate the online version of the context-adaptive, energy-aware security problem by mapping it to the online version of the multiple-choice knapsack problem. This is the first study to provide such a formulation. We call this formation CONTEXT-SEC-ONLINE. We also develop two algorithms to solve CONTEXT-SEC-ONLINE.
- We demonstrate that the theoretical competitive ratios under certain assumptions previously proved for MCKP-Online are also achieved for this problem under similar assumptions.

– We also demonstrate through simulated experiments that our algorithms are scalable to more general scenarios.

2 Related Work

We begin by introducing the notation and terminology used in describing the offline problem closely related to the problem we consider in this paper. Our description of the offline problem here follows [14]. We assume that a single mobile device user travels through n different locations. Each of these locations may be allocated a security level from out of a possible m levels. The security levels are denoted by $S = \{S_1, S_2, \cdots, S_m\}$, and each security level S_i is represented by an ordered pair $(p_i, b_i)_{i=1}^m$, where p_i is the power consumption or the energy requirement and b_i is the benefit associated with security level S_i. Assuming that all (p_i, b_i) are known beforehand, and assuming that it is possible to allocate the same security level to more than one location, the (offline) context-adaptive, energy-aware security allocation problem is to find the optimal allocation of the m security levels to the n travel locations of the user such that the total energy consumed stays within a pre-specified energy budget E, while the total security benefit associated with the allocation is maximized. This version of the problem is referred to in the literature as CONTEXT-SEC [14, 15] and for our purposes we rename this problem CONTEXT-SEC-OFFLINE. We formally define this problem as follows:

Definition 1. CONTEXT-SEC-OFFLINE

INPUT: User's energy budget E
           m ordered pairs $(p_j, b_j)_{j=1}^m$, where
           p_j: power consumed for security level j
           b_j: benefit from security level j
OUTPUT: For each location $i \in \{1, 2, \cdots, n\}$,
           allocate a security level j_i, where
           $j_i \in \{1, 2, \cdots, m\}$, so that the total
           benefit $\sum_{i=1}^n b_{j_i}$ is maximized,
           subject to the condition $\sum_{i=1}^n p_{j_i} \leq E$.

Roy et al. [14] observed the interesting one-to-one correspondence between the decision versions of CONTEXT-SEC-OFFLINE and the well-known multiple-choice knapsack problem [11] and concluded that the decision version of CONTEXT-SEC-OFFLINE is NP-Complete. For ease of reference later in this paper, the statement of the offline multiple-choice knapsack problem is provided below.

Definition 2. MULTIPLE-CHOICE-KNAPSACK-OFFLINE

INPUT: *A knapsack of capacity W*
m ordered pairs $(w_j, v_j)_{j=1}^{m}$, where
w_j is the weight of item j, and
v_j is the value of item j.

OUTPUT: *Choose n items such that the total*
value $\sum_{i=1}^{n} v_{j_i}$ is maximized,
subject to the condition $\sum_{i=1}^{n} w_{j_i} \leq W$,
where $j_i \in \{1, 2, \cdots, m\}$.

Thus, the power consumption p_i corresponds to the weight w_i, the benefit b_i corresponds to the value v_i, and the energy budget E corresponds to W, the capacity of the knapsack. Several variants of the knapsack problem have been studied extensively. Among these, the classical knapsack problem (KP) and the multiple-choice knapsack problem (MCKP) have been shown to accept an FPTAS [11].

As mentioned previously, the offline formulation of context-adaptive, energy-aware mobile security is not always realistic as the security levels available are not known beforehand, and only become available as the mobile device user travels to new locations. There exist other applications which are formulated as online problems in a manner similar to the problem we consider in this paper. One such application arises in keyword-based ad auctions [8,13]. The *Adwords problem*, as it is commonly known in the literature, is an online assignment problem that requires allocating from a stream of queries, each item as it arrives, to one of several bidders. Each query has a value and a cost associated with it, and the goal of the allocations is to maximize the value for each bidder while remaining within their budget. Guided by these studies and due to the correspondence we have just established between CONTEXT-SEC-OFFLINE and MULTIPLE-CHOICE-KNAPSACK-OFFLINE, we were motivated further to developing algorithms for the solution of CONTEXT-SEC-ONLINE.

Further investigation into the online versions of KP and MCKP [12] has revealed that there exist no non-trivial competitive algorithms for the general case of the online knapsack problem, unless certain simplifying assumptions are made [5]. For instance, [5,17] have presented competitive deterministic algorithms for solving the online version of the classical knapsack problem, by making the assumptions of $w_i \ll W$ and $L \leq v_i/w_i \leq U$ (for some L and U). They report a competitive ratio of $\ln(U/L) + 2$.

In this paper, we advance the state-of-the-art by providing a model for online context-adaptive, energy-aware mobile device security allocation (CONTEXT-SEC-ONLINE), presenting two novel algorithms for its solution, and by testing our approaches on some realistic datasets.

3   Problem Formulation

As we have already established a rationale for using the online multiple-choice knapsack problem formulation as a basis of our proposed model, we begin by providing a statement of this problem namely MULTIPLE-CHOICE-KNAPSACK-ONLINE, based on the descriptions of [5,17]. We assume that at time instant t, a set N_t of m_t items arrives from which at most one item must be selected to be put in the knapsack, whose current unfilled capacity is W_t.

Just as CONTEXT-SEC-OFFLINE has been mapped to MULTIPLE-CHOICE-KNAPSACK-OFFLINE, we identify the elements of an online version of CONTEXT-SEC-OFFLINE that appropriately map to the different elements of MULTIPLE-CHOICE-KNAPSACK-ONLINE, formulate the online version of CONTEXT-SEC-OFFLINE, and call the resulting online problem CONTEXT-SEC-ONLINE.

Definition 3. MULTIPLE-CHOICE-KNAPSACK-ONLINE

INPUT: *A partially filled knapsack whose unfilled capacity is W_t at time instant t*
m_t ordered pairs $(w_j^t, v_j^t)_{j=1}^{m_t}$, where w_j^t is the weight of item j arriving at time t, and v_j^t is the value of item j arriving at time t.

OUTPUT: *Choose at most one item r with value v_r and weight w_r such that v_r is maximized, while $w_r \le W_t$, and $r \in \{1, 2, \cdots, m_t\}$.*

We assume that when the mobile user reaches location ℓ, a set $\mathbf{S}^\ell$ of m_ℓ security levels is available from which at most one security level must be allocated without exceeding the current unused energy budget of E_ℓ. Therefore, the unfilled capacity W_t at time instant t in MULTIPLE-CHOICE-KNAPSACK-ONLINE corresponds to the unused energy budget E_ℓ when the user arrives at location ℓ in CONTEXT-SEC-ONLINE. Similarly, the set N_t of items arriving at time instant t corresponds to the set $\mathbf{S}^\ell$ of the m_ℓ security levels available at location ℓ. The weight w_j and the value v_j of each item in MULTIPLE-CHOICE-KNAPSACK-ONLINE correspond to the power requirement p_j and the benefit b_j associated with security levels as before. Just as MULTIPLE-CHOICE-KNAPSACK-ONLINE requires the selection of at most one of the items from N_t, CONTEXT-SEC-ONLINE requires the selection of at most one security level from $\mathbf{S}^\ell$. We present below this formulation of CONTEXT-SEC-ONLINE as a definition.

Definition 4. CONTEXT-SEC-ONLINE

INPUT: *User's unused energy budget E_ℓ*
m_ℓ ordered pairs $(p_i^\ell, b_i^\ell)_{i=1}^{m_\ell}$, where p_i^ℓ is the power consumed for security level i at location ℓ, and b_i^ℓ is the benefit from security level i at location ℓ.

OUTPUT: *For location ℓ, allocate at most one security level r with power requirement p_r and benefit b_r such that b_r is maximized, while $p_r \le E_\ell$, and $r \in \{1, 2, \cdots, m_\ell\}$.*

---

4   Algorithms

It is well known that no non-trivial competitive algorithms exist for the general case of the online knapsack problem [12]. In other words, if we make no assumptions regarding the weights and values involved in the knapsack problem, then there is no algorithm with constant competitive ratio. On the other hand, under suitable assumptions, deterministic algorithms with provable competitive ratios that depend on the value-to-weight ratio have been developed for a variety of online knapsack problems [5]. The assumptions made in [5] for MULTIPLE-CHOICE-KNAPSACK-ONLINE translate to the following assumptions for CONTEXT-SEC-ONLINE:

1. The power requirement for each level of security is very small compared to the energy budget. In other words, $p_i \ll E$ for all i; equivalently, there exists a positive ε and very close to zero such that $p_i/E \leq \varepsilon$ for all i.
2. The benefit-to-power ratio of each security level is bounded from below and above by two constants L and U. In other words, $L \leq b_i/p_i \leq U$ for all i.

Under these assumptions, we have experimented with two different approaches to handling CONTEXT-SEC-ONLINE.

A Greedy Approach. First, we take a greedy approach. As the mobile device user moves to a new location, among the security levels that become available, the level that offers the maximum benefit to energy consumption ratio while staying within the available energy budget is allocated. We assume that the unused energy budget when the user reaches location ℓ is E_ℓ. We denote by $\mathbf{S}^\ell = \{S_1^\ell, S_2^\ell, \cdots, S_{m_l}^l\}$ the security levels available at location ℓ. Also, $S_i^\ell \in \mathbf{S}^\ell$ is characterized by (p_i^ℓ, b_i^ℓ), where p_i^ℓ is the power requirement for the security level S_i^ℓ, and b_i^ℓ is the benefit offered by the security level S_i^ℓ. The greedy algorithm is then described as shown below:

Algorithm CONTEXT-SEC-ONLINE-GREEDY
Allocate security level $S_k^\ell \in \mathbf{S}^\ell$ such that b_k^ℓ/p_k^ℓ is the largest, and $p_k^\ell \leq E_\ell$.

An online algorithm A for an optimization problem is said to be *c-competitive*, if for any input sequence s of input items it is true that $OPT(s) \leq cA(s)$, where $OPT(s)$ is the optimal solution obtained by an offline algorithm with prior knowledge s, and $A(s)$ is the solution obtained by A without prior knowledge of s. We also say that A has a competitive ratio of c. The greedy algorithm has a theoretical competitive ratio of U/L [17].

An Efficient Approach. Our second approach to the solution of CONTEXT-SEC-ONLINE is to adapt the algorithm of [5] for MULTIPLE-CHOICE-KNAPSACK-ONLINE. The general idea behind this approach is to use an efficiency function, and be increasingly selective as the energy budget gets used. Under this approach, a security level is allocated to a location if and only if its benefit-to-power ratio exceeds the efficiency determined by a monotonically increasing function of the fraction of the energy budget utilized so far. The precise function has been determined by linear program and otherwise in [5,17]. This function, denoted $\psi(z)$, where z is the fraction of the energy budget utilized so far, is defined by [5,17] as

$$\psi(z) = (Ue/L)^z (L/e),$$

in which e is the base of the natural logarithm. Also, when the mobile device user reaches location ℓ, the fraction of the energy budged used so far is denoted z_ℓ and can be calculated as $z_\ell = 1 - E_\ell / E$, where E_ℓ is the unused budget. With these in place, the algorithm of [5,17] takes the following form when applied to CONTEXT-SEC-ONLINE.

Algorithm CONTEXT-SEC-ONLINE-EFFICIENT

1. Determine $\mathbf{S} = \left\{ w \in [m_\ell] \;\middle|\; \dfrac{b_w}{p_w} \geq \psi(z_\ell) \right\}$.

2. Allocate security level $w \in \mathbf{S}$ such that b_w is the largest, and p_w does not exceed E_ℓ.

In other words, the security level to be allocated to location ℓ is chosen using a greedy strategy, but only from among those levels whose benefit-to-power ratio exceeds the efficiency $\psi(z_\ell)$. The algorithm based on this strategy has a competitive ratio of $\ln(U/L) + 2$ [5].

5 Evaluation

In this section, we discuss the evaluation strategy and the results obtained by running the proposed approaches on a synthetic yet realistic dataset.

5.1 Settings

To test the performance of our proposed approaches, we implement CONTEXT-SEC-ONLINE-GREEDY and CONTEXT-SEC-ONLINE-EFFICIENT on a desktop computer with a 4.6 GHz. Intel core i7-8700 Processor and a 16 GB RAM. Each algorithm, implemented using the Python programming language, allocates at most one security level from a given set of preferred security levels for each location revealed only when the mobile device user reaches the location. On all our tests, we set the energy budget E at 100, representing 100% of the energy set aside for being spent on the security of the mobile device.

We ran two sets of experiments. The first set focused on comparing the two online algorithms with an offline brute force algorithm that produces an optimal solution. Assuming that m security levels were available, the brute force algorithm considered all $(m + 1)$ possible allocations to each location (including allocating no security level), and found the allocations that yielded the maximum total benefit, which is the exact optimal solution. Because of the exponential growth of the possibilities to examine for the brute force algorithm, we restricted n to be in the range $[4, 12]$, and m in $[2, 10]$. We ran the two online algorithms for these choices of m and n with the same randomly generated $(p_i, b_i)_{i=1}^m$ values. We selected the parameters consistent with the assumptions $p_i \ll E$ and $L \leq p_i/b_i \leq U$, so that we could compare the results obtained by the two algorithms with the corresponding optimal benefit obtained by the brute force algorithm. With $p_i \in [0.1, 1]$, we selected b_i to vary according to a normal distribution with a mean of $100p_i/\max p_i$ and a standard deviation of $1.67n$. This choice was made after rigorous testing to realistically represent the fact that some security levels with higher level of energy consumption might have lower level of benefit and vice versa. The values of L and U were then calculated from the selected values of p_i and b_i. To be specific, L was set as $\min b_i/\max p_i$, and U as $\max b_i/\min p_i$. These settings allowed us to determine the actual competitive ratios and compare them with the corresponding theoretical bounds obtained by [17] and [5] in relation to the online adwords and multiple-choice knapsack problems. We also experimented by relaxing the assumption $p_i \ll E$ and choosing $p_i \in [1, E/n]$ to study the algorithms for their performance for $n \in [4, 12]$.

The second set of experiments was conducted for the purpose of comparing the two online algorithms among themselves on their performance. For these experiments, we set $n \in [10, 100]$ and $m \in [10, 100]$, and chose the (p_i, b_i) defining the security levels as done with the first set of experiments. Additionally, in order to ensure that the randomly selected data reflected the real-life scenario more accurately, for the second set of experiments, we set the total number of security levels at m, but varied the number of preferred security levels m_ℓ at each location ℓ according to the normal distribution with a mean of $m/2$ and a standard deviation that ranged from $0.1n$ to $0.4n$. Table 1 summarizes the above-described data settings we used for all the tests. Each test was run 10 times and the average of the results were obtained for each test. However, we did not compare the results for the second set of experiments with those that could have been produced by the offline algorithm as it is not practical to run the brute force algorithms for such large values of n and m.

Table 1. Parameters and their values usedfor testing the proposed solutions.

Variables	Notations	Values
Number of locations	n	$[4, 12], [10, 100]$
Number of security levels	m	$[2, 10], [10, 100]$
Energy budget	E	100
Energy consumption	p_i	$[0.1, 1], \mathcal{U}(1, \frac{E}{n})$
Benefit	b_i	$\mathcal{N}(p_i \cdot \frac{100}{\max p_i}, [1.67n])$
Threshold	Ψ	Decided from p_i and b_i
Number of security levels available in each location	m_l	$\mathcal{N}(\frac{m}{2}, [0.1n, 0.4n])$

5.2 Results

For the first set of tests, our aim was to compare the theoretical bounds of U/L for the CONTEXT-SEC-ONLINE-GREEDY algorithm and $\ln(U/L) + 2$ for the CONTEXT-SEC-ONLINE-EFFICIENT (ψ-function-based) algorithm by running both against a brute force offline algorithm assuming all security of levels were known beforehand. Varying p_i in $[0.1, 1]$ to ensure that the condition $p_i \ll E$ is satisfied, we considered the number of locations $n \in [4, 12]$. Summarized in Table 2 are the ranges of competitive ratios (**CR**) obtained and the corresponding theoretical bounds (**Bound**) for comparison.

Table 2. Comparison of competitive ratios

Algorithm	CR	Bound
CONTEXT-SEC-ONLINE-GREEDY	$[1, 2.63]$	$[198, 495]$
CONTEXT-SEC-ONLINE-EFFICIENT	$[1, 2.63]$	$[6.9, 7.2]$

The execution time for the offline brute force algorithm grew exponentially from around 2.5 ms for $n = 4$ to around 1200 ms for $n = 12$; correspondingly, CONTEXT-SEC-ONLINE-GREEDY took from around 0.5 ms for $n = 4$ to around 0.8 ms for $n = 12$; and CONTEXT-SEC-ONLINE-EFFICIENT took from around 0.01 ms for $n = 4$ to around 0.5 ms for $n = 12$. As the results do not vary significantly with different values of m, we only show the average of the results obtained using different values of m in all our plots.

Next, we compare the total benefit obtained by the two algorithms with the optimal solution obtained by the brute force algorithm. The average solution resulting from CONTEXT-SEC-ONLINE-EFFICIENT coincides with the average optimal solution (total benefit) obtained using the brute force method, and the average solution from CONTEXT-SEC-ONLINE-GREEDY ranges from around 55% to 63% of the average optimal solution. Figure 1 shows this comparison. The competitive ratios obtained over all our experiments range from $[1, 2.63]$, as shown in Table 2.

From these results, we conclude that the theoretical bounds on the competitive ratios obtained for other applications are too conservative for the CONTEXT-SEC-ONLINE problem. Also, when the security levels satisfy $p_i \ll E$ and $L \le b_i/p_i \le U$, both CONTEXT-SEC-ONLINE-EFFICIENT and CONTEXT-SEC-ONLINE-GREEDY are about 1000 times faster than brute force searching for the optimal solution, with CONTEXT-SEC-ONLINE-EFFICIENT performing roughly 1.6 times faster than CONTEXT-SEC-ONLINE-GREEDY for the range of parameter values we tested. Thus, CONTEXT-SEC-ONLINE-EFFICIENT produces superior results in less time compared to CONTEXT-SEC-ONLINE-GREEDY.

Next, we relax the assumption $p_i \ll E$ and choose p_i in the range $[1, E/n]$, varying n in the same range of $[4, 12]$ as before. This allows us to empirically

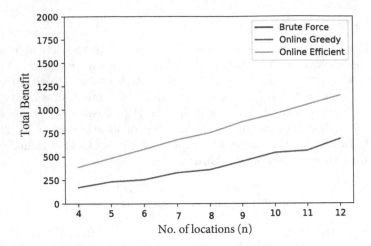

Fig. 1. Comparison of total benefits for $p_i \in [0.1, 1]$. Note that the blue line (result from brute force searching) is not visible as the green line (result from CONTEXT-SEC-ONLINE-EFFICIENT) coincides with the blue line. (Color figure online)

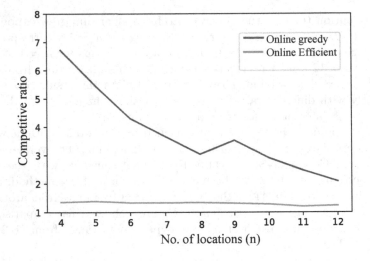

Fig. 2. Comparison of competitive ratios for $p_i \in [1, E/n]$.

compare the competitive ratio and the total benefit produced by the online algorithms as the offline results were also available. Figure 2 shows a comparison of the competitive ratios of CONTEXT-SEC-ONLINE-GREEDY and CONTEXT-SEC-ONLINE-EFFICIENT. The average competitive ratio for CONTEXT-SEC-ONLINE-EFFICIENT stays close to 1 and varies from 1.25 to 1.35 as n ranges from 4 to 12. On the other hand, the competitive ratio for CONTEXT-SEC-ONLINE-GREEDY decreases from a value of 6.8 to a value of 2 as n is increased.

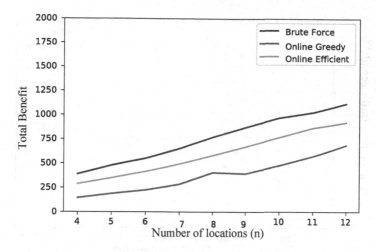

Fig. 3. Comparison of total benefit for $p_i \in [1, E/n]$.

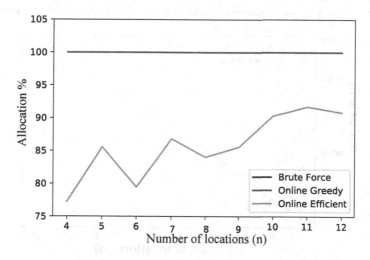

Fig. 4. Comparison of allocation percentage for $p_i \in [1, E/n]$. Note that the blue line (result from brute force searching) is not visible as the red line (result from CONTEXT-SEC-ONLINE-GREEDY) coincides with the blue line. (Color figure online)

The execution times for both CONTEXT-SEC-ONLINE-GREEDY and CONTEXT-SEC-ONLINE-EFFICIENT didn't change significantly when the assumption $p \ll E$ was relaxed. Both algorithms took from around 0.01 ms to 1 ms for all cases from $n = 4$ to $n = 12$. Finally, we compared the total benefit obtained by CONTEXT-SEC-ONLINE-GREEDY and CONTEXT-SEC-ONLINE-EFFICIENT with the optimal solution produced by brute force. Figure 3 shows that CONTEXT-SEC-ONLINE-EFFICIENT produced results closer to the optimal solution when compared to the solutions produced by CONTEXT-

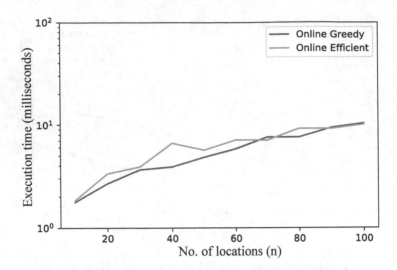

Fig. 5. Comparison of execution times for $p \in [1, E/n]$ and $n \in [10, 100]$

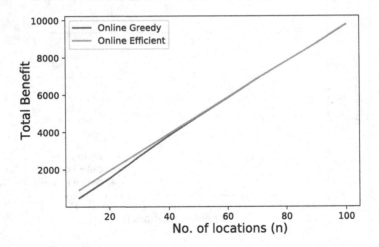

Fig. 6. Comparison of total benefits for $p \in [1, E/n]$ and $n \in [10, 100]$.

SEC-ONLINE-GREEDY. Specifically, the solution produced by CONTEXT-SEC-ONLINE-EFFICIENT was between 75% and 77% of the optimal solution, while CONTEXT-SEC-ONLINE-GREEDY produced roughly between 52% and 65% of the optimal solution.

We also study the percentage of locations which are allocated security levels, as it is possible that some of the locations may not be allocated any security level to remain within the energy budget constraint. For the case when p_i varied in the range $[0.1, 1]$, all algorithms allocated security levels to all locations. However, the percentage of locations allocated security levels varied widely when p_i varied in the range $[1, E/n]$, as shown in Fig. 4. There is defi-

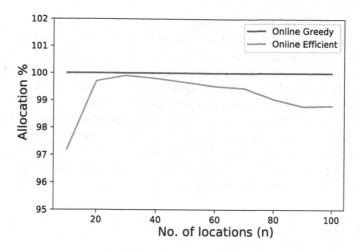

Fig. 7. Comparison of allocation percentages for $p \in [1, E/n]$ and $n \in [10, 100]$.

nitely a trade-off between CONTEXT-SEC-ONLINE-GREEDY and CONTEXT-SEC-ONLINE-EFFICIENT in this regard, because CONTEXT-SEC-ONLINE-EFFICIENT achieves a superior solution with only 77.5% to 92% of the locations allocated security levels, whereas CONTEXT-SEC-ONLINE-GREEDY allocates security levels to 100% of the locations while achieving 25% less benefit compared to CONTEXT-SEC-ONLINE-EFFICIENT.

For the second set of tests, our aim is to compare CONTEXT-SEC-ONLINE-GREEDY and CONTEXT-SEC-ONLINE-EFFICIENT by choosing larger numbers of locations and security levels for which brute force testing was infeasible. This will also give an insight into the scalability of the proposed algorithms.

For the range of values of n in $[10, 100]$, we set $E = 100$ and test the proposed algorithms for a wide variety of (p_i, b_i) as described in Table 1. We have varied p in $[0.1, 1]$ as well as in $[1, 100/n]$. We obtain the total benefit, percentage of locations that were allocated security levels, and execution times comparing the two online algorithms for $n \in [10, 100]$.

As seen from Figs. 5, 6, and 7, both CONTEXT-SEC-ONLINE-GREEDY and CONTEXT-SEC-ONLINE-EFFICIENT scale easily to as many as 100 locations, and their performance characteristics follow the same trends as were observed for smaller number of locations $n \in [4, 12]$. CONTEXT-SEC-ONLINE-EFFICIENT produces solutions that yield higher benefits, while not necessarily allocating security levels to all locations. CONTEXT-SEC-ONLINE-GREEDY produces solutions that yield lower benefits compared to CONTEXT-SEC-ONLINE-EFFICIENT while allocating security levels to 100% of the locations.

6   Conclusions and Future Work

In this paper, we have studied the context-adaptive, energy-aware security allocation methods for new locations to which a mobile device user may travel

Although the offline version of the problem has previously been studied, to the best of our knowledge, this is the first work that formulates the online version of the problem where the available security levels are not known *a priori* and only revealed when the user reaches a particular location. We have shown that this problem can be mapped to the online multi-choice knapsack problem and therefore no provably competitive solution is possible unless certain conditions are satisfied. To this end, we have proposed two novel solutions to solve the online problem. Our proposed solutions provide provable competitive ratios if certain conditions are met, are fast, and also scale well to a large number of locations. In the future, we plan to work on tightening the theoretical bound for this solution such that it matches the empirical bound found through experiments.

References

1. Abowd, G.D., Dey, A.K., Brown, P.J., Davies, N., Smith, M., Steggles, P.: Towards a better understanding of context and context-awareness. In: Gellersen, H.-W. (ed.) HUC 1999. LNCS, vol. 1707, pp. 304–307. Springer, Heidelberg (1999). https://doi.org/10.1007/3-540-48157-5_29
2. Al-Turjman, F., Alturjman, S.: Context-sensitive access in industrial internet of things (IIoT) healthcare applications. IEEE Trans. Ind. Inform. **14**(6), 2736–2744 (2018)
3. Ben-Asher, N., Kirschnick, N., Sieger, H., Meyer, J., Ben-Oved, A., Möller, S.: On the need for different security methods on mobile phones. In: Proceedings of the 13th International Conference on Human Computer Interaction with Mobile Devices and Services, pp. 465–473. ACM (2011)
4. Botezatu, N., Manta, V., Stan, A.: Self-adaptability in secure embedded systems: an energy-performance trade-off. In: The 2011 International Conference on Information Security and Internet Engineering, World Congress on Engineering (2011)
5. Chakrabarty, D., Zhou, Y., Lukose, R.: Online knapsack problems. In: Workshop on Internet and Network Economics (WINE) (2008)
6. Fischer, G.: Context-aware systems: the 'right' information, at the 'right' time, in the 'right' place, in the 'right' way, to the 'right' person. In: Proceedings of the International Working Conference on Advanced Visual Interfaces, AVI 2012, pp. 287–294. ACM, New York (2012). https://doi.org/10.1145/2254556.2254611
7. Ghahramani, M., Zhou, M., Hon, C.T.: Mobile phone data analysis: a spatial exploration toward hotspot detection. IEEE Trans. Autom. Sci. Eng. **16**, 351–362 (2018)
8. Goel, G., Mehta, A.: Online budgeted matching in random input models with applications to adwords. In: Proceedings of the Nineteenth Annual ACM-SIAM Symposium on Discrete Algorithms, pp. 982–991. Society for Industrial and Applied Mathematics (2008)
9. Hager, C.T.: Context aware and adaptive security for wireless networks. Ph.D. thesis, Virginia Polytechnic Institute and State University (2004)
10. Jameson, A.: Modelling both the context and the user. Pers. Ubiquitous Comput. **5**(1), 29–33 (2001). https://doi.org/10.1007/s007790170025, http://dx.doi.org/10.1007/s007790170025
11. Kellerer, H., Pferschy, U., Pisinger, D.: Knapsack problems 2004 (2003)
12. Marchetti-Spaccamela, A., Vercellis, C.: Stochastic on-line knapsack problems. Math. Program. **68**(1–3), 73–104 (1995)

13. Mehta, A., Saberi, A., Vazirani, U., Vazirani, V.: Adwords and generalized on-line matching. In: 46th Annual IEEE Symposium on Foundations of Computer Science (FOCS 2005), pp. 264–273. IEEE (2005)
14. Roy, S., Sankaran, S., Singh, P., Sridhar, R.: Modeling context-adaptive energy-aware security in mobile devices. In: 2018 IEEE 43rd Conference on Local Computer Networks Workshops (LCN Workshops), pp. 105–109. IEEE (2018)
15. Sankaran, S.: Lightweight security framework for IoTs using identity based cryptography. In: 2016 International Conference on Advances in Computing, Communications and Informatics (ICACCI), pp. 880–886, September 2016. https://doi.org/10.1109/ICACCI.2016.7732156
16. Sankaran, S., Sridhar, R.: User-adaptive energy-aware security for mobile devices. In: 2013 IEEE Conference on Communications and Network Security (CNS), pp. 391–392. IEEE (2013)
17. Zhou, Y., Chakrabarty, D., Lukose, R.: Budget constrained bidding in keyword auctions and online knapsack problems. In: Papadimitriou, C., Zhang, S. (eds.) WINE 2008. LNCS, vol. 5385, pp. 566–576. Springer, Heidelberg (2008). https://doi.org/10.1007/978-3-540-92185-1_63
18. Zhu, K.: Phone usage pattern as credit card fraud detection trigger, 26 February 2013. US Patent 8,386,386

A Framework Towards Generalized Mid-term Energy Forecasting Model for Industrial Sector in Smart Grid

Manali Chakraborty[1]([✉]), Sourasekhar Banerjee[2], and Nabendu Chaki[3]

[1] Università Ca' Foscari, Venice, VE, Italy
manali.chakraborty@unive.it
[2] Department of Computer Science and Engineering,
Indian Institute of Technology Patna, Bihta, India
1821cs12@iitp.ac.in
[3] Department of Computer Science and Engineering,
University of Calcutta, Kolkata, India
nabendu@ieee.org

Abstract. Smart Grid is emerging as one of the most promising technologies that will provide several improvements over the traditional power grid. Providing availability is a significant concern for the power sector, and to achieve an uninterrupted power supply accurate forecasting is essential. In the implementation of the future Smart Grid, efficient forecasting plays a crucial role, as the electric infrastructure will work, more and more, by continuously adjusting the electricity generation to the total end-use load. Electricity consumption depends on a vast domain of randomly fluctuating influential parameters, and every region has its own set of parameters depending on the demographic, socioeconomic, and climate conditions of that region. Even for the same set of parameters, the degree of influence on power consumption may vary over different sectors, like, residential, commercial, and industrial. Thus it is essential to quantify the dependency level for each parameter. We have proposed a generalized mid-term forecasting model for the industrial sector to predict the quarterly energy usage of a vast geographic region accurately with a diverse range of influential parameters. The proposed model is built and tested on real-life datasets of industrial users of various states in the U.S.

Keywords: Smart Grid · Forecasting · Data mining · Parametric modelling

1 Introduction

Technological progressions in recent years lead us to a more advanced, comfortable, and machine-dependent society, where the majority of these machines are fueled by electricity. As a result, the demand for electricity increases rapidly. To meet this demand, several distributed renewable energy sources are incorporated

© Springer Nature Switzerland AG 2020
D. V. Hung and M. D'Souza (Eds.): ICDCIT 2020, LNCS 11969, pp. 296–310, 2020.
https://doi.org/10.1007/978-3-030-36987-3_19

into the supply chain of electricity. Simultaneously, electricity usage pattern also fluctuates throughout the day based on several driving factors, such as temperature, working hours of commercial, industrial and educational establishments, festivals, etc. [13]. Balancing the supply-demand ratio in the Smart Grid considering all these odds, is far from being an easy job and requires additional technological support. Smart Grid incorporates a parallel data communication network along with the electricity network. This combined system can offer a two-way data exchange facility, where utilities can share supply related information with users. Users can also share their demands, usage history, as well as additional information (e.g., data on locally produced electricity using solar panel or bio-fuel.) with utilities.

In this paper, we are going to deliver a generalized model for forecasting industrial energy demand on Smart Grid. In [15], a generalized mid-term load forecasting model has been proposed for residential and commercial sectors in Smart Grid. The same can be applied to various geographical regions, having different socio-economic, demographic, and weather parameters. The model in [15] was tested on various states of the U.S and even on some other regions in India. However, in the industrial sector, it was not performing as expected. Analyzing the results further, we have found that the energy demand in the industrial sector is guided by a different set of parameters than the other two sectors. Besides, even the common influential parameters show different effects on residential, commercial, and industrial sectors. As an example, weather variations and festivities do not affect the energy usage of the industrial sector as much as the residential sector. U.S. Energy Information Administration (EIA) categorized the industrial sector in three distinct industry types [9]:

- *energy-intensive industries* generally consist of iron and steel manufacturing, petroleum refineries, nonferrous metals, and nonmetallic minerals industries.
- *non energy-intensive industries* including various pharmaceuticals, electronic, and electrical gadget manufacturing industries.
- *non manufacturing industries*, such as agricultural, forestry, fishing, construction, etc.

The energy demand in the industrial sector varies across regions and countries, depending on the combination of the industries mentioned above. Hence, we have selected industrial energy usage as the primary driving factor, that can be used to distinguish different regions for our proposed model. The purpose of this model is to predict the quarterly energy demand of any large geographic region, e.g., a state of a particular country. We have used six various data mining techniques and identified the most suitable one depending on the results. Then we have tried to find a multiplier variable that can be multiplied by the forecasted value to introduce accuracy in prediction. Here, we have categorized different geographical regions based on their average electricity usage in the industrial sector. For each region, we have tried to find out a range of multipliers.

The rest of the paper is organized as: in Sect. 2, we have discussed the motivations behind this work, and a brief literature review has given. Our proposed model is explained in Sect. 3. Finally, Sect. 4 concludes our paper.

2   Literature Review

Energy forecasting is about estimating future consumption based on various available information and as per consumer behavior. Forecasting models can be categorized into three groups depending on the period of prediction [17]:

- Short Term Load Forecasting (STLF): It refers to forecasting models that are used to predict the demand over hourly or day by day data.
- Mid-Term Load Forecasting (MTLF): It refers to the forecasting model that predicts demand over one week or several months or quarter.
- Long-Term Load Forecasting (LTLF): This type of model predicts the demand for several years.

This paper mainly focused on Mid-Term Load Forecasting. It is generally used to find peak load within several weeks or months. It can also be used to analyze the impact of different factors on electrical demand profile, such as weather profile, demographic profile, number of energy-intensive industrial establishments, etc. [20]. Compared to the other two forecasting models, MTLF provides a better insight, which in turn helps utilities to cope with any sudden changes in energy demand [15].

Over decades several forecasting techniques have been evolved to predict electrical load. Most of them are either from time series literature [30] or soft computing framework [25]. Different soft computing based technique viz. artificial neural network, fuzzy logic, genetic algorithm-based methods have taken proper attention in the field of forecasting. These methods provide high accuracy in their results even though there is non-linearity in data. But the problem is most of the time; these techniques act as a black box. It is quite challenging to find out the relationship between the explanatory variable and the response variable.

On the other hand, regression-based techniques provide both accuracy and interpretability of dependent and independent variables. In [11,18], the authors have used additive regression techniques to build their model. The performance of regression models depends on the quality of data sets and computing capability of machines [18,26].

In [23], authors have proposed a fuzzy regression technique to efficiently forecast long-term energy consumption in the industrial sector of Iran. They have introduced four independent variables, such as energy price, energy intensity, gross domestic production, and employment as inputs to the model. The prediction accuracy is better than the traditional ANOVA and ARIMA model.

A short-term load foresting model based on wavelet decomposition and the random forest has proposed in [19]. The traditional data mining algorithms have some drawbacks, viz. They can fall into local optimum, or they have poor generalization capability. Wavelet decomposition algorithm is a valid method to extract the load of the different components as the training set, and random Forest regression algorithm suffers less from the problem of overfitting and determining the difficulty of model parameters.

The authors in [22] have proposed this energy management problem for the industrial sector as a bigdata problem. They have introduced a multidimensional hybrid architecture that can handle the integration of locally stored structured energy-related data and external unstructured big data. They have shown a comparative study on different data mining techniques such as Decision Tree (C4.5), MLP, SVM, Linear Regression, and conclude that the decision tree gives higher accuracy in results.

Lee et al. proposed a hybrid model based on dynamic and fuzzy time series for midterm load forecasting in [21]. They have evaluated their model with the koyck and ARIMA model. The MAPE was less than 3% for consecutive four months of load forecasting. So this concludes that their proposed model gives a substantial reduction in the forecasting errors.

Another forecasting approach is presented in [24], where the authors proposed a new bagging based ensemble learning approach named Remainder Sieve Bootstrap (RSB) and applied it to enhance univariate forecasts for monthly electricity demand across different countries. Deep Neural networks can also be applied to forecasting energy usage in the smart grid. Some works on Deep learning has given in [10,14,16,27]

The industrial sector represents almost 54% [9] of global energy consumption, which makes it the largest energy consuming end-user sector in the economy. Besides, studies show that industrial energy usage will increase by as much as 40% by the next 15 years [9], especially in developing countries. Since the industrial sector is generally dominated by heavy types of machinery and mostly nonshiftable loads, it can have a significant contribution to high peak demands, that can challenge the generation process of utilities. In order to avoid these situations, it is necessary to acquire prior knowledge regarding the future energy demand of this sector. There exist some good works [11,12,18,19,23,29,30], which propose various methods to forecast future energy usage in industrial sectors, as well as other sectors, such as, residential and commercial. However, most of these methods were developed for a small geographical region. The underlying algorithms and procedures were trained and tested on the dataset of that particular region. As a result, these methods can be useful as long as we apply these to regions that have the same socio-economic, demographic characteristics as the region, based on which the model has been developed. Otherwise, every time we have to build a new model from scratch, depending on the characteristics of our application region. To solve this problem, we have proposed a generalized forecasting model for industrial sector users of Smart Grid. We have tested our model for various states across the U.S.

3   Proposed Methodology

The construction of our proposed model consists of two primary phases:

1. **Select underlying data mining algorithm:** using **training** and **testing** of various data mining algorithms and comparing the results.

2. **Construct multiplier database:** this phase helps us to generalize our proposed model so that we can apply it to a large geographical region.

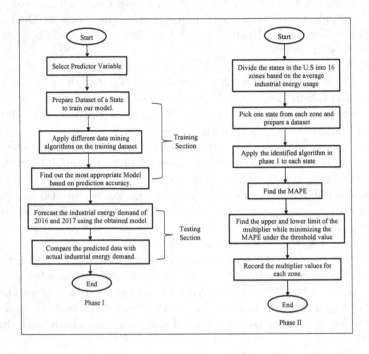

Fig. 1. Block diagram for proposed forecasting model.

Figure 1 depicts the basic block diagrams for the two phases separately. To justify the correctness of our multiplier values, we have tried to predict the multipliers and compared the obtained values with our calculated multipliers and found that they belong to the same range.

3.1 Select Underlying Data Mining Algorithm

The following series of steps will describe the methodology of selecting proper data mining techniques for predicting industrial electricity usage briefly.

1. Selection of the predictor variables for the industrial sector.
2. Data collection.
3. Data Preprocessing.
4. Experimental Setup and results.
5. Verify the result using the data of 2015.
6. Predict the quarterly demand for energy for the year 2016 and 2017.

Selection of the Predictor Variable for the Industrial Sector: We have selected ten industry-related influential parameters as follows:

1. **Previous quarterly energy usage (Thousand megawatts) history,** an average of 10 years' usage data for each quarter.
2. **Number of Energy Intensive Industry,** Here, we mainly focused on petroleum refinery, heavy metal, and manufacturing industries [3].
3. **Number of Energy Non-intensive Industry** consists of wood, plastic, rubber, computers, and electronic equipment manufacturing, etc. [3].
4. **GDP growth rate** for each quarter of each state.
5. **Population density** of each state for each quarter.
6. **Average Maximum Temperature** of each state.
7. **Average Minimum Temperature** of each state.
8. **Average Mean Temperature** of each state.
9. **Industrial load share** determines what percentage of electrical energy is used for the industrial sector amongst all sectors.
10. **Retail sale of energy (cents per kilowatt-hour)** for each quarter to industries of each state.

Data Collection: We have collected quarterly data from 2000 to 2017 for different states of the USA. All the dataset contains the same previously mentioned demographics and socio-economic parameters. Data for parameters 1, 9, and 10 have been collected from the US Energy Information Administration (EIA) [4]. The establishment of the energy-intensive and nonintensive industry has been collected from the Bureau of Labor Statistics (BLS) [5]. The GDP and population data have been collected from the Bureau of Economic Analysis (BEA) [1] and [6], respectively. Parameter 6, 7 and 8 have been collected from national centers for environment Information (NOAA) [2]. We have trained our model on the dataset of North Carolina (2000–2017). Other datasets are divided into 9 decade long sets, i.e.: 2000–2009, 2001–2010, 2002–2011, 2003–2012, 2004–2013, 2005–2014, 2006–2015, 2007–2016, 2008–2017 for different states of USA. These datasets are used as test sets.

Data Preprocessing: It is a common requirement for many machine learning estimators to standardize datasets. Here we scale features to lie between a range of 0 to 1. In this paper, we calculate x_i_norm, the normalized value for each predictor variable x_i for i = 1, 2, ..., n, as 1:

$$x_i\_norm = \frac{(x_i - x_i\_min)}{(x_i\_max - x_i\_min)} \tag{1}$$

where, x_i_max and x_i_min are the maximum and minimum values for the vector x_i, and n is the total number of predicted variables.

Experimental Setup and Results: All experiments have been performed on WEKA-3.8.3: Waikato Environment for Knowledge Analysis [7]. It is a suite of machine learning software written in Java to perform data mining tasks.

Selection of appropriate data mining algorithms: We have selected four regression-based data mining approaches: *Additive Regression, Random Forest, M5P Tree, and SMOReg* to identify which approach gives better results than other methods.

As mentioned previously, we have taken a quarterly dataset (2000–2017) of North Carolina as training set and applied 4 different machine learning techniques on the training set with 10 fold cross validation to prepare models. We have compared the performances of these four models based on 6 metrics, [28] such as *Correlation Coefficient (CC), Mean Absolute Error (MAE). Root Mean Square Error (RMSE), Relative Absolute Error (RAE), Relative Root Square Error (RRSE), Mean Absolute Percentage Error (MAPE)* The results of our experiments are given in Table 1. After analyzing all these data and taking consideration of every comparison metrics, we have found that the ensemble learning-based algorithm Random Forest gives better accuracy in forecasting than other techniques.

Table 1. Performance metrics

Methods	CC	MAE	RMSE	RAE (%)	RRSE (%)	MAPE
Additive Regression	0.9017	84.96	107.465	42.425	42.9074	4.131
Random Forest	0.9544	60.3091	79.0997	30.1177	31.5821	3.349
M5P	0.91	76.7695	102.903	38.3369	41.086	3.686
SMOReg	0.947	61.806	79.7712	30.8685	31.8502	3.516

Predict Quarterly Usages of Energy for the Year 2016 and 2017: Here we have predicted the quarterly usage of energy in the industrial sector of North Carolina for the years 2016 and 2017 using the model based on Random Forest. We have compared our results with the actual usage of energy. Figure 2 shows the comparison of actual and predicted usage of energy. The pattern of the prediction curve has a similarity with the actual curve.

3.2   Construct Multiplier Database:

In this Sect. 3.1, we have created a model based on Random Forest to forecast the energy usages of North Carolina. Here we will measure the performance of the proposed model using the datasets of the different geographic regions of the same country, which have the same socio-economic parameters. We have studied 17 years long quarterly data for average energy usages in the industrial sector

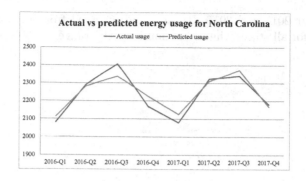

Fig. 2. Comparison results using Random Forest for North Carolina.

Table 2. Division of region based on Average energy usage in previous 15 years

Region	Average industrial energy usage (Gigawatt)	States
A	0–500	Maine, New Hampshire, Rhode Island, Vermont, North-Dakota, South Dakota, Delware, Montana, Alaska, Hawaii
B	500–1000	New Jersey, Kansas, Nebraska, Idaho, New Mexico, Utah, Wyoming
C	1000–1500	Massachusetts, New York, Missouri, Florida, Virginia, West-Virginia, Mississippi, Arkansas, Oklahoma, Arizona, Colorado, Nevada, Oregon
D	1500–2000	Wisconsin, MInnesota
E	2000–2500	North Carolina, South Carolina, Tennessee, Louisiana
F	2500–3000	Michigan, Georgia, Alabama
G	3000–3500	Illinois, Kentucky
H	3500–4000	Pennsylvania, Indiana, California
I	4000–4500	Ohio
J, K, L, M, N, O	4500-...-7500	NIL
P	>7500	Texas

of all states of the U.S; then we have divided the country into 16 regions based on average industrial energy usage. This division is given in Table 2.

We have selected datasets of New Hampshire, New Jersey, New York, Wisconsin, Lousiana, Michigan, Indiana, Ohio, and Texas from zone A-I and P, respectively, taking at least one state from each region and have applied our proposed model on them. Figure 3(a)–(d) shows the comparison between actual and predicted quarterly energy usage for the year 2014 and 2015 and Fig. 4(a)–

(e) for the year 2015 and 2016. It has been observed from Figs. 3(a)–(d) and 4(a)–(d) that for all states, the prediction is in the range of 2000–3000.

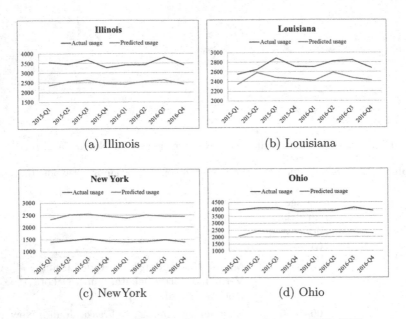

Fig. 3. Actual vs Previous energy usage for year 2015–2016

However, interestingly, there is some similarity in patterns. In most cases, the actual energy usage curve and the prediction curve are similar. Thus, the work reduces to find a constant to be multiplied by the predicted value to improve prediction accuracy. In the next section, we will produce a multiplier database, which we have calculated after doing experiments on states of the different regions. We have also predicted multiplier for each quarter of the year 2015 for a state and verified it with its multiplier range. There is an upper and lower limit of multiplier for each region. By using an appropriate multiplier from this range, we can improve the accuracy of the predicted result.

Multiplier Database: In this section, we have tried to find a multiplier database that can be used to improve the accuracy and scalability of the proposed forecasting model. We have applied our model on the datasets of each state representing each zone and calculated MAPE. If the value of MAPE is less than 10, then we can say that prediction has higher accuracy. If the MAPE is not below 10, then we have to minimize the value of MAPE by changing the predicted value. Here our main objective is to find out a range of multipliers say x for each zone. Algorithm 1 describes the procedure for finding x, for which the minimum value of MAPE is less than 10. Using Algorithm 1 in various states, we have found the upper and lower limit of the multiplier. The results are given in Table 3 and Fig. 5.

(a) Florida

(b) Indiana

(c) Michigan

(d) Texas

(e) Wisconsin

Fig. 4. Actual vs Previous energy usage for year 2014–2015

Table 3 clearly shows that Louisiana-North Carolina and Indiana-California both are from region E and H respectively, and both have similar multiplier range. So by calculating the average of individual multiplier limits of all states belonging to the same region, we can produce the approximate range of multiplier for that region. It has also been observed from Fig. 5 that the actual energy usage curve belongs within the prediction range. Further, we have taken seven decade-long datasets of Ohio from the region I and has found that both upper and lower limits are almost same for all dataset. Figure 6 depicts the results.

Verification of Proposed Model: We have tried to predict the multiplier for a state and compared it with our calculated values. We have collected 15 years of long quarterly data of actual energy usage and predicted energy demand, which has been calculated by applying the proposed model, discussed in [8]. We have selected the dataset of Florida for experimental purposes and calculated

---

Algorithm 1: *Find_Multiplier*

Input: Quarterly data of Predicted and Actual usages of energy.

Output: mul_L and mul_U:Lower and Upper limit of multiplier respectively.

1 Start;

2 let x = 0 ,min_mape = 0, flag = 2;

/* flag determines the upper and lower limit of the multiplier.   */

3 **while** *(flag ≠ 0)* **do**

4 $\quad min\_mape = \frac{\sum_1^n abs((actual_i - x \times predicted_i)/actual_i)}{n} \times 100$;

5 $\quad$ **if** *(min_mape < 10 && flag == 2)* **then**

6 $\quad\quad mul_L = x;$

7 $\quad\quad$ flag = 1;

8 $\quad$ **else**

9 $\quad\quad$ **if** *(min_mape ⩾ 10 && flag == 1)* **then**

10 $\quad\quad\quad mul_U = (x - 0.001);$

11 $\quad\quad\quad$ flag = 0;

12 $\quad\quad$ **end**

13 $\quad$ **end**

14 $\quad x+ = 0.001;$

15 **end**

16 End;

Table 3. Upper and Lower Limit of Multiplier for different states

Region	State	Upper limit of Multiplier	Lower limit of Multiplier
A	New Hampshire	0.06	0.08
B	New Jersey	0.28	0.31
C	Florida	0.57	0.7
C	New York	0.52	0.7
D	Wisconsin	0.77	1
E	Louisiana	0.9	1.1
E	North Carolina	0.9	1.1
F	Michigan	1.01	1.2
H	Indiana	1.4	1.7
H	California	1.5	1.8
I	Ohio	1.7	2.1
P	Texas	3	3.7

the multiplier for each quarter where MAPE is minimum. The result has been shown in Table 4.

Now, we have done time series forecasting in WEKA [28] using these obtained multiplier values in Table 4. In time series forecasting, we have applied Random Forest as a base learner, and Maximum Lag creation is 12. We have forecast

Table 4. Minimum MAPE and corresponding Multiplier (Florida 2000–2014).

Year with quarter	Actual energy usages	Predicted energy usages	Multiplier	Minimum MAPE
2000-Q1	1527.33	1526.16	0.578	0.077
2000-Q2	1578.33	1579.34	0.584	0.064
2000-Q3	1575.33	1576.51	0.577	0.075
2000-Q4	1502.33	1503.61	0.577	0.085
...	...	...	...	...
2014-Q1	1338	1338.56	0.618	0.042
2014-Q2	1440.33	1439.21	0.622	0.078
2014-Q3	1483.67	1482.65	0.637	0.069
2014-Q4	1374.33	1374.44	0.613	0.007

Table 5. Multiplier prediction and Actual vs. Predicted energy usage (Florida)

Year with quarter	Predicted multiplier	Actual energy	Predicted energy
2015-Q1	0.615	1317.33	1334.4
2015-Q2	0.621	1448.67	1478.697
2015-Q3	0.624	1470	1479.654
2015-Q4	0.619	1400.33	1445.74

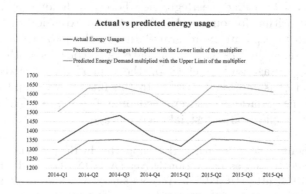

Fig. 5. Actual vs predicted energy demand of Florida (2014–2015)

energy usage for each quarter of 2015 for Florida. The output of the predicted multiplier has given in Table 5. It has been observed that predicted multipliers are in the range of region C, as mentioned in Table 3 in Sect. 3.2. These results, in turn, justify the effectiveness and correctness of our multiplier database, as well as our proposed forecasting model.

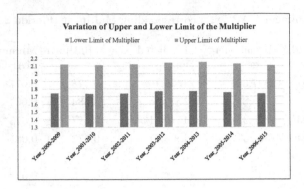

Fig. 6. Variations of Upper and Lower limits of multiplier for Ohio

4 Conclusions

In order to plan the generation, transmission, and distribution in a Smart Grid, the energy consumption pattern of individual sectors must be known in advance. Especially in the industrial sector, quarterly demand forecasting can motivate the utilities to design the supply side of the process accordingly, so that peak demands can be reduced and an uninterrupted flow of electricity can be maintained with optimized economic gain for both users and utilities.

In this paper, our main objective is to find a generalized model that can be able to predict industrial energy demand for a vast geographic region. We have achieved our goal by using the Regression Forest technique as an underlying data mining algorithm for our model. As a future extension of this work, we are planning to incorporate more granularity in the parametric modeling for forecasting. Besides, in this paper, we have only considered the variation of industrial energy usage and its effect on the dependencies between influential parameters and consumption patterns. In the future, we would like to study the impact on the variations of several economic factors, like GDP, the price of electricity, and its effect on industrial energy usage.

Acknowledgments. This research work is supported by the projects "ADditive Manufacturing & Industry 4.0 as innovation Driver (ADMIN 4D)" and TEQIP Phase 3 in University of Calcutta (UCT-CU). Authors sincerely acknowledge and thank the projects for providing the support required for carrying out the research work.

References

1. Bureau of Economic Analysis (BEA) U.S. Department of Commerce. https://www.bea.gov
2. National Centers for Environmental Information, NOAA. https://www.ncdc.noaa.gov
3. U.S. EIA, Today in Energy. https://www.eia.gov/todayinenergy/detail.php?id=8110

4. U.S. Energy Information Administration, Electricity. https://www.eia.gov/electricity/monthly/backissues.html
5. U.S. Bureau of Labor. https://www.bls.gov/
6. U.S. Census Bureau. https://www.census.gov/
7. Weka 3.8.1: Data mining software in java. https://www.cs.waikato.ac.nz/ml/weka/
8. Weka 3: data mining software in java, Class Random Forest. http://weka.sourceforge.net/doc.dev/weka/classifiers/trees/RandomForest.html
9. U.S. Energy Information Administration: Industrial sector Energy Consumption. International Energy Outlook, pp. 113–126 (2016)
10. Agrawal, R.K.: Long-term load forecasting with hourly predictions based on long-short-term-memory networks. In: IEEE Texas Power and Energy Conference (TPEC), March 2018
11. Ali, S.M., Mehmood, C.A., Khan, B., Jawad, M.: Stochastic and statistical analysis of utility revenues and weather data analysis for consumer demand estimation in smart grids. PLoSONE 11(6), e0156849 (2016)
12. Ang, B.W., Xu, X.Y.: Tracking industrial energy efficiency trends using index decomposition analysis. Energy Econ. 40, 1014–1021 (2013)
13. Bakker, V.: Triana a control strategy for smart grids forecasting, planning and real-time control. Ph.D thesis. ISBN 978-90-365-3314-0, ISSN 1381-3617. https://doi.org/10.3990/1.9789036533140
14. Barger, D.J.: MGE experience with INSITE spatial load forecasting. In: IEEE Power and Energy Society General Meeting, October 2011
15. Chakraborty, M., Chaki, N., Das, S.K.: A medium-term load forecasting model for smart grid with effect quantification of socio-economic predictor parameters. In: Revision resubmitted to Sustainable Energy, Grids and Networks (SEGAN) Journal. Elsevier, April 2019. ISSN 2352–4677
16. Dong, X., Qian, L., Huang, L.: Short-term load forecasting in smart grid: a combined CNN and k-means clustering approach. In: IEEE International Conference on Big Data and Smart Computing (BigComp), pp. 119–125, March 2017
17. Ghalehkhondabi, I., Ardjmand, E., Weckman, G.R.: an overview of energy demand forecasting methods published in 2005–2015. Energy Syst. 8(2), 411–447 (2017)
18. Hong, T., Gui, M., Baran, M.E., Willis, H.L.: Modeling and forecasting hourly electric load by multiple linear regression with interactions. In: Power and Energy Society General Meeting, USA, pp. 1–8 (2010)
19. Huang, Q., Li, Y., Liu, S., Liu, P.: Short term load forecasting based on wavelet decomposition and random forest. In: Workshop on Smart Internet of Things, SmartIoT, p. 2 (2017)
20. Khodayar, M.E., Wu, H.: Demand forecasting in the smart grid paradigm: features and challenges. Electr. J. 28(6), 51–62 (2015)
21. Lee, W., Hong, J.: A hybrid dynamic and fuzzy time series model for mid-term power load forecasting. Electr. Power Energy Syst. 64, 1057–1062 (2015)
22. Mate, A., Peral, J., Ferrandez, A., Gil, D., Trujillo, J.: A hybrid integrated architecture for energy consumption prediction. Future Gener. Comput. Syst. 63, 131–147 (2016)
23. Mehr, M.N., Samavati, F.F., Jeihoonian, M.: Annual energy demand estimation of Iran industrial sector by fuzzy regression and ARIMA. In: Eight International Conference on Fuzzy Systems and Knowledge Discovery, vol. 1, pp. 593–597. IEEE (2011)
24. Oliveira, E.M., Oliveira, F.L.C.: Forecasting mid-long term electric energy consumption through bagging ARIMA and exponential smoothing methods. Energy 144, 776–788 (2018)

25. Socares, L.J., Mederios, M.C.: Modeling and forecasting short-term electricity load: a comparison of methods with an application to Brazilian data. Int. J. Forecast. **24**(4), 630–644 (2008)
26. Song, K., Baek, Y., Hong, D.H., Jang, G.: Short-term load forecasting for the holidays using fuzzy linear regression method. IEEE Trans. Power Syst. **20**(1), 96–101 (2005)
27. Wang, Y., Liu, M.: Short-term load forecasting with multi-source data using gated recurrent unit neural networks. Energies **11**, 1138–1157 (2018)
28. Witten, I.H., Frank, E., Hal, M.A.: Data Mining: Practical Machine Learning Tools and Techniques, 3rd edn. Morgan Kaufmann, Burlington (2004)
29. Xu, X.Y., Ang, B.W.: Multilevel index decomposition analysis: approaches and application. Energy Econ. **44**, 375–382 (2014)
30. Zafer, D., Hunt, L.C.: Industrial electricity demand for Turkey: a structural time series analysis. Energy Econ. **33**(3), 426–436 (2011)

An Online Low-Cost System for Air Quality Monitoring, Prediction, and Warning

Rishi Sharma[1] ⓘ, Tushar Saini[1](✉) ⓘ, Praveen Kumar[1] ⓘ, Ankush Pathania[1] ⓘ,
Khyathi Chitineni[1] ⓘ, Pratik Chaturvedi[1,2] ⓘ, and Varun Dutt[1] ⓘ

[1] Applied Cognitive Science Lab, Indian Institute of Technology Mandi, Mandi,
Himachal Pradesh, India
tushar.saini1285@gmail.com, varun@iitmandi.ac.in
[2] Defence Terrain Research Laboratory, Deference Research and Development Organization,
New Delhi, India

Abstract. Air-quality is degrading in developing countries and there is an urgent need to monitor and predict air-quality online in real-time. Although offline air-quality monitoring using hand-held devices is common, online air-quality monitoring is still expensive and uncommon, especially in developing countries. The primary objective of this paper is to propose an online low-cost air-quality monitoring, prediction, and warning system (AQMPWS) which monitors, predicts, and warns about air-quality in real-time. The AQMPWS monitors and predict seven pollutants, namely, PM1.0, PM2.5, PM10, Carbon Monoxide, Nitrogen Dioxide, Ozone and Sulphur Dioxide. In addition, the AQMPWS monitors and predicts five weather variables, namely, Temperature, Pressure, Relative Humidity, Wind Speed, and Wind Direction. The AQMPWS has its sensors connected to two microcontrollers in a Master-Slave configuration. The slave sends the data to the API in the cloud through an HTTP GET request via a GSM Module. A python-based web-application interacts with the API for visualization, prediction, and warning. Results show that the AQMPWS monitor different pollutants and weather variables within range specified by pollution control board. In addition, the AQMPWS predict the value of the pollutants and weather variables for the next 30-min given the current values of these pollutants and weather variables using an ensemble model containing a multilayer-perceptron and long short-term memory model. The AQMPWS is also able to warn stakeholders when any of the seven pollutants breach pre-defined thresholds. We discuss the implications of using AQMPWS for air-quality monitoring in the real-world.

Keywords: Air-quality · Machine learning · Warning

1 Introduction

Air quality is at its worst currently in developing countries like India [11]. For example, India accounts for 22 of the top 30 cities of the world with the most air pollution [7]. Here, the Particulate Matter (PM) levels for PM10, PM2.5, and PM1.0 are particularly worrisome [7]. PM10, PM2.5, and PM1.0 levels are defined as the fraction of particles

D. V. Hung and M. D'Souza (Eds.): ICDCIT 2020, LNCS 11969, pp. 311–324, 2020.
https://doi.org/10.1007/978-3-030-36987-3_20

with an aerodynamic diameter smaller than 10, 2.5, and 1 μm, respectively. When it comes to comparing PM10 (in μg/m^3) measurements of the world's largest cities, India's capital Delhi comes in with an annual average of 292, ahead of Cairo (284), Dhaka (147), Mumbai (104), and Beijing (92) [6]. This pollution level is significantly higher compared to the WHO air quality guideline value of 50 μg/m^3 [26]. For PM2.5, the world mean annual exposure stands at 45.522 μg/m^3, whereas in India, the value is as high as 91 μg/m^3 [2] (the PM2.5 levels should not be more than 10 μg/m^3 [26]).

Poor air quality is detrimental to human health, with a number of studies finding short-term and long-term pulmonary and cardiovascular health effects of PM10 and PM2.5 [21]. In fact, pollutants such as particulate matter with an aerodynamic diameter smaller than 2.5 μm (PM2.5), nitrogen oxides (NO$_X$), and tropospheric ozone (O3) continue to be a cause of cancer, respiratory and cardiovascular disease, and premature death [4]. Furthermore, long exposure to poor air quality can increase the chances of stroke, heart diseases, lung cancer and both chronic and acute respiratory diseases. These diseases of the respiratory tract cause coughing, mucus secretion, aggravation of asthma and chronic bronchitis and make people more prone to other infections [25]. In addition, air pollution also incurs major economic costs on the order of billions of Euros a year in the form of premature deaths, damage to buildings, health problems and hospital costs and reduced agricultural yields. [4].

Currently, India has about 731 manual (offline) air quality monitoring stations [17]. Air quality is measured at specific prescribed times during the day at these stations. However, the problem with manual air quality monitoring is that air quality depends on various environmental and human factors and it can change drastically over a short period of time. Thus, manually measured air-quality values are only true over a short period of time and these values may not be indicative of short-term changes in air-quality throughout the day. As air quality monitoring systems must be able to timely warn people about deteriorating air-quality, there is a need for real-time (online) air-quality monitoring. India currently has 150 real-time air quality monitoring stations across the country, which along with the manual air quality monitoring stations cover about 70 cities. Among these 150 systems, 48 systems are installed in Delhi itself and the Indian government is planning to increase the real-time monitoring systems to 450 and manual stations to 1,500 by 2024 [17]. However, the real challenge is the high cost of real-time air quality monitoring systems: the average cost for a real-time air quality monitoring station is about 1.04 crore and, for a manual monitoring station, it is about 14.5 lakhs [16].

Beyond monitoring, one also needs to predict air-quality ahead of time to give lead-time to people to protect themselves against deteriorating quality of air. Currently, a number of machine-learning (ML) approaches have been proposed for monitoring air-quality in the real world [22]. For example, reference [22] has used time-series regression to analyze and predict the trends in SO$_2$, NO$_2$, CO, and O$_3$ in Delhi. However, the use of an ensembling of ML models along with the time-series forecasting for air-quality prediction has been less explored.

The primary objective of this research is to develop a new solution for low-cost, real-time monitoring of air quality. Such a novel solution requires the system to be self-reliant to be deployed even in the remote regions. Hence, we design a new low-power circuit that can run perpetually on solar power. The circuit has been tuned in a way such that the average energy consumption of the system is smaller compared to the charging provided by the solar energy.

In what follows, first, we detail past works on air quality monitoring. Next, we describe the development of a new IoT-based system with the description of its circuit, system architecture and hardware design. Furthermore, we shed light on the programming of the microcontrollers and the predictive analytics of air quality values for the purpose of generating warning. We close this paper by discussing the implications of this new technology for real-time air-quality monitoring on a large-scale in the real-world.

2 Literature Review

2.1 Air Quality Monitoring

Reference [24] proposed an indoor air-quality monitoring system for monitoring of temperature, humidity, PM2.5, PM10, total VOCs, CO_2, CO, illuminance, and sound levels. However, sensors were limited to indoors and there was no benchmark used. Prior research proposed an air-quality monitoring system for urban areas in Italy where measurements were limited to CO, NO_2, O_3, temperature, and humidity values. Also, sensors used costly proprietary nodes and comparison with benchmarks was limited [3]. Reference [10] proposed an air-quality system where the measurements were restricted to CO, SO_2, O_3, temperature, and humidity values with a limited comparison to benchmarks. References [1, 18] and [12] have proposed environmental air-pollution monitoring system prototypes for CO, CO_2, SO_2 and NO_2; however, a comparison to benchmarks was not present. In this research, we propose a system that monitors seven pollutants (PM1.0, PM2.5, PM10, Carbon Monoxide, Nitrogen Dioxide, Ozone and Sulphur Dioxide) and five weather variables (Temperature, Pressure, Relative humidity, Wind speed, and wind direction) and we benchmark the values measured against hand-held meters or other real-time air-quality devices.

2.2 Predictive Analysis

In preliminary research, reference [19] has investigated the use of auto-encoders and regression to understand PM2.5, PM10, SO2, NO2, CO, and O3 concentrations every hour. However, several other machine-learning (DL) techniques were left unexplored. Furthermore, a number of classical ensemble methods to predict O3 levels in Spain over a two-year period have been proposed [14]. However, the methods used were limited and time-series forecasting was not touched. Authors of reference [29] have used decision-tree methods for forecasting of PM2.5 levels over three years 2013–2015 in Shenyang, China. There was limited use of methods and limited time-period. Some authors have also used ANNs for air-quality predictions [23, 28]. But these authors have limited time-periods and locations and no applications of recurrent machine-learning methods. In this research, we propose an ensemble machine-learning architecture consisting of both a recurrent and a feed-forward neural network for predicting the values of seven pollutants (PM1.0, PM2.5, PM10, Carbon Monoxide, Nitrogen Dioxide, Ozone and Sulphur Dioxide) and five weather variables (Temperature, Pressure, Relative humidity, Wind speed, and Wind direction) via a single model.

3 Air Quality Monitoring System

3.1 Circuit Design

The sensors to be used in the circuit need to be carefully chosen to cover pollutant levels within and beyond the ambient air quality standards. Table 1 specifies the ranges of different pollutants and weather variables covered by the air-quality monitoring, prediction, and warning system (AQMPWS). The range of pollutants covers the norms specified by Central Pollution Control Board of India [15].

Table 1. Ranges of the AQMPWS.

Sensors	Range
Temperature	−40 °C to 80 °C
Humidity	0 to 100%
Pressure	300 to 1100 hPa
Sulfur dioxide	0 to 20 ppm
Ozone	0 to 10 ppm
Carbon monoxide	1 to 1000 ppm
NO_X	5 to 10 ppm
Particulate matter	0 to 500 $\mu g/m^3$
Wind speed	0 to 50 m/s
Wind direction	N, NE, E, SE, S, SW, W, NW

Considering the number of sensors and other accessories being controlled by microcontrollers, 2 microcontrollers are needed. These two microcontrollers work in a master-slave configuration. The master controls the humidity and temperature sensor, pressure sensor, ozone sensor and a cooling fan. The master writes the sensor values to the slave in a string format via the I^2C protocol [9]. The slave controls the particulate matter sensor, CO sensor, NOX sensor, SO2 sensor, anemometer and wind vane. The slave uses the GSM Module which is supported by a capacitor to send data to the cloud via an HTTP GET Request. The Solar Panel charges a 10,000 mAh battery through a charge controller. A voltage booster delivers the required voltage of 5 V to the circuit. The supply to the components is controlled by the microcontrollers using an NPN transistor as a switch.

3.2 System Architecture

Figure 1 shows the working of the AQMPWS. The master reads the temperature, pressure, humidity and ozone values from the sensors in the ambient air. It activates the fan if the temperature inside exceeds the external temperature by 10 °C. These sensed data are next sent to the slave. The slave obtains the readings for sulfur dioxide, carbon monoxide, nitrogen oxides and particulate matter sensors. Next, the slave makes an

HTTP request to an API using the GSM Module with the data recorded. The data along with the location reaches the cloud-based API via an HTTP GET request. The request arguments are extracted and inserted into the database. The values in the database can be requested using another GET request. At each request to the API, the values are checked against the ambient air quality standards. If they cross the standard thresholds, the warning system is triggered.

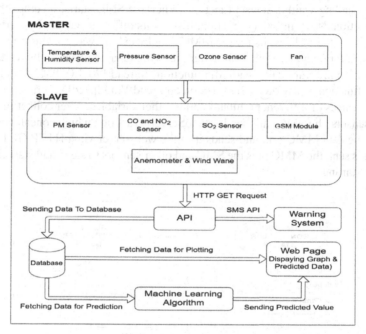

Fig. 1. The AQMPWS' architecture.

The warning system triggers a custom SMS message containing the pollutant names and the current concentrations for each pollutant that crossed its threshold. This message is then sent to all the registered users as an SMS alert. The same alert is also sent to the local authorities so that preventive measures may be immediately taken. A separate Web Interface is designed to visualize the pollution levels across locations from anywhere around the globe. This interface is equipped to interact with different machine learning models to display the air quality predictions.

3.3 Microcontroller Programming

The setup() function is called when the microcontroller starts. It is used to initialize variables and pin modes. The setup() function will only run once, after each powerup. After creating a setup() function, which initializes and sets the initial values, the loop() function does precisely what its name suggests, and loops consecutively.

Figure 2 shows the flowchart of the program, first the master microcontroller (MMC) setups the interval of sleep and pin modes. Then in loop() function, the system sleeps for a preset interval which is 28 min. The sleep for 28 min ensures that the system saves energy and measures pollution and weather parameters about 48 times in the day. After sleeping for the preset interval, it switches on the slave microcontroller (SMC) and its sensors. The MMC then calls the readSensors() function which collects data from sensors by calling readTempHumid() function, readPressure() function and readOzone() function. After collecting data, the MMC calls sendToSlave() function which sends data to SMC as a string using the serial output. The MMC then waits for the SMC to complete its tasks by calling waitForSlave() function. When the SMC starts, it setups the pin in setup() function. Next, in loop() function, it starts its different sensors by startSensor() function. Then, the SMC waits for the MMC data by calling waitForMaster() function, which listens for data on serial input. After receiving data, the SMC calls readSensor() function which in return calls readPM() function (to read PM 1.0, PM2.5 and PM10), readSo2() function, readCo&No2() function and readWindSpeedDir() function to read the current values of different pollutants and weather variables. After collecting the data from the sensors, the SMC calls sendDataToServer() function which concatenates SMC data with the data MMC sent and sends it to the web-server via a HTTP GET request. After data is sent, the MMC puts the SMC and other sensors to sleep and start executing loop from starting.

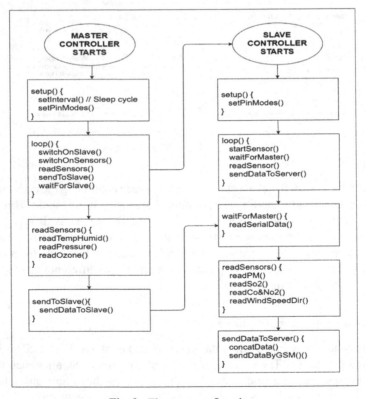

Fig. 2. The program flowchart.

3.4 Power Consumption

The AQMPWS was designed for outdoor use on solar power with no dependence upon grid-connected power supply. As the cost of solar panel and charging circuit increases the overall cost of the system, we wanted to decrease the power consumed by the system. The reduction in power consumption in the system was executed via a customized bootloader and a power-down library [13]. The customized bootloader turned off the potentially costly analogue to digital conversion (which can use power even when idle) and the brown out detection that stops the running code when its input voltage gets too low. The brown out detection was not needed as we ensured adequate voltage to the circuit via a voltage booster.

Based upon the customized bootloader and code optimizations, the system consumed 0.3 mA in sleep mode and 320 mA in wake-up (on) mode. In contrast, popular microcontrollers (like ATmega 2560 and ATmega328p) consume 50 mA in sleep mode and about 360–450 mA in wake-up (on) mode. For our study, we used a 10AH lithium-ion battery with 3.2 W solar panel charging it and observed that our system could work without discharging the battery during its operation over a two-month period. For this experiment, we setup the AQMPWS via our customized bootloader on the microcontroller as well as the AQMPWS via the ATmega 2560 and ATmega328p microcontrollers with their respective bootloaders side-by-side. Figure 3 shows the relation between the charge remaining in the battery over a 60-days period from the three systems. As can be observed from Fig. 3, while the ATmega2560 and ATmega328p completely discharged the battery after the tenth day and ATmega328p after the 20th day, respectively, the AQMPWS never discharged the battery below the 9000 mAh mark. Overall, the battery hardly lost any charge and the AQMPWS could run for an extended period.

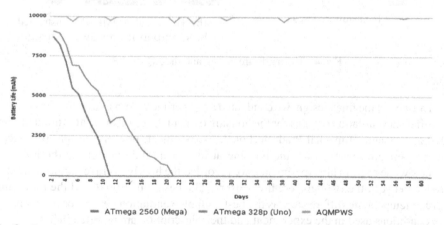

Fig. 3. Graph showing power consumption of different microcontrollers and AQMPWS over time.

3.5 Designing the External Housing

Figure 4(a) shows the design of the AQMPWS box. In addition, Fig. 4(b) shows the actual AQMPWS developed based upon its design. The housing for the AQMPWS (a letter-box shape) was designed to protect the circuit from external agents, and at the same time, ensure similarity of temperature inside and outside the box. The box was also painted white for minimum absorption of heat. Figure 4 shows the design of the box. Since the AQMPWS would work in the real-world, the box was closed to protect the circuit from environmental factors like rain.

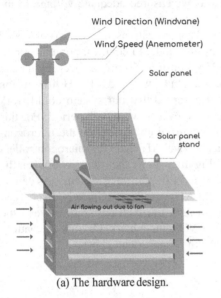

(a) The hardware design.

(b) The actual AQMPWS constructed based upon its hardware design.

Fig. 4. The hardware design and the AQMPWS.

To arrive at the final design, we conducted an experiment with five conditions involving different ventilation designs for the housing over a 1-h period on an afternoon in May 2019 at Kamand, Himachal Pradesh. For this experiment, in every design, we placed one temperature sensor inside the housing at its center, and one outside the housing, just below the roof. In all experiments, we recorded the hourly average temperature difference between the two temperature sensors. The design that produced the minimum average temperature difference was the best suitable ventilation design for the housing. The conditions used in the experiment and their description are reported in Table 2.

Figure 5 shows the temperature difference between the inside and outside of the housing across the five conditions. As shown in the Figure, in all-closed condition, the average temperature difference was found to be 1.95 °C. In Left-Front-Open condition, the average temperature difference was found to be 2.46 °C. In Left-Right-Open condition, the average temperature difference was found to be 2.07 °C. In All-Open condition, the average temperature difference was found to be 4.50 °C. In All-Open-Fan condition,

Table 2. Different ventilation conditions for the housing and their description.

Condition	Description
All-closed	Completely closed housing with no ventilation. The housing was closed from all sides so that no air flow could occur. This condition served as a control in the experiment
Left-Front-Open	Left and front ventilators open in the housing for air flow to take place. All other ventilators closed
Left-Right-Open	Left and right ventilators open in the housing for air flow to take place. All other ventilators closed
All-Open	Left, front, and right ventilators were open
All-Open-Fan	Left, front, and right ventilators were open. A DC fan was placed at the front side of the box to improve the ventilation system

the average temperature difference was found to be 1.82 °C. Thus, the All-Open-Fan condition (see the Fig. 4(a)), gave the minimum temperature difference and it was the one selected as the final design (see Fig. 4(a) for the finalized design). In the All-Open-Fan condition, the air flows from one or two ventilators and exits from the third ventilator. The circuit and sensors are exposed to the pollutants in the air flow. To optimize the design further, the circuit is mounted on a platform inside the housing such that sensors are in the housings centre. This placement ensured an optimal interaction with the pollutants.

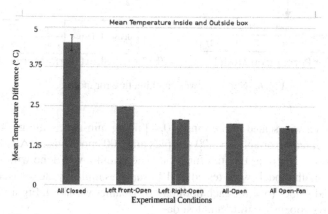

Fig. 5. Mean Temperature Difference inside and outside the box.

The optimal solar angle changes from place-to-place and from month-to-month in a year. Thus, the solar panel stand in the housing was made adjustable where the platform could rotate 0–360° in the horizontal plane and 0–90° in the vertical plane.

4   Predicting Air Quality

The AQMPWS not only monitors seven pollutants and five weather variables, it also predicts the future values of these pollutants and weather variables. In the AQMPWS, artificial neural networks are designed to predict the pollutants and weather variables at the next timestep by analyzing the values of these variables at the current time. The data is available in the form of a multi-variate time series.

The prediction module is an ensembling of two separate models, namely Long-Short Term Memory (LSTM) [27] and Multi-Layer Perceptron (MLP) [5]. The LSTM model comprises of an LSTM layer and a fully connected layer. The LSTM layer has 50 units and a look-back period of 4. The fully connected layer contains 12 neurons (one for each predicted value of the pollutant and weather variable). The MLP model consists of a hidden fully connected layer of 50 neurons which accepts a vector of shape (1, 12) and the output layer again comprises of 12 neurons (similar to the LSTM model). The outputs of both the models are ensembled by simply averaging their individual predictions. Figure 6(a) and 6(b) represent the model structures for MLP and LSTM models respectively.

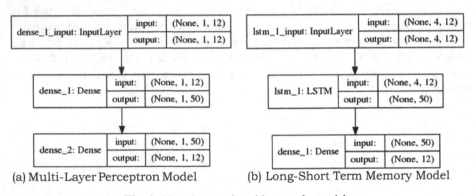

(a) Multi-Layer Perceptron Model   (b) Long-Short Term Memory Model

Fig. 6. Neural network architecture for models.

First, the data was scaled in the range [0, 1] using min-max scaling [20]. Both the models were trained separately for 200 samples and 200 epochs using Adam Optimizer and Mean Absolute Error as the loss function. The training was done without shuffling the data. Later, both models were tested on 120 samples multivariate dataset containing the 12 predicted values (one for each pollutant or weather variable). Figure 7 shows the graph of loss v/s epochs for train and test data.

The output vector of both models was averaged and scaled back to original range using inverse min-max scaling. Figure 8 depicts the predictions of the ensemble model along with the actual values recorded by the system in training and test data (RMSEs are shown individually for both training and test data). As seen in the Fig. 8, the model does a reasonable job in predicting different pollutant and weather variables.

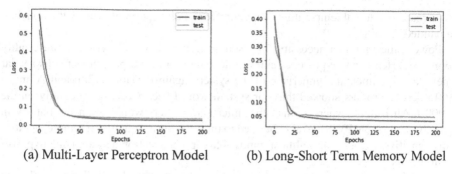

(a) Multi-Layer Perceptron Model   (b) Long-Short Term Memory Model

Fig. 7. Loss curves for the Models.

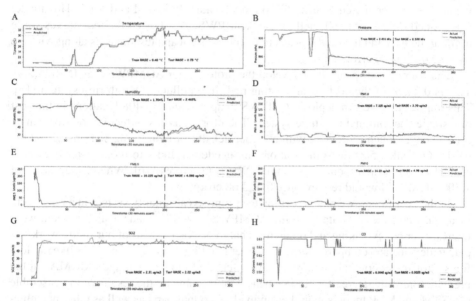

Fig. 8. Model predictions on Train and Test Data.

5 Discussion and Conclusion

Causing damage to crop, buildings, ecological sensitive regions and pulmonary and cardiovascular diseases in humans, the deteriorating air-quality inflicts heavy economic costs to the countries around the world, especially the developing ones [28]. Being able to monitor, predict and generate warning about the poor air-quality is of the utmost importance today [16]. Therefore, we designed a novel low-cost, online system for monitoring, predicting and warning (AQMPWS).

While designing the housing, we considered the facts that the pollutants are carried with the flowing air and that the system needs to be deployed in places with scorching heat. The experiment to determine the most appropriate ventilation concluded that the best scenario was to keep the three ventilators open and a fan to effectively minimize the increase in internal temperature. To minimize the absorption of heat by the housing, we painted it white.

Power efficiency is a necessity for a self-sufficient, low-cost system to air-quality monitoring. Hence, a low-power circuit was designed for the purpose powered by a solar panel. An experimental comparison of the system against ATmega328p and ATmega 2560 microcontrollers showed that our system would keep working efficiently on the 10,000 mAh battery; whereas, the other micro-controllers would drain the battery in about 20 days. AQMPWS can also be used to monitor the air-quality in remote, ecologically sensitive regions that is almost impossible for a conventional system due to power requirements.

Apart from real-time monitoring of air quality, we developed a prediction module to predict future air quality. We used an ensembling approach to design the module, where we average the predicted values of two models, namely LSTM and MLP. This model was trained on the data collected by the AQMPWS. We showed the loss curves while training the data and the model predictions for the train and test datasets along with the root mean squared error.

The overall cost incurred to develop the prototype of AQMPWS was INR 24,500. This is 0.245% of the cost of an existing real-time pollution monitoring system [16]. This implies that we can deploy AQMPWS in approximately 408 locations in the cost of a single conventional real-time system. Therefore, this cost-effective solution can be used to cover much more area with a higher density of monitoring stations across the world. Overall, 1,500 real-time stations are needed in India to monitor air quality at critical points, which would cost about INR 3,000 crores [16]. Whereas, an array of 1,500 AQMPWS would require only INR 3.68 crores.

In the near future, we plan to deploy the proposed air-quality system in a real-world location. The collected data from the AQMPWS would be made available via a web-interface for policymaking and predictive analytics. Also, as part of our future work, we plan to develop and compare a variety of other machine learning techniques like random forests for regression and auto regressive integrated moving average (ARIMA) in the prediction module. Here, it would be beneficial to compare the results of the ensemble of LSTM and MLP models with their individual counterparts as well as other machine-learning models. One interesting analysis would be the ability of the machine-learning models to produce long-term predictions without observing a high degradation of the accuracy of the predictions. Finally, we plan to replicate the AQMPWS in a number of poor air-quality locations for monitoring, warning, and predictions. This replication will allow us to make AQMPWS useful for society in years to come.

Acknowledgement. We are thankful for the generous funding from Department of Environment, Science & Technology, Government of Himachal Pradesh for the project IITM/DST-HP/VD/240 to Varun Dutt and Pratik Chaturvedi. We appreciate the help of Khyati Agrawal in developing the machine learning models. We thank Jhalak Choudhary and Roshan Sharma for helping in designing and developing the circuit and helping in programming microcontroller. Moreover, the experiment for ventilation was conducted with the help of Aman Raj and Amit Chauhan who also helped in designing the external housing.

References

1. Ayele, T., Mehta, R.: Air pollution monitoring and prediction using IoT. In: 2018 Second International Conference on Inventive Communication and Computational Technologies (ICICCT), pp. 1741–1745 (2018)
2. Brauer, M., et al.: The Global Burden of Disease Study 2017 (2017)
3. Brienza, S., et al.: A low-cost sensing system for cooperative air quality monitoring in urban areas (2015)
4. European Environment Agency: Air Quality in Europe (2016)
5. Goodfellow, I., Bengio, Y., Courville, A.: Deep Learning, 2nd edn. MIT Press, Cambridge (2016)
6. Gowen, A.: As China cleans up its act, Indias cities named the world's most polluted (2019). https://wapo.st/2KFabc3
7. Griffiths, J.: 22 of the top 30 most polluted cities in the world are in India (2019). https://cnn.it/2TdTUQY
8. How air pollution is destroying our health (2019). https://bit.ly/2ryRjRH
9. I2C Bus, Interface and Protocol. https://i2c.info/
10. Ikram, J., et al.: View: implementing low cost air quality monitoring solution for urban areas. Environ. Syst. Res. 1(1), 10 (2012)
11. Irfan, U.: Why India's air pollution is so horrendous (2019). https://bit.ly/2CU7ShD
12. Kiruthika, R., et al.: Low cost pollution control and air quality monitoring system using Raspberry Pi for Internet of Things. In: 2017 International Conference on Energy, Communication, Data Analytics and Soft Computing (ICECDS), pp. 2319–2326 (2017)
13. Lightweight Low-Power Arduino Library. https://bit.ly/2Zd72UG
14. Martnez-Espaa, R., et al.: Air-pollution prediction in smart cities through machine learning methods: a case of study in Murcia, Spain. J. Univ. Comput. Sci. 24(3), 261–276 (2018)
15. National Ambient Air Quality Standards (2009). https://bit.ly/2ZbYVId
16. Nandi, J.: Study hints at bias in India's air pollution monitoring stations (2018). https://bit.ly/2O2c4BL
17. NDTV Report: Centre To Install 1,500 Manual Air Quality Monitoring Systems By 2024 (2019). https://bit.ly/2P1mZxC
18. Parmar, G., et al.: An IoT based low cost air pollution monitoring system. In: 2017 International Conference on Recent Innovations in Signal processing and Embedded Systems (RISE), pp. 524–528 (2017)
19. Qi, Z., et al.: Deep air learning: interpolation, prediction, and feature analysis of fine-grained air quality. IEEE Trans. Knowl. Data Eng. 30(12), 2285–2297 (2018)
20. Raschka, S.: About feature scaling and normalization and the effect of standardization for machine learning algorithms (2014). https://bit.ly/2U0DJlG
21. Rückerl, R., Schneider, A., Breitner, S., Cyrys, J., Peters, A.: Health effects of particulate air pollution: a review of epidemiological evidence (2011)
22. Sharma, N., et al.: Forecasting air pollution load in Delhi using data analysis tools. Procedia Comput. Sci. 132, 1077–1085 (2018)
23. Subramanian, V., et al.: Data analysis for predicting air pollutant concentration in Smart city Uppsala (2016)
24. Tiele, A., et al.: Design and development of a low-cost, portable monitoring device for indoor environment quality (2018). Article 5353816
25. WHO Ambient Air Quality Facts (2019). https://bit.ly/2FlSZpw
26. World Health Organization: WHO air quality guidelines for particulate matter, ozone, nitrogen dioxide and sulfur dioxide (2005)

27. Yan, S.: Understanding LSTM and its diagrams (2016). https://bit.ly/2z5kdir. Accessed 18 Aug 2019
28. Zhang, J., et al.: Prediction of air pollutants concentration based on an extreme learning machine: the case of Hong Kong (2017)
29. Zhao, C., et al.: Application of data mining to the analysis of meteorological data for air quality prediction: a case study in Shenyang (2017)

Word2vec's Distributed Word Representation for Hindi Word Sense Disambiguation

Archana Kumari$^{(\boxtimes)}$ ⓘ and D. K. Lobiyal ⓘ

Jawaharlal Nehru University, New Delhi, India
archan49_scs@jnu.ac.in, dkl@mail.jnu.ac.in

Abstract. Word Sense Disambiguation (WSD) is the task of extracting an appropriate sense of an ambiguous word in a sentence. WSD is an essential task for language processing, as it is a pre-requisite for determining the closest interpretations of various language-based applications. In this paper, we have made an attempt to exploit the word embedding for finding the solution for WSD for the Hindi texts. This task involves two steps - the creation of word embedding and leveraging cosine similarity to identify an appropriate sense of the word. In this process, we have considered two mostly used word2vec architectures known as Skip-Gram and Continuous Bag-Of-Words [2] models to develop the word embedding. Further, we have chosen the sense with the closest proximity to identify the meaning of an ambiguous word. To prove the effectiveness of the proposed model, we have performed experiments on large corpora and have achieved an accuracy of nearly 52%.

Keywords: Natural Language Processing · Hindi Word Sense Disambiguation · Word2vec · Word embedding

1 Introduction

WSD is regarded as a Holy Grail of Natural Language Processing (NLP) as most of the words in natural language are ambiguous. In spite of the multiple meanings of the words, a human being can identify the correct meanings of the words from a context. In 2009, [1] described WSD as the "ability to identify the meaning of words in context in a computational manner". In other words, WSD is the task of automatically identifying the sense of a word in a sentence in the given context. The solutions of WSD task can be split into two categories - All-words WSD, which performs disambiguation on all words in a sentence, and Lexical-sample WSD, which carries out disambiguation on one target word in the sentence.

Over the past few years, most of the research works focus on representing the words in a multidimensional space in the form of vectors. However, word embedding, due to its incredible ability to express the words in the Low-dimensional vector space, is achieving more attention of the researchers. A word embedding is a continuous representation of words in a pre-defined vector space. Word Embedding uses real numbers to collate the characteristics and relationship between the words in a natural language. Word2vec is one of the techniques available for generating word embedding. This technique uses unsupervised training. Using large amounts of unannotated plain

D. V. Hung and M. D'Souza (Eds.): ICDCIT 2020, LNCS 11969, pp. 325–335, 2020.
https://doi.org/10.1007/978-3-030-36987-3_21

text, word2vec learns associations between words automatically. The two most used models for word embedding are CBOW and Skip-gram models, which are proposed by [2] (Figs. 1 and 2).

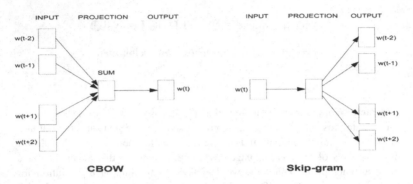

Fig. 1. Word2Vec learning model [2]

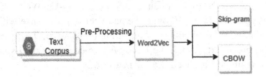

Fig. 2. Learning word vectors

The majority of the work for the word embedding reported in the literature pertains to the English language [11, 12] and [13] and various other languages such as Chinese [20], Japanese [19], Arabic [21]. However, some of the researchers have also attempted research work related to vector representation for the Hindi language. We aim to create a model of word embedding using both CBOW and Skip-Gram techniques. This paper summarizes all the different steps to develop the word embedding model using both methods. Initially, we have collected the corpus and applied the required pre-processing. The word embeddings is then created for pre-processed data. The sense definition is accessed using any knowledge-base or machine readable dictionaries. Next, we induce the created word embeddings to generate Context-Vector and Sense-Vectors for the ambiguous word given in the test sentence. These generated vectors will help to find the semantic similarity. We employ Cosine similarity to find the semantic relatedness between the vectors. In our work, we choose the sense definition having the highest semantic score as the sense of an ambiguous word.

The remaining paper is structured as follows: Sect. 2 describes the related work. In Sect. 3, we explain the proposed work. Section 4 presents detailed account of the proposed model. Section 5, covers the experimental results. Section 6 concludes the presented work and Sect. 7 covers the suggestions for future work.

2 Related Work

In distributional semantics, word embedding is the most eminent technique as this technique supports neural networks to represent the contexts of a word in which it is supposed to exist. Due to its capability to learn the semantics of words, it becomes the backbone of various NLP downstream applications. These representations are beneficial for NLP systems because they could be employed as the extra word feature and can be fed into multiple learning algorithms. These word representations place similar words in the vector space models based on their similarity.

[3] in 1986, proposed distributed representations for words which were successfully utilized by [4] and [5] in language models. Moreover, these representations were employed for various tasks, such as by [6], in 2010, for NER (Named Entity Recognition), for word sense disambiguation by [7] in 2011, for word representation learning by Mikolov [8], 2012, for tagging by [9] and for parsing by [10].

A considerable amount of research has been carried out to evaluate the performance of word embedding for word sense disambiguation. These include the works done by [11] in 2010, and by [12]. In 2015, [12] used word embedding based on feed-forward neural networks for supervised WSD. They observed that the integration of word embedding into supervised WSD has significantly improved the performance of WSD. [13], in 2015, introduced a method called AutoExtend, in which word embeddings are used effectively to develop embedding for synsets and lexemes. Their experimental results indicate that they have achieved state-of-art performance on WSD and Word Similarity. In 2014, [14] introduced a unified model which integrates word sense disambiguation with word sense representation. Their model represents one sense per word. They have shown that competitive performance on coarse gained WSD outperforms supervised all words WSD and improves the performance of contextual word similarity when compared to existing WSR system. In 2013, [2, 18] proposed two models, CBOW and Skip Gram, which is used to learn word representations. Further, they showed that syntactic and semantic information between words could be captured by these models. However, most of the works on word sense disambiguation were performed for the English language.

In this work, we present the influence of various training parameters on our proposed system. Further, in this work, we put forth an architecture for an extensive evaluation of multiple methods which use word embedding as WSD features. We have also investigated the effect of various parameters while training word embedding on the WSD.

3 Proposed Work

Based on the motivation from word embedding work for English, we have introduced a model for Hindi Word Sense Disambiguation using word embedding. In our proposed system, we use IndoWordnet to access the senses for words. Further, our system measures existing semantic relations amid the context of the target word and its gloss. Then, we choose the sense with the closest proximity to identify the sense of an ambiguous word. In this method, we first train the word vectors from the corpus using

Mikolov's word2vec models. Secondly, it represents the context of the target word and all its possible senses in a vector space. Finally, cosine similarity plays a role of a measure for calculating the similarity of the Context-Vectors with their (target word) Sense-Vectors. For WSD, the sense with the highest similarity provides the sense of an ambiguous word.

4 Methodology

The idea of utilizing word vectors for NLP tasks have obtained notable accomplishments. They have the potential to retain the semantic information from a large amount of data. Due to these characteristics, Word Sense Disambiguation has become eminent, as it can be solved efficiently using word embedding. The objective of the proposed work is to map words from Hindi text to the real number in the form of vectors. In pursuance of best configuration to find preferable embedding model for Hindi WSD, we need to assess the word representations using both the models of word embedding. Figure 3 outlines the framework of the proposed method.

To solve Hindi Word Sense Disambiguation using word embedding, we present a 3-step based method, (i) create Word embeddings, (ii) generation of context and (iii) sense vectors, and similarity computation.

Step 1: Word Representation: In this step, vectors are generated for words from the prepared corpus using following steps.

Corpus Creation and Pre-processing: In this step, we need to train our model from the collected corpus. For this purpose, we have chosen the Indian Corpora from NLTK [22]. Additionally, we have incorporated 500 texts extracted from Wikipedia. Initially, we apply pre-processing to remove punctuation, non-Hindi words and other diacritics from the corpus.

Word Embedding Creation: In order to create the word embedding, we employ Skip-Gram and CBOW architecture to create the word embeddings for the prepared input corpus. Further, we utilize these vector representations to generate Context-Vector and Sense-Vector.

Step 2: Generation of Context and Sense Vectors: In this step, we build two vectors. The former is called the context vector, which represents the context of the words while the latter is named as sense vectors carries the sense of the target word.

Context Vector Generation: Now, we utilize the created word embeddings in step 1 to compute the context vector of the test input sentence. The context vector is formed by summing up all the vectors of the words in the context window of the ambiguous word in the input sentence.

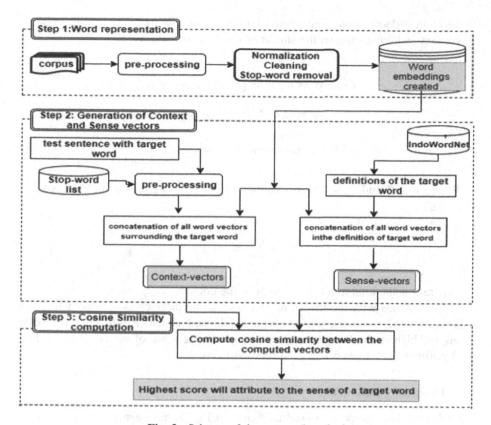

Fig. 3. Schema of the proposed method

Sense Vector Generation: This vector is also named as definition vector, which represents the various possible definitions of the ambiguous word. To extract the definitions (glosses) of the target word, we utilize IndoWordNet developed by Bhattacharyya [16]. Once armed with the definitions of the target word, we represent each word into their vector using Word embeddings created step1. Afterwards, to generate the sense vector, we find the sum of vectors of all the words in the glosses of the target word.

Step 3: Compute Similarity: The idea of computing similarity is motivated by the fact that embedding places the word vectors with similar semantics closer together. Our framework measures the semantic relation between the context of the target word and its definitions.

Cosine Similarity Computation: To find the similarity between computed context and sense vectors in step 2, we employ cosine distance technique [15]. We delineate the sense of the target word having its nearest semantic similarity to its local context.

Sense Disambiguation: Finally, we associate an ambiguous word with its appropriate senses, i.e. to perform disambiguation, we select the meaning with the nearest semantic similarity in its local usage. This approach uses a similarity metric as a basis between the context and senses where, the similarity metric is defined as:

$$Context\ vector\ C = \{c_1, c_2 \ldots, c_k\}\ of\ w$$

$$Sense\ vector\ s^w = \{s_1, s_2, \ldots, s_n\}$$

$$Sim(s, c) = argmaxsim(s_i, c_w) = argmax \frac{s_i \cdot c_w}{\|s_i\| \cdot \|c_w\|} \tag{1}$$

Where $s_i \in s^w$ and c_w is the summation of word vectors representing each word in context C:

$$c_w = \sum_{i=1}^{n} vec_w(c_i)$$

Where n is the total number of words in the context.

In consonance with the preceding steps, semantic distance is measured for each ambiguous word using the similarity metric defined above. Resultantly, the sense having the highest similarity represents the appropriate sense of the target word. Figure 3 outlines the framework of the proposed method.

4.1 Illustrative Example

The schema of the proposed model as shown in Fig. 3, has been explained with the help of an example as follows:

(1) Word Representation: Here, we find the word embedding representations for the given input dataset as explained in Sect. 3.

(2) Generation of Context and sense vector: After creation of word embeddings, we aim to generate the context-vector and the Sense-Vector.

Consider the Target word (A): "आम".

C is the context used for an ambiguous word A.

C: बड़े शहरों में तो यह समस्या आम इंसान की है |

Context Vector: Here we are generating the context vector by concatenating all the vectors of the words surrounding the ambiguous word.

$$V_0 = V(बड़े) + V(शहरों) + V(समस्या) + V(आम) + V(इंसान)$$

Sense Vectors: For each definition extracted from IndoWordNet, we are creating Sense-Vector by the summation of the all word vector in the definition.

The glosses of the target word are:

Gloss 1: जो पका हुआ न हो |
Gloss 2: जो कम पका हुआ हो |
Gloss 3: जिसमें कोई विशेषता न हो या अच्छे से कुछ हल्के दरज़े का |
Gloss 4: प्रायः सभी व्यक्तियों, अवसरों, अवस्थाओं आदि में पाया जाने वाला या उनसे संबंध रखने वाला|
Gloss 5: लोगों के विशाल समुदाय का या उससे संबंधित |

where glosses are the definition for the target word that has been extracted from the IndoWordNet. For each definition extracted from IndoWordNet, we are creating Sense-Vector by the summation of the all word vector in the definition.

$V_1 = V(पका)+V(हुआ)$
$V_2 = V(कम(+V(पका)+V(हुआ)$
$V_3 = V(जिसमें)+V(विशेषता)+V(अच्छे)+V(कुछ)+V(हल्के)+V(दरज़े$
$V_4=V(प्राय)+V(व्यक्तियों)+V(अवसरों)+(अवस्थाओ)+V(पाया)+V(जाने))+V(संबंध)+V(रखने)$
$V_5 = V(लोगों)+V(विशाल)+V(समुदाय)+V(संबंधित)$

(3) Similarity Computation: We delineate the sense having the nearest semantic similarity to its local usage. The Sense-Vector having highest cosine distance score with the context vector will attribute to the real sense of the target word.

$$Sim(V_0, V_1) = cos(V_0, V_1) = 99.42$$

$$Sim(V_0, V_2) = cos(V_0, V_2) = 99.42$$

$$Sim(V_0, V_3) = cos(V_0, V_3) = 99.71$$

$$Sim(V_0, V_4) = cos(V_0, V_4) = 96.47$$

$$Sim(V_0, V_5) = cos(V_0, V_5) = 72.23$$

Above example explains the working of the proposed system step by step. In this example, it comes out that, sense 3 (Sense Vector V_3) gives the highest similarity and therefore, represents the sense of the ambiguous word in the given context.

5 Experimental Results

The results presented in the paper emanate from the study of the various parameters of word embedding, which in turn affects the WSD performance.

Our Hindi WSD model requires a Lexical Knowledgebase for the disambiguation of Hindi language. This knowledgebase can easily provide various meanings of the target word. We have chosen IndoWordNet [16] for this purpose. We have evaluated the performance of our WSD system (which is developed based on embedding) using the test dataset. For the test dataset, we use Hindi corpus [17] built by CIIL (Central Institute of Indian Languages). This corpus includes 1233 text documents. These text documents consist of various domains. For the experiments, we have employed word2vec toolkit from Genism library to train our vectors. From the test data, we have tested 100 sentences, 10 for each ambiguous word for the evaluation of our proposed system.

Table 1 shows the analysis of results obtained from both the architectures using their best configurations for the evaluation of WSD system.

From the comparison between Skip-gram and Continuous Bag-of-word model (Table 1), it is observed that CBOW has performed better than Skip-Gram. Our analysis depicts the effect of various parameters on the performance of our proposed model. Hindi corpus with the configuration as size = 150, window = 10 and negative = 5 provides an optimum result.

Table 1. WSD performance by varying parameters of word embedding models

Embedding model	Different configuration			WSD precision
	Size	Window	Negative	
Skip gram	100	15	0	45.00
	150	10	5	47.00
	200	5	10	36.00
CBOW	100	15	0	41.00
	150	10	5	52.00
	200	5	10	46.00

Due to the shortage of freely available data for Hindi text, lack of tested samples and various resources for the disambiguation task of Hindi Language, the comparison is a difficult task. Figures 4, 5, and 6 below demonstrate the effect of various parameters on the performance of our proposed WSD model while training uses CBOW Model.

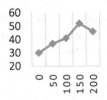

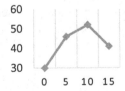

Fig. 4. Dimensionality   **Fig. 5.** Window size   **Fig. 6.** Negative examples

Lastly, we present the disambiguation of some ambiguous words. We have tested seven sentences for different ambiguous words. Table 4 shows the accuracy of the disambiguation of some ambiguous words. From the results shown in Table 2, we can observe that the word with the maximum number of sense definitions having an insufficient number of words gives the lowest precision.

Table 2. Performance of our method based on some ambiguous words

Ambiguous words	Number of senses	Precision(%)	Translation
आम	4	85.71	Mango /Common
उत्तर	7	14.28	Answer/Direction
सोना	3	28.57	Sleep/Gold
शाखा	4	71.42	Branch/Department
रंग	5	100.0	Hue/Deception
मंगल	5	57.14	Tuesday/Auspicious
फल	9	85.71	Fruit/Result
अंग	5	71.42	Organ/Part
दल	12	0.00	Group/Side

6 Conclusion

In this paper, we have proposed a model to solve the problem of word sense disambiguation for Hindi text using word embedding. The proposed model has been solved in two phases: creation of word embeddings from the collected corpora. We have exploited the two mostly used word embedding models, CBOW (Continuous Bag-Of-Word) and SG (Skip-Gram) techniques. Further, we have computed cosine similarity was computed between Context-Vector and Sense-Vector to find the appropriate meaning of an ambiguous word. To evaluate the proposed model, we have performed experiments on test data set and have achieved an accuracy of 52%.

Through various experiments and ablations, we have found that CBOW architecture with the arrangement of window-size 10, vector dimension of 150 and 5 negative examples configuration achieves better results against all the tested parameter configurations. From the experiments, we have observed that Continuous Bag-Of-Word architecture provides the best result for Hindi WSD on the given corpus.

7 Future Work

In future work, we will utilize various semantic relations like hypernyms, hyponyms etc. to develop more efficient sense vectors. Moreover, we believe that the size of context of an ambiguous word can significantly impact the quality of disambiguation. We consider that our proposed is generic and with required configuration could be adapted to solve various NLP applications like Machine Translation, Information Retrieval, Sentiment Analysis, Question Answering etc. Our research affords some considerable insights into the determination of the performance of proposed models for Indian languages.

References

1. Navigli, R.: Word sense disambiguation: a survey. ACM Comput. Surv. (CSUR) **41**(2), 10 (2009)
2. Mikolov, T., Chen, K., Corrado, G., Dean, J.: Efficient estimation of word representations in vector space. In: Proceedings of Workshop at ICLR. arXiv:1301.3781v1 (2013)
3. Rumelhart, D.E., Hintont, G.E., Williams, R.J.: Learning representations by back-propagating errors. Nature **323**, 533–536 (1986)
4. Bengio, Y., Schwenk, H., Senécal, J.S., Morin, F., Gauvain, J.L.: Neural probabilistic language models. In: Holmes, D.E., Jain, L.C. (eds.) Innovations in Machine Learning. STUDFUZZ, vol. 194, pp. 137–186. Springer, Heidelberg (2006). https://doi.org/10.1007/3-540-33486-6_6
5. Mnih, A., Hinton, G.: A scalable hierarchical distributed language model. In: Proceedings of the 21st International Conference on Neural Information Processing Systems, pp. 1081–1088. Curran Associates Inc., Vancouver (2008)
6. Turian, J., Ratinov, L., Bengio, Y.: Word representations: a simple and general method for semi-supervised learning. In: Proceedings of the 48th Annual Meeting of the Association for Computational Linguistics, pp. 384–394. Association for Computational Linguistics, Uppsala (2010)
7. Collobert, R., Weston, J., Bottou, L., Karlen, M., Kavukcuoglu, K., Kuksa, P.: Natural language processing (almost) from scratch. J. Mach. Learn. Res. **12**, 2493–2537 (2011)
8. Mikolov, T.: Statistical language models based on neural networks. Ph.D. thesis, Brno University of Technology (2012)
9. Socher, R., et al.: Recursive deep models for semantic compositionality over a sentiment treebank. In: Proceedings of the 2013 Conference on Empirical Methods in Natural Language Processing, pp. 1631–1642 (2013)
10. Socher, R., Lin, C.C., Manning, C., Ng, A.Y.: Parsing natural scenes and natural language with recursive neural networks. In: Proceedings of the 28th International Conference on Machine Learning (ICML 2011), vol. 2, pp. 129–136 (2011)
11. Zhong, Z., Ng, H.T.: It makes sense: a wide-coverage word sense disambiguation system for free text. In: Proceedings of the ACL 2010 System Demonstrations, pp. 78–83 (2010)
12. Taghipour, K., Ng, H.T.: Semi-supervised word sense disambiguation using word embeddings in general and specific domains. In: Proceedings of the 2015 Conference of the North American chapter of the Association for Computational Linguistics: Human Language Technologies, Denver, Colorado, pp. 314–323 (2015)
13. Rothe, S., Schütze, H.: AutoExtend: extending word embeddings to embeddings for synsets and lexemes. In: Proceedings of the 53rd ACL, Beijing, China, vol. 1, pp. 1793–1803 (2015)
14. Chen, X., Liu, Z., Sun, M.: A unified model for word sense representation and disambiguation. In: Proceedings of the 2014 Conference on Empirical Methods in Natural Language Processing (EMNLP), pp. 1025–1035. ACM, Qatar (2014)
15. Biemann, C., Panchenko, A., Einreichung, T.D., Master-Thesis, E.Z.: Unsupervised Word Sense Disambiguation with Sense Embeddings (2016)
16. Bhattacharya, P.: IndoWordNet. In: Proceedings of Lexical Resources Engineering Conference 2010, Malta (2010)
17. Hindi Corpus. http://www.cfilt.iitb.ac.in/Downloads.html. Accessed 17 May 2019
18. Mikolov, T., Sutskever, I., Chen, K., Corrado, G.S., Dean, J.: Distributed representations of words and phrases and their compositionality. In: Advances in Neural Information Processing Systems, pp. 3111–3119 (2013)

19. Suzuki, R., Komiya, K., Asahara, M., Sasaki, M., Shinnou, H.: All-words word sense disambiguation using concept embeddings. In: Proceedings of the Eleventh International Conference on Language Resources and Evaluation (LREC 2018) (2018)
20. Orkphol, K., Yang, W.: Word sense disambiguation using cosine similarity collaborates with Word2vec and WordNet. Future Internet 11(5), 114 (2019)
21. Laatar, R., Aloulou, C., Belghuith, L.H.: Word2vec for Arabic word sense disambiguation. In: Silberztein, M., Atigui, F., Kornyshova, E., Métais, E., Meziane, F. (eds.) NLDB 2018. LNCS, vol. 10859, pp. 308–311. Springer, Cham (2018). https://doi.org/10.1007/978-3-319-91947-8_32
22. Wagner, W., Bird, S., Klein, E., Loper, E.: Natural language processing with python, analyzing text with the natural language toolkit. Lang. Resour. Eval. 44, 421–424 (2010)

Text Document Clustering Using Community Discovery Approach

Anu Beniwal, Gourav Roy, and S. Durga Bhavani[✉]

University of Hyderabad, Hyderabad, India
sdbcs@uohyd.ernet.in

Abstract. The problem of document clustering is about automatic grouping of text documents into groups containing similar documents. This problem under supervised setting yields good results whereas for unannotated data the unsupervised machine learning approach does not yield good results always. Algorithms like K-Means clustering are most popular when the class labels are not known. The objective of this work is to apply community discovery algorithms from the literature of social network analysis to detect the underlying groups in the text data.

We model the corpus of documents as a graph with distinct non-trivial words from the whole corpus considered as nodes and an edge is added between two nodes if the corresponding word nodes occur together in at least one common document. Edge weight between two word nodes is defined as the number of documents in which those two words co-occur together. We apply the fast Louvain community discovery algorithm to detect communities. The challenge is to interpret the communities as classes. If the number of communities obtained is greater than the required number of classes, a technique for merging is proposed. The community which has the maximum number of similar words with a document is assigned as the community for that document. The main thrust of the paper is to show a novel approach to document clustering using community discovery algorithms. The proposed algorithm is evaluated on a few bench mark data sets and we find that our algorithm gives competitive results on majority of the data sets when compared to the standard clustering algorithms.

Keywords: Social networks · Louvain community discovery algorithm · Clustering

1 Introduction

Every day we deal with huge amount of text data on the internet or on our computer systems. It will be very helpful for us if text data is structured well because handling it and using it for analysis purposes will then be easy. One way of structuring the data set is by clustering similar documents together. One of the major problems in information retrieval is detection of relevant documents, a challenge faced every day by news editors and scientists trying to retrieve

© Springer Nature Switzerland AG 2020
D. V. Hung and M. D'Souza (Eds.): ICDCIT 2020, LNCS 11969, pp. 336–346, 2020.
https://doi.org/10.1007/978-3-030-36987-3_22

documents pertaining to their interest. The traditional approach to represent a document is using a bag of words [17] (BOW) approach in which each document is represented as a binary vector denoting the presence or absence of a word or by the TF-IDF score of the respective word. Text clustering is done in order to group similar documents together when the labels of the documents are not known. In this work, we propose a novel approach to text clustering, by building a network of words and using community discovery algorithms from the literature of social network analysis in order to obtain a clustering of the documents.

2 Related Work

Several problems like text classification, text categorization, document classification, topic modeling are related tasks in natural language processing. Immense research is reported every day in these areas, latest being deep learning approaches [9] and graph convolutional neural networks [11]. The conventional approach to document clustering is via the standard approaches like K-means [8] and Agglomerative [18] clustering. Some of the latest research in these areas pertain to analysis of volumes of textual data available on social media and this forms a major subarea in social network analysis. Twitter sentiment analysis [12] and detection of fake news [15] are extremely popular problems. Recently, algorithmic approaches from social network analysis have started being applied for these problems. We take an approach similar to that of Kido et al. [10] who apply community detection for topic modeling. We apply community detection algorithm in order to obtain clustering of documents.

Community Discovery is the detection of subgraphs called communities in a network, such that the nodes within a community are highly connected with one other as compared to the nodes outside the community. We used the Louvain [2] algorithm for community discovery. Louvain algorithm works based on the modularity [5] maximization approach. The Louvain algorithm uses an agglomerative approach where at the initial stage number of communities is equal to a number of nodes in the network and then merging is carried out in order to improve modularity.

3 Community Discovery Approach

We are carrying out document clustering by modeling the problem using graphs. A graph is created in which nodes are non-trivial words of the documents and edge weight between two nodes denotes the number of documents in which the pair of words occur together. It is to be noted that if we use documents instead of words as nodes for the graph creation, then the approach would not be scalable. Using the standard approaches followed in NLP, significant distinct words are obtained after stop word removal. The

Our proposed approach involves the following steps:

Step 1: First carry out the preprocessing of the data in order to obtain significantly distinct words which would be considered as vocabulary V underlying the documents.

Step 2: The words in V are considered as nodes of the graph and the nodes are connected by an edge if the corresponding pair of words occur in at least one common document.

Step 3: A community discovery algorithm is applied to the graph in order to obtain communities.

Step 4: Carry out the merging procedure if the number of communities obtained is more than required.

The algorithm for the proposed approach is given here.

Algorithm 1

> *Input: Graph $G = (V, E)$ (built from Vocabulary V)*
>   *Set_of_Communities $C \leftarrow$ Louvain_Algo(G)*
> $C = \{C_1, C_2, \ldots C_k \}$
>   **for** *each i and j, $1 \leq i, j \leq K$* **do**
>   **if** *Wu-Path_Similarity$(C_i, C_j) >$ threshold* **then**
>   *Merge (C_i, C_j)*
>   **end if**
>   **end for**
>   **for** *each test document d given as a set of words* **do**
>   *Compute $l = argmax\{j : C_j \cap d\}$*
>   **Return:** *d belongs to community C_l*
>   **end for**

end

The proposed approach is depicted as a flowchart in the Fig. 1. Each block in the flowchart is explained in detail in the following sections.

3.1 Preprocessing Using NLTK

For preprocessing of the text documents, NLTK library is used for computing word count, tokenization, stemming, stop words removal, lemmatization and for finding synsets and path-similarity using Wordnet [17]. Text data needs to be represented as numerical vectors which can be done using the Bag of Words (BOW) approach. There are many words like stop words, punctuations, email addresses, numbers etc. in the documents which are not helpful for clustering. These words are removed during preprocessing step and all the words are converted into lower case using NLTK package available in Python. Stemming is applied to the processed words in order to convert them into their respective root forms because

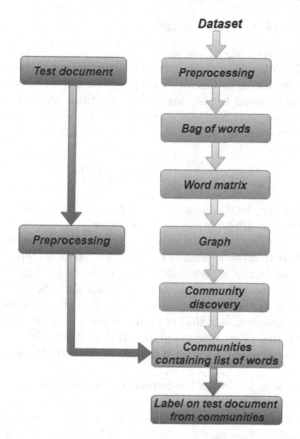

Fig. 1. Flow chart of our proposed approach

all the morphological forms of a word represent the same meaning. Vocabulary V represents the unique words obtained after pre-processing.

Bag of words is just a collection of binary vectors in which each document is represented as a binary vector of length $|V|$, by considering whether a word from vocabulary is present in the document or not. If it is present then the corresponding position in the vector is 1 otherwise 0. Thus we obtain a matrix of size $|V| \times D$ where D is the number of documents.

3.2 Graph Creation

We construct a graph G_V by taking the words of vocabulary V as vertices. Two nodes i and j in V are joined by an edge if both the words occur in at least one common document. Let the length of vocabulary V be N. The word_matrix M is a weighted adjacency matrix of size N in which each entry M_{ij} represents the number of documents in which the pair of words i and j occur together.

3.3 Clustering of Text Documents

This is the important step of the proposed approach in which a community discovery algorithm from social networks literature is used to carry out the clustering task. Clustering is an unsupervised procedure in which the labels of the documents are not passed to the clustering algorithm. Most of the community discovery algorithms use a heuristic measure called Newman's modularity measure [6] which is defined as follows.

$$Q = \frac{1}{2m} \sum_{i,j \in V} \left[M_{ij} - \frac{k_i k_j}{2m} \right] \delta(c_i, c_j)$$

where k_i denotes the degree of node i and $\delta(c_i, c_j) = 1$ if the words i and j belong to the same community and zero otherwise.

Louvain [2] algorithm is an iterative procedure that uses the measure Q to evaluate the quality of the communities obtained at each step. This is considered as one of the fastest algorithms that is scalable for large networks. The algorithm follows a bottom-up approach with each node being given a distinct community label in the initialization step. In the first step, the community label of each node is reassigned with that of its neighbours and Newman's modularity measure is computed. The assignment is retained if it yields an improvement in the modularity measure. The two steps are repeated until no improvement is seen.

We apply Louvain algorithm for detecting communities lying in the network G_V. The intuition is that documents belonging to a specific class contain many common words leading to clustering of the words in the network. In the ideal case each document class may be represented by one cluster in the network. In practice, the algorithm yields many more communities than the number of classes.

3.4 Merging of Communities

If the number of communities obtained is more than the required number then a procedure for merging needs to be designe d. Merging is carried out based on degree centrality in two ways (Fig. 2):

Path Similarity by Taking a Single Centroid per Community. For each community, the word with highest degree (max degree node) is considered as a centroid. Similarity between every pair of centroids is calculated by using a path similarity measure as proposed in [14]. Find the *synsets*, that is, the set of synonyms of the two centroids from *Wordnet*[17]. The path similarity is based on the length of the shortest path that connects the synsets in the taxonomy. Scores returned by path similarity are in the range of 0 to 1. We use Wu-Palmer Similarity implemented in NLTK for our algorithm.

We propose that the centroids that are having high path similarity values represent similar clusters and hence may be merged.

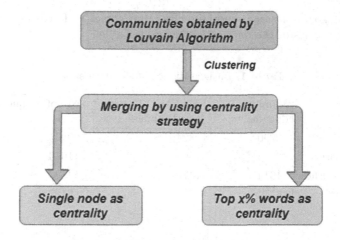

Fig. 2. Merging of communities

Mean Path Similarity by Taking Top $x\%$ Words from Each Community. Consider top $x\%$ (x an integer $0 < x <= 100$) words from each community and compute path similarity between all pairs of words for each pair of communities. That is, say, n_1 and n_2 words are obtained from communities C_1 and C_2, compute path similarity between all the $n_1 \times n_2$ pairs of words. The results are stored in a matrix T where the row and column lengths are n_1 and n_2 respectively. Mean of this matrix is calculated and that mean is taken as similarity value between the two communities C_1 and C_2. This process is carried out for every pair of communities. Pairs of those communities are merged whose mean value is high.

3.5   Document Class

Finally, how do we use the clustering to assign a class label to a test document? Consider the BOW vector corresponding to the document and assign the document to the cluster that yields the maximum overlap.

4   Experimental Evaluation

For the experiments we choose four data sets, namely, CD review [3], BBC [1], SMSSpamCollection [16]. CD_review data set [3] contains reviews of customers and it is a challenging data set because common people write their thoughts about a product and these are unedited texts. All the data sets other than BBC have two classes. BBC data set consists of five classes, namely, sports, business, politics, technology and entertainment. We extract two data sets from the BBC data set: (i) 2-class data set by choosing Sports and Business documents and (ii) 3-class data set constituting the three classes of Sports, Entertainment and Politics. SMSSpamCollection data set consists of two type of documents: spam class holding spam messages and ham class that consists of non-spam messages. The basic statistics of the data sets is given in Table 1.

Table 1. Basic statistics of the data sets

Data sets	Number of documents	Avg. No. of words per document	No. of unique words
CD_Review	10000	82	30495
Buss_Sports	944	150	11056
Buss_Spo_Enter	1314	147	14322
SMSSpam	5574	12	5127

4.1 Performance Evaluation Measures

Performance is evaluated by using three standard measures [7] used, namely, NMI, Rand-index and F1-score for checking the goodness of our model against the ground truth class information.

NMI. Normalized Mutual Information is used to check the amount of overlap between the predicted and the actual communities. NMI is a good measure to check the quality of clustering. The value of NMI is between 0 and 1, with higher values of NMI denoting good predictions of clustering.

$$NMI(Y;C) = \frac{2 * J(Y;C)}{H(Y) + H(C)} \tag{1}$$

where Y is the set of class labels, C is the set of community(cluster) labels, and $H(.)$ is entropy function. $J(V_1, V_2)$ gives the mutual information between V_1 and V_2. $J(Y;C) = H(Y) - H(Y/C)$, where $H(Y/C)$ gives the entropy of class label within each community.

Rand-Index. Rand-Index is similar to accuracy but it is used in unsupervised approach. Rand Index is based on the percentage of decisions that are taken correctly. For finding Rand index a confusion matrix is created containing TP, TN, FP, FN, where TP = True Positive, TN = True Negative, FP = False Positive, FN = False Negative.

$$Rand - index = \frac{TP + TN}{TP + TN + FP + FN} \tag{2}$$

F-Measure. Rand-Index gives equal weightage to FP and FN. But since grouping similar documents into different clusters is worse than inter-mixing of dissimilar documents, different weightage should be assigned to FP and FN. F1 measure is used for this purpose. Penalization of false ositives is done by taking $\alpha > 1$, thus giving more weightage to recall.

$$P = \frac{TP}{TP + FP}, \quad R = \frac{TP}{TP + FN}, \quad F_\alpha = \frac{(\alpha^2 + 1)P \cdot R}{\alpha^2 P + R} \tag{3}$$

5   Experimental Results

The proposed algorithm based on community discovery is implemented on four benchmark data sets and the results are tabulated. The performance is compared with the traditional unsupervised approaches [7] of K-Means and Agglomerative Clustering using the implementations available in NLTK. The results are tabulated in Table 2.

As can be seen in Table 2, in the case of CD_reviews data set, the proposed approach for document clustering gives a much higher accuracy of 62.62% in comparison to K-means [8] that shows 46.96% and agglomerative clustering with 52.04% accuracy.

Similarly, for the other binary class data sets of BBC (Buss_Sports) and SMSSpam, the results obtained by the proposed algorithm are slightly better or on par with K-Means.

In the case of the 3-class data set of BBC [1] (sports_ politics_entertainment) data set, our algorithm is not doing so well by yielding 90.94% in comparison to K-means which shows 98.09% accuracy. On the other hand, agglomerative clustering performs very poorly by giving only 42.16% accuracy. We find that agglomerative clustering divides the corpus into only two classes, thus mixing the class information, yielding a low accuracy. It is important to note that F1-score which is a better measure of accuracy, penalizing false positives, is higher for the proposed algorithm for all the data sets.

Table 2. Experimentation results of the proposed approach in comparison to the standard clustering approach, with best Rand_index, NMI and F1 measure on the four data sets.

Performance	Proposed approach			K-means			Agglomerative		
Data sets	Rand index	F1-score	NMI	Rand index	F1-score	NMI	Rand index	F1-score	NMI
CD_Review	62.62	0.62	0.04	46.96	0.43	0.00	52.04	0.44	0.00
Buss_Sport	99.50	0.99	0.96	99.36	0.99	0.95	98.09	0.98	0.86
Spo_Ent_Pol	90.94	0.91	0.73	98.90	0.98	0.95	42.16	0.33	0.26
SMSSpam	92.06	0.94	0.45	91.7	0.85	0.45	95.47	0.90	0.59

6   Complexity Analysis

The complexity analysis of K-Means algorithm is compared with that of the proposed algorithm.

Let D be the number of documents, N be the size of the vocabulary V, K denote the number of centroids and I be the number of iterations. Then the time complexity of K-means algorithm is $\mathcal{O}(D * N * K * I)$.

The graph G_V is created in $\mathcal{O}(N^2.D)$ time. And the complexity of Louvain community discovery is $\mathcal{O}(NlogN)$; and $O(K^2)$ is involved for look-up of Word-net and path similarity calculation required for merging of communities. Hence total complexity for the proposed algorithm is

$$\mathcal{O}(N^2.D) + \mathcal{O}(NlogN) + \mathcal{O}(K^2) = \mathcal{O}(N^2.D)$$

as $K << N$. Hence, complexity of the proposed algorithm is $\mathcal{O}(N^2.D)$. Even though the proposed algorithm may not be as fast as K-Means algorithm whose complexity is $\mathcal{O}(N * D * K * I)$, since D can be potentially unbounded the proposed algorithm based on community discovery may turn out to be as fast as the K-means algorithm for large data sets.

7   Conclusion

In all of the 2-class data sets on which the experimentation has been carried out, the proposed model is giving better results for clustering when compared to standard clustering algorithms. At the time of merging, in the proposed clustering approach, the case of taking single node from each community as a centrality node, yields better results than choosing $x\%$ nodes as centrality nodes. The reason is, when we take $x\%$ nodes as the centrality nodes, we observe that the similarity values between all the pair of communities come out to be high, so the choice of communities to be merged turns out to be a difficult task since most of the similarity values of cluster pairs are close to each other. Accuracy of the proposed approach also depends on the number of words in a document. We note that if the set of words in the corpus is large, accuracy is higher when compared to the corpus with less number of words. In the case of 3-class data set of Spo_Ent_Pol, the performance of the proposed algorithm is not as good as that of K-Means algorithm, which needs to be investigated further through experimentation on other multi-class data sets.

8   Future Work

In this work we have only compared the results against the classical algorithms of K-Means and Agglomerative clustering. In order to establish this approach, clearly, it needs to be compared against some of the state-of-the-art methods for document clustering which is part of our future work. The proposed approach can be extended in several ways. The size of the network can be made more economical by considering hypernyms of the words as nodes, so that many similar words can be compressed into one node, thus making the algorithm much faster. Along with each centroid, we can take the top five or more synonyms for the word so that separation of communities may be better. The proposed approach does not depend upon the choice of the community discovery algorithm. The experiments have been done using only Louvain community discovery algorithm, which can be replaced by any other state-of-the-art community discovery algorithms. Another interesting idea would be to carry out text summarization first for each document and then on summarized data apply our approach. By doing so, the number of computations decreases and so does the size of the network.

References

1. Dataset:BBC (2019). http://mlg.ucd.ie/datasets/bbc.html. Accessed 29 Apr 2019
2. Blondel, V.D., Guillaume, J.-L., Lambiotte, R., Lefebvre, E.: Fast unfolding of communities in large networks. J. Stat. Mech. Theory Exp.t **2008**(10), 100–108 (2008)
3. CD_review (2019). https://gist.githubusercontent.com/kunalj101corpus. Accessed 29 Apr 2019
4. Chen, Z., Liu, B.: Mining topics in documents: Standing on the shoulders of big data. In: Proceedings of the 20th ACM SIGKDD International Conference on Knowledge Discovery and Data Mining, KDD 2014, pp. 1116–1125, New York. ACM (2014)
5. Fortunato, S.: Community detection in graphs. Phys. Reports **486**(3–5), 75–174 (2010)
6. Girvan, M., Newman, M.E.J.: Community structure in social and biological networks. Proc. Natl. Acad. Sci. **99**(12), 7821–7826 (2002)
7. Han, J., Kamber, M., Pei, J.: Data Mining: Concepts and Techniques. Series in Data Management Systems. Morgan Kaufmann, San Francisco (2012)
8. Hartigan, J.A., Wong, M.A.: Algorithm AS 136: a k-means clustering algorithm. J. Roy. Stat. Soc. Ser. C (Appl. Stat.) **28**(1), 100–108 (1979)
9. Johnson, R., Zhang, T.: Semi-supervised convolutional neural networks for text categorization via region embedding. In: Advances in Neural Information Processing Systems (NIPS), vol. 28, pp. 919–927 (2015)
10. Kido, G.S., Igawa, R.A., Barbon, S.: Topic Modeling based on Louvain method in Online Social Networks, XII Brazilian Symposium on Information Systems, Florianópolis, SC, 17–20 May 2016
11. Kiph, T.N., Welling, N.: Semi-Supervised Classification with graph convoluional networks. In: ICLR (2017)
12. Liu, X., Li, K., Zhou, M.: Collective semantic role labeling for tweets with clustering, IJCAI, pp. 1832–1837, (2011)
13. Papadopoulos, S., Kompatsiaris, Y., Vakali, A., Spyridonos, P.: Community detection in social media. Data Min. Knowl. Disc. **24**(3), 515–554 (2012)
14. Sarkar, K., Law, R.: A novel approach to document classification using wordnet. ArXiv preprint arXiv:1510.02755 (2015)
15. Shu, K., Sliva, A., Wang, S., Tang, J., Liu, H.: Fake news detection on social media: a data mining perspective. ACM SIGKDD Explor. Newsl. **19**(1), 22–36 (2017)

16. Dataset: SMSSpamCollection. https://archive.ics.uci.edu/ml/datasets/sms+spam +collection
17. Wordnet: https://wordnet.princeton.edu (2010)
18. Zhao, Y., Karypis, G.: Evaluation of hierarchical clustering algorithms for document datasets. In: Proceedings of the Eleventh International Conference on Information and Knowledge Management, pp. 515–524. ACM (2002)

Data Processing and Blockchain Technology

An Efficient and Novel Buyer and Seller's Distributed Ledger Based Protocol Using Smart Contracts

Priyanka Kumar[✉], G. A. Dhanush, D. Srivatsa, S. Nithin Aakash,
and S. Sahisnu

Department of Computer Science and Engineering, Amrita School of Engineering,
Amrita Vishwa Vidyapeetham, Coimbatore, India
k_priyanka@cb.amrita.edu,
{cb.en.u4cse17415,cb.en.u4cse17459,cb.en.u4cse17443,
cb.en.u4cse17450}@cb.students.amrita.edu

Abstract. The emergence of Distributed Ledger systems has made us rethink things that are possible to be digitized. A lot of tedious man labour requiring systems can be converted to digital systems for various benefits. With this new technology, we have a new means to record transactions and the system inherently preserves the integrity of it. With these benefits, we could design systems that primarily deal with transactions in ease. In this paper, we have discussed the advantages of using a distributed ledger system for performing transactions and propose and implement a buyer-seller protocol for land transactions to show the advantages of using this system.

Keywords: Land registry · Distributed ledger · Blockchain · Ethereum · Smart contract

1 Introduction

The advent of new software technologies has shaped the way for traditional systems that rely on paper-based documentation become more efficient and reliable. Many systems working under the government require and collect physical documentation. For example, to issue a birth certificate to a person, one makes a physical record in paper and hands it over to whomsoever to would belong to. When computers came into the picture, we saw an attempt to digitize all the records by making digital copies of the physical records available and storing information about them in digital repositories like a database. This did not stop the issuing of physical records because there were several problems with traditional database systems. With the emergence of Distributed Ledger Technology, we find means to convert these traditional paper-based systems into full-fledged digital systems that maintain the records similar to a database and extends further by providing ways to trace the history of the records and securing the records in previously unachievable ways. Government systems that use physical

© Springer Nature Switzerland AG 2020
D. V. Hung and M. D'Souza (Eds.): ICDCIT 2020, LNCS 11969, pp. 349–363, 2020.
https://doi.org/10.1007/978-3-030-36987-3_23

records like banking and finance department, chambers of commerce, healthcare department etc. would very much benefit if they could find ways to store their records in a distributed digital ledger. In this paper, we present a way to implement traditional land registry system which is paper-based and stores its records in a conventional database and convert it into a full-fledged digital system by using distributed ledger technology.

2   Technologies Used

To understand how we have implemented our land registry system, we need to understand the technologies that we have used to make it. Blockchain is fundamentally a distributed ledger system and one can use its properties to digitize land registry. Many blockchain platforms are existing but the platform that we have chosen is Ethereum.

2.1   Ethereum

Ethereum is an open-source, public, blockchain-based distributed computing platform and operating system featuring smart contract functionality [1]. Ethereum, as a platform, supports various features that we require to implement our land registry system and makes the development experience free of hassle. Here are a few notable mentions in the way it helps:

- **Open source:** Ethereum being open source means that developers who work on that platform are free to view the platform's source code, so they can come up with ways in helping the platform get better collaboratively. This aspect helps our project as the platform is available free of cost for us to work on and we could provide the report of bugs in the platform if we find any while developing our project.
- **Public:** This platform is hosted online and there is no restriction for any user to join in this platform. It also helps us to keep the information transparent as anyone knowing the hash address to the block can view the contents in it. All the land transaction records will be made publicly available so that everyone will be informed to whom each land belongs to.
- **Blockchain based:** As explained in the previous section, blockchain is a distributed ledger technology. To implement our land registry system, we need a platform that inherently supports distributed ledger and blockchain is the perfect fit for this. All the land transactions made are recorded in the ledger and once entered they become immutable, meaning the transactions cannot be erased or rolled back.
- **Smart contracts:** Smart contract used in blockchain essentially refers to a piece of code that runs on the above-mentioned platform. To run these smart contracts on the blockchain, Ethereum contains a stack-based virtual machine called EVM [2]. Smart contracts can be used to write business logic and once fired up, can execute a set of instructions that write transaction

records on the blockchain. This helps us to write the business logic of our implementation and make our work easier by automatically recording each state change in a program as a transaction.

Ethereum brings in certain constraints to execute smart contracts in its platform. Since Ethereum virtual machine code is Turing complete [2], its execution must be controlled in an environment like a distributed ledger. If a program does not halt, then its state would remain to change forever. Since all the miners in the network need to work to mine a block, it becomes computationally expensive to record all these state changes. So, Ethereum introduces a *gas* cost to execute a particular instruction. This prevents the continuous execution of a program without halting and for a person to execute a smart contract, he needs to pay the *gas* amount for the contract to run. Thus, one must think about the design and efficiency of smart contract that is designed by him/her.

There are two ways that a smart contract is written can be tested out. One way is to test the smart contract that in the test nodes available in the Ethereum network. These test nodes are a fork of Ethereum blockchain, but developers can request free tokens which are used to pay for the gas cost incurred. Also, smart contract once deployed will exist in the platform forever. So, it is necessary to test the smart contracts before deploying. Another way is to create a local development server which hosts a fork of Ethereum blockchain and allows a person to execute his smart contract on the created local server. There are preexisting software solutions available that help us to do the same. Truffle Suite is a set of applications that are available to locally host a blockchain and provide templates of code that helps us to bootstrap the process of writing smart contracts [3]. From the truffle suite, we worked with Truffle, a development framework for Ethereum [4], and Ganache, a personal Ethereum blockchain to run tests [5].

2.2 Truffle

Truffle, being a development framework, provides an easy way to test and deploy smart contracts that we write. It uses JavaScript to write code that helps us deploy a smart contract on the blockchain (called as migration files). To use Truffle, we need to add the following directories and files in our project directory:

contracts/ We add all the smart contracts that we write in this directory. We can add one or more smart contracts in the directory and we need to add corresponding migration file to deploy the smart contract in the blockchain.

migrations/ For the smart contract to be deployed on the blockchain, we need to write migration files that instruct to deploy it. The sequence of deployment is controlled by indexing the filenames in a particular sequence. All the migration files necessary for the deployment of smart contracts reside in this directory.

tests/ We can write specialized tests for our smart contract to check whether it performs valid transactions. All the tests that are required to test our smart contracts are stored in this directory. We can write these tests in a variety of languages like JavaScript, Typescript and Solidity.

truffle.config.js. As the name suggests, this file is used to configure the properties of the deployment. In our project, we specifically used it to configure network requirements like host address and port number.

Truffle provides command-line utilities to create a project. It has pre-made templates called boxes that contain standard boilerplate code. Using truffle's CLI utilities, we can download a standard template.

2.3 Ganache

Ganache enables us to locally run Ethereum blockchain in our machine. This enables us to test the smart contract program that we write. Deployment of the smart contract on the blockchain is done with the help of Truffle's command-line utilities. We can choose the port in which our local blockchain instance is hosted on. We are also presented with few user accounts, their hash identities and each user has 100 ETH (ETH stands for Ether, Cryptocurrency of Ethereum platform, also used as a token for gas spent by smart contracts) in the platform. Ganache also allows us to visualize blocks created, transactions incurred and contracts deployed in our blockchain. With all these functionalities, Ganache is the correct tool to deploy and test our smart contracts (Fig. 1).

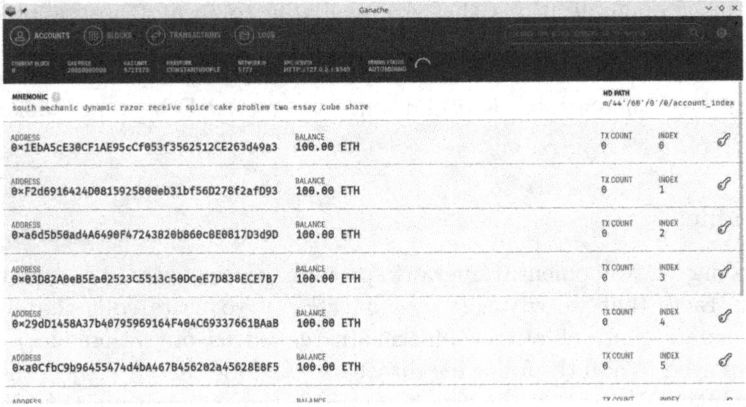

Fig. 1. The interface of Ganache Application

3   System Architecture

Utilizing the platforms that we have mentioned in the above sections, we implement our theoretical model of buyer and seller protocol for a land registry system. Our implementation is discussed in detail in this system architecture section. We discuss our implementation in three sections. The first section explains how the data is organized in our implementation. The second section explains how the transactions occur and how they are reflected in our system. Finally, the third section explains how the smart contract code that we write responds to each process that needs to occur in our system.

3.1 Data Organization

In our system, we need to store the details of two entities: Land and the user. To store details of the land, we create a separate data structure that can hold the following fields:

- *LandId:* It is a uniquely identifiable hash address that is used as a key to identify our land.
- *LandCoordinates:* This field holds the coordinates of the location of the land. Can be used to precisely identify pieces of land in the same address. May be replaced in future with a unique land identifiable token provided in real life.
- *LandAddress:* this field holds the real-world address of the land.
- *LandOwnerId:* It holds the uniquely identifiable hash address of a person who is the current owner of this land.
- *LandPreviousOwners:* This field holds the LandOwnerId of previous land-owners of this land.
- *LandStatus:* It is used to identify whether the land is 'on sale' or 'owned' by a person.
- *LandPrice:* It is used to store the price of the land. It will be updated when the land status changes to 'on sale' and will be updated to the current price of the land.

Details of the user are stored in another data structure. It holds the following fields:

- *UserId:* Similar to LandId, it is a uniquely identifiable hash address that is used as a key to identify a user.
- *UserName:* This field is used to store the name of the user.
- *UserWalletId:* This field holds the wallet address of our user. The user is free to change the wallet he/she uses.
- *UserPrivilege:* This field classifies user into one of three types; admin, registrar and Customer. The need and functionality of these user types are explained in the next section.

These are the two entities that are created and interact in our system. The interactions in the system are modelled based on real-world requirements. In the next section, we describe how a user and land is registered in our system, how a user can avail to purchase land and finally how the transfer of land is recorded as a transaction.

3.2 Real World Interactions

As mentioned in the previous section, a user is categorized into one among the three types:

- *Admin:* This user has the highest privilege in our system. He/she has access to the creation of new lands and the creation of new users with desired privileges. We use admin to create registrars in the system.
- *Registrar:* This user holds the second privilege level. He/she is the person who is authorized to create new lands similar to admin. He/she cannot administer the creation of new users.
- *Customer:* This user holds the least privilege in the system. This privilege is assigned to user accounts who possess the land and can only perform land transactions. They cannot administer the creation of other users or the addition of new lands into the system.

In the real-life, registrars would be people who work under the government in the department related to the land registry. These people can physically verify the presence of the land and update their details into the system. Admin privilege would be given to higher authorities present in the government institutions who assign registrars who work under them. By categorizing privileges into three different levels, we achieve the separation of functionality that is held by each person using this application.

Furthermore, the lands in our system hold a separate field to denote the status. It can be in two possible states:

- *On Sale:* This states that the land can be transacted to another person. If the land is in this particular state, calling a transaction land function would result in an error.
- *Owned:* This states that the land is held by a particular person and cannot be transacted. If the land is in this particular state, land transaction function would transfer the land from the current landowner to the new buyer.

Now that we have described most of the terminologies used in our system, we further provide insights on how a user could register into the system and perform land transactions. Initially, a user is supposed to register into the system by filling in user credentials. User's credentials will be handled by the application layer logic of the system. In our smart contract, we generate a new ID corresponding to the user and assign privilege of the user as 'Customer'. An admin account is created and fed into the system before the smart contract is deployed. We also provide the functionality to the admin account to create new admins. Now, these admins could create new registrars that add land details to our system. Registrars verify the presence of land in real life and feed the necessary details of the land into our system. Again, only necessary details mentioned in the data organization section are stored in the smart contract. Other details are abstracted out and handled by application-layer logic. When registrar assigns land to the user, the land status is essentially assigned as 'Owned' state. The status of the land can be later changed to 'On Sale' state either by the user (or) if the user becomes absent in the system, a registrar (or) an admin have the privilege to change the status of the land. Once the status of the land is changed to 'On Sale', the land can be transacted. By initiating a method in the smart contract, the particular land referred by its LandId would be transacted to the user referred by his/her UserId. As the changes in detail occur in a smart contract, it gets recorded as a transaction in our blockchain. More about this is explained in the next section.

In the next section, we describe the logic that is used in our smart contract to perform all the above-mentioned actions.

3.3   Smart Contract Logic

A smart contract that runs on blockchain essentially records the state changes in the program as individual transactions. This gives the program the ability to stop anywhere and resume from the state previously left anytime the contract is invoked. The data that we store in our smart contract holds the data of Land and User details. As new users and new lands are added into the system, the state of the data structure changes and it is recorded as an individual transaction in our blockchain. Also, when we transact the land, the land details get mutated and change its state. Since our blockchain record state changes as a series of transactions, the previous state of data could be traced back. By recording state changes as transactions, we get two advantages; each state change is recorded as a transaction and the previous history of the data is obtainable.

Now, we explain the smart contract logic that we have incorporated into our model. Firstly to register a new user, we receive the details of the user as parameters. Then, based on the name and an auto-incrementing index, we generate UserId that can uniquely identify the user. Then, we store the details of the user with assigning the privilege of the user as 'Customer'. Registration of registrar and admin is done differently. The first admin created during the deployment of the smart contract has access to the creation of other admins and registrars. This admin can create new users using a function call. This function call first checks whether the person is an admin. If he/she is an admin, they can create a user with necessary privileges. The process of creation of this user will follow the same as creating a user with 'Customer' privilege.

To register new lands into the system, the parameters required for the creation of new land is obtained from the user (in this case, a registrar). Then, based on the land coordinates and an auto-incrementing index, we generate LandId which uniquely identifies the land. These details are stored and the status of the land is set as 'Owned'. We have a separate function which changes the status of the land. This function initially checks whether the user is either the owner of the land or is either a registrar or an admin. If they fall into any of those categories, then the status of land can be changed from 'Owned' to 'On Sale' by the user.

Finally, the transaction of land can occur in two different methods. Either the person who wants to purchase the land requests for a transaction or registrar forces the transaction to happen forcefully for a land which is on sale to be transacted to another user. For the first method, the user provides the details of the land as the parameter. Now, this function checks whether the person has sufficient wallet balance to purchase the land. The cost of the land is obtained from LandPrice field. If the user has sufficient balance, it checks for the status of the land. If the land is set to 'on sale' status, then further steps follow.

The landowner detail is updated to hold the id of the new landowner. LandPreviousOwner list is appended with the id of the previous landowner. Wallet balance of the new owner is deducted and transferred to the previous owner. Status of the land is set to 'Owned'. This finalizes the transaction of land. Now the previous user loses ownership of the land and the new user gains ownership. For the second method, during emergencies, one needs to forcefully transfer land from one person to another. This transfer is initiated by the registrar. This method checks for the privilege of the user and performs its action when the user is either a registrar or an admin. It checks whether the buyer has sufficient balance to purchase the land and proceeds if true. We provide a separate parameter in our implementation to override the condition checking of balance. Then, it receives LandId and the UserId to whom the land should be transferred to as the parameters. After this, it changes the ownership of the land to the new user, updates PreviousOwner list and finally changes the status of the land to 'Owned'. If the parameter to check for the balance is set to true, then an amount equal to the price of the land is deducted from the user's wallet. This finalizes the second type of transaction occurring in our system.

Model Diagram:

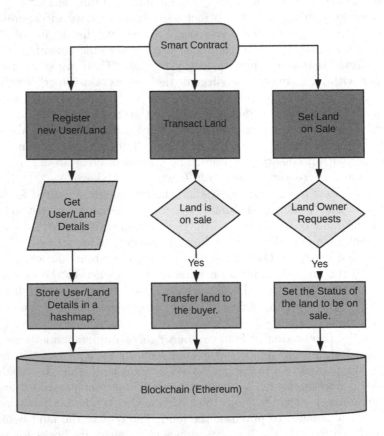

Fig. 2. Architecture diagram

These are the logic that we implement in our smart contract to perform transactions between a buyer and a seller in our application. Following contains a simplified diagram which explains each part explained above is handled by our smart contract (Fig. 2).

4   Our Contribution

We had explained the smart contract logic that we require in our program in the previous section. In this section, we mention how we incorporate them as functions in the program. Each smart contract logic is described by a corresponding function in our program. We can broadly classify the functions into three categories; functions that perform user and land registrations, functions that update the status of land and functions that transfer the ownership of land from one person to another. We explain each function that we have incorporated into our program under each category in further sections of the paper (Fig. 3).

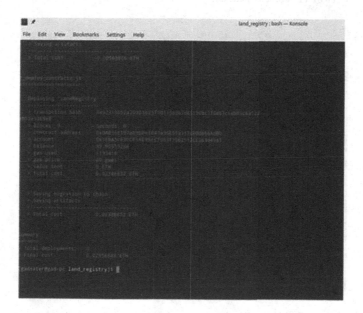

Fig. 3. Successful migration of smart contract to the local blockchain

4.1   Registration

This category explains the functions that perform user and land registration. Each of the functions receives detail as parameters which are passed to it by the application layer logic. These details then get stored into the corresponding data structure in our smart contract.

User Registration. To register a user, we implement two different functions. Function *registerCustomer* runs with a low level of privilege and is used to register 'Customers' into the system. Function *registerUser* is used to register a user by an admin. This admin can set the privileges of the user by passing it as a parameter to the function.

1. *registerCustomer:* This function receives UserName and UserWalletId as parameters. It then adds these details into the User details data structure. It generates new UserId by combining an auto-incrementing index value and the name of the person. Finally, it sets the privilege level of the user as a customer.
2. *registerUser:* Additional to the arguments received by the previous function, it receives user privilege as an argument. This function, before execution, checks whether the person who executes this method is an admin or not. It only performs the actions if the user is an admin. Also, it follows everything that *registerCustomer* does but sets the privilege from the parameter passed to the function (Figs. 4, 5 and 6).

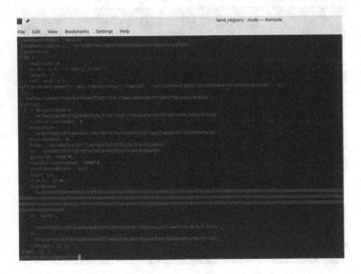

Fig. 4. Calling registerLand function

Land Registration. To register a new land into our system, we create a function called *registerLand*. This function can be invoked by a registrar or an admin and it creates a new entry in our land data structure.

1. *registerLand:* This function receives the required land details as the parameter from application-layer logic. Then it checks whether the user is an admin or a registrar. If they fall into either one of the categories, the function starts

to execute. It creates a new entry in the land data structure. A unique LandId is calculated by combining LandCoordinates and an auto-incrementing index value. It sets the status of land as 'Owned' by default.

Fig. 5. Calling registerUser function

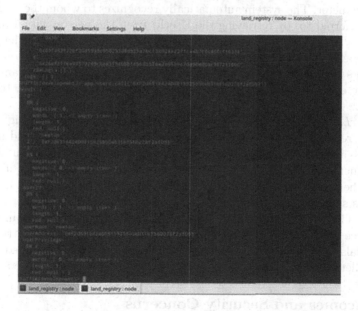

Fig. 6. Showing the registration of user in the platform

4.2   Land Status Update

These functions are used to update the status of the land. In order to perform this we include a function called *updateLandStatus*.

1. *updateLandStatus:* This function receives the LandId and LandStatus as parameters. Before updating the status of the land, it checks whether the user is the owner of the land or he/she is a registrar or an admin. If it is true, then it changes the status of the land if the LandStatus parameter provided is either 'Owned' or 'On Sale'.

4.3   Land Transaction

To perform land transactions, we create two functions that serve two different purposes. The first function is named *transactLand*. This function can be invoked by a user with Customer privilege. It transfers the ownership of land from the seller to the buyer. Also, the seller has the price of land added to his wallet and the buyer loses the same price in his wallet. The second function is named *transferLand*. This forces the transfer of land from one user to another with/without paying the price of land. This can only be invoked by admin or registrar and is included for emergencies where the customer owns the land is unavailable or leaves the system.

1. *transactLand:* This function is invoked when the user present in the system wants to purchase a land that is set in on sale status. It receives LandId as the parameter. The system automatically recognizes to whom the land should be transferred to, by retrieving the UserId from the person who invoked the function. Then, the user is checked for wallet balance. If the wallet balance is sufficient, it checks for the status of the land. If the land is 'on sale', it transfers the ownership of land from the seller to buyer and transfers the amount equivalent to the price of the land from buyer's wallet to seller's wallet.
2. *transferLand:* This function can only be invoked by users' with higher privilege. It receives LandId, UserId of person to whom the land should be transacted to and a truth value to know whether the wallet balance of buyer should be deducted or not, as parameters. First, this function checks for user privilege. Then, if the truth value is set to true, it checks for the wallet balance. If there is sufficient wallet balance, the ownership of land is transferred to the buyer. The wallet balance deducted from the buyer, which is equivalent to the price of land, is added to the registrar/admin account. If the truth value is set false, the land gets transferred to the buyer without any deduction in his wallet balance. Finally, it updates the status of land as 'Owned'.

5   Outcomes and Security Concerns

In our implementation, we were able to register new users and lands in our system and define a smart contract logic to transfer ownership of land from the buyer to seller. We have also put our thought on edge cases and included certain functions like *transferLand*, that force the transfer of ownership of land if the user is not present in the system. This would overcome the problem of inability to perform the land transaction in the long absence of landowner. The smart contract logic defines the buyer and seller protocol. Since we have used smart contracts, the protocol is strictly enforced and there can be no failure until the Ethereum platform that we run our smart contract on gets compromised. Since blockchain is inherently fool-proof to many of the security issues that we worry about and many developers are emerging who build their application for Ethereum platform, we believe that many of the security concerns would be alleviated. Another main security concern that can be only taken care by application layer logic is safeguarding admin account. If the credentials of the admin account get compromised, then all the land and user details can be altered. But, our blockchain records the history of these values. If we come to know that the system gets compromised, we could deploy a new smart contract with new admins and resume adding data from the place where the data got compromised. This ensures that the integrity of data can be recovered went it gets compromised. Finally, this system is scalable, meaning, it could work for any land registry system that deals with the buyer and seller and flexible enough to handle edge cases that can occur (Figs. 7 and 8).

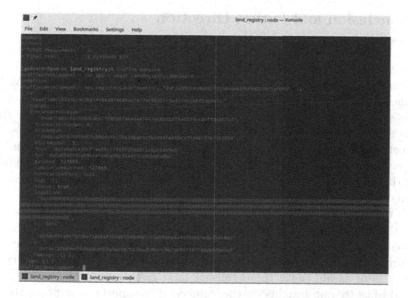

Fig. 7. Deploying a smart contract and interfacing with it

Fig. 8. Showing a successful transfer of ownership of land

6   Conclusion and Future Direction

To conclude, we have understood the merits of a Distributed Ledger system, embraced the architecture of blockchain and utilized a blockchain platform called Ethereum to implement our Buyer - Seller protocol for land registration. We have explained about the various tools that we have used in our project namely the Truffle suite and Ganache. We have also given a strong reason to use smart contracts by discussing them in detail. Then, we have discussed the system architecture, in which, we have explained how land transactions occur and how our smart contracts need to respond. Then we have discussed the implementation details by providing a brief description of the functions that we have created in our smart contract. Finally, we discuss briefly security concerns in the results section to understand how vulnerabilities might occur in our system. We have stated that the system we made is scalable, but we wanted to extend it further. We would like to store the land records in a separate file called land document and store them in a distributed file system called IPFS (Inter-Planetary File System). This would make the details of land easily accessible. Furthermore, we would like to gain insights on the vulnerability aspects to improve the user registration process in our system. Also, we are developing an application that interfaces with the smart contract to make the functionalities easily accessible by any user.

References

1. Wikipedia, Ethereum. https://en.wikipedia.org/wiki/Ethereum. Accessed on 10 Jan 2018
2. Wood, G.: ETHEREUM: a secure decentralised generalised transaction ledger, Technical Report, 2014. http://gavwood.com/Paper.pdf
3. Truffle Suite. https://www.trufflesuite.com
4. Truffle. https://www.trufflesuite.com/truffle
5. Ganache. https://www.trufflesuite.com/ganache
6. Nakamoto, S.: Bitcoin: A peer-to-peer electronic cash system (2008)
7. Tschorsch, F., Scheuermann, B.: Bitcoin and beyond: a technical survey on decentralized digital currencies. IEEE Commun. Surv. Tutorials **18**(3), 2084–2123 (2016)
8. Bahga, A., Madisetti, V.K.: Blockchain platform for industrial Internet of Things. J. Softw. Eng. Appl. **9**(10), 533 (2016). https://solidity.readthedocs.io/en/v0.4.24/
9. Sato, T., Yosuke H.: Smart-contract based system operations for permissioned blockchain. In: 2018 9th IFIP International Conference on New Technologies, Mobility and Security (NTMS), IEEE (2018)
10. Mohanta, B.K., Panda, S.S., Jena, D.: An overview of smart contract and use cases in blockchain technology. In: 2018 9th International Conference on Computing, Communication and Networking Technologies (ICCCNT) (2018)
11. Buchmann, N., Rathgeb, C., Baier, H., Busch, C., Marian, M.: Enhancing breeder document long-term security using blockchain technology. In: IEEE 41st Annual Computer Software and Applications Conference (2017)
12. Chen, Y., Hui L., Li, K., Zhang, J.: An improved P2P file system scheme based on IPFS and blockchain. In: IEEE International Conference on Big Data (BIGDATA) (2017)
13. Lo, S.K., Xu, X., Chiam, Y.K., Lu, Q.: Evaluating suitability of applying blockchain. In: International Conference on Engineering of Complex Computer Systems (2017)
14. Nomura Research Institute, Survey on Blockchain Technologies and Related Services (2016)
15. Thompson, S.: The preservation of digital signatures on the blockchain - Thompson - See Also, University British Columbia iSchool Student Journal, vol. 3, no. Spring (2017)
16. Schmidt, P.: Certificates Reputation and the Blockchain. MIT Media Lab, Cambridge (2015)
17. Shah, M., Kumar, P.: Tamper proof birth certificate suing blockchain technology. Int. Journal of Recent Technol. Eng. (IJRTE), 7(5S3) (2019)

Distributed and Lazy Auditing
of Outsourced Data

Amit Kumar Dwivedi$^{(\boxtimes)}$, Naveen Kumar$^{(\boxtimes)}$, and Mayank Pathela

IIIT Vadodara, Gandhinagar, India
{amit_dwivedi,naveen_kumar,mayank_pathela}@iiitvadodara.ac.in

Abstract. Data outsourcing is useful for ICT organizations who need cost-effective management of resources. Auditing of outsourced data is an essential requirement for the data owner who outsources it to the untrusted third party storage service provider. It is a posterior mechanism for data verification. In this work, we propose a distributed auditing scheme for verifying the integrity of the outsourced data as compare to the existing centralized auditing schemes. To the best of our knowledge, this is the first such scheme uses distributed auditing. The proposed scheme avoids intense computing requirement at the data owner or the auditor. We classify the existing auditing schemes into generic classes, analyze them, and compare them with the proposed scheme. The performance evaluation of the auditing operation in the proposed scheme is carried out and verified with the analytical results.

Keywords: Data integrity · Auditing · Distributed cloud

1 Introduction

Data outsourcing provides data storage-as-a-service to the ICT organizations dealing with a large amount of data and limited resources. It allows the organizations to focus on their core work and left other issues such as storage management, data availability and system scalability to the service provider. We consider a data outsourcing scenario with three entities [1,2]: a data owner, a cloud service provider and the end-users. The data owner can be an enterprise who seeks storage-as-a-service, the cloud service provider (CSP) is an organization who provides the data storage-as-a-service to the data owner, and the end-users are the registered users with the data owner authorized to access a subset of data files. The data owner is responsible for enforcing data access control and distributes access credentials among the registered users. Knowing their access credentials, the authorized users can access the data files directly from the CSP avoiding any possibility of the bottleneck at the data owner. We consider access permissions such as read, write, or both. The data owner can read and write any data file.

The CSP is a third-party organization and can not be fully trusted by the data owner. Therefore, the security of the outsourced data would be a major concern for the data owner. To ensure data confidentiality, data files are encrypted

© Springer Nature Switzerland AG 2020
D. V. Hung and M. D'Souza (Eds.): ICDCIT 2020, LNCS 11969, pp. 364–379, 2020.
https://doi.org/10.1007/978-3-030-36987-3_24

before they are outsourced. The decryption keys are distributed among the authorized user by the data owner. A user with the decryption key can download the file, decrypt and use it. Since a user is allowed to write a data file directly to the server without interacting with the data owner, we consider Malicious-But-Cautious CSP [3]. Such CSP may involve in performing active attacks on the outsourced data without leaving any evidence of their malicious behavior.

Since the CSP is untrusted, it may involve in the unauthorized modification of outsourced data files for personal benefits. It may also collude with the users (such as revoked users) to modify the existing data files. Such unauthorized modification may harm the image of the data owner or damage the valuable data. To this extent, the data integrity of the outsourced data will be another major security concern for the data owner to be addressed. Data integrity ensures that only authorized users can modify or update a data file.

On the other hand, as the outsourced data files are modified directly at the server by a user without interacting with the data owner, the data owner needs some posterior mechanism to verify the integrity of the outsourced data. Such posterior mechanism is known as auditing [4,5]. Auditing will be a continuous process. For practical reasons, it can be performed after a fixed interval of time. The time-period of auditing is decided based on the sensitivity of the data and computation complexity. The outcome of such auditing schemes will be an assurance (known as *proof*) about the integrity of the outsourced data. Proof of integrity generated by verifying all the data files is called deterministic proof and a proof generated by verifying a random subset of data files is called probabilistic proof. Auditing is usually done by the data owner or a third party auditor in the supervision of the data owner.

1.1 Motivation

There are several auditing schemes [6–19] have been proposed in the literature for outsourced data verification. The important characteristics of an auditing scheme are deterministic or probabilistic auditing, computation cost at the auditor, communication cost between the auditor and the CSP, and storage cost at the auditor. To the best of our knowledge, all the existing auditing schemes are centralized in nature. Majority of them [6–9] uses probabilistic auditing for efficiency reasons. In many schemes [13,18], the auditing process is outsourced by the data owner to a trusted third party auditor to reduce the computation cost at the data owner.

In this work, we propose a distributed auditing scheme to counter the issues in the existing auditing schemes. It is a lazy scheme as the auditing of data is done during the read-only. The proposed scheme will reduce the computation cost at the data owner and discourage the involvement of any third-party auditor. The scheme uses deterministic auditing with no communication cost between the data owner and the CSP. The important contribution of this work is as follows:

– Existing auditing schemes are classified into newly proposed generic auditing schemes.

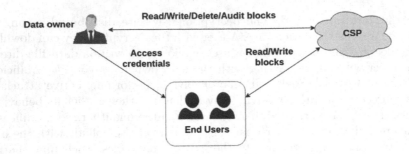

Fig. 1. Data outsourcing scenario

– A distributed auditing scheme is proposed in contrast to the existing centralized auditing scheme.
– The proposed distributed scheme is analyzed and compared with the generic schemes.

1.2 Data Outsourcing Scenario

There are three parties involved in the considered data outsourcing scenario [1,2,9,20]: the data owner, the CSP and the end-users as shown in Fig. 1.

Data owner is the owner of the outsourced data. It does an initial agreement with the CSP that defines the authentication policy for the data seekers. It will define the data access policies for its registered data users and may revoke user access if needed. It can read, write, delete, and audit any outsourced data files.

CSP is a third party organization provides data storage-as-a-service to the data owner and may not be fully trusted by the data owner. We consider malicious-but-cautious CSP which may involve in active attacks. The CSP is bound to follow the service level agreement created initially with the data owner. Upon receiving a read or write request, it authenticates the request and fulfils it if initiated by an authorized user.

End-users are first registered with the data owner. The data owner returns the access credentials through a secure channel to the end-users. Using their access credentials the end-users can read or write the authorized data files directly from the CSP. End-users are assumed to be trusted by the data owner.

In what follows, we first classify the existing auditing schemes into newly created generic auditing schemes. In Sect. 3, we discuss the proposed novel and efficient distributed auditing scheme, in detail. Section 4 discusses and compares the proposed distributed auditing scheme with the proposed generic auditing schemes. Experiment evaluation of proposed distributed auditing scheme is discussed in Sect. 5. We conclude this work in Sect. 6.

2   Generic Auditing Schemes

There is a number of auditing schemes [6–19] proposed in the literature. They can be divided broadly into two types: deterministic and probabilistic schemes. A deterministic auditing scheme verifies each outsourced data file before concluding a proof whereas probabilistic schemes verify a subset of files. Although auditing all the outsourced data files before creating proof gives maximum assurance to the auditor, it requires a significant computation overhead. A probabilistic auditing scheme reduces the computation cost by auditing a limited number of data files but gives a probabilistic guarantee.

Some of the existing schemes [5,10] are restricted to the auditing of static data, few use attribute-based cryptosystem [19], few adopt identity-based cryptosystem [14], and few addresses privacy requirement [21]. Erway et al. uses rank-based skip list data structure in auditing [15]. Auditing scheme for batch processing is proposed by Yamamoto et al. [22].

These schemes can be further classified according to the data storage cost at the auditor, communication cost between the auditor and the CSP, computation cost involved, etc. This type of classification will help the users or the researchers working in this area to select the optimal scheme for their use. It will also provide an analytical understanding of these schemes. In what follows, we define and classify the existing auditing schemes into generic auditing schemes according to their auditing methodology and basic characteristics.

2.1   A Trivial Scheme

In trivial auditing scheme, the data owner computes the metadata corresponding to each data file to be outsourced and store it locally. The stored metadata will be used later by the data owner at the time of auditing. During auditing, the auditor downloads all the outsourced data files, re-computes the metadata and verifies it with the stored metadata. If every file is verified successfully, the integrity is intact and the proof is successful else proof fails. In case the proof is failed, the necessary action will be taken by the data owner. The auditing process is repeated after every fixed interval of time.

It is a deterministic scheme since every outsourced data file is audited in each time interval. Therefore, a significant cost towards communication between the auditor and the CSP is involved. Another disadvantage with this scheme is that it requires significant local storage at the auditor to store the metadata against each outsourced data file. Maintaining the local storage is an issue since each data update requires updating of the corresponding local metadata.

2.2   A Deterministic Scheme with Constant Communication Cost

In the trivial scheme, the auditor is supposed to download the entire data and compute the proof locally. Whereas in this scheme, for each challenge by the data owner, the CSP computes the proof and sends it to the auditor. The proof send by the CSP is of constant size. Therefore, the communication cost is reduced significantly as compared to the trivial scheme. It is assumed that n number of data files are outsourced along with n number of encrypted hash (tags). These tags are computed in such a way that they are unique for each file.

In this scheme, at the start of each auditing phase, a random key is generated by the auditor and sent to the CSP as a challenge. Using the challenge key, the auditor and the CSP will generates n random values (as Set X) by using a public pseudo-random function. Now, the CSP will computes a pair (T, P) as a proof of storage. T (a combined tag) is computed using X and the outsourced tags along with the outsourced files. P is computed using the outsourced data files and X. The CSP then returns the pair (T, P) to the auditor. The auditor verifies the proof pair (T, P) using locally computed X. Since the challenge key (used in the computation of X and the proof generation) is distinct in every auditing interval, the proof will also be unique.

Barsoum et al. [16] have proposed a similar scheme where the list of data files (or one data file) can be divided into a set of blocks. The data owner computes a Message Authentication Code (MAC [23]) for each data block (called tag) and sends all the file blocks to the CSP along with their tags. At the time of auditing, the auditor sends a challenge containing a fresh random key to the CSP used by both the auditor and the CSP to compute a set of random numbers using a pseudorandom function. The random numbers set and the respective data tags are used by the CSP for computing an integrity proof which is then sent to the auditor. Upon receiving the proof, the auditor verifies it using a similar set of random numbers generated locally. If proof is successfully verified, it infers the integrity is intact, else necessary action will be taken by the data owner.

A major advantage of this scheme is that the communication cost between the auditor and the CSP is constant as compared to the trivial scheme. However, the local storage requirement at the auditor is still high to store the random numbers used in the generation of the proof. Also, a significant computation cost is involved to generate the proof and its verification.

2.3   A Probabilistic Scheme with Reduced Local Storage

The above generic schemes are deterministic as proof of outsourced data is computed based on every outsourced data file. The proof is prepared by the CSP and verified by the auditor. It increases the computation cost at the auditor and the CSP. Storage cost at auditor is also significantly more.

To reduce the computation cost of the auditor and the CSP, probabilistic schemes can be used. A probabilistic scheme generates a probabilistic proof of auditing, i.e., more the number of challenges more is the assurance. Idea is to audit less number of files but assuring the whole set of data files with a high probability.

This scheme considered static outsourced data. The data owner computes tag for each data file, encrypts it and outsources it along with the file. During the auditing phase, the auditor sends a key as a challenge to the CSP. The key is used to generate a fixed number c of random file identifiers (IDs). Using the files corresponding to the given IDs (instead of all the outsourced files), the CSP computes a pair (T, P) of values as in the above scheme. The proof (T, P) is then sent to the auditor for verification. The auditor decrypts T and uses it to verify P. As in the above scheme, since the challenge key is distinct in every auditing interval, the proof will be unique.

This scheme requires reduced local storage cost (order c) at the auditor as compare to order n in the above schemes. Ateniese et al. [7] show that the c will be equal or more than 4.6% to get 99% probability to find the defective file considering 1% files are defective. It infers that c is significantly less than the total number of files n in practice so as the computation cost. The communication cost is still constant as in the above schemes.

Ateniese et al. [7,8,24] describe a similar scheme also called as Provable Data Possession (PDP). In this scheme, the auditor verifies the integrity of whole outsourced data with a high probability without retrieving it. Each file is divided into several blocks as in [16]. A homomorphic tag is computed for each file block. A homomorphic tag T_{m1+m2} (corresponding to the message $m1 + m2$) is efficiently computed using two tags T_{m1} and T_{m2}. The challenge-response protocol is used between the auditor and the CSP during auditing. Let a file f_i is divided into four blocks $B1$, $B2$, $B3$ and $B4$ and their corresponding tags are $T1$, $T2$, $T3$ and $T4$, respectively. During the challenge phase, the auditor sends a challenge for the file f_i with a subset of blocks $B2$, $B3$ and $B4$. Upon receiving the challenge, the CSP will compute a homomorphic block $B5$ corresponding to the challenged blocks. It also computes a homomorphic tag $T5$ corresponding to the respective tags $T2$, $T3$, and $T4$. Upon receiving the response, the auditor verifies the $B5$ and $T5$. Similar challenges will be executed for a randomly selected subset of data files and respective tags are verified during each auditing time interval for any data integrity violation.

This gives a probabilistic proof since a subset of files (or blocks) are only verified in each auditing time interval in contrast to the deterministic schemes. Due to the probabilistic proof, communication between the auditor and the CSP is reduced. This scheme will work only for the static data as the auditor has to redo the tag computation and outsourcing of data files against any dynamic operation such as insert, delete, append or update.

2.4   A Probabilistic Scheme for Dynamic Data

The above-discussed auditing (deterministic or probabilistic) schemes support static data. But in practice, data may be highly dynamic in nature. The above probabilistic scheme is also based on asymmetric key cryptography that forces huge computation overhead at the auditor and the CSP. Therefore, we need an auditing scheme which should provide dynamic data support and preferably uses symmetric key cryptography.

To support dynamic data all kind of dynamic operations on the outsourced data like insert, delete, append should be defined. After every dynamic operation on a data file, new metadata for the same is computed and stored. Old metadata related to the updated data file should be replaced by the new one. This scheme will pre-compute several challenges (C) for a random combination of data files

(F). Each challenge is an encrypted hash value computed using a fix (r) number of files. These challenges are outsourced along with the data files. At the time of auditing, the CSP computes proof for a given challenge and sends it to the auditor along with the outsourced pre-computed challenge (C_i). The auditor first decrypts each challenge (C_i) and compares it with the received one from the CSP. If both are same then an audit is successful.

In order to insert, delete, or modify a file, the data owner downloads the all pre-computed challenge from the server. Re-compute the challenges, as per the updated file and outsources it along with the updated file.

One such scheme was proposed by Ateniese et al. [6] supports data integrity audit for dynamic data. Each data file is divided into a set of blocks. This approach has three phases: setup phase, verification phase, and update phase. In the Setup phase, the data owner generates a fixed set of challenges and their corresponding proofs (as tokens) before outsourcing the data. The data owner encrypts each token and outsources it along with the data blocks. In the verification phase, the auditor sends a randomly selected challenge (from the list of pre-computed challenges) to verify proof of possession. The auditor sends a random nonce will be used later to ensure freshness of the proof computed by the CSP. The CSP computes the proof of possession corresponding to the challenge and sends it along with the encrypted token uploaded by the auditor. Now, the auditor decrypts the encrypted token and verify it with the received proof. If both match the outsourced data integrity is intact.

In the update phase, suppose the data owner wants to change a kth data block. An update request is sent to the CSP. The CSP will return all the uploaded encrypted tokens to the data owner. The data owner computes all the tokens again over updated data blocks, encrypts them, and send them to the CSP.

Advantages of this scheme are that it uses symmetric cryptosystem and supports dynamic data. The local storage at auditor is approximately the same as in the above scheme. One of the limitations of this approach is that it only supports the limited number of challenges (or tokens). This is due to the fixation of the number of tokens in the setup phase. If the data owner increases the number of challenges, then it is necessary to re-execute the setup phase. The insertion operation is also costly in this scheme as it needs renumbering of data blocks and re-computation of the tokens. Also, at every update, the CSP has to send all the respective tokens back to the data owner and the data owner returns newly updated tokens to the CSP which increases the communication cost. As the number of updates increases, the computation and communication cost also increases.

2.5   Priority-Based Scheme

All the above schemes consider same sensitively level for all the data files. However, in practice, some of the files are comparatively more sensitive than others. Therefore, in a probabilistic auditing scheme, sensitive files must be audited more frequently than the others. It will give more confidence to the data owner about the integrity proof. The auditing of less sensitive files may be delayed, if necessary.

A priority-based auditing scheme is a probabilistic scheme, i.e., it will audit a subset of data files in each time interval. A fixed number of priority levels are defined. A priority is assigned to each outsourced data file. The highest priority data files are audited more frequently than the less priority data files.

An example scheme is proposed by Popa et al. [9]. In this scheme, a probability (or priority) is assigned to each outsourced data file based on its sensitivity level. They used four sensitivity levels. Highly sensitive blocks are assigned a higher probability and are audited in each auditing-interval. Let's assume that a file $B2$ is the most sensitive therefore given the highest probability value. This file will be audited in every audit cycle whereas a file $B3$ is of lowest probability and audited rarely. There are three parties involved: data owner, CSP and the end-users. End-users are frequently performing read and write operation on the outsourced data files. In every read (or write) operation, the CSP is providing consent to the reader (or writer) confirming the operation. After receiving the consent the end-user forward it to the auditor. Upon receiving all the consents, the auditor verifies and arranges them according to their sensitivity levels. Now the consents are audited or verified considering the sensitivity of the data files.

Advantage of this scheme is that it supports dynamic data. However, it provides the probabilistic proof, uses asymmetric cryptosystem, and requires significant storage at the data owner to store the attestations. Also, since every attestation is communicated to the data owner, a significant communication cost is involved.

Third Party Auditor(s): The above schemes use centralized auditing, i.e., there is only one auditor which involved in tedious auditing job. Since the auditing process requires significant computation cost, it may create a bottleneck at the auditor. Avoiding the situation, the data owner may hire a third-party organization for the auditing. They are skilled and known as Third-party auditors (TPA) [11–13]. When using TPA, the data owner is relaxed from the auditing burden. The TPA may distribute the auditing task among multiple servers.

There can be single TPA or multiple TPAs. Saxena et al. [13] assume that a TPA can be compromised and considers a setup with multiple TPAs to nullify the effect of the compromised TPA (s). It gives confidence to the data owners in the auditing proof. However, it will increase the financial cost. Therefore, there is a trade-off between increasing the number of TPAs and the cost involved.

In a nutshell, auditing burden should be reduced from the data owner. The auditing scheme should preferably be deterministic, uses symmetric cryptosystem, requires less storage and computation cost. Keeping all these facts in mind a distributed auditing scheme is proposed in the next section.

3   Proposed Distributed Auditing Scheme

The above section describes various generic auditing schemes covering all the existing schemes to the best of our knowledge. The deterministic schemes increase the communication cost between the auditor and the CSP. The number of challenges sent by the auditor to the CSP depends upon the number of file data blocks [25]. Probabilistic schemes reduce the communication cost but give probabilistic proof of integrity. Probabilistic schemes for dynamic data requires a constant amount of local storage at the auditor and constrained the number of challenges per auditing time interval. Priority-based auditing considers the sensitivity of data files for efficient auditing.

We can summarize the essential auditing requirements from the above schemes and look forward to a generic integrity auditing scheme with the following features: deterministic, constant storage requirement at the data owner, less processing at auditor, suitability to dynamic data, and less communication cost between the auditing entities.

Looking at the currently distributed databases used in many real-world applications, we look forward to an auditing scheme which audits in a distributed fashion for efficiency reasons. It may help the auditors to audit possibly all the files in an efficient manner. An advantage of distributed auditing is that it reduces the processing burden at the auditor.

In what follows, we propose a distributed auditing scheme considering the above requirements. We assume that each outsourced data file is frequently accessed by the end-users and every communication between the auditor and the CSP is done through a secure channel. We show how auditing load can be distributed in the considered setup. In the considered scenario, end-users are accessing the outsource data files as and when needed. They frequently perform read and write operations as per their authorization. Since end-users are the registered users (for example, employees of an organization), they cannot be fully untrusted by the data owner. We assume that the end-users are partially trusted, i.e., they will follow the instructions given by the data owner however tasks may be delayed.

Read is the most frequent and basic operation performed by the authorized end-users. During a read operation, an end-user, in general, will verify the integrity of the downloaded content before using it. This motivates our idea of distributed auditing. Each end-user is expected to audit their downloaded data file during the read operation. If the audit fails, the failure report is expected to be communicated to the data owner. In this way auditing of the outsourced data would be distributed among registered end-users by the data owner. The distributed auditing scenario is shown in Fig. 2. The figure shows that the data owner only receives the failure reports. Upon receiving a failure report, the data owner cross-verifies it by accessing the file from the CSP. If verification fails, the necessary action will be taken.

This type of auditing is called *lazy auditing* as the data files are audited as and when they are accessed by the authorized users. A file not accessed for a long time by any authorized user will not be audited. We believe that a file accessed more frequently is more important for the system. Therefore, the files which are not accessed or audited for a long time will impact on the system. However, whenever it is accessed by a user it will be audited.

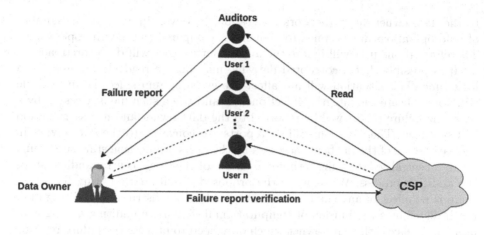

Fig. 2. Distributed auditing scenario

a) **Record Structure**

ID	V_i	E(K, X)	MAC(K_M, E(K, X))	...

b) **Failure Report**

U	E(K_U, ID ‖ V_i)

Fig. 3. Outsourced data record and failure report structures

Auditing Protocol

We consider an outsourced data record (shown in Fig. 3(a)) which contains file identifier ID, file version number V_i, encrypted file $E(K,X)$ where $E()$ is symmetric encryption function, X is the data file, K is the shared encryption key between read and write authorized users including the data owner. $MAC(K_M, E(K,X))$ is Message Authentication Code (MAC) computed over $E(K,X)$ using key K_M. K_M is known to the same set of users knowing K. MAC is used for verifying the integrity of the encrypted data at the time of record read operation.

During a read operation, the authorized user accesses the whole file record. Now, knowing key K_M and received $E(K,X)$ the reader first computes $MAC(K_M, E(K,X))$. Then compares it with the received MAC. If both match then there is no integrity violation. Otherwise, the user creates a failure report (as shown in Fig. 3(b)) and send it to the data owner. The failure report contains user's id (U) and data file details (i.e., file identifier ID and version number V_i) encrypted with a secret shared key (K_U) known to the data owner and the user. Upon receiving the failure report, the data owner decrypts it and re-verifies it with the CSP. If verification fails, the necessary action will be taken.

In the proposed approach, the end-user may not always audit the outsourced data record during a read operation or may not send the failure report to the data owner due to efficiency reasons. Also, some of the failure reports may not reach to the data owner due to network congestion. However, in general, the number of read operations are assumed to be more as compared to the write operations. Therefore, If one user will ignore the audit another user will do before read.

It is possible that a corrupted data file may not be read by any user for a long time. This situation will not affect the given system since the unread file will not replicate the integrity infections. As and when such file is accessed by a user, the failure report will be reported to the data owner and necessary action will be taken. Therefore, the failure reports are conveyed to the data owner in the early stage of the file being accessed by the users or infection start spreading.

In a centralized auditing technique, failure of the single central auditor stops the auditing process. Whereas, in the proposed distributed auditing technique there is no effect of any single point failure. Also, the distributed auditing approach distributes the burden of computationally-intensive auditing among end-users and relaxed the data owner which only need to process the failure reports. It is to be noted here that, in practice, the failure reports are limited in number.

The proposed auditing scheme is a cycle-free approach where auditing is done round the clock. Every file is given the same priority however most accessed files are audited more frequently by default. In practice, important files are accessed more frequently. It is a deterministic scheme as every file is accessed with the same probability. A constant size local storage is needed to store the secret keys. It supports dynamic operations since auditing of a file will start immediately after it is committed at the server. Therefore, the proposed scheme works well with both static and dynamic scenarios.

4   Comparison of Auditing Schemes

In this section, we analyze and compare the above discussed generic auditing schemes with the proposed distributed scheme. We consider the following properties in the comparison: proof type, i.e., deterministic or probabilistic, computation cost at the auditor, computation cost at the CSP (excluding data access time), communication cost between the CSP and the auditor, local storage needed at the auditor in an auditing cycle, extra storage needed at the CSP for auditing, preferred cryptosystem, whether supports dynamic data or not, number of auditors auditing the data, and auditing type, i.e., aggressive or Lazy [26]. Comparison of the generic schemes is given in Table 1. The abbreviation used for the generic scheme is as follows: TS (Trivial Scheme), DSwCCC (Deterministic Scheme with Constant Communication Cost), PSRLS (Probabilistic Scheme with Reduced Local Storage), PSDD (Probabilistic Scheme for Dynamic Data), PbA (Priority-based Auditing), and proposed DS (Distributed Scheme). To improve the readability, the list of abbreviations used for different operations is given in Table 2.

Details of other notations used are: A is the signed message called Attestation (see [9]), F is the data file, n is the number of files, t is the number of pre-computed challenges, c is the number of files or blocks in a challenge, $\#X$ defines the number of operations X, k is the number of files failed in audit, $Digest$ is the outcome of hash function H, K is symmetric key, and K' is asymmetric key.

As shown in Table 1, TS, DSwCCC, and proposed DS are deterministic schemes whereas others are probabilistic schemes. In practice, $c < n$ and $k < c$. Therefore, DS scheme requires comparatively minimum computation cost at the data owner, i.e., it requires k (the failure reports) number of MAC computations. The DS scheme does not require any additional computation cost at the CSP as in TS scheme. However, it incurs additional communication cost of the order of failure reports in comparison to the DSwCCC, PSRLS, and PSDD schemes which require constant communication cost.

Storage cost at the data owner is constant in the DS scheme along with the PSRLS and PSDD schemes. Storage cost at the CSP is however comparable with the other schemes. It uses symmetric cryptosystem in comparison to the comparatively inefficient asymmetric cryptosystem-based schemes. DS trivially supports dynamic operations since every new or modified data files can be audited immediately after it is outsourced. Auditing is decentralized in the proposed DS scheme in comparison to the other schemes as every user (as an auditor) is auditing only their authorized data files. All the schemes use aggressive auditing other than the DS scheme which uses lazy auditing, i.e., a file is audited as and when it is required and accessed by a user.

PbA scheme was the only data-sensitive auditing scheme, i.e., most sensitive files are audited in every auditing cycle whereas least sensitive files are rarely audited. In the proposed DS scheme it is assumed that the sensitive data file would be frequently read by the users. Therefore, auditing of important files would be frequent in the DS scheme as compared to the least important files.

An end-user may have low configured device (e.g., PDA, smartphone, etc.). Therefore, the failure report may be sent late to the auditor by the end-user. Since read is a very frequent operation, if one end-user fails to send the failure report another will send it. Also, since the data owner is not involved in computational intensive auditing operations, it can efficiently audit a small subset of sensitive data files, if needed.

5   Experimental Evaluation

In the proposed auditing processes, the data owner receives only failure reports. Although end-users are partially-trusted, the data owner may re-verify the failure reports. In this section, we evaluate the computation cost at the data owner for verifying the failure reports. Since the auditing task in the proposed protocol is distributed among end-users, computation cost at end users are not the concern.

Setup: To audit the failure reports, an experimental setup is laid out. The setup consists of two machines where one machine is used as the data owner and other machine works as CSP. The protocol is implemented in Python version 3.6.8. The configuration of each machine is as follows: Operating system (OS): Ubuntu 14.04 LTS; OS Type: 64 bits, hard disk: 500 GB; RAM: 8 GB, Processor: intel core i5 3.30 GHz*4, Graphics: Intel Haswell Desktop.

Table 1. Comparison of proposed auditing scheme with generic schemes

Scheme → ↓ Properties	TS	DSwCCC	PSRLS	PSDD	PbA	Proposed DS
Proof Type	Deterministic	Deterministic	Probabilistic	Probabilistic	Probabilistic	Deterministic
Computation cost at the data owner	$n*H$	$n(RG + 2*Add) + 1Mul + H$	$c*(D' + H + Div)$	$c*D$	$(\#R + \#W)D' + (2*n-1)H$	$k*H$
Computation cost at the CSP (except data access)	Nil	$n(RG + 2Mul + Add)$	$c*RG + H$	$c*RG + H$	$(2*n-1)H$	Nil
Communication cost between the CSP and the Data owner	$n*|F|$	$2*|Digest|$	$2*|Digest|$	$2*|Digest|$	$\#W*|F|$	$k*(|F| + |Digest|)$
Communication cost between the End user and the Data owner	NA	NA	NA	NA	$(\#R+\#W)* (|A| + |Digest|)$	$k*(2*|ID| + |V|)$
Storage at auditor	$n*|Digest|$	$n*|Digest|$	$3*|K'|+|\#c|$	$3*|K|$	$(\#R+\#W)* (|A| + |Digest|)$	$2*|K|$
Storage at CSP (other than files)	NA	$n*|Digest|$	$n*|Digest|$	$t*|Digest|$	NA	$n*|Digest|$
Preferred Cryptosystem	Symmetric Key	Asymmetric Key	Asymmetric Key	Symmetric Key	Asymmetric Key	Symmetric Key
Dynamic Data Support	No	No	No	Yes	Yes	Yes
Decentralized Auditing	No	No	No	No	No	Yes
Aggressive/ Lazy Auditing	Aggressive	Aggressive	Aggressive	Aggressive	Aggressive	Lazy

Table 2. Notations used for operations

Symbol Used	Name of operation	Symbol Used	Name of operation	Symbol Used	Name of operation
Mul	Multiplication	Div	Division	R	Read
D	Symmetric decryption	D'	Asymmetric decryption	W	Write
Add	Addition	RG	Random Number Generation	H	Hash

Failure Reports Verification Cost at Data Owner: To verify a failure report, the data owner sends a download request as a challenge to the CSP. The challenge is based on the data record mentioned in the failure report. The CSP responds it by sending the data record corresponding to the challenge by the data owner. Upon receiving, the data owner computes MAC of the received data and compares it with the received MAC. The total verification time includes communication time between the data owner and the CSP along with the computation time at the data owner.

In the experiment, we consider files with variable size, i.e., 100 KB, 500 KB, and 1 MB. With each fixed file size, the variable number of files are verified at a time, i.e., 10, 50, and 100 files. Times are measured in microseconds (ms). Each experiment is repeated 20 number of times and an average value is computed. The experimental results (containing the average values) are shown in Table 3.

Table 3. Experimental result for Auditing cost (in microseconds)

S. No	File Size	Number of Files	Auditing Time	Communication Time	Computation Time
1	100 KB	10	6.735301	5.933166	0.802135
		50	26.691451	24.553943	2.137508
		100	47.032347	44.022326	3.010021
2	500 KB	10	91.005945	36.131525	54.87442
		50	308.251367	161.044116	147.207251
		100	712.635765	491.023674	221.612091
3	1 MB	10	178.08311	52.243328	125.839782
		50	696.996789	313.613744	383.383045
		100	1179.622054	451.44356	728.178494

The Table 3 shows the total auditing time and the respective communication time between the data owner and the CSP considering the variable file sizes and the variable number of files for each fixed file size. We can see from the table that with 100 KB file, nearly 90% of the time is consumed in communication and only 10% of the time is used in the computation. With the 500 KB file the communication time is nearly as same as the computation time and with 1 MB file, the computation time is slightly more than the communication time. As we go to cloud setup instead of the existing local setup, the communication time will increase significantly without an increase in computation time. Therefore, in general, the computation time is less than the communication time in the verification process. The relative increase in computation time is shown in Fig. 4 corresponding to the Table 3.

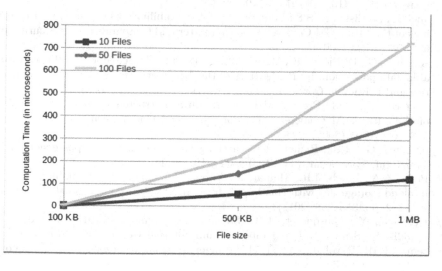

Fig. 4. Computation cost of failure reports verification at the data owner

6   Conclusions and Future Work

This work discusses the existing integrity auditing schemes and classifies them into newly defined generic auditing schemes. This classification work on auditing schemes is the first of its kind to the best of our knowledge. A symmetric key based distributed auditing scheme is proposed to address the efficiency issues in the existing scheme. As best of our knowledge this will be the first scheme that uses distributed auditing. The proposed distributed scheme is compared with the generic schemes. As compared to the existing schemes, the proposed scheme requires minimum computation time at the data owner, needs no communication cost between the CSP and the data owner, incurs no additional computation cost at the CSP, does deterministic auditing, requires constant storage cost at the data owner, and supports dynamic operations.

As future work, accountability of the end-users and the CSP needs to be explored. It may help the data owner to defend against bogus auditing and encourage action against misbehaving parties.

References

1. Barsoum, A., Hasan, A.: Enabling dynamic data and indirect mutual trust for cloud computing storage systems. IEEE Trans. Parallel Distrib. Syst. **24**(12), 2375–2385 (2013)
2. De Capitani Di Vimercati, S., Foresti, S., Jajodia, S., Paraboschi, S., Samarati, P.: Over-encryption: management of access control evolution on outsourced data. In: Proceedings of the 33rd International Conference on Very Large Data Bases, pp. 123–134. VLDB endowment (2007)
3. Arapinis, M., Bursuc, S., Ryan, M.: Privacy-supporting cloud computing by in-browser key translation. J. Comput. Secur. **21**(6), 847–880 (2013)
4. Shacham, H., Waters, B.: Compact proofs of retrievability. In: Pieprzyk, J. (ed.) ASIACRYPT 2008. LNCS, vol. 5350, pp. 90–107. Springer, Heidelberg (2008). https://doi.org/10.1007/978-3-540-89255-7_7
5. Juels, A., Kaliski Jr., B.S.: Pors: proofs of retrievability for large files. In: Proceedings of the 14th ACM Conference on Computer and Communications Security, pp. 584–597. ACM (2007)
6. Ateniese, G., Di Pietro, R., Mancini, L.V., Tsudik, G.: Scalable and efficient provable data possession. In: Proceedings of the 4th International Conference on Security and Privacy in Communication Netowrks, p. 9. ACM (2008)
7. Ateniese, G., et al.: Provable data possession at untrusted stores. In: Proceedings of the 14th ACM Conference on Computer and Communications Security, pp. 598–609. ACM (2007)
8. Ateniese, G., et al.: Remote data checking using provable data possession. ACM Trans. Inf. Syst. Secur. (TISSEC) **14**(1), 12 (2011)
9. Popa, R.A., Lorch, J.R., Molnar, D., Wang, H.J., Zhuang, L.: Enabling security in cloud storage slas with cloudproof. In: USENIX Annual Technical Conference, vol. 242, pp. 355–368 (2011)
10. Deswarte, Y., Quisquater, J.-J., Saïdane, A.: Remote integrity checking. In: Jajodia, S., Strous, L. (eds.) Integrity and Internal Control in Information Systems VI. IIFIP, vol. 140, pp. 1–11. Springer, Boston, MA (2004). https://doi.org/10.1007/1-4020-7901-X_1

11. Zhang, Y., Chunxiang, X., Li, H., Liang, X.: Cryptographic public verification of data integrity for cloud storage systems. IEEE Cloud Comput. **5**, 44–52 (2016)
12. Zhang, Y., Chunxiang, X., Liang, X., Li, H., Yi, M., Zhang, X.: Efficient public verification of data integrity for cloud storage systems from indistinguishability obfuscation. IEEE Trans. Inf. Forensics Secur. **12**(3), 676–688 (2017)
13. Saxena, R., Dey, S.: Cloud audit: a data integrity verification approach for cloud computing. Procedia Comput. Sci. **89**, 142–151 (2016)
14. Liu, C., Yang, C., Zhang, X., Chen, J.: External integrity verification for outsourced big data in cloud and iot: a big picture. Future Gener. Comput. Syst. **49**, 58–67 (2015)
15. Chris Erway, C., Küpçü, A., Papamanthou, C., Tamassia, R.: Dynamic provable data possession. ACM Trans. Inf. Syst. Secur. **17**(4), 15:1–15:29 (2015)
16. Barsoum, A.F., Anwar Hasan, M.: Provable possession and replication of data over cloud servers. Centre For Applied Cryptographic Research (CACR), University of Waterloo, Report, 32:2010 (2010)
17. Chunxiang, X., Zhang, Y., Yong, Y., Zhang, X., Wen, J.: An efficient provable secure public auditing scheme for cloudstorage. KSII Trans. Internet Inf. Syst. **8**(11), 4226–4241 (2014)
18. Hussain, Md., Al-Mourad, M.B.: Effective third party auditing in cloud computing. In: 2014 28th International Conference on Advanced Information Networking and Applications Workshops (WAINA), pp. 91–95. IEEE (2014)
19. Yu, Y., Li, Y., Yang, B., Susilo, W., Yang, G., Bai, J.: Attribute-based cloud data integrity auditing for secure outsourced storage. IEEE Trans. Emerging Topics Comput. 1 (2019)
20. Kumar, N., Mathuria, A.: Improved write access control and stronger freshness guarantee to outsourced data. In: Proceedings of the 18th International Conference on Distributed Computing and Networking, Hyderabad, India, January 5–7, 2017, p. 19 (2017)
21. Wang, C., Chow, S.S.M., Wang, Q., Ren, K., Lou, W.: Privacy-preserving public auditing for secure cloud storage. IEEE Trans. Comput. **62**(2), 362–375 (2013)
22. Yamamoto, G., Oda, S., Aoki, K.: Fast integrity for large data. In: Proceedings of the ECRYPT Workshop Software Performance Enhancement for Encryption and Decryption, pp. 21–32 (2007)
23. Krawczyk, H., Bellare, M., Canetti, R.: Hmac: Keyed-hashing for message authentication. Technical report (1997)
24. Ateniese, G., et al.: Remote data checking using provable data possession. ACM Trans. Inf. Syst. Secur. **14**(1), 12:1–12:34 (2011)
25. Oprea, A., Reiter, M.K., Yang, K., et al.: Space-efficient block storage integrity. In: NDSS (2005)
26. Fu, K.E.: Group sharing and random access in cryptographic storage file systems. Technical report, MASTER'S THESIS, MIT (1999)

HealthChain: A Secure Scalable Health Care Data Management System Using Blockchain

T. P. Abdul Rahoof[(⊠)] and V. R. Deepthi

Department of CSE, College of Engineering Trivandrum, Thiruvananthapuram, India
rahoof086@gmail.com, deepthi@cet.ac.in

Abstract. Electronic Health Records (EHRs) are designed to manage the complexities of multi-institutional and lifetime medical records. As patients move among providers, their data become scattered across different organizations, losing easy access to past records. The records should be kept in digitized format with required protection from unauthorized access. There are many schemes to solve these issues, which includes central server based systems, cloud based systems and blockchain based systems. The trending solutions are cloud based and blockchain based solutions. Even though cloud based system provides much scalability through various mechanisms, it is trusted as a secure system in which data may be corrupted with or without the knowledge of cloud provider. The blockchain technology overcomes the barrier of trusting an agent. But the blockchain based system lacks scalability and requires huge storage space. The proposed system, HealthChain, provides a secure health care record management system with scalability and low storage space. HealthChain divides the whole system into regions and uses two kinds of blockchains, Private Blockchain: for intra-regional communication and, Consortium Blockchain: for inter-regional communication. The proposed system utilizes a consensus mechanism for mining.

Keywords: Health care · Blockchain · Electronic Medical Record · Smart contracts · Data sharing · IPFS

1 Introduction

Securing health care records is an important part of laws like HIPAA (Health Insurance Portability and Accountability Act) rules enacted by United States Congress. Health care is now witnessing various approaches in disease prevention and treatment. The health care technology provides large databases and tools to track the intended health care data. The challenging issue is that as patient moves among doctors, the patient needs to bring his or her previous medical records and should be submitted to the newly assigned doctor. Maintaining these records physically is very difficult to patients. Getting such medical records repeatedly will delay the treatment and is very costly. Thus keeping medical records in digitized form will be a promising solution and it will help the doctors to give proper treatment efficiently. Maintaining digital documents securely and controlling access to these records is also an upcoming issue in the present years. One solution is to store the medical records in the cloud with proper authorization mechanism. Then the records will be available to users by proving the legitimacy. The system needs to be trusted since it has a centralized control, but malfunction happening to the medical records can not be identified. The malfunctions may include corrupting records, changing authorization, selling medical records for individual benefit etc. Another solution to secure medical records is by using blockchain technology in its backend [1]. The blockchain technology provides the functionalities like immutable log, decentralized management, data provenance, robustness, availability and privacy. But it has an issue of high storage space and lack of scalability. Detailed review about blockchain is listed in the subsection. Most implementations use Electronic Medical Record (EMR) standard for health care records [2]. It is a standardized and inter-operable format, developed based on the objective of storing and controlling access to patient's health care records. It includes information regarding episodes of care provided by different care providers.

1.1 Blockchain

Blockchain is a decentralized distributed technology which is widely used for transaction management. Issues with the current transaction management systems are the existence of transaction fee and control by centralized control system. All these issues disappears if blockchain is used as it has decentralized control and immutability. Blockchain was invented by Satoshi Nakamoto in 2008 to serve as a public ledger of the cryptocurrency, bitcoin. Blockchain maintains an append only distributed ledger which will be updated on each transaction. Sometimes the blockchain is also called an append only distributed ledger. Each block in the blockchain contains a summary of transactions happened during a particular time interval, previous block's hash and a nonce which is used by miners to solve puzzle. Blockchain can be classified into permissioned and permission-less blockchains. The permissioned blockchains can be used as private blockchain, in which blocks can only be created by authorized users and the users are not freely able to join in the network as opposite to the permission-less blockchain. The inter-chain communication concept in the blockchain enable users to transfer valuable assets between different blockchains. It also reduces number of global users and the size of distributed shared ledger, since each user needs to store ledger of transactions within a specific region only. Untangling blockchain [3] describes an overview of data processing in blockchain. In Bitcoin technology, blockchain stores coins as the system states. The nodes implement a state machine model which transfer coins from one address to other. Ethereum [4] enables decentralized smart contracts which plays a way to permissioned blockchain. Applications include higher education credit platform [5], banking and insurance [6], asset and finance management and personal data protection [7].

In a blockchain based health care application [8], patient's records are treated as the block data and the access control is maintained by smart contracts. The users of blockchain are classified as patients and providers (doctors). The provider can store records related to a patient while consulting and the patient can authorize and control access to their records. The patient can also give record permissions to a third party, which may be another doctor or a relative of the patient.

2   Related Works

Modern technologies brief the idea of Pervasive Social Network (PSN) [9] based health care. A PSN based health care system [10] proposes two protocols, initial one is an improved version of IEEE 802.15.6 display authentication. It establishes secure link with mobile devices and resource limited sensor nodes. The other one uses blockchain strategy to share health care data among PSN nodes. It uploads addresses of sensors and mobile devices to the blockchain which allows a PSN node to access health care data from other nodes.

MedRec [11] is a blockchain based record management system to handle EMRs. The framework gives an immutable log to patients and effectively access medical records among doctors. The block content represents the data ownership and viewership permissions, which includes pointers to the medical records instead of records itself. It also appends hash values of records to protect against tampering. The MedRec utilizes Ethereum smart contracts to intelligently handle medical data stored in individual databases. The MedRec has three contracts: Registrar contract, Patient-Provider Relationship contract and Summary contract. Registrar contract is a global contract which stores user's Ethereum address together with a string ID. The Patient-Provider Relationship contract represents relationship between provider and patient. It includes ownership, EMR queries and hashes. The Summary contract stores details of relationships among providers or patients representing all the previous and current engagements. The proposed HealthChain framework utilizes these concepts of MedRec.

Ancile [12], a newly proposed work, has additional functionalities over MedRec. It utilizes proxy re-encryption technique to transfer encrypted records between nodes without sending symmetric key. A group of proxy nodes are selected randomly and the message is encrypted with a master public key. The associated decryption key is distributed among proxies. Each proxy now select a random blind value to provide a blindness and apply a homomorphic multiplication with the piece of decryption key. The message can only be decrypted by the intended receiver. The MedRec and Ancile both stores the records itself into the intended hospital databases, and the host name and port address are uploaded into the blockchain for requesting the data. There is a risk of intrusion attack into the hospital database. The HealthChain prevents this intrusion by using a decentralized storage technique, IPFS.

Secure Attribute based Signature (ABS) scheme [13] has proposed an electronic health care system with multiple authorities for blockchain. Combining the advantage of ABS with the blockchain technology, the system provides privacy for patients while maintaining immutability of EHRs. The main contributions of the system are as follows:

- Combines the blockchain technology and ABS scheme.
- To avoid collision attack, a pseudorandom function seed is shared between every two authorities.
- The private key of each authority is enclosed in the private key of patient.

The system utilizes bilinear pairing for signing and it is linearly dependent on number of authorities. A work by We and Tsai [14] proposes simple bilinear pairing computation in blockchain.

MedShare [15] is a cloud based medical data sharing system with blockchain. The system needs cryptographic primitives such as Requestor private-public key pair and Authenticator contract key, which is generated by the authenticator and is attached to smart contracts. The user requests medical data through the query system, which processes the query into a format applicable to the data structuring and provenance layer. Results of every action completed is added to the blockchain for trustless and fair auditing.

BSPP [16] is a blockchain based secure and privacy preserving personal health information sharing scheme. Two kinds of blockchains are proposed in this system namely, private blockchain and consortium blockchain. The private blockchain stores PHI (Personal Health Information) while consortium blockchain keeps secure index of the PHI. The framework used keyword search algorithm for fetching encrypted records. The keywords are the indexes for the records and will be stored in the consortium blockchain. TKSE [17] approach provides a trustworth keyword search over encrypted data in the blockchain. The proposed system, HealthChain, also uses the inter-blockchain concept. In HealthChain, the private blockchain belongs to a particular region instead of a single hospital. The consortium blockchain interconnects the regional private blockchains.

2.1   Preliminaries

IPFS. Inter Planetary File System (IPFS) [18] is a peer-to-peer distributed file system. It is known as content addressed block storage model since the link to stored file is the hash of the content of that file. IPFS is a recently grown up technology. It is similar to the technologies like Git, BitTorrent, etc, which is now mostly combined with blockchain for storing large data. HealthChain stores the encrypted record into the IPFS. The IPFS ensures the availability of records. The records can be fetched easily by knowing only ipfs-hash (link) of that file. Instead of storing the host-name and port address, the HealthChain stores ipfs-hash to the blockchain.

Mining. HealthChain authorizes the number of doctors by using Proof of Authority (PoA) scheme. In this scheme, the miners are also the users of the blockchain, but have an additional role to verify the doctors. It uses consensus mechanism, in which a registered doctor can add a block only when he/she gets 50% or more votes. This can reduce fake doctors from creating malicious blocks (malicious records) into the blockchain.

3   Proposed Framework: HealthChain

HealthChain uses the concept of inter-blockchain communication, which divides the whole system into various regions. The users are partitioned into regions and hence the global transactions. This system greatly reduces ledger memory, as it appends only the transactions in a particular region. Two kinds of blockchain are used in the system, private blockchain and consortium blockchain. The private blockchain is used for the purpose of intra-regional communication and the consortium blockchain for inter-regional communication.

3.1   Smart Contracts

Smart contracts are the set of rules or protocols which should be obeyed by the members of the blockchain. HealthChain uses ethereum blockchain for implementation. There are four smart contracts used in the system. The Fig. 1 shows the logical structure of these contracts.

Registrar Contract (RC) and Global Registrar Contract (GRC). Users of the HealthChain are registered into the private blockchain using the RC contract. RC contracts includes user's name, unique ID, public key and a link to the corresponding Summary Contract of the user. A unique ID is dynamically generated for a patient during his first registration. The providers are uniquely identified by Unique Physician Identification Number (UPIN). Providers must be registered into the consortium blockchain for accessing inter-regional medical records, patients are only part of private blockchain. The Global Registrar Contract (GRC) is similar to RC. It is used by the providers to register in the consortium blockchain. The providers must be verified by the miners to add blocks into the blockchain in the respective private blockchain.

Patient-Provider Contract (PPR). The meta data about the medical records are handled using PPR contract. The PPR contract is created for each medical record. The details like the owner ID, cryptographic hash, record name, reference to the record, key, and permissions are added into the blockchain using the PPR contract. The owner ID is always the unique Id of patient. The references to the record is the ipfs-link used to fetch the corresponding encrypted record. The key is the record key encrypted with the public key of patient or provider, which will be used by the user to decrypt the record. The permissions are recorded in a separate contract called Permission Contract.

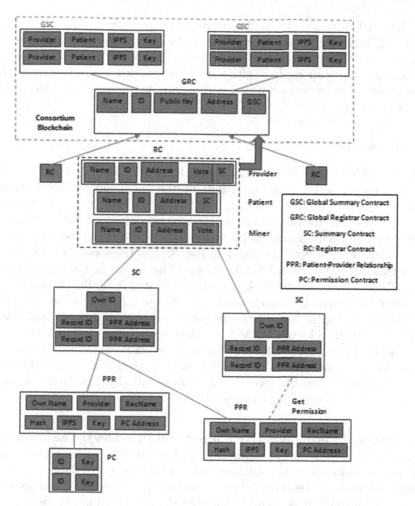

Fig. 1. Smart contracts of proposed system HealthChain

Summary Contract (SC) and Global Summary Contract (GSC). Summary Contracts maintain a history of patient provider relationships. It holds a record ID and a reference to the corresponding PPR contract. During each patient provider engagement, a PPR contract will be created. The corresponding SC of both patient and provider will be updated with the new PPR address. The SC also gets updated when a new permission is granted for a particular record. Thus the SC provides a quick look up list of relationships. In the consortium blockchain the GSC stores the references to the record and the record key encrypted with the public key of third party. It helps the third party to fetch the record without further communication.

Permission Contract (PC). The third party permissions are handled using the PC. It includes the third party ID and the record key encrypted with the public key of third party. Using the contract the record owner and the corresponding provider can easily identify the permissioned users. Only the owner of the record (the patient) can add permissions to the corresponding medical records.

3.2 Procedure

Adding a Medical Record (By Provider). The flow diagram of adding a medical record is shown in Fig. 2. Initially the patient and provider must be registered into the private blockchain. The miners also must verify the providers. The step 1 and 2 in the diagram shows the selection of a particular EMR record and encrypting it with a random key (record key). The encrypted record is then added to the IPFS network as shown in step 3. The IPFS node returns an ipfs-link of that particular record for future use. The record key is encrpyted with provider's and patient's public key as shown in step 4. Later the patient and provider can decrypt the encrypted record key using their respective private key. The cryptographic hash of the file computed at step 6, encrypted key and the ipfs-link returned by the ipfs node are then uploaded to the blockchain. Upon receiving the details, the blockchain creates a new PPR contract with the record details and adds the address of the PPR in both patient's and provider's SC. Also, PC is created for the record with no data initially. Similarly the records can be retrieved by reversing the procedure.

Inter Regional Permission (By Patient and Provider). The permission is given only by the patient. The permission adding concept is similar in both intra-regional communication and inter-regional communication. There is an additional work done by the provider in the inter-regional record permission management. In the patient side, the patient gets the encrypted key of the particular record from the blockchain, and decrypt the key using the patient's private key. This record key is then encrypted with third party public key. The third party public key will be obtained from the provider. For inter-regional blockchain, the provider can fetch the third party public key from consortium blockchain. In case of intra-regional communication, the third party public key will be fetched directly by the patient from the private blockchain. Initially the patient gives his own private key as shown in Fig. 3. The private key is used for decrypting the encrypted record key. The encrypted record key can be fetched from the blockchain. The patient encrypts record key with the public key of third party and uploaded into the private blockchain as depicted in steps 3 to 5. The permission contract in the private blockchain will be updated with the third party address and encrypted key.

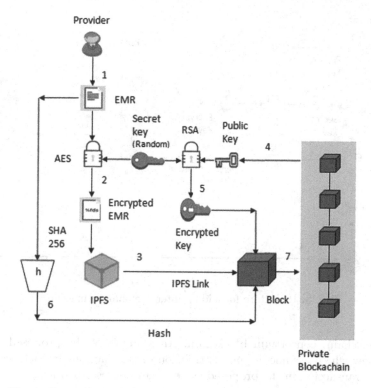

Fig. 2. Procedure for adding a medical record into the blockchain

For inter regional communication, the provider takes record key encrypted with the public key of third party and ipfs-link from the private blockchain. The provider then adds these two details into the consortium blockchain. The step 6 in figure represents the process of adding the patient details into the consortium blockchain by provider.

4   Analysis and Comparison

Every transaction in the network is broadcasted in a typical blockchain system. Ledger memory required for each user is dependant on the number of transaction in the respective region or blockchain. Ethereum requires an average block size of 200 KB for every transaction. In the existing systems (single blockchain based systems), every action is considered as a transaction and added to ledger memory. But in the HealthChain system, the transactions are partitioned among various regions. Thus the ledger memory and transaction execution time required for the proposed system differ from existing systems.

Even though the total transaction in the HealthChain system is larger, the system efficiently manages and reduces the ledger memory since the blockchains are independent. The users in a particular region need to store only the transactions in that region. The inter regional blockchain will be stored in the upper

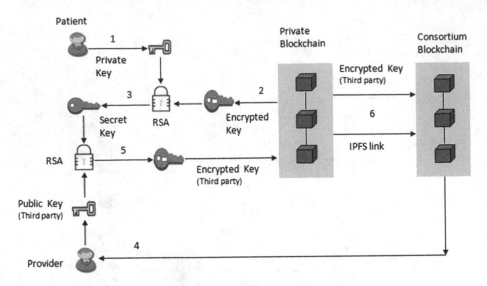

Fig. 3. Procedure for adding inter regional permission

layer blockchain, consortium blockchain. An analysis of the proposed work is given below which assumes equal distribution of transactions in each region.

Total transaction in the proposed system can be described as,

$$t_T = t_{inter} + t_{intra} * r_T \tag{1}$$

where,
t_T - Total transactions
t_{inter} - Inter regional transactions
t_{intra} - Intra regional transactions
r_T - Number of regions

In the case of existing system, there will be a single region comprising of r_T regions in the proposed system. Then the ledger memory required for each user in the existing system is,

$$ledger\_memory_{exsys} = r_T * t_{intra} * 200\,\text{KB} \tag{2}$$

Let n be the number of regions where a patient has registered, then the total number of transactions stored by the patient, t_{pat}, can be calculated as follows.

$$t_{pat} = t_{intra} * n \tag{3}$$

From Eq. (3), the amount of ledger memory required for patient is,

$$ledger\_memory_{pat} = t_{pat} * 200\,\text{KB} \tag{4}$$

Normally a patient may not be registered in all regions. In that case, $n * t_{intra} < r_T * t_{intra}$ and subsequently, $ledger\_memory_{pat} < ledger\_memory_{exsys}$.

Similarly, total number of transactions stored by the provider, t_{pro}, can be calculated as follows.

$$t_{pro} = t_{intra} + t_{inter} \tag{5}$$

From Eq. (5), the amount of ledger memory required for provider is,

$$ledger\_memory_{pro} = t_{pro} * 200\,\text{KB} \tag{6}$$

In every region, inter regional transaction will be normally less than intra regional transactions. In that case, $t_{intra} + t_{inter} < r_T * t_{intra}$ and subsequently, $ledger\_memory_{pro} < ledger\_memory_{exsys}$.

Hence, the ledger memory required for each user is greatly reduced in proposed system compared to existing system. But the provider may have larger ledger memory if the inter regional transactions are larger than intra regional transactions.

The average time to add a transaction into a block depends on the number of transaction in the region and the time required to create a block.

Transaction execution time in existing system can be calculated as,

$$T_{exsys} = \frac{r_T * t_{intra}}{t_b} * T_b \; sec \tag{7}$$

where,
T_b - Block creation time
t_b - Transactions per block

Transaction execution time in HealthChain, where transactions in different blockchain are executed in parallel, can be represented as,

$$T_{proposed} = \frac{t_{intra}}{t_b} * T_b \; sec \tag{8}$$

Hence, the total time required for adding transactions in a single blockchain based system is very high when compared to HealthChain.

In the existing systems, the records are stored in the respective hospital database and the port number and database id is passed to the requestor. It is not very secure as the intruder may find the storage system. HealthChain stores the encrypted records in the IPFS, which replicates the records in various nodes and provide quick access. The system prevents intruders since no information regarding the location of record is communicated.

Table 1 shows a comparison of different health care related systems. With the various metrics derived from the careful analogy of data usage and data accumulation, a conclusion can be drawn that the proposed HealthChain framework as compared to other blockchain based systems has greater advantages including reduction in ledger memory, enhancement in scalability and prevention of intrusion attack.

Table 1. Comparison between health care related systems

Metric	MedRec [11]	Ancile [12]	BSPP [16]	HealthChain (Proposed)
Confidentiality	No	Yes	Yes	Yes
Data Integrity	Yes	Yes	Yes	Yes
Preventing intruder	No	No	Yes	Yes
Time requirements	High	High	High	Low
Space requirements (Ledger-memory)	High	High	High	Low
Scalability	Low	Low	Low	High

5   Conclusion and Future Work

Handling health care data is a challenging task and many solutions have been developed so far to store and access these health records. Centralized health care systems are easily vulnerable to attacks like medical records being changed by authorized or unauthorized users. Blockchain based ideas overcome these issues by keeping meta data of records immutable. But they need high time and storage requirements. To avoid these barriers, this paper proposes an inter blockchain concept. The number of users and transactions in a single blockchain is reduced and hence the ledger memory. The proposed system also prevents intruders which was an issue in the existing blockchain based ideas, by incorporating IPFS. To make the record key more secure, the re-encryption scheme can be included in future.

References

1. Tschorsch, F., Scheuermann, B.: Bitcoin and beyond: a technical survey on decentralized digital currencies. IEEE Commun. Surv. Tutor. **18**, 2084–2123 (2016)
2. Lesk, M.: Electronic medical records: confidentiality, care, and epidemiology. IEEE Access **11**, 19–24 (2017)
3. Dinh, T.T.A., Liu, R., Zhang, M.: Untangling blockchain: a data processing view of blockchain systems. IEEE Trans. Knowl. Data Eng. **30**, 1366–1385 (2018)
4. Wood, G.: Ethereum: a secure decentralized transaction ledger (2014). http://gavwood
5. Turkanovic, M., Holbl, M., Kosic, K., Hericko, M., Kamisalic, A.: EduCTX: a blockchain-based higher education credit platform. IEEE Access **6**, 5112–5127 (2018)
6. G. S. Group: Blockchain: putting theory into practice (2016)
7. Zyskind, G., Nathan, O., Pentland, A.S.: Decentralizing privacy: using blockchain to protect personal data. In: IEEE Security and Privacy Workshops, pp. 180–184 (2015)
8. Laure A.L., Koo, M.B.: Blockchain For Health Data and Its Potential Use in Health IT and Health Care Related Research

9. Varshney, U.: Pervasive healthcare and wireless health monitoring. Mob. Netw. Appl. **12**, 113–127 (2007)

10. Zhang, J., Xue, N., Huang, X.: A secure system for pervasive social network-based health care. IEEE Access **4**, 9239–9250 (2016)

11. Azaria, A., Ekblaw, A., Vieira, T., Lippman, A.: MedRec: using blockchain for medical data access and permission management. In: International Conference on Open and Big Data (2016)

12. Dagher, G.G., Mohler, J., Milojkovic, M., BabuMarella, P.: Ancile: privacy preserving framework for accesscontrol andinteroperability of electronic health records using blockchain technology. Elsevier Int. J. **39**, 283–297 (2018)

13. Guo, R., Shi, H., Zhao, Q., Zheng, D.: Secure attribute-based signature scheme with multiple authorities for blockchain in electronic health records systems. IEEE Access **6**, 11676–11686 (2018)

14. Wu, H.-T., Tsai, C.-W.: Toward blockchains for health-care systems: applying the bilinear pairing technology to ensure privacy protection and accuracy in data sharing. IEEE Consum. Electron. Mag. **7**(4), 65–71 (2018)

15. Xia, Q., Sifah, E.B., Asamoah, K.O., Gao, J., Du, X., Guizani, M.: MeDShare: trust-less medical data sharing among cloud service providers via blockchain. IEEE Access **5**, 14757–14767 (2017)

16. Zhang, A., Lin, X.: Towards secure and privacy-preserving data sharing in e-health systems via consortium blockchain. Springer Int. J. (2018)

17. Zhang, Y., Deng, R.H., Shu, J., Yang, K., Zheng, D.: TKSE: trustworthy keyword search over encrypted data with two-side verifiability via blockchain. IEEE Access **6**, 31077–31087 (2018)

18. Benet, J.: IPFS - Content Addressed, Versioned, P2P File System (2014)

Transcript Management Using Blockchain Enabled Smart Contracts

Kirtan Patel[✉] and Manik Lal Das

DA-IICT, Gandhinagar, Gujarat, India
kirtan24399@gmail.com, maniklal@gmail.com

Abstract. Blockchain has demonstrated immense potential leading to act as one of the key catalysts in the 4th Industrial revolution. Smart Contract is the programmable transactions, which enables and enforces complex transactions on Blockchain. Blockchain-enabled Smart Contracts are driving force for ubiquitous applications of Blockchain across the fields of Health, Education, Banking and many more. In this paper, we discuss one such use case of Blockchain in the field of Education, called it Transcript Management. Whenever students move from one institute to another, they are expected to submit an official transcript from the previous institute. Currently deployed conventional method of operation is highly inefficient, lacks transparency and leaves data susceptible to forgery or tampering. This paper presents a new method involving Blockchain-enabled smart contracts for sharing and managing transcripts across different institutions. We have proposed algorithms for different modules, namely transcript issuance, verification, acceptance, and the analysis and implementation results of these modules assure both security and efficiency required for this application.

Keywords: Blockchain · Smart Contract · Merkle Tree · Security

1 Introduction

Student's credentials of his/her earned degree are being communicated to others via a piece of paper called Transcript, which is demanded by the institute where the student will be pursuing further studies for authentication of various details. Currently deployed conventional method of operation for this entire sharing of transcript across the two Institutions is as shown in Fig. 1. Initially, a student submits a soft copy of his/her transcript for the Academic Administration via admission portal or via an email. After admission is confirmed, student is expected to submit a hard copy of the transcript directly sent by his/her current institute. Student goes to examination office of his/her current institute and requests them to send hard copy of transcript to the institute he or she will be joining. Student specifies the address of that university for courier delivery and pays a fee for the same. Examination department then collects data and hard copy of transcript is sent in a sealed courier to the address specified by the

D. V. Hung and M. D'Souza (Eds.): ICDCIT 2020, LNCS 11969, pp. 392–407, 2020.
https://doi.org/10.1007/978-3-030-36987-3_26

student. Received courier is forwarded to Admission block, where transcript is verified and cross-checked with the one submitted by the student on admission portal or an email. All the verified data is entered into the student registration system and referred to whenever needed in the future.

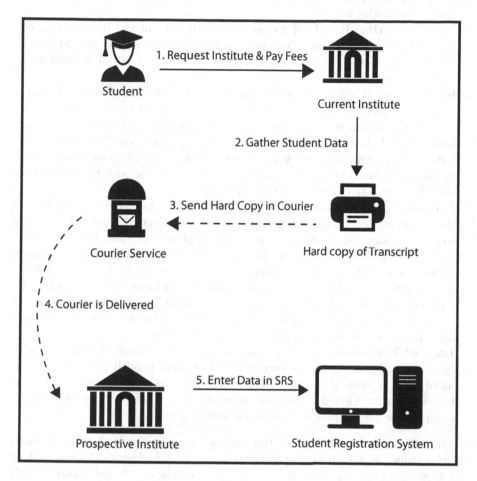

Fig. 1. Conventional deployed transcript verification system

Most of the institutions employ above mentioned process for accepting transcripts. Lately, some of them started transcript using online services similar to My eQuals [1] in New Zealand/Australia and CHESICC [2] in China instead of courier service. These service providers of specific regions collaborate with each other to accomplish task of verification. Major problems in using any of these conventional paper based process are as follows:

1. **Lack of Authentication**: It is not possible to authenticate the identity of the sender in the current courier service protocol. Even if a protocol is designed by courier service providers for authentication of sender, it is difficult to share that information with the universities. Moreover, it is always possible to breach the protocol by the presence of even a single venal person in the position of authority.

2. **Data Integrity**: It is hard to verify the integrity of the delivered parcel. Person with ample resources can bribe any of the involved entity and replace the original courier. Forgery of stamps and signatures is not a challenging task as it was before.

3. **Inefficiency**: When both the universities are far off it might take at least 2 days and considerable amount of money. Employees of the institute sending the parcel perform mundane tasks like gathering data and packaging courier. Employees of the institute receiving the parcel perform similar tasks like collecting and forwarding courier, cataloguing courier and cross verification with previously submitted data. It is wastage of resources for both the universities as well as students in terms of time and money.

4. **No Guarantee**: Even today with advanced tracking technology, posts around the world are lost, misplaced, returned or delayed. Student might miss chance to secure admission at university he/she is applying because of such an unreliable system. Such mishaps are also troublesome for administration department of university he/she is applying too because they do not want students to suffer unnecessarily. At the same time, they cannot afford to delay the admission process. Because of involvement of humans, process is prone to mistakes like writing wrong address on courier, delay in processing request for sending courier or losing track of received courier.

5. **Lack of Transparency**: There are a lot of entities involved in the transfer of a transcript. Basis for the success of this system is faith of the receiver in all of these entities. It is naive to trust all of them as it also involves unknown entities. As mentioned earlier, the presence of a single venal person might compromise the faith of receiver in the entire system.

Existing digital solutions involves third party violating the fundamental principle of transparency. Considering the importance of this document for a student and inefficiency of this system, we propose a blockchain based solution with smart contracts to facilitate Transcript Management. Blockchain's fundamentals guarantee immutability of data, smart contract eliminates third party and therefore, assuring transparency in the entire process. We proposed two different protocols using smart contracts each for uploading transcripts on the blockchain and verification of transcript. We have implemented the proposed solution in Hyperledger Framework and the results demonstrate its practically.

Previously some of the papers [3–5] have described blockchain based solutions for record keeping of degree certificates. Other research works [6,7] have given hint that smart contracts can be used for similar purposes, although none of them provides detailed architecture and logic for those smart contracts leaving readers wondering about the details. We have provided details surrounding the

blockchain-empowered transcript management system using smart contracts.
The remaining of the paper is organized as follows: Sect. 2 provides some preliminaries of blockchain, smart contract and Merkle tree. In Sect. 3, we present the proposed transcript management scheme. Section 4 provides the implementation of the proposed scheme. We conclude the paper in Sect. 5.

2   Preliminaries

2.1   Blockchain

Nakamoto [8] introduced blockchain as a distributed public ledger with peer-to-peer network in order to solve double spending problem. Although with time, diverse applications are proposed using the same technology in the field of Governance [9,10], agriculture [11,12], healthcare [13,14] and so on. Blockchain is a contiguous set of virtual blocks that are chained with each other using cryptographic hashes. Each block contains its index, its transactions, hash of its own and hash of the previous block. First block of any blockchain is known as genesis block of the chain. This block has index 0 and has previous hash set as 0. As more and more blocks are added, security of data stored in previous blocks keeps increasing because of cryptography based chaining. If one of the block is altered, then none of the blocks after that will be acceptable. Blockchain's security relies upon cryptography and state of the art consensus mechanism for peer-to-peer network. Every node of the blockchain has a copy of the current state of the Blockchain. Having a peer-to-peer network eliminates the possibility of single point of failure and provides immutability to the data. In order to update blockchain, many distributed consensus mechanisms like proof-of-stake, proof-of-work, etc. are designed as described in [15]. Blockchain can be visualized as shown in Fig. 2.

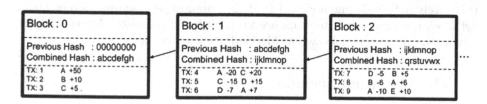

Fig. 2. Blockchain visualization

Blockchain has certain inherent features because of its novel architecture such as provenance and immutability of data. All of them combined provides finality which ensures necessary trust in untrustworthy environment without the need of any third party. In short, it is an immutable ledger of transactions that is shared between all the peers of the networks.

2.2 Smart Contracts

Smart contracts [16,17] are designed in order to provide more dynamic facilities on the blockchain. Blockchains without smart contracts host a distributed ledgers and they can only handle transfer of assets from one entity to another. Smart contracts are Turing Complete programs that enables users to use contractual transfer of assets as well as mechanisms to provide more dynamic processing of transactions. They are enabled by each node hosting virtual operating system apart from maintaining a ledger and designing protocols for contractual transfer of assets. Smart contracts are analogous to the cheque system in the context of banking system. Every bank holds the ledger which contains list of funds available in each user account similar to blockchain. For example, is user X of Bank x gives a cheque to user Y of Bank y, there is a legal contract between both the users and banks. Here, a cheque is a smart contract and based upon the type of cheque there are certain contractual agreements between all of them. For example in the case of account payee cheque user X guarantees that there will be sufficient funds in his account on the mentioned date. In the same manner Bank X guarantees that if there are sufficient funds in X's account it will transfer it to bank Y. Then, Bank Y guarantees as soon as it receives funds from X, and it credits it to user Y. Similarly, Bearer cheques will have different contracts and so on. As a result, all the four parties have to legally abide by this contracts for complete transaction of a cheque.

2.3 Merkle Tree

Merkle Tree [18] is a cryptographic integrity-preserved data structure, which looks similar to the structure of a binary tree. Data/Hash of Data acts as a leaf nodes for Merkle tree, parent nodes are created by pairing two of the children of lower level nodes. Starting with leaf nodes, value of parent node is determined by hashing concatenation of data of children nodes. This process is repeated recursively until only one node is left at the topmost level known as root node. Set of all the hash values that are needed in order to calculate Merkle Root for a particular leaf node is known as Merkle Path for that node.

3   The Proposed Scheme

We use blockchain enabled smart contracts for the entire process of transcript management. In the proposed scheme we use certain symbols throughout the text and their representation is as shown in Table 1.

3.1   Proposed Protocols

We have designed two different protocols: one for *Uploading TS* on the blockchain and another for *Verifying the TS*.

Table 1. Symbol and Meaning

Symbol	Meaning
A	Institute where a student pursued education
B	Institute where a student is applying for further education
S	Student who has studied at A and is applying to B for further education
TS	Transcript of S that is to be sent from A to B

Protocol for Uploading TS on Blockchain: The protocol for uploading TS on blockchain can be visualized as shown in Fig. 3. Entities involved in this protocol are Controller of Examination, Professors and Students. We can divide the entire protocol into four different steps as follows:

1. Collection of Data: A can store individual transcript of every student on blockchain. However, it is not an efficient choice considering the computational power consumed by blockchain for each transaction. Therefore, we suggest constructing a Merkle Tree for each batch of students separately and store only the Merkle root of these trees on the blockchain. By storing the Merkle root, we indirectly make data of all the students immutable. University's Database already hold student's grades for the period of time student is studying in the institute. We need to reformat that stored data in order to form Merkle tree and simplify the protocol. Controller of Examination will accumulate data of all the students of a particular batch, put it in a file using specific format and send the same file to all the Professors who taught that particular batch. Batch ID should consist of a year and batch identifier as its part. Each student's should be listed in the following format in a file:

```
{
    "firstName": "John",
    "lastName": "Cooper",
    "DOB": "26/02/1980",
    "BatchID": "BTECH1998",
    "height_cm": 185.4,
    "identification_mark":"Blue eyes",
    "sha256_hash_of_image_file":"1684...",
    "Transcript": [
    {
        "CourseID":"IT101",
        "CourseName": "Introduction to ..",
        "Grade": "AA",
        "Comments": "Excellent skills"}
        {....}
        ...
    ]
}
```

2. Generating Merkle Tree: TS of each student of a particular batch will be hashed using SHA256 [19]. Controller of Examination will generate a Merkle Tree using these hashes where each of them will act as a leaf node for the Merkle tree. Once Merkle tree is generated, TS and Merkle path of each student will be stored back into the database temporarily. Some Merkle paths might be intentionally obscured, so that B can verify only using the smart contract and maintain privacy.

3. Publishing Data on Blockchain using Smart Contract: After Controller of Examination of A has formed Merkle tree of a particular batch, it can simply store Merkle root of that batch on the blockchain. In order to avoid data tampering during formation of Merkle tree and ensure transparency in the process, we need a contractual agreement between all the professors and Controller of Examination that uploaded data is correct for the particular batch. Therefore, a smart contract can be used for this contractual transaction. This smart contract, termed as upload transcript contract will be invoked by the Controller of Examination. All the Professors who taught this batch will sign it after individually computing Merkle roots from the data they have of their own subjects as well as data of others which they received in the mail. This ensures a completely transparent and trustworthy protocol for uploading data on blockchain.

4. Emailing Data to Students: After data is successfully published on blockchain, all the students of the particular batch will receive email from Controller of Examination containing their TS with Merkle path corresponding to their TS and Merkle root of their batch. This data can be encoded in a QR-code and then university can attach this QR code with the digital or physical transcript for easier retrieval of data on verification end.

Protocol for Verifying TS on Blockchain: The protocol for verification of TS on blockchain can be visualized as shown in Fig. 4. Entities involved in this protocol are S and Academic administration of B. S can simply submit a soft copy of TS with QR code to B. Academic administration of B can verify submitted data by simply computing Merkle root and comparing it with value stored on the blockchain. However, searching for individual Merkle roots on the blockchain becomes a cumbersome process. Furthermore, it is also possible that person searching for this Merkle root corrupts transparency of the process. Instead, we can deploy a smart contract that takes TS and Merkle path from the B, computes Merkle root, compares it with the stored Merkle root for that batch and stores result permanently on the blockchain. Having this smart contract can also help to create revenue model by obscuring some of the default Merkle path values as discussed before. With all these, academic administration of B can simply scan the QR code and invoke this smart contract, which termed as Verify Transcript and it verifies the given data and record will be permanently added to blockchain.

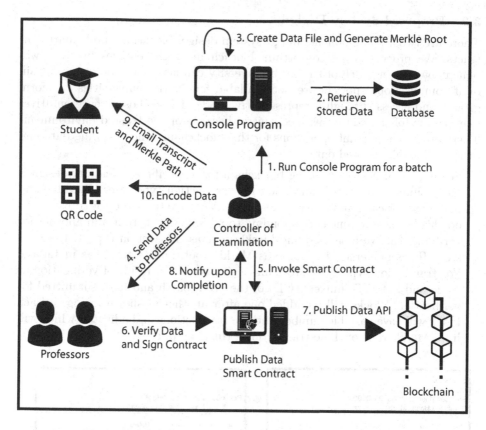

Fig. 3. Proposed Scheme for publishing data on Blockchain

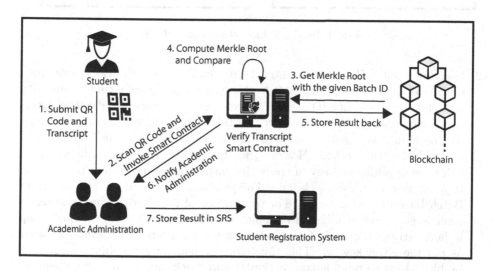

Fig. 4. Proposed scheme for verifying transcript

3.2 Proposed System Design

There are two key components in our system design: blockchain and smart contracts. We propose using consortium blockchain as the entities involved will benefit by trusting each other. Each university can act as a node of blockchain or if computational powers are not available few of the universities can form groups and access through a representative node. These chosen representatives can use any of the consensus mechanism, because of the trusted environment. There are two important operations for this blockchain. One is storing data and other is searching stored data.

1. Storing Data: As we are using blockchain for a specific application, design is fairly simple. We store transaction ID, transaction type, user ID, value and metadata for each and every Transaction. We have two types of transactions on this blockchain, one corresponding to adding Merkle root and another for verifying TS. We assign adding Merkle root as transaction type 1. Here, we store ID as university ID, value as Merkle root, and BatchID as metadata. For transaction type 2, we store university ID as ID, result of verification as value and BatchID, university ID of the given batch and hash submitted for verification. Blocks will be added one after another as shown in Fig. 5. Each block will have variable number of these transactions and a header which will have Merkle root of these transactions, timestamp, etc.

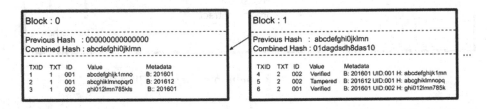

Fig. 5. Proposed blockchain-enabled TS

2. Searching Data: We add an entry corresponding to each transaction in a multilevel hash map. Adding data to this hash map will be in time complexity of $O(1 + \alpha)$. University ID acts as a level 1 key. We store two different trees, one each corresponding to one type of transaction, hence, transaction type will be level 2 key. After that year and batchID acts as level 3 and 4 keys for both the transactions. However, for transaction of type verification, we will have an additional key of transcript hash. University ID and transaction type are stored on the blockchain. The year and batch can be retrieved from Batch ID stored in metadata. For transaction of type verification, transcript hash is also part of metadata (depicted in Fig. 6). Searching in hash map is fairly straightforward, $O(1 + \alpha)$, as we move from one node to another as per the given key set. This time-efficient searching capability is utilized by blockchain to provide transactionID and block number quickly whenever verify transcript smart contracts ask for it.

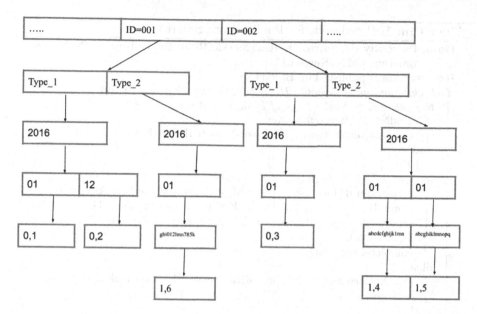

Fig. 6. Multilevel HashMap for proposed TS system

Smart Contracts: We present two different smart contract - one corresponding to Publishing Data and another for Verification of Transcript.

1. Publish Data Smart Contract: Pseudocode for this smart contact is shown in Algorithm 1. This smart contract takes University ID, Batch ID, Year, Merkle root, List of public keys of Professors and public key of requester as the arguments. Variables used are self explanatory and explanation for functions used are as follows:

   (a) checkPermission (UniversityID, public_Key_Of_Requester): This function checks if given user has permission to publish Merkle root corresponding to the given UniversityID from an existing Access control rule (refer Algorithm 2 for Pseudocode).

   (b) sendNotification(public_Key, Message): Each account will have a List of Notifications which is shown to user upon login. This function sends specified message to the specified account (refer Algorithm 3 for Pseudocode).

   (c) generateNotificationForProfessors(BatchID, MerkleRoot): This function returns a message for professors to notify them to sign the contract (refer Algorithm 4 for Pseudocode).

   (d) waitFor(time): This function puts smart contract to sleep for specified time (refer Algorithm 5 for Pseudocode).

   (e) signedByAll(list_Of_Public_Keys): This function checks if all the listed Professors have signed the contract. Refer Algorithm 6 for Pseudocode.

Algorithm 1: Pseudocode for Publish Data Smart Contract

Data: University_ID, Batch_ID, Year, Merkle_Root, Public_Keys_of_Professors,
          timeOut, public_Key_Of_Requester;
Result: Data is published on Blockchain
if *checkPermission(University_ID, public_Key_Of_Requester)* **then**
  for *public_Key: Public_Keys_of_Professors* **do**
    sendNotification(public_Key,
    generateNotificationForProfessors(Batch_ID,Mekle_Root));
  end
  waitFor(timeOut);
  if *signedByAll(Public_Keys_of_Professors)* **then**
    transactionID,blockNo = publishDataOnBlockChain(Merkle_Root,
    Batch_ID, University_ID, Public_Key_of_Requester, Type_1);
    sendNotification(public_Key_Of_Requester, transactionID +"
    "+blockNo);
    completeContract();
  else
    sendNotification(public_Key_Of_Requester,"Request Failed");
    terminateContract();
  end
else
  sendNotification(public_Key_Of_Requester,"Request Failed");
end

Algorithm 2: Function for checking if User has permission to Publish
Data on Blockchain

Result: Check-pointing permission
Input: UniversityID, public_Key;
if *is_permission[UniversityID]== public_Key* **then**
  | return true;
else
  | return false;
end

Algorithm 3: Function to send Notification to a User

Result: Notification is sent to the User
Input: public_Key, Message;
notificationList=getNotificationList(public_Key);
notificationList.add(Message);

(f) publishDataOnBlockChain(): This function can be thought of as an API
    by blockchain to add transaction. This function is only accessible by pub-
    lish data smart contract account in order to maintain access control. This
    function finds the newest block, adds data to it, adds search key to the
    hashmap and returns back to the called function.

Algorithm 4: Function for Generating Message for Professors

Result: A Message is Generated and Returned
Input: Batch_ID, Merkle_Root;
Message= "Please sign transaction for batch " + BatchID + " with Merkle Root " + Merkle Root;
return Message;

Algorithm 5: Function to Pause Smart Contract

Result: Smart Contract goes to Sleep
Input: time;
contract.state=Sleep(time);
return;

Algorithm 6: Function for checking if Professors have approved

---

Result: Check pointing approval of Professors
Input: List_Of_Public_Keys;
for *public_Key : List_Of_Public_Keys* **do**
    if *hasNotSigned(public_Key)* **then**
      | return false;
    end
end
return true;

(g) completeContract(): This is analogous to return 0 for main function in C programming language to log successful completion event.

(h) terminateContract(): This is analogous to return not equal to 0 for main function in C as this logs unsuccessful completion with a reason.

2. Verify Transcript Smart Contract: Pseudocode for this smart contract is shown in Algorithm 7. This smart contract takes transcript, UniversityID, BatchID, Merkle path for transcript and public key of user as arguments. Variables used are self explanatory and explanation for new functions used in this pseudo code is as follows:

(a) ComputeMerkleRoot(Transcript,Merkle Path): This function returns Merkle root computed using transcript and Merkle path. Merkle path is an array of the subsequent elements needed to compute Merkle root (refer Algorithm 8 for Pseudocode).

(b) getBlockNoFromHashMap(UniversityID, Year, BatchID): This function is an API function provided by Blockchain that returns block number and TransactionID from hash map using BatchID, Year and UniversityID.

(c) getValueFrom(blockNo,TXID): This function is an API function provided by blockchain that probes through the block with given block number and returns value corresponding transaction along with metadata.

Algorithm 7: Pseudocode for verify transcript Smart Contract

Result: Transcript is verified
Inputs: Transcript, UniversityID, BatchID, Merkle_Path,
,public_Key_Of_Initiator;
rootComputed=ComputeMerkleRoot(Transcript,Merkle_Path);
Year=extractYear(BatchID);
TXID, blockNo = getBlockNoFromHashMap (UniversityID, Year, BatchID);
rootSored, MetaData=getValueFrom(blockNo,TXID);
if *rootComputed == rootStored* **then**
   | transactionID,blockNo = publishDataOnBlockChain(Merkle_Root,
   | Batch_ID, University_ID, Public_Key_of_Requester, Type_2);
   | sendNotification(Initiator,Verified+transactionID+blockNo);
else
   | transactionID,blockNo = publishDataOnBlockChain(Merkle_Root,
   | Batch_ID, University_ID, Public_Key_of_Requester, Type_2);
   | sendNotification(Initiator,Tampered+transactionID+blockNo);
end
completeContract();

Algorithm 8: Function to Compute Merkle Root

Result: Merkle Root is Computed
Input: Transcript, Merkle_Path; MerkleRoot=sha_256(Transcript);
for *i=0; i <Merkle_Path.size() ; i++* **do**
   | MerkleRoot=MerkleRoot + Merkle_Path[i];
   | MerkleRoot=sha_256(MerkleRoot);
end
return MerkleRoot;

---

4   Implementation of the Proposed Scheme

In order to experiment the proposed scheme, we have implemented the scheme on Hyperledger framework [20]. Blockchain on hyperledger framework uses PBFT [21] consensus mechanism and is suitable in a permissioned blockchain. Assume that a student studying at University of AType in 2016 batch. He/she is applying for further studies at University of BType. First step would be University of AType uploading Merkle root of batch 2016. Controller of Examination of University of AType will follow the protocol for uploading Uploading TS of 2016 batch on blockchain. After creating Merkle tree, Controller of Examination invokes upload Transcript Smart Contract on blockchain as shown in Fig. 7. For simplicity, consider that there is only one student in Batch 2016. Hence, Merkle root is equivalent to the hash of transcript of that student, which will add Merkle root on blockchain, but its status is still unverified as the Professors who taught this batch has not signed signature contract approving this Merkle root. After Professors has approved this transaction using signature smart contract, its status changes to verified as shown in Fig. 8. Once status is changed to verified, Controller of Examination of University of AType sends the details to students and embed encoded details in a QR Code. Now, Academic administration of University of BType scans it to retrieve data. Assuming data is retrieved, it invokes verify Transcript Smart Contract, which follows embedded logic and store result on blockchain. As shown in Fig. 9, result will be either verified or unverified, which is stored in the form of an Asset Verification Request.

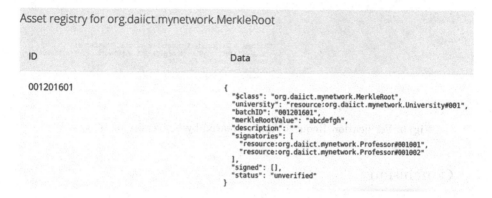

Asset registry for org.daiict.mynetwork.MerkleRoot

ID	Data
001201601	

```
{
 "$class": "org.daiict.mynetwork.MerkleRoot",
 "university": "resource:org.daiict.mynetwork.University#001",
 "batchID": "001201601",
 "merkleRootValue": "abcdefgh",
 "description": "",
 "signatories": [
   "resource:org.daiict.mynetwork.Professor#001001",
   "resource:org.daiict.mynetwork.Professor#001002"
 ],
 "signed": [],
 "status": "unverified"
}
```

Fig. 7. Merkle root Asset of Batch 2016 signed by Controller of Examination of University of AType and to be signed by Professors of University of AType.

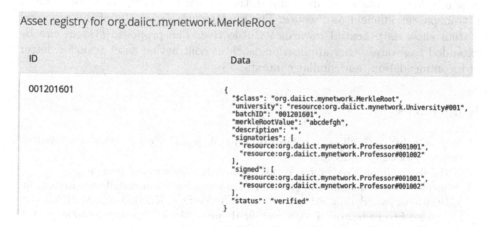

Asset registry for org.daiict.mynetwork.MerkleRoot

ID	Data
001201601	

```
{
 "$class": "org.daiict.mynetwork.MerkleRoot",
 "university": "resource:org.daiict.mynetwork.University#001",
 "batchID": "001201601",
 "merkleRootValue": "abcdefgh",
 "description": "",
 "signatories": [
   "resource:org.daiict.mynetwork.Professor#001001",
   "resource:org.daiict.mynetwork.Professor#001002"
 ],
 "signed": [
   "resource:org.daiict.mynetwork.Professor#001001",
   "resource:org.daiict.mynetwork.Professor#001002"
 ],
 "status": "verified"
}
```

Fig. 8. Merkle root Asset of Batch 2016 signed by Professors of University of AType and Controller of Examination of University of AType

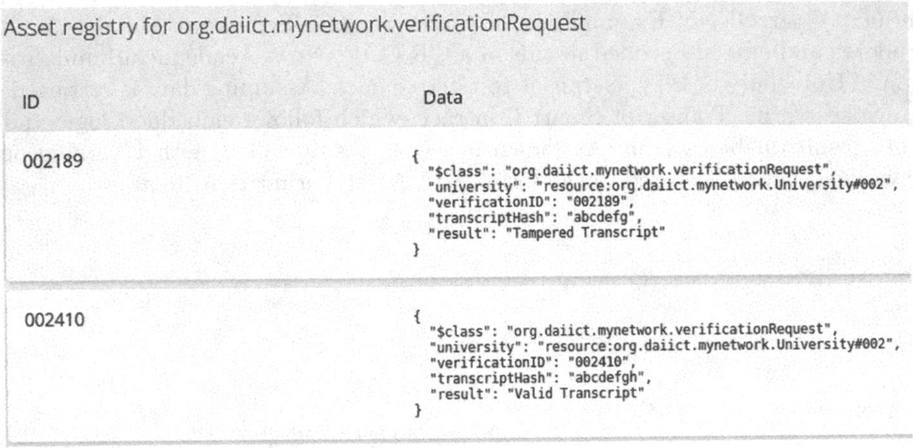

Asset registry for org.daiict.mynetwork.verificationRequest

ID	Data

002189	`{`
	`  "$class": "org.daiict.mynetwork.verificationRequest",`
	`  "university": "resource:org.daiict.mynetwork.University#002",`
	`  "verificationID": "002189",`
	`  "transcriptHash": "abcdefg",`
	`  "result": "Tampered Transcript"`
	`}`

002410	`{`
	`  "$class": "org.daiict.mynetwork.verificationRequest",`
	`  "university": "resource:org.daiict.mynetwork.University#002",`
	`  "verificationID": "002410",`
	`  "transcriptHash": "abcdefgh",`
	`  "result": "Valid Transcript"`
	`}`

Fig. 9. Verification Request Assets created by University of BType.

5   Conclusion

We discussed issues in sharing transcripts using current system and proposed an efficient transcript management system using blockchain-enabled smart contracts. Lack of authentication in the currently deployed conventional transcript sharing system is addressed by using secure public/private key mechanism and storing immutable metadata for verification. Because of absence of third party or single decision maker at any point in the proposed system, the whole process is transparent, efficient and secure. The implementation results of the proposed system show its potential towards its objective. The proposed system can be extended to several other applications such as contractual asset transfer, letter of recommendation, and similar contexts.

References

1. My eQuals: The Official Platform of Australian and New Zealand Universities. https://www.myequals.edu.au/
2. CHESICC: China Credentials Verification. https://www.chsi.com.cn/en/
3. Sharples, M., Domingue, J.: The Blockchain and Kudos: a distributed system for educational record, reputation and reward. In: Verbert, K., Sharples, M., Klobučar, T. (eds.) EC-TEL 2016. LNCS, vol. 9891, pp. 490–496. Springer, Cham (2016). https://doi.org/10.1007/978-3-319-45153-4_48
4. Hoy, M.B.: An introduction to the Blockchain and its implications for libraries and medicine. Med. Ref. Serv. Q. **36**(3), 273–279 (2017)
5. Skiba, D.J.: The potential of Blockchain in education and health care. Nurs. Educ. Perspect. **38**(4), 220–221 (2017)
6. Lemieux, L.: Blockchain and distributed ledgers as trusted record-keeping systems. In: Proceedings of Future Technology Conference, pp. 41–48 (2017)

7. Victoria, L.L.: A typology of Blockchain recordkeeping solutions and some reflections on their implications for the future of archival preservation. In: Proceedings of IEEE International Conference of Big Data, pp. 2271–2278 (2017)
8. Nakamoto, S.: Bitcoin: a peer-to-peer electronic cash system. http://www.bitcoin.org/bitcoin.pdf
9. Pilkington, M.: Blockchain technology: principles and applications. In: Handbook of Research on Digital Transformations. Edward Elgar Publishing, London, United Kingdom (2015)
10. Swan, M.: Blockchain: Blueprint for a New Economy. O'Reilly Media Inc. (2015)
11. Feng, T.: An agri-food supply chain traceability system for China based on RFID and Blockchain technology. In Proceedings of International Conference on Service Systems and Service Management, pp. 1–6 (2016)
12. Tse, D., Zhang, B., Yang, Y., Cheng, C., Mu, H.: Blockchain application in food supply information security. In: Proceedings of IEEE International Conference on Industrial Engineering and Engineering Management, pp. 1357–1361 (2017)
13. Azaria, A., Ekblaw, A., Vieira, T., Lippman, A.: MedRec: using Blockchain for medical data access and permission management. In: Proceedings of International Conference on Open Big Data, pp. 25–30 (2016)
14. Xia, Q.I., Sifah, E.B., Asamoah, K.O., Gao, J., Du, X., Guizani, M.: MeDShare: trust-less medical data sharing among cloud service providers via Blockchain. IEEE Access 5, 14757–14767 (2017)
15. Tschorsch, F., Scheuermann, B.: Bitcoin and beyond: a technical survey on decentralized digital currencies. IEEE Commun. Surv. Tutor. 18(3), 2084–2123 (2016)
16. Delmolino, K., Arnett, M., Kosba, A., Miller, A., Shi, E.: Step by step towards creating a safe smart contract: lessons and insights from a cryptocurrency lab. In: Clark, J., Meiklejohn, S., Ryan, P.Y.A., Wallach, D., Brenner, M., Rohloff, K. (eds.) FC 2016. LNCS, vol. 9604, pp. 79–94. Springer, Heidelberg (2016). https://doi.org/10.1007/978-3-662-53357-4_6
17. Blockcerts : The Open Standard for Blockchain Credentials. https://www.blockcerts.org/
18. Merkle, R.C.: A digital signature based on a conventional encryption function. In: Pomerance, C. (ed.) CRYPTO 1987. LNCS, vol. 293, pp. 369–378. Springer, Heidelberg (1988). https://doi.org/10.1007/3-540-48184-2_32
19. Menezes, A.J., Vanstone, S.A., Van Oorschot, P.C.: Handbook of Applied Cryptography. CRC Press, Boca Raton (1996)
20. Androulaki, E., et al.: Hyperledger fabric: a distributed operating system for permissioned Blockchains. In: Proceedings of EuroSys Conference, Article no. 30 (2018)
21. Castro, M., Liskov, B.: Practical byzantine fault tolerance andproactive recovery. ACM Trans. Comput. Syst. 20(4), 398–461 (2002)

Short Papers

Identifying Reduced Features Based on IG-Threshold for DoS Attack Detection Using PART

Deepak Kshirsagar[✉] and Sandeep Kumar[✉]

Department of Computer Science and Engineering,
Indian Institute of Technology Roorkee, Roorkee, Uttarakhand, India
kdeepak83@gmail.com, sandeepkumargargiitr@gmail.com

Abstract. Benchmark datasets are available to test and evaluate intrusion detection systems. The benchmark datasets are characterized by high volume and dimensionality curse. The feature reduction plays an important role in a machine learning-based intrusion detection system to identify relevant and irrelevant features with respect to the classification. This paper proposes a method for the identification of reduced features for the classification of Denial of Service (DoS) attack. The reduced feature technique is based on Information Gain (IG) and Threshold Limit Value (TLV). The proposed approach detects DoS attack using a reduced feature set from the original feature set with PART classifier. The proposed approach is implemented and tested on CICIDS 2017 dataset. The experimentation shows improved results in terms of performance with a reduced feature set. Finally, the performance of the proposed system is compared with the original feature set.

Keywords: Feature reduction · Information Gain · Threshold · Denial of Service · PART

1 Introduction

Denial of Service (DoS) is an attack that occurs when an intruder targets towards network resources to interrupt, degrade or to make services unavailable to genuine users in cyberspace. The attacker typically generates a large number of malicious network traffic targets towards systems, servers or networks through generation which results in a state of denial to genuine users. The attack can be generated by flooding of partial requests, large connections pools; cache enabled keep-alive connections or requesting unrelated port and services using programs or software tools. The attacker can target the network, transport or an application layer of the TCP/IP model.

A report published in 2019 by Akamai Technologies [1] suggests that more than 800 types of DoS attacks are tracked in the domain of financial industries. These attacks mainly disturb the financial service to steal account credentials of the user or exploit vulnerability towards the web. The attacker generates a flood of malicious network traffic in different ways in a short span of time to launch a DoS attack. Intrusion Detection

© Springer Nature Switzerland AG 2020
D. V. Hung and M. D'Souza (Eds.): ICDCIT 2020, LNCS 11969, pp. 411–419, 2020.
https://doi.org/10.1007/978-3-030-36987-3_27

System (IDS) is used for the detection of such types of attacks and which add an extra layer of security for the network.

Many approaches such as misuse, anomaly, and machine learning are employed for the detection of DoS attacks. Many research organizations contributed benchmark datasets for DoS attack which are publicly available to use for research purposes. These datasets suffer from the curse of dimensionality. The problem of high dimensional dataset affects the overall computation time of the system. It is possible to identify relevant and irrelevant features present in the dataset for classification. To identify optimal features for the classification is vital task in machine learning-based intrusion detection.

The key contributions of this work are summarized as below:

1. The proposed feature reduction is based on Information Gain (IG) and Threshold Limit Value (TLV) is employed.
2. The proposed approach uses reduced features with PART classifier for the efficient multilevel classification of DoS attack.
3. The proposed approach is tested with reduced features on DoS CICIDS 2017 dataset and compares the performance with original features.

The rest of this paper is organized as follows. The relevant work in the domain of feature reduction-based intrusion detection is described in Sect. 2. The proposed approach for DoS attack detection is explained in Sect. 3. Evaluation and Result analysis with CICIDS 2017 dataset are presented in Sect. 4. Finally, the conclusion of the present work and future scope are provided in Sect. 5.

2   Related Work

Salih and Maiwan [2] propose the best feature selection technique in intrusion detection. The best feature reduction technique is based on gain ratio, information gain, and correlation methods. The system uses K-Nearest Neighbor (KNN), Naïve Bayes, and Multilayer Perceptron classifiers for binary classification. The system is tested on KDD CUP 99 dataset for evaluation. KNN produces higher accuracy and precision as 99% and 98.9% respectively compared to other classifiers with 6 reduced features.

Shrivastava et al. [3] propose attack detection and forensics for DoS, malicious, SSH and Spying attacks in IoT. The system uses the best-first search and subset evaluation for feature extraction. After feature extraction, the proposed system uses J48, SVM, and Random Forest, etc. The proposed system is tested on 40 days collecting data in the laboratory with the help of honeypot Cowrie. The experimentation results show SVM which produces a higher accuracy of 97.39% among all other classifiers.

Shubhangi and Meenu [4] propose a feature selection technique for DoS attacks. This study proposes heuristic feature reduction with the help of filter methods such as information gain, correlation and gain ratio. This system employs filter-based feature selection techniques and analyzes with the help of C4.5 classifier. The experimental results show the gain ratio filter method provides maximum accuracy of 98.02% on the KDD99 dataset for binary classification on KDD dataset with 30 features.

Salo et al. [5] propose a hybrid feature reduction technique with an ensemble classifier for intrusion detection. The feature reduction technique combines information gain and principal component analysis for dimensionality reduction. The system is tested on Kyoto2006+, NSL KDD and ICSX 2012 datasets. The system uses ensemble classifiers based on Multilayer Perceptron (MLP), Support Vector Machine (SVM) and Instant based learning algorithms for binary classification. The system produces a higher accuracy of 99.011% for ISCX 2012 dataset with 7 reduced features compared to NSL KDD and Kyoto2006+ datasets.

Xiao et al. [6] propose a feature reduction-based intrusion detection model with convolutional neural networks. The system initially uses principal component analysis for feature reduction. The autoencoder is used for the concept of reconstruction error to convert reduced data into image data. The system uses convolutional neural networks for classification and tests on KDDCUP99 dataset. The accuracy of the model is high as 94%, but it produces a lower detection rate as 18.96% and 20.61% for R2L and U2R respectively.

Wang et al. [7] propose an Efficient Correlation-based Feature Selection (ECOFS) with support vector machine in IDS. The ECOFS is based on mutual information and the Pearson correlation coefficient feature selection algorithms. The system is tested in KDD CUP 99 and NSL-KDD datasets. The experimentation results show that the system produces better results in terms of accuracy, precision and recall for KDD CUP 99 with 9 reduced features as compared to NSL-KDD dataset with 10 reduced features.

3 Proposed Approach

In this study, the proposed approach uses Information Gain (IG) and Threshold Limit Value (TLV) with rule-based classifiers based on PART (Partial Decision Trees) which are presented to enhance the performance of the system. Figure 1 represents the proposed framework, which consists of four stages namely pre-processing, feature reduction, build and train the rule-based classifier based on PART and attack classification.

The existing datasets do not support for efficient detection of intrusion or normal data which needs data pre-processing before training the machine learning model. The key actions of the data pre-processing to be performed with the elimination of duplicate records, replace missing and infinite values to zero and map labels into numeric values.

Feature reduction algorithms [8] can be grouped into two categories: Filter, and Wrapper. In filter method, statistical tests are applied on the dataset and score is calculated for each feature. This score helps to select or discard the feature. In wrapper method, the set of features is selected from the original feature set and different combinations of the selected features are evaluated on a predictive model. The wrapper method involves training of the selected features on a predictive model which results into more computation time. This paper mainly uses the concept of filter method in feature reduction.

Information Gain (IG) is a filter method used for feature selection or reduction which measures the importance of an attribute or feature present in the dataset. Entropy represents an uncertainty of samples. Entropy is calculated by Eq. 1.

$$Entropy = -\sum_{i=0}^{K} P_i \log_2 P_i \tag{1}$$

where P_i represents the proportion of samples belonging to class K

The IG value of each feature is the difference between the total entropy and entropy of each feature. This algorithm calculates the importance of each feature ranging from 0 to 1. The high IG value represents higher importance of the feature and zero IG value represents an irrelevant feature. This algorithm uses a ranker method that ranks each feature based on the value of IG.

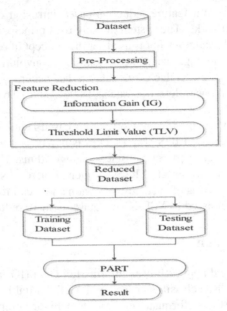

Fig. 1. The proposed approach for DoS attack detection

In statistics, Threshold Limit Value (TLV) is used to distinguish ranges of values by which behavior of predicted model changes. The selection of TLV is important to help intrusion detection which makes the best decision for the classification of network traffic into normal or attack. It is difficult to identify TLV for classification. The incorrect TLV results in increase in False Alarm Rate (FAR) in intrusion detection. The work presented in [9] and [10] has proposed and implemented a threshold mechanism for the detection of DDoS attacks. These works motivated to use the concept of threshold in the domain of feature reduction in intrusion detection. Therefore, this paper uses the concept of TLV for feature reduction based on information gain.

The reduced dataset is obtained from TLV based Information Gain (IG) which is used to train and test the machine learning model. This machine learning model uses the PART classifier to detect a DoS attack. The PART classifies six attack states present in the dataset. These attack states consist of Slowloris, SlowHTTPTest, GoldenEye, Hulk, Heartbleed and Benign. The performance of the proposed system is measured with the classification result in the terms of accuracy, precision, TPR, FPR and build up time on the test dataset.

4 Evaluations and Result Analysis

The experimentation is performed on Intel Xeon e3 v3 CPU coupled with 32 GB of RAM. The paper mainly works on the identification of the reduced features for the DoS attack. Therefore, the proposed system is evaluated with DoS dataset which was created on Wednesday in CICIDS2017. DoS CICIDS2017 dataset consists of a total record of 692703 including 440031 and 252672 normal and DoS attack records respectively with the presence of 78 features. The DoS attack consists of 11, 5499, 231073, 5796, and 10293 records of Heartbleed, SlowHTTPTest, Hulk, Slowloris, and GoldenEye respectively.

4.1 Data Pre-processing and Feature Reduction

The evaluation dataset comes from different platforms and may be noisy, incomplete or inconsistent. The dataset is preprocessed as mentioned in the proposed approach. The preprocessed dataset is used for further feature reduction process. The information gain is calculated as shown in Table 1.

Table 1. Information Gain (IG) of features in DoS CIC-IDS-2017

F No	Name	IG	F No	Name	IG
66	"Init_Win_bytes_Fwd	0.879866	74	Idle_Mean	0.496838
19	Flow_IAT_Max	0.792137	72	Active_Max	0.494164
41	Packet_len_Mean	0.780143	70	Active_Mean	0.493598
40	Max_Packet_len	0.779578	4	Total_Backward_Packets	0.492886
53	Average_Packet_Size	0.776777	64	Subflow_Bwd_Packets	0.492886
55	Avg_Bwd_Seg_Size	0.775973	73	Active_Min	0.480593
13	Bwd_Pkt_len_Mean	0.775973	28	Bwd_IAT_Sd	0.415681
6	Total_len_of_Bwd_Packets	0.765311	30	Bwd_IAT_Minimum	0.384905
65	Subflow_Bwd_Bytes	0.765311	39	Min_Packet_len	0.362246
2	Flow_Duration	0.761665	8	Fwd_Packet_len_Minimum	0.342785
17	Flow_IAT_Mean	0.753414	25	Fwd_IAT_Minimum	0.341150
16	Flow_Pkts/s	0.750844	3	Total_Fwd_Pkets	0.324505
37	Fwd_Pkts/s	0.741006	62	Subflow_Fwd_Packets	0.324505
42	Pkt_len_Std	0.736916	12	Bwd_Packet_len_Min	0.311014
43	Pkt_len_Variance	0.735987	20	Flow_IAT_Min	0.277351
24	Fwd_IAT_Max	0.735003	68	act_data_pkt_fwd	0.116844
11	Bwd_Pket_len_Max	0.719882	48	ACK_Flag_Count	0.10496
22	Fwd_IAT_Mean	0.699619	44	FIN_Flag_Count	0.100002

(continued)

Table 1. (*continued*)

F No	Name	IG	F No	Name	IG
7	Fwd_Pkt_len_Max	0.696415	75	Idle_Std	0.096836
21	Fwd_IAT_Total	0.691670	52	Down and Up_Ratio	0.089728
38	Bwd_Pkts/s	0.678572	69	min_seg_size_Fwd	0.071862
15	Flow_Bytes/s	0.673218	47	PSH_Flag_Count	0.067642
1	Dest_Port	0.668724	71	Active_Std	0.061591
5	Total_len_of_Fwd_Pktets	0.638729	49	URG_Flag_Count	0.040829
63	Subflow_Fwd_Bytes	0.638729	31	Fwd_PSH_Flgs	0.031103
36	Bwd_Header_len	0.620591	45	SYN_Flag_Count	0.031103
18	Flow_IAT_Std	0.616739	51	ECE_Flag_Count	0.000222
14	Bwd_Packet_len_Std	0.598547	46	RST_Flag_Count	0.000221
23	Fwd_IAT_Std	0.575131	32	Bwd_PSH_Flags	0
67	Init_Win_bytes_backward	0.572642	33	Fwd_URG_Flgs	0
29	Bwd_IAT_Max	0.55987	34	Bwd_URG_Flgs	0
35	Fwd_Header_len	0.54659	57	Fwd_Avg_Packets/Bulk	0
9	Fwd_Packet_len_Mean	0.525852	50	CWE_Flag_Count	0
54	Avg_Fwd_Segment_Size	0.525852	56	Fwd_Avg_bytes/Bulk	0
26	Bwd_IAT_Total	0.521834	59	Bwd_Avg_bytes/Bulk	0
10	Fwd_Packet_len_Std	0.507887	60	Bwd_Avg_pkets/Bulk	0
76	Idle_Max	0.506876	61	Bwd_Avg_bulk_rate	0
27	Bwd_IAT_Mean	0.500196	58	Fwd_Avg_bulk_rate"	0
77	Idle_Min	0.499655			

Static and dynamic techniques are used to determine TLV. Dynamic techniques are difficult to determine the TLV, because prior knowledge of network traffic is required. Therefore, static TVL is determined based on the values of IG. Table 1 shows that Information Gain (IG) values range from 0 to 1. Therefore, it is decided to assign TLV as 0, 0.25, 0.50, and 0.75. The TLV 0.75 indicates that the features having information gain value equal or higher than 0.75 are considered for feature selection and other features are eliminated and so on for 0, 0.25, and 0.50. The TLV of 0 consist of all features which are present in the dataset. Table 2 shows the TLV and its corresponding feature set. The TLV 0, 0.25, 0.50, and 0.75 consist of 77, 54, 38 and 12 features respectively.

Table 2. Feature set w.r.t TVL

TLV	Features	Count
0.25	1, 2, 3, 4, 5, 6, 7, 8, 9, 10, 11, 12, 13, 14, 15, 16, 17, 18, 19, 20, 21, 22, 23, 24, 25, 26, 27, 28, 29, 30, 35, 36, 37, 38, 39, 40, 41, 42, 43, 53, 54, 55, 62, 63, 64, 65, 66, 67, 70, 72, 73, 74, 76, 77	54
0.50	1, 2, 5, 6, 7, 9, 10, 11, 13, 14, 15, 16, 17, 18, 19, 21, 22, 23, 24, 26, 27, 29, 35, 36, 37, 38, 40, 41, 42, 43, 53, 54, 55, 63, 65, 66, 67, 76	38
0.75	2,6, 13, 16,17, 19, 40, 41, 53, 55, 65, 66	12

4.2 Results and Discussion

The performance of the proposed approach is measured in terms of [11] True Positive Rate (TPR), False Positive Rate (FPR), Precision, Recall and Accuracy. The proposed approach uses a reduced dataset for training and testing. The reduced dataset uses TLV of 0.5 which consists of 38 features. Initially, the system is trained with 10% dataset and the remaining 90% dataset is used for testing. Similarly, the system is trained with 20% of dataset and the remaining 80% dataset is used for testing and so on up to 90% training at the interval of 10%.

The system is tested for these classifiers and tested for the best percentage of the split for training and testing with all features. It is found that PART provides the best accuracy and precision of 99.97%, TPR of 99.98% and FAR of 0.05% in 50% training and testing split with nine-minute model built up time. PART produces the best performance compared to the decision table, JRip, and OneR. Therefore, the proposed approach further uses PART with 50% training and testing for classification.

Table 3 shows the evaluation of the proposed approach in terms of performance on the DoS CICIDS2017 dataset with a reduced feature set. The experimental results show that PART produces higher precision for GoldenEye, Hulk, SlowHTTPTest, and Slowloris with 38 reduced features compared to original features. PART produces a slight decrease in precision for the classification of benign records.

Table 3. Performance of PART on DoS CICIDS2017 dataset with the reduced feature set

	Benign	Slowloris	SlowHTTPTest	Hulk	GoldenEye	Heartbleed
TPR (%)	99.9691	99.2083	99.0906	99.9809	99.7091	57.1429
FPR	0.0341	0.0041	0.0052	0.0234	0.0076	0.0003
Precision (%)	99.9805	99.5166	99.3435	99.9532	99.4969	80.0000
Recall (%)	99.9691	99.2083	99.0906	99.9809	99.7091	57.1429
Accuracy (%)	99.9680	99.9893	99.9876	99.9781	99.9882	99.9988

The dataset consists of only 11 samples for Heartbleed attack. The proposed approach produces a decrease in precision for this attack due to a few numbers of Heartbleed samples are unable to learn the system. The performance comparison of PART in terms of accuracy and FPR is resented in the form of graphs as shown in Fig. 2. It shows that PART produces a slight increase in accuracy of GoldenEye, Slowloris, and Hulk. On the other hand, it slightly decreases for benign, SlowHTTPTest and Heartbleed compared to the original feature set.

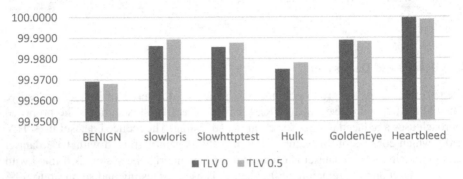

Fig. 2. Accuracy of PART with TLV 0 and 0.5

5   Conclusion and Future Scope

This work proposes a reduced feature reduction technique for the efficient classification of DoS attack at the application layer. The approach identifies reduced features using concepts of information gain and threshold. The approach identifies 38 reduced features from the original 77 features. The implemented system with PART using reduced features shows encouraging results. The experimentation results on DoS CICIDS 2017 dataset show better results for GoldenEye, Hulk, SlowHTTPTest, and Slowloris in terms of precision with reduced features.

The present work can be extended to identify the optimal feature set and improve the performance of the Heartbleed attack classification.

References

1. Shuster, E., LaSeur, L., Katz, O., Ragan, S.: Financial Services Attack Economy. Akamai Technologies (2019)
2. Salih, A.A., Abdulrazaq, M.B.: Combining best features selection using three classifiers in intrusion detection system. In: 2019 International Conference on Advanced Science and Engineering, pp. 94–99. IEEE (2019)
3. Shrivastava, R.K., Bashir, B., Hota, C.: Attack detection and forensics using honeypot in IoT environment. In: Fahrnberger, G., Gopinathan, S., Parida, L. (eds.) ICDCIT 2019. LNCS, vol. 11319, pp. 402–409. Springer, Cham (2019). https://doi.org/10.1007/978-3-030-05366-6_33
4. Dongre, S., Chawla, M.: Analysis of feature selection techniques for denial of service (DoS) attacks. In: 2018 4th International Conference on Recent Advances in Information Technology, pp. 1–4. IEEE (2018)

5. Salo, F., Ali, B., Aleksander, E.: Dimensionality reduction with IG-PCA and ensemble classifier for network intrusion detection. Comput. Netw. **148**, 164–175 (2019)
6. Xiao, Y., Xing, C., Zhang, T., Zhao, Z.: An intrusion detection model based on feature reduction and convolutional neural networks. IEEE Access **7**, 42210–42219 (2019)
7. Wang, W., Du, X., Wang, N.: Building a cloud IDS Using an efficient feature selection method and SVM. IEEE Access **7**, 1345–1354 (2018)
8. Selvakumar, B., Muneeswaran, K.: Firefly algorithm based feature selection for network intrusion detection. Comput. Secur. **81**, 148–155 (2019)
9. David, J., Ciza, T.: Efficient DDoS flood attack detection using dynamic thresholding on flow-based network traffic. Comput. Secur. **82**, 284–295 (2019)
10. Faizal, M., Zaki, M.M., Shahrin, S., Robiah, Y., Rahayu, S.S., Nazrulazhar, B.: Threshold verification technique for network intrusion detection system (2009). arXiv preprint: arXiv: 0906.3843
11. Manzoor, I., Neeraj, K.: A feature reduced intrusion detection system using ANN classifier. Expert Syst. Appl. **88**, 249–257 (2017)

Uniform Circle Formation by Swarm Robots Under Limited Visibility

Moumita Mondal[1(✉)] and Sruti Gan Chaudhuri[2(✉)]

[1] Techno Main Saltlake, Kolkata, India
mmoumi@gmail.com
[2] Jadavpur University, Kolkata, India
sruti1947@gmail.com

Abstract. This paper proposes a distributed algorithm for uniform circle formation by multiple autonomous, asynchronous, oblivious mobile swarm robots. Each robot executes cycle of *look-compute-move* repeatedly. All robots agree upon a common origin and axes. Eventually an uniform circle of a given radius and center is formed without any collision or deadlock.

Keywords: Uniform circle formation · Autonomous · Oblivious · Swarm robots · Limited visibility

1 Introduction

Swarm robot is a collection of tiny autonomous mobile robots who collaboratively perform a given task. One of the interests of the investigations on cooperative swarm robotics is *distributed motion coordination*, which allows the robots to form certain patterns. The significance of positioning the robots based on some given patterns may be useful for various tasks, such as operations in hazardous environments, space mission, military operations, tumor excision etc. This paper addresses one such geometric problem, uniform circle formation. Each robot is capable of sensing its immediate surrounding, performing computations on the sensed data, and moving towards the computed destination. The robots are free to move on the 2D plane and are anonymous, oblivious and can only interact by observing others position. They have uniform limited visibility range and can be inside or outside the given circle. Based on this model, we study the problem of uniform circle formation, i.e., positioning the robots equidistant apart on the circumference of a circle with given radius and center.

A large body of research work exists in the context of multiple autonomous swarm robots exhibiting cooperative behavior. The aim of such researches is to study the issues as group architecture, resource conflict, origin of cooperation, learning and geometric problems [3]. Traditional or conventional approach to swarm robots involves artificial intelligence in which most of the results are based on experimental study or simulations. Recently a new emerging field of robot

D. V. Hung and M. D'Souza (Eds.): ICDCIT 2020, LNCS 11969, pp. 420–428, 2020.
https://doi.org/10.1007/978-3-030-36987-3_28

swarm looks at the robots as distributed mobile entities and studies several coordination problems and proceed to solve them deterministically. Flocchini et al. [4], solved the uniform circle formation problem for any initial configuration of $n \neq 4$ anonymous, autonomous, oblivious, disoriented point robots. Mamino and Viglietta [5] solved the uniform circle formation for four point robots. All of these algorithms assume the robots to be a point which neither creates any visual obstruction nor acts as an obstacle in the path of other robots. Obviously such robots are not practical. However small they might be, they must have certain dimensions.

Czyzowicz et al. [1] extend the traditional weak model [2] of robots by replacing the point robots with unit disc robots. They named these robots as fat robots. Dutta et al. [6] have proposed a circle formation algorithms for fat robots in limited visibility. Mondal et al. [7] have proposed an uniform circle formation algorithm for fat robots considering full visibility.

In this paper, we propose an algorithm to form a *convex regular polygon* in other words a *uniform circle* by fat robots under limited visibility. The algorithm works without encountering any collision and deadlock.

2   Algorithm

In this section, we first describe the robot model used in this paper and present an overview of the problem. Then we move to the solution approach and present the algorithms with the proofs of their correctness.

Underlying Model. We use the basic structure of weak model [2] of robots and add some extra features which extend the model towards real time situation. Let $R = r_1, r_2, .., r_n$ be a set of unit disc shaped autonomous robots referred as *fat robots*. A robot is represented by its center, i.e., by r_i we mean a robot whose center is r_i. The set of robots R deployed on the 2D plane is described as follows:

- The robots are autonomous, non-transparent, i.e opaque.
- Robots are anonymous and homogeneous in the sense that they are unable to uniquely identify themselves, neither with an unique identification number nor with some external distinctive mark (e.g. color, flag).
- Each robot executes a cycle of look-compute-move asynchronously.
- The robots are oblivious in the sense that they can not recollect any data from past cycle.
- A robot can see up to a fixed distance around itself on the 2D plane.
- Robots can not communicate explicitly. Each robot is allowed to have a camera which can take picture over 360° and up to a fixed radius. The robots communicate only by means of observing other robots within its visibility range with the camera.
- The robots have a common origin, common x-y axis, common sense of direction and common unit distance.

Overview of the Problem. A set of robots R (as described above) is given. Our objective is to form a circle (denoted by CIR) of radius k and centered at

C by moving the robots from R. Following assumptions and definitions are used in this paper:

Definition 1: Each robot can see up to a fixed distance around itself. This distance is called visibility range of that robot. The visibility range of $r_i \in R$ is denoted by R_v. Visibility Range is equal for all robots in R.

Definition 2: The circle, centered at robot r_i 2 R and having radius R_v is called the visibility circle of the robot r_i, denoted by $VC(r_i)$. r_i can see everything within and on the circumference of $VC(r_i)$. r_i cannot see beyond $VC(r_i)$.

Assumptions:

- All robots in R agree on a common origin, axes, sense of direction and unit distance. C, the center of the circle CIR is considered as the origin of the coordinate system.
- The radius (k) of the circle to be formed (CIR) is given. The length of k is such that CIR can accommodate all the robots in R.
- Initially the robots in R can be either inside, outside or on the CIR.

Notations: The following notations are used throughout the paper.

- $T(r_i)$: Destination point for robot r_i.
- dist(p1, p2): Euclidean distance between two points p1 and p2.
- cir(r_i, C): A circle centered at centered at C and having radius of dist(r_i, C).
- projpt(r_i, A): The projected (radially outward) point of the robot position r_i on circle A.
- arc(a, b): The arc of a circle between the points a and b on the circumference of that circle.

Definition 3: If the circular area of radius 2 and centered at point p does not contain the center of any other robot, then p is called a vacant point.

   Two constraints have been put on the movement of any robot r_i.

Constraint 1. Let $r_j \in R$ be any robot inside $VC(r_i)$ (the visibility circle of r_i). r_i is eligible to move if—-

- r_i is inside CIR, dist(C; r_i) $\geq$ dist(C; r_j) and dist(C; r_j) $<$ k.
- r_i is inside CIR, and dist(C; r_i) $<$ dist(C; r_j) and dist(C; r_j) $=$ k.
- r_i is outside CIR, dist(C; r_i) $\leq$ dist(C; r_j) and dist(C; r_j) $>$ k.
- If r_i is outside CIR, and dist(C; r_i) $>$ dist(C; r_j) and dist(C; r_j) $=$ k.
- If r_i is at C, then r_i is eligible to move. (An example in Fig. 1(ii))

   Note: For all other cases r_i will not move.

Constraint 2. $r_i \in R$ moves only in any of the following fixed directions.

- Radially outwards following the ray starting from C, directed towards r_i.
- Radially inwards following the ray starting from r_i, directed towards C.

- Right side of the ray, starting from C and directed towards r_i.
- Right side of the ray, starting from r_i and directed towards C.

This following sections present the description of algorithms ComputeTargetPoint, ComputeRobotPosition, ComputeDestination(r_i) and UniformCircleFormation required for uniform circle formation by computing the destination for the robots.

2.1   Description of the Algorithm ComputeTargetPoint

Let L be the line parallel to the Y axis and passing through the center C of CIR. If the north-most intersection point of L and CIR be o then, o is the first target point. The next target point is computed as $\frac{2\pi k}{n}$ distance apart from o at both sides of L. Similarly all other target points are counted such that the distance between two consecutive target points is $\frac{2\pi k}{n}$.

2.2   Description of the Algorithm ComputeRobotPosition

This algorithm decides the position of robot r_i, either inside CIR or outside CIR or on the CIR. The inputs to the algorithm are n and rad_c. Let co-ordinates of the center of CIR, c is (0,0) and position of r_i is (x, y). For all r_i, if $\sqrt{(0-x)^2 + (0-y)^2} = CIR$, then r_i is on the CIR. Else if $\sqrt{(0-x)^2 + (0-y)^2} < CIR$, then r_i is inside CIR. Otherwise, r_i is outside CIR.

2.3   Description of the Algorithm ComputeDestination

We categorize different configurations depending on the position of visibility circles of r_i and r_j. We denote these configurations as $\Phi 1$, $\Phi 1$, $\Phi 3$ and $\Phi 4$.

- $\Phi 1$: $V(r_i)$ and $V(r_j)$ do not touch or intersect each other (Fig. 1).
- $\Phi 2$: $V(r_i)$ and $V(r_j)$ touch each other at a single point say q. If there is a robot at q say rq, then r_i and rq and r_j and rq are mutually visible (Fig. 1).
- $\Phi 3$: $V(r_i)$ and $V(r_j)$ intersect each other at two points such that r_i and r_j can not see each other (Fig. 2). Let Δ be the common visible region of r_i and r_j. If there is a robot in the region Δ, say r_k, then r_k can see r_i and r_j, and both r_i and r_j can see r_k.
- $\Phi 4$: $V(r_i)$ and $V(r_j)$ intersect each other at two points such that r_i and r_j can see each other.(Fig. 2) Let Δ be the common visible region of r_i and r_j. If there is a robot in the region Δ, say r_k, then r_k, r_i and r_j can see each other.

There are nine configurations depending on the position of r_i inside or outside CIR. We denote these configurations as Ψ_1, Ψ_2, Ψ_3, Ψ_4, Ψ_5, Ψ_6, Ψ_7, Ψ_8 and Ψ_9.

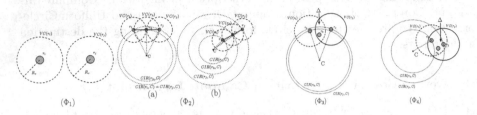

Fig. 1. Example of configurations $\Phi1$ and $\Phi2$ **Fig. 2.** Example of configurations $\Phi3$ and $\Phi4$

- Ψ_0: When r_i is on the CIR circumference and vacant space is available, radially outside CIR, then r_i moves radially outward to the available vacant space, else r_i does not move until vacant space is available outside CIR.
- Ψ_1: When r_i is on a target point, on the circumference of CIR, it does not move any further (Fig. 3).
- Ψ_2: When r_i is inside the CIR and VC(r_i) touches CIR (at some point say h) (Fig. 3). If h is vacant and is a target position, then $T(r_i)$ moves to h. Otherwise, r_i moves to the midpoint of the line joining r_i and h.
- Ψ_3: When r_i is inside the CIR but not at C and VC(r_i) does not touch or intersect the circumference of CIR (Fig. 4). Let t be projpt(r_i, $VC(r_i)$, If t is a vacant point, then r_i moves to t. Otherwise, r_i moves to the midpoint of line joining r_i and t.
- Ψ_4: When r_i is at C (Fig. 4), it moves to intersection point of positive X-axis of robot r_i and $VC(r_i)$ (Say m). If m is a vacant point then $T(r_i)$ moves to m, else $T(r_i)$ moves to the midpoint of the line joining r_i and m.
- Ψ_5: When r_i is inside the CIR and VC(r_i) intersects CIR (at two points say g and l) (Fig. 5).
  Here, we can visualize the configuration of robots as m concentric circles whose center is C. We consider that the robots of Ψ_5 are in concentric circle $C(m-1)$ and they can either jump to $C(m)$[as in Case Ψ_5(a) and Case Ψ_5(b)]

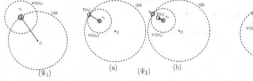

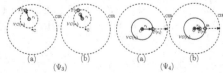

Fig. 3. Example of the configuration Ψ_1 and Ψ_2 **Fig. 4.** Example of the configuration Ψ_3 and Ψ_4

or remain in the same circle $C(m-1)$ to move rightwards [as in this Case $\Psi_5(c)$].

Possible cases for Ψ_5:

$\Psi_5(a)$ - There is a target position $T(r_i)$ on the radially outward projpt(r, C) of the arc gl.
- If $T(r_i)$ is vacant then r_i moves to $T(r_i)$.
- Else Check for next target point on the right of it upto l.

$\Psi_5(b)$ - There is no target point on the radially outward projpt(r, C) but there is target position on the arc gl.
- If $T(r_i)$ is vacant then r_i moves to $T(r_i)$.
- Else Check for next target point on the right of it upto l.

$\Psi_5(c)$ - There is no vacant target position at all on the arc tl.
- If the next position on the right on the same concentric circle $C(m-1)$ is vacant, the robot on $C(m-1)$ moves rightwards to the next position.
  * If $T(r_i)$ is found on $C(m)$ then move to $T(r_i)$ and exit Ψ_5;
  * If $T(r_i)$ not found then repeat $\Psi_5(c)$.
- If the next position on the right on the same concentric circle $C(m-1)$ is not vacant: The robot, $r_i i$ on $C(m-1)$ does not move until the robot on the next right position of r_i, has moved to $C(m)$.

- Ψ_6: When r_i is outside the CIR and VC(r_i) touches CIR (at some point say h) (Fig. 6). If h is a vacant point, then r_i moves to h (Fig. 7(a)). Otherwise, r_i moves to the midpoint of the line joining r_i and h.
- Ψ_7: When r_i is outside the CIR and VC(r_i) does not touch or intersect the circumference of CIR (Fig. 6). Let, t be projpt$(r_i, VC(r_i))$. If t is a vacant point, then r_i moves to t (Fig. 7(a)). Otherwise, r_i moves to the midpoint of line joining r_i and t.
- Ψ_8: When r_i is outside the CIR and VC(r_i) intersects CIR (at two points say g and l) (Fig. 7).

Here, we can visualize the configuration of robots as m concentric circles whose center is C.

We consider that the robots of Ψ_5 are in concentric circle $C(m+1)$ and they can either jump down to $C(m)$ [as in Case $\Psi_5(a)$ and Case $\Psi_5(b)$] or remain in the same circle $C(m+1)$ to move rightwards [as in this Case $\Psi_5(c)$].

Possible cases for Psi_8:

$\Psi_8(a)$ - There is a target position $T(r_i)$ on the radially inward projpt(r, C) of the arc gl.

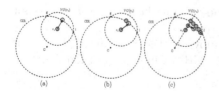

Fig. 5. Example of the configuration Ψ_5

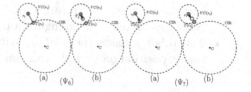

Fig. 6. Example of the configuration Ψ_6 and Ψ_7

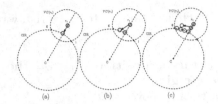

Fig. 7. An example of the configuration Ψ_8

- If $T(r_i)$ is vacant, r_i moves to $T(r_i)$.
- Else Check for next target point on the right of it upto l.

$\Psi_8(b)$ - **There is no target point on the radially inward projpt(r, C) but there is target position on the arc gl.**

- If $T(r_i)$ is vacant, r_i moves to $T(r_i)$.
- Else Check for next target point on the right of it upto l.

$\Psi_8(c)$ - **There is no vacant target position at all on the arc tl.**

- If the next position on the right on the same concentric circle $C(m+1)$ is vacant, the robot on $C(m+1)$ moves rightwards to the next position.
  * If T(ri) found on C(m), move to T(ri) and exit Ψ_8;
  * If T(ri) not found, repeat $\Psi_8(c)$.
- If the next position on the right on the same concentric circle $C(m+1)$ is not vacant: The robot, r_ii on $C(m+1)$ does not move until the robot on the next right position of r_i, has moved down to $C(m)$. $\Psi_8(c)$ - **There is no vacant target position at all on the arc tl.**

- Ψ_9: **(i) - When r_i is outside the CIR with $VC(r_i)$ touching CIR at a point and there is a target position T at that point. Also, another robot r_j is inside the CIR with $VC(r_j)$ touching CIR at the same point. (Fig. 8).**
  - The robots r_i moves radially inwards and r_j moves radially outwards towards the CIR till the target point T is visible to both r_i and r_j.
  - The robot inside the CIR r_j will move to the target position T and the robot outside CIR, r_i will move to the next vacant target position on its right.

(ii) - When r_i is outside the CIR with $VC(r_i)$ intersecting CIR (at two points say g and l) and r_j is inside the CIR with $VC(r_j)$ intersecting CIR (Fig. 9).

- The robot inside CIR, r_j will move radially outwards towards the CIR and occupy the vacant target position, T, on the CIR. If $T(r_i)$ is not vacant r_j moves as in configuration $\Psi_8(c)$.
- The robot outside the CIR, r_i will move to the next available vacant target position on its right side, on the CIR as in configuration $\Psi_8(c)$.

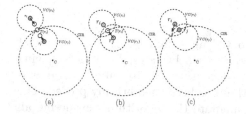 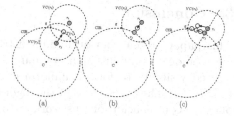

Fig. 8. An example of the configuration $\Psi_9(\text{i})$

Fig. 9. An example of the configuration $\Psi_9(\text{ii})$

Correctness of ComputeDestination(r_i):

Observation 1. r_i never goes outside of VC(r_i).

Observation 2. If two robots r_i and r_j are in $\Phi 1$ (Fig. 1), their movements are not affected by each other.

Observation 3. If two robots r_i and r_j are in $\Phi 2$ (Fig. 1), and there is a robot (say r_k) at the touching point of VC(r_i) and VC(r_j) (r_k is visible by both r_i and r_j), then the movements of r_k, r_i and r_j are not affected by each other.

Observation 4. If two robots r_i and r_j are in $\Phi 3$ (Fig. 2), and there is any robot (say r_k) in common visible region (r_k is visible by both r_i and r_j), namely Δ, the movements of r_k, r_i and r_j are not affected by each other.

Observation 5. If two robots r_i and r_j are in $\Phi 4$ (Fig. 2), (they are mutually visible) and there is any robot (say r_k) in common visible region Δ (r_k is visible by both r_i and r_j), then the movements of r_k, r_i and r_j are not affected by each other.

Lemma 1. The destination $T(r_i)$ computed by the robot r_i 2 R using Compute destination(r_i) is deterministic.

2.4 Description of the Algorithm UniformCircleFormation

Each robot executes the algorithm **UniformCircleFormation(r_i)** and places itself on the circumference of CIR in finite number of execution of the algorithm. In this algorithm, if r_i is not eligible to move according to Constraint 1, then r_i does not move. Otherwise, $T(r_i)$ is computed by ComputeDestination(r_i) and r_i moves to $T(r_i)$.

Correctness of UniformCircleFormation(r_i)

Lemma 2. The path of each robot is obstacle free.

Theorem 1. Circle formation(r_i) forms circle CIR by R in finite time.

3   Conclusion

This paper presents an outline of distributed algorithm which allows a set of autonomous, oblivious, non communicative, asynchronous, fat robots having limited visibility to form a uniform circle executing a finite number of operation cycles. The correctness of the algorithm has been theoretically proved. The ongoing continuation of this work is to simulate the algorithm considering all real time scenarios. In theoretical point of view one of the extensions would be to study the same problem considering the robots having non uniform visibility ranges which is quite practical for the issue of battery decay. Incorporating faulty robots is another future scope.

References

1. Czyzowicz, J., Gasieniec, L., Pelc, A.: Gathering few fat mobile robots in the plane. Theor. Comput. Sci. **410**, 481–499 (2009)
2. Efrima, A., Peleg, D.: Distributed algorithms for partitioning a swarm of autonomous mobile robots. Theor. Comput. Sci. **410**, 1355–1368 (2009)
3. Uny, C.Y., Fukunaga, A.S., Kahng, A.B.: Cooperative mobile robotics: antecedents and directions. Auton. Robot. **4**, 1–23 (1997)
4. Flocchini, P., Prencipe, G., Santoro, N., Viglietta, G.: Distributed computing by mobile robots: solving the uniform circle formation problem. In: Aguilera, M.K., Querzoni, L., Shapiro, M. (eds.) OPODIS 2014. LNCS, vol. 8878, pp. 217–232. Springer, Cham (2014). https://doi.org/10.1007/978-3-319-14472-6_15
5. Mamino, M., Viglietta, G.: Square formation by asynchronous oblivious robots. In: Proceedings of the 28th Canadian Conference on Computational Geometry, CCCG 2016 (2016)
6. Dutta, A., Gan Chaudhuri, S., Datta, S., Mukhopadhyaya, K.: Circle formation by asynchronous fat robots with limited visibility. In: Ramanujam, R., Ramaswamy, S. (eds.) ICDCIT 2012. LNCS, vol. 7154, pp. 83–93. Springer, Heidelberg (2012). https://doi.org/10.1007/978-3-642-28073-3_8
7. Mondal, M., Gan Chaudhuri, S.: Uniform circle formation by mobile robots. In: Proceedings of the Workshop Program of the 19th International Conference on Distributed Computing and Networking, Article No. 20 (ICDCN 2018) (2018)

Histopathological Image Classification by Optimized Neural Network Using IGSA

Himanshu Mittal, Mukesh Saraswat[✉], and Raju Pal

Jaypee Institute of Information Technology, Noida, India
saraswatmukesh@gmail.com

Abstract. The histopathological image classification is a vivid application for medical diagnosis and neural network has been successful in the image classification task. However, finding the optimal values of the neural network is still a challenging task. To accomplish the same, this paper considers a two-layer neural network which is optimized through intelligent gravitational search algorithm. Further, the optimized two-layer neural network is applied for the histopathological tissue classification into healthy and inflamed. The proposed method is validated on the publicly available tissue dataset, namely Animal Diagnostic Laboratory (ADL). The experimental results firm the better performance of the proposed method against state-of-the-art methods in terms of seven performance measures, namely recall, specificity, precision, false negative rate (FNR), accuracy, F1-score, and G-mean.

Keywords: Histopathological image classification · Two layer neural network · Intelligent gravitational search algorithm

1 Introduction

The manifestation of a disease from the surgical samples or biopsy through the microscopic examination is termed as histopathology. In histopathology, structure of the tissue, cell count within the tissue, or variation in the cell shape are analyzed for the disease diagnostic. Normally, this study is carried out manually which requires expert pathologists which makes this costly, biased, and time-consuming process [17]. Thus, its automation is essential for the fast and unbiased diagnosis of the disease [18]. For the same, computerized histopathological image analysis is done wherein the histopathology procedures are performed on the histopathological images that are captured by the microscopic mounted cameras. In literature, histopathological image classification poses a challenging problem due to their complex structure [13], as illustrated in Fig. 1.

Generally, neural networks have been quite successful for image classification application. In fact, the 2-layer architecture of neural network is most widely preferred network architecture for classification problems as it can easily approximate any continuous and discontinuous function [3]. For illustration, Fig. 2 represents an architecture of a two-layer neural network which consists of two hidden

© Springer Nature Switzerland AG 2020
D. V. Hung and M. D'Souza (Eds.): ICDCIT 2020, LNCS 11969, pp. 429–436, 2020.
https://doi.org/10.1007/978-3-030-36987-3_29

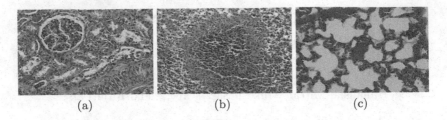

(a)   (b)   (c)

Fig. 1. Representative histopathological images of tissues [20].

layers and one output layer. Learning of a neural network is a critical part which involves the fine-tuning of the network parameters i.e., weights and biases. The essence of learning is to minimize the error function as low as possible. Usually, back-propagation (BP) method or its variants are popular resort for the learning of network parameters. However, this learning procedure suffers from a number of drawbacks namely, tendency of producing local optimal solutions, slow convergence, and dependence over parameter settings of the BP method [6]. To mitigate the same, meta-heuristic algorithms have been efficient in obtaining optimal solutions [3,4,14]. Meta-heuristic algorithms mimic the nature's behavior to attain optimal solution [1,7]. In literature, these algorithms have been employed in various engineering applications such as image segmentation, software testing, clustering, controller design [21]. Gravitational search algorithm (GSA), one of the well accepted meta-heuristic algorithm [16], has been used to tune neural networks and attained effective results [2,5].

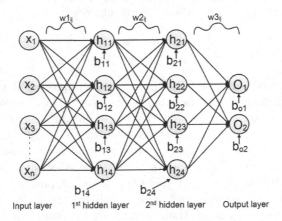

Fig. 2. A two-layer neural network architecture.

GSA explores the search space by considering the current fitness and gravitational force. It is a population based algorithm in which each individual cooperate and compete with each other. Moreover, every individual of GSA searches for the global optimal solution under the influence of gravitational law. In GSA, three operations are mainly performed for individual: mass computation, gravitational force, and position updation. GSA has a number of advantages such as fast convergence rate, low computational cost, and dependency over distance [9,11]. However, it sometimes traps into local optima and results in lack of solution precision [8]. To alleviate such problems, a novel variant of GSA, intelligent gravitational search algorithm (IGSA), has been proposed in [10] which has shown good solution precision and enhanced convergence rate. Therefore, this paper investigates the efficiency of the IGSA for the optimal learning of two-layer neural network.

The paper made following contributions: (i) A two-layer neural network is used for the classification of the histopathological tissue images into two classes, i.e. healthy and inflammatory and (ii) IGSA optimizes the parameters of the considered neural network. The experimental results are conducted on the histopathological tissue images taken from the publicly available Animal Diagnostic Laboratory (ADL) dataset [20]. This dataset consists of inflamed and healthy images for three organs, namely Kidney, Lung, and Spleen. Moreover, the proposed method has been compared with state-of-the-art classification methods for ADL dataset in terms of confusion matrix and other classification performance matrices, namely recall, specificity, precision, false negative rate (FNR), accuracy, F1-score, and G-mean.

The remaining paper is organized as follows: Sect. 2 discusses the two layer neural network architecture and IGSA. The proposed IGSA-based neural network classification method is detailed in the Sect. 3 followed by the experimental analyses in Sect. 4. Finally, the conclusion is drawn in Sect. 5.

2   Preliminaries

2.1   Two-Layer Neural Network

In literature, it has been validated that a two-layer neural network (one input, two hidden, and one output layer) can solve almost every linear and non-linear problem. Figure 2 illustrates a representative two layer neural network. Consider a two layer neural network where the number of nodes at input layer, both hidden layers and output layer are n, h, and m, respectively. The activation function is sigmoid function. At every epoch of learning, the output at the first hidden layer is calculated as per Eq. (1).

$$f(s_q) = \frac{1}{[1 + exp(-(\sum_{a=1}^{n} w_{aq} \cdot x_a + b_q))]} \tag{1}$$

where, w_{aq} is the weight of the edge between a^{th} input node and q^{th} hidden node and b_q corresponds to the bias value for the qth hidden node of first layer. $f(s_q)$ signifies the output of the qth hidden node which is further passed to the next hidden layer to compute $f(s_p)$ which is equated in Eq. (2).

$$f(s_p) = \frac{1}{[1 + exp((\sum_{q=1}^{h} w_{qp} \ f(s_q) + b_p))]} \tag{2}$$

where, $w_q p$ is the weight of the edge between q^{th} hidden node and p^{th} hidden node and b_p corresponds to the bias value for the pth hidden node. Finally, the output at the output layer is computed as Eq. (3).

$$g_k = \sum_{j=1}^{h} (w_{pk} \cdot f(s_p) + b_k) \tag{3}$$

where, $w_p k$ is the weight of the edge between p^{th} hidden node and k^{th} output node and b_k corresponds to the bias value for the kth output node. Therefore, $f(s_p)$ signifies the output of the pth hidden node.

2.2 Intelligent Gravitational Search Algorithm (IGSA)

Intelligent GSA [10] is an improved variant of GSA [15] in which the position equation has been modified. In GSA, the Newton's law of gravity and law of motion guides the position updation. GSA considers each solution as an object and best solution corresponds to the position of the heaviest object. Besides a single parameter and fast convergence algorithm, GSA has he possibility of getting trap into local optima. To achieve better solution precision, IGSA considers the global best ($gBest$) and global worst ($gWorst$) solutions in the updation of the position. The position equation is formulated as Eq. (4).

$$x_i^d(t+1) = x_i^d(t) + v_i^d(t+1) + r(t) \times \underbrace{\frac{(gBest^d(t) - x_i^d(t))}{|(\rho \times gWorst^d(t)) - x_i^d(t)|}}_{Intelligent\ component} \tag{4}$$

where, $r(t) \in [0,1]$ is a random number at iteration t and ρ is a constant which is taken as 0.99. In [10], the optimality achieved through IGSA has been validated against a number of benchmark functions belonging to different categories, namely unimodal, multi-modal and real-parameter CEC2013.

3 Proposed Method

This paper presents an optimized neural network using IGSA for histopathological image classification. In the first step, the histopathological image is processed to extract features. The extracted features are input to the considered neural network. The considered architecture for the two layer neural network is diagrammed in Fig. 2. There are two hidden layers and one output layer. As number of nodes in a hidden layer is a hyper-parameter, it is considered as four for both hidden layers in the considered network. Moreover, the number of nodes in the output layer is two as the considered problem is a binary classification problem. The activation function defined for the neural network is sigmoid. This neural network process the extracted features and classify the image based on the optimized weight and bias values. To achieve the optimal weights and biases, IGSA has been used. To encode the weights and biases of the considered network, the

---

Algorithm 1. Proposed Histopathological Image Classification Method

---

Input: Assume an image (X).
Output: Image label.

Extract feature from X;
for Till the stopping criteria **do**
    Initialize IGSA population randomly over the $k + t$ dimensions where k and t
    corresponds to the weights and bias parameters, respectively.
    Using considered neural network, compute fitness (fit).
    Update the parameters according to IGSA.
end for
Perform classification by tuning considered neural network according to the optimal
solution of the IGSA.

---

vector encoding strategy has been used in this paper. Thus, every individual of
IGSA represents the weights and biases as a vector. Furthermore, the objective
function considered for this problem is the error which is represented in Eq. (5).

$$Argmin \sum_{i=1}^{q} \frac{E_i}{q} \tag{5}$$

where, q is the number of samples and E corresponds to the average error over
the samples which is calculated as Eq. (6).

$$E_i = \sum_{k=1}^{m} \left(g_k^i - a_k^i\right)^2 \tag{6}$$

where, g_k^i and a_k^i are generated and actual output at the kth node of the output
layer. The proposed method is detailed in Algorithm 1.

4 Experimental Results

Experiments analysis the proposed method against state-of-the-art methods on
publicly available histopathological dataset, namely Animal Diagnostic Laboratory (ADL) dataset [20]. This dataset contains inflamed and healthy images
of three organs, namely Kidney, Lung, and Spleen. The images are labeled by
expert pathologists of Pennsylvania State University. The inflamed category represents the diseased images which contain special type of white blood cells know
as eosinophils. Each organ contains a total of 240 images in which 120 images
are of inflamed organ and other 120 images are of healthy organ. The dataset
contains a total of 720 images of all three organs. The images are generated
after using Hematoxylin-Eosin (H&E) die to color the tissues for each organ.

Table 1. The confusion matrix returned by each considered method over different organ images.

Classes	Kidney		Lung		Spleen		Method
	Healthy	Inflammatory	Healthy	Inflammatory	Healthy	Inflammatory	
Healthy	0.6925	0.3075	0.8687	0.1125	0.5232	0.4880	WND-CHARM
	0.8750	0.1250	0.7520	0.2750	0.6948	0.2917	SRC
	0.8250	0.1750	0.7601	0.2500	0.6140	0.3500	SHIRC
	0.8800	0.1200	**0.8900**	0.1100	**0.7510**	0.2490	Proposed
Inflammatory	0.2812	0.7188	0.3720	0.6238	0.1275	0.8725	WND-CHARM
	0.2500	0.7500	0.2417	0.7853	0.2083	0.7917	SRC
	0.1667	0.8333	0.1500	0.8500	0.1167	0.8833	SHIRC
	0.1550	**0.8450**	0.1500	**0.8500**	0.1100	**0.8900**	Proposed

The bluish purple regions represent the inflammation. For training 60 images per category per organ is randomly selected and rest of the images are used for validation.

For the simulation and experimental analysis, the proposed method is implemented in MATLAB 2016a. A computer system with the i7 processor (Intel core 3.30 GHz) and 8 GB RAM is used for simulation. The results are validated against other state-of-the-art methods namely, WND-CHARM [12], SRC [22], and SHIRC [19]. In WND-CHARM, the extracted features from the medical images are directly used to train the SVM classifier while in the SRC method, the RGB images are first converted to sparse representation then feature are extracted from these images for the classification. However, the sparse representation is based on the single channel which is further extended for multiple channels by the SHIRC method.

Table 1 depicts the confusion matrices between inflamed and healthy categories for each organ images. For kidney, the proposed method correctly identify 84.5% of inflamed images which is better than other considered methods. Moreover, the 88% of the healthy images are correctly identified by the proposed methods. The accuracy returned by other methods on Kidney, Lung, and Spleen images are depicted in Table 1. From the tables, it can be observed that the true positives returned by proposed method is better than other considered methods in every scenario. Furthermore, the efficiency of the proposed method is also analyzed in term of various classification performance matrices, namely recall, specificity, precision, false negative rate (FNR), accuracy, F1-score, and G-mean. The performance values returned by each considered method of these parameters have been depicted in Table 2. From the table, it is observed that the proposed method outperforms other considered methods in every performance parameter.

Table 2. Performance analysis of considered methods.

Organ	Methods	Recall	Specificity	Precision	FNR	Accuracy	F1 score	G-mean
Kidney	WND-CHARM	0.6900	0.7200	0.7100	0.2800	0.7100	0.7000	0.7000
	SRC	0.8750	0.7500	0.7778	0.2500	0.8125	0.8250	0.8235
	SHIRC	0.8250	0.8333	0.8319	0.1667	0.8292	0.8284	0.8284
	Proposed	**0.8800**	**0.8450**	**0.8502**	**0.1150**	**0.8625**	**0.8649**	**0.8650**
Lung	WND-CHARM	0.8875	0.6264	0.7046	0.3736	0.7572	0.7908	0.7856
	SRC	0.7250	0.7647	0.7500	0.2353	0.7451	0.7374	0.7373
	SHIRC	0.7500	0.8500	0.8333	0.1500	0.8000	0.7906	0.7895
	Proposed	**0.8900**	**0.8500**	**0.8557**	**0.1500**	**0.8700**	**0.8725**	**0.8727**
Spleen	WND-CHARM	0.5116	0.8725	0.8004	0.1275	0.6921	0.6399	0.6242
	SRC	0.7083	0.7917	0.7727	0.2083	0.7500	0.7398	0.7391
	SHIRC	0.6500	0.8833	0.8478	0.1167	0.7667	0.7423	0.7358
	Proposed	**0.7510**	**0.8900**	**0.8722**	**0.1100**	**0.8205**	**0.8071**	**0.8094**

5 Conclusion

This paper focuses on the optimization of the two-layer neural network architecture. Mainly, the neural network parameters, i.e. weights and biases, have been optimized by a recent variant of gravitational search algorithm, namely IGSA. The performance of optimized neural network has been validated on the classification of histopathological tissue images into healthy and inflamed classes. For the experimental analyses, the publicly available Animal Diagnostic Laboratory (ADL) dataset is considered. The efficiency is analysed in term of confusion matrix and classification measures. The proposed method outperformed the considered three state-of-the-art methods, namely WND-CHARM, SRC, and SHIRC. The possible extension of this work is the inclusion of multiple objectives while the parameter optimization.

Acknowledgment. Authors are thankful to the Science and Engineering Research Board, Department of Science & Technology, Government of India, New Delhi for funding this work as part of the project (ECR/2016/000844).

References

1. Ashish, T., Kapil, S., Manju, B.: Parallel bat algorithm-based clustering using mapreduce. In: Perez, G.M., Mishra, K.K., Tiwari, S., Trivedi, M.C. (eds.) Networking Communication and Data Knowledge Engineering. LNDECT, vol. 4, pp. 73–82. Springer, Singapore (2018). https://doi.org/10.1007/978-981-10-4600-1_7
2. Azali, S., Sheikhan, M.: Intelligent control of photovoltaic system using BPSO-GSA-optimized neural network and fuzzy-based PID for maximum power point tracking. Appl. Intell. **44**(1), 88–110 (2016)
3. González, B., Valdez, F., Melin, P., Prado-Arechiga, G.: Fuzzy logic in the gravitational search algorithm for the optimization of modular neural networks in pattern recognition. Expert Syst. Appl. **42**(14), 5839–5847 (2015)
4. Gupta, V., Singh, A., Sharma, K., Mittal, H.: A novel differential evolution test case optimisation (DETCO) technique for branch coverage fault detection. In: Satapathy, S.C., Bhateja, V., Das, S. (eds.) Smart Computing and Informatics. SIST, vol 78, pp 245–254 Springer, Singapore (2018) https://doi org/10 1007/ 978-981-10-5547-8_26

5. Jadidi, Z., Muthukkumarasamy, V., Sithirasenan, E., Sheikhan, M.: Flow-based anomaly detection using neural network optimized with GSA algorithm. In: 2013 IEEE 33rd International Conference on Distributed Computing Systems Workshops, pp. 76–81. IEEE (2013)
6. Mirjalili, S., Hashim, S.Z.M., Sardroudi, H.M.: Training feedforward neural networks using hybrid particle swarm optimization and gravitational search algorithm. Appl. Math. Comput. **218**(22), 11125–11137 (2012)
7. Mittal, H., Pal, R., Kulhari, A., Saraswat, M.: Chaotic Kbest gravitational search algorithm (CKGSA). In: 2016 Ninth International Conference on Contemporary Computing (IC3), pp. 1–6. IEEE (2016)
8. Mittal, H., Saraswat, M.: cKGSA based fuzzy clustering method for image segmentation of RGB-D images. In: Proceedings of International Conference on Contemporary Computing, pp. 1–6. IEEE (2018)
9. Mittal, H., Saraswat, M.: An optimum multi-level image thresholding segmentation using non-local means 2D histogram and exponential Kbest gravitational search algorithm. Eng. Appl. Artif. Intell. **71**, 226–235 (2018)
10. Mittal, H., Saraswat, M.: An automatic nuclei segmentation method using intelligent gravitational search algorithm based superpixel clustering. Swarm Evol. Comput. **45**, 15–32 (2019)
11. Mittal, H., Saraswat, M.: Classification of histopathological images through bag-of-visual-words and gravitational search algorithm. In: Bansal, J.C., Das, K.N., Nagar, A., Deep, K., Ojha, A.K. (eds.) Soft Computing for Problem Solving. AISC, vol. 817, pp. 231–241. Springer, Singapore (2019). https://doi.org/10.1007/978-981-13-1595-4_18
12. Orlov, N., Shamir, L., Macura, T., Johnston, J., Eckley, D.M., Goldberg, I.G.: WND-CHARM: multi-purpose image classification using compound image transforms. Pattern Recogn. Lett. **29**(11), 1684–1693 (2008)
13. Pal, R., Saraswat, M.: Histopathological image classification using enhanced bag-of-feature with spiral biogeography-based optimization. Appl. Intell., 1–19 (2019)
14. Pandey, A.C., Rajpoot, D.S., Saraswat, M.: Twitter sentiment analysis using hybrid cuckoo search method. Inf. Process. Manage. **53**(4), 764–779 (2017)
15. Rashedi, E., Nezamabadi-Pour, H., Saryazdi, S.: GSA: a gravitational search algorithm. Inf. Sci. **179**(13), 2232–2248 (2009)
16. Rashedi, E., Rashedi, E., Nezamabadi-Pour, H.: A comprehensive survey on gravitational search algorithm. Swarm Evol. Comput. **41**, 141–158 (2018)
17. Saraswat, M., Arya, K.: Automated microscopic image analysis for leukocytes identification: a survey. Micron **65**, 20–33 (2014)
18. Saraswat, M., Arya, K., Sharma, H.: Leukocyte segmentation in tissue images using differential evolution algorithm. Swarm Evol. Comput. **11**, 46–54 (2013)
19. Srinivas, U., Mousavi, H., Jeon, C., Monga, V., Hattel, A., Jayarao, B.: SHIRC: a simultaneous sparsity model for histopathological image representation and classification. In: 2013 IEEE 10th International Symposium on Biomedical Imaging (ISBI), pp. 1118–1121. IEEE (2013)
20. Srinivas, U., Mousavi, H.S., Monga, V., Hattel, A., Jayarao, B.: Simultaneous sparsity model for histopathological image representation and classification. IEEE Trans. Med. Imaging **33**(5), 1163–1179 (2014)
21. Tripathi, A.K., Sharma, K., Bala, M.: A novel clustering method using enhanced grey wolf optimizer and mapreduce. Big Data Res. **14**, 93–100 (2018)
22. Zhang, Y., Jiang, Z., Davis, L.S.: Learning structured low-rank representations for image classification. In: Proceedings of the IEEE Conference on Computer Vision and Pattern Recognition, pp. 676–683 (2013)

Author Index

Printed in the United States
By Bookmasters